COOKING
A TO Z

The Complete
Culinary Reference Tool

Jane Horn
Editor/Writer

Janet Fletcher
Contributing Writer

Gary Hespenheide
Interior Designer

Jane Horn, a Bay area cookbook writer and editor, is a graduate of Cornell University, with a master's degree in communication from Stanford University. In the California Culinary Academy series of cookbooks, she is the author/editor of *The Art of Eating In* and has contributed to *Chicken and Other Poultry, Microwave and More*, and other titles in the series. She also is the co-author of *The New Harvest* (published by The Cole Group/101 Productions), a guide to exotic and specialty produce. Her column on culinary equipment, "Cook's Tools," appears regularly in *Bay Food* magazine.

Janet Fletcher, a Bay area food and wine writer and editor, holds a degree in economics from Stanford University and attended the Culinary Institute of America in Hyde Park, New York. She has cooked in several west coast restaurants, including the highly acclaimed Chez Panisse, and writes a weekly restaurant column for the Oakland *Tribune*. She also writes for the food and wine industry. She co-authored *Appetizers & Hors d'Oeuvres* and *Italian Cooking* and was contributing writer for *Cookies*, all part of the California Culinary Academy cookbook series.

The California Culinary Academy In the forefront of American institutions leading the culinary renaissance in this country, the California Culinary Academy, founded in San Francisco in 1977, has gained a reputation as one of the world's outstanding professional chef-training schools. With a teaching staff recruited from among the best restaurants of Western Europe, the Academy educates students from around the world in the preparation of classical cuisine. The recipes in this book were created in consultation with the chefs of the Academy. For information about the Academy, write the Office of the Dean, California Culinary Academy, 625 Polk Street, San Francisco, CA 94102.

Copyright © 1988, 1992 The Cole Group

All rights reserved under international and Pan-American copyright conventions.

1 2 3 4 5 6 7 8 9
92 93 94 95 96 97

ISBN 1-56426-003-8

The Cole Group
4415 Sonoma Highway, PO Box 4089, Santa Rosa, CA 95402-4089

CONTRIBUTORS

Cakes, Pastries, and Breads
Tina Salter

Cooking Technique
Daniel Strongin

Equipment
Bill Hughes

Food Processor
Greg Patent

General Recipe Development
Susan Walter

Ice Cream and Frozen Desserts
Leonard D. Grotta

Jams, Jellies, Preserves, and Condiments
Katie Millhiser

Microwave Cooking
Lorinda Moholt

Additional Recipes and Text
Bruce Aidells
John Phillip Carroll
Ron Clark
Hallie Donnelly
Olivia Erschen
Lonnie Gandara
Michael Goodwin
Jay Harlow
Faye Levy
Susan E. Mitchell
Julie Renaud
Cynthia Scheer
Vicki Barrios Schley
Angelo Villa
Charlotte Walker
Naomi Wise

Consultants
Ron Clark
Joyce Jue
Julie Renaud

Illustrator
Edith Allgood

The Cole Group
Publisher
Brete C. Harrison

Associate Publisher
James Connolly

Director of Operations
Linda Hauck

Director of Production
Steve Lux

Senior Editor
Annette Gooch

Address all inquiries to
The Cole Group
4415 Sonoma Highway, PO Box 4089
Santa Rosa, CA 95402-4089

Distributed to the book trade
by Publishers Group West.

Copy Chief
Melinda E. Levine

Copyeditors
Andrea Y. Connolly
Judith Dunham

Proofreader
Lorna Cunkle

Editorial Assistants
Karen K. Johnson
Kass Kapsiak
Tamara Mallory
Raymond F. Quinton

Layout Editor
Linda M. Bouchard

Typographer
Robert C. Miller

Indexer
Elinor Lindheimer

Production by
Studio 165

Special Thanks to
Joanne Bautista
John A. Brown Kitchenwares
Vivianne Coles
Cuisinarts
Peggy Fallon
Jane Frorath
Sylvia Hajak
Robert L. Iacopi
Rebecca Johnson
Sam Kellogg
Tricia Reuter O'Brien
Darryl Salter
Paula Schlosser
Mark Zielinski
    and
    Ted Evans
    Christine Robertson
    Sally W. Smith
    Ernie S. Tasaki

COVER DESIGN
Glenn Martinez & Associates

PHOTOGRAPHY

Cover
Deborah Jones, photographer
Sandra Cook, food stylist

Recipes
Kevin Sanchez, photographer
Susan Massey-Weil, food stylist
Liz Ross, photographic stylist
Chris Coughlin, photographer's assistant

Technique
Marshall Gordon, photographer
Kathleen Prisant, food stylist
Diana Torrey, stylist's assistant

Equipment, Chefs (at left)
Kit Morris, photographer
Carol Haagens, photographer's assistant

Additional Photographers
Patricia Brabant, pp. 7, 78, 81, 82, 86, 112, 125, 126, 127, 161, 162, 163, 164, 165, 186, 239, 260, 400, 421, 423, 431, 437, 454, 483, 484, 486, 495, 498; Victor Budnik, pp. 312, 313; Ed Carey, pp. 133, 206, 237, 270, 273, 328, 388, 582 (left); David Fischer and Patrick Lyons, pp. 25, 75, 111, 231, 563, 611; Joel Glenn, pp. 114, 122, 233, 358, 445, 447, 485, 595, 602; Dennis Gray, pp. 53, 134, 194, 199, 201, 202, 253, 450, 467, 527, 598; Michael Lamotte, pp. 6, 13, 14, 26, 27, 28, 39, 42, 56 (left), 61, 64, 92, 139, 141, 143, 144, 146, 147, 150, 159 (right), 169, 182, 185, 188, 234, 286, 293, 298, 300, 341, 395, 397, 424, 427, 458, 463, 496, 509, 514, 528, 541, 565, 631; Fred Lyon, pp. 46, 176, 219, 221, 265, 280, 335, 346, 357, 452, 453, 510, 519, 531, 581, 591, 597, 609, 610; Doug Manchee, page 131 (right); Bob Montesclaros, pp. 68, 174, 198, 296, 350, 417, 472, 474, 476, 513, 533, 557; Allan Rosenberg, pp. 91, 179, 181, 374, 491, 614, 618, 623, 624, 625, 629, 630; Tom Tracy, page 303; Jackson Vereen, pp. 224, 295, 392, 532, 536, 537, 538, 542, 544, 546.

Additional Stylists
Allison Anthony, Roz Baker, M. Susan Broussard, Sandra Cook, Joanne Dexter, Olivia Erschen, Amy Glenn, Sandra Griswold, Carol Hacker, Karen Hazarian, Robert Lambert, Sandra Learned, Bunny Martin, Cherie Miller, Amy Nathan, Janet Nusbaum, Jan Rhodes, Cynthia Scheer, Sara Slavin, Carla Tavaras, Kathleen Volkmann, Doug Warne, Maria Winston.

PREFACE

Cooking A to Z is a practical, comprehensive culinary reference book. It is also a collection of more than 600 specially selected recipes covering the basics and more. And it is a beautiful book that anyone who loves food will read with pleasure.

If you are a novice cook, through this book you can learn the fundamentals — the terms, techniques, and equipment you need to prepare any recipe with success. *Cooking A to Z* will also guide you through the constantly changing marketplace: it tells you how to shop for and cook with fresh ingredients and processed foods; how to stock pantry and cupboard; and how to identify, select, and care for kitchen equipment. More experienced cooks will appreciate the convenience of finding all the basic food and cooking information in one up-to-date volume, as well as a wealth of reliable and creative recipes. With so much to offer, *Cooking A to Z* will prove invaluable to cooks and (noncooking) food enthusiasts alike, both as a workbook and as a source of hours of fascinating reading.

The information presented on these pages reflects the expertise of consultants drawn from all aspects of cooking. Equipment entries offer the most current information on the range of basic culinary tools and appliances. You will learn how to use the equipment, how to decide whether or not it should be part of your personal *batterie de cuisine*, and which pieces are interchangeable. Each of the equipment entries is accompanied by a photograph that clearly shows the item. Cooking terminology, the culinary shorthand that is the foundation for every recipe, is fully explained; terms are often illustrated. More than 35 sets of step-by-step photographs, plus detailed text, demonstrate important techniques such as boning, beating egg whites, carving, filleting, and decorating cakes. For each ingredient, you are provided with specific information for use, availability, selection, and storage. Throughout the book you will find over 75 special features that offer highlights and tips. The recipes are wide ranging, from sauces to cookies to roasts, and include exciting ways to use familiar ingredients and those that are new to you.

You will refer to this book when you come across something you don't know in a recipe, or when you hear of a recipe and want to know what it is or how to prepare it. For instance, perhaps you recently tasted the following dessert: an apple tart composed of a pastry base with a filling of sliced apples, finished with an apricot glaze and presented in a pool of custard sauce. Open *Cooking A to Z* and look up: *apple, tart, tart pan, tart pastry, glaze,* and *custard.* You will find information on selecting, storing, and using apples; on what a tart is and how to make one; on what a tart pan is and what different kinds there are; on the types of tart pastry and which one to use; on the definition of *glaze* and several representative types of glazes; and on custards and how to make a custard sauce. You will find a number of recipes for tarts, as well as one for apple pie (just in case, even after learning all about tarts, you still prefer pie).

Cooking A to Z is organized alphabetically; the encyclopedia format makes it easy to locate any subject. You can also use the thorough index. While each of the almost 500 entries tells a complete story, many will also direct you elsewhere in the book for further information or additional recipes. Hundreds of full-color photographs of both recipes and techniques complement the clear, straightforward text and also make browsing a pleasure.

Whether this is your first cookbook or the latest addition to an extensive culinary library, *Cooking A to Z* will prove indispensable, so give it a good spot on your shelf or kitchen counter.

A popular Chinese restaurant dessert, meltingly tender Chinese Almond Cookies, uses both almond extract and whole blanched almonds to impart nutty flavor. The recipe is on page 145.

ACHIOTE

The hard, brick red seed of the annatto tree is called achiote. The seeds are valued more for the golden yellow color they impart to other foods than for their flavor, which is somewhat dusty.

Use   The seeds, typically, are soaked in water or heated in oil or lard, then discarded, and the oil or water is used to color food. Latin American cooks often add ground achiote to the water when cooking rice; and they use it in spice pastes for stews and sprinkle it on meats before roasting. The seed is also used commercially in this country to color butter, margarine, and cheese.

Availability   Check Latin American, Caribbean, and Philippine markets for achiote. It is available as whole seeds, ground powder, paste, and liquid extract.

Selection   Achiote seeds should have a lively brick red color; a brownish color indicates age.

Storage   Both seeds and powder should be stored in a tightly covered jar in a cool, dark place. Seeds will keep indefinitely; powder will keep up to six months. The paste should be refrigerated after opening; it will keep indefinitely.

Preparation   To color cooking fat, heat 2 parts oil or lard with 1 part achiote seed over moderately low heat until fat turns a golden orange (5 to 10 minutes). Cool, strain into a jar, and refrigerate. To prepare seeds for grinding, cover with water, bring to a boil and simmer 5 minutes, then remove from heat and let soak until cool. Drain and grind with a mortar and pestle, clean coffee grinder, or electric minichopper.

ACIDULATED WATER

The flesh of certain fruits and vegetables, such as apples and pears, will darken when exposed to air unless used immediately after cutting or unless they are dropped into acidulated water, a dilute solution of 5 or 6 parts water to 1 part acid. Typically the acid is lemon juice or vinegar.

ADJUST, TO

In cooking, this term means to taste a dish after it has cooked for a while, or just before serving, and then add more seasoning if needed.

AL DENTE

The literal meaning of this Italian term is *to the tooth*. It describes the consistency of pasta and vegetables when cooked just to the point of doneness. At this stage food still offers some resistance when chewed (the technical term is *percussion*) and has developed a fuller and richer flavor than when raw.

ALLSPICE

The allspice berry resembles an oversized, reddish brown peppercorn. Its flavor and aroma suggest a pungent and spicy blend of cloves, cinnamon, and nutmeg.

Use   Allspice adds zest to both savory and sweet dishes, including stews, sauces (particularly tomato-based ones), marinades, relishes and preserves, cooked fruit, and baked goods of all kinds. It combines well with other spices. One of the pickling spices, it is sometimes part of the French blend *quatre épices* (four spices) used in pâtés. If necessary substitute a mixture of equal amounts of cloves, cinnamon, and nutmeg for allspice.

Availability   Buy it packaged or bulk, whole or ground.

Selection Packaged seasonings lose quality after a while; try to buy from a store that restocks its spice section fairly often.

Storage Keep in an airtight container away from light and heat. Ground spice stays pungent up to six months, whole berries even longer.

Preparation Grind whole berries in a pepper mill, clean coffee grinder, electric minichopper, or with a mortar and pestle.

Recipes and Related Information
Carrot Spice Cake, 86; Honeyed Chicken With Apricots, 557.

ALMOND

Encased in a light-tan pitted shell, the almond is a white, oval, flat nut covered with a brown skin. Both bitter and sweet varieties exist. Raw bitter almonds contain toxic prussic acid, which is harmful except in small amounts, and so only sweet almonds are sold in the United States. Because the acid is destroyed by heat, commercial processors can use oil from the more intensely flavored bitter nut for extracts and liqueurs. For more flavor, European recipes may add a touch of bitter almond to the sweet almond.

Use Extremely versatile, the almond is used as both ingredient and garnish. It adds texture and crunch to poultry, fish, rice, sauces, vegetables, salads, breads, desserts, cake and pastry fillings, and candy.

Availability Almonds come packaged in cans or clear bags, or in bulk; in the shell or shelled; unblanched or blanched; whole, chopped, sliced, or slivered.

Selection Buy nuts that are as fresh as possible.

Storage Unshelled nuts can be stored in a cool place for up to six months. Shelled nuts will keep in an airtight container in the refrigerator for several months or in the freezer for up to six months (thaw before using).

Preparation See NUT.

ALMOND PASTE AND MARZIPAN

Made from finely ground blanched almonds, sugar, and egg whites, marzipan and almond paste can be molded to form flowers, stems, leaves, and other fanciful shapes, or rolled out into sheets to decorate cakes and pastries. They have been used for making confections for centuries. They were originally two distinct products, but now have become essentially interchangeable, both in use and in name. If a difference must be stated: Marzipan is cooked and firmer and more pliable than almond paste, which is not cooked. They can be found in better supermarkets or gourmet shops, or you can make your own (see right).

To roll out either almond paste or marzipan, dust work surface lightly with confectioners' sugar and roll out with a rolling pin. Tint almond paste or marzipan by kneading in a few drops of food coloring. Pale tints are usually the most appetizing on pastry.

■ **HOMEMADE ALMOND PASTE**
   2 cups very finely ground blanched almonds
2¼ cups sifted confectioners' sugar
   1 to 2 egg whites, beaten until foamy
      Fondant (optional)

1. Combine almonds and sugar in a bowl. Stir well to blend. Gradually stir in enough egg whites to moisten almond mixture. Gather mixture into a ball; knead until smooth. Wrap well and refrigerate. Keeps for 1 week.

2. To make almond paste more pliable and easier to roll out, work a little fondant into it. Fondant is a sticky white icing available at bakeries or stores that sell cake-decorating supplies (see page 96). To roll out almond paste, dust work surface with confectioners' sugar.

Makes about 1 pound.

Food Processor Version Use metal blade to process almonds and sugar until almonds are very finely ground. Add 1 unbeaten egg white and process 20 seconds. If paste does not form a ball, add more egg white.

■ **HOMEMADE MARZIPAN**
   2 cups sugar
  ¾ cup water
3½ cups very finely ground blanched almonds
   2 egg whites, beaten until foamy
      Confectioners' sugar, for dusting

1. Combine sugar and the water in saucepan. Cook to 240° F (soft-ball stage; see CANDY AND CONFECTION, Stages of Sugar Syrup). Remove from heat; stir until cloudy. Then stir in almonds.

2. Stir in egg whites and cook over low heat until mixture firms slightly. Dust work surface with confectioners' sugar. Knead marzipan until pliable. Wrap well and store in refrigerator for up to 1 month.

Makes 1¾ pounds.

Food Processor Version Use metal blade to grind almonds in 2 batches. Add to recipe as directed. Process cooked mixture until pliable (30 to 45 seconds).

Recipes and Related Information
Almond Meringue Cake, 361; Almond Torte 89; Apricot-Almond Squares, 143; Chinese Almond Cookies, 145; Panforte, 186; Raspberry-Almond Tart, 496; Ricotta Cheesecake, 119; Your Own Bridge Mix, 59.

Green-tinted marzipan was rolled out and then applied to a leaf mold. The marzipan takes the shape of a leaf, even the detailing of the veins. After removal from the mold, it can be placed on a cake for decoration.

ANGELICA

A large perennial herb native to the northern hemisphere and New Zealand, angelica is valued principally for its roots and stalks.

Use Fresh angelica is eaten as a vegetable in the world's northernmost regions, such as Iceland, Norway, and Siberia. Because of its pungent flavor and alleged digestive properties, angelica root is used in the production of cordials and liqueurs, such as Benedictine and Chartreuse. The leaves and stalks may be used to flavor custards. When processed commercially, the green celerylike stalks are generally candied in sugar syrup for decorative use in breads, cookies, cakes, and fruitcakes. Candied angelica is expensive, and occasionally counterfeits made of dyed substitutes appear in the market.

Availability Fresh angelica is not grown commercially in the United States. Some home gardeners cultivate it, and it may be found wild. Angelica stalks candied in sugar syrup are available packaged or in bulk from specialty food markets or a bakers' supply outlet.

Storage Keep fresh stalks in a plastic bag in refrigerator crisper and use within a couple of days. Store candied angelica in a cool, dark place for two to three months, or freeze indefinitely.

Preparation Wash and trim fresh angelica. Halve lengthwise to be sure hollow stalks are clean. Cut stalks in smaller lengths and steep in milk for custards, or dice and candy in sugar syrup. Candied angelica can be marinated in brandy or liqueur for several hours before using.

> *Recipes and Related Information*
> *Candied Fruit, 93; Candy, 93.*

ANISE

An annual herb in the parsley family, anise yields small, pungent leaves and greenish gray seeds; both have a licoricelike flavor.

Use Add anise leaves sparingly to salads and vegetable dishes. Anise seed (also spelled *aniseed*) is popular in German and Scandinavian cookies, cakes, and breads, and in Italian twice-baked cookies (*biscotti*). Add it to pickles, cabbage slaw, or ground-pork mixtures. Anise oil is used as a flavoring agent in cough medicines.

Availability Whole anise seed is packaged in glass jars. It is rarely available ground but may be ground at home. Anise leaves are not available commercially.

Selection Packaged seasonings lose quality after a while; try to buy from a store that restocks its spice section fairly often.

Storage Keep in an airtight container away from light and heat. Anise seed will stay pungent up to one year.

Preparation Leaves are used whole; rub them lightly between the fingers to release oils. Seed may be used whole, or ground in a pepper mill, clean coffee grinder, electric minichopper, or with a mortar and pestle.

■ BISCOTTI

Almost every Italian bakery sells several varieties of dry *biscotti*, twice-baked (*bis cotto*) cookies that are meant to be dunked in coffee or wine. They keep for weeks in an airtight container; offer them with afternoon tea or coffee or with a late-night glass of sweet wine. Note that the dough must chill at least overnight.

    ¼ cup dried currants
    2 tablespoons Marsala
    ½ pound unsalted butter, softened
    2 cups sugar
    4 eggs
    1 teaspoon vanilla extract
    1 tablespoon anise-flavored liqueur
    4 cups flour
    1 teaspoon baking powder
    1 teaspoon baking soda
    ½ teaspoon salt
    2 teaspoons grated lemon rind
    1 teaspoon anise seed
    ½ cup half-and-half
    1 cup coarsely chopped, toasted walnuts
    1 cup coarsely chopped, toasted hazelnuts

1. Put currants in a bowl with Marsala; soak for 20 minutes.

2. Cream butter; add sugar gradually and beat until light. Add eggs one at a time, beating until light and fluffy. Add vanilla, liqueur, and currants with their soaking liquid.

3. Sift together flour, baking powder, baking soda, and salt. Stir in lemon rind and anise seed. Add to creamed mixture alternately with half-and-half. Stir in walnuts and hazelnuts by hand. Cover and chill dough for at least 2 hours or overnight.

4. Divide dough into quarters and place each quarter on a length of waxed paper. Form into a roll about 15 inches long and 1½ inches thick. Wrap in waxed paper, then in aluminum foil. Chill overnight (dough can be frozen at this point for up to 1 month; bring frozen dough to refrigerator temperature before proceeding).

5. Preheat oven to 350° F. Unwrap rolls and place them on ungreased baking sheets. Bake until very lightly browned (20 to 25 minutes). Carefully transfer rolls to a cutting board and cut on a 45-degree angle into slices about ½ inch thick. Place slices cut side up on baking sheets and return to oven. Bake until golden (8 to 12 minutes). Cool cookies thoroughly on racks. Store in airtight containers.

Makes about 4 dozen cookies.

Food Processor Version As a timesaver, use standard shredding disk to process nuts.

> **Recipes and Related Information**
> *Florentine Grape Coffee Cake, 279; Spiced French Honey Bread, 304.*

APPLE

The sweet, round, thin-skinned fruit of a tree that grows in temperate zones, the apple is presumed a native of southwest Asia. Of the thousands of classified varieties, fewer than 20 are commercially important in the United States. Skin color of most varieties is green, yellow, or red; the moist, crisp flesh is white to creamy white, sometimes with yellow, green, or red tints.

Use Raw apples are commonly eaten out of hand or in fruit salads. Apples may be stewed and puréed for applesauce, baked whole, or used as an ingredient in a wide variety of baked desserts. Cooked apples are a popular garnish for savory pork dishes; they also figure in some classic French chicken and veal preparations. Apples may be pressed for juice, which, in turn, may be fermented into cider or distilled into brandy (also known as applejack and Calvados).

Availability Early varieties such as the Gravenstein and Astrachan are harvested in July and August. Late varieties begin in September and continue through November. Controlled-storage apples are available the rest of the year. Fresh apples are sold in bulk, overwrapped trays, or plastic bags. Cooked apples are available as canned or bottled applesauce or as canned apple-pie filling. Sliced apples are also available dried.

Selection Choose firm apples without bruised spots. Scald (irregularly shaped tan or brown area) has tougher texture than unblemished skin but does not seriously affect eating quality.

The following are suggested pairings of apple varieties and uses; eating apples such as Golden Delicious, Granny Smith, or Newtown pippin are fine eaten out of hand but also are good, all-purpose cooking apples. These groupings are offered for optimum flavor; or use what your recipe suggests.

For Eating Try Golden Delicious (gold), Granny Smith (green), Jonathan (brilliant red), McIntosh (red to green), Newtown pippin (green), Red Delicious (red), Stayman (red), or Winesap (red).

For Pies and Applesauce Use tart or slightly acidic varieties: Gravenstein (yellow-green with red stripes), Grimes Golden (gold), Jonathan (brilliant red), McIntosh (red to green), Newtown pippin (green), Northern Spy (red); Rhode Island Greening (green), Stayman (red), Winesap (red), and York Imperial (red).

For Baking Use firmer-fleshed varieties preferably over 3 inches in diameter: Northern Spy (red), Rome Beauty (red), Winesap (red), York Imperial (red).

Storage Refrigerate apples until use; hardy varieties will last a month or more. Dried apples will keep indefinitely when stored in a plastic bag in the refrigerator.

Preparation Peel apples or not, as desired. For cooked dishes, halve or quarter apples and remove core. To core whole apples, use an apple corer, or use a small, sharp knife to cut all the way around the core and lift it out.

Homey Apple Crisp (see page 10) is an early American baked fruit dessert with a sweetened crumb topping. Whipped cream or vanilla ice cream is the perfect, cool complement to the warm, fragrant fruit.

A smooth, buttery sauce is an easy way to transform asparagus into a festive dish. Hollandaise Sauce (see page 516) and asparagus are a classic pairing.

ARUGULA

Also known as rugola, rocket, Italian cress, and roquette, arugula is a delicate salad green popular in Mediterranean countries. When young its slender, dark green leaves are tender and nutty, with a subtle peppery flavor; mature arugula has an unpleasantly hot, mustardlike character. The four-petaled, white blossoms are edible.

Use Arugula is enjoyed as a salad green, alone, garnished with the delicate flowers, or in combination with other greens. As part of a sandwich filling, it lends an appealing nutty flavor; small whole leaves can be added to potato or lentil soup at the last minute.

Availability It is sold loose or in clear bags, and is at its best in spring and fall.

Selection Buy fresh greens that are not limp and do not show any signs of decay.

Storage Keep in a plastic bag in refrigerator crisper for several days; wash just before using.

Preparation Trim away roots; wash leaves well and dry thoroughly.

ASPARAGUS

The asparagus plant is a member of the lily family. Its edible part is the long, slender shoot, which can range from pencil thin to about one half inch thick. Mostly asparagus is harvested green. White asparagus is harvested when the tip just breaks the ground; lack of exposure to the sun keeps the spear pale.

Use Steamed or boiled asparagus is served at room temperature or chilled as a salad, often with mayonnaise, vinaigrette, or other salad dressing; served hot, it is generally dressed with butter or oil or Hollandaise sauce and offered as a first course or side dish. Asparagus tips are a popular garnish for salads, soup, rice, and pasta dishes; for omelet and quiche fillings; and for Asian stir-fries.

Availability Asparagus is available fresh, frozen, or canned; whole spears or tips. The fresh crop is harvested between March and June.

Selection Choose bright green or white spears that are brittle, not limp, have tightly closed tips, and stalks that are at least two-thirds green.

Storage Refrigerate spears, upright, with stem ends in water; or wrap cut ends in wet paper towels or cloth, cover with a plastic bag, and refrigerate. Refrigerated asparagus keeps up to one week.

Preparation Break asparagus spears by hand where they snap easily. Alternatively, use a small knife or vegetable peeler to remove tough outer peel at stem end; tips are tender and do not require peeling. Leave whole or cut diagonally into 1- to 2-inch pieces.

Cooking See BOIL, STEAM, STIR-FRY.

■ ASPARAGUS WITH LEMON, TOMATO, AND ONIONS

When asparagus and new onions turn up in Italian markets at the same time, the chefs of Bologna prepare this dish and put it in their windows.

> 1½ pounds medium asparagus
> 2 small, sweet new onions *or*
>   4 green onions, minced
> 2 tablespoons fresh lemon juice
> ½ cup extravirgin olive oil
>   Grated rind of 1 lemon
> 2 tablespoons snipped fresh chives
> 2 tomatoes, peeled, seeded, and diced
>   Salt and freshly ground pepper, to taste

1. Bring a large pot of salted water to a boil. Add asparagus and cook until barely tender (about 5 minutes). Transfer with tongs to a bowl of ice water. When cool, drain and dry well. Transfer to a serving platter with all tips facing the same direction.

2. Combine onion, lemon juice, olive oil, lemon rind, and half of the chives. Whisk well, then stir in tomatoes. Season to taste with salt and pepper. Spoon sauce over asparagus, then garnish with remaining chives. Serve at room temperature.

Serves 4.

Food Processor Version Use metal blade to process onion, cut in 1-inch pieces, 10 seconds. Add lemon juice, olive oil, lemon rind, and half the chives; process 5 seconds. If you have a French-fry disk, process tomatoes, halved and squeezed to remove excess juice, into dressing in work bowl.

Recipes and Related Information
Beef With Asparagus, 558; Cream of Any Vegetable Soup, 563; Pasta Primavera, 414.

AVOCADO

The avocado is the pear-shaped fruit of a tropical tree. Some varieties, such as the common Fuerte, have a thin, dark green skin; others, such as the Hass, have a thick, rough, pebbly skin that changes from green to black as they ripen. The yellow-green flesh surrounds a large dark seed; when ripe, the flesh is smooth and buttery with a nutty flavor.

Use Avocados are generally eaten raw as a salad or first course. Halved avocados can be stuffed with seafood or eaten plain with lemon or vinaigrette. Sliced avocados add a buttery texture to green salads, seafood salads, sandwiches, and omelet fillings. They are commonly used to garnish Mexican tostadas, tacos, and other Latin American dishes, and are the major ingredient in guacamole. Seasoned mashed avocado makes a rich, creamy smooth, and delicious sandwich spread.

Availability The supply of winter varieties peaks in January; summer varieties appear in the market from June through late August. Because the fruit can be held on the tree for months without becoming overripe, avocados are generally available the year around.

Selection Choose avocados with full necks and with flesh that gives slightly to pressure. Dark-skinned varieties should be very dark; light-skinned varieties should have a soft, dull-looking skin with a velvety feel.

Storage If using within a few days, ripe avocados will keep at cool room temperature; or store in refrigerator for up to one week. Ripen at warm room temperature, preferably in a dark spot; ripening takes from three to five days (refrigeration will slow process). To ripen quickly, place in a paper bag. To store partially used avocados, rub cut surfaces with lemon juice, cover tightly with plastic wrap, and refrigerate.

Preparation Cut avocado in half, lengthwise, around seed. Twist halves apart. To remove seed, either slide tip of a spoon gently underneath and lift it out or carefully strike seed with a sharp knife, embedding knife in seed. Rotate knife to lift out seed. To slice or cube avocado, hold one half, cut side up, in one hand and use a large spoon to scoop flesh out of skin in one piece. Put half, pit side down, on a cutting surface and slice or cube. Sprinkle cut surfaces with lemon or lime juice to keep them from browning.

■ GUACAMOLE

Avocado is used extensively in Mexico. Often just sliced and served as a garnish, it provides one of the important textural contrasts so typical of the cuisine. Certainly its best known and most popular use is in guacamole.

Guacamole is a versatile dish. In Mexico it is most often served on lettuce as a salad or side dish, but it is used also as a garnish for tacos, burritos, tostadas, or *flautas* and, of course, as a dip accompanied by fried tortilla wedges or assorted raw vegetables.

    2 large avocados
    2 teaspoons fresh lime or lemon juice
    ¼ cup sour cream (optional)
    1 small clove garlic, crushed
    1 small tomato, diced
    1 canned jalapeño chile, seeded and finely
      chopped (optional)
    ¼ cup finely minced onion
      Few sprigs cilantro, coarsely chopped

1. Halve avocados; remove pit, scoop out pulp, and mash with a fork.

2. Add lime juice, sour cream (if used), garlic, tomato, jalapeño (if used), onion, and cilantro, mixing after each addition.

Makes approximately 2½ cups.

Food Processor Version Use metal blade to process garlic and 1 small onion until finely chopped (10 to 15 seconds). Add avocado and process to desired consistency. Add lime or lemon juice, sour cream, jalapeño, and cilantro sprigs; process 5 seconds. Stir in tomato.

Quick Guacamole Follow Guacamole recipe through step 1. Mix mashed pulp with ⅓ cup prepared salsa. *To make in a food processor:* Use metal blade to process avocados to desired consistency. Add salsa and process a few seconds to combine.

Makes approximately 2 cups.

Recipes and Related Information
Avocado Bacon Burger, 44; Avocado, Jicama, and Grapefruit Salad, 281; Guacamole Burger, 44.

BAIN-MARIE

A hot water bath or bain-marie provides a constant, even source of heat to delicate foods such as custards, cheesecakes, and sauces. Restaurant kitchens use a bain-marie to hold sauces at serving temperature for long periods of time. The home cook will also use a  water bath for this purpose, but more typically will use it to insulate oven-cooked foods. The cooking dish is set in a larger pan filled partway with water that is almost, but not quite, boiling and then placed in the oven. Any pan can be used as the bottom container, as long as it is large enough to hold the cooking dish with a few inches of clearance on all sides. Roasting pans or cake pans, found in most home kitchens, are commonly used for this purpose. A large saucepan is suitable for stove-top service. A double boiler is a form of bain-marie.

> ***Recipes and Related Information***
> *Cheesecake, 117; Custard, 168; Sauce, 512.*

BAKE, TO

The process of baking, as well as that of roasting, its twin, involves cooking raw food in an oven with currents of dry, hot air. For all practical purposes, to bake and to roast mean the same thing. See ROAST.

BAKE BLIND, TO

To bake a pastry crust for a pie or tart, partially or completely, before it is filled. To keep pastry from puffing up during baking, it is pricked evenly with a fork, lined with aluminum foil or parchment paper, filled with dried beans or metal or ceramic pie weights, then baked until set (10 to 15 minutes). Foil and beans are removed and pastry is returned to oven until it is partially or completely baked, as needed.

Partially baked crusts are used for some custard and cream fillings, which tend to be soggy or undercooked if filled raw. Fully prebaked shells are used to hold an uncooked filling (fresh fruit), a cold filling (mousse, Bavarian cream, pastry cream), or a filling that is cooked on top of the stove and added later (lemon curd, pudding).

> ***Recipes and Related Information***
> *Cake and Pastry Tools, 92; Pie and Tart, 434.*

BAKER'S PEEL

Professional bakers use wooden shovels called peels to slide yeast breads and pizzas into the oven and to retrieve them when done. The amateur pizza maker can find scaled-down peels in cookware stores. Use the peel for the final rising of pizza and bread dough, after  first sprinkling with cornmeal to prevent sticking. To transfer pizza or loaf to oven, give peel a few preliminary shakes to make sure the pizza glides freely, then set far edge of peel at far edge of baking surface (either baking stone or baking sheet); give peel a sharp jerk, and slowly pull back as pizza or loaf slides off.

Baker's peels are made of smooth, pale basswood and are commonly available in three sizes: 12 by 14 inches, 14 by 16 inches, and 16 by 18 inches. Buy the size that fits your oven and suits your needs. If you make single loaves, or pizzas for one or two, the smaller ones are sufficient. Giant breads need a giant board. If you have two ovens and bake several pizzas or breads at one time or in succession, and if you plan on cutting and serving on the peels, consider buying several. They also make wonderful bread and cheese boards.

After using, wipe peel clean with a damp cloth; scrape off any pieces of food. Don't wash under running water or wood will warp and eventually split.

> ***Recipes and Related Information***
> *Baking Stone and Tile, 24; Pizza, 445; Yeast Bread, 613.*

BAKING PANS, FOR BATTER AND DOUGH

Selecting bake ware can be confusing. Often the same baking pan is sold under different names and in a variety of materials. As a primary guideline, consider the function of the pan, and then buy the one that will do the job best, regardless of what it is called. See MATERIALS FOR COOKWARE for more information.

Increasingly, professional-quality bake ware is available for home use. Although these pans usually cost more, in the long run they will prove their worth and justify their higher price. The superior materials and craftsmanship mean a better-looking, higher-quality final product. Professional pans have a longer life expectancy as well.

Should you purchase every pan described here? Hardly. Before buying, ask yourself the following questions. What do I bake most often? What is the yield of favorite recipes?

Bake ware is available for home use in a range of shapes, sizes, and materials. Shown top row, from left: ring mold, angel food cake pan, miniature savarin rings, panettone pan, charlotte mold, loaf pans, brioche molds, cake pans. Middle row, from left: savarin mold, ladyfinger pan, madeleine pan, muffin and popover pans, flan rings, tart pans, quiche pan. Bottom row, from left: pizza pans, Kugelhopf pan, baking cloche, bundt pan, cake pans, pie tins, baking sheet, and baking pan.

Do I need more than one of each pan? What are the dimensions of my oven? How much storage space do I have? Then purchase what best suits your needs.

ANGEL FOOD CAKE PAN

This pan with high sides has a center tube that promotes even distribution of heat and supports the delicate air-leavened batter as it rises. As angel food cakes must cool upside down, these pans usually have small metal feet spaced around the rim or a tube higher than the pan sides for added stability and to allow air circulation. Pans are typically 10 inches in diameter by 4 inches tall and are made of aluminum, often with a nonstick coating. They have a 9-cup capacity. Most have removable bottoms.

BABA MOLD

These small, thimble-shaped, aluminum molds are used for baking the sweet, yeast-leavened French cake known as baba. The molds are as tall as they are wide—2¼ inches. Miniature savarin rings are often substituted for baba cups (see Savarin Mold).

BAGUETTE PAN

Adapted from professional bake ware, these black steel or stainless steel troughs hold the long, slender loaves of crusty bread known as baguettes during their final rise and in the oven. Most bread recipes yield two loaves, so that is the configuration commonly found in cookware stores;

other sizes are available by special order. Pans are 17 inches long, with 2-inch-wide troughs. Some have a vented band between each pair of troughs for circulation of heat.

BAKING CLOCHE

Commercial bakery ovens produce breads with superior crusts by injecting a fine spray of water into the oven cavity. The bell-shaped stoneware baking cloche re-creates this environment for home-baked breads. To use, the porous dome is first soaked in water. The dough is set on the base, which has been sprinkled with cornmeal to prevent sticking, then covered with the dome, and put in the oven. Steam forms within the dome and blankets the dough. If you bake bread often and have a lot of storage space (dome is 10 inches high and base is 11 inches in diameter), you may want to buy one. A covered, unglazed clay casserole will work as well; only the shape is different.

BAKING PAN AND BAKING SHEET

Baking pans have straight sides, ¾ inch tall or higher, all the way around. Baking sheets have a low lip on one or more edges for easy handling. Baking pans are designed to contain runny batters. Baking sheets, also called cookie sheets, work for any freestanding baked product—stiff cookie doughs, rolls and free-form yeast breads, biscuits, cream puffs, and meringues, for example.

Both pans and sheets are kitchen workhorses. Sheets are used to support bottomless flan rings and delicate tartlet pans. Pans set under pies keep ovens clean by catching bubbling juices. They can help organize setup by serving as a catchall for ingredients and equipment.

Buy baking pans or baking sheets of the heaviest weight and best quality available. Aluminum and heavy-gauge black steel are good choices. A typical baking pan measures 11 by 16 by 1 or 2 inches. A standard jelly-roll pan measures approximately 11 by 15 by ¾ inches. Baking sheets vary in size, but a 14- by 17-inch sheet should fit most home ovens. Consider buying several sheets if you have two ovens, or if you bake in big batches.

A relative newcomer, the air-cushioned cookie sheet, sandwiches a layer of air between two sheets of aluminum. Inspired by the professional baker's trick of double sheeting—baking on two stacked sheets as a way of controlling heat distribution—this design keeps dough from browning too quickly on the bottom. Sheets measure 9½ by 14 inches and 14 by 16 inches. An air-cushioned jelly-roll pan is also available.

PAN SUBSTITUTION

Whenever possible, use the size and shape pan recommended in the recipe you are using. Measure pan depth on the outside of one side, bottom to top; measure length and/or width across top of pan between inside edges. If you do not have the right size pan or wish to vary the shape, you can consult the chart below to find a reasonable substitute. Choose a pan that has the same volume and similar depth as the pan in the recipe. The depth may vary up to ½ inch as long as the volume remains the same. The volume of a pan is measured by the amount of liquid it holds when filled to the rim. (This does not refer to the amount of batter the pan holds.) You may need to bake your cake, pie, or bread a little longer if you choose a deeper pan than the one recommended.

Pan Measurements Sides × Depth	Shape of Pan	Volume of Pan
2¾″ × 1⅜″	Muffin cups	Scant ½ cup
9″ × 1¼″	Pie plate	1 quart (4 cups)
8″ × 1½″	Round	1 quart (4 cups)
8″ × 8″ × 1½″	Square	1½ quarts (6 cups)
7″ × 11″ × 2″	Rectangular	1½ quarts (6 cups)
4½″ × 8½″ × 2½″	Loaf	1½ quarts (6 cups)
10″ × 2″	Deep-dish pie	1½ quarts (6 cups)
8″ × 2″	Round	1½ quarts (6 cups)
9″ × 1½″	Round	1½ quarts (6 cups)
8″ × 8″ × 2″	Square	2 quarts (8 cups)
9″ × 9″ × 1½″	Square	2 quarts (8 cups)
5″ × 9″ × 3″	Loaf	2 quarts (8 cups)
9″ × 2″	Round	2 quarts (8 cups)
9″ × 3″	Bundt	2¼ quarts (9 cups)
9″ × 4″	Kugelhopf (tube)	2¼ quarts (9 cups)
8″ × 3¼″	Tube	2¼ quarts (9 cups)
9″ × 9″ × 2″	Square	2½ quarts (10 cups)
9½″ × 2½″	Springform	2½ quarts (10 cups)
9″ × 13″ × 2″	Rectangular	3 quarts (12 cups)
10″ × 2½″	Springform	3 quarts (12 cups)
10″ × 3½″	Bundt	3 quarts (12 cups)

BRIOCHE PAN

An egg-rich French yeast bread with a characteristic topknot of dough, a brioche is traditionally made in a flared, fluted tinned steel mold.

Molds range from individual ones, 3½ inches in diameter by 1½ inches high, to those sized to serve a whole dinner party, 8 inches by 2½ inches. Brioche pans also make charming soup bowls or containers for condiments and preserves.

BUNDT PAN

These deep tube pans are used to bake the popular, densely textured bundt cakes. Pan sides have curves and indentations that produce a cake with an attractive, sculptured exterior. The center tube allows heat to reach more of the batter and also shapes the cake into a ring, which is easier to slice. Typically, these pans are made of cast aluminum with a nonstick interior coating and measure 10 inches in diameter by 3½ inches high, with a 12-cup capacity. Also available is a tray of six miniature bundt cake molds. Each mold holds 1 cup of batter.

CAKE PAN

Every kitchen probably has at least one of these baking pans. They are basic equipment and very versatile. Round pans are used for layer and other types of cakes and for breads; square and rectangular ones for sheet cakes, bar cookies, and breads. Most recipes call for round or square pans 8 or 9 inches by 1½ inches high. The standard rectangular pan is 9 by 13 by 1½ to 2 inches. Deep cake pans with 3-inch sides, formerly only available from restaurant suppliers, are now sold at well-stocked cookware stores. Also called cheesecake pans, these produce a cake with more volume than one baked in a shallower pan, because the batter has more surface to grab on to as it rises. Often the cake is sliced horizontally to produce additional layers.

The best-quality cake pans are made of heavy-gauge aluminum. If square or rectangular, they have sharply angled corners that make a more professional-looking product. Other materials are tinned steel, black steel, stainless steel, and ovenproof glass. Round pans often have removable bottoms.

CHARLOTTE MOLD

Like jelly-roll and bundt pans, this round mold with slightly flared sides gets its name from what is traditionally baked in it. A charlotte is a type of sweet dessert with an outside shell of bread or cake fingers and a center of cooked fruit or chilled cream. The pan is well-suited for making any molded dish: baked entrées, soufflés, and bombes (molded ice cream), for example. The mold is of tinned steel, with heart-shaped handles and a lid. The better ones still come from France. Sizes range from ¾- to 8-cup capacity.

CORN-STICK PAN

Making cornbread in corn-shaped, cast-iron molds adds a homey, country touch. These pans make seven corn sticks and need seasoning so they won't rust. In addition to the traditional ears of corn, molds now come in many designs.

CRUMPET AND ENGLISH MUFFIN RINGS

Crumpets are flat, round, griddle-cooked English yeast breads made in molds because the batter is too liquid to hold its shape. English muffins are similar to crumpets but are made with a stiffer batter, so using rings is optional. The stainless steel, 4-inch by 1-inch rings are packaged in sets of four. If you don't make these breads often enough to warrant the purchase of special equipment, use well-scrubbed tuna fish cans, with tops and bottoms removed.

FLAN FORM

See Tart Pan.

KUGELHOPF PAN

This turban-shaped tube pan is used for *Kugelhopf,* a sweet yeast bread studded with raisins and almonds. It most closely resembles a bundt pan, with swirls and ridges molded into the sides. A 9-inch pan with a 9-cup capacity is standard. Materials used are tinned steel, black steel, aluminum, and ovenproof glass. Some have nonstick interiors. This attractive pan can do alternative service as a mold for layered salads.

LADYFINGER AND LANGUES-DE-CHAT PAN

Strictly speaking, ladyfinger molds have straight sides, and those for making the crisp French cookie known as *langue-de-chat* (cat's tongue) have slightly pinched middles, but they look enough alike to be used interchangeably. The tinned steel trays have 10 molds, each about 3¾ inches tall and about 1 inch wide. Both ladyfingers and langues-de-chat can also be formed without a mold, using a pastry bag and plain tip; directions are usually given in the recipe.

LOAF PAN

Another kitchen essential, loaf pans are multipurpose—for breads, pound and fruit cakes, meat loaves, and pâtés. The standard loaf pan for bread is 5 by 9 by 3 inches. Smaller pans measure 4½ by 8½ by 2½ inches. Miniatures are about 2 inches wide by 4 to 5 inches long. Other pans are longer, or shallower, or narrower, or taller, but whatever their proportions, all are rectangular. They are made of tinned or black steel, aluminum, ovenproof glass, or ceramic. Some have a nonstick interior finish.

Crinkle-Edged Loaf Pan   This rectangular pan with accordion-pleated ends resembles a stretched brioche mold. Several sizes are available.

Pullman Pan   Because it bakes with a lid, this specialty bread pan produces a loaf with a dense texture and thin crust. Used for sandwiches or canapés, it is known as a pullman loaf or *pain de mie.* Long and narrow, this pan usually measures 4½ by 12½ by 4 inches.

MADELEINE PAN

This tinned-steel tray has slightly elongated, shell-shaped molds used to prepare madeleines, the buttery, French sponge cookie-cakes. Full-sized madeleines are 3 inches long; miniature madeleinettes measure 1⅝ inches.

MUFFIN PAN

The standard muffin pan has 6 or 12 cups, each 2¾ inches wide at the top and 1½ inches deep. Large cups produce a product 4 inches in diameter by 2 inches deep. These come in 2-, 4-, and 6-cup trays. Miniatures (also called gems) are bite-sized, a mere 1⅞ inches across by ¾ inch deep. Gem trays have 12 or 24 cups. Buy a muffin pan made of a heavyweight metal of good quality, whether aluminum (coated or uncoated), tinned steel, or cast iron. Muffins and cupcakes will rise higher and bake more evenly if you do.

PANETTONE PAN

Tall and cylindrical with straight sides, this mold is used for an Italian holiday fruited yeast bread. Although not authentic, the bread will taste just as good if baked in a coffee can, charlotte or soufflé mold, or even a tall tube pan. The panettone pan is 7½ inches in diameter, with 4-inch sides.

PIE PAN

American pie pans have sloping sides, in contrast to European tart pans, which have straight sides. As with any bake ware, heavyweight metal pie pans produce a more evenly browned product, but ovenproof glass and ceramic make good, versatile pans as well. Standard sizes are 8, 9, and 10 inches in diameter by 1 inch deep; consider buying one in each size. Deep-dish pans are 1½ to 2 inches tall.

A note on recipe style: Some directions call for pie pans or tins, others for pie plates. Generally, the former are metal, the latter glass or ceramic. Regardless, use what you have as long as it's the correct size.

PIZZA PAN

Pizza is more popular than ever. In addition to the familiar round metal pans, several other choices are available to the home pizza maker.

Deep-Dish Pizza Pan Aficionados of thick Chicago-style pizza can try their hand at home with the same high-sided pan that restaurants use. Made of aluminum or black steel, the round pan measures 15 by 2 inches. Some even come with a metal gripper, for purists the only way to rush the pizza from oven to table. Aluminum pans will darken and season with use, which will improve their heat conductivity and produce an even better crust. Wash black steel and darkened aluminum with warm sudsy water and wipe dry. Don't scrub to remove baked-on food or the seasoning will wear away.

Perforated Pizza Pan As dough bakes, it produces steam. Unless this moisture is drawn away, the crust will be soggy instead of desirably crisp. One solution is to use this aluminum pan pierced with hundreds of holes that allow steam to escape and heat to penetrate crust. The pan does wonders for frozen pizza as well and is dishwasher-safe. It is available in 13-, 14-, and 15-inch rounds; buy the size that fits your oven.

POPOVER PAN

The pan for the American cousin to Yorkshire pudding must absorb heat well. Popover batter needs a quick shot of heat to convert its moisture to steam, which then forces batter to expand into a light, airy bread. Cast iron is the traditional material, but tinned and black steel are good alternatives. Most pans have 6 cups. Popovers can also be made in individual porcelain custard cups (see MOLD).

QUICHE PAN

Although many baking dishes can be used to prepare the savory custard pie known as quiche, the one most associated with it is a fluted, straight-sided ceramic or metal pan with a removable bottom. Quiche pans are usually 10 to 12 inches in diameter by 1½ inches tall. Quiches are often baked in shallower tart pans if they are to be used as a first course. A porcelain dish is an attractive choice if you are serving the quiche in its pan.

RING MOLD

The center hole of this pan is larger than that of a tube pan. It is typically made of aluminum, comes in a range of sizes, and is suitable for breads, cakes, molded rice, and gelatin desserts.

SAVARIN MOLD

A savarin is a sweet, yeast-leavened French cake similar to a baba, but is larger and baked in a shallow ring mold, as opposed to the tumbler-shaped cup used for the baba. After baking, the cake is drenched with liqueur, painted with an apricot glaze, and served with a mound of whipped cream, custard, or fresh fruit placed in the center. The mold, 7 to 10 inches in diameter, is made of tinned steel. As a variation, miniature savarin rings for single servings are also available (see Baba Mold).

SPRINGFORM PAN

Most cheesecake recipes call for this round baking pan with high sides, but it is also used for other dense cakes that need special handling to be unmolded. A clamp releases the sides from the base, ensuring that the cake can be removed intact from the pan. Sizes range from 6 to 12 inches, in half-inch increments. Standard height is 2½ inches, and most are made of tinned steel.

TART PAN

Tarts are baked in shallow, fluted, straight-sided pans that usually have removable bottoms or in bottomless metal bands called flan forms or rings, which are set on baking sheets for support. Tinned or black steel are the most common materials. Round tart pans range from 8 to 12 inches in diameter and are 1 to 2 inches deep. Other sizes include a 14-inch square and an 8- by 12-inch rectangle. Flan forms, which are round, rectangular, or scalloped, come in sizes corresponding to tart pans. Tartlet pans are miniature tart pans; some are shaped like diamonds, ovals, circles, or rectangles, with fluted, rounded bottoms. Boat-shaped tartlet pans are called barquette tins.

TUBE PANS

These cake pans have a center tube that supports delicate batters as they rise in the oven. This design also gives a boost of heat to the core of the cake, which promotes more even baking. Angel food cakes, bundt cakes, and yeast breads such as *Kugelhopf* are baked in tube pans. Most of these pans can hold a large amount of batter, anywhere from 9 to 12 cups. Some have a nonstick interior, although these should also be greased and floured if that step is called for in the recipe.

Recipes and Related Information

Angel Food Cake, 82; Apple Charlotte, 10; Babas au Rhum, 623; Baking Stone and Tile, 24; Cake, 77; Cheesecake, 117; Christmas Panettone, 628; Classic Brioche, 622; Cookie, 139; French Baguettes, 617; Kugelhopf, 628; Ladyfingers, 84; Madeleines, 147; Muffin, 374; Old-Fashioned Buttermilk Corn Sticks, 270; Pie, 431; Pizza, 445; Plump Popovers, 29; Quiche Lorraine, 443; Savarin, 623; Tart, 431; Yeast Bread, 613.

Currant-studded Irish Soda Bread (see page 24) is distinctively marked with a cross-shaped surface. Like all quick breads, it is quickly assembled. Serve it sliced and spread with fresh butter and homemade marmalade.

BAKING POWDER

A chemical leavening agent used for making baked goods, baking powder is a carefully balanced mixture of an acid or acid-reacting salt, or a combination of acid-reacting salts, and sodium bicarbonate. Most baking powders also contain a small amount of dry starch, such as cornstarch, to prevent absorption of moisture. In the presence of moisture or heat, the acid acts upon the alkaline component—sodium bicarbonate—to produce carbon dioxide gas. Single-acting baking powders release gas quickly upon contact with moisture. Double-acting baking powder, the most widely used today, releases a small amount of gas upon contact with moisture but requires heat for full reaction.

Use Baking powder leavens a variety of commercial and home-baked goods. It gives volume and an appetizing texture to cakes, quick breads, muffins, biscuits, pancakes, waffles, crackers, and cookies.

Availability Baking powder is packaged in tins.

Storage Keep in an airtight container in a cool, dry place. Routinely replace old baking powder every three to four months.

Preparation Baking powder is usually sifted with the other dry ingredients of a recipe to disperse it evenly before adding it to a batter. Because baking powder is activated in part by liquid, baking powder batters should be baked immediately after liquid is added.

> ***Recipes and Related Information***
> *Baking Powder Biscuits, 49; Baking Soda, 23;*
> *Leaven, 338.*

BAKING SODA

Also known as sodium bicarbonate or bicarbonate of soda, baking soda is a chemical leavening agent used for a variety of baked goods. In combination with an acid ingredient, such as buttermilk or molasses, it releases carbon dioxide gas and causes expansion of a batter.

Use Because it is an alkaline substance, baking soda is used to neutralize and leaven batters with acid ingredients. It also absorbs odors; an open box in the refrigerator will keep air fresh. A tablespoon of baking soda dissolved in 2 cups warm water is an effective cleanser.

Availability Baking soda is packaged in boxes.

Storage Keep in a cool, dry place.

Preparation If used in excess, baking soda can impart a soapy taste to a finished product. To avoid unpleasant flavors, the rule of thumb is to use no more than 1 teaspoon of soda per cup of acidic liquid. If additional leavening power is needed, it should come from baking powder. This explains why many recipes call for baking powder in addition to baking soda. Baking soda is usually sifted with the other dry ingredients of a recipe to disperse it evenly before adding it to a batter. Because baking soda is activated immediately by liquid, batters leavened only by baking soda should be baked immediately after liquid is added.

■ IRISH SODA BREAD

This currant-studded bread is really a giant biscuit. It is immediately recognizable because of its distinctive cross-shaped surface. This design is formed by marking an *x* on the top of the dough before baking. It makes an inviting breakfast when slathered with butter and marmalade—and also goes well with a main-dish soup. It's as easy to make your own spread as it is to make a quick bread; see page 320 for a recipe for Classic Orange Marmalade.

2¾	cups unbleached flour
¼	cup wheat germ
3	tablespoons sugar
1	teaspoon *each* baking soda and baking powder
½	teaspoon salt
3	tablespoons cold butter or margarine
½	cup dried currants or raisins
1¼	cups buttermilk
2	teaspoons milk

1. Preheat oven to 375° F. In a large bowl stir together flour, wheat germ, sugar, baking soda, baking powder, and salt. Cut in butter until mixture is the consistency of coarse crumbs. Stir in currants.

2. Add buttermilk and stir only enough to moisten dry ingredients.

3. Turn dough out onto a floured surface and knead lightly until it is smooth enough to shape into a flattened ball about 1½ inches high. Place on a greased baking sheet and brush with milk. With a floured knife cut an *x* into top of loaf (cutting from center to within about 1 inch of edge) about ¼ inch deep.

4. Bake until loaf is golden brown (40 to 45 minutes). Test by inserting a wooden skewer in thickest part.

5. Slide loaf onto a wire rack to cool slightly. Cut into thick slices and serve warm or at room temperature.

Makes 1 loaf.

Food Processor Version Use metal blade to process flour, wheat germ, sugar, baking soda, baking powder, salt, butter, and currants (10 seconds). Transfer to bowl and mix in buttermilk as directed.

> ***Recipes and Related Information***
> *Baking Powder, 23; Biscuit, 49; Leaven, 338.*

BAKING STONE AND TILE

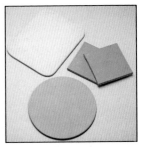

A commercial brick baker's oven produces light, wonderfully crispy breads, cookies, and pizzas because its porous stone floor and side walls absorb moisture from the dough and distribute heat efficiently. To achieve similar results with a home oven, use round or rectangular baking stones made of smooth, unglazed, high-fire stoneware or unglazed, square quarry tiles. The former, also sold as pizza stones, are sold at cookware stores; the latter can be purchased from suppliers of floor tile. Buy enough individual tiles to cover oven rack or floor.

Stones are available in 13- and 15-inch rounds or 12- by 15-inch rectangles. Some are packaged with a stainless steel rack for carrying and serving. Which size should you buy? First of all, the one that fits your oven. Then, the size and shape that accommodate what you bake most often. Round stones are best suited for single pizzas or breads. Up to four small pizzas or several loaves can fit on a rectangular stone at one time, and they needn't be round.

To be effective, stone must preheat with oven, usually at 400° F or higher, on lowest rack. Pizza or loaf is transferred to stone with a wooden paddle (baker's peel). After baking, stone stays in oven to cool. If stone is used frequently, store it on oven rack.

Baking stones are fragile and apt to crack if exposed to sudden changes of temperature. Clean by wiping with a damp cloth, not in the dishwasher, as the porous material will absorb soap or detergent. With use, pale color will darken and stain, a superficial change that in no way affects performance.

> ***Recipes and Related Information***
> *Baker's Peel, 18; Pizza, 445; Yeast Bread, 613.*

BAMBOO SHOOT

The young, spring shoots of the tropical bamboo plant are a popular Asian vegetable. The ivory-colored shoots are conical, usually about 3 inches wide and 4 inches long, and covered with a multilayered brown husk. When harvested they may be sweet, but they quickly become bitter when out of the ground. Lengthy boiling in the husk removes the bitterness. Flavor of the cooked, husked shoot is mild and refreshing; texture is fibrous and crisp.

Use Bamboo shoots add texture and sweetness to Asian soups, stews, and stir-fried dishes. Japanese diners prize fresh bamboo shoots as a first sign of spring.

Availability Water-packed, canned bamboo shoots are available whole or sliced. Occasionally "fresh-cooked" bamboo packed in water in plastic bags is exported to the United States. Sun-dried bamboo shoots are sometimes available in Asian markets.

Storage Once opened, canned bamboo shoots will stay fresh for 1 week to 10 days if stored properly; place in fresh water in a covered container, refrigerate, and change water daily. Store fresh bamboo shoots in water, cover the container, refrigerate, and change water daily. Bamboo shoots may be covered with water and frozen for several months, but they will lose some crispness.

Preparation Rinse canned bamboo shoots well, washing off any grainy white calcium (a residue from commercial processing) caught in the ridges. If a canned flavor persists, blanch briefly in fresh water before using. Fresh-cooked bamboo packed in water should be parboiled 15 minutes.

Recipes and Related Information
Mu Shu Pork, 378; Pork and Cabbage Wontons, 192; Shanghai Spring Rolls, 389.

BANANA

The common yellow banana is generally about 7 to 9 inches long and about 1½ inches in diameter. The red banana is shorter and slightly fatter. When ripe, the flesh is moist, slightly sticky, soft, and sweet. Unripe bananas are hard, rather dry, and starchy.

Use Ripe raw bananas are eaten out of hand, or sliced and used in fruit salads or as a topping for breakfast cereals. Bananas are baked as a dessert or blended with other ingredients to flavor cakes, quick breads, puddings, pies, or ice cream. Use slightly underripe bananas for baking with butter and brown sugar; save overripe bananas for cakes and breads.

Availability Fresh bananas are sold all year.

Selection Choose plump, well-filled fruit with unblemished skin and no signs of decay.

Storage Bananas continue to ripen after harvest. Ripe yellow bananas have a solid yellow skin with brown speckles. Ripe red bananas have dark red skin with black speckles and feel slightly soft. With both varieties, the skin will continue to darken as the banana ages. To ripen bananas further after purchase, store at room temperature. A bright yellow fruit with a green tip will reach ideal ripeness in two to three days. After ripening, bananas may be refrigerated for several days.

Preparation Peel. For use in fruit salads, sprinkle bananas with lemon or lime juice to prevent browning.

■ BANANAS FOSTER

This impressive flaming dessert from New Orleans is simple but must be prepared at the last minute in small batches; do not attempt it for a large dinner party. Flaming desserts are easier to prepare over a gas burner (see the directions in step 2). If you are cooking on an electric burner, heat the rum in a small saucepan until it just begins to boil. Then pour it over the bananas and use a match to ignite it. The liqueur and rum can also be warmed in a microwave oven. Use 100 percent power and heat 30 to 45 seconds.

> 2 tablespoons unsalted butter
> 2 tablespoons light or dark brown sugar
>   Pinch ground cinnamon
>   Pinch freshly grated nutmeg
> 2 small, firm bananas, cut in half lengthwise
> ¼ cup Drambuie liqueur
> ¼ cup dark rum
> 2 scoops vanilla ice cream

1. In a 10-inch omelet or saute pan over medium heat, melt butter. Add sugar, cinnamon, and nutmeg; mix well. Add bananas and sauté until they begin to soften (about 1 minute on each side).

2. Pour in liqueur and rum. Turn up heat and tilt pan to ignite liquor. Shake pan slightly to prolong flames. When flames burn out, place 2 banana halves on each serving plate. Place a scoop of ice cream between the banana halves and spoon the sauce over all.

Serves 2.

Recipes and Related Information
Banana Cream Pie, 440; Banana Split, 311; Toasted Coconut-Banana Bread, 491.

BARD, TO

To cover meats, poultry, or fish with thin slices of fat—usually bacon or pork fat—before cooking (see photograph, page 593). This technique developed as a way of keeping faster-cooking, lean parts moist and juicy until fattier areas are done, or to keep roasts with little internal fat moist. For example, the breast meat of chicken or turkey is lower in fat than the dark meat of the legs or thighs and thus is finished sooner. Barding the breast will keep it from drying out before the bird is fully cooked. Veal is another meat that also benefits from barding or the application of another type of baste.

Barding and larding are similar techniques in that they both use applied fat to maintain or add moisture; they differ in where the basting fat is placed. Barding adds surface fat. Larding bastes by inserting strips of fat into the meat's interior mass (see LARD).

Bananas Foster makes an impressive grand finale to any meal. The bananas may be cut in chunks, as shown here, or halved, as in the recipe at left. Other fruits, such as fresh peaches, pears, or papayas, can be substituted for the bananas; you can also pour the delicious sauce over angel food cake.

Beef Soup au Pistou gets its name from the pungent paste of puréed basil and garlic that is stirred into the soup just before the tureen is brought to the table.

BASIL

A native of India, basil is cultivated as an annual culinary herb in temperate climates. Its soft green leaves are intensely aromatic, with a pungent, licoricelike flavor.

Use Fresh basil flatters tomato salads and sauces. It is the principal ingredient in Italian pesto and French *pistou,* which are used as a pasta sauce and soup garnish respectively. Fresh basil leaves enhance mixed green salads, pasta and pizza, Mediterranean squash and eggplant salads and cooked dishes, vegetable soups, egg dishes, veal, lamb, fish, and chicken. To substitute dried basil for fresh, see HERB.

Availability Fresh commercial garden basil is most plentiful in summer. Fresh hothouse basil is available all year. Dried basil is packed in airtight jars or tins.

Selection Choose fresh, aromatic bunches that aren't limp and don't show signs of decay. Packaged seasonings lose quality after a while; try to buy from a store that restocks its spice section fairly often.

Storage Fresh basil will last three or four days if wrapped first in damp paper towels, then in plastic wrap, and refrigerated. To freeze fresh basil, snip leaves finely and freeze in plastic bags. To dry fresh basil, hang bunches upside down in a warm, dry place. Store dried basil in a cool, dark place in an airtight container. Replace every six months.

Preparation Wash leaves and dry thoroughly. Use whole or mince. Leaves cut with a knife discolor quickly; use only in cooked dishes. For uncooked dishes, tear leaves by hand.

■ BEEF SOUP AU PISTOU
This traditional French soup is usually made without meat, but ground beef makes it even better. The word *pistou* refers to the pestolike paste of basil and garlic that flavors the soup.

> 2 tablespoons olive oil
> 1½ pounds lean ground beef, crumbled
> 1 large onion, thinly slivered
> 1 clove garlic, minced
> 1 large can (28 oz) tomatoes, coarsely chopped; reserve liquid
> 3½ cups Beef Stock (see page 560) *or* 2 cans (14½ oz each) regular-strength beef broth
> 2 cups water
> 2 teaspoons salt
> ¼ teaspoon freshly ground pepper
> 2 medium potatoes (about 1 lb), cut in ½-inch cubes
> 1 pound green beans, cut in 1-inch pieces
> ¼ pound vermicelli, broken in half
> ½ cup finely grated Gruyère or Swiss cheese
> Grated Gruyère or Swiss cheese, for garnish

Pistou

> ¼ cup olive oil
> 3 cloves garlic, minced
> ½ cup loosely packed, fresh basil leaves *or* 2 tablespoons dried basil and ½ cup loosely packed, chopped parsley
> ¼ teaspoon *each* salt and sugar
> 1 tablespoon red wine vinegar

1. In a 5- to 6-quart kettle, heat oil. Add ground beef and cook over medium heat, stirring often. As meat begins to brown, stir in onion and continue cooking until onion is soft. Stir in garlic. Add tomatoes and their liquid, broth, the water, salt, pepper, and potatoes.

2. Bring to a boil, cover, reduce heat, and simmer for 1 hour. Meanwhile cook green beans uncovered in a large quantity of boiling, salted water until they are tender-crisp (6 to 8 minutes). Drain and rinse immediately with cold water to stop cooking; drain and set aside.

3. After soup has cooked for 1 hour, add vermicelli and boil gently, uncovered, stirring occasionally, until pasta is just tender (10 to 12 minutes). Add green beans and cook just until beans are heated through.

4. Add the ½ cup Gruyère cheese, about 2 tablespoons at a time, stirring after each addition until cheese melts.

5. Place Pistou in a warm tureen, add soup, and stir until soup and Pistou are well blended. Serve at once, garnishing each serving with additional grated cheese to taste.

Makes about 16 cups, 6 to 8 servings.

Pistou   In blender or food processor, combine olive oil, garlic, basil, salt, sugar, and vinegar. Whirl until smooth.

Makes about ⅓ cup.

◼ PESTO

A summer sauce, pesto is made when basil is abundant and inexpensive. Its pungent aroma is unforgettable, whether it's tossed with hot linguine or stirred into steaming minestrone. For Genoese sailors long at sea, a fragrant *pasta al pesto* is the traditional welcome home.

> 2 **cups loosely packed, fresh basil leaves,**
> ½ **cup light olive oil**
> 2 **tablespoons pine nuts, toasted**
> 4 **large cloves garlic, minced**
> 1 **teaspoon coarse salt**
> ½ **cup freshly grated Parmesan cheese**
> 2 **tablespoons freshly grated Pecorino Romano cheese**
> 3 **tablespoons unsalted butter, softened**

Put basil, olive oil, pine nuts, garlic, and salt in a blender or food processor. Blend or process until smooth. Transfer to a bowl and stir in Parmesan, Pecorino Romano, and butter.

Makes 1 cup.

Make-Ahead Tip   Pesto may be made up to 1 week ahead, covered with a thin film of olive oil, and refrigerated in an airtight container. Pesto may be frozen for up to 1 month, covered with a thin film of olive oil; if you plan to freeze it, make pesto without garlic and stir in minced garlic just before using. It is also possible to freeze pesto in ice-cube trays; each cube will provide sauce for 1 portion of pasta. In this case, wait to incorporate Parmesan, butter, and garlic until you are ready to serve it.

Recipes and Related Information
Northern-Style Tomato Sauce, 412; Osso Buco, 58;
Pizza Margherita, 446; Tomatoes With Mozzarella
and Basil, 507.

BASTE, TO

This term, usually associated with meats and poultry, means to brush on or pour liquid over foods while they are cooking to keep them moist and flavorful and to develop an attractive finish. Usually the basting liquid is a combination of pan drippings and fat. Seasonings or other ingredients may be added to enhance taste.

Recipes and Related Information
Bulb Baster, 67; Cake and Pastry Tools, 89.

BATTER

A batter is a mixture of flour and a liquid, such as milk, beer, or wine, plus eggs and other leavening or flavoring ingredients. The proportion of flour to liquid determines the thickness and end use of the batter, although by definition all batters must be thin enough to pour or drop from a spoon. Pourable batters, which have an equal amount of flour and liquid, are used for pancakes, popovers, and cakes. Thicker drop batters contain twice as much flour as liquid and are the basis for muffins, drop biscuits, fritters, and coatings for fried foods.

Batter coatings act as a puffy, protective barrier between oil and food. Coatings also improve the taste, appearance, and texture of fried foods. Quick-cooking foods that can hold their shape, such as fish, boned poultry, vegetables, and fruits, give the best results when dipped in batter and fried. *Frittered, French-fried,* and *batter-fried* are all terms used for batter-coated foods.

Batters have a wonderful flavor, but are not as convenient a coating for fried foods as a simple dip in flour or crumbs. It is a messy process, and one that allows little time between setup and cooking—once a food has been dipped in the batter, it must be fried at once, or batter will slide off. Although batter-coated foods cook quickly, preparation takes time. Most batters should rest at least 30 minutes to 1 hour before use to allow flour to blend completely with liquid, to give leavening a chance to activate, and to allow gluten to relax. But, this isn't always necessary, and usually a recipe will guide you. Remember to dry food thoroughly before coating or batter won't adhere. Dusting with flour (or confectioners' sugar in the case of fruit) is often recommended as a first step. Flour dries the surface of the food and gives the batter something to cling to.

For all batters, be sure the oven or frying fat is heated to the proper temperature. Deep-fried batter-coated foods cook at approximately 365° F. Test temperature with a deep-fat thermometer (see THERMOMETER); another test is to drop a cube of bread in the hot fat and slowly count to 60. The fat is ready to use if the bread is golden brown. For more information about cooking oils and frying, see DEEP-FRY and FRY.

Basting adds moisture and flavor to food. The best basting brushes are made of natural boar bristles. Make sure the bristles are securely attached to the handle.

■ FLAGEOLETS WITH HERBS

Small, pale green flageolets are used frequently in French cuisine, particularly as a flavorful accompaniment to roast leg of lamb. Note that the beans must soak overnight, or quick-soak 1 hour (see Preparation).

   2 cups (about 1 lb) dried flageolets or
      small navy beans
10 cups water
   1 bay leaf
   4 carrots, sliced
   1 onion, sliced
   2 cloves garlic, quartered
  1½ teaspoons dried rosemary
   1 teaspoon dried thyme
   2 tablespoons olive oil
   2 cups Beef Stock (see page 560)
   2 teaspoons salt
   1 teaspoon freshly ground pepper

1. Soak beans as directed on page 30, using 6 cups water. Add the remaining water, bay leaf, carrots, onion, garlic, rosemary, thyme, and oil.

2. Increase heat, and boil 10 minutes; reduce heat, and simmer 1½ hours; drain. Add stock, salt, and pepper, and continue cooking 30 minutes.

Serves 8 to 10.

GREAT NORTHERN BEAN

The Great Northern is a large white shell bean with a mild flavor. Dried Great Northern beans are packaged in plastic bags or sold in bulk. Use within a year of purchase. Cooked Great Northern beans are also available in cans and jars. Use in soups, stews, baked bean dishes, and salads.

GREEN BEAN

See Snap Bean.

HARICOT VERT

The haricot vert is an exceptionally slender, stringless green bean. Although long popular in France, this sweet, tender bean has only recently been commercialized in America. Now specialty markets generally have fresh haricots verts from July through September. Choose firm pods, ⅛ inch or less in diameter, with solid green color. To prepare, remove stem ends. Store beans in a perforated plastic bag in the refrigerator crisper; use within one or two days of purchase. Steam briefly, then sauté in butter or oil, and serve hot, or dress steamed beans with vinaigrette and serve at room temperature or chilled.

ITALIAN ROMANO (GREEN) BEAN

See Snap Bean.

KIDNEY BEAN

The kidney bean is the kidney-shaped seed of a common shell bean. Both red and white varieties exist, although the white kidney bean is more commonly called a *cannellini* bean. Dried red and white kidney beans are packaged in plastic bags or sold in bulk; use within a year of purchase. Canned kidney beans are widely available. The meaty flavor and mealy texture are appealing in soups, stews, chili, and salads.

■ RED BEANS AND RICE

This is the traditional Monday-night dinner of New Orleans. The custom probably began because folks had spent all their money on the weekend and needed a cheap but substantial way to feed themselves. Although it is an inexpensive meal, it does not lack in flavor and appetite appeal, and it makes an ideal dish for informally entertaining a large group. Note that the beans first have to soak overnight, and then when cooked should be refrigerated at least overnight.

   1 pound dried red beans
   4 quarts water
   2 meaty ham hocks
   8 cups Beef Stock (see page 560) or
      Chicken Stock (see page 560)
   4 bay leaves
  ½ teaspoon thyme
   1 teaspoon cayenne pepper
   1 teaspoon freshly ground pepper
   1 pound andouille (sausage)
  ¼ pound tasso (sausage), chopped (optional)
   2 cups chopped onion
  ½ cup chopped celery
   1 green bell pepper, chopped
   1 bunch green onions, chopped
   1 tablespoon minced garlic
   8 chaurice sausages (approximately 2 lb) or
      other fresh, hot sausages
      Salt and freshly ground pepper, to taste
      Red wine vinegar, to taste (optional)
   4 cups cooked rice
      Hot-pepper sauce, to taste

1. Wash beans and soak overnight in the water. The next day drain beans and wash well under cold running water. Place beans, ham hocks, and stock in a heavy, 6- to 8-quart stockpot or Dutch oven. Beans should be covered by about 2 to 3 inches of liquid; add more if necessary. Bring to a boil and skim any scum that collects on the surface. Reduce heat to simmer and add bay leaves, thyme, cayenne, and pepper. Simmer for 30 minutes while you prepare vegetables.

2. Chop ¼ pound of the *andouille* into ¼-inch pieces. Place in a 12-inch cast-iron frying pan (or other heavy frying pan) with *tasso* (if used). Fry for 5 minutes to render fat and brown meat. Add chopped onion and celery and cook until vegetables are soft (about 10 minutes). Add bell pepper, green onions, and garlic. Cook an additional 5 minutes, then add to simmering pot of red beans. Continue to cook beans until they are soft and some begin to break apart (about 1 hour). Allow beans to cool; refrigerate, covered, overnight or for up to 4 days.

3. When ready to serve, bring beans to a simmer. Place *chaurice* whole in a heavy frying pan, cover, and fry over medium heat for about 15 minutes, checking sausages frequently and turning them as they brown. Meanwhile, slice remaining andouille into ¼-inch slices and add to beans. Cook in beans for about 10 minutes. Taste beans for salt and pepper and correct if necessary; add a little vinegar (if desired). To serve, place about ½ cup hot rice in center of each plate, spoon beans over rice, and accompany with 1 chaurice. Serve with hot-pepper sauce.

Serves 8.

Food Processor Version Use metal blade to process vegetables, one after the other. Cut 2 large onions into eighths, put in work bowl, and turn motor on and off 3 to 4 times. Cut 1 stalk celery into 1-inch chunks and process same way. Cut bell pepper into 1-inch pieces and process same way. Cut green onions into 1-inch pieces and process 5 to 10 seconds.

LENTIL

The flat, disklike seeds of a leguminous plant, lentils are native to Asia Minor. Today lentils are marketed only dried, either packed in plastic bags or boxes or sold in bulk. Lentils are available in several different colors, including yellow, pink, and greenish brown. Store all varieties in a cool, dry place and use within a year.

Add lentils to soups and stews; boil until tender, drain, and dress with vinaigrette for a cool salad; or boil until tender, drain, and reheat with oil, butter, or bacon fat for a side dish.

LIMA BEAN

Also known as butter bean, the lima bean is a relatively large, kidney-shaped, light-green bean in an inedible green pod. Limas are occasionally available fresh in summer; choose solid-green, pliable pods without evidence of drying. To prepare, pull on string to open pod and remove beans. Limas are also available canned, frozen, and dried; dried limas are packed in plastic bags or sold in bulk. Store fresh limas in a plastic bag in refrigerator crisper; use quickly. Use dried limas within a year of purchase.

Add limas to soups and stews; boil until tender, drain and dress with butter or oil, and serve hot; or boil until tender, drain and dress with vinaigrette, and serve at room temperature or chilled as a salad.

The classic Monday-night dinner of New Orleans, Red Beans and Rice, is embellished with Louisiana sausages and smoked meats. The hot sausage here, called chaurice, is flavored with fresh onions, parsley, and chiles and lightly smoked. Also pictured is tasso, a Cajun seasoning meat, which is more spicy and smoky than ham. If tasso is unavailable, you can use a smoked ham.

■ SUCCOTASH

The name succotash derives from an Indian word, *m'sickquatash,* meaning corn not crushed or ground. Colonists learned from Native Americans the land-saving practice of planting corn and beans together, then training the bean vines up the corn stalks. At the harvest they simply combined the two in cooking. Today we usually make succotash with corn and lima beans, but many New England cooks prefer cranberry beans, and the Pennsylvania Dutch often add green bell peppers, tomatoes, and other vegetables. Some early recipes also called for fowl or meat plus potatoes or turnips, thus making more of a stew. This modern recipe is simple, colorful, and delicious, and it is very good made with frozen vegetables.

  ¼ **cup butter**
  2 **cups fresh corn kernels or frozen corn kernels, thawed**
  2 **cups cooked lima beans**
  ¼ **teaspoon salt**
  ¼ **teaspoon freshly ground pepper**
  ½ **cup whipping cream**
  2 **tablespoons chopped parsley**

1. In a medium saucepan over medium heat, melt butter. Add corn, beans, salt, and pepper; stir to combine.

2. Add cream and simmer gently, uncovered, for about 5 minutes.

3. Stir in parsley and serve.

Serves 6.

"Never saw a man so tired he couldn't eat some beans," said the old prospector in Treasure of Sierra Madre. *Probably he was thinking of that southwestern indispensable, Frijoles, shown here, and its variation, Refried Beans.*

MUNG BEAN

The small cylindrical seed of a leguminous plant, the mung bean is most commonly green, but brown and black varieties exist. When shelled and split in half, the green mung bean yields a rectangular yellow bean called the split golden gram or *moong dal*. Both mung beans and split golden gram are highly valued by Indian cooks as a source of protein. Sprouted mung beans, an even finer source of protein, are used frequently in Asian cooking.

Fresh mung bean sprouts are widely available all year. Select firm white sprouts without brown areas. Refrigerate in a plastic bag and use immediately. If not using right away, blanch bean sprouts in boiling water for 30 seconds, then transfer to ice water. Refrigerate, covered with water, and change water daily. Blanched bean sprouts will stay fresh for five or six days. Mung bean sprouts are also available canned; rinse under cold water before using. Dried mung beans are packaged in plastic bags or sold in bulk. Use within a year of purchase.

Use whole mung beans in soups, stews, and pilafs. Mung bean sprouts add texture to salads, stir-fries, and omelets. Mung bean starch is the basis for the transparent "cellophane" noodles used by Chinese cooks. Indian cooks use mung bean flour for breads and sweets.

NAVY BEAN

The navy bean is a small, oval, white bean so named because it has long been a staple of the diet of the U.S. Navy. Dried navy beans are packaged in plastic bags or sold in bulk. Use within a year of purchase. Navy beans are also widely available canned; they are the variety used for most canned and home-cooked versions of pork and beans or baked beans. Use navy beans in soups, stews, and salads.

■ BOSTON BAKED BEANS

In colonial times, it was customary to begin cooking baked beans early Saturday, so they would simmer quietly all day and evening and be ready for an effortless Saturday supper, Sunday breakfast, or noontime dinner. Today, beans are no longer considered strictly Sabbath food (although they still take all day to cook). If you wish, add a little catsup to the recipe; it's not traditional, but it adds color and tang. Otherwise, pass catsup at the table.

> 2 cups (1 lb) dried navy beans
> 1½ teaspoons salt
> 3 tablespoons *each* molasses and brown sugar
> 1 tablespoon dry mustard
> ¼ cup catsup (optional)
> 1 onion, peeled and left whole
> ¼ pound salt pork

1. Pick over beans to remove pebbles or bits of dirt, then rinse well in a colander. Place in a large pan, add 1 teaspoon salt and enough water to cover beans by about 3 inches. Bring to a rolling boil over high heat, and boil for 2 minutes. Remove from heat, cover pan, and let stand 1 hour.

2. Uncover pan, bring back to a boil, reduce heat, and simmer until beans are tender (1 to 1½ hours). Add more water if necessary to keep beans well covered.

3. Drain well, reserving liquid. In a bean pot or casserole of about 2½-quart capacity, combine molasses, brown sugar, mustard, catsup (if desired), and ½ teaspoon salt. Add drained beans, and stir in enough reserved cooking liquid to cover beans; mix well. Push whole onion down one side of beans. Cut several gashes in salt pork and bury it on the other side.

4. Cover pot, place in oven, and turn heat to 350° F. Bake until beans are bubbling (about 1 hour). Reduce heat to 250° F and bake for 6 to 8 hours more, stirring every hour or so. As beans cook, they will absorb liquid; continue adding reserved cooking liquid (or water), a little at a time, to keep them moist but not soupy. Baked beans are done when thick, fragrant, and a deep brownish red. They can remain in a 200° F oven for 1 or 2 hours longer if you wish; just remember to add liquid occasionally so they do not dry out. Beans also reheat well the next day. Remove and discard onion before serving. Serve with sliced salt pork if you wish.

Serves 4 to 6.

B

Te
co
be
tou
be

pr
br
re
ch
the
En

alt
Cr
co

W
Q
Di
on
m
fla
So
fla
le
so

ity
an
ca
to

ity
ca
hu
be
in
the
me
be

V
Tl
an
on

th
ha
to
wl
ri

PINTO BEAN

The pinto bean is the mottled oval seed of a common shell bean. Dried pinto beans are sold in plastic bags or in bulk; use within a year of purchase. Canned pinto beans are also widely available. Pinto beans appear in many southwestern and Mexican soups, stews, and chilis.

▨ FRIJOLES

Homemade beans do taste better than beans from a can. Note that the beans have to soak overnight, or quick-soak 1 hour (see Preparation).

  1 pound dry pinto beans
16 cups cold water
  1 large onion, coarsely chopped (about 1½ cups)
  1 tablespoon (about 2 cloves) minced garlic
  ¼ teaspoon red pepper flakes
  1 medium onion, finely chopped (about 1 cup)
  3 tablespoons bacon fat or lard
  1 large tomato, peeled, seeded, and
    coarsely chopped (about 1 cup)
    Salt and freshly ground pepper, to taste

1. Soak beans overnight in 8 cups of the cold water.

2. Drain and add 8 cups fresh water, the coarsely chopped onion, garlic, and red pepper. Bring to a boil, lower heat, cover, and simmer until beans are tender (about 90 minutes).

3. In a medium skillet over moderate heat, sauté finely chopped onion in bacon fat until wilted; add tomato and sauté until soft. Place ½ cup drained beans in small bowl and mash well with a fork. Add mashed beans to skillet along with a little of their liquid (about ¼ cup); stir over low heat until a thick paste.

4. Spoon contents of skillet into bean pot. Simmer, stirring frequently, until liquid thickens (about 30 minutes). Season to taste with salt and pepper.

Serves 6 to 8.

Texas Jalapeño Pinto Beans Complete steps 1 through 3. Spoon contents of skillet into bean pot and add canned or pickled jalapeño chiles to taste—up to an entire 4-ounce can for a very, very spicy dish. Continue with step 4.

Refried Beans Complete steps 1 and 2. Drain cooked beans, reserving liquid. Mash well with a fork or a potato masher (not a food processor). In a large, heavy skillet, heat 3 tablespoons of rendered bacon fat with 4 tablespoons of lard until aromatic and almost smoking. Very carefully add mashed beans (they will spatter) and lower heat. Cook over medium-low heat, stirring frequently, until fat is absorbed. Thin to desired consistency with some of the reserved cooking liquid, stirring it in by tablespoons. Add ¼ pound Monterey jack cheese, coarsely grated, and cook about 15 minutes longer, until cheese is completely absorbed. Season with salt and pepper.

RUNNER BEAN

Also known as the scarlet runner bean, the runner bean has a flat, broad, green pod and small scarlet seeds. The edible blossom may be red or white. The runner bean is available fresh in summer and fall. Choose firm pods that have solid color, do not show signs of drying, and have beans that are not too pronounced. Steam and serve hot, with butter or oil, or cold with vinaigrette. Add to vegetable soups or mixed vegetable salads. To prepare, cut along each side of bean to remove strings and ridges. Slice across pod on the diagonal between each seed.

SNAP BEAN

Immature *Phaseolus vulgaris*, at the stage when entire pod is edible, is called snap bean. Snap beans include the common green or string bean, the Italian Romano bean, the yellow wax bean, and the purple-podded bean. Snap beans are available fresh, frozen, and canned. Some fresh varieties are available the year around, but the supply peaks in summer. Choose fresh snap beans that are firm, with smooth pods, and do not show signs of browning or drying. To prepare for cooking, remove strings and brown tips (see GADGETS, Bean Slicer). Snap beans may be steamed, braised, sautéed, stir-fried, or pickled. Serve hot, with butter or oil, or cold as a salad. They may be added to soups or hot, mixed vegetable combinations.

SOYBEAN

Fresh soybean pods are dark green with a soft outer fuzz; inside are two or four small oval beans. Soybeans can be yellow, green, brown, black, or mottled. When cooked their texture is firm, their flavor mild.

Because of their high protein content, soybeans are a valuable food source. They are made into a wide variety of products, from bean curd (tofu) to soy milk to soy sauce to soy flour.

Shell and boil fresh soybeans as you would English peas, or substitute soybeans for lima beans or fava beans in recipes that have a comparable flavor and texture. Dried soybeans can be sprouted for use in salads, stir-fries, and sandwiches, or boiled and served hot as a side dish. The salted black beans widely used in Chinese cooking are soft black soybeans that have been cooked, inoculated with a mold, and brined for about six months. Salted black beans are used to flavor steamed fish, pork ribs, clams, and many other dishes.

Fresh soybeans are available occasionally in Japanese markets and specialty markets in summer and fall; dried soybeans can be bought in bulk at Asian markets and health-food stores. Salted black beans are sold in Chinese markets in cans or small bags usually labeled "salted black beans." Do not confuse them with the uncooked variety, which is sold in similar packages.

Choose firm, well-filled soybean pods, without brown edges or spots.

Beets with their greens and young turnips make a distinctive winter salad. Serve as a first course before a hearty roast.

with a slotted spoon to a bowl of ice water. Drain and pat thoroughly dry. Boil stems 1 minute in same water; transfer to ice water and, when cool, drain and dry them. Coarsely chop both beet greens and stems.

3. In a large bowl, combine lemon juice, vinegar, mustard, and anchovy paste. Whisk in the ½ cup olive oil. Stir in 1 tablespoon of the Parmesan. Add beet greens and stems and marinate 15 minutes.

4. Bring another large pot of salted water to a boil. Wash turnips, then boil until tender. Very small turnips may take only 10 minutes, larger turnips up to 45 minutes. Drain and dry. While still warm, peel turnips, slice into rounds, then into thin matchsticks. Very small turnips may be left whole or halved.

5. Add beets, turnips, and remaining 2 tablespoons oil to marinating beet greens; let marinate 20 minutes. Add salt and pepper to taste. Line a serving platter with green-leaf and romaine leaves. Top with salad. Combine remaining Parmesan and parsley and sprinkle over salad.

Serves 4.

Recipes and Related Information
Budapest Borscht, 76; Red-Flannel Hash, 45.

BELGIAN ENDIVE

Also known as French endive, or Belgian or witloof chicory, Belgian endive is the blanched shoots of a chicory root. To produce blanched (white) shoots, the roots are dug up and removed to a cool, darkened location or to forcing beds where they are covered with sand. The resulting shoots, harvested when 4 to 6 inches long and about 1½ inches wide, are made of compact, tightly furled, white leaves shading to yellow or light green tips.

Use   Belgian endive is eaten raw as a salad green or is braised in butter or cream sauce as a vegetable side dish. Braised with ham slices and cream sauce, it is a main course. Belgian endive leaves are perfect edible containers for cheese spreads or all kinds of hors d'oeuvres.

Availability   Fresh Belgian endive is sold in late fall and winter.

Selection   Choose bright white Belgian endive heads that are firm and unblemished.

Storage   Keep endive in a plastic bag in the refrigerator. Use within three or four days.

Preparation   Cut away bitter core with a knife. Rinse with cold running water. To braise, cook heads whole in butter in a covered pot, adding lemon juice to prevent discoloration. For salads, use raw leaves whole or cut into rings or strips.

Cooking   See BOIL, BRAISE.

■ WINTER SALAD OF BEETS AND TURNIPS

Beet greens are mixed with beets and turnips for a hearty first course. Note that beets must bake for 1½ hours.

> 3 or 4 medium beets with greens attached
> 7 or 8 small turnips
> 2 tablespoons *each* fresh lemon juice and red wine vinegar
> 1 tablespoon Dijon mustard
> ½ tablespoon anchovy paste
> ½ cup plus 2 tablespoons olive oil
> 3 tablespoons freshly grated Parmesan cheese
> Salt and freshly ground pepper, to taste
> ½ head *each* green-leaf and romaine lettuce, washed and dried
> 2 tablespoons minced parsley

1. Preheat oven to 375° F. Remove beet greens and stems and set aside. Wash beets and put them in an ovenproof bowl or baking dish. Add water to come halfway up sides of beets, then cover tightly with a lid or aluminum foil and bake until beets can be easily pierced with a knife (about 1½ hours). Remove from oven and let cool. While beets are still warm, peel them and slice into rounds, then into thin matchsticks.

2. Wash beet stems and greens, then separate stems from greens. Bring a large pot of salted water to a boil and blanch greens for 30 seconds. Transfer greens

BRAISED BELGIAN ENDIVE

Small heads of lettuce can also be braised.

    8 small Belgian endives
    3 tablespoons unsalted butter
    ½ cup Chicken Stock (see page 560)
       Juice of 1 lemon
    2 tablespoons parsley, minced
       Pinch sugar

1. Trim dry ends from endive. Remove any brown or shriveled leaves. In a heavy-bottomed, 10-inch skillet, place endives, butter, stock, lemon juice, parsley, and sugar.

2. Simmer over medium heat 8 minutes; turn and simmer 7 minutes more. Endive will be tender when pierced with a knife.

Serves 4.

BIND, TO

To cause ingredients to thicken and form a cohesive mass by adding another ingredient, called the binding agent. For example, Hollandaise sauce and mayonnaise are bound by egg yolks, puddings by tapioca, Bavarian cream by gelatin, some cream soups by potato, and many sauces, soups, and stews by flour, cornstarch, crackers, or bread crumbs.

BISCUIT

A biscuit is a quick bread made with a soft dough (3 parts flour to 1 part liquid), rather than the fairly moist batter used for quick loaf breads and muffins.

The ideal biscuit is uniform in shape, with straight sides and a level top, and has doubled its height during baking. The crust is crisp, tender, and golden brown, with lighter sides. The crumb is generally creamy white and fine grained, and pulls off in flaky sheets.

When shaping biscuits, use a floured, sharp-edged cutter or knife and cut by pressing downward. A dull edge will pinch top and bottom together, and the biscuits won't rise properly. Twisting the cutter produces lopsided biscuits.

Drop biscuit dough, too sticky to roll, is spooned directly onto an ungreased baking sheet. For dumplings, dough is dropped into boiling water or stock, or on a simmering stew, and gently steamed. Deep-dish fruit cobblers use either rolled or dropped biscuit dough for a top crust.

Biscuits are at their best served hot from the oven. If they must be reheated, wrap them in aluminum foil and heat in a 350° F oven for 10 minutes. To freeze, let cool and protect with freezer wrap, or tray-freeze: Set biscuits on a baking sheet, freeze just until firm, then package in plastic freezer bags labeled with the date. Frozen biscuits will keep for two to three months. Thaw in wrapping at room temperature; if wrapped in aluminum foil, place in a low oven.

BAKING POWDER BISCUITS

Although biscuits are traditionally shaped with a round biscuit cutter, the dough can also be cut with a knife into squares, rectangles, or diamonds. Whichever tool you use, flour the cutting edge so the dough will release easier.

    2 cups flour
    4 teaspoons baking powder
    ½ to 1 teaspoon salt, to taste
    6 tablespoons solid vegetable shortening
    ¾ cup milk
       Flour or beaten egg, for topping (optional)

1. Preheat oven to 425° F. Butter and flour a baking sheet or line with baking parchment.

2. Mix flour, baking powder, and salt; then sift into a medium bowl. With a pastry blender or with fingertips, cut vegetable shortening into dry ingredients until mixture is the consistency of fine crumbs. Pour in milk all at once and stir to mix. As soon as mixture holds together, turn out onto a floured work surface and knead lightly.

3. Roll or pat dough to a thickness of ½ to ¾ inch (depending on use); cut into 2½-inch rounds with a floured cutter.

4. For crustier biscuits place rounds about 1 inch apart on prepared baking sheet. For softer sides set touching or ¼ inch apart. Finish with a dusting of flour (for a soft surface) or brush with a beaten egg for a shiny surface. Bake until golden brown (12 to 15 minutes). Biscuits are best served hot from the oven.

Makes about 16 biscuits.

Drop Biscuits   Prepare as for Baking Powder Biscuits with these changes: Increase shortening to ½ cup and milk to 1 cup. For pebbly biscuits, scoop out a tablespoon (or more) of dough with a floured spoon, drop batter onto a baking sheet, leaving a few inches between each biscuit, and dust each with flour. For a smoother surface, scoop out batter with floured hands, roll lightly between hands to the size and shape of an egg, dip all sides in flour, and place on baking sheet; do not crowd. Bake until puffed and golden brown (10 to 12 minutes).

Cheese Biscuits   Add 1 teaspoon dry mustard to dry ingredients. After fat has been cut in, add ½ cup grated Cheddar or Swiss cheese and ¼ cup freshly grated Parmesan cheese and combine.

Herb Biscuits   Add 1½ teaspoons crushed dried dill or other herb and 1 teaspoon freshly ground pepper to dry ingredients.

TIPS

MIXING BISCUIT DOUGH

When mixing the dough be gentle and work quickly, or the biscuits will be tough. On the other hand, don't undermix the dough. Kneading further distributes the leaven and develops the gluten in the flour just enough to support the biscuit as it rises. Undermanipulated biscuits are squatty and will have yellow spots in the crumb and brown spots on the crust—the result of undissolved or poorly distributed leaven. With experience you will sense when the dough is ready.

■ CREAM BISCUITS

Using cream instead of milk will produce a richer biscuit. A topping of flour makes a soft crust, cream a browner one.

    2 cups flour
    1 tablespoon baking powder
    ½ teaspoon baking soda
    1 tablespoon sugar
    1 teaspoon salt
    2 tablespoons butter
    1¼ cups whipping cream
       Flour or whipping cream, for topping

1. Follow instructions for Baking Powder Biscuits (see page 49).

2. Brush lightly with flour or whipping cream and bake until golden brown (12 to 15 minutes).

Makes about 16 biscuits.

■ BUTTERMILK BISCUITS

These biscuits have a slightly tangy flavor and tender crumb because of the buttermilk. To create carbon dioxide, the gas that makes biscuits rise, the acid in the buttermilk must be balanced with an alkali, usually baking soda.

    2 cups flour
    2 teaspoons baking powder
    ½ teaspoon baking soda
    ½ teaspoon salt
    1 tablespoon sugar
    6 tablespoons unsalted butter
    ⅔ cup buttermilk
       Flour or buttermilk, for topping

1. Follow instructions for Baking Powder Biscuits (see page 49).

2. Brush lightly with flour or buttermilk and bake until golden brown (10 to 12 minutes).

Makes about 16 biscuits.

Orange Buttermilk Biscuits Increase baking powder to 1 teaspoon and sugar to ¼ cup. Reduce buttermilk to ½ cup; combine with ¼ cup fresh orange juice and grated rind of 2 oranges; add to fat-flour mixture as directed.

■ BERRY SHORTCAKE

Strawberries are traditional, but a mixture of fresh berries is also wonderful for this classic American dessert.

Shortcake

    2 cups flour
    1 tablespoon baking powder
    ½ teaspoon salt
    3 tablespoons sugar
    6 tablespoons butter
    ¾ cup whipping cream
       Cream, for brushed topping

Filling

    2 pints strawberries, hulled and sliced
    2 cups whipped cream, flavored with sugar,
       to taste, and 1 teaspoon vanilla extract

1. *For the shortcake:* Follow instructions for Baking Powder Biscuits (see page 49). Brush with cream and bake until golden brown (about 12 minutes).

2. To serve, split a biscuit in half horizontally. Place the bottom on an individual serving plate. Spoon on whipped cream and prepared fruit. Cover with biscuit top. Repeat with remaining biscuits and filling. For a marbled effect, purée half the fruit; just before serving fold purée into whipped cream.

Serves 12.

■ SCONES

The English upper classes pronounce this word as if it rhymes with "on" rather than "own." Webster's dictionary, a product of the colonies, says either way is acceptable. Traditionally, scones are split in two and eaten with butter, preserves, and, if available, Devonshire clotted cream (or substitute whipped cream). If etiquette is followed, the butter and preserves should be spooned on the plate, the scone sliced in half, and then only enough butter and preserves spread on for a mouthful. If cream is served, it is spooned on top of the preserves.

    3½ cups flour
    1 tablespoon baking powder
    1 teaspoon baking soda
    ½ teaspoon salt
    ¾ cup sugar
    ½ cup butter
    ½ cup buttermilk
    2 eggs, lightly beaten
       Butter, preserves, and clotted cream or
       whipped cream, for accompaniment (optional)

1. Follow instructions for Baking Powder Biscuits (see page 49). Before adding buttermilk, whisk with eggs.

2. Or, halve dough and knead gently to form 2 balls. Flatten each ball to a thickness of ½ to 1 inch. With a sharp knife, cut each round into 8 triangles. Arrange on prepared baking sheet and bake at 400° F until golden brown (20 to 30 minutes). Serve hot with butter, preserves, and cream (if desired).

Makes about 16 rounds or triangles.

Orange or Lemon Scones With buttermilk-egg mixture, add 1 tablespoon grated orange or lemon rind.

Raisin Scones With buttermilk-egg mixture, add 1 cup dark or golden raisins, dried currants, or a combination.

Spice Scones To dry ingredients, add 1 teaspoon mixed spices (equal amounts of ground cinnamon, nutmeg, cloves, and allspice).

Whole Wheat Scones For the 3½ cups all-purpose flour, substitute a blend of 2 cups all-purpose flour and 1½ cups whole wheat flour. Increase butter to ¾ cup.

◼ FRUIT COBBLER

Grunt, slump, buckle, roly-poly, flummery, pandowdy, and cobbler—all are old-fashioned regional desserts of cooked fruit with a biscuit, dough, or bread topping of some type. In New England the fruit might be blueberries, in the South, peaches. Any juicy fruit or a combination of fruits would be equally delicious. Use the Cream Biscuit variation of Baking Powder Biscuits for the topping.

> **2 to 3 pints fresh blueberries or other juicy fruit or berry**
> **½ cup sugar, or more, to taste**
> **Grated rind and juice of 1 lemon**
> **2 tablespoons water**
> **Cream Biscuits (see page 50)**
> **Cream and sugar, for topping**
> **Ice cream or whipped cream, for accompaniment**

1. Preheat oven to 400° F. Wash blueberries and drain; pick over to remove any soft or bruised ones. Place blueberries in a shallow, 1½-quart, ovenproof baking dish. Sprinkle with sugar, lemon juice and rind, and the water; toss to combine.

2. After preparing Cream Biscuits, shape dough in one of the following ways: drop by tablespoons onto fruit; *or* roll out ½ inch thick, cut into 2-inch rounds, and set on fruit; *or* roll out ½ inch thick and just slightly smaller than baking dish, crimp edges, and set on fruit. Brush dough with cream and dust with sugar. Bake until biscuit dough is golden brown (30 to 40 minutes).

3. Serve hot straight from the oven, or at room temperature, with ice cream or whipped cream.

Serves 4 to 6.

> **Recipes and Related Information**
> *Baking Powder, 23; Baking Soda, 23; Cut In, 171; Drop, 187; Dumpling, 189; Quick Bread, 490.*

BLACKBERRY

A member of the rose family, the blackberry has black or deep purple, seedy fruit similar to raspberries, boysenberries, dewberries, olallieberries, loganberries, and youngberries in structure. The berries are composed of numerous small sacs on a fleshy stem. Ripe berries are sweet and very juicy.

Use Fresh uncooked berries are enjoyed as is, or with milk or cream and sugar, as a breakfast dish, snack, or dessert. Blackberries are used in tarts, pies, ice cream, fruit salads and compotes, shortcakes, crisps and cobblers, puddings, and preserves.

Availability Fresh, frozen, and canned. Fresh blackberries are in season from May through August, with peak supply in June and August. They are packed loosely in cardboard or plastic baskets with cellophane covers.

Selection Look for relatively bright berries with uniform dark color and plump, tender sacs. Stem caps should not be attached. Avoid stained containers, which may indicate spoilage and either unripe or oversoft berries.

Storage Pick berries over, discarding overripe or moldy ones. Spread remaining berries on a paper-towel–lined tray and refrigerate; use within two or three days.

Preparation Wash berries gently just before use.

Biscuits and berries are a classic summer dessert. Strawberries are the usual choice, but try a combination of strawberries, raspberries, and blueberries for an appealing mix of color, flavor, and texture.

> **Recipes and Related Information**
> *Basic Berry Pie, 437; Fruit Cobbler, 51.*

BLANCH, TO

To cook foods—most often vegetables—briefly in boiling water and set briefly in cold water until completely cool. Food is blanched for one or more of the following reasons: to loosen and remove skin (almonds, peaches, tomatoes); to enhance color and reduce bitterness (raw vegetables for hors d'oeuvres); to extend storage life (raw vegetables to be frozen); to draw out excess salt from meats such as bacon and salt pork.

Parboiling and blanching are identical processes, but although blanched foods boil only a short time, parboiled foods are cooked almost halfway. Parboiling is a great timesaving technique for stir-fries and sautés. It tenderizes longer-cooking ingredients so that all foods cook in the same amount of time, and it can be done in advance of final preparation, another convenience.

HOW TO BLANCH

Almost any vegetable can be blanched successfully in boiling water, and most can be blanched over steam. Steaming better maintains the shape of the vegetables and conserves more nutrients than water-blanching, but it takes a bit longer. Blanching in a microwave oven is quick and easy, and protects both nutrients and color. Time varies with specific vegetables and end use. In general, boil just until vegetable is tender-crisp. For peeling, usually 1 or 2 minutes is all the boiling time needed.

Microwave-Blanching   You'll need appropriate oven-proof dishes. Prepare 1 pound of vegetables as for conventional cooking. Place in a glass casserole, add ⅓ cup water, and cover. Cook at 100 percent power until evenly cooked (4 to 6 minutes). When done, cool and drain as directed for water-blanching.

Steam-Blanching   Use a large pot with a tight-fitting lid and a steaming rack that fits the pot. Fill pot with about 2 inches water and place rack in pot. Water should not touch rack. Bring water to a boil, loosely pack vegetables on rack in a single layer no more than 2 inches deep, and cover pot. When done, cool and drain as directed for water-blanching.

Water-Blanching   Use a large pot with a tight-fitting lid, ideally one equipped with a strainer for lifting the vegetables in and out of boiling water. If your pot doesn't have its own strainer, use a basket, colander, or wire-mesh strainer that is large enough to allow the food to move around in boiling water. Bring lightly salted water to a hard boil; lower vegetable-filled strainer or basket into pot; return water to boiling point as quickly as possible; stir vegetables again once boiling resumes. Stir vegetables into ice water or hold under running water until completely cooled; drain immediately.

BLEND, TO

To mix two or more ingredients together by hand or with a machine until smooth or until they combine to produce uniform texture, color, or flavor.

BLENDER, IMMERSION BLENDER

The blender is often compared with the food processor, and often suffers in the comparison. Although it has slipped in popularity, its virtues should be kept in mind. The blender purées, makes mayonnaise and silky sauces, and mixes the best drinks. Its tall, narrow container is better designed for some jobs than the work bowl of the food processor. The shape also allows the machine to process small batches, sometimes a problem with the wider processor bowl. Processor bowls may have a problem with liquid seeping from the base. This can't happen with a blender. However, it cannot whip egg whites, which a processor can do if it has a whisk attachment, and the processor is better for chopping, shredding, and grating.

Blenders may have as many as 16 speeds, including an on-off pulse function designed to give more control over food consistency. Most cooks will use only a few settings and ignore the rest. Some models come with small jars that substitute for the standard container. These jars are a good size for small portions (including homemade baby food and salad dressings), and they come with covers so they can be stored in the refrigerator.

Do you need a blender? If you make a lot of purées for soups, sauces, ice creams, and sorbets, and have space for the blender, you'll find it useful. If you have room for only one appliance of this type—in your budget or on your kitchen counter—the food processor, although more expensive, is more versatile and therefore a better buy. An alternative is a relatively new (for the home cook) machine called the immersion blender.

IMMERSION BLENDER

Just making its debut in home kitchens, the immersion blender (also called a hand blender) has been a valued chef's tool for years. Essentially it is a blender without a container. It is a tall, narrow, handheld machine with rotary blades. Like a conventional blender, it excels at making sauces and purées. Unlike a conventional blender, this machine is portable. This means it can be used right in the cooking pot and can handle more food at a time because it is not limited by the size of the container. As another benefit, there are fewer dirty bowls to clean.

Why has a home version of this machine appeared only recently if it's been in restaurant kitchens for so long? The time is right. This appliance very much complements contemporary cuisine with the emphasis away from caloric, starch-thickened sauces, toward fresh purées and vegetable reductions—the types of preparations the immersion blender makes best.

Choose a model with variable speeds for optimum control. Soft foods blend at low speeds, but thick ingredients such as whole tomatoes or cooked potatoes need more mixing to work into a smooth purée. High speed also does a better job at creating emulsion sauces. If you have a blender with a whisk attachment, you can whip and beat as well as blend and purée. Other accessories include beakers for mixing drinks and blending small quantities, a strainer, and a wall mount.

The food processor will still perform more culinary chores than either type of blender, and if you only want one small appliance in this general category the processor should be it. If the portability and easy storage of the immersion blender appeal to you, you might consider acquiring one as a companion to the processor.

> ### Recipes and Related Information
> *Food Processor, 240; Hollandaise Sauce, 516; Ice Cream and Frozen Dessert, 308; Mayonnaise, 519; Purée, 487; Sauce, 512; Stock and Soup, 558.*

BLUEBERRY

The blueberry is a round, dark blue berry that grows wild in Scandinavia, the British Isles, Russia, and North and South America. Cultivated varieties date only from the early twentieth century and are larger than the wild berries. Ripe blueberries are sweet and juicy.

Use Fresh uncooked blueberries are enjoyed as is, or with milk or cream and sugar, as a breakfast dish, a snack, or dessert. When blueberries are blended with other berries, such as raspberries and strawberries, they make a simply prepared, visually appealing, and delicious fruit cup. Blueberries also add color and flavor to fruit salads, fools, yogurt, ice creams, muffins, and pancakes. They add sweetness to pies, tarts, cobblers, puddings, coffee cakes, tea breads, and other baked desserts. Blueberries make excellent preserves.

Availability Blueberries are marketed fresh, frozen, and canned. Blueberries are harvested from May to September, with peak supplies in July and August. They come to market in cardboard containers with cellophane covers. Frozen blueberries are packed in plastic bags or cardboard freezer packages. Canned blueberries, both cultivated and wild, are packed in water or sugar syrup.

Selection Choose firm, plump berries with a silvery bloom; they should not have stems attached. Avoid juice-stained containers and soft berries.

Storage Refrigerate fresh blueberries for up to two weeks; wash just before using. To freeze fresh blueberries, do not wash. Dry them thoroughly, repack in cardboard container, and overwrap tightly with plastic wrap, covering air holes at bottom of container. Alternatively, tray freeze: Spread blueberries out in a single layer on shallow metal pans and put directly in freezer. When berries are frozen solid, pack airtight in plastic bags or containers and refreeze. Frozen berries will keep at least a year. They do not have to be defrosted before using in baking recipes.

Preparation Wash berries just before using; discard any berries that appear moldy.

Served warm or at room temperature, Blueberry Coffee Cake is inviting for breakfast or as a midday treat with coffee or tea. The recipe is on page 54.

▩ BLUEBERRY COFFEE CAKE

Dust confectioners' sugar over this almond-crusted fresh blueberry cake to dramatize its luscious appearance.

¼ cup *each* sliced almonds and
　　firmly packed brown sugar
1½ cups flour
¾ cup granulated sugar
1 tablespoon baking powder
½ teaspoon salt
¼ teaspoon freshly grated nutmeg
⅓ cup butter
1 cup fresh blueberries
1 egg
½ cup milk
1 teaspoon vanilla extract
　　Confectioners' sugar, for dusting

1. Preheat oven to 350° F. Generously grease a 9-inch tube pan with a capacity of 6 to 7 cups. Combine almonds and brown sugar; sprinkle mixture in pan; set aside.

2. In a large bowl mix flour, granulated sugar, baking powder, salt, and nutmeg; cut in butter until mixture resembles coarse crumbs. Lightly stir in blueberries.

3. In a small bowl beat egg lightly with milk and vanilla. Stir milk mixture into blueberry mixture just until combined. Spread batter gently in prepared pan.

4. Bake until coffee cake is well browned and a long skewer inserted in thickest part comes out clean (45 minutes to 1 hour).

5. Let stand in pan for about 5 minutes, loosen edges, and invert onto a serving plate. Serve warm or at room temperature, dusted with confectioners' sugar.

Serves 6 to 8.

Recipes and Related Information
Blueberry Buttermilk Pancakes, 600; Blueberry Muffins, 375; Fruit Cobbler, 51.

BOIL, TO

The process of heating a liquid to the boiling point (212° F at sea level). When it reaches the boiling point, all of the liquid will be in motion, with bubbles constantly rising and breaking on the surface.

Once water reaches 212° F, its temperature won't increase, but it will be more agitated and will evaporate faster. The following terms should help you create a type of boil by identifying the appearance of the surface of the water.

Shake　Surface begins to shake, but bubbles have not yet appeared (for stocks).

Smile　Small bubbles begin to pop up on the surface (for delicate sauces, poaching, stocks).

Simmer　A continuous stream of small bubbles slowly rises to the surface (for slow cooking; soups, stews).

Moderate Boil　Water surface is agitated but not rolling on top of itself (for most cooking).

Rolling Boil　A great deal of turbulence is produced as bubbles form rapidly and rise to the surface, but break before reaching the surface (for green vegetables, pasta, reducing liquids).

BOILING VEGETABLES

An American cookbook from the turn of the century directed that string beans (cut in pieces) needed to boil one to three hours to tenderize. Few of us have probably been subjected to three-hour beans, but vegetables boiled to a dull, mushy, nutrient-depleted mass most likely were typical fare as we grew up. Today's emphasis on fresh, quality ingredients has resulted in a greater understanding of how to cook these foods to preserve their appearance, flavor, and nutrition.

Boiling is one of the principal cooking techniques for fresh vegetables. There are two approaches: using a large amount of water or using very little (usually ½ to 1 inch or enough water to cover). Green vegetables cooked uncovered in a pot full of water will keep their color better than if boiled in a small amount of liquid, but can lose important nutrients. When cooked in 1 or 2 inches of water in a covered pan, these vegetables retain nutrients but can turn dull and unappealing.

The challenge is to prepare vegetables so that nutrients are conserved and visual appeal maintained; most recipes will provide specific cooking instructions. In general, to avoid loss of nutrients, cook as briefly as possible in a small amount of water. To hold color, add a little salt to the water and begin cooking uncovered to allow gases that have a negative effect on color to escape, then finish in a covered pan; or lift cover several times during cooking to release gases. Bring water to a boil first, then add vegetables; quickly return to a boil and cover. Remember that vegetables cut in pieces of similar size will cook more evenly. To preserve the color of green vegetables, it's best to cook them uncovered in a large amount of boiling, salted water. Bring salted water to a boil and add vegetables. Stir vegetables until water returns to a boil, then let boil until done. Drain immediately and serve.

Cooking time depends upon freshness and maturity of vegetables and whether they are whole or cut up, and is usually measured from the point at which water returns to a boil after vegetables have been added. As a measure of comparison, broccoli spears will boil tender-crisp in about 7 to 10 minutes; florets need only 3 to 5 minutes to be ready. A head of cauliflower should cook 15 to 20 minutes; florets 5 to 10 minutes; slices only 3 to 5 minutes.

BONE, TO

A basic preparation technique used to separate the flesh of meat, poultry, and fish from the bones, and to trim away sinews, gristle, and fat in order to make eating easier and more enjoyable. All cooks, even those who prefer to have the butcher perform this service for them, should learn how to bone certain cuts, such as chicken breasts. Whole and bone-in poultry and other meats are less expensive per pound and will allow the cook last-minute flexibility when deciding what to prepare. Boned breasts are well suited to poaching, sautéing, and frying. Boneless legs and thighs are elegant when served with a savory stuffing. See FISH, for a discussion of filleting. See DISJOINT for a description of cutting up a whole chicken.

You will bone with less damage to the piece of meat if you use your hands to learn, by feel, the anatomy of the animal. That way you will get to know where the bones and joints are and then be able to cut in order to expose them. These preliminary cuts are exploratory ones that show you where subsequent cuts should be made. Use a sharp knife and a cutting board. Remember to wash the preparation surface thoroughly before and after it comes in contact with raw poultry.

BONING A CHICKEN BREAST

For a whole breast, remove skin and place breast skin side down. With tip of knife cut through membrane covering breastbone. Pick up breast with both hands and press back on ribs to break them away from breastbone, which will pop out. Pull out breastbone, including cartilage.

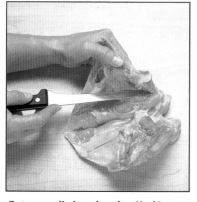

Cut away ribs by using tip of knife to make shallow cuts as close to rib bones as possible. Or, slip fingers between ribs and meat and work meat free from bones. Work wishbone free with fingers. Split breast in half, removing tough membranes lying along breastbone.

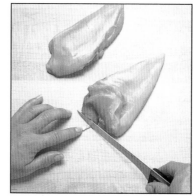

Locate white tendon on smaller muscle of each breast half. Place tendon side down on work surface and hold end with fingernail. With knife held vertically, scrape from end of tendon inward, removing meat from tendon. Trim into neat fillet shape.

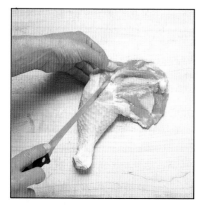

BONING A CHICKEN LEG AND THIGH

Do not separate leg and thigh. With boning knife, cut along thigh bone, to expose it, and then down drumstick.

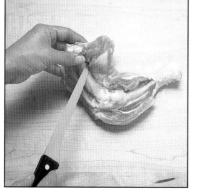

With hand, push meat away from bone. Then hold by exposed end of thigh bone so that leg and thigh hang down. Cut meat away from bone by making little cuts around the bone. Continue around knee joint to free leg bone.

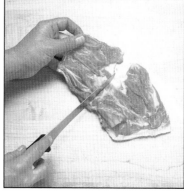

If a larger piece of meat is desired, pound to flatten before stuffing. To separate into boneless leg and thigh, cut through at point where thigh and leg bone are joined.

Bouquet garni is a classic seasoning mixture made of fresh herbs that are tied in a bundle or wrapped in cheesecloth. The herbs will vary depending on usage and the cook's preference.

BORAGE

A hardy, highly ornamental, annual herb native to southern Europe and North Africa, borage has a stout stem, bristly gray-green leaves, and delicate, star-shaped, blue-violet flowers. The leaves have a cucumberlike flavor.

Use   Young borage leaves may be eaten raw as a salad or added to salads. Older leaves may be cooked and served like spinach. Fresh borage flowers make a colorful garnish for salads or iced drinks; dried borage flowers may be added to potpourri; candied flowers are used to decorate cakes and desserts.

Availability   Found in specialty markets from May through October.

Selection   Choose fresh leaves that are not limp and do not show any signs of decay.

Storage   Keep leaves and flowers loosely in plastic bags in the refrigerator. Use within a couple of days.

BOUQUET GARNI

A bundle of aromatic herbs and vegetables, bouquet garni is used to flavor soups, stocks, poaching liquids, stews, and braised dishes. It is always removed after cooking. The herbs are tied together with a string or gathered together in a cheesecloth bag to facilitate their retrieval from the finished dish. Traditional bouquet garni herbs include bay leaf, thyme, and parsley, although other herbs and vegetables such as tarragon, chervil, peppercorns, celery, and leeks may be included to enhance the flavor of a particular dish.

For a small bouquet garni, tie together with string three sprigs fresh parsley, two sprigs fresh thyme, and one bay leaf. If using dried or loose herbs, wrap all ingredients in a square of cheesecloth and tie with a string.

Recipes and Related Information
Bay, 29; Cheesecloth, 119; Herb, 299; Parsley, 406; Stock and Soup, 558; Thyme, 578.

BOWL CHOPPER

The bowl chopper is easy to recognize. It has a single stainless steel blade which is curved along the bottom at the cutting edge, and an easy-to-grip wooden knob as the handle. It chops and minces like a chef's knife, food processor, or electric minichopper, and is efficient for small tasks—a few tablespoons of garlic, herbs, or onion. Although it can be bought separately, most often it is paired with a small hardwood bowl whose curve matches the curve of the chopping blade.

A bowl chopper has homey appeal and is also practical. The bowl keeps the food contained so that it doesn't hop around when hit by the blade. Consider buying a chopper and matching bowl if you cook for one or two persons most of the time.

Select a blade that fits its bowl, or it won't be as effective. After each use, rinse the chopper in warm, sudsy water and wipe dry. Don't wash bowl; wipe away remaining food. Periodically treat wood with mineral oil. To protect blade, store chopper in bowl.

A *mezzaluna* is a large, double-handled, curved chopper, used on a flat chopping surface. A more serious piece of kitchen equipment than the bowl chopper, it has been referred to as the Italian chef's knife.

Recipes and Related Information
Food Processor, 240; Knife, 328.

BRAISE, TO

Braising is a combination of cooking methods designed to render tough cuts of meat and fibrous vegetables succulent and tender. Usually, food is first sautéed or browned for color and flavor, then cooked slowly in a small amount of liquid in an airtight pot. This creates a moist, steamy cooking environment that gently breaks down hard-to-chew connective tissue and muscle and releases the food's own juices. The browned meat is often set on a bed of chopped aromatic vegetables (*mirepoix*), which later may be puréed, mixed with pan juices, and used as a sauce. About ¼ to ½ inch of liquid—water, stock, wine, hard cider, tomato purée—is added to the bottom of the pot, which is tightly covered to prevent evaporation. Cooking is completed either on top of the stove or in the oven. Stewing is almost identical to braising, but uses smaller pieces of meat and requires more liquid.

Any casserole with a tight-fitting lid is suitable for braising. It is important that the vessel be of a material that conducts heat evenly and efficiently to prevent scorching and hot spots. The pot should not be much larger than the meat plus its liquid, so that the heat will be directed to the meat rather than the empty spaces.

The best foods for braising are shoulder cuts of beef (often called chuck), lamb, veal, and pork. Other good cuts are beef brisket, beef round, beef rump, veal shanks, and lamb shanks. Boneless cuts that are rolled and tied in a neat cylinder are ideal for braising because they are easy to carve. Whole chickens and Rock Cornish game hens are also delicious when braised.

BRAISING VEGETABLES

Although vegetables are commonly part of a meat or poultry braise for their wonderful flavor, they are also braised alone and served as a side dish. Root vegetables and leafy greens are superb when braised. Butter, or butter with some water, stock, or wine, plus seasonings, is a typical mixture for braising vegetables. Sugar is frequently added for flavor and to help develop a shiny syrup. Browning vegetables adds to their taste, but isn't always called for in many braised vegetable recipes. Often the first step is to toss vegetable pieces briefly in hot oil or melted butter; more liquid is then added and the vegetables cooked until tender. Alternatively, after slowly cooking in a small amount of liquid just until tender, vegetables can be finished in butter and seasonings for a short period of time until coated. Sometimes all ingredients are added at once.

Cooking times depend upon the size and shape of vegetables, their freshness, and maturity. As a rough guideline and comparison for other vegetables, celery hearts should braise for 10 to 15 minutes; Belgian endive needs about 15 to 20 minutes; blanch whole leeks to tenderize, then braise anywhere from 15 to 25 minutes, depending upon thickness; braise halved leeks 10 to 15 minutes without blanching (they will separate if precooked); braise carrots until tender and glazed with the reduced cooking liquid, anywhere from 8 to 15 minutes depending upon size of the pieces; braise greens just until wilted along with some sautéed onions and a small amount of liquid.

▌ ROLLED BEEF WITH PROSCIUTTO

Braciole is the Italian word for boneless meat cutlets, which are almost invariably stuffed, rolled, and tied. Here, in a Roman version, the cutlets are wrapped around a filling of prosciutto and celery, then gently braised with tomatoes and aromatic Italian mushrooms.

> 1 **pound bottom round of beef**
> 1½ **ounces dried porcini mushrooms**
> ⅓ **pound prosciutto, sliced paper-thin**
> 1 **cup coarsely chopped celery leaves**
> 3 to 4 **tablespoons olive oil**
> 1 **tablespoon minced garlic**
> 1 **cup minced onion**
> 2 **cups peeled, seeded, and diced tomatoes, fresh or canned**
> **Salt and freshly ground pepper, to taste**

1. Have butcher slice meat into eight 2-ounce slices, or freeze it briefly and slice it yourself with a sharp knife. Place slices between 2 sheets of lightly oiled waxed paper and pound with a mallet or bottom of a skillet until they are paper-thin. Soak *porcini* mushrooms in hot water to cover for 1 hour.

2. Place beef slices on a flat surface. Divide prosciutto slices evenly among them and sprinkle chopped celery leaves over prosciutto. Roll each beef slice into a neat bundle and tie securely with kitchen string.

3. Heat 3 tablespoons oil in a heavy skillet over medium-high heat until a light haze forms. Brown beef rolls on all sides, in batches if necessary, then set aside. If necessary, add a little more oil to coat surface of pan, then add garlic and onion and sauté over moderate heat until softened but not browned.

4. With a slotted spoon, remove mushrooms from soaking liquid and squeeze dry. Strain liquid through cheesecloth to remove any grit or sand. Add mushrooms, tomatoes, and reserved soaking liquid to skillet. Season with salt and pepper to taste. Return meat to skillet and bring sauce to a simmer. Cover, reduce heat to maintain a slow simmer, and cook 2 hours. Check meat after 1 hour, adding a little water if sauce has reduced too much. When meat is quite tender, transfer rolls to a warm serving plate, cut strings carefully with a small knife, and cover with sauce.

Serves 4.

Food Processor Version Use metal blade to process 3 to 4 cloves of garlic for 10 seconds. Cut 1 large onion into eighths and add to work bowl. Turn motor on and off 3 or 4 times. Scrape bowl and pulse 2 to 3 more times until onion is minced.

Serve Osso Buco with buttered fettuccine and a tiny spoon for scooping the soft marrow out of the veal shank bones. The hollow bone gives the dish its name.

2. When all shanks have been browned, pour off excess fat, add wine to Dutch oven, and bring to a boil. With a wooden spoon, scrape up any browned bits clinging to bottom of pot. Add stock and simmer 2 minutes. If using canned beef stock, dilute with water to taste, to reduce strength and saltiness.

3. Place thyme, parsley, and bay leaves in a cheesecloth bag. Add to pot along with basil. Return shanks to pot and set aside.

4. In a large skillet over moderate heat, melt butter. Add onion, celery, carrots, and garlic, and cook until vegetables are slightly softened (about 5 minutes). Add tomatoes and simmer 5 minutes. Transfer mixture to Dutch oven, cover tightly, and bring to a simmer over moderately high heat. Reduce heat to maintain simmer and cook gently for at least 2 hours. (Dish may also be baked in a 325° F oven for 2½ to 3 hours; bring it to a simmer on top of stove first.) Check occasionally to make sure liquid has not reduced too much; add a little wine, stock, or water if necessary.

5. When meat is fork-tender, transfer shanks to a warm serving platter. Place pot briefly over high heat to reduce sauce slightly. Add Gremolata during final 30 seconds, then spoon sauce over meat.

Serves 8.

Gremolata   In a small bowl combine parsley, lemon rind, and garlic; mix to blend well.

Food Processor Version   Use metal blade to process 3 or 4 cloves garlic for 10 seconds. Cut 2 large onions, 2 celery stalks, and 2 medium carrots into 1-inch pieces. Add half to work bowl. Turn motor on and off 3 to 4 times to chop coarsely. Add to skillet in step 4. Repeat with remaining onion, celery, and carrot and add to skillet.

▨ GAME HENS COQ AU VIN

Classic coq au vin uses an old rooster. The tender game hens are a tasty alternative and speed the cooking time considerably.

> 2   Rock Cornish game hens (1 to 1½ lb each), cut into serving pieces
>   Salt and freshly ground pepper
> ½   cup butter
> ¼   cup brandy
> 4   cups (approximately) dry red wine
>   Bouquet garni (3 sprigs parsley, 1 bay leaf, 1 teaspoon dried thyme, 1 teaspoon dried marjoram, wrapped in 4-in. square of cheesecloth)
> 3   slices (each ½ in. thick) salt pork
> 12 small boiling onions, peeled
> 12 mushroom caps
>   Beurre manié (3 tablespoons each flour and butter kneaded together)

▨ OSSO BUCO

Meaty veal shanks turn fork-tender when braised slowly with wine and vegetables, and they yield a delectable dividend: a nugget of marrow in each hollow bone (*osso buco*).

> 3   veal shanks, each sawed into 6 to 8 pieces about 2½ inches long
>   Salt and freshly ground pepper
> 2   cups flour, for dredging
> ½ to ¾ cup safflower oil
> 1¼ cups dry white wine
> 2   cups Brown Veal Stock or Beef Stock (see page 560) or canned stock
> 4   sprigs fresh thyme
> ½   cup parsley sprigs and stems
> 3   bay leaves
> 1   cup whole fresh basil leaves
> 5   tablespoons butter
> 1½ cups chopped onion
> 1   cup diced celery
> 1   cup diced carrots
> 1   tablespoon minced garlic
> 2   cups peeled, seeded, and chopped tomatoes

Gremolata

> 2   tablespoons finely minced Italian parsley
> 1   tablespoon grated lemon rind
> 1   teaspoon finely minced garlic

1. Salt and pepper shanks well, then dredge lightly in flour and shake off excess. In a large Dutch oven over medium-high heat, heat oil. Add shanks and brown well on all sides, in batches if necessary. Transfer shanks to a plate as they are browned.

1. Wash game hens and pat dry; season with salt and pepper. In a large, heavy-bottomed sauté pan over medium-high heat, melt butter. Add game hens and sauté until golden brown (about 5 minutes per side). Drain fat from pan.

2. Pour brandy over game hens and flame it. When flame dies down, add enough red wine to cover hens. Add bouquet garni and cook, covered, over medium heat until game hens are tender when pierced with a fork (about 30 minutes).

3. After 15 minutes, brown salt pork in a medium, heavy-bottomed sauté pan over medium-high heat. Add onions and sauté until a rich brown color (about 10 minutes). Add mushrooms and continue cooking until just tender (about 1 minute). Set aside.

4. When chicken is tender, remove bouquet garni. Add vegetables. Drop beurre manié into sauce and whisk to blend; cook over medium heat until sauce has thickened.

Serves 4.

■ LEEKS BRAISED WITH TASSO

This dish demonstrates a typical and flavorful use of the Cajun seasoning meat called *tasso,* which imparts a smoky tang to the leeks and adds a contrast of color. Tasso is usually made from lean pork shoulder cut into chunks. It is richly seasoned with cayenne. Smoked ham can be substituted for tasso, but it is less smoky.

> 3 **medium-sized leeks**
> 1 **carrot, diced**
> 2 **shallots, finely chopped**
> 2 **cloves garlic, minced**
> ¼ **pound tasso, finely chopped**
> 2 **cups Beef Stock (see page 560)**
> 2 **tablespoons butter**

Split leeks and wash thoroughly. Place in a heavy pan over medium heat with carrot, shallots, garlic, tasso, stock, and butter. Cover, reduce to simmer, and cook until leeks are tender when pierced (30 to 40 minutes). Remove to a warm serving dish and reduce liquid until it turns syrupy. Pour over leeks and serve.

Serves 4 to 6.

BRAZIL NUT

The Brazil nut is the fruit of the tall bertholetia tree, which grows wild in Paraguay and Brazil. The tree yields 3- to 4-pound pods with thick shells that must be broken open with a machete. Inside are 12 to 20 three-sided Brazil nuts, with a dark brown shell that is rough and hard and has sharp edges. The large kernel inside has a thin brown skin and ivory meat; it is oily, with a flavor reminiscent of hazelnut and coconut.

Use   Shelled Brazil nuts are used in candies, cakes, and salted nut mixes. They add texture and nutty flavor to stuffings, chicken salad, and grain dishes.

Availability   Whole shelled nuts are packed in cans or plastic bags, or are sold in bulk. Unshelled nuts are available in bulk.

Selection   Buy as fresh as possible.

Storage   Keep unshelled nuts in a cool place for up to six months. Shelled nuts go stale quickly; store them in an airtight container in the refrigerator and use within three months. Shelled nuts may be frozen for up to six months, although they will lose some crispness.

Preparation   See NUT.

■ YOUR OWN BRIDGE MIX

Trail mixes, party mixes, bridge mixes, cocktail mixes— whatever the name, they are an addicting munchie, and best when you make your own. Fill small bowls with this nutty mix, which is naturally sweetened with raisins and dried apricots and spiked with wine. Place the bowls strategically around the room: on the bar, on the mantel, on the piano, or wherever guests are likely to gather. This recipe yields a large batch, enough for a crowd; store any extra in an airtight container.

> 1 **pound Brazil nuts, unskinned**
> 1 **pound almonds, unskinned**
> 1 **pound blanched cashews**
> ½ **pound shelled pine nuts**
> ¼ **pound muscat raisins or**
>   **seedless dark raisins**
> ⅓ **pound golden raisins**
> ⅓ **cup Marsala or sweet vermouth**
> ½ **pound shelled pistachio nuts**
> ¼ **cup shredded unsweetened coconut**
> ¼ **cup lightly salted sunflower seeds**
> ¼ **cup finely minced dried apricots**
>   **Kosher salt**
>   **Worcestershire sauce (optional)**

1. Preheat oven to 350° F. In separate batches, toast Brazil nuts, almonds, cashews, and pine nuts on cookie sheets until lightly browned and fragrant. Set nuts aside to cool.

2. In a medium saucepan combine muscat and golden raisins with Marsala. Bring to a boil, reduce heat, and simmer gently until liquid has evaporated (20 to 30 minutes). Set aside to cool.

3. Combine cooled toasted nuts with raisins, pistachios, coconut, sunflower seeds, and apricots. Add salt and Worcestershire sauce (if used) to taste.

Makes about 10 cups.

HOW TO BREAD FOOD

Holding food with fingers, dip food in flour and turn to coat on all sides; shake off excess flour.

Dip food in egg mixture, coating evenly with liquid. Do not get liquid on fingers. Remove food with a slotted spoon or wire skimmer, allowing excess liquid to drip off.

Set food in crumbs. Shake dish to coat food with some crumbs. Turn food and pat with fingers to firmly set top crumbs. Turn again and pat to set crumbs on other side; shake off excess.

BREAD, TO

To coat with bread or other crumbs, mostly to foods that will be fried. During cooking, the crumbs form a pleasantly crunchy crust that acts as a protective barrier between food and cooking oil. Often a layer of flour and then egg precedes the crumbs. The flour dries the outside of the food and gives the egg something to adhere to. The egg acts as glue for the crumbs. To develop an attractive, crisp crust, it is important to shake off excess coating before applying the next. The above directions will ensure that the crumbs coat the food and not your hands by keeping your hands free of egg wash, a very effective binder.

> ***Recipes and Related Information***
> *Deep-fry, 174; Fry, 254.*

BROCCOLI

A vegetable in the cabbage family, broccoli has a thick, rigid, green stalk, grayish green leaves, and a flowering dark green or purplish green head. All parts are edible.

Use The flowering heads of young broccoli may be eaten raw, dressed with vinaigrette, or accompanied by a dipping sauce. More mature broccoli is generally boiled or steamed and eaten cold as a salad or hot as a side dish. It is flattered by cheese sauce and cream sauce. Chopped broccoli may be made into soup, soufflé, or baked pudding. A variety of Chinese broccoli with more leaf than flower is used in Chinese stir-fried dishes.

Availability Fresh and frozen. Fresh broccoli is sold all year, with peak supplies in fall through winter. Frozen broccoli is available whole or chopped.

Selection Choose broccoli with tightly closed florets that do not show signs of yellowing. Avoid spears with tough, woody stems and wilted leaves.

Storage Keep broccoli in a plastic bag in the refrigerator for three or four days. It also freezes well.

Preparation Wash carefully. Trim butt end. If desired, peel tough green outer skin of stalks down to moist, pale green part. Flower heads cook more quickly than stalks; to cook heads and stalks evenly, split stalks lengthwise in halves or quarters, slicing all the way up to but not through flower heads.

Cooking See BOIL, STEAM, STIR-FRY.

■ BROCCOLI SAUTEED WITH GARLIC

Italian vegetables are often parboiled—partially cooked in water until almost tender—then sautéed in olive oil or butter, sometimes both.

> 1   **bunch of fresh broccoli or**
>   **1 package (10 oz) frozen sliced broccoli**
> 2   **cloves garlic, minced**
> ¼   **cup olive oil**
>   **Salt, to taste**

1. Slice off and discard ends of fresh broccoli stalks; peel stalks if broccoli is tough. Split stalks in half or into quarters with florets left attached, or slice whole stalks horizontally into bite-sized pieces. Steam or drop into boiling salted water and cook until just fork-tender. Drain well. (Cook frozen broccoli according to package directions until barely tender.)

2. Over medium heat, sauté garlic in olive oil until golden. Add broccoli and salt and sauté about 3 to 4 minutes.

Makes 4 servings.

A quick, easy-to-make white sauce combined with grated Parmesan cheese transforms blanched broccoli into a golden gratin.

■ BROCCOLI GRATIN

A gratin is a popular way of preparing any vegetable that tastes good with cheese. The vegetable is cooked until tender, then baked with cheese sauce—try one flavored with grated Parmesan. Gratins can be made with one vegetable or with a mixture of cooked vegetables or vegetable purées.

    ¾ **pound broccoli**
       Pinch salt
    1 **cup Cheese Sauce (see page 513), finished**
       with 1 egg yolk
    2 **tablespoons grated Parmesan cheese**

1. Preheat oven to 425° F. Divide broccoli into medium florets. (Reserve stalks for soup.)

2. In a large saucepan boil enough water to cover broccoli generously and add a pinch of salt. Add broccoli and boil, uncovered, until just tender when pierced with a sharp knife (about 5 minutes). Drain broccoli, rinse with cold water, and drain thoroughly.

3. Butter a 4- or 5-cup shallow baking dish.

4. Arrange broccoli in one layer in baking dish. Spoon sauce over broccoli, covering it completely. Sprinkle with cheese. Broccoli can be kept, covered, up to 1 day in refrigerator.

5. Bake until hot (about 5 minutes if broccoli and sauce were hot, or about 15 minutes if they were cold).

6. If surface is not brown by the time mixture is hot, broil for about 1 minute. Serve hot.

Serves 4.

Recipes and Related Information
Beef With Asparagus, 558; Cream of Any Vegetable Soup, 563; Vegetable Purées, 487.

BROCCOLI RAAB

This leafy green member of the cabbage family figures prominently in Italian cooking. It has slender but firm stalks about 12 inches long, bright green leaves with jagged edges, and small green florets with yellow flowers. Its flavor is pleasantly bitter. It is marketed under a variety of similar names, including *cima di rapa, cima di rabe, broccolirab, broccoli di rape, rape, raab,* and *rapini.*

Use Broccoli raab may be steamed and served cool or chilled, as a salad with lemon and oil. Italian cooks briefly boil broccoli raab, then sauté it with oil and garlic for use as an accompaniment to pork roast. Alternatively, it may be very slowly sautéed in oil without preblanching.

Availability Fresh broccoli raab is most widely available fall through spring.

Selection Choose stalks with dark green, fresh-looking leaves and sturdy stems.

Storage Keep in a plastic bag in refrigerator crisper for three to four days.

Preparation Trim away any large wilted or bruised leaves; peel tough outer layer of stalk or cut away tough stem ends entirely.

Cooking See PARBOIL, SAUTE, STEAM.

▥ ROMAN-STYLE BROCCOLI RAAB

The full flavor of broccoli raab stands up to garlic and cheese and is an excellent foil for pork or tomato-sauce dishes. Substitute Swiss chard if broccoli raab is not available.

> 2 **pounds broccoli raab**
> ¼ **cup olive oil**
> ½ **tablespoon minced garlic**
>   **Coarse salt and freshly ground pepper**
> 3 **tablespoons fresh lemon juice**
> 2 **tablespoons grated Romano cheese**

1. Wash broccoli raab and trim away any woody stems. Bring a large pot of salted water to a boil. Blanch broccoli raab 2 minutes. Drain and refresh in a bowl of ice water. Drain again and gently towel-dry.

2. Heat olive oil in a large skillet over moderate heat. Add garlic and sauté, stirring constantly, for 1 minute. Add broccoli and cook, turning often with tongs, until greens are coated with oil, hot throughout, and tender (about 2 minutes). Season to taste with salt and pepper; add lemon juice. Transfer to a warm serving platter. Sprinkle with cheese and serve at once.

Serves 4.

BROIL, TO

A cooking method which uses dry, radiant heat. It is appreciated for its convenience, speed, and simplicity. The goal for all broiled foods is to have the surface perfectly browned when the interior is cooked to taste. For a moist and tender final product, a delicate balance must be maintained between rapid surface cooking and slower internal heat transfer. The farther food is from the heat source, the more time it can stay under the broiler before overcooking. Thus larger pieces of meat, requiring a longer broiling time than thin fillets or skewered foods, may need to be set on a low oven rack to ensure a nicely browned surface and properly cooked interior.

Experiment with your broiler's temperature controls and rack settings. With experience you will develop an understanding of how to control the variables of this technique. As a general rule of thumb, however, place food about 4 to 6 inches from the broiler element. Broiled items should be uniform in size and at room temperature, so all will cook evenly and quickly.

SOME HINTS TO KEEP IN MIND

- Always preheat your broiler. If it's electric, have the door ajar when the unit is in operation.
- Line the inside of the broiler pan with aluminum foil to ease cleanup.
- Trim excess fat from meats and poultry before broiling since fat can ignite from high heat. For the same reason, drain off oil-based marinades and pat meat dry.
- Use tongs, not a fork, to turn meat; pricked meat loses its juices and becomes dry.
- Broiling *Fish:* Broiled fish is done when the meat is opaque and no longer clings to the bone. Cook 8 to 10 minutes per inch of thickness.
- Broiling *Meat:* See Timetable for Broiling Meat, opposite page. Any timetable should be considered merely a guideline, because so many variables should be taken into account when computing broiling time— shape of meat, amount of fat and bone, whether it was at room temperature, accuracy of your oven. Other ways than time for judging doneness include color of meat and touch. A few minutes before the estimated end of cooking time, make a small cut in the meat (near the bone if it has one; near center if boneless) to view the inside. Another way, used by professional chefs, takes into account how meat changes consistency as it cooks (see GRILL, When Is It Done?). When broiling steak, trim away most fat, leaving about ¼ inch; slash fat to keep from curling. For very thick steaks, use an instant-read thermometer to judge internal temperature. Very lean meats such as veal benefit from a baste or marinade to keep them moist.
- Broiling *Poultry:* See Timetable for Broiling Meat, opposite page. Broiled poultry is done when a meat thermometer inserted in the thickest part of the flesh reads 170° F to 175° F, or when the juices run slightly pink, or when the flesh springs back slightly when touched.
- Broiling *Vegetables:* Because they lack fat to keep them from drying out, baste vegetables with fat (oil or butter) or marinate them before broiling. Also ahead of time, blanch fibrous vegetables, such as leeks or celery, to soften slightly. Don't use the most intense heat, as vegetables may char before they cook completely. Broil until tender when pierced and slightly streaked with brown. Suggested for broiling: Japanese eggplant, leek, mushroom, onion, peppers, squash, tomato.

BROWN, TO

To expose food to high temperature in order to deepen surface color and intensify flavor. This is done under a broiler, in the oven, or by cooking in fat on top of the stove. Browned foods, properly cooked, have a crisp and pleasing texture without being brittle and burnt.

BROWNIE

How to define a brownie? Most often it's described as a square of rich, thin chocolate cake. Technically, however, it's a bar cookie, and it isn't always chocolate. Even the dictionary hedges in its definition of this extraordinarily popular sweet; Webster's describes it as "usually" chocolate and "often" made with nuts. What about texture? Brownie lovers argue whether the best is fudgy and chewy, or light and cakelike.

Actually there isn't a single, standard brownie recipe. There are numerous approaches, which have all evolved from the many techniques of making cakes. What is important is the final product, not what you had to do to make it or whether you've chosen to use solid chocolate, chocolate syrup, or cocoa powder to infuse the batter with its characteristic flavor.

Traditionally brownies are flat and square, although few of us would refuse one cut in a wedge or something even more unorthodox. The texture is either moist, chewy, and dense, or moist and cakey. Most often they are brown, but butterscotch brownies (blondies) are golden, those made with white chocolate quite pale, and marbled ones two-tone. The addition of chopped nuts is common, but controversial. Even more contentious is the inclusion of fruit, which some recipes may suggest.

In sum, a brownie is square or rectangular, made of chocolate, with nuts or other additions, and has a moist texture. But not always.

Note These delicate formulations are created to produce a particular result. Varying proportions of ingredients, size of pan, and, most important, oven temperature and baking time even slightly will alter the final product. So, if you find *the* brownie recipe, follow it to the letter each time and you will be rewarded batch after batch.

CUTTING BROWNIES WITH PRECISION

Although even brownie crumbs taste wonderful, these bars look best when cut cleanly. For best results, refrigerate brownies in the pan to firm the chocolate before cutting. Turn out onto a dry, clean work surface and cut upside down to keep the top from crumbling. Use a sharp, serrated knife; for very fudgy brownies, dip knife in hot water before cutting. Wipe after each cut to prevent dragging. For brownies made in a square pan, cut in half each way, then halve each half. For larger rectangular pans, mark cuts lightly on the surface of the brownie using a ruler and sharp knife, and then cut along these lines. To make straight cuts, lay the ruler along the marked line and use the ruler's edge to guide the knife. If the brownie is especially moist, wipe the knife blade between cuts.

TIMETABLE FOR BROILING MEAT

A timetable such as this one can help you estimate how long a particular cut will take to broil to a particular degree of doneness. Keep in mind that the times are approximate and are based on a preheated broiler and meat at room temperature. Depending upon thickness and tenderness, cuts cook from 2 to 6 inches from the heat. Thicker cuts (1 inch thick or more) need to broil farther from the heating element and will need the longer cooking time. See also TEMPERATURE, Guide to Internal Temperatures.

Type of Meat	Thickness	Rare	Total Cooking Time (in minutes) Medium	Well Done
Beef				
Flank steak	1 inch	4–5	6–8	
Hamburger	1 inch	3–5	9–11	13–15
	2 inches	4–6	11–13	15–17
Rib eye	1 inch	3–5	6–7	10–12
	2 inches	5–7	6–7	12–14
T-bone, porterhouse,	1 inch	5–6	9–11	13–16
club steak	2 inches	7–8	11–13	15–18
Tenderloin	1 inch	3–5	6–7	
	2 inches	5–7	9–11	
Top sirloin steak	1 inch	5–6	9–11	13–16
	2 inches	7–8	11–13	15–18
Lamb				
Loin chop	1 inch	5–7	8–10	12–14
	2 inches	7–8	10–12	14–16
Rack chop	1 inch	5–7	8–10	12–14
	2 inches	7–8	10–12	14–16
Shoulder chop	1 inch	5–7	8–10	12–14
Pork				
Loin chop	1 inch	8–10	12–14	
	2 inches	10–12	14–16	
Shoulder chop	1 inch	8–10	12–14	
	2 inches	10–12	14–16	
Tenderloin		10–12	14–16	
Poultry				
Boned breast				5–10
Chicken, turkey (bone-in pieces)				50–70
Halved game hen				12–15
Small whole bird				25
Veal				
Loin chop	1 inch	8–10	12–14	
Rack chop	1 inch	8–10	12–14	

Children of all ages love brownies, those ultimate bar cookies. Chewy or cakelike, nutty or plain, solid or layered, there's a brownie recipe to please every taste.

STORING AND FREEZING BROWNIES

Because brownies are so moist, they keep extremely well. When cool, remove bars from pan and wrap individually or leave in pan, tightly covered. Store in a cool, dry place. Moist, dense brownies will keep up to one week, drier, cakelike brownies one to two days. In warm weather you may want to store brownies in the refrigerator, where they will keep for three to four days. For longer storage wrap well and freeze for up to two months. Thaw slowly at room temperature.

CLASSIC FUDGE BROWNIES

These brownies have a moist texture and an intense, chocolate flavor. For a taste of mocha, try the Espresso Brownies variation.

   4 **ounces unsweetened chocolate, chopped**
  ½ **cup butter**
  3 **large eggs**
1⅓ **cups sugar**
  2 **teaspoons vanilla extract**
  ¾ **cup flour**
     Pinch salt
  1 **cup chopped pecans or walnuts**

1. Preheat oven to 350° F. Line bottom of an 8-inch-square cake pan with parchment paper; butter pan and dust with flour.

2. In a small, heavy-bottomed saucepan, melt chocolate and butter over low heat. Let chocolate mixture cool and continue with step 3.

3. In a large bowl beat eggs and sugar until thickened and lemon-colored; blend in vanilla. Sift flour and salt together and fold in; blend in chocolate mixture, then nuts.

4. Spread into prepared pan; bake until toothpick inserted near edge comes out clean (30 to 35 minutes).

5. Cool in pan. Refrigerate at least 2 hours before cutting. Serve chilled or at room temperature.

Makes 16 brownies.

Espresso Brownies   Add 1 teaspoon instant coffee powder to chocolate-butter mixture as it melts.

WHITE-CHOCOLATE AND CHIP BROWNIES

The cocoa butter in white chocolate makes this brownie even richer; the color—dotted with dark bits of chocolate chips—makes it elegant.

   3 **ounces white chocolate**
  ½ **cup butter or margarine**
1½ **cups flour**
  ½ **teaspoon baking powder**
  ¼ **teaspoon salt**
  3 **eggs, at room temperature**
1½ **cups sugar**
  1 **teaspoon vanilla extract**
  1 **package (6 oz) semisweet or milk chocolate chips**
  ½ **cup sliced almonds**

1. Preheat oven to 350° F. Line bottom of a 9- by 13-inch pan with parchment paper; butter pan and dust with flour. In a small, heavy saucepan, melt white chocolate and butter over low heat; stir well to blend. Remove chocolate mixture from heat and let cool while continuing with step 2.

2. In a medium bowl combine flour, baking powder, and salt; set aside.

3. With an electric mixer beat eggs and sugar at high speed until thick and lemon-colored. Blend in vanilla. Gradually add white chocolate mixture, then flour mixture; beat well until combined. Stir in chocolate chips and ¼ cup almonds.

4. Spread batter in prepared pan, and sprinkle with remaining ¼ cup almonds. Bake until edges begin to pull away from sides of pan and center is nearly set when tested with a toothpick (30 to 35 minutes).

5. Let cool in pan on a wire rack for 10 minutes, then cut into bars. Remove from pan when cool.

Makes 3 dozen bars.

■ **CAKE-LOVER'S BROWNIES**

Not as dense and gooey as fudgy brownies, these bars have more in common with a rich chocolate cake.

> 4 **ounces unsweetened chocolate, chopped**
> ½ **cup butter, softened**
> ¾ **cup sugar**
> 3 **eggs**
> 1 **tablespoon vanilla extract**
> ½ **cup flour**
>   **Pinch salt**
> 1 **cup chopped pecans or walnuts**
> ¼ **cup chocolate chips** *or* ½ **cup raisins (optional)**

1. Preheat oven to 350° F. Line bottom of an 8-inch-square cake pan with parchment paper; grease and flour.

2. In a double boiler over hot, but not boiling, water, melt chocolate; remove from heat and cool.

3. In a medium bowl cream butter and sugar until the consistency of whipped cream. Add eggs, one at a time, beating well after each addition. Stir in vanilla.

4. Sift flour and salt, and fold into egg mixture; gently blend in chocolate, then nuts and chocolate chips (if used). Spread into prepared pan; bake until toothpick inserted 2 inches from edge comes out clean (25 minutes; center may still look a little soft). Cool in pan.

5. Refrigerate at least 2 hours before cutting. Serve chilled or at room temperature. Best eaten within 2 days.

Makes 16 brownies.

■ **BUTTERSCOTCH SAUCEPAN BROWNIES**

The pecan-studded batter for these buttery blond brownies can be mixed in one saucepan to simplify preparation.

> 1 **cup flour**
> ¾ **teaspoon baking powder**
>   **Pinch salt**
> ⅓ **cup butter or margarine**
> 1 **cup firmly packed brown sugar**
> 1 **egg**
> 1 **teaspoon vanilla extract**
> ½ **cup chopped pecans**

1. Preheat oven to 350° F. Line bottom of an 8-inch-square cake pan with parchment paper; butter pan and dust with flour. In a medium bowl thoroughly combine flour, baking powder, and salt; set aside.

2. In a 2-quart saucepan melt butter over medium heat. Add brown sugar, stirring until sugar dissolves and mixture bubbles. Remove from heat and let stand 5 minutes to cool slightly.

3. Beat in egg and vanilla, then gradually stir in flour mixture. Stir in pecans. Spread batter in prepared pan.

4. Bake until edges begin to pull away from sides of pan and center is nearly set when tested with a toothpick (25 to 30 minutes).

5. Let cool in pan on a wire rack 10 minutes, then cut into bars. Remove from pan when cool.

Makes 18 bars.

■ **MARBLED CREAM CHEESE BROWNIES**

Two batters—one made with cream cheese, the other with melted semisweet chocolate and chopped nuts—are swirled together to make these unusual brownies.

Cream Cheese Mixture

> 2 **tablespoons butter or margarine, softened**
> 1 **small package (3 oz) cream cheese, softened**
> ¼ **cup sugar**
> 1 **egg**
> 1 **tablespoon flour**
> ½ **teaspoon vanilla extract**

Chocolate Mixture

> 4 **ounces semisweet chocolate**
> 3 **tablespoons butter or margarine**
> ½ **cup flour**
> ½ **teaspoon baking powder**
> ¼ **teaspoon salt**
> 3 **eggs**
> ¾ **cup sugar**
> 1 **teaspoon vanilla extract**
> ½ **cup chopped walnuts**

1. Preheat oven to 350° F. Line bottom of an 8-inch-square cake pan with parchment paper; butter pan and dust with flour.

2. *For Cream Cheese Mixture:* In a medium bowl beat butter and cream cheese until well mixed. Add sugar and beat well. Add egg and beat until fluffy. Blend in flour and vanilla; set aside.

3. *For Chocolate Mixture:* In a small, heavy saucepan melt chocolate and butter over low heat; stir well to blend and set aside to cool. In a small bowl combine flour, baking powder, and salt; set aside. In a medium bowl beat eggs at high speed with an electric mixer until light-colored. Gradually beat in sugar, then vanilla. Gradually add flour mixture, mixing until well combined. Blend in chocolate mixture. Stir in walnuts.

4. Spread half of Chocolate Mixture in prepared pan. Pour Cream Cheese Mixture over it, lightly spreading to pan edges. Cover with remaining chocolate mixture. Swirl a thin spatula through all 3 layers to create a marbled effect.

5. Bake until edges begin to pull away from sides of pan and center is nearly set when tested with a toothpick (40 to 45 minutes).

6. Let cool in pan on a wire rack 5 minutes, then cut into bars. Remove from pan when cool.

Makes 18 bars.

Brussels Sprouts With Fresh Chestnuts is at its appealing best during the winter months, when chestnuts are in season.

BRUISE, TO

To partially crush a food—such as a clove of garlic—with the heel of a knife or with a mortar and pestle to release flavor. Bruising also facilitates removal of garlic's papery peel. When used for a sauce, berries are often bruised so they will absorb sugar more easily.

BRUNOISE

A mixture of aromatic vegetables cut in an even, fine dice, *brunoise* is used to flavor soups, stews, and sautés. Commonly included are onions, celery, carrots, and leeks, and less often turnips and parsnips; the choice is up to the cook. *Mirepoix* is a similar vegetable mixture used in the same way, but cut in coarser pieces.

BRUSH, TO

To apply a coating with a brush. Most often what is spread on is a flavoring agent, such as a glaze or a basting liquid; a fat, such as butter or oil; or a protective layer, such as an egg wash or aspic. A natural-bristle brush is recommended, as plastic bristles will melt and distort upon contact with heat.

> ### Recipes and Related Information
> *Baste, 27; Cake and Pastry Tools, 89; Glaze, 268.*

BRUSSELS SPROUT

The Brussels sprout is a member of the cabbage family, native to northern Europe. Instead of one large head, the plant produces numerous small heads arranged in neat rows around a thick stalk.

Use   Cooked Brussels sprouts may be eaten cold as a salad but are generally eaten hot as a side dish, dressed with butter, oil, or meat-roasting juices. Their nutty flavor is flattered by sliced almonds, braised chestnuts, and cream sauces.

Availability   Fresh and frozen. The domestic fresh crop is harvested from mid-August through the first week of May. Imported Brussels sprouts from Mexico are available in late spring and summer. Brussels sprouts are generally removed from their stalk and sold in bulk (by the pound) or in cardboard buckets overwrapped with cellophane. However, they are increasingly coming to market still attached to their stalks. These sprouts have superior flavor; remove the heads from their stalk just before cooking.

Selection   Choose Brussels sprouts that are small and odorless, tightly closed, and bright green, without yellowing or loose leaves around base.

Storage   Refrigerate fresh Brussels sprouts in a plastic bag for three to five days.

Preparation   Wash; trim stem ends and remove wilted or discolored leaves. Cut an *x* in stem ends for faster and more even cooking.

Cooking   See BOIL, SAUTE, STEAM.

▨ BRUSSELS SPROUTS WITH FRESH CHESTNUTS

The European custom of roasting chestnuts and selling them on street corners is a romantic tradition that dates from antiquity. Brussels sprouts and chestnuts make a classic pairing for a holiday side dish.

> 2 **pounds fresh chestnuts** *or*
>   **1 can (16 oz) chestnuts, drained**
> 2 **pounds fresh Brussels sprouts**
> 2 **cups Beef Stock (see page 560)**
> ¼ **teaspoon salt**
>   **Freshly ground pepper**

1. On the rounded side of each chestnut, make a deep *x* through outer shell and inner shell underneath. Place chestnuts in a 2-quart saucepan, cover with water, and boil for about 15 minutes; drain. Peel shell and inner skin. (If chestnuts are too hot to handle, cool briefly, but not for more than 1 or 2 minutes or they will be hard to peel.)

2. Trim the Brussels sprouts of dried stems and leaves. Cut an *x* into stem end of each so that they will cook more evenly and be less apt to separate.

3. In a large skillet combine stock and Brussels sprouts, and bring to a boil. Reduce heat and simmer 15 minutes. Add cooked chestnuts, salt, and pepper to taste, and cook 10 minutes more.

Makes 8 servings.

BULB BASTER

Bulb basters look like over-sized eyedroppers and work in the same way. They are used to keep meats moist and flavorful by drenching them with pan juices or other liquid.

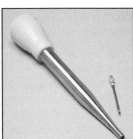

Their shafts are made of either nylon or stainless steel, both with a removable rubber bulb. Metal basters come with a long-handled cleaning brush to push out any food trapped in the narrow tip. Some are also packaged with a hollow metal injecting needle for internal basting and flavoring, which screws onto the shaft. Most basters measure about 10 inches from tip to top of bulb.

Nylon basters are considerably cheaper than metal ones; they also let you see how much liquid is drawn up into the shaft. Metal, however, is more durable and should last a lifetime. Both materials are safe to be put in a dishwasher. Remove bulb to clean. To reassemble, wet edge of shaft and bulb will slide on easily.

BURNET

A perennial herb native to Europe, burnet has rounded, toothed leaves that grow close to the ground, a tall flower stem, and rose-colored flowers. The leaves have a mild, cucumberlike flavor.

Use Add whole burnet leaves to salads or float in iced drinks. Mince and add to mayonnaise or when using fines herbes. The leaves are a refreshing addition to salads, iced drinks, and herb vinegars.

Availability Fresh burnet can be found in specialty markets from May through October.

Selection Buy burnet that looks fresh and sprightly, without signs of wilting or decay.

Storage Keep in a plastic bag in refrigerator crisper for one or two days.

Preparation Wash just before using.

BUTTER

A solid fat, butter is made by agitating or churning cream (the fatty portion of cow's milk). It takes about 10 quarts of milk to yield 1 pound of butter. Most of the butter available commercially is sweet cream butter made from fresh (not sour) cream; it may be salted or unsalted. Sour cream butter, churned from cream that has been allowed to mature and sour slightly, is now hard to find commercially due to changing tastes; however, many who have grown up on sour cream butter prefer its pronounced flavor. It is probably still made for home use by many of those who keep dairy cows.

Although some consumers and cookbook writers use the term sweet butter to refer to unsalted butter, that term is misleading. A supermarket package labeled sweet cream butter may or may not be salted. If the butter does contain salt, it will be listed as an ingredient on the label. Unsalted butter is usually identified as such on the label. Salt adds flavor to butter and prolongs its refrigerated shelf life. However, many cooks prefer the delicate, fresh taste of unsalted butter. Vegetables sautéed in unsalted butter with a pinch of salt have a different flavor than those sautéed in salted butter. Because it is more perishable, unsalted butter is more expensive. Except in certain delicate cookies and pastries, it is rarely essential to the success of a dish.

Whipped butter is sweet cream butter, salted or unsalted, which is whipped with air or inert gas to make spreading easy.

Use Butter adds flavor and richness to a variety of cooked foods and prepared dishes. Pouring melted butter on cooked vegetables; spreading softened butter on breads, muffins, biscuits, or other baked goods; swirling butter into a soup; and dotting butter on the top of a casserole before baking are all ways to use the nutty flavor of butter to enrich a dish.

It is the base of several important sauces, garnishes, and frostings. Both the classic Hollandaise sauce and its variations and the classic beurre blanc (white butter sauce) and its variations are butter-based sauces for savory foods. Compound Butters are classic garnishes for grilled meats, poultry, and fish. Butter provides the basis for buttercream frosting and hard sauce, the traditional accompaniment for steamed puddings.

Butter is also valued as a cooking medium. Cooking fish, meat, poultry, eggs, bread, vegetables, and batters in butter adds flavor and an appetizing brown surface.

As an ingredient in baked goods, butter adds tenderness and flavor and prolongs shelf life. Butter can also help leaven a baked product. Thoroughly creaming butter for a cake batter traps air and moisture; when cake is baked, hot air and steam expand and so does the cake. Similarly, layers of butter folded into a puff pastry dough will release steam in the oven, causing the pastry to rise.

Clarified butter has a clearer taste than whole butter and is preferred for light sauces. As it doesn't burn easily, it is often used for sautéing.

Availability   In retail markets butter is packaged in ¼-pound sticks or 1-pound blocks, wrapped in pure vegetable parchment or parchment-laminated metal foil to prevent absorption of other flavors or odors during storage. For added protection, it's usually packaged in waxed-paper cartons. Whipped butter is most commonly sold in 8-ounce tubs.

Selection   High-quality butter should have a sweet, not stale, aroma. It should have a semisoft consistency at room temperature and should not sweat, which would indicate excessive water content. It should melt smoothly on the tongue without leaving a deposit. Salted butter should not taste oversalted.

Storage   Salted butter will keep for several weeks in its original package in the coldest part of the refrigerator. Unsalted butter loses its delicate flavor after a week or two of refrigeration. Keep partially used butter in a covered dish in the refrigerator to prevent absorption of other odors. Store only what will be used within three days in the butter-storage compartment of the refrigerator. Butter freezes well—up to one month in its original package and up to nine months in freezer paper.

■ BROWN BUTTER (BEURRE NOISETTE) AND BLACK BUTTER (BEURRE NOIR)

The nutty flavor of both of these butter sauces complements poached fish, fried eggs, brains and other variety meats, green beans, cauliflower, and asparagus. To make Brown Butter, cook clarified butter over low heat until amber and fragrant. For Black Butter, cook clarified butter until very dark brown, almost black.

■ CLARIFIED BUTTER

Also known as drawn butter, clarified butter is butter with the milk solids removed. The clear yellow fat that remains can withstand high heat without burning. It will keep several weeks in the refrigerator or longer in the freezer.

To clarify butter: In a heavy pan, melt 1 pound of butter over low heat. Skim off froth and carefully pour clear yellow liquid from pan, leaving milky residue behind. Discard residue.

Makes about 1½ cups.

■ COMPOUND BUTTERS

Compound butters (also known as composed butters or flavored butters) are a mix of softened butter plus flavoring used as a sauce on grilled meats, fish, and poultry. They are also wonderful for basting. Compound butters freeze well, up to two months wrapped in waxed paper. Shape butter into a block or roll before chilling or freezing. To use, cut desired amount off block and store remainder.

Prepare butters as follows: In a medium bowl combine ingredients either by hand or with an electric mixer until well blended. Use immediately, or wrap in waxed paper.

Ancho Chile Butter
Adds heat to grilled meat, fish, or poultry. *Makes ½ cup.*

   2 large dried ancho chiles (or use New Mexico, pasilla, or California variety)
   ½ cup butter

Cover chiles with boiling water. When they are rehydrated, drain and finely chop in a food processor or blender. Mix with butter.

Bercy Butter
Classically used for grilled beef and fish. *Makes ½ cup.*

   ½ cup dry white wine
   1 tablespoon minced shallots
   1 tablespoon minced parsley
   1 tablespoon fresh lemon juice
   ¼ cup cubed poached marrowbone
      Salt and freshly ground pepper, to taste

Boil wine and shallots until reduced to about 3 tablespoons; cool, then mix with parsley, lemon juice, marrowbone, salt and pepper.

Garlic Butter
Spread on bread or melt on meat, fish, or vegetables. *Makes ½ cup.*

   5 cloves garlic, peeled
   2 cups water
   ½ cup butter, softened

Boil garlic in the water about 5 minutes. Drain, cool, then crush garlic and mix with butter.

Herb Butter
Pair with fish, poultry, or vegetables. *Makes ½ cup.*

   4 tablespoons herbs of choice (chives, oregano, parsley, thyme, tarragon)
   ½ cup butter, softened

Maître d'Hôtel Butter
Classically served with grilled meats, fish, or vegetables. *Makes ½ cup.*

   2 tablespoons chopped parsley
   1 teaspoon fresh lemon juice
   ½ cup butter, softened

Nut Butter
Use as a garnish for soups or toast, or as a sauce for fish or poultry. *Makes ¾ cup.*

   ½ cup finely chopped, toasted hazelnuts, almonds, or pistachios
   ½ cup butter, softened

Orange Butter

Use with fish, poultry, vegetables, breads, pancakes, or waffles. *Makes ½ cup.*

> 2 teaspoons freshly squeezed orange juice
> Grated rind of 1 orange
> ½ cup butter, softened

Red Pepper Butter

Use with fish and poultry. *Makes 1 cup.*

> 2 shallots, finely chopped
> 2 large red bell peppers, peeled, seeded, and finely chopped
> 1 tablespoon balsamic vinegar
> 1 tablespoon butter
> ½ cup unsalted butter, softened

Cook shallots, red pepper, and vinegar in 1 tablespoon butter until peppers soften; cool, then mix with butter.

Recipes and Related Information
Beurre Blanc, 518; Broiled Porterhouse Steak With Savory Butter, 41; Buttercream Frosting, 248; Butter Curler, 69; Hollandaise Sauce, 516.

BUTTER CURLER, MOLD, PADDLES, PRINT

Butter doesn't taste any better when it's curled, rolled, or pressed out of a mold, but it's certainly prettier and more fun to use. For all the butter shapes, store and serve over ice. Some of these shapes are tricky to produce. You may want to practice with each of these tools before attempting anything elaborate for a special dinner party. If you have time, prepare the shapes in quantity and freeze, well-wrapped. Then use the amount you need and leave the rest for another occasion.

BUTTER CURLER

The curved stainless steel blade has one notched edge that produces shell-like, ribbed curls of butter. To use, dip blade in warm water and draw across a block of butter that is soft enough to peel without falling apart, yet cold enough to hold its shape, but not shatter, when pressed.

BUTTER MOLD

Use this wooden cup to shape rounds of butter charmingly imprinted with a bird, flower, or other motif. Immerse mold in ice water for about 10 minutes. Fill cavity of mold with softened butter and refrigerate until butter firms. Press out butter by pushing down on plunger.

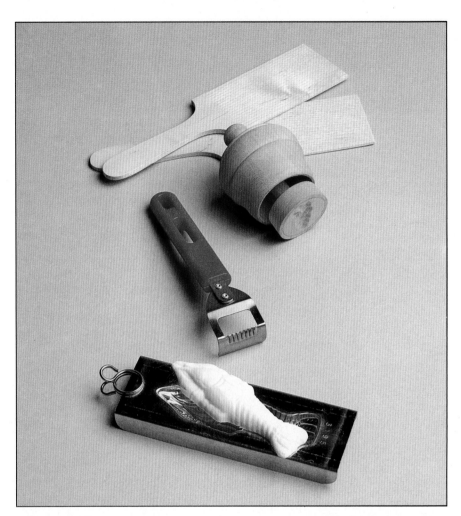

BUTTER PADDLES

To make butter balls, soak wooden paddles in water for about 10 minutes. Set a lump of cold butter about the size of a large marble on the ribbed surface of one paddle. Lay the other paddle, ribbed side down, on butter at a 90-degree angle and rotate until a ridged ball is formed.

BUTTER PRINT

This wooden or ceramic disk embosses a design on single servings of butter. Dip print in ice water, then press on a slightly softened pat or round of butter.

Whether rolled into balls, curled, or molded, shaped butter adds a decorative note to the table. Shown from top to bottom are: butter paddles, wooden mold with grape design, butter curler, metal mold with fish pattern.

BUTTERFLY, TO

This butcher's technique involves halving food horizontally, without cutting all the way through it, so that the two halves can be opened like the wings of a butterfly or the pages of a book. Often this is the first step when preparing a roast that is to be stuffed and rolled.

Braised Chinese Cabbage and Garlic, a richly seasoned vegetable side dish, is shown in a special earthenware casserole known as a clay pot or sand pot. This type of pot has been used in China for centuries for slow, gentle cooking over very low heat.

CABBAGE

One of the oldest vegetables cultivated by man, cabbage grows well in almost any climate and is appreciated in almost all of the world's cuisines. The cabbage or brassica family is quite large and includes such common vegetables as cauliflower, broccoli, mustard, kale, horseradish, radish, rutabaga, and turnip.

The members of the brassica family that go by the name cabbage are many and varied. Most are characterized by large round heads of tightly packed leaves, although some varieties are elongated, flattened, or loosely packed. Most varieties are white to light green, although red varieties exist.

Use   Raw and cooked cabbages are employed in many countries throughout the world. Raw cabbage can be shredded, dressed, and eaten as a salad, as in American cole slaw. It can be steamed, sautéed, braised, or baked, added to soups and stews, stuffed whole, or creamed. Steamed cabbage leaves can be filled with a stuffing, rolled, and braised. Thai diners often use whole cabbage leaves as a wrapper for spicy salads. Cabbage also makes a popular pickle: German sauerkraut, Japanese cabbage pickle, and the spicy Korean kimchee are all variations on the same theme.

Availability   Fresh cabbage is in the produce section all year, except for savoy cabbage, which is plentiful from fall until spring. Chinese cabbage is available at Asian markets, specialty produce markets, and well-stocked supermarkets. This entry details specific varieties of commercial importance.

Selection   See specific cabbages.

Storage   Western varieties may be stored in a plastic bag in the refrigerator crisper for at least two weeks. Chinese cabbage keeps, under similar conditions, for up to one week. Do not wash cabbages before storing.

Preparation   This varies depending upon variety; check specific types for preparation information.

Cooking   See BOIL, BRAISE, SAUTE, STEAM, STIR-FRY.

CHINESE CABBAGE

Several varieties of Chinese cabbage are available on the commercial market. Some form relatively compact, elongated heads. Others are open, leafy, flowering cabbages.

Bok Choy   This elongated, non-head-forming cabbage has long white ribs with dark green leaves; it resembles chard. Choose bok choy (also known as *pak choy* or *pak choi*) that has good color and firm white ribs; avoid wilting leaves. To prepare, trim stem and discard any discolored or ragged leaves. Bok choy is usually sliced across the ribs and stir-fried, but it may be eaten raw as a salad. A miniature version called baby bok choy or *bok choy sum* is occasionally available in specialty markets; it is particularly attractive when braised whole.

Napa Cabbage   Also called Chinese cabbage or celery cabbage, Napa cabbage has elongated, tightly furled leaves with wide white ribs and soft, pale green tips. Mild in flavor, it may be eaten raw or cooked. Choose heads that are heavy for their size, without bruised or ragged leaves; avoid very large heads, which may be bitter. To prepare, trim away any brown or bruised leaves. Slice and add raw to salads, or use in soups and stir-fries.

BRAISED CHINESE CABBAGE AND GARLIC

Braised and simmered dishes allow you to put together a Chinese dinner at a leisurely pace. The cabbage simmers unattended for the last 15 or 20 minutes, allowing plenty of time to prepare the rest of the meal. Lily buds are the dried, unopened buds of a tiger lily. Soaked in water and drained, they add a pleasant texture and slightly tart and tealike flavor to certain Chinese dishes. They are available at Asian markets, as are Chinese clay pots (see CASSEROLES AND BAKING DISHES, Chinese Clay Pot).

½ cup dried lily buds
  Oil, for stir-frying
1 large head garlic, separated into cloves
  and peeled
1 medium carrot, peeled and sliced
  on the diagonal
1 tablespoon minced fresh ginger
1 pound bok choy or other large-ribbed Chinese
  cabbage, cut crosswise into 1½-inch slices
2 or 3 green onions, trimmed and
  cut into 2-inch lengths
1 cup Rich Chicken Stock (see page 560) or
  duck stock, salted to taste
1 tablespoon black soy sauce

1. In a small bowl soak lily buds in lukewarm water until soft. Drain, squeezing out excess liquid. Cut or pinch off hard ends, and set lily buds aside.

2. Have ready a 1½-quart or larger Chinese clay pot (see CASSEROLES) or other flameproof, covered casserole. If using a clay pot, preheat it with hot water and dry it. Heat a wok or skillet over medium heat. Add a tablespoon or so of oil, and stir-fry garlic cloves and carrot until lightly browned. Add ginger and stir-fry until fragrant. Transfer contents of wok to casserole. Add a little more oil to wok, and stir-fry cabbage and green onions until just heated through. Transfer to pot. Add stock, soy sauce, and lily buds to wok and bring just to a boil. Pour over vegetables in pot.

3. Place casserole over medium-low heat, bring to a simmer, and cover. Simmer 15 to 20 minutes. Serve directly from pot.

Serves 6 to 8 with other dishes.

GREEN CABBAGE

The most common cabbage in American markets is the large round-headed variety with pale green or green leaves overlapping tightly around a central core. Select head cabbage that is heavy for its size, without drying around the core. To prepare, discard any wilted or damaged outer leaves and remove core with a sharp paring knife. Cabbage may be shredded and eaten raw as a salad or coleslaw; it may be steamed, braised, added to soups, or preserved as sauerkraut. The whole head may be blanched, then stuffed between the leaves and braised, or hollowed, stuffed, and baked. Individual leaves may be blanched to soften, then stuffed and braised. See Cabbage Preparation, page 76.

QUICK BUTTERED CABBAGE

This simple, basic technique is useful for cooking all green vegetables. They should be cooked until tender with just a touch of crispness; the easiest way to check is by tasting. When cooked in this way, cabbage remains bright green and has a delicate flavor. Serve it with any meat or poultry, or even with seafood.

1 medium (about 2 lb) green cabbage
¼ cup butter
  Salt and freshly ground pepper, to taste

1. Cut hard core from cabbage and discard. Rinse cabbage and cut in thin strips.

2. In a large saucepan boil enough lightly salted water to cover cabbage generously. Add cabbage and boil, uncovered, until just tender (about 5 minutes); check by tasting.

3. Drain cabbage, rinse with cold water, and drain thoroughly. Gently squeeze dry in a colander. Cabbage can be kept, covered, for 1 day in refrigerator.

4. Melt butter in a large skillet over medium heat. Add cabbage, salt, and pepper. Cook, stirring, until butter is absorbed (about 3 minutes). Taste and add more salt and pepper, if needed.

Serves 4 to 6.

STEAMED CABBAGE WEDGES

A very simple but delicious and attractive preparation for cabbage, the wedges can be dressed with a flavored butter, such as lemon butter, and served with a poultry or meat stew. See BUTTER, Compound Butters, for a selection of recipes for flavored butters. See STEAM for more information about steaming vegetables.

1 medium (about 2 lb) green cabbage

1. Trim any battered outside leaves from cabbage. Cut head in half lengthwise; cut each half into wedges, each including part of core. Steam until just tender (5 to 8 minutes).

2. Transfer wedges to a cutting board, cut away core, and transfer intact to plates (slide knife blade under wedge to lift it in one piece).

Serves 4 to 8.

Microwave Version   For 1 pound of cabbage, prepare for cooking as directed in step 1. Place in a glass container and add 2 tablespoons water. Cook at 100 percent power 5 to 7 minutes. Let stand 2 minutes before dressing with lemon butter; serve.

▨ BOHEMIAN CABBAGE ROLLS

Plump cabbage-wrapped packets of ground ham and pork are steamy and delicious. Serve with fluffy white rice.

> 1 egg
> ⅓ cup whipping cream
> ¼ cup soft bread crumbs
> ¼ teaspoon salt
> ⅛ teaspoon *each* ground allspice, dill, and white pepper
> 2 cups ground smoked pork picnic shoulder or leftover ham
> ½ pound ground pork
> 1 large (2½ to 3 lb) green cabbage
>   Paprika
>   Flour
> 2 tablespoons butter or margarine
> 1 medium carrot, thinly sliced
> 1 medium tomato, peeled and chopped
> 1 medium onion, finely chopped
> ½ cup *each* dry white wine and tomato juice
>   Sour cream and chopped parsley, for garnish

1. Preheat oven to 375° F. To prepare filling, beat egg with cream; mix in bread crumbs, salt, allspice, dill, and pepper. Lightly combine with ground meats; set aside.

2. To prepare cabbage, cut out core and carefully separate outer 6 leaves (reserve remainder for salad or other uses). Cut out thickest part at base of each leaf. Place leaves loosely in a large, deep frying pan; add just enough water to cover bottom. Cover and steam just until leaves are wilted and bright green (2 to 3 minutes). Remove cabbage from pan and drain.

3. Divide filling among the 6 prepared cabbage leaves. For each cabbage bundle, fold in sides, roll up loosely, and fasten with a toothpick (see Cabbage Preparation, page 76). Sprinkle cabbage rolls lightly with paprika, then coat with flour.

4. Pour out water from pan in which cabbage was steamed; in same pan brown cabbage rolls lightly on all sides in butter. Transfer rolls to a 2- to 3-quart casserole as they brown. Surround with carrot and tomato.

5. In same pan cook onion until it begins to brown. Mix in wine and tomato juice. Bring to a boil and cook, stirring, 3 minutes. Pour over cabbage rolls. (At this point casserole may be covered and refrigerated overnight.)

6. Bake, uncovered, for 1 hour. Uncover and continue cooking for 15 minutes longer. To serve, spoon vegetables and sauce over cabbage rolls, and top with a dollop of sour cream and a sprinkling of parsley.

Serves 6.

Food Processor Version With slicing disk slice carrot and set aside until needed. Cut onion into quarters, put in work bowl, and with metal blade, turn motor on and off 3 or 4 times; remove from work bowl and set aside.

To grind meat: Cut lean pork and smoked pork into 1-inch pieces. Pulse motor about 10 times to chop. Add egg, cream, bread crumbs, salt, and spices. Process 5 seconds to combine.

Microwave Version *To wilt leaves:* Place 6 cabbage leaves in a dish in the microwave oven; cover and cook at 100 percent power for about 2 minutes. Let stand, covered, if additional time is needed to soften the leaves; drain any liquid.

▨ STUFFED WHOLE CABBAGE

Instead of stuffing individual cabbage leaves, try stuffing the whole head and cutting it into wedges to serve. When cabbage is sliced, the filling contrasts attractively with the subtle green of the leaves.

> 1 large (2½ to 3 lb) green cabbage
> 1 small onion, diced
> 1 clove garlic, minced
> 2 tablespoons vegetable oil
> 4 tablespoons unsalted butter
> ½ pound ground veal
> ½ pound ham, minced
> 3 sprigs parsley, minced
> ½ teaspoon salt
> ⅛ teaspoon freshly ground pepper
> 1 egg
> ¼ cup Beef Stock (see page 560)
> ½ cup soft bread crumbs
> ½ cup whipping cream

1. Remove tough outer leaves from cabbage, reserve 2 or 3 to cover top, and discard remainder. Slice off top of cabbage and scoop out interior, leaving a shell about ¾ inch thick and a cavity approximately 4 inches in diameter (see Cabbage Preparation, page 76). Place cabbage in a 4-quart saucepan; cover with boiling water, reduce heat, and simmer until just tender (about 20 minutes). Drain upside down in a colander; let cool.

2. Preheat oven to 350° F. In a large skillet sauté onion and garlic in oil and 2 tablespoons butter over medium heat until soft but not browned (about 5 minutes). Add veal and ham, and sauté, stirring constantly and breaking up clumps as they form, until thoroughly cooked (about 10 minutes).

3. Mix in parsley, salt, pepper, egg, Beef Stock, bread crumbs, and cream. Cook briefly (2 to 3 minutes), stirring to combine. Stuff filling into hollowed cabbage. Cover stuffed cabbage with reserved cabbage leaves.

4. Grease a 3-quart casserole with remaining 2 tablespoons butter and set stuffed cabbage in dish. Cover casserole tightly with lid or aluminum foil and bake 90 minutes. Remove from oven, let rest 10 minutes, discard loose top leaves, and cut into 6 to 8 wedges to serve.

Serves 6 to 8.

■ CHOUCROUTE GARNI

Alsace is a region of France near Germany. Alsatian food often reflects both French and German cuisines. *Choucroute* is French for sauerkraut: the word gives this dish its name—sauerkraut with accompaniments. This recipe is easily made ahead for a gathering. Bring the piping hot casserole to the table and serve guests some meat, potatoes, and sauerkraut. Accompany with a glass of Riesling or dry white wine. Many cooks reserve duck, goose, or chicken fat to use here in place of vegetable oil.

   1 tart apple, diced
   2 medium onions, diced
   4 tablespoons vegetable oil
   ½ cup parsley, minced
   4 slices bacon, diced
  10 juniper berries, crushed
   1 teaspoon thyme
   1 bay leaf
  1⅔ cups Chicken Stock (see page 560)
  1⅓ cups Riesling or dry white wine
   3 to 4 skinless ham hocks
   2 pounds sauerkraut, rinsed
  12 small potatoes
   6 veal sausages
   3 smoked pork chops or pork steaks

1. In a 6-quart Dutch oven, sauté apple and onions in oil over medium heat until soft (10 minutes). Stir in parsley, bacon, juniper berries, thyme, bay leaf, stock, wine, and ham hocks. Cover and simmer 45 minutes.

2. Rinse sauerkraut in colander under cool water; pat dry. Scrub potatoes and cut each in half. Add sauerkraut, potatoes, and veal sausages to Dutch oven. Stir to combine, cover, and simmer another 15 minutes.

3. Remove pork chop meat from bone and cut into 2-inch cubes. Stir in pork cubes, cover, and cook another 40 minutes. Make sure each portion has a serving of meat, potatoes, and sauerkraut.

Serves 8 to 10.

Recipes: Crispy Coleslaw, 506; New England Boiled Dinner, 42.

RED CABBAGE

Ranging from reddish purple to dark purple, the firm, round red cabbage has tightly packed, overlapping leaves around a white central core. It is available the year around. Select compact cabbages that feel heavy for their size and do not have wilted outer leaves. To prepare, discard any damaged outer leaves and remove core with a sharp paring knife. Red cabbage may be pickled or eaten raw as a salad, braised, steamed, or sautéed. Adding vinegar or lemon juice to the cooking water (about 1 tablespoon per cup of water) will help preserve the bright color.

■ RED CABBAGE WITH APPLES

Apples and cabbage are a traditional pairing of flavors, sparked by a sweet-and-sour mixture of cider vinegar and brown sugar. Serve this alongside bratwurst or with any pork or beef dish.

   2 tablespoons vegetable oil
   1 onion, coarsely chopped
   ¼ cup cider vinegar
   2 tablespoons brown sugar or honey
     Salt and freshly ground pepper, to taste
   1 green apple, cored and thinly sliced
   1 small red cabbage, coarsely shredded

1. In a large frying pan, heat oil. Add onion and sauté until softened (5 minutes). Add vinegar, sugar, and salt and pepper to taste; stir to mix.

2. Add apple and cabbage. Bring liquid to a boil, reduce heat to medium, cover, and cook until cabbage wilts (about 10 minutes). Stir occasionally to coat cabbage with vinegar-sugar mixture.

Serves 4.

Microwave Version Prepare cabbage for cooking. Place shredded cabbage in a glass container and add 2 tablespoons water. Cover and cook at 100 percent power for 6 to 8 minutes. Add to recipe in step 2, after apple has cooked. Toss to coat with vinegar-sugar mixture.

Red Cabbage With Apples is part of a traditional German wurst supper. Shown with the cabbage dish are pan-fried bratwurst, sautéed onion, Spätzle (see page 190), and dark pumpernickel bread.

Flour, sugar, milk, butter, eggs, nuts, raisins, fruits, and spices are just some of the ingredients that are transformed into cakes and pastries of all sorts. Using the freshest, best-quality ingredients will make a noticeable difference in the final product.

Flour   Along with eggs, flour gives a cake its structure by forming an elastic network that traps expanding gas and steam. Use cake flour when indicated for a lighter, more tender cake. Sifting is recommended for most cakes, especially for more delicate ones such as angel food, sponge, and chiffon. Sifting results in a finer end product; it aerates the flour, removes specks of foreign material, and breaks up lumps. Cake flour should always be sifted; follow recipe directions about sifting before or after measuring. If you wish to substitute all-purpose flour for cake flour in a recipe, substitute 2 tablespoons cornstarch for the same amount of flour per 1 cup cake flour specified. It's unnecessary to sift all-purpose flour before measuring, although some older recipes may call for it. It's a good idea to sift after measuring to blend the flour with the other dry ingredients. For more information about sifting, see FLOUR.

Fat   From fat, a cake gets tenderness, richness, and fluidity. Select a fat that is plastic (pliable) and easily beaten. Butter is preferred for its flavor, but is limited in the range of temperatures at which it can be beaten. Hydrogenated vegetable shortening is plastic at a wider range of temperatures than butter, but is tasteless. Some recipes compromise by calling for half shortening (for its superior creaming ability) and half butter (for excellent flavor). Butter creams best at room temperature. Let chilled butter warm on the counter until it is cool to the touch, but soft enough that a finger pressed into the surface leaves an impression. When oil is specified, use a light one such as safflower oil. Lard should be avoided because it doesn't cream well.

Sugar   To balance the toughness contributed by flour and eggs, sugar is added to the batter to tenderize and, of course, to sweeten. When sugar is creamed with fat, its crystalline structure carries air into the mixture and contributes to the volume of a cake. Use granulated sugar unless otherwise indicated. Angel food cake recipes often specify superfine sugar which, like cake flour, is finely granulated and makes a finer crumb.

Eggs For foam cakes, eggs are the primary or only source of leavening and, along with flour, provide structure for all baked goods. They are a source of liquid and function as emulsifiers, which make the batter more uniform and stable. Unless otherwise directed, always use eggs graded large. Separate eggs when cold. Use whole eggs, egg yolks, and egg whites at room temperature. If desired, eggs may be measured by volume and weight. An egg is two-thirds white and one-third yolk. See EGG, Beating Eggs, for information about beating whole eggs, egg yolks, and egg whites.

Liquid In a cake batter, liquid adds moisture, which converts to steam with heat. Common liquids for cakes include milk, cream, sour cream, buttermilk, yogurt, fruit juices, and water. Recipes for foam cakes don't require liquids, other than what is provided by eggs or, in the case of chiffon cakes, by oil.

Acid Cream of tartar and lemon juice, both acids, help to stabilize an egg foam until it sets in the oven. Cream of tartar is commonly beaten into egg whites for this reason, especially if they are not whipped in a copper bowl. Acids help develop a finer texture and more tender crumb; for an angel food cake, they enhance its characteristic white color.

ABOUT CAKE PANS AND OTHER EQUIPMENT

By custom, an angel food cake has a hole in its center and a layer cake is round. We expect to see them that way and so most are, but angel food cakes in loaf form taste just as wonderful, as do square layers. The point is that any one of a number of baking pans will do a particular job well. Don't be compelled to buy every specialty pan you come across unless you have a lot of storage space, you bake a particular cake often, or different shapes appeal to you. Whichever you choose is up to you as long as the pan meets these criteria: it is of the proper volume and height for the recipe (regardless of shape); it is of good quality; it is made of a material that will conduct heat evenly and well. For information on specific pans and materials, see BAKING PANS, FOR BATTER AND DOUGH and MATERIALS FOR COOKWARE.

Other equipment useful for cake making includes such kitchen staples as wooden spoons, spatulas, measuring spoons and cups, mixing bowls, cooling racks, and a quality portable or stand electric mixer with a strong motor. Additional specialized tools, particularly those used for cake decorating—pastry bags, combs, turntables—are optional. See CAKE AND PASTRY TOOLS.

PREPARING PANS

Greasing and flouring baking pans aren't always necessary, but most recipes suggest that you do because it is less likely that the cake will stick. Some recipes call for greasing the bottom and sides, some only the bottom. Some recipes recommend adding a lining of parchment or waxed paper, others don't. Most call for dusting a pan with flour, but a few might suggest using sugar or crumbs. This powdery coat develops a thin, crisp crust and also keeps a cake from absorbing fat from the pan. Follow the directions in the recipe. If you are using a nonstick pan, grease and flour anyway if you are instructed to do so.

A few cakes need special treatment. Dense butter cakes such as pound cakes and heavy fruitcakes, which must bake slowly and for a long time, are baked in greased and paper-lined pans to protect the sides of the cake from overbrowning. Many bakers prefer parchment paper because it can withstand high oven temperatures and is very easy to peel off. Rich batters (those with a lot of sugar or eggs) and those with a large quantity of fruit should bake in greased and floured pans, even pans with nonstick interiors. Angel food cakes and chiffon cakes bake in ungreased pans so the delicate batter can cling to the sides as it rises.

When greasing pans, only a thin layer of fat is necessary, but it should be evenly applied. Use butter, solid shortening, oil, or vegetable cooking spray, and apply with a paper towel, pastry brush, or fingers. To make a paper liner, use bottom of cake pan as a guide, and trace around pan onto a piece of parchment or waxed paper. Cut paper to fit, and place it on the greased bottom of the pan. Grease the paper. If using paper, don't flour pan until after paper is in place. For dusting, place a few tablespoons flour, sugar, or other powder in greased pan, and tilt pan in each direction until entire surface is covered with a thin layer of flour. Invert pan and tap it on a counter or with your fist to remove excess flour (see PREPARING PAN FOR BAKING).

FILLING PANS

Cake batter should fill the pan from one-half to three-quarters full depending upon cake. The pan should never be so full that when the batter rises it overflows. For batters that rise high, such as angel food and sponge cakes, use deeper pans and less batter per pan. For heavier batters such as layer and pound cakes, pans are filled two-thirds to three-quarters full. When dividing a batter among several pans, as for layer cakes, use a ladle or spoon, rather than pouring from the mixing bowl, in order to maintain control and divide batter equally.

ABOUT BAKING CAKES

Place a cake in the oven as soon as possible. Leavening agents begin their action even before a cake is baked and need oven heat to finish the job or they will lose some of their power. Always bake in a preheated oven. Turn oven

SUCCESSFUL CAKE BAKING

If you are well organized and have thoroughly read the recipe before you begin, you will find baking a pleasure and will produce more successful baked products. Look up any unfamiliar terms or techniques. Assemble all of the equipment and ingredients in advance (a baking pan is a good catchall; the French call this process *mis en place*—all in place). Measure all ingredients precisely and carefully; have them at the specified temperature and in the condition indicated in the recipe. Finally, get into the habit of checking oven temperature and turning on the oven before you do anything else. Even the best bakers fail to achieve perfect results every time. Consult the following if you experience difficulties.

IF BUTTER CAKE BATTER CURDLES

- Each egg was not sufficiently mixed in before the next one was added.
- Batter was beaten at too high a speed. If it starts to curdle, ignore it or reduce the mixer speed to medium or medium-low and add 1 tablespoon flour per egg.

IF CAKE FALLS IN THE MIDDLE

- Batter was overbeaten, creating excess aeration which cake was unable to contain.
- Too much sugar was added to the batter.
- Too much baking powder was added.
- Too much liquid was added.
- Cake was undercooked.
- Oven door was opened before cake was set or cake was disturbed because oven door was closed with too much force.

IF CAKE PEAKS IN THE CENTER

- A hard (high-gluten) flour was used instead of soft flour (cake flour).
- Batter was overbeaten after flour was added. (This overactivates the gluten in the flour, creating a tough cake.)
- Oven was too hot. Cake rose too quickly.

IF CAKE IS TOUGH, FLAT, AND HEAVY

- Batter was underbeaten, causing insufficient aeration.
- Not enough sugar was added.
- Not enough baking powder was added.

on at least 10 to 15 minutes before you need to use it. Baking at the proper temperature and maintaining that temperature throughout the process are critical to the success of the final product. Cakes need to bake relatively fast to give their structure some rigidity. Without this framework, they would rise and then collapse because the leavening gases could not be maintained. Avoid opening the oven door during the first half of baking, which is the rising period. If the door is opened, the temperature will drop and the cake will fall; if you must open the door, do so quickly and close it gently without banging it shut.

Know your oven and how it bakes. Test it at several different temperatures with an oven thermometer to see if it is accurately calibrated. If it is off by 25° F or less, you can compensate by raising or lowering the oven temperature. If it is off by as much as 50° F, have it recalibrated. If you have two ovens and you often use both at one time for baking, you may find it convenient and helpful to leave an oven thermometer in each oven. See THERMOMETER.

In a standard oven, bake cakes on the center rack unless otherwise directed. Leave 1 to 2 inches between pans, and between pans and walls of oven. Try not to bake on more than one rack at a time; if you do, the goods baked on the bottom rack will tend to burn because they are close to the heating element and the heat will reflect from the pan on the upper shelf. If you are baking in quantity and need to employ more than one rack, use the middle rack and stagger the pans; once the cake is set rotate pans so they will bake evenly.

You can bake any of the recipes in this book in a convection oven, but you may need to adjust the oven temperature or baking time; see manufacturer's instructions.

USING A MICROWAVE OVEN

Baking cakes in a microwave oven produces mixed results. They won't brown and can bake unevenly; however, they can be moist, airy, and light, and they can have greater volume than those baked in a conventional oven because they don't develop a crust and therefore can rise more. The best cakes for baking in a microwave are rich cakes made with whole eggs, pudding cakes, and cakes made with oil. Boxed cake mixes also can be baked in a microwave with good results—just omit one egg when making the mix to improve texture and volume.

Round and ring shapes bake most evenly. Cakes often bake more evenly on the bottom when elevated on a plastic trivet or inverted glass dish. Rotating the cake dish once or twice, a quarter to a half turn, also facilitates even baking, especially in older ovens.

Experiment with several recipes to see if cakes from a microwave are to your liking; that's the best way to determine which ones are suited for this type of cooking.

WHEN IS THE CAKE DONE?

Experienced cooks rely not only on baking time to know when a cake is ready to come out of the oven, but also on how it looks, smells, sounds, and feels. A cake is done when it springs back lightly when touched in the center with a fingertip and when it begins to pull away from the sides of the pan. It will have developed an aroma, and the popping and sizzling of the batter will have slowed down (if these sounds have stopped completely, cake may be overdone). Start checking about 10 minutes before the end of the recommended baking time. A cake tester, toothpick, or wooden skewer should come out clean when inserted into the center of the cake.

COOLING AND TURNING OUT OF THE PAN

Cool the cake as directed in the recipe. Sponge cakes and butter cakes are often left to sit in their pans on wire cooling racks for 5 or 10 minutes before turning out. During this brief period they will continue to shrink from the sides of the pan. In addition, steam builds between cake and pan, which will help release the cake. Before unmolding, run a knife around the cake to loosen it from the sides of the pan, then sandwich it between two cooling racks and invert. Remove pan, sandwich cake gently between two racks, and flip again. Cool completely at room temperature before icing or storing.

Angel food cakes and chiffon cakes cool by hanging upside down in their pans. Set the angel food cake pan on its legs, or invert and place on the neck of a bottle or a funnel. Chiffon cakes in their pans can be inverted and set directly on a cooling rack because they don't rise as high as angel food cakes and won't be crushed by the rack.

STORING AND FREEZING CAKES

Cakes with fat, such as butter cakes and chiffon cakes, have the best keeping qualities; sponge cakes taste freshest when eaten the day they are baked or within a day or two. Ideally, cakes should be frozen unfrosted and unfilled, then frosted or filled after thawing. Butter-based icings can be frozen successfully for up to two months in rigid containers; thaw in the refrigerator, then bring to room temperature to make spreadable. If icing curdles during thawing, add a little hot, clarified butter and whip at high speed until it comes together. Icings based on egg whites or whipped cream do not freeze well. If you must frost a cake before freezing, select a butter-based icing. Always allow cake to cool completely before freezing. Certain spices, such as nutmeg and cloves, intensify in flavor when they are frozen, so use slightly less than the amount called for in the recipe.

Wrap cakes well with plastic wrap and aluminum foil, date, and freeze for time indicated. Cakes stored longer than the recommended period will suffer a loss of quality but will still be safe to eat. The freezing times are for goods stored at 0° F. Storing foods at temperatures higher than 0° F shortens the storage period considerably.

Angel, Chiffon, and Sponge Cakes Wrap first in plastic wrap and then airtight in a plastic storage bag: angel food cake—four to five days; chiffon cake—up to two weeks; sponge cake—two to three days. To freeze, follow directions for butter cakes. For added protection, store in a box or rigid container, sealing edges with freezer tape; label. Freeze unfrosted cakes up to six months, frosted cakes up to two months.

Butter and Pound Cakes Wrap well and store airtight, five to seven days. To freeze unfrosted, wrap, label, and date. Freeze for up to four months. To thaw, loosen wrapping and thaw at room temperature. To freeze a frosted cake, chill on a tray in freezer (uncovered) until firm. Wrap, label, and date. Freeze for up to two months. To thaw, remove wrapping and thaw at room temperature or in refrigerator.

Cheesecakes Refrigerate, loosely covered with aluminum foil, up to three days. To freeze, chill on a tray in freezer (uncovered) until firm. Wrap, label, and date. For added protection, store in a box or rigid container, sealing edges with freezer tape; label. Freeze for up to four months. Thaw in wrapping in refrigerator.

Fruitcakes Store in an airtight container; will keep up to three weeks when cut; freeze after that. To freeze, wrap, label, and date. Freeze for up to 12 months. Thaw in wrapping at room temperature.

FREEZING CAKE BATTER

As a timesaver, batter for butter cakes can be frozen, unbaked, for up to four weeks, and baked just as it comes from the freezer.

Prepare batter and spoon into pan in which it will be baked, first lining pan with heavy-duty foil. Freeze, uncovered, until solid (this usually takes 6 to 12 hours). Remove batter from pan, wrap it completely, label and date package, and return it to freezer. To bake, grease baking pan in which batter was frozen, peel away foil around batter, and place batter back in pan. Add at least 5 to 10 minutes to normal baking time; cake is done when a wooden pick inserted in center comes out clean.

Proper packaging is important for protecting batters during storage. Package materials must be resistant to both moisture and air. Aluminum foil is excellent; use either heavy-duty foil or a double thickness of regular foil. Heavy plastic bags designed for freezer storage are suitable for packaging cupcakes. Be sure to check the label on the package—if it does not say the bags are suitable for freezing, choose another bag.

Air pockets between food and package material collect moisture, resulting in frost and freezer burn. When wrapping frozen batters, press out as much air as you can and mold wrappings as close to food as possible. To extract air from plastic bags, insert a drinking straw in the opening, squeeze the opening shut around the straw, inhale to draw out air, and fasten tightly. Label and date all packages.

Most batters will keep up to four weeks at 0° F. If your freezer doesn't maintain a temperature of 0° F (and many combination refrigerator-freezers don't), do not keep the batter frozen more than two weeks.

CAKE DECORATION

Some cakes look and taste fine when unadorned. Others require a finish, whether simple or elaborate. The process of cake decoration ranges from the texturing of icing spread on a cake to the application of intricate patterns. When cakes are baked to celebrate an occasion or event, you can tailor their shape and decorations accordingly. Rectangular cakes are good picnic fare because they can be simply iced and easily carried. The same cake base can be baked in layers and elegantly adorned with buttercream rosettes or piped scrolls to serve at a dinner party. See FROSTING, ICING, AND FILLING for specific techniques.

FINISHING THE CAKE

The outside of a cake can be covered with one of the following treatments.

Almond Paste Almond paste or marzipan can be rolled out and used to form the top layer or outside covering of a cake. Almond paste can also be molded or shaped to form cake decorations (roses, flowers, leaves, stems, animals, fruits).

Confectioners' Sugar For a simple, quick finish, sift a light layer of confectioners' sugar over the cake. Create a design by laying a stencil, a fancy paper doily, a cutout snowflake, or strips of paper on the surface of the cake. Sift confectioners' sugar over the pattern, and carefully

With an easy-to-make paper piping cone (see page 246), you can decorate any cake, cookie, or pastry with all types of designs or messages. Lines 1 through 4 are typical borders. Line 5 shows a sample of script. Line 6 is a classic repeating design.

Elegant, sugar-dusted Ladyfingers are a classic example of the pastry maker's art. To shape them into even lengths, the cake batter is piped onto a baking sheet with a pastry bag.

2. In bowl of heavy-duty mixer or other medium bowl, beat yolks and ¼ cup sugar together until mixture falls from beater in a ribbon and leaves a slowly dissolving trail on surface (ribbon stage). In a copper or stainless steel bowl, beat egg whites to soft peaks (if bowl is stainless steel, add cream of tartar when whites are just foamy); add remaining sugar and beat until stiff peaks form.

3. Stir one-fourth beaten egg whites into yolk mixture to lighten; sift in half the flour and fold into batter. Add remaining flour, then most of remaining beaten egg whites. Fold in rest of whites and vanilla.

4. Fill a pastry bag fitted with a ½-inch plain tip half full with batter. Pipe 4-inch-long fingers onto paper-lined baking sheet, about 1 inch apart (see Note). Sprinkle with confectioners' sugar and bake until edges are just beginning to brown (15 to 18 minutes). Cool on wire racks.

Makes 3 dozen ladyfingers.

Note If ladyfingers are to be used to line a charlotte mold, you can pipe fingers ½ inch apart so that as they bake they will expand and touch. To line mold, don't separate ladyfingers. Trim them to proper height, then lift in a sheet and set around inside of mold. For a variation, pipe rows of ladyfingers on the diagonal.

▨ GENOISE

A sponge cake is leavened with a foam made of separately beaten egg yolks and egg whites, and without fat; a génoise uses whole eggs and is enriched with butter. It is the classic French cake, and the foundation for almost all of the French *gâteaux*. Eggs will beat to greatest volume if utensils and ingredients are at room temperature.

> 4 **eggs**
> ⅔ **cup sugar**
> 1 **cup cake flour, sifted twice**
> **Pinch salt**
> 3 **tablespoons unsalted butter, melted and cooled**

1. Preheat oven to 350° F. Lightly grease and flour an 8-inch-diameter cake pan; line bottom with a circle of parchment paper.

2. *To prepare in a heavy-duty mixer:* In warmed bowl of mixer (fill bowl with hot water and drain), beat eggs at medium speed to break up; add sugar and beat until mixture falls from beater in a ribbon and leaves a slowly dissolving trail on surface (ribbon stage). *To prepare with a portable electric mixer or balloon whisk:* Beat eggs and sugar to ribbon stage in a large mixing bowl set over a pan of hot, but not boiling, water (make sure that pan does not touch water).

3. Gently fold in one third of flour, then another third. Mix some batter with melted butter; continue mixing until butter is incorporated, then fold into batter with last third of flour.

▨ LADYFINGERS

These soft, spongy fingers of cake are probably best known as the shell for Charlotte Russe (see page 170). They are also delicious eaten alone. Quick to make, they store well in an airtight container for one week. For longer storage and in damp, wet weather, they should be frozen.

> 1 **cup cake flour**
> **Pinch salt**
> 4 **eggs, separated**
> ½ **cup sugar**
> ¼ **teaspoon cream of tartar (optional)**
> 1 **teaspoon vanilla extract**
> **Confectioners' sugar, for dusting**

1. Preheat oven to 350° F. Line a baking sheet with parchment paper; butter paper and lightly dust with flour. Sift flour and salt together and set aside.

4. Pour batter into prepared pan and smooth surface, making a slight hollow in center. Bake until a pale gold color, the center springs back when gently pressed with finger, and a wooden skewer inserted in the center comes out clean (25 to 30 minutes). Cool in pan 10 minutes; turn out onto a wire rack to cool completely.

5. Slice horizontally into 2 layers with a long, serrated knife (see photograph at right). To moisten and flavor cake layers, brush with a soaking syrup (see SUGAR AND SYRUP), then fill with fruit, buttercream, or any of the frostings or icings in FROSTING, ICING, AND FILLING.

Serves 8.

LEMON CHIFFON CAKE

An American creation of the 1920s, the chiffon cake is a cross between a foam cake and a shortened cake. Because it uses oil instead of butter, it is extremely moist and stores well. Chiffon cake has a pleasing light texture and keeps its shape well, so it can travel to a potluck or picnic without damage. The cake tastes equally delicious if made with fresh orange juice and orange instead of lemon (see Orange Chiffon Cake variation). Glacé icing is extremely simple to prepare and apply.

  2 cups cake flour
1½ cups sugar
  1 tablespoon baking powder
  ½ teaspoon salt
  ½ cup vegetable oil
  ¼ cup fresh lemon juice
  ½ cup milk
  1 teaspoon finely grated lemon rind
  6 eggs, separated
  ½ teaspoon cream of tartar (optional)
     Citrus Glacé Icing (see page 250)

1. Preheat oven to 325° F. In a large bowl sift flour, sugar, baking powder, and salt. Add oil, lemon juice, milk, and grated rind.

2. In a copper or stainless steel bowl, beat egg whites to soft peaks (if bowl is stainless steel, add cream of tartar to whites when just foamy). Gently fold one third of whites into flour mixture to lighten, then gently fold in remaining whites.

3. Pour batter into 10-inch bundt or tube pan. Bake until wooden skewer comes out clean and top springs back when gently pressed with finger (about 1 hour). Cool upside down on wire rack.

4. When cool, remove from pan and decorate with Citrus Glace Icing.

Serves 8 to 10.

Orange Chiffon Cake   Substitute grated orange rind and fresh orange juice for the lemon rind and juice. Prepare icing with orange flavoring.

BASIC YELLOW LAYER CAKE

The American counterpart to the French genoise, the versatile layer cake appears at all celebrations. It can be dressed up or down, and is rich and moist. This is a butter or creamed cake, which means that fat and sugar are beaten together to incorporate air. The creaming step gives the cake its characteristic velvety texture. Remember that fats cream to best volume at room temperature. A chocolate variation follows. The batter can also be used for cupcakes. Fill and frost with any of the frostings in FROSTING, ICING, AND FILLING.

2½ cups cake flour
2½ teaspoons baking powder
  1 teaspoon salt
1⅓ cups sugar
  ¾ cup solid vegetable shortening or butter
  3 eggs
  1 teaspoon vanilla extract
  ½ cup milk

1. Preheat oven to 350° F. Lightly grease bottoms of two 9-inch-diameter cake pans; line bottoms with circles of parchment paper; lightly grease and flour pans and paper.

2. Sift together flour, baking powder, and salt; set aside. In a large bowl cream sugar and shortening until combined. Add 1 egg; beat until light, fluffy, and a pale, ivory color. Add remaining eggs, beating well after each addition. If using a heavy-duty mixer, stop beating as soon as eggs are incorporated and mixture is light and fluffy. Blend in vanilla.

3. Remove beater from mixture. By hand, gently fold in sifted flour mixture in 3 stages, alternating with milk, and beginning and ending with flour.

4. Divide batter evenly between 2 prepared pans. Bake until golden brown, top springs back when gently pressed with finger, and a wooden skewer inserted in center comes out clean (20 to 25 minutes). Cool in pan 10 minutes, then turn out onto wire rack and cool completely. Decorate as desired.

Serves 8.

For an 8-Inch Layer Cake   Use two 8-inch cake pans. Bake 25 to 30 minutes. Each layer can be split in half to make a 4-layer cake.

Basic Chocolate Layer Cake   Substitute ½ cup unsweetened cocoa powder for ½ cup flour; sift cocoa powder and flour together to blend.

Basic Cupcakes   Spoon batter into lightly greased and floured muffin pans or line pans with paper cupcake liners. Bake 15 to 20 minutes.

Makes 18 to 24 cupcakes.

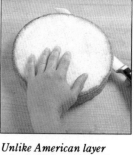

Unlike American layer cakes, which are formed from two separately baked rounds, a layered génoise is created from a single layer sliced in half horizontally. Use a sharp, serrated bread knife, longer than the diameter of the cake, to make a clean slice.

This scrumptious Carrot Spice Cake is topped with Cream Cheese Frosting, partly piped on with a pastry bag, and walnut halves. The sides are covered with chopped, toasted walnuts.

▮ DEVIL'S FOOD CAKE

Perhaps this rich, dark chocolate layer cake got its name because it contrasts dramatically with the snowy whiteness of angel food cake. Split the layers, if desired, to create a four-layer extravaganza.

   ¾ cup unsweetened cocoa powder
   ¾ cup boiling water
   ½ cup solid vegetable shortening or butter
   2 cups sugar
   2 eggs
   1 teaspoon vanilla extract
   ¼ teaspoon salt
 1½ teaspoons baking soda
   1 cup buttermilk
   2 cups sifted cake flour
   2 cups Chocolate Buttercream Frosting
     (see page 248)

1. Preheat oven to 350° F. Lightly grease bottoms of two 8-inch-diameter by 2-inch-deep cake pans; line bottoms with circles of parchment paper; lightly grease and flour pans and paper. Stir cocoa into the boiling water until dissolved; set aside.

2. In a large bowl cream shortening and sugar together until light and fluffy. Add eggs, one at a time, beating after each addition. Beat in vanilla and salt.

3. Stir baking soda into buttermilk. Add ½ cup flour to egg mixture; then add ⅓ cup buttermilk mixture. Continue to add flour and buttermilk alternately, beating well after each addition. Stir in cocoa mixture.

4. Divide batter evenly between the 2 prepared pans. Bake until top springs back when gently pressed with finger and a wooden skewer inserted into center comes out clean (30 to 35 minutes). Cool in pans 5 minutes, then turn out onto wire racks and cool completely. Frost with Chocolate Buttercream.

Serves 8.

▮ CARROT SPICE CAKE

For a simple finish to this delicious cake, follow the directions given in the recipe. For a more elaborate presentation, see photograph at left.

 1⅓ cups unsalted butter
 1¾ cups sugar
   4 eggs
   2 cups flour
   2 teaspoons baking soda
   1 teaspoon ground cinnamon
   ½ teaspoon ground allspice
   ¼ teaspoon freshly grated nutmeg
   ¼ teaspoon ground cloves
   3 cups (about 1 lb) grated carrots
 1¼ cups chopped walnuts
   ¼ cup golden raisins
   ¼ cup coarsely chopped walnuts, for decoration

Cream Cheese Frosting

   ¼ cup unsalted butter, softened
   6 ounces cream cheese, softened
   2 cups sifted confectioners' sugar
   2 teaspoons fresh lemon juice

1. Preheat oven to 325° F. Lightly grease and flour a 9- by 13-inch baking pan.

2. In a large bowl cream butter to lighten; gradually add sugar and cream until light, fluffy, and a pale, ivory color. Add eggs, one at a time, beating well after each addition.

3. Sift together flour, baking soda, cinnamon, allspice, nutmeg, and cloves. Add to butter mixture and blend well. Stir in carrots, the 1¼ cups walnuts, and raisins.

4. Spread batter evenly in pan. Bake until top springs back when gently pressed with finger and a wooden skewer inserted into center comes out clean (45 to 55 minutes). Cool in pan on wire rack. Spread Cream Cheese Frosting on cool cake. Sprinkle the ¼ cup walnuts on top.

Serves 10 to 12.

Cream Cheese Frosting Cream butter and cream cheese. Add confectioners' sugar and lemon juice; beat until smooth.

PECAN APPLESAUCE CAKE

Chunks of homemade applesauce keep this cake moist for days. If you are looking for a healthier snack, replace the flour and sugar with whole wheat flour and honey.

    ½ cup unsalted butter or corn oil
    ½ cup firmly packed brown sugar
    2 eggs
    ½ cup honey
    ½ cup apple juice
    2½ cups sifted unbleached flour
    1½ teaspoons baking soda
    1 teaspoon salt
    ¼ teaspoon baking powder
    1 teaspoon ground cinnamon
    ½ teaspoon ground cloves (optional)
    ¼ teaspoon ground allspice (optional)
    ½ cup dried currants
    1 cup chopped pecans
       Pecan halves, for decoration

Chunky Applesauce

    4 apples
    ¼ cup sugar
    2 tablespoons water

Whipped Cream Icing

    6 ounces cream cheese, softened
    ⅓ cup firmly packed light brown sugar
    1 teaspoon vanilla extract
    1 cup whipping cream

1. Preheat oven to 350° F. Lightly grease and flour a 9- by 13-inch baking pan. Make Chunky Applesauce; cool to room temperature.

2. In a large bowl cream butter with brown sugar until light and fluffy. Add eggs and beat. Combine honey with apple juice; set aside.

3. Sift together flour, soda, salt, baking powder, cinnamon, and cloves and allspice (if used). Add to egg mixture alternately with honey–apple juice mixture, beating after each addition. Stir in currants, pecans, and Chunky Applesauce.

4. Bake until cake tester comes out clean (40 to 50 minutes). Cool in pan on wire rack.

5. Spread Whipped Cream Icing over top of cake. Decorate each serving with a pecan half.

Serves 10 to 12.

Chunky Applesauce Peel, core, and slice apples. In a medium saucepan combine apples with sugar and the water; cover and cook until apples are just tender but not mushy (do not overcook).

Makes 1½ cups.

Whipped Cream Icing Beat cream cheese with brown sugar until smooth. Add vanilla. Whip cream until it holds peaks, and gently fold into cream cheese mixture.

GINGER-PEACH UPSIDE-DOWN CAKE

Spicy gingerbread makes a delicious partner to peaches or nectarines in this unusual version of the classic American dessert—upside-down cake. The cake batter is spooned on a layer of sliced fruit. When turned upside down after baking, the fruit slices glow under a buttery brown-sugar glaze that drips delicately down the sides of the cake.

    1 cup firmly packed light brown sugar
    6 tablespoons unsalted butter, melted
    3 peaches or nectarines
    2½ cups flour
    2 teaspoons baking soda
    ½ teaspoon ground cinnamon
    2 teaspoons ground ginger
    ⅛ teaspoon freshly grated nutmeg
    ⅛ teaspoon ground cardamom (optional)
    ½ teaspoon salt
    ½ cup dark molasses
    1 cup boiling water
    1 scant cup unsalted butter, melted,
       or safflower oil
    1 cup granulated sugar
    2 eggs, lightly beaten
    2 teaspoons finely grated orange rind (optional)

1. Preheat oven to 350° F. Butter sides of a 10- by 3-inch springform pan. Stir brown sugar into the 6 tablespoons melted butter; spread evenly in bottom of pan. Peel and pit peaches; cut into ½-inch-wide slices. (If using nectarines, do not peel.) Arrange slices (packed closely together) in concentric circles on sugar in bottom of pan.

2. Sift together flour, baking soda, cinnamon, ginger, nutmeg, cardamom (if used), and salt; set aside. Combine molasses and the water in a bowl; set aside.

3. In a large bowl beat the 1 cup melted butter and granulated sugar until light. Beat in eggs and orange rind (if used). Add the molasses mixture. Stir in dry ingredients; beat until well blended. Pour batter into the peach-lined pan. Bake until cake tester comes out clean or cake springs back when lightly touched in center (about 1 hour). Cover top of cake with aluminum foil if it begins to burn at the edges.

4. Allow cake to cool in pan for 30 minutes. Invert cake on serving platter, remove cake pan, and allow glaze to drip down sides of cake. Serve while still warm or at room temperature with whipped cream.

Serves 10 to 12.

CHOCOLATE MARBLE CREAM CAKE

Here's a chocolate marble cake designed to be eaten with your fingers. It's perfect fare for picnics or box lunches.

> 4 ounces semisweet chocolate, coarsely chopped
> 2¼ cups sifted cake flour
> 1½ teaspoons baking powder
> ¾ cup granulated sugar
> 1 cup whipping cream
> 2 tablespoons fresh lemon juice
> 2 extralarge eggs
> Confectioners' sugar, for decoration

1. Preheat oven to 375° F. Lightly grease bottom of a 5- by 9- by 3-inch loaf pan. Line bottom of pan with parchment paper; lightly grease and flour pan and paper.

2. Melt chocolate in a bowl over hot, not boiling, water. When chocolate is just melted, remove from heat; cool 10 minutes.

3. Sift flour with baking powder twice; set aside. Combine granulated sugar, cream, and lemon juice in a medium bowl. Add eggs, one at a time, beating well after each addition.

4. Divide batter evenly between 2 medium bowls. Stir melted chocolate into half of batter. Stir half of flour into each half of batter. Fill loaf pan, alternating layers of chocolate and vanilla batter. To create a marbled effect, run a knife through batter in a figure-eight pattern.

5. Bake 20 minutes. Reduce oven to 350° F and bake until golden brown, top springs back when gently pressed with finger, and a wooden skewer inserted in center comes out clean (20 to 30 minutes). Turn out onto wire rack to cool. When cool, sift a light layer of confectioners' sugar on top.

Serves 8 to 10.

POUND CAKE

A very rich creamed cake, pound cake was originally made with 1 pound *each* butter, sugar, eggs, and flour. The eggs were the sole leavening. Today, a little baking powder is often added for additional lightness. If you prefer a less sweet version, omit the 3 tablespoons sugar.

> 1½ cups flour
> ½ teaspoon baking powder
> 1 cup butter
> 1 cup plus 3 tablespoons sugar
> 4 eggs

1. Preheat oven to 350° F. Lightly grease and flour a 4½- by 8½- by 3-inch loaf pan. Sift flour and baking powder together; set aside.

2. In a medium bowl cream butter and sugar together until light, fluffy, and a pale, ivory color. Add eggs, one at a time, beating well after each addition (if mixture begins to curdle, add 1 tablespoon flour).

3. Fold in flour and pour immediately into prepared pan. Bake until golden brown and a wooden skewer inserted into center comes out clean (25 to 30 minutes). Cool in pan 10 minutes, then turn out onto wire rack and cool completely. Serve sliced with fresh fruit or ice cream.

Serves 8.

RICH FRUITCAKE

Although the English may not have invented fruitcake, it is certainly associated with that country. There, fruitcakes are made for all sorts of celebrations, from Christmas to weddings to birthdays. Compared with an American version, this is more cakelike. It is dark, rich, and very traditionally English. The fruits mixed into the spiced batter are a combination of dried and candied—raisins and currants, glacé cherries, and candied citrus peel. For more flavor, let fruits macerate in either sherry or brandy several hours or overnight.

> 2½ cups flour
> 1 teaspoon baking powder
> ½ teaspoon *each* ground cinnamon and nutmeg
> ¼ teaspoon *each* ground allspice and cloves
> 1½ cups dark raisins
> 1½ cups golden raisins
> 1½ cups dried currants
> 1 cup glacé cherries
> ½ cup candied citrus peel
> ½ cup slivered or sliced almonds
> ½ cup sherry or brandy
> 1 cup butter, softened
> 1⅓ cups firmly packed brown sugar
> 4 eggs
> ½ cup milk
> Grated rind and juice of 1 lemon

1. Preheat oven to 350° F. Lightly grease a deep, 8-inch-diameter cake pan; line with a double layer of parchment paper. Lightly grease and flour paper. Into a medium bowl sift flour, baking powder, cinnamon, nutmeg, allspice, and cloves; set aside.

2. In a large bowl combine dark raisins, golden raisins, currants, cherries, citrus peel, and almonds. Sprinkle with sherry and set aside (preferably several hours or overnight).

3. In a large bowl cream together butter and sugar until light, fluffy, and a pale, ivory color. Add eggs, one at a time, beating well after each addition. Fold in flour mixture alternately with milk. Drain fruit if any liquid is left and fold into batter.

4. Spoon batter into prepared pan. Bake 1 hour. Reduce heat to 300° F and bake until golden brown and a wooden skewer inserted into center comes out clean (1½ hours). Should cake begin to overbrown before it is done, cover with aluminum foil.

Serves 10 to 12.

■ ALMOND TORTE

In the winter this very moist cake is delicious with cooked fruit compotes. In the summer accompany it with fresh fruits and fruit sauces.

1¼ cups flour
1 teaspoon baking powder
¾ cup sugar
¾ cup butter
1 package (7 oz) soft almond paste
4 eggs
½ teaspoon almond extract
Raspberry Sauce, for accompaniment (see page 522)

1. Preheat oven to 350° F. Lightly grease bottom of a 9-inch-diameter cake pan; line with a circle of parchment paper; lightly grease and flour pan and paper. Sift flour and baking powder together and set aside.

2. In a large bowl cream together sugar, butter, and almond paste until light and fluffy. Add eggs, one at a time, beating well after each addition; stir in almond extract. Fold in flour mixture.

3. Pour batter into prepared cake pan. Bake until golden and a wooden skewer inserted into center comes out clean (40 to 50 minutes). Cool 10 minutes in pan, then remove from pan and cool on rack to room temperature. Serve accompanied with Raspberry Sauce.

Serves 8.

Recipes and Related Information

Cheesecake, 117; Chocolate Ruffle Torte, 127; Gingerbread, 267; Greek Walnut Torte, 605; Lemon Roulade Charlotte, 171; Poppy Seed Cake With Cream Cheese Frosting, 454.

CAKE AND PASTRY TOOLS

Having every tool and utensil described here does not guarantee that your pie crust will be flaky or that your angel food cake will rise light and airy, but the better equipped you are, the easier baking will be. On the other hand, buy only what you need and have room to store.

BOWL SCRAPER

This thin, flat, flexible piece of nylon has one edge that is curved to fit the curve of a mixing bowl. Many cooks prefer it to a rubber spatula for getting at the last bit of batter left in a bowl or for scooping up frosting, cream puff paste, or other light mixtures. Usually either kidney-shaped or rectangular, it has a general overall measurement of 5¾ inches by 3¾ inches. It is dishwasher-safe.

BRUSHES: PASTRY AND BASTING

Use a pastry brush if you need to apply a delicate jelly glaze to a fruit tart or cake; coat breads, rolls, and pastries with an egg wash, milk, or butter; or wipe away excess flour or other crumbs on a pie or a serving plate. These brushes tend to have short handles (1½ to 4 inches long), and the best are made of long-lasting boar bristles rather than nylon. They are either flat (½ inch to 4 inches wide) or round (usually about 1 inch in diameter). Round brushes and wide flat ones make fast work of buttering pans and wide sheets of filo dough. For laying on the thinnest glaze or liqueur bastes, some pastry makers use a brush made of goose feathers, which are braided at the ends to form a handle.

Brushes with longer handles are used for basting meats and poultry or for buttering pans. Handles average about 12 inches long and bristles are often offset, at an angle. This design lets the cook stand back at a safe distance from a hot oven or grill, yet still be able to reach the food.

Select a brush with bristles that fit deep into the handle and are connected securely to it so they stay on the brush and do not end up in the food. Some nylon and plastic brushes can go in the dishwasher. Natural-bristle brushes should be washed by hand with warm, soapy water right after using and air-dried.

CAKE COMB

The swirls and grooves that texture the frosting of many cakes are easily made with this tool, which is also known as a decorating comb or comb scraper. It is a rigid metal triangle with serrated teeth on all three sides; each row of teeth is of a different size. Made of stainless steel, the comb measures approximately 5 by 5 by 4 inches.

Fresh fruit best complements the rich, buttery flavor of Almond Torte. Try a summery sauce of puréed and whole raspberries.

Many specialty tools are available to assist the home baker. Clockwise from bottom left are: pie weights, pastry bag and tips, dough scraper, cooling racks, pastry blender, pastry brushes, flour dredger, cardboard cake trays, cake tester, cookie press, pastry crimper and wheels, rolling pin, cookie cutters, and a marble board.

CAKE-DECORATING TURNTABLE

By elevating a cake above the counter, this device allows more room for your hand to maneuver. Because the platter rotates, you can apply frosting, chopped nuts, or other surface decoration more evenly and with a more professional-looking result. Plates come in 12-, 14-, and 16-inch rounds or 12- by 16-inch rectangles; all sizes sit on a 4-inch-high base. The better ones are metal, with a cast-iron base and an aluminum alloy disk. For the occasional user, a less expensive plastic version with a shorter base will serve the same purpose.

CAKE TESTER

A cake is considered done if crumbs or batter does not adhere to a tester inserted into the center. For this task you can use a special tool made of a rigid stainless steel wire with a plastic-coated loop handle, or, perhaps more handily, a toothpick, bamboo skewer, broom straw, or sharp knife.

CARDBOARD CAKE TRAYS

These are invaluable aids for cake-decorating. Set under cakes to give them support so they can be easily maneuvered, these trays are especially helpful when applying frosting or other finishing touches. The trays are coated and are available in standard cake sizes, in rounds, rectangles, and squares. Look for them at better cookware stores and at cake-decorating supply stores. You can make your own tray by cutting cardboard slightly smaller than the cake and wrapping it smoothly and tightly with aluminum foil.

COOKIE PRESS

With this hand-operated machine you can transform butter-rich spritz cookie dough into dozens of fanciful shapes. The body is an aluminum and chrome cylinder that you fill with chilled dough. A removable aluminum collar at one end holds one of over a dozen accompanying pattern disks; a mechanism at the other end—either a lever, screw, or plunger—forces the dough through the disk. A press can also function like a pastry bag if you use one of the decorating tips. Look for a cookie press that allows you to regulate the amount of dough ejected through the disk. Even with the best presses, it takes some practice to produce uniform results, but you can always recycle the rejects and try again. After use, wash each part thoroughly in warm, sudsy water, and dry immediately before storing.

COOLING RACK

Wire cooling racks allow air to circulate around baked goods as they cool so steam won't build up underneath and cause them to get soggy. Round racks are good for a single layer of cake; rectangular ones hold two layers, a sheet cake, several loaves of bread, or a big batch of cookies. A good assortment would be two or three round racks and two rectangular ones. Select rectangular racks as large as you can store; these allow you to cool several baking sheets' worth of cookies at a time. Buy racks made of sturdy, heavy-gauge wire strong enough to support cakes and breads without sagging. Larger racks should have feet in the center as well as the corners. Round ones measure 11½ inches in diameter; well-sized rectangular ones are 10½ by 17 inches and 13 by 19 inches.

DREDGER

A cup-shaped dredger is a handy way to coat a cake or pastry with confectioners' sugar, cinnamon sugar, or cocoa, or to flour a work surface. Flour dredgers have about a 2-cup capacity, with a perforated metal screw-on cover and a handle. Sugar dredgers are smaller, holding no more than ½ cup, have a mesh cover, and do not have a handle.

FLOUR SIFTER

See COLANDER, STRAINER, AND SIEVE.

ICING SPATULA

See SPATULA, SCRAPER, AND TURNER.

PASTRY BAG AND TIPS

With a pastry bag you can inscribe a cake with a special message or adorn it with chains of stars, shape delicate ladyfingers and elegant éclairs, or border a roast with a ribbon of mashed potatoes. To use, the cone-shaped bag is filled with batter or icing; when pressure is applied to the bag, the filling is pushed out through a decorative tinned or chromed steel tip held at the pointed end of the bag.

Pastry bags are made of lightweight nylon, canvas, or plastic-lined cloth. Nylon is preferred because it doesn't retain odors, is flexible, and is easy to care for. Most useful sizes are 12, 14, and 16 inches long. Smaller bags are better suited for small designs and for decorating cakes and cookies. Larger bags hold more and can pipe a larger

surface without needing a refill. They can be purchased alone or in a set with an assortment of the most common tips: *plain* for writing and for making lines, stems, dots, or line drawings; *open-star* for small or large rosettes, stars, and border designs; *closed-star* for rosettes and flowers; *leaf* for piping leaves; *slit* for ribbons. Hundreds of specialty tips can be bought singly or in sets. A plastic coupling unit allows you to change tips without switching to a new bag or to use tips that would otherwise not fit the bag. If you don't want to bother with the coupler, consider buying several sizes of bags and a selection of tips for each.

After use, wash pastry bag, tips, and coupling unit in hot, sudsy water; rinse well and air-dry completely or bag will mildew and tips rust.

For information on how to use a pastry bag, see FROSTING, ICING, AND FILLING.

PASTRY BLENDER

To cut fat into flour when making pastry or biscuit dough, most people use a pastry blender. This hand tool has six U-shaped, thin stainless steel wires that are held in place by a wooden or plastic handle. The wires evenly distribute the cold fat, which is worked until the flour-fat mixture is the desired consistency, usually described as coarse crumbs. The more rigid the wires, the better the tool will work. Make sure wires are fastened securely to handle.

PASTRY BOARD

For rolling out pastry and for making candies, you want a surface that stays cool. Marble is considered best because it naturally maintains a surface temperature 20° F cooler than air. It is nonporous and therefore won't absorb moisture from the dough and cause it to stick. Marble, however, is heavy and expensive. A less costly, less weighty, but quite effective alternative is a board made of a dense, white, synthetic polycarbonate. Like marble, this material stays cool; it has the additional attribute of being dishwasher-safe.

Portable marble boards weighing about 20 pounds are ½ inch thick and measure 18 inches square. Boards of synthetic materials come in many sizes; 16 by 18 inches and 16 by 20 inches are practical dimensions. Choose the largest board that will easily fit your work space and allows you to roll out dough comfortably.

PASTRY CLOTH

Made of canvas, pastry cloths are used as a surface for rolling out pastry. Some are printed with guides representing standard diameters of pie crusts; others are set in a frame that keeps the cloth taut and wrinkle-free. Before use, flour is rubbed into the weave, which creates a somewhat nonstick finish. Before storing, the cloth should be shaken out; occasional washing will keep it sanitary. Cloths measure 17 by 18 inches or 21 inches square.

▦ PEANUT BRITTLE

Peanuts are synonymous with this hard, richly flavored candy, but other nuts, such as almonds, pecans, or hazelnuts—or a mixture—will be equally delicious.

>   2 cups sugar
>   1 cup light corn syrup
>   ¾ cup water
>   2 cups raw peanuts (whole or halved),
>   skins removed
>   2 tablespoons butter

1. Oil or butter a baking sheet. In a large, heavy-bottomed saucepan, combine sugar, corn syrup, and the water; stir over low heat until sugar has completely dissolved. Increase heat to medium and cook without stirring until a rich golden brown (300° F on a candy thermometer, hard-crack stage).

2. Immediately remove from heat, add nuts and butter, and stir until nuts are coated. Pour onto prepared sheet, spreading quickly with a buttered spatula to about ½-inch thickness. Cool, break into pieces, and serve. Or store airtight; brittle keeps for about 2 weeks.

Makes about 1½ pounds brittle.

▦ FONDANT

Crystalline, creamy fondant is a foundation or base for other confections, including some frostings. When making fondant the goal is to develop sugar crystals that are fine enough that the candy won't have a gritty texture (see To Control Crystal Formation). After kneading, fondant should be stored for several days before using. Making fondant is hard work and many cooks prefer to purchase it ready-made from cake-decorating supply stores.

>   2 cups sugar
>   2 tablespoons liquid glucose (available at
>   cake-decorating supply stores)
>   ⅛ teaspoon cream of tartar
>   ½ cup water
>   ¼ to ½ teaspoon vanilla or almond extract (optional)

1. In a large, heavy-bottomed saucepan combine sugar, liquid glucose, cream of tartar, and the water and dissolve over low heat, washing down any crystals that may form on the sides of the pan with a brush dipped in hot water.

2. Bring to a boil and cook without stirring to 238° F on a candy thermometer (soft-ball stage). Immediately remove from heat and pour onto a marble slab or other smooth work surface. Cool undisturbed to 110° F. With a dough scraper or 2 metal spatulas that have been dipped in hot water, lift fondant from edges and push back to center.

3. Work fondant continuously, lifting and folding from edges to center, until it becomes white in color and smooth, pliable, and satiny. If desired, the final kneading can be done with buttered hands. If the fondant

becomes too stiff to work, cover with an inverted metal bowl and let sit briefly to soften; work again when ready.

4. Before using, let fondant ripen in an airtight container for several days to become more pliable. *To flavor:* Knead in vanilla or almond extract. *To tint:* Pierce mass and sprinkle a few drops of food coloring (pastel colors are most appropriate, so don't add too much coloring) into holes; let color seep into fondant, then knead to distribute evenly. Fondant keeps for up to 3 months if well wrapped and stored airtight in a cool place.

Makes ¾ to 1 pound.

▦ DIVINITY

Divinity is creamy, like fondant, but is fluffier because the sugar syrup is beaten into whipped egg whites. If made with brown sugar, the candy is called seafoam. Wrapped airtight, Divinity will keep one to two weeks.

>   3 cups sugar
>   ¾ cup light corn syrup
>   ¼ cup water
>   2 egg whites
>   1 tablespoon vanilla extract
>   1½ cups chopped toasted nuts, chopped
>   candied citrus peel, or chopped glacé cherries

1. Oil or butter an 8-inch baking pan or set out sheets of parchment paper. In a medium, heavy-bottomed saucepan combine sugar, corn syrup, and the water; stir over low heat until sugar has dissolved completely. Increase heat to medium and cook without stirring until 250° F on a candy thermometer (hard-ball stage).

2. While syrup is cooking, beat egg whites until soft peaks form. When sugar syrup reaches temperature, slowly pour in a thin stream onto egg whites, beating continuously at high speed. Fold in vanilla and nuts.

3. Continue to beat until mixture cools slightly; pour immediately into prepared pan or drop by tablespoonfuls onto parchment paper. Let stand until firm. If made in pan, cut into squares to serve.

Makes about 5 dozen candies.

▦ CHOCOLATE FUDGE

In older cookbooks, fudge recipes are often named for one of the New England women's colleges, because making this candy was such a popular pastime with students at these schools—Smith, Vassar, and Wellesley all have their own versions.

>   1½ cups sugar
>   1 cup whipping cream
>   1 jar (7 oz) marshmallow cream
>   ¼ cup butter, cut in pieces
>   1 pound semisweet chocolate, chopped
>   1 teaspoon vanilla extract
>   1 cup chopped nuts (optional)

1. Oil or butter an 8-inch baking pan. In a large, heavy-bottomed saucepan, combine sugar, whipping cream, and marshmallow cream; stir over low heat until sugar has dissolved completely. Increase heat to medium and cook without stirring until 238° F on a candy thermometer (soft-ball stage).

2. Remove from heat and add butter and chopped chocolate; stir until completely melted and smooth. Stir in vanilla and nuts (if used).

3. Pour into prepared pan and cool until firm. Cut in 1-inch squares and serve. Stored airtight between layers of parchment paper, fudge keeps for 2 to 3 weeks.

Makes about 5 dozen candies.

■ CHOCOLATE TRUFFLES

Truffles are extremely easy to make because they have few ingredients and aren't dependent upon a temperamental sugar syrup for their base. Note that the truffle mixture must chill overnight before shaping.

  1¼ **cups whipping cream**
    1 **pound semisweet chocolate, chopped**
  ½ **cup unsalted butter, cut in small pieces**
      Unsweetened cocoa powder or chopped nuts, for coating

1. In a large, heavy-bottomed saucepan, bring cream to a boil. Add chocolate in small bits. Then add butter a little at a time. Stir until all is smooth. Cover and chill 8 hours or overnight.

2. If using cocoa, sift onto a plate. If using nuts, place in a layer on a plate. Scoop up chocolate mixture in teaspoonfuls. With hands, shape into ¾-inch balls (chocolate will melt a bit when handled). Roll in cocoa or nuts and set on another plate. Store, covered, in refrigerator until ready to serve. Truffles keep up to 1 month.

Makes about 6 dozen truffles.

Grand Marnier Truffles Before chilling and shaping chocolate mixture, add ¼ cup Grand Marnier and 1 teaspoon grated orange rind.

Recipes and Related Information
Icing Fondant, 251; Pralines, 424; Sugar and Syrup, 567.

CAPE GOOSEBERRY

Despite its name, the cape gooseberry is not a gooseberry at all, but a relative of the husk tomato (or tomatillo) and the ground cherry. It is also known as Chinese lantern, golden gooseberry, or strawberry tomato. Of Peruvian origin, it was later cultivated and highly regarded in South Africa, especially around the Cape of Good Hope. Today it is a commercial crop in New Zealand.

The small, golden, oval fruit is concealed by a brown, papery, outer husk, which must be removed. Its texture is firm and moist, its flavor mild.

Use Cape gooseberries are eaten raw as part of a fruit salad and cooked as an ingredient in a fruit compote. They may be added to stuffings of bread and fruit, made into jams or dessert sauces, used for pie and tart fillings, or added to gingerbread.

Availability Fresh cape gooseberries are available in specialty markets from March through June.

Selection Choose fruit with undamaged husks.

Storage Refrigerate in a plastic bag in crisper for up to two days.

Preparation Remove husk and rinse fruit. Slice, halve, or leave whole.

Perhaps not since the introduction of fudge has a confection appealed to the American sweet tooth as much as the French candy, truffles. Set in individual foil cups, they make a glamorous dessert.

CARDOON

Although the cardoon resembles celery, it's actually a thistle, like the artichoke. It has foot-long, pale green stalks, a tender white heart, and a flavor reminiscent of both artichoke and celery. Cardoon is much appreciated by both French and Italian cooks.

Use   Cardoon heart (inner stalks) may be steamed or boiled, then drained and buttered or dressed with anchovy sauce, or baked with cheese sauce. Italian cooks steam it, then coat it with egg and bread crumbs, and deep-fry it. It is also a traditional component in an Italian *bagna cauda.*

Availability   Fresh cardoon is a winter vegetable. Peak season is October through December.

Selection   Choose bunches with sturdy, pale green stalks and fresh-looking leaves, and without signs of wilting or decay.

Storage   Refrigerate in a plastic bag in crisper for one to two days.

Preparation   Remove and discard tough outer stalks. Trim spurs and leaves from inner stalks. String outside surfaces of stalks as you would celery by scraping with a paring knife. Cut stalks into ½-inch or larger lengths and keep in water acidulated with vinegar or lemon juice to prevent discoloration before cooking.

Cooking   See BOIL, BRAISE, DEEP-FRY, STEAM.

CAROB

Also called St. John's bread, carob is the pod of a tree native to Syria. According to legend, carob sustained St. John in the wilderness. Although carob is unrelated to chocolate, it has a vaguely similar sweet flavor.

Use   Mediterranean children eat dried carob pods as a sort of candy. In the United States, the seeds are sold in health-food stores and enjoyed as an out of hand snack. The seeds are also ground to produce carob powder or flour, for use in beverages, cakes, cookies, and breads. Carob chips are used as a substitute for chocolate chips in cookies and health-food snacks. Because carob does not contain caffeine and has a naturally sweet taste, some consider it a nutritious alternative to chocolate.

Availability   Carob is sold in most health-food stores as whole seeds, unsweetened chips, toasted powder, or chunks sweetened with dates.

Storage   Refrigerate carob seeds. Store carob chips, chunks, and powder in an airtight container in a cool place; they will keep indefinitely.

CARROT

A root vegetable, carrots have feathery green tops; commonly cultivated varieties are a deep orange color and average about 7 to 8 inches long and ¾ inch in diameter; they get larger and less sweet with age. Baby carrots are increasingly available commercially and are especially attractive on raw vegetable platters.

Use   Carrots have the highest sugar content of any vegetable after beets. They are delicious raw—whole, in sticks, or grated in salads. Carrot sticks are a nutritious addition to a child's lunchbox or an appetizer assortment of raw vegetables. Steamed and buttered or sugar-glazed carrots are a common side dish. Carrots may be creamed or pickled, added to stews, baked in a pudding, made into soup, or added to soups; because of their natural sweetness, they are an essential ingredient in a good basic stock. One of the most popular American desserts—spiced carrot cake with cream cheese frosting—depends on grated raw carrots for its moist, appealing texture and distinctive flavor.

Availability   Fresh carrots are sold all year, in bulk or in plastic bags. Frozen and canned carrots are also available.

Selection   Choose small, slender carrots that are rigid, not rubbery. If tops are attached, they should be fresh looking and bright green. Avoid carrots that are split, pale, or deeply discolored around the stem, which indicates age.

Storage   Remove carrot tops, if attached. Store fresh carrots in a plastic bag in the refrigerator crisper. They will keep for several weeks but will gradually lose sweetness and rigidity.

Preparation   Peel if desired; trim ends.

Cooking   See BOIL, BRAISE, GRILL, STEAM.

▪ GLAZED CARROTS
Baby vegetables are charming, especially when dressed up with a buttery glaze. This very simple preparation is one to remember for an impromptu dinner.

    16 baby carrots, scrubbed and trimmed
    ¼ cup butter
    2 tablespoons brandy or fresh lemon juice
    1 tablespoon brown sugar or honey

1. In a large skillet bring salted water to a boil. Add carrots, cover, and simmer until tender-crisp (10 to 15 minutes). Do not overcook. Drain.

2. Push carrots to one side and add butter, brandy, and sugar, stirring to combine. Sauté carrots over medium-high heat, shaking skillet, until carrots are well coated and lightly browned. Serve immediately.

Serves 4.

When combined with white wine and dark raisins, simple root vegetables such as carrots and baby onions become a sophisticated vegetable side dish.

CARROT AND BABY ONION STEW WITH RAISINS

Raisins and white wine give this vegetable stew a delicate, sweet-and-sour flavor. When the vegetables are tender, their cooking liquid becomes a buttery glaze. Serve this stew as an accompaniment to any roast, broiled meat, or poultry, especially beef, pork, chicken, and duck. Note that the stew can be prepared as much as two days ahead of serving and stored in the refrigerator until needed.

   ¼ **cup butter**
   1 **pound carrots, quartered and cut in 2-inch pieces**
   ½ **pound baby onions, peeled (see Note)**
   ½ **cup dark raisins**
   ⅓ **cup dry white wine**
   ⅓ **cup water**
     Salt and freshly ground pepper, to taste
   1 **bay leaf**

1. Melt butter in a large frying pan over medium heat. Add carrots and onions and sauté until lightly browned.

2. Add raisins, wine, the water, salt and pepper to taste, and bay leaf. Bring to a boil. Reduce heat to low, cover, and simmer, stirring occasionally, until vegetables are tender (about 35 minutes).

3. Raise heat to medium, uncover, and cook until liquid forms a syrupy glaze (about 10 minutes). If mixture is too watery and vegetables are beginning to fall apart, remove them carefully with a slotted spoon and boil liquid until it thickens; return vegetables to liquid and heat gently. Stew can be kept, covered, up to 2 days in refrigerator; reheat in a covered frying pan over low heat.

4. Taste and add more salt and pepper, if needed; best if served hot.

Serves 4.

Note To peel the baby onions, drop them into a saucepan of boiling water and boil 1 minute. Drain, rinse with cold water until cool, then peel with a paring knife.

Recipes and Related Information
Carrot-Raisin Salad, 507; Carrot Spice Cake, 86; Cream of Any Vegetable Soup, 563; Vegetable Purées, 487.

CELERIAC

Grown primarily for its swollen root, celeriac is a type of celery. About the size of a baseball, the knobby, brown-skinned root has long, celerylike stalks that are usually removed in processing for the retail market. The appearance of this vegetable gave rise to its other common names: celery root, celery knob, and turnip-rooted celery. It has firm, crisp white flesh with a flavor that very much resembles that of celery.

Use   Celeriac may be eaten raw in salads or cooked in soups, stews, and casseroles. Boiled celeriac may be whipped with butter and cream, or mixed with whipped potatoes. Sliced celeriac may be baked in a cream or cheese sauce. French cooks cut raw celeriac into fine matchsticks and dress it with a mustard mayonnaise to make *céleri-rave rémoulade,* a salad popular with both home cooks and chefs.

Availability   Fresh celeriac is most readily found fall through winter.

Selection   Choose small to medium celery root that is firm, not spongy.

Storage   Celeriac will stay fresh in a plastic bag in the refrigerator crisper for up to one week.

Preparation   Peel with a small, stainless steel paring knife (carbon knives discolor celeriac). Plunge immediately into acidulated water to prevent discoloration. Slice, grate, or cube as recipe directs. Celeriac may also be washed and boiled in its skin, then peeled.

Cooking   See BOIL.

▇ CELERY ROOT SALAD
Céleri-rave rémoulade

The unglamorous celery root, when peeled and shredded, can be transformed into an elegant salad, often served as a first course in French restaurants. A creamy dressing made of mustard and shallot coats the crunchy pieces. Use a food processor, if you have one, fitted with a shredding disk, for the tedious shredding job. A food processor also makes quick work out of emulsifying the ingredients for the piquant dressing.

>   1 large (1 to 1½ lb) celery root
>   2 tablespoons fresh lemon juice
>   1 egg yolk
>   2 tablespoons tarragon wine vinegar
>   1 tablespoon Dijon mustard
>   ½ teaspoon salt
>   Pinch cayenne pepper
>   1 shallot, finely chopped
>   ¼ cup *each* olive oil and vegetable oil
>   Butter or Boston lettuce leaves
>   Chopped parsley, for garnish

1. Peel celery root thoroughly, cutting out any deep bits of peel. Shred quickly, using a food processor or grater (you should have 5 to 6 cups). Immediately mix well with lemon juice to prevent discoloration. Cover and refrigerate for about 1 hour.

2. In a medium bowl beat egg yolk with vinegar, mustard, salt, cayenne, and shallot. Using a whisk or fork, gradually beat in oils, a small amount at a time, until dressing is thick and creamy.

3. Shortly before serving, mix celery root lightly with dressing to coat.

4. Serve celery root mixture on lettuce leaves, sprinkled with parsley.

Serves 6.

Food Processor Version   Use a metal blade to process egg yolk, vinegar, mustard, salt, cayenne, and 1 tablespoon oil for 1 minute. Slowly add remaining oil. Add shallot and process 10 seconds more.

Recipes and Related Information
Sherried Oxtail Soup, 501; Vegetable Purées, 487.

CELERY

A member of the same vegetable family as carrots and parsley, celery has long, crisp stalks that may reach a foot in length. Some varieties are forcibly blanched and are white or very pale green throughout. Most commercial celery, however, has green outer stalks and pale green inner stalks furled around a central heart. Celery has pungent green leaves that are often removed in processing for the retail market.

Use   The crisp texture of raw celery is appealing in salads or as an hors d'oeuvre, often stuffed with a creamy cheese. It adds texture and flavor to soups, stuffings, and stews. Its flavor is important, if not essential, to stock-making. It is also a required ingredient in a classic French *mirepoix,* the mixture of diced aromatic root vegetables used to flavor sauces, soups, and stews. Braised celery hearts (the tender, innermost stalks) are a good companion to game, duck, or pork.

Availability   Fresh celery is sold the year around, either loose or packed in cellophane bags.

Selection   Choose celery that looks moist and crisp, and does not show signs of limpness or drying. Generally speaking, the darker the color, the stronger the flavor.

Storage   Refrigerate celery in a plastic bag in crisper for up to 10 days.

Preparation   Trim ends, remove leaves, and peel away any tough outer strings. Save leaves for use in stock.

Cooking   See BOIL, BRAISE, STIR-FRY.

BRAISED CELERY WITH WALNUTS

Although usually thought of as a salad vegetable in this country, celery is delicious cooked and served as a side dish. As celery is fibrous and won't cook tender with a brief sauté, it must first be parboiled to cook partway.

1 head celery, separated into stalks and washed
2 tablespoons butter
1 small onion, finely chopped
⅓ cup walnuts, coarsely chopped
Grated rind of 1 lemon

1. Cut celery diagonally into 1½-inch pieces. In a medium saucepan bring to a boil enough salted water to cover celery; add celery and parboil 5 minutes. Drain.

2. Meanwhile, in a large frying pan melt butter. Add onion and walnuts and sauté briefly. Add lemon rind and celery. Toss to coat celery.

Serves 4.

CELERY SEED

This tiny, pungent seed is the fruit of wild celery, which is also known as smallage.

Use Celery seed adds a celerylike flavor to soups, salad dressings, pickling mixtures, tomato juice, potato salad, cole slaw, stuffings, meat loaf, and shellfish stews. It is ground and mixed with salt to make celery salt.

Availability Celery seed is packaged in airtight jars or plastic bags.

Selection Packaged seasonings lose quality after a while; try to buy from a store that restocks its spice section fairly often.

Storage Keep in a cool, dry, dark place; replace celery seed once a year.

CHAYOTE

Also known as mirliton, vegetable pear, *chocho,* and christophine, the chayote is a pear-shaped, tropical squash native to Central America. It has been grown in North Africa and exported to Europe for years as a gourmet vegetable. Chayote is becoming increasingly available in markets throughout the United States. Its skin is smooth, thin, pale green to green with slight ridges; its flesh is moist and creamy white, with a delicate, slightly sweet flavor often compared to that of a cucumber. The single flat seed is edible with a nutty taste. On the average chayotes measure 4 to 6 inches in length and weigh about 1 pound.

Use Chayote may be used like any other squash: baked, steamed, boiled, stuffed, or fried. Its mild flavor is a good counterpoint to spicy stuffings and other spicy treatments, although it is often simply steamed and buttered or cooled and dressed in vinaigrette.

Availability Peak availability for fresh chayote is October through April. If you cannot find chayote, try a large pattypan squash.

Selection Choose small unblemished chayotes with dark green skins.

Storage Refrigerate in a plastic bag in crisper for up to two weeks.

Preparation Young chayotes with tender skins do not need to be peeled; peel mature squash. Halve or quarter and remove seed.

Cooking See BOIL, SAUTE, STEAM.

Céleri-rave rémoulade is the French name for this very popular salad made of shredded celeriac (celery root) tossed in a tangy mustard-shallot dressing.

TIPS

COOKING
WITH CHEESE

Cheese adds distinctive flavor to countless savory and sweet dishes, from the simple grilled cheese sandwich to cheesecake. Cheeses cannot, however, be used interchangeably in recipes; differences in protein, fat, and moisture content make them react differently to heat. A high-fat cheese such as fontina browns nicely on top of a casserole, but a low-fat ricotta or goat cheese does not. If substitution is required, be sure to substitute a cheese of comparable fat and moisture content.

Sauces containing cheese should not be heated too long or at too high a temperature. Excessive cooking causes the casein in the cheese to coagulate and separate from the fat and water, producing a stringy mass with an oily slick. Add grated cheese slowly to a sauce over low or moderate temperature; stir constantly to blend. Remove from heat or set pot over simmering water once cheese has melted.

■ STUFFED MIRLITON

The mild flavor of chayote takes well to the spicy stuffing given in this recipe from Louisiana, where the vegetable is known as mirliton.

      2 **chayotes, cut in half lengthwise**
      4 **cups water**
    ¼ **cup unsalted butter**
    ½ **pound andouille (sausage), chopped**
      1 **cup chopped onion**
    ½ **cup chopped celery**
    ½ **cup chopped green bell pepper**
      1 **tablespoon minced garlic**
    ½ **pound raw shrimp, shelled, deveined, and chopped**
    ½ **cup chopped green onions**
    ½ **teaspoon basil**
    ¼ **teaspoon thyme**
    ½ **teaspoon cayenne pepper**
      1 **teaspoon Worcestershire sauce**
    ¾ **to 1 cup dry bread crumbs**
         Salt and freshly ground pepper, to taste

1. Place halved chayotes in a pan large enough to hold them in a single layer, cover with the water, and bring to a boil. Boil over medium heat until flesh of squash is tender (about 30 minutes). Remove from pan and cool under cold water. Remove seeds and scoop out pulp, being careful not to break through skin of chayotes. Chop pulp; reserve pulp and shells.

2. Preheat oven to 350° F. In a 12-inch frying pan over medium heat, melt butter. Add *andouille* and cook until slightly browned (about 5 minutes). Add onion and celery and cook until vegetables are soft (about 10 minutes). Add green pepper and garlic and cook for another 2 minutes. Add chopped shrimp and cook until shrimp turns pink (1 to 2 minutes). Add green onion, basil, thyme, cayenne, Worcestershire, and chopped chayote pulp. Add enough bread crumbs to bind the stuffing. Taste for salt and pepper; correct if necessary. Fill chayote shells with stuffing and bake for 30 minutes.

Serves 4.

Food Processor Version   Use metal blade to chop 1 medium onion and 1 stalk celery. Add to andouille. With metal blade process 1 small green pepper, cut in 1-inch pieces, and 3 cloves garlic; add to pan.

CHEESE

Despite their remarkable variety, almost all cheeses start out as coagulated milk. The milk is coagulated by adding bacteria that cause it to curdle—to separate into solid curds and liquid whey. The vast differences in taste and texture depend on three factors: the source of the milk, the treatment after coagulation, and the aging process.

Most of the world's cheeses are made from cow's, goat's, or sheep's milk. Italian buffalo-milk mozzarella is one notable exception. Not only do the different types of animals yield milk of very different character, but the flavor of the milk is affected by the season and the region. Summer milk from cows that have grazed on pastureland tastes different from—many say better than—winter milk from grain-fed cows. Microorganisms in a given region also contribute to the flavor of a cheese, which partly explains why cheeses made by the same methods in different regions will not taste the same.

PROCESSING

Cheeses may be made from whole milk, skimmed milk, or milk with added cream (such as the French double and triple creams). The higher the fat portion of the milk or milk and cream mixture, the creamier and smoother the final cheese.

Cheese may also be made from either pasteurized or unpasteurized (raw) milk. Pasteurizing kills bacteria that impart flavor to cheese, which is why many consumers claim that a raw-milk cheese has better flavor than the same cheese made from pasteurized milk. Raw-milk cheeses are strictly regulated because raw milk is a potential carrier of disease-causing bacteria. Raw-milk cheeses, both imported and domestic, must be aged at least 60 days. Many cheeses—such as Maytag Blue from Iowa and Parmesan and Fontina Val d'Aosta from Italy—are made from raw milk and meet this aging requirement. Others, such as French Camembert and Brie, are aged less than 60 days and must be made from pasteurized milk if intended for sale in this country.

Raw-milk cheeses depend on natural bacteria to produce lactic acid, which curdles the milk by coagulating its protein (casein). Pasteurized milk does not contain these acid-producing bacteria; they must be introduced with a culture or starter. Sometimes rennet, an enzyme extracted from the stomachs of young calves, is added to speed coagulation. For some cheeses, coloring is added at this point; to make blue-veined cheeses such as Gorgonzola, the milk is inoculated with mold spores.

After coagulation the curd is cut into smaller pieces to encourage draining of the whey—the liquid, noncoagulating portion. The size of the cut and the length of the draining period determine the texture and moisture content of the finished cheese. Curds cut into large pieces and left to drain briefly produce a moist, soft cheese. Smaller cuts and a longer draining period yield a firmer cheese. Sometimes the curd is cooked or briefly heated with the whey before draining; this process produces a firm hard cheese such as Gruyère.

Some curds are ladled into molds and allowed to drain naturally. Others are molded and pressed, either lightly or heavily, to establish a shape and expel even more whey. Pressed cheeses have a firmer, more solid texture than unpressed cheeses.

After molding, cheeses may be soaked in brine or repeatedly washed with water, brine, or alcohol. They may be sprayed with spores to produce an exterior mold; they may also be waxed, smoked, wrapped with herbs or leaves, coated with ashes, or soaked in oil.

Lastly, some cheeses are aged or ripened under controlled temperature and humidity. Aging develops flavor and causes moisture loss. Generally, the longer a cheese has been aged, the stronger in flavor and drier it will be. Young Parmesan can be sliced and has a smooth, nutty flavor; aged Parmesan, best for grating, has a sharp flavor.

TYPES OF CHEESE

To make sense of the enormous variety of cheeses, it helps to classify or categorize them in some way. One helpful system is to classify them by texture: Are they hard or soft? Sliceable? Spreadable? Another system is to classify them by the source of the milk: cow, sheep, goat. Some cheeses are traditionally grouped together because they're made by a common process, such as the blue-veined and *pasta filata* cheeses.

Some of the more traditional classifications are outlined below. Categories inevitably overlap, and placement of a cheese in a particular category is somewhat arbitrary. A cheese may be semihard when young but hard when aged. Blue cheeses may be classified by texture—Gorgonzola is semisoft, Stilton is semihard—but they are generally grouped together because of their color.

CLASSIFICATION BY TEXTURE: SOFT CHEESE

Soft-textured cheeses, also known as fresh cheeses, include such popular varieties as cottage cheese, cream cheese, and French *fromage blanc*. They are uncooked and unripened or barely ripened; they are often not molded, but simply spooned into tubs. Soft cheeses are usually very mild and creamy.

Use Fresh cheeses such as cream cheese may be spread on crackers or bread. Cottage and pot cheeses may be salted and eaten with crisp vegetables as a salad, or sugared and eaten with fruit for breakfast or dessert. Serve slightly chilled. *Mascarpone* or whipped, sweetened cream cheese may be used to fill crêpes or fruit tarts. Fresh cheeses may also be made into cheesecakes and cheese pies.

Selection Buy soft cheeses from a market that has a rapid turnover.

Storage Because of their high moisture content, soft cheeses are highly perishable; all should be refrigerated in a covered container and most should be eaten within one week.

Cheeses in This Category Cottage cheese, pot cheese, farmer cheese, cream cheese, Neufchâtel, Gervais, *fromage blanc*, ricotta, *stracchino, mascarpone.*

■ COEUR A LA CREME

This charming molded cheese dessert is traditionally made in a heart-shaped basket or porcelain dish that is pierced on the bottom so the mixture can drain as it sets. The molds are available at better cookware stores.

> 1 **pound cottage cheese**
> 1 **pound cream cheese, softened**
> 1 **teaspoon vanilla extract**
>   **Pinch of salt**
> 1 **cup confectioners' sugar, sifted**
> 2 **cups whipping cream**
> 1 **pint whole strawberries** *or* **1 cup Raspberry Sauce (see page 522), for garnish**

1. Have ready a heart-shaped, 8-cup *coeur à la crème* mold. Dampen a towel and press into mold, leaving towel ends free.

2. Press cottage cheese through a sieve or whirl briefly in food processor; place in a 2-quart mixing bowl. Stir in cream cheese, vanilla, and salt. Add confectioners' sugar.

3. Whip cream to soft peaks; fold into cheese mixture. Pour mixture into prepared mold and cover with towel ends. Place mold in a shallow dish and chill 8 to 12 hours.

4. To unmold, fold back towel. Set serving plate over cheese and invert. Remove mold and towel from cheese. Garnish with whole strawberries or Raspberry Sauce.

Serves 8 to 10.

Recipes: Buttermilk Blintzes, 600; Cheese Roulade, 206; Figs With Flavored Ricotta, 220; Gnocchi Verde, 190; Marbled Cream Cheese Brownies, 65; New York–Style Cheesecake, 117; Ricotta Cheesecake, 119; Unbaked Cheesecake, 118.

A simple, but appealing dinner finale in the European tradition features a variety of cheeses in wedges, slices, or balls, served with fruits, nuts, and crackers. Offer a selection of fruit liqueurs or serve a dessert wine such as a late-harvest Zinfandel, a port, or a Muscat Canelli.

BRIE IN PUFF PASTRY

Center wheel of Brie on top of smaller puff pastry circle. Brush water on pastry from cheese to pastry edge. Cover with larger circle of pastry and press gently on top piece of dough at edges to seal the two circles together. Freeze until dough is firm but not frozen (about 10 minutes).

Cut a scallop pattern around edge of dough. Cut a ¼-inch hole in center of pastry (do not puncture cheese). Roll a 1-inch by 1½-inch piece of foil into a tube; set in hole in pastry (will serve as a steam vent).

Brush pastry decorations with water and apply to top. Freeze 20 minutes. Remove from freezer. Brush top of pastry with egg wash. Bake 20 to 25 minutes at 425° F.

CLASSIFICATION BY TEXTURE: SOFT-RIPENED CHEESES

Soft-ripened cheeses have not been cooked or pressed. Instead they are cut in large curds and allowed to drain naturally. They are then sprayed with spores or washed with brine, water, or alcohol to promote development of a rind. Sprayed cheeses develop a powdery white rind; washed cheeses develop an orange-hued rind.

These cheeses ripen from the rind inward. When fully ripe, they have a smooth, almost spreadable texture and range in flavor from mild to quite strong.

Use   Soft-ripened cheeses are delicious dinner cheeses, served after the main course but before dessert. They are traditionally offered with bread or crackers and wine. The rind is edible, although some prefer to cut it away. Serve soft-ripened cheeses at room temperature.

Selection   These cheeses should give slightly to pressure. They should feel supple but not liquid. Avoid any that have a chalky white center (they are underripe) or a strong ammonia odor (they are overripe). The rind should be evenly colored and slightly moist.

Storage   Keep them in the refrigerator, wrapped airtight in plastic; change wrapping every few days. Use within a couple of weeks.

Cheeses in This Category   Boursault, Brie, Brillat-Savarin, Camembert, *Caprice des Dieux, Carré de l'Est, Chaource,* Coulommiers, Liederkranz, Limburger, Muenster, Pont l'Eveque.

▣ BRIE OR CAMEMBERT IN PUFF PASTRY

Soft-ripened cheeses, such as a round of Brie or Camembert, are a special treat when baked in puff pastry (see photographs at left). Wedges of the pastry served with a glass of wine and fresh fruit are delicious after dinner. You can enclose any size wheel of Brie or Camembert in puff pastry. Allow 2 ounces of cheese per person for a small serving. One recipe of puff pastry can easily enclose a 1-pound wheel of cheese. You can make circles of puff pastry from 1½ pounds virgin puff pastry and use trimmings to decorate the outside of the pastry.

> 1½ recipes (2 lb) Classic Puff Pastry
> with 6 turns (see page 482)
> 2 wheels (8 oz and 4 in. diameter each)
> Brie or Camembert, well-chilled, *or*
> 1 wheel (16 oz and 8 in. diameter)
> 1 egg, lightly beaten with 1 teaspoon water

1. Roll out Classic Puff Pastry a little less than ¼ inch thick. Chill sheet of dough until firm. If using two 4-inch wheels of cheese, cut out two 6-inch circles and two 7-inch circles of puff pastry. If using one 8-inch wheel, cut out one 10-inch circle and one 11-inch circle. Cover and refrigerate 30 minutes. Gather scraps of dough into a ball; refrigerate 30 minutes.

2. Roll out trimmings of dough as thin as possible (less than ⅛ inch thick); freeze until very cold but not frozen. Use pastry cutters or a sharp knife to make cutouts for decorating top of puff pastry (stems, leaves, flowers, grapes, etc.). Freeze decorations until firm. Freeze wheels of cheese no longer than 20 minutes.

3. Place two 6-inch circles (or one 10-inch circle) of puff pastry on a parchment-lined baking sheet. Place a wheel of cheese in center of each. Brush water around the border from cheese to edge of pastry. Cover each wheel with a 7-inch circle of puff pastry dough (or an 11-inch circle if using larger wheel). Press down on dough around base of cheese with fingertips to seal edges of dough together. Firm dough in freezer 10 minutes.

4. When dough is well chilled but not frozen, cut a scallop pattern at edge of pastry with a sharp knife. Create a hollow aluminum foil tube (a chimney) by wrapping a 1-inch by 1½-inch strip of foil 2 or 3 times around a pencil; butter exterior of foil tube and remove pencil. Cut a ¼-inch hole in center of top layer of pastry and fit buttered tube into it. This will allow steam from inside pastry to escape. Brush cutout decorations with water and apply in an attractive pattern on top. Return to freezer for 20 minutes. Preheat oven to 425° F.

5. Remove pastry rounds from freezer, and brush top of each with egg wash (take care not to drip any down sides of pastry). Bake until golden brown (20 to 25 minutes). Cool for 30 to 45 minutes before cutting. If served immediately, cheese will run out after pastry is cut. Cut each pastry into 4 (or 8 if using a large wheel) wedges.

Serves 8.

CLASSIFICATION BY TEXTURE: SEMISOFT CHEESES

The cheeses in this category have generally been pressed but not cooked. Ranging in flavor from very mild to strong, they have a soft texture but can be sliced. Many of these cheeses were originally made by European monks and are known as monastery cheeses.

Use   Serve semisoft cheeses as part of a cheese board, with bread or crackers and wine. Bring to room temperature before serving. Because they can be sliced, they may be used for sandwiches. Because they melt well, they may be used in grilled sandwiches or as a topping for many types of casseroles.

Selection   Choose semisoft cheeses that give slightly to pressure. They may smell strong, but they should not smell rank or ammoniated.

Storage   Keep semisoft cheese in the refrigerator, wrapped airtight in plastic; change wrapping every few days. Semisoft cheeses keep for up to one month.

Cheeses in This Category   Bel Paese, brick, Esrom, Gouda, Havarti, Livarot, Monterey jack, *morbier*, Oka, Port Salut, *reblochon*, Saint Paulin, Samsoe, Sonoma jack, *taleggio*, Tilsit.

Recipes: Cheese Roulade, 206; Chiles Rellenos, 428; Refried Beans, 35; Tiropita, 223.

CLASSIFICATION BY TEXTURE: SEMIFIRM CHEESES

These cheeses have been cooked and pressed to eliminate excess moisture. They may or may not have a rind. Texture is firm but smooth and allows cheeses to be sliced; flavor ranges from mild to sharp.

Use   Serve semifirm cheeses as part of a cheese board, with bread or crackers and wine. Bring to room temperature before serving. Because they can be sliced, they may be used for sandwiches. Most semifirm cheeses also melt well and may be grated for use in a range of cooked dishes, such as omelets, soufflés, sauces, breads, puddings, pies, and casseroles.

Selection   Avoid semifirm cheese with a cracked rind or a dry, crumbly texture.

Storage   Keep in refrigerator, wrapped airtight in plastic; change wrapping every few days. For long storage, overwrap plastic with aluminum foil and store in bottom of refrigerator. Coating cut side of cheese with butter or hot paraffin before wrapping prevents drying and the development of surface mold. Semifirm cheeses keep for several months under these conditions. They may also be frozen for up to two months. Wrap tightly in plastic, then in foil, and freeze quickly. Thaw slowly in refrigerator.

Cheeses in This Category   Appenzeller, Asiago, Caerphilly, Cantal, Cheddar, Cheshire, Danbo, Derby and Sage Derby, Double Gloucester, Edam, Emmentaler, fontina, Gjetost, Gruyère, Jarlsberg, *raclette*.

■ FONTINA FRITTERS

Golden brown outside and molten within, these fritters are a heavenly mouthful. The batter may be made ahead, but the cheese must be fried at the last minute. Serve with a crisp, white Italian wine, such as an Orvieto or a Soave.

  ¾   **pound chilled fontina, not too ripe**
  ¼   **cup dry white wine**
  2   **eggs, separated**
  1   **teaspoon minced garlic**
  1   **teaspoon baking powder**
1½   **cups flour**
  1   **teaspoon salt**
2½   **tablespoons olive oil**
  ½   **to ⅔ cup ice water**
    Vegetable oil, for deep-frying
  ½   **cup minced fresh basil**
    Salt, to taste

1. Cut cheese into 1-inch cubes. In a bowl whisk together wine, egg yolks, and garlic. Whisk in baking powder, flour, and 1 teaspoon salt. Whisk in oil, then add enough of the ice water to make a thick but pourable batter, about the consistency of pancake batter. Let rest at room temperature for 2 hours.

2. When ready to serve, heat 2 inches of vegetable oil in a frying pan to 360° F. Beat egg whites with a pinch of salt until stiff but not dry. Fold into batter along with minced basil.

3. Dip cheese chunks into batter. Allow excess batter to drip off; fry chunks in oil until uniformly golden. Drain fritters on paper towels and salt lightly. Serve fritters immediately.

Serves 8 with other hors d'oeuvres.

CLASSIFICATION BY TEXTURE: FIRM CHEESES

These pressed, cooked cheeses have been aged until dry and hard. When young, they can be sliced; when aged, they must be grated.

Use   Hard cheeses are rarely used as table cheeses, except when young. Young Parmesan, dry jack, and Asiago can be sliced and may be served after dinner with fruit or nuts. Dry, aged cheeses are designed for grating. Use

Dip cubes of fontina cheese in batter, then fry until crisp and brown. The piping-hot Fontina Fritters makes a fine appetizer, served with chilled white wine and herbed olives.

A crock of English Stilton cheese mixed with mellow port makes a royal spread for small toasts or crackers.

CLASSIFICATION BY PROCESS: BLUE-VEINED CHEESES

Inoculating cheese with mold spores will, with time, produce a blue-veined interior. Blue-veined cheeses are generally pungent; they range in texture from the moist creaminess of Gorgonzola to the firm, slightly crumbly Stilton.

Use   Blue-veined cheeses are a pleasing addition to an after-dinner cheese board. Complemented by apples, pears, and walnuts, they should be served with crackers or bread and a rich red wine or port. Bring to room temperature before serving. Crumbled blue cheese makes a piquant addition to salads and salad dressings. Blue cheese may be whipped half and half with butter to make a cracker spread or a topping for grilled meats.

Selection   Blue cheeses may smell strong but should not smell rank or ammoniated. If possible, sample before buying; avoid cheeses that are overly salty or chalky.

Storage   Small pieces may be stored in the refrigerator, wrapped in plastic, for up to one month; change plastic wrap every few days. Large pieces or whole wheels keep longer if covered with a damp towel; cut cheese as needed and rewrap carefully.

Cheeses in This Category   Bleu de Bresse, Danablu, Fourme d'Ambert, Gorgonzola, Maytag Blue, Oregon Blue, *Pipo Crem'*, Roquefort, Stilton.

▨ STILTON CROCK WITH PORT WINE

A wedge of blue-veined Stilton cheese and a decanter of port are a venerable British tradition, usually served in the drawing room at the end of a formal meal. This pair can also be packed into a handsome crock for a predinner spread, the flavors melding during the course of a week-long aging. If you are hosting a large party, you can order a whole wheel of Stilton (usually in 10- or 16-pound pieces). Slice off the top and scoop out the cheese, leaving a sturdy wall all around. Then mash the cheese with about one bottle of port, refill the wheel, and replace the cover for aging. It makes an impressive buffet centerpiece, especially at holiday time.

> 2 **pounds Stilton cheese**
> ⅓ **to ½ cup imported port**
>   **Crackers, for accompaniment**

1. Trim any rind from cheese; place cheese in a bowl. Add port. With back of a wooden spoon, blend port and cheese. Pack into a 4-cup crock, cover with plastic wrap, refrigerate, and let age 1 week.

2. Bring cheese to room temperature and serve with crackers.

Makes 4 cups, or enough for 20 to 30 cocktail servings.

Recipes: Blue Cheese Soufflé, 205; Stilton Snow Peas, 419.

them in pasta, on soups, in casseroles, on pizzas, and in rice or egg dishes. Because hard cheeses go stale quickly after grating, it is preferable to buy them in blocks and grate them at home just before using.

Selection   Firm cheeses should be hard but not dried out. If possible, sample before buying and reject any that taste overly salty or bitter.

Storage   Because of their exceptionally low moisture content, hard cheeses store well. Follow storage and freezing advice for semifirm cheeses.

Cheeses in This Category   Aged Asiago, *Grana Padano*, Parmesan, Pecorino Romano, Sapsago, Sbrinz.

Recipes: Gnocchi di Patate, 189; Pesto, 27.

CLASSIFICATION BY PROCESS: PASTA FILATA CHEESES

A specialty of Italy, *pasta filata* (spun paste) cheeses are made by washing the curd in hot water or whey, then kneading and stretching it to the desired consistency and shape. The process produces a pliable cheese that can be molded by hand; occasionally these cheeses are formed into animal or pear shapes. The finished cheese should be smooth and elastic but not rubbery. Pasta filata cheeses are usually mild in flavor and are occasionally smoked.

Use In Italy fresh mozzarella is drizzled with olive oil and served as a first course, often with sliced tomatoes or roasted peppers. Fresh or factory-made mozzarella may be used in baked pasta dishes, such as lasagne, or layered in vegetable casseroles.

Selection Fresh mozzarella should be purchased and used within two or three days of its manufacture. Other pasta filata cheeses have a longer shelf life. Avoid any that have a rubbery texture.

Storage Refrigerate, wrapped airtight in plastic. These cheeses keep for several weeks. Serve at room temperature.

Cheeses in This Category *Cacciocavallo,* mozzarella, Provolone, Scamorza.

Recipes: Deep-fried Zucchini Blossoms, 238; Pizza, 445; Tomatoes With Mozzarella and Basil, 507.

CLASSIFICATION BY PROCESS: WHEY CHEESES

Most cheeses are made from coagulated milk curds, but a very few are made from the liquid whey. To make a whey cheese, the whey is heated until its solid matter coagulates. The best-known examples are Italian ricotta, made from the whey drained from provolone and mozzarella, and Norwegian Gjetost.

Use Ricotta may be sugared and eaten with fresh berries or sliced fruit. It may be salted and eaten as a salad with crisp vegetables, olives, and olive oil. Seasoned ricotta is used as a filling for baked pasta dishes, as a stuffing for breast of veal, and in cheesecakes.

Norwegian Gjetost is usually sliced thin and eaten with toast for breakfast or with spiced fruit cake.

Selection Fresh ricotta is very perishable; it should be purchased and used within a few days of its manufacture.

Storage Keep in a covered container in the refrigerator. It is moist and creamy, with a very mild, almost sweet flavor. Domestic factory-made ricotta has a slightly longer shelf life but lacks the creamy texture and pure flavor of the fresh version.

Gjetost, an unusual cheese, is made from whey heated slowly until the water evaporates and the natural sugars caramelize. Lactose and brown sugar may be added. The result is a golden brown cheese with a smooth, creamy texture and a pronounced caramel flavor. It stores well, wrapped in plastic and chilled; change wrap often.

OTHER CLASSIFICATIONS: PROCESSED CHEESES

Most processed cheeses derive from a natural cheese that has been ground and mixed with emulsifiers to make it uniformly smooth, then is pasteurized and packed. Some processed cheeses contain preservatives and colorings. Products labeled cheese spread or cheese food may contain flavorings as well as liquid or powdered milk for added moisture and spreadability.

These cheeses generally have a mild flavor and a uniformly smooth texture. Although they keep well and are often conveniently packaged, they lack the distinctive character and complexity of natural cheeses.

OTHER CLASSIFICATIONS: CHEESES FOR SPECIAL DIETS

Today's market is full of cheeses made to comply with special diets. Low-fat and low-salt or low-sodium cheeses are widely available and are identified as such on their labels. Because fat adds richness and texture to cheese, low-fat cheeses may lack the full flavor and good melting qualities of the comparable full-fat cheeses. Part-skim mozzarella, for example, does not melt as well as whole-milk mozzarella but may be preferred by those counting calories.

CLASSIFICATION BY MILK SOURCE: GOAT CHEESES

Also known as *chèvre* (French for goat), goat's milk cheese has a distinctive chalky color and tangy flavor. Young, fresh goat cheese is mild and creamy. As it ages, it gets stronger and drier. Goat cheeses are made in a variety of shapes and sizes. They may be coated with ash or dried herbs or sprayed with mold spores to produce a rind.

Use Goat cheeses are a pleasing addition to a cheese board; offer them with crackers or bread and wine. Small, round goat cheeses may be coated with soft bread crumbs and sautéed or baked until warm throughout. Goat cheese adds a creamy tang to stuffings, salads, pizza toppings, souffles, and omelets.

Selection Young, highly moist goat cheeses have a short shelf life. Buy them from a shop that has a rapid turnover and try to sample before purchase. Reject any that have a sour or ammoniated flavor.

Storage Keep moist goat cheese in refrigerator, covered with plastic wrap; it will keep for one or two weeks. Change plastic wrap every few days. Aged goat cheese keeps slightly longer.

Cheeses in This Category Banon, *bûcheron*, California chévre, *caprino*, Chabichou (or *Cabécou*), feta (some feta is made from sheep's milk or part sheep's milk), Montrachet, Sainte-Maure.

ENTERTAINING WITH WINE AND CHEESE

Cheese and wine are ancient foods that go back to the earliest days of agriculture. It is not surprising, then, that they pair very well. There is probably not a wine that cannot be matched to one cheese or another, nor a single cheese that cannot be served with some wine. But some combinations of wine and cheese go together better than others.

A wine and cheese buffet can make excellent party fare, as long as you avoid the familiar "Cheddar, Swiss, and Brie, burgundy and chablis." A good cheese board can consist of as few as three or four cheeses, or a dozen or more, depending on the number of guests. The key is to provide a variety of flavors and textures. Wines should also be chosen for variety, so that at least one wine will suit every guest's personal taste.

Here are some pointers on assembling a selection of wines and cheeses:

- For a party at which dinner will not be served, allow about ¼ pound of cheese per person and one bottle of wine for every three or four guests. Allow half as much for a before-dinner cocktail hour. Remember, cheese is filling; don't overwhelm appetites before dinner.
- Try for a balanced selection of cheeses by choosing one example from each category. To get you going, you might want to plan around one soft-ripening cheese (such as Brie, Camembert), one semisoft cheese (consider Port-Salut, Monterey jack), one firm cheese, either of the Swiss or Cheddar type, and one blue-veined cheese. With

more guests, for variety add a stronger soft or semisoft cheese (two are Pont l'Evêque, Esrom), a hard cheese (such as quality Parmesan, aged Gouda), a goat's-milk cheese, a double- or triple-cream cheese (such as Boursault, Saint-André), an herbed or spiced cheese (including Havarti with dill or Cumminost), or whatever other types you like.

- Follow the same approach with the wines. Start with one dry red, say a Zinfandel or a lighter-style Cabernet, and one white wine that is slightly sweet, such as Chenin Blanc or Riesling. Next, add both a dry white (Chardonnay or Sauvignon Blanc) and a different style of red (such as Gamay Beaujolais). Unless the purpose of the party is to provide an opportunity for tasting as many wines as possible with a variety of cheeses, keep the wine selection simple.
- Serve an assortment of breads or crackers. Avoid highly seasoned crackers if you want the flavor of the cheese and wine to come through. With really fine cheeses, thin, unsalted crackers or matzos are best.
- Other nice accompaniments to a cheese board are crunchy raw vegetables, nuts, olives, and fresh fruits, especially apples and grapes. Some guests might also enjoy a few condiments like fancy mustards, chutney, and gherkins.
- To show cheeses at their best, serve them at room temperature. Provide plenty of knives or cheese slicers, at least one for each cheese, to facilitate serving.

▤ BAKED GOAT CHEESE SALAD

The richness of the goat cheese complements the pungent winter greens and a tangy wine vinegar. When baked, the cheese becomes creamy. This is a good company dish as the cheese must marinate one hour before baking, so preparation is completed before guests arrive.

1	small goat cheese log (about 5 oz)
9½	tablespoons olive oil
⅓	cup dry bread crumbs
1½	tablespoons red wine vinegar
¼	teaspoon salt
⅛	teaspoon pepper
¼	cup snipped fresh chives
10	to 12 cups washed, dried, and torn salad greens (endive, chicory, watercress, arugula)
½	red bell pepper, cored, seeded, and cut into thin strips
	Freshly ground black pepper
	French bread, for accompaniment

1. Slice goat cheese into ½-inch-thick rounds. Pour 4 tablespoons olive oil into a shallow bowl; place bread crumbs on a sheet of waxed paper. Dip goat cheese rounds into olive oil to coat completely, then into bread crumbs; shake off excess crumbs. Set breaded rounds on a tray and chill for 1 hour. Toward the end of chilling period (or about 30 minutes before serving), preheat oven to 375° F.

2. In a small bowl whisk together 3 tablespoons oil, vinegar, salt, pepper, and chives; reserve. Thirty minutes before serving, let salad greens come to room temperature, if chilled.

3. Pour remaining olive oil into an 8-inch square baking dish. Set chilled goat cheese rounds in dish and bake until a light golden crust forms (about 8 minutes). Turn with a spatula (handle rounds gently so that they don't break) and bake on second side for 2 minutes.

4. To serve, toss salad greens with two thirds of the dressing; divide among 6 individual salad plates. Remove cheese from baking pan and place one breaded round in the center of each nest of greens. Arrange red peppers around goat cheese, drizzle with remaining dressing, and grind black pepper over top. Serve immediately with French bread.

Serves 6.

Recipes: Deep-fried Zucchini Blossoms (goat cheese and sun-dried tomato variation), 238.

CLASSIFICATION BY MILK SOURCE: SHEEP'S MILK CHEESES

Sheep's milk cheeses have a sharp tang that immediately distinguishes them from cow's milk cheeses. Most sheep's milk cheeses are made in countries and regions that have too little pasturage to support cattle—such as Greece, Spain, the Pyrenees, and the Middle East.

Use Depending on their moisture content, sheep's milk cheeses may be sliced for use in sandwiches, snacks, and salads, or grated for use as a flavor accent on salads and cooked dishes.

Selection If possible, ask for a sample before buying. Sheep's milk cheeses may be sharp but should not be excessively salty or bitter.

Storage Keep them in plastic wrap in the refrigerator, changing the wrapping every few days. Highly moist cheeses deteriorate more quickly than varieties with low moisture.

Cheeses in This Category Feta (some feta is made from goat's milk), *kasseri*, Liptauer, *manchego*, *pecorino*, Romano, Ricotta Pecorino (also known as *ricotta salata*), Roquefort.

Recipes: Greek Salad, 507; Tiropita, 223.

CHEESECAKE

This rich, creamy confection has achieved an enduring popularity that seems to transcend food fads and concern for calories. A cheesecake is a cake or pie with a custard-like filling whose main ingredient is cream cheese, cottage cheese, ricotta cheese, or some combination, contained in a cookie or crumb crust, or baked without a crust.

In New York, "real" cheesecake is a tall, dense, lemony, cream cheese–based cake. Elsewhere, preference might be for something lighter, perhaps flavored with liqueur or finished with a coat of sour cream or a layer of fresh fruit. Then there's marble, mocha, pumpkin, savory, chocolate chip, Italian, no-bake, and many, many others.

PREPARING CHEESECAKE

Regardless of the version you prefer, there are a few points to remember that apply to all. Packaged cream cheese usually contains gum, which makes a cake denser. Natural cream cheese, available at cheese and specialty food stores and well-stocked supermarkets, is free of gum and will produce a lighter-textured cake. Whichever type you favor, have the cream cheese at room temperature before using; it will mix easier and blend more quickly with the other ingredients.

Most recipes specify using a springform pan, whose sides release for easier removal of the cake. If the cheesecake is to bake in a hot water bath (bain-marie), wrap the outside of the pan with foil. The foil acts as a barrier to keep the water from seeping through the seams of the pan and into the cake, making it soggy. An alternative is to use a cheesecake pan, which is a deep layer-cake pan preferred by commercial bakers. Because it is made in one piece, it stays watertight, but for that reason the cake is more difficult to unmold.

■ NEW YORK–STYLE CHEESECAKE

This is always a dense, rich cake, served in thin slices because it is so filling. To suit today's taste for lighter desserts, cottage cheese has been added, but the texture is classic. Serve it as it comes from the oven or top with a lemon or raspberry glaze. The thick batter may strain the motor of some portable electric mixers. Use a heavy-duty mixer if possible; first beat by hand completely or partway to soften and blend the ingredients, then finish mixing with the machine.

    1 pound whole-milk cottage cheese
    1½ pounds natural cream cheese,
        at room temperature
    1½ cups sugar
        Grated rind and juice of 1 lemon
    5 eggs
    ¼ cup cornstarch
    1 pint sour cream
    2 tablespoons vanilla extract

Lemon Custard Glaze (optional)

    1 egg
    2 egg yolks
    6 tablespoons sugar
    ¼ cup fresh lemon juice
    1 teaspoon finely grated lemon rind
    4 tablespoons unsalted butter, softened
        Cookie crumbs (optional)

Raspberry Glaze (optional)

    1 package (10 oz) frozen raspberries
    2 tablespoons sugar
    1 tablespoon cornstarch
    2 teaspoons raspberry liqueur or kirsch

1. Preheat oven to 300° F. Butter bottom and sides of a 10-inch springform pan.

2. To refine texture of cottage cheese, force cheese through a wire-mesh sieve or purée in a blender or food processor. In a large bowl blend softened cream cheese and cottage cheese purée with a heavy-duty mixer and paddle attachment, or by hand with a wooden spoon. Add sugar and lemon rind; mix well to incorporate.

3. Add eggs, one at a time, beating well after each addition. Sift in cornstarch; beat to combine. Stir in sour cream, vanilla, and lemon juice. Pour into prepared pan and bake 50 minutes (it will be pale yellow—not at all brown—set around the edges, and still wobbly under the surface in the center). Turn off oven, leave door slightly ajar, and allow cheesecake to cool completely. When cool, spread with either glaze (if desired) or leave plain; refrigerate at least 6 hours, or overnight. Before serving, bring cake to room temperature. To slice cleanly and evenly, use a sharp, thin- and narrow-bladed knife. It may be necessary to dip blade in hot water and wipe clean after each slice, so knife draws easily through cake without drag.

Serves 12 to 16.

Lemon Custard Glaze In a medium stainless steel bowl, combine egg, egg yolks, sugar, lemon juice, and lemon rind. Immediately place over a pot of boiling water (double-boiler fashion) and whisk egg mixture until it thickens to the consistency of mayonnaise (do not boil or mixture will curdle). Remove from heat and immediately whisk in butter. Spread on cake while custard is still warm. If desired, sprinkle cookie crumbs around border of cake to decorate top.

Raspberry Glaze Thaw raspberries; drain, reserving juice. In a small saucepan combine juice with sugar, cornstarch, and about half of the berries. Bring to a boil, stirring, and cook until thickened and clear. Strain to remove seeds. To strained sauce add liqueur and reserved berries. Cool to room temperature, then spoon on cake, letting some glaze spill over top onto sides, if desired.

TIPS

WHAT CAUSES CRACKS?

Probably the most frequent complaint by home bakers about cheesecakes is that they often crack. Usually this is the result of baking at a temperature that is too high, which causes the outside of the cake to set before the interior has had time to expand and settle. Cheesecakes should bake slowly; check the accuracy of your oven frequently with an oven thermometer. Creating humidity inside the oven will keep the surface of the cake moist and also combat cracking. To do this set a pan of water on the rack below the cheesecake, or bake the cake in a hot water bath.

Overbeating dense batters can also cause cracks. When too much air is incorporated into the mixture, it will rise, then collapse and split. If using a heavy-duty mixer, beat with the flat paddle and not the whisk. A food processor fitted with the steel blade will work well. You may need to process in two batches, depending on the size of the work bowl. You can also beat by hand. A final recommendation: If cracks appear despite all precautions, ignore them. The cake will taste just as wonderful and disappear just as fast as one that is crack-free.

A specialty of southern Italy, Ricotta Cheesecake has a ricotta filling encased in pastry. Raisins, pine nuts, almonds, and a hint of chocolate enrich the filling.

■ UNBAKED CHEESECAKE

This mildly flavored cheesecake benefits from the addition of one of the fruit variations. Because the filling sets with gelatin, only the crumb crust needs to be baked.

    1 **pound natural cream cheese,
       at room temperature**
    ½ **cup superfine sugar**
    2 **tablespoons vanilla extract
       Grated rind and juice of 2 lemons**
    3 **egg yolks**
    1 **envelope unflavored gelatin**
    1 **cup whipping cream**
    3 **egg whites**
    ¼ **cup granulated sugar**

Graham Cracker Crumb Crust

    2 **cups fine graham cracker crumbs**
    2 **tablespoons granulated sugar**
    ¼ **cup melted butter**

1. Preheat oven to 350° F. Butter bottom and sides of a 10-inch springform pan. Prepare Graham Cracker Crumb Crust.

2. In a large bowl beat cream cheese until smooth; add sugar, vanilla, and lemon rind, and beat well. Add egg yolks, one at a time, beating well after each addition. In a small saucepan dissolve gelatin in lemon juice over low heat. Pour into cream cheese mixture.

3. Whip cream to soft peaks and fold into cheese mixture. Whip egg whites to soft peaks; add ¼ cup granulated sugar and beat briefly just to incorporate sugar. Stir one third of beaten egg whites into cream cheese mixture; gently fold in remaining whites.

4. Pour filling over cooled crust. Smooth surface with a spatula. Refrigerate until set (2 to 3 hours, or overnight). To serve, decorate top and sides with whipped cream or one of the fruits suggested in the variation.

Serves 8 to 12.

Graham Cracker Crumb Crust In a medium bowl combine graham cracker crumbs and sugar; add melted butter and mix thoroughly. Press into prepared pan. Bake 10 minutes. Cool on a wire rack.

Food Processor Version Use metal blade to process cream cheese, lemon rind, vanilla, and superfine sugar until smooth, scraping work bowl as necessary. Add all egg yolks at once and process 15 seconds. With motor running, pour dissolved gelatin through feed tube and process 10 seconds. Transfer to large mixing bowl and complete recipe as directed.

Fruit Cheesecake   Mix in any of the following fruits with whipped cream in step 3: 1 pound fresh ripe, pitted cherries poached in ½ cup water and puréed in food processor or blender; *or* 1 cup dried apricot purée (soak in water for several hours or overnight, then poach in soaking water until tender, about 15 minutes; sweeten to taste and purée); *or* 1 package (10 oz) frozen raspberries, thawed, drained, puréed, and strained through a fine sieve to remove seeds.

▓ RICOTTA CHEESECAKE

Cheesecakes in southern Italy are made with ricotta, raisins, and pine nuts, and are commonly flecked with chocolate and flavored with rum. This version incorporates crunchy pine-nut brittle, a delicious candy to savor on its own. Offer this rich *torta* in the afternoon with a glass of Marsala, or serve it as the luscious finish to a light meal. Note that the raisins must macerate in the rum for 1 hour.

> 1 cup superfine sugar
> 3 tablespoons water
> 5 tablespoons pine nuts
> 4 tablespoons golden raisins
> 2 tablespoons rum
> 3¼ cups flour
> 1 tablespoon baking powder
> ½ cup firmly packed dark brown sugar
> 1¼ cups ground almonds
> 4 tablespoons chilled unsalted butter,
>   cut in small pieces
> 1 egg
> 1 teaspoon vanilla extract
> 1½ pounds whole-milk ricotta cheese
> 1 teaspoon grated lemon rind
> 2 ounces milk chocolate, coarsely chopped

1. In a 1-quart saucepan heat ¼ cup superfine sugar and the water over high heat. When mixture boils and sugar dissolves, add pine nuts. Continue cooking, swirling pan often, until sugar turns light brown. Turn mixture out onto an oiled baking sheet and let cool. Break up into small chunks. Combine raisins and rum in a small bowl and set aside for 1 hour.

2. *To make dough in a food processor:* Combine flour, baking powder, brown sugar, and almonds; process 5 seconds. Add butter and process until mixture resembles coarse meal, about 10 seconds. Whisk egg and vanilla together, then add to food processor with motor running. Process just until dough nearly holds together. Turn dough out onto a board, gather into a ball, and wrap in plastic. Do not knead or work dough, even if it doesn't hold together well. Refrigerate at least 1 hour. *To make*

dough by hand: Stir together flour, baking powder, brown sugar, and almonds. Cut in butter with a pastry blender until mixture resembles coarse crumbs. Whisk egg and vanilla together, then add to flour mixture. Toss lightly with a fork, just until dough holds together. Gather into a ball and wrap in plastic; refrigerate 1 hour.

3. In a large bowl combine ricotta, remaining sugar, lemon rind, raisins, and rum. Add chocolate bits and pine-nut brittle; mix well.

4. Preheat oven to 350° F. Line bottom and sides of a 10-inch springform pan with aluminum foil. Place a little more than half the pastry dough on bottom of pan, patting it into place and pushing it up sides. Spoon in ricotta filling. Roll out remaining pastry into a 10-inch round and lay over top of filling. Bake until top colors slightly (50 to 55 minutes).

5. Transfer cheesecake to a rack and cool in pan. Release sides of springform pan and gently peel back foil from sides. Lift bottom of cake gently with a spatula and pull out foil. Serve barely warm or at room temperature.

Serves 12.

Make-Ahead Tip   Pastry dough may be made 1 day ahead and refrigerated. If stored airtight, brittle can be made up to 2 weeks ahead.

CHEESECLOTH

Soft, lightweight, and porous, cheesecloth is woven of natural cotton, which won't fall apart in hot liquids or add flavor to food. It is used as a neutral, porous wrap. Flavoring infusions such as bouquet garni and mulling spices are bundled in cheesecloth so they can be easily dropped into and retrieved from soups, stews, and beverages. Delicate poached foods such as whole fish and pasta rolls are wrapped in this material to preserve their shape while they cook. Some baked goods, such as fruitcakes, which benefit from slow soaking in liquor, are swaddled in alcohol-soaked cheesecloth to season. It also serves as a flexible strainer for stocks and other liquids.

Cheesecloth is sold in both coarse and fine weave. Each has its place in the kitchen. Coarse cheesecloth resembles bandage gauze. Inexpensive and widely available in supermarkets and cookware stores, it can be cut, used, and thrown away without too much concern for cost. Better quality, fine-mesh cheesecloth is harder to find and seems expensive in comparison with the coarse type, but because it can be washed and reused, it lasts longer.

CHERIMOYA

A heart-shaped fruit native to Ecuador and Peru, the cherimoya is now cultivated in southern California. Its dull green skin has thumbprintlike indentations edged in brown. The fruit inside is creamy white with large black seeds; it has a creamy, custardlike texture and a flavor reminiscent of banana, pineapple, and pear. Its other common names—custard apple and sherbet fruit—attest to its flavor and texture. Cherimoyas range in weight from ¼ pound to 2½ pounds.

Use   Cherimoya is refreshing when eaten chilled "on the half shell." The flesh is scooped out with a spoon and the seeds discarded. The peeled, diced fruit may be added to fruit salads or puréed for sherbet, ice cream, or daiquiris.

Availability   Fresh cherimoyas are in season from November through May. Because they must be hand-pollinated and handpicked and because the trees are low-yielding, cherimoyas are always expensive.

Selection   Choose green cherimoyas that give slightly to pressure; brownness indicates overripeness.

Storage   Hard cherimoyas may be ripened at room temperature. Ripe cherimoyas should be refrigerated and used within one or two days.

Preparation   Scoop from skin and remove seeds.

CHERRY

Although wild cherries are a prehistoric fruit, cherry cultivation probably originated in Asia Minor. Today cherries are cultivated throughout the world's temperate zone. Most of the many cherry varieties can be classified as either sweet (for eating raw) or sour (for cooking). The most commercially important sweet varieties in America are the yellow-orange Royal Ann and the dark red Bing; other varieties include Black Republican, Black Tartarian, Chapman, Lambert, early Burlat, and Schmidt. The most important sour varieties in America are red Montmorency and English Morello.

Use   Sweet cherries may be eaten out of hand or added to fruit salads, fruit compotes, tarts, or ice cream. They may be preserved in brandy for use as a garnish for ice cream or cake. Sour cherries are best for pies, cobblers, preserves, jams, dessert sauces, and pickles. Vinegared sour cherries are a piquant garnish for pâtés and other cold meats. Sour cherries are also used for commercial maraschino liqueur and syrup and for distilling.

Availability   Depending on the variety and the area, fresh sweet cherries are available late spring through August. June is the peak month for most varieties. Sour cherries are harvested from mid-June to mid-August but are rarely available fresh outside the immediate area of cultivation. Most domestic sour cherries are canned whole, in light or heavy syrup, often identified as cherry-pie filling. Wild cherries called *amarena* are imported from Italy packed in syrup or brandy. Dried sour cherries and wild cherry preserves are occasionally available in Greek markets.

Selection   With the exception of Royal Anns, dark color is the best indication of good flavor. Cherries should have a bright, glossy, plump appearance and fresh-looking stems. Avoid soft cherries or any with brown discoloration.

Storage   Handle fresh cherries carefully; refrigerate and use within a few days of purchase. Transfer leftover canned cherries to a covered plastic container; refrigerate for up to two weeks.

Preparation   For compotes and fruit salads, remove fresh cherry stems; remove pits with a cherry pitter, if desired. Fresh sour cherries should be pitted before cooking.

▮ SOUR-CHERRY PIE

A lattice-top cherry pie shows off the ripe, red fruit to perfection. A cherry pitter (see opposite page) will make quick work of ridding the cherries of hard-to-remove pits.

> 1   **9-inch double-crust Flaky Pastry or Egg Pastry (see pages 434, 435)**
> 1¼ **cups sugar**
> 5   **tablespoons flour**
> ⅔   **cup cherry juice or other red fruit juice**
> ½   **teaspoon ground cinnamon**
> ⅛   **teaspoon almond extract**
> 1   **tablespoon fresh lemon juice**
> 5   **cups pitted tart red cherries**
> 1   **egg white, lightly beaten**
> 1½ **tablespoons unsalted butter**

1. Preheat oven to 425° F. Roll out pastry for bottom crust and line a 9-inch pie plate. Roll out remaining pastry to form top crust or lattice top (see page 433).

2. In a saucepan combine sugar, flour, cherry juice, cinnamon, almond extract, lemon juice, and cherries. Cook over low heat, stirring frequently, until mixture thickens; set aside to cool.

3. Brush inside of bottom crust with egg white to moistureproof the crust. Pour in cooled filling. Dot with butter.

4. Moisten edges of bottom crust and cover with top crust or lattice top; finish edges. Bake for 20 minutes. Lower heat to 400° F and continue baking until crust is golden brown (40 minutes). Cover edges of crust with strips of aluminum foil, if necessary, to prevent excessive browning.

Serves 8.

CHERRY CLAFOUTI

Buttery pastry, sweet red cherries, and custard are baked together to create a French *clafouti*, a type of custard tart. A clafouti can be made from a batter, something like a fruit-dotted puffy pancake or popover, or with a pastry dough that is covered with fruit. If made with a batter, the dish is served from its baking pan. When baked in pastry, it is served in wedges. This version is a combination of a soft filling contained in a tart pastry crust. Although cherries are traditional, when the fresh fruit is unavailable, you can substitute sliced fresh kiwis, poached pears or peaches, or fresh berries. Boysenberries, loganberries, or olallieberries make delicious clafouti.

1 (9½-in.) Sweet Tart Pastry (see page 441)
½ cup milk
½ cup whipping cream
2 whole eggs
2 egg yolks
½ cup sugar
  Pinch freshly grated nutmeg
1 tablespoon kirsch
1 egg white, lightly beaten
2¼ cups pitted sweet red cherries
¼ cup confectioners' sugar

1. Place pastry dough on a lightly floured surface and roll out to form a circle ⅛ inch thick and large enough to line a 9½-inch tart tin with removable bottom. Blind bake until partially baked (see page 18); cool in tart tin on a wire rack.

2. Preheat oven to 400° F. In a heavy-bottomed saucepan bring milk to a simmer over medium-low heat; add cream. In a mixing bowl whisk together eggs, egg yolks, sugar, and nutmeg. Add a little of the milk-cream mixture to gently raise the temperature of the eggs and keep them from curdling; stir well to blend. Blend in remaining milk-cream mixture; cool. Stir in kirsch. Set custard aside.

3. To prevent crust from getting soggy, gently brush tart shell with a thin layer of lightly beaten egg white. Arrange cherries (whole or cut in half; if halved, arrange cut side down) in an even layer over bottom of tart shell. Carefully pour custard over cherries (do not fill tart shell more than three fourths full).

4. Bake for 10 minutes at 400° F. Reduce heat to 325° F and bake until custard is set (about 35 minutes).

5. Sift confectioners' sugar over tart. Place under preheated broiler to caramelize sugar. Watch carefully—sugar burns easily. Serve slightly warm.

Serves 6 to 8.

Recipes and Related Information
Cherries Jubilee, 315; Fruit Cheesecake, 119.

CHERRY PITTER

Like a hole puncher, which this hand tool resembles, a cherry pitter makes quick work out of a most tedious chore—removing pits from cherries and olives. All the models are variations of a basic press system: the device holds the round or oval fruit in place while pressure is applied to a plunger that pushes out the pit. The simplest model handles one or two cherries at a squeeze and must be continually reloaded. If this procedure seems too time-consuming, look for an automatic pitter with a built-in container that can hold up to 3 cups of cherries. A funnel feeds the stored fruit to the pitter each time you press the plunger. It *is* child's play. If you have a junior chef who wants to help with meal preparation, this is exactly the type of repetitious work that young hands love to do.

Recipes and Related Information
Cherry, 120; Olive, 398.

CHERVIL

An annual herb native to Asia and Eastern Europe, chervil resembles a very delicate form of parsley. It has soft, feathery, green leaves atop slender stems and umbrella-shaped clusters of tiny white flowers. The leaves have a faint anise flavor.

Use   The aniselike flavor of chervil complements egg, tomato, and fish dishes. Add it to green salads and potato salads, cream soups, mayonnaise, and herb butters and sauces. Chervil is an ingredient in the classic French fines herbes mixture.

Availability   Fresh chervil, tied in bunches or packed in plastic bags, is occasionally available in specialty markets. Dried chervil is sold in airtight jars.

Selection   Buy chervil that is fresh-looking without signs of wilting or decay. Packaged seasonings lose quality after a while; try to buy from a store that restocks its spice section fairly often.

Storage   Keep fresh chervil in refrigerator, wrapped in damp paper towels then in plastic, for up to three days. Store dried chervil in an airtight container in a cool, dry, dark place.

Preparation   Mince fresh chervil leaves just before using. For cooked dishes, add chervil at the last moment; its delicate flavor dissipates with cooking.

Sidewalk chestnut vendors are a familiar winter sight in New York and the cities of Europe. They tuck the steaming nuggets into paper cones for shoppers and strollers, who probably appreciate the warmth as much as the rich, nutty taste. Chestnuts become harder to peel as they cool, so serve them hot from the cooking container or in a napkin-lined basket.

CHESTNUT

The chestnut is the fruit of a tree native to several continents. Chestnut trees flourished in America until the early twentieth century, when they were destroyed by a fungus blight. They still have not been reestablished, although efforts are being made.

The golden chestnut is encased in both a fine, reddish brown membrane and an inedible hard, brown shell. The shelled, cooked chestnut is simultaneously sweet and starchy, with a moist, crumbly texture.

Use Fresh chestnuts may be roasted in their shells, then peeled and eaten whole as a snack. Peeled chestnuts may be simmered in stock or milk and served as an accompaniment to game or rich meats or made into soup. Whole chestnuts are often braised with red cabbage or Brussels sprouts. Cooked and puréed chestnuts may be seasoned with butter, salt, and pepper for a savory side dish, or sweetened with sugar and cream and used for dessert. French and Italian cooks use sweetened chestnut purée as a filling, garnish, or ingredient for a variety of desserts. Whole candied chestnuts are a popular Christmas confection in Western Europe and an autumn treat in Japan. Chopped candied chestnuts may be added to ice cream, dessert sauces, or confections. Americans add chopped cooked chestnuts to holiday poultry stuffings. Japanese steam autumn chestnuts with rice. In northern China, dried chestnuts are added to stews.

Chestnut flour, made from dried, ground chestnuts, is used in Europe for breads, soups, and desserts.

Availability Fresh chestnuts are available in winter. Whole peeled chestnuts packed in water are imported from France. Unsweetened chestnut purée, packaged in cans and identified as *purée de marrons*, is imported from France and Switzerland. Sweetened chestnut purée, labeled as *crème de marrons*, is imported from France in cans and tubes. Also from France come whole candied chestnuts (*marrons glacées*) and chestnut pieces (*marrons débris*) in vanilla-flavored syrup, packed in cans and jars. Dried chestnuts are available in Italian and Chinese markets. Chestnut flour is sold in health-food stores and some Italian markets.

Selection Choose glossy chestnuts that fill their shells and feel heavy for their size. Those with air pockets are likely to be older and dried out. Chestnuts can appear fresh and still be spoiled inside, so it's a good idea to buy a few more than you need.

Storage Fresh chestnuts will keep up to one week in a cool place or up to two weeks in a plastic bag in the refrigerator. Unused chestnut purée or tinned candied chestnuts will keep in a covered plastic container in the refrigerator for several months. Dried chestnuts will keep in an airtight container in a cool place for two months or in the refrigerator or freezer indefinitely. Chestnut flour keeps one month in the refrigerator.

Preparation To shell fresh chestnuts, cut an *x* in the flat side. Roast in a preheated 350° F oven for 10 minutes, then peel. Alternatively, blanch them in boiling water for 3 to 4 minutes. Remove from water one at a time and peel (easiest when chestnuts are hot).

ROASTED CHESTNUTS

Cook chestnuts at home in the oven as described below, or wrap them in heavy-duty aluminum foil and roast them outdoors over coals. You can also roast them on a grate in the fireplace or over an open fire, using a heavy, lidded skillet with a long handle or a popcorn popper; shake the pan repeatedly until the shells pop open.

> 2 dozen chestnuts
> Olive oil
> 2 tablespoons water

1. Preheat oven to 425° F. With a small, sharp knife, cut a cross in the flat side of each chestnut. Place chestnuts in a casserole with a tight-fitting lid; add a few drops of oil, toss nuts to coat lightly, add the water, and cover.

2. Bake until chestnuts feel tender when squeezed and peel easily (25 to 30 minutes). Remove to a napkin-lined basket or serve from the casserole.

Makes 2 dozen.

CHICORY

A variety of mostly perennial plants go by the family name *chicory*. Some chicory is grown for its leaves, some for its roots. Chicory grown for its roots is rarely seen in retail markets; the roots are dried, ground, and used as a coffee substitute or additive, popular in New Orleans.

The chicory family includes Belgian endive, escarole, and radicchio, as well as the salad green often labeled chicory in retail markets. The latter chicory is also sometimes labeled *frisé* or curly endive.

Because several of the major members of the chicory family are described in separate entries, this entry deals primarily with the salad green commonly called chicory. A head of chicory contains loosely grouped leaves that are frizzy and have spiky edges. Outer leaves are dark green; inner leaves are pale green, becoming yellow at the heart.

Use Chicory adds texture and a slightly bitter flavor to green salads. Because of its coarse texture, it is often mixed with other greens.

Availability Fresh chicory is sold all year but may be more abundant in early spring or late fall.

Selection Select chicory without evidence of wilting or browning on leaf tips.

Storage Keep chicory in a plastic bag in refrigerator crisper; use within two or three days.

Preparation Wash well just before using. Trim root end and discard any dark or ragged leaves.

CHIFFONNADE

A French term, *chiffonnade* refers to leafy greens and herbs cut into thin ribbons. A chiffonnade of basil, for example, can serve as a flavoring mixture or as a bed for other foods. Shredded lettuce or sorrel is a classic garnish for soups. To prepare a chiffonnade, trim leaves of their stems and any woody parts. Then roll leaves together into narrow tubes and slice into fine strips.

Chiffonnade is also a salad dressing that is based on a French dressing with the addition of chopped hard-cooked egg and strips of green bell pepper, chives, and other vegetables.

CHILL, TO

To make something cold by placing it in the refrigerator or by stirring it over ice water. Salads, gelatin-based dishes, pâtés, soups, mayonnaise-based sauces, custards, pastry dough, and fruit desserts are examples of foods that may require chilling.

CHIVE

A member of the onion family, chives grow in long, thin, hollow green shoots.

Use Snipped chives add a delicate onion flavor to soups, salads, vegetable dishes, eggs, fish, and cheese spreads. They are frequently used as a topping for baked potatoes, along with sour cream. Because of their delicate flavor, they are best as a raw garnish; if possible, add them to cooked dishes at the last minute. Chives are one ingredient in the classic French fines herbes mixture.

Availability Whole fresh chives are sold the year around, tied in bunches or packaged in plastic bags. Snipped freeze-dried chives are packed in airtight jars or tins. Snipped frozen chives are also available in supermarket freezer cases.

Selection Buy fresh shoots without evidence of wilting or decay. Dried seasonings lose quality after a while; try to buy from a store that restocks its spice section often.

Storage Wrap fresh chives in damp paper towels, then in a plastic bag, and refrigerate; use within three or four days. Store freeze-dried chives in an airtight container in a cool, dry, dark place and use within three months. Use frozen chives within six months.

Preparation Mince fresh chives with a knife or snip with kitchen scissors just before using. There is no need to reconstitute freeze-dried chives or thaw frozen chives before using.

CHIVE POTATO SALAD

In this version of a popular salad, tiny whole potatoes are tossed in a creamy dressing, punctuated by the oniony flavor and bright green color of fresh chives. Note that the potatoes cook a day in advance, and that, once tossed in dressing, they will keep another 24 hours.

    2 pounds small new potatoes
    ¾ cup Mayonnaise (see page 519)
    ¾ cup Crème Fraîche (see page 161) or sour cream
    1 bunch fresh chives, snipped

1. The day before the salad is prepared, peel off a strip of skin from around the middle of each potato. Bring a 4-quart pot of salted water to a boil. Add potatoes and cook, covered, until easily pierced with the tip of a sharp knife (20 to 30 minutes). Drain and cool completely. Refrigerate, covered.

2. The next day, combine Mayonnaise and Crème Fraîche in a medium bowl. Add potatoes and toss to cover with sauce. Sprinkle with snipped chives. Serve immediately or refrigerate, covered, up to 24 hours before serving.

Serves 6.

MAKING CHOCOLATE RUFFLES

To make a thin chocolate sheet for a ruffle Refrigerate a piece of marble for several hours or place a rimmed baking sheet filled with ice on top of marble for 30 minutes to chill it. (Chocolate can be spread on the back of a baking sheet but ruffles will not look as shiny when finished.) Dry marble with paper towels. Pour a 1-inch-wide strip of melted and tempered chocolate on ice-cold marble. Use a flexible metal spatula and swift, smooth, even strokes to spread chocolate into a thin sheet about 3 inches wide and 10 inches long.

To form a fan-shaped ruffle When chocolate begins to set but is still pliable, slide a wide-bladed putty knife under right edge of chocolate. To form a fan-shaped ruffle, push chocolate toward left side of marble by moving putty knife from right to left (flexing wrist back and forth as you push). Use index finger and thumb of left hand to gather chocolate into a ruffle as you go along. Transfer ruffle to a waxed paper–lined baking sheet and immediately place in refrigerator.

For the Chocolate Ruffle Torte Make enough ruffles to cover the top of the cake in an overlapping design of rose petals. Rechill marble as necessary. Store ruffles between pieces of waxed paper in a pan in refrigerator until ready to place on cake, after cake has been wrapped with chocolate ribbon (see below). Cover top of pan with plastic wrap.

MAKING CHOCOLATE RIBBONS

Cut out a sheet of waxed paper that is slightly wider than cake is tall and as long as circumference of cake. With a flexible metal spatula, spread a thin layer of melted and tempered chocolate on waxed paper. When chocolate begins to set but is still pliable, place one end of strip against cake (with wet chocolate toward cake). Wrap rest of chocolate strip around cake so it rests smoothly against sides of cake. Press top edge of chocolate down onto top of cake. Chill in refrigerator until chocolate is firm and waxed paper peels away easily.

MAKING CHOCOLATE LEAVES

Choose thick, waxy plant leaves with visible veins. Paint melted and tempered chocolate evenly on undersides of leaves. Chill in refrigerator until chocolate is firm. Slide fingernail between leaf and chocolate near stem to loosen chocolate from leaf. Pull leaf away from chocolate. Use these delicate leaves to decorate all sorts of cakes.

MAKING CHOCOLATE CURLS

It is easiest to produce chocolate curls from a 4-ounce or larger bar of chocolate (at room temperature). Scrape long side of bar with a potato peeler. When chocolate is just the right temperature, this will produce chocolate curls. If chocolate is too cold, you will end up with short chocolate shavings or shredded chocolate.

CHOCOLATE RUFFLE TORTE

This stunning chocolate mousse torte requires some knowledge of the properties of chocolate and a little experience in working with melted chocolate. If you are a beginner to chocolate work, see Working With Chocolate.

  ¾ **cup unsalted butter, softened**
  ¾ **cup sugar**
  ¾ **cup (3 oz) finely ground almonds**
  6 **ounces bittersweet chocolate,
       melted and cooled**
  6 **egg yolks**
  6 **egg whites**

Chocolate Mousse

  1¼ **cups whipping cream**
  6 **ounces semisweet chocolate,
       melted and cooled**
  ½ **cup water**
  7 **tablespoons sugar**
  4 **egg yolks**

Chocolate Ribbons and Ruffles

  1 **pound semisweet chocolate**

1. Preheat oven to 350° F. Butter and lightly flour 2 round cake pans 2 inches tall and 8 inches in diameter (see Pan Substitution Chart, page 20, if you don't have pans this size). Line bottom of each with a circle of waxed paper.

2. In large electric mixer bowl, cream butter with half of the sugar until light. Add almonds and beat until light. Beat in melted chocolate.

3. Add egg yolks, one at a time, beating well after each addition; beat until light and fluffy.

4. Beat egg whites in a separate bowl until they begin to hold peaks. Gradually add remaining sugar and beat until stiff but still glossy.

5. Stir one fourth of egg whites into chocolate mixture to lighten batter. Gently fold in remaining whites. Whites should be completely incorporated but not deflated.

6. Divide batter equally between the 2 pans and gently smooth top of batter. Bake for 30 to 40 minutes, or until done. Cool in pans 10 minutes, then turn out onto wire racks to finish cooling. This cake tends to sink in the middle as it cools. Trim top with serrated knife to create even layers.

7. Place one layer on a cardboard cake circle that is ⅛ inch smaller than the cake. Spread half of the Chocolate Mousse over this layer. Set next layer on top of mousse. Spread remaining Chocolate Mousse on sides and top of cake. Refrigerate until mousse is firm (about 45 minutes).

8. Decorate cake with Chocolate Ribbons and Ruffles.

Serves 8.

Chocolate Mousse Whip cream until it holds soft peaks. Refrigerate. Melt chocolate; cool to tepid. Combine the water and sugar in saucepan. Bring to a boil to dissolve sugar. Boil 1 minute. Measure out ½ cup hot syrup. Place egg yolks in a deep, 4- to 5-quart stainless steel bowl. Whisk in hot syrup. Continue whisking in one direction (either clockwise or counterclockwise) over a double boiler until mixture holds soft peaks (5 to 7 minutes). Beat yolks off heat with electric mixer or by hand until they are cool. Stir in melted, tepid chocolate. Fold in one eighth of whipped cream. Gradually fold in remaining whipped cream. If you fold in cream too quickly, it will cause chocolate to harden and form chocolate chips.

Chocolate Ribbons and Ruffles Melt and temper (see page 125) 1 pound of semisweet chocolate. Follow step-by-step instructions on opposite page to form ruffles and ribbons.

Chocolate Ruffle Torte, adorned with pleats of rich chocolate, is a cake that borders on being a work of art. Inside the chocolate case are both chocolate cake and chocolate mousse—a chocoholic's fantasy.

CHOCOLATE-DIPPED FRUIT

When dipping fruits in chocolate, first dry the fruits completely. Any residual moisture will cause the chocolate to seize, or become stiff. Strawberries, glacé apricots, candied ginger, candied citrus peels, dried figs, and prunes look fabulous half-dipped. Fruits that tend to darken when exposed to the air, such as bananas, apples, and pears, are best totally coated. Moist fruits, such as orange sections, raspberries, and seedless grapes, should also be completely coated. The amount of chocolate required depends on the size of the pieces of fruit being coated. A dipping fork, with two or three thin prongs or a loop, is useful, although many professional candy makers use the tips of their fingers. Have ready a baking sheet covered with aluminum foil or parchment paper to set the fruit on after dipping. Fruits completely covered in chocolate can be refrigerated, loosely covered, up to 48 hours, or layered in a container between sheets of waxed paper or parchment paper. Partially covered moist fruits such as strawberries should be served within 12 hours.

    1 orange, sectioned
    1 apple
    1 box (8 oz) raspberries
   14 ounces semisweet chocolate, tempered
        (see page 125)

1. Section orange. Using a sharp knife, remove skin and white membrane of orange, exposing flesh beneath. Carefully cut out each section by cutting next to membrane from edge to core on each side of section. Place sections on paper towels to dry.

2. Wash apple and pat dry. Core apple and cut into 12 pieces. Pat sections dry. Wash and dry raspberries. Discard any that are moldy or bruised.

3. Using a dipping fork or 2 fingers, dip orange sections and apple slices into tempered chocolate. Coat fruit completely, lift from bowl of chocolate, shake gently to remove excess chocolate, and place on a baking sheet lined with aluminum foil or parchment paper. Dip raspberries in same manner, being extremely gentle. Store dipped fruit in the refrigerator if not serving immediately.

Makes about 4 dozen coated fruits.

STRAWBERRIES IN WHITE CHOCOLATE

White chocolate is very perishable due to the milk solids that are combined with sugar and cocoa butter to make this product. The best method for melting and tempering white chocolate requires a bain-marie (hot water bath). Water is boiled in a large pan while the chocolate is finely chopped and placed in a metal mixing bowl. The heat is then turned off under the water, and the bowl of white chocolate is placed in the hot water. The chocolate is stirred constantly as it melts, and the tempering process continues as for semisweet chocolate (see page 125). Many American companies make a confectioners' coating, or summer coating, which is similar to white chocolate but uses vegetable fat instead of cocoa butter.

   30 large strawberries, with long stems
   10 ounces white chocolate

1. Wash strawberries and thoroughly pat dry. Temper chocolate according to instructions in the introduction and on page 125.

2. Hold strawberries by their stems. Dipping one at a time, lower tip of strawberry into chocolate to cover half of the fruit. Gently shake strawberry to remove excess chocolate and place on a baking sheet lined with aluminum foil or parchment paper. Repeat with remaining strawberries, setting berries about ½ inch apart on baking sheet. Place fruit in refrigerator if not serving immediately. Refrigerate for up to 12 hours. Because strawberries are perishable, they are best eaten within hours after dipping.

Makes 30 strawberries.

DIPPED AND STUFFED STRAWBERRIES

Strawberries in white chocolate are taken one delicious step further—they are filled with rich cream cheese.

   20 large strawberries, with long stems
    ½ cup natural cream cheese
   10 ounces semisweet or white chocolate,
        tempered (see preceding recipe)

1. Wash strawberries and thoroughly pat dry. Cut a slit in each strawberry from tip almost to stem. Gently pry slit apart until it is about ¼ inch wide at tip.

2. Taking about 1 teaspoon of cream cheese, fill opening. Smooth edges with a knife to conform to the contour of strawberry.

3. Dip as directed in step 2 of Strawberries in White Chocolate (preceding).

Makes 20 strawberries.

Recipes and Related Information
Baked Chocolate Custard, 169; Cake-Lover's Brownies, 65; Chocolate Doughnuts, 180; Chocolate Fudge, 96; Chocolate Fudge Frosting, 248; Chocolate Glaze, 250; Chocolate Ice Cream, 312; Chocolate Mousse Torte, 373; Chocolate-Pecan Waffles, 599; Chocolate Pretzels, 146; Chocolate Soufflé, 207; Chocolate Sponge Cake, 83; Chocolate-Swirled Babka, 630; Chocolate Truffles, 97; Classic Fudge Brownies, 64; Devil's Food Cake, 86; Hot Fudge Sauce, 522; Marbled Cream Cheese Brownies, 65; Old-fashioned Chocolate Sauce, 523; Pain au Chocolat, 626; Philadelphia-Style Chocolate Ice Cream, 313; Ricotta Cheesecake, 119; White-Chocolate and Chip Brownies, 64.

Minced can(
some supern
candied fruit
preservative

Storage C
mail-order s
servatives a
supermarket
refrigerated,

Preparation

CITRU

The intense,
of freshly s(
juice can't b
the bottled
rus reamer i
tract juice f(
Many designs
but in fact all
variations of
an upright, p
cone, shaped
the flesh of a
releases the ju

At its mos
handle. Juice,
more elabora
reamer is att
juice to drip t
pulp and seed
tainer, which
Both mani
ease the chor
food process(
long-popular,
features a rea
a horseshoe-sl
fits over the re
through a stra
been set bene
A citrus sp(
Inserted into u
spoonfuls of ju
and salads. Fr
serted. In addi
because fruit
longer. Avoid :
the skin of the

CHOP, TO

To cut food into small, but not necessarily even, pieces with a knife, a bowl chopper, in a food processor, or in an electric minichopper. Chopped pieces are larger than those that are minced or diced, and can be evenly or ran- domly shaped. See KNIFE, Cutting Techniques, for informa- tion on proper hand position when chopping with a knife and specifics on chopping particular foods. Also see spe- cific entries on other chopping equipment.

CHOPPING AND CUTTING BOARD

A cutting surface must be soft enough to cushion the edge of a knife blade so that it will not dull the knife, but hard enough to resist splintering or otherwise dis- integrating into the food. Wood is the favorite cutting surface of most cooks. Lam- inated hardwood cutting

boards and end-grain butcher blocks are both excellent choices. Wooden boards have some disadvantages, how- ever. They require a lot of care, including periodic sanding and oiling. They also tend to absorb odors from food and are harder to sterilize and deodorize than nonporous ma- terials. For this reason, some cooks prefer a synthetic surface for cutting meats, poultry, and especially seafood. The best synthetic boards are made of a dense, opaque white polycarbonate and have a slightly uneven surface that gives under the knife blade much as wood does. They are easy to clean with dishwashing detergent (which should never be used on a wooden board). Do not confuse these boards with decorative boards of shiny, clear plastic or any other hard surface, which will dull knives.

Whether you use a wooden or synthetic cutting board, choose the largest size that will easily fit your work space. Nothing is more frustrating than trying to cut a lot of foods on a tiny board. Although sizes may vary from one manu- facturer to another, boards are typically available sized 15 by 20 by 3/8 inches, 18 by 24 by 3/8 inches, and 16 by 9 by 3/8 inches.

HOW TO CLEAN WOODEN CUTTING SURFACES

After each use, scrape wooden boards clean with a metal dough scraper. Never soak with water. If a film remains, sprinkle with coarse salt and scour with a plastic or wire scrub brush; wipe with a clean, damp sponge. For minor stains, rub with the cut side of a lemon half. Deep stains

can only be removed by sanding. Occasionally, sanitize the wood by cleaning with a solution of equal parts of bleach and water; rinse away solution with a clean, damp sponge. To keep wood from drying out and splintering, oil occa- sionally with mineral oil, or special wood oil available at hardware stores, home improvement stores, and better cookware stores.

Recipes and Related Information
Cake and Pastry Tools, 92; Knife, 328.

CILANTRO

Also known as coriander or Chinese parsley, cilantro is a pungent herb often used in Latin American and Asian cooking. It has small, fragile green leaves and thin stems. Although cilantro resembles parsley, its slightly musty aroma and flavor are entirely different. The aromatic seeds, which have a sweet flavor far removed from the flavor of the leaves, are an important and ancient season- ing marketed as coriander seed.

Use Cilantro leaves and stems add pungent flavor to Latin American soups, salads, and stews; they are an aro- matic, all-purpose garnish for countless Latin American dishes, used in much the same way minced parsley is in French or American cooking. Chinese steamed fish and shellfish, noodle dishes, soups, and stews are also com- monly garnished with fresh cilantro leaves. Fresh cilan- tro is also used in Indian chutneys, Moroccan stews, and Thai salads.

Coriander seed is an ingredient in most commercial curry powders and pickling spice mixtures. Ground cori- ander is added to hot dogs and other sausages, to ginger- breads, coffee cakes, Danish pastry, and Swedish butter cookies, and to lamb, pork, chicken, and cheese dishes.

Availability Fresh cilantro, tied in small bundles, is available all year. Coriander seed is available whole or ground, in bulk or prepacked in airtight containers or plastic bags.

Selection Buy fresh-looking bunches without evidence of wilting or decay. Packaged seasonings lose quality af- ter a while; try to buy from a store that restocks its spice shelves fairly often.

Storage Keep fresh cilantro, root ends down, in a jar of water. Cover with a plastic bag and refrigerate up to one week. Store coriander seed in an airtight container in a cool, dry, dark place. Replace ground coriander every six months. Whole coriander seed will last longer, anywhere from one to two years.

Preparation Trim root ends of fresh cilantro; mince or add whole to dishes. Toast whole coriander seed briefly in a dry skillet to bring out its flavor.

Decorating gingerbread people, a holiday tradition, is one of the pleasures of childhood that even the youngest artists can do.

1. In a small bowl combine raisins and brandy; let stand 30 minutes. Add walnuts, sugar, and cinnamon; stir to blend; set aside.

2. Preheat oven to 425° F. Divide Cream Cheese Pastry in half. On a lightly floured surface, roll each half into a thin round. With a sharp knife cut 10-inch-diameter circles from each round of dough by placing bottom of a 10-inch tart tin (or a 10-inch-diameter pattern cut from paper) on dough and cutting around it. Roll scraps from both circles into another thin round, and make an 8-inch-diameter circle.

3. Sprinkle surface of each 10-inch circle with ⅔ cup raisin-nut filling; use ½ cup filling for 8-inch circle (a few tablespoons of filling will be left over). Press filling lightly with your hands to make it adhere to dough.

4. With a floured knife cut 10-inch circles into 12 wedges and cut 8-inch circles into 8 wedges. Starting with wide edge, roll each wedge toward tip, encasing filling.

5. Arrange rolls on ungreased baking sheets. Place sheets in oven and immediately reduce heat to 400° F. Bake until lightly browned (12 to 14 minutes). Transfer to wire racks; when cool sprinkle cookies with confectioners' sugar.

Makes 32 cookies.

Cream Cheese Pastry   In a bowl beat cream cheese, butter, salt, sugar, and vanilla until light and smooth. Add flour and beat until just blended. Gather dough into a ball and enclose in waxed paper or plastic wrap; refrigerate several hours or overnight.

■ GINGERBREAD PEOPLE

These little cookie people, cut from a thick slab of spicy molasses dough, are wonderful for a children's party. Make a batch and allow children to decorate their own. School-age children can maneuver an icing-filled paper piping cone. Provide younger children with a confectioners' sugar glaze, sprinkles, and decorating sugar.

> ½ **cup unsalted butter, softened**
> ½ **cup firmly packed brown sugar**
> ½ **cup molasses**
> 1 **egg**
> 2½ **cups flour**
> 1 **teaspoon baking soda**
> ½ **teaspoon salt**
> 2 **teaspoons ground ginger**
> 1 **teaspoon ground cinnamon**
> ½ **teaspoon freshly grated nutmeg**
> ½ **teaspoon ground cloves**
> **Dried currants, for decorating**
> **Royal Icing (see page 250)**

1. In large mixer bowl cream butter; gradually add sugar and beat until light. Add molasses and egg and beat to blend well; set aside.

■ RUGELACH

Although Jewish delicatessens sell Rugelach throughout the year, these cream cheese crescents are a Hanukkah tradition. They may be stuffed with nuts and raisins, as they are here, or with jam or poppy seed filling if preferred. They do not keep well and should be eaten within a few hours of baking.

> ½ **cup raisins, coarsely chopped**
> 1 **tablespoon brandy**
> 1 **cup finely chopped, toasted walnuts**
> ½ **cup granulated sugar**
> 1 **teaspoon cinnamon**
> **Confectioners' sugar, for dusting**

Cream Cheese Pastry

> 1 **package (8 oz) cream cheese, at room temperature**
> ½ **cup unsalted butter, at room temperature**
> ¼ **teaspoon salt**
> 1 **tablespoon sugar**
> 1 **teaspoon vanilla extract**
> 1 **cup flour**

2. In a bowl stir together flour, baking soda, salt, ginger, cinnamon, nutmeg, and cloves. Gradually add flour mixture to butter mixture, beating until just blended. Gather dough into a ball and enclose in plastic wrap; refrigerate at least 1 hour.

3. Preheat oven to 325° F. On a lightly floured board, roll out gingerbread to a thickness of ¼ inch. Cut out cookies with a floured, 4½-inch-long cutter and transfer to greased baking sheets. Bake until cookies are lightly browned around edges and feel barely firm when touched gently (about 10 minutes). Transfer to wire racks. While each cookie is hot, press in currants to create eyes, mouth, and buttons. When cool, decorate with Royal Icing piped from a paper cone.

Makes about 1 dozen 4-inch-long cookies.

Recipes and Related Information
Baking Pans, 18; Biscotti, 8; Cake and Pastry Tools, 89; Linzer Hearts, 298; Macadamia Crisps, 346.

COOKWARE (POTS AND PANS)

In simplest terms, cookware permits controlled exposure of food to heat. The best pots and pans conduct heat evenly and efficiently and are most responsive to changes in temperature, usually due to their material and construction (see MATERIALS FOR COOKWARE). Size and shape are adaptations that have evolved over time for specific purposes; these features are subjective ones, having less to do with performance than with personal cooking styles or manufacturers' preferences.

Quality cookware is an investment that will return long-term dividends of reliability and durability. How do you judge quality? Price is a clue; better cookware costs more. But with proper care, each piece can be a one-time purchase. Resist the prepackaged appeal of a set. More than likely these collections include at least one pan that you wouldn't buy if you didn't have to. What appears to be a bargain, then, really isn't. If you don't need it, you don't want it. Resist, too, the seduction of surface flash—color and pattern don't keep a sauce from burning or make water boil faster. A material with good heat-conducting qualities offers those attributes. If it's pretty, consider its appearance a secondary bonus. Today's home cooks have come to appreciate and even prefer the clean, spare, utilitarian lines of commercial cookware, choosing a decorative pan only if it will go to the table.

BUTTER WARMER

This is a very versatile little pan, despite its single-purpose name. It is perfectly sized for melting jellies and preserves for glazes; warming syrups, single portions of soups,

and baby foods; softening honey and ice cream sauces; and heating alcohol for flambés. Most hold about 2 cups. Choose one with a wide, stable, flat bottom. A pan this small should also have a long handle, so the cook's hand is at a distance from the burner. Most cookware lines offer a version, in the usual materials. Some are enameled steel or cast iron—decorative enough to come to the table.

CARAMELIZING POT

If you make sugar syrups and candies more than occasionally, you might consider investing in this heavyweight, straight-sided pot traditionally used for sugar work. Copper is the metal of choice because it is extremely sensitive to heat; this affords important control of sugar syrup, which can quickly deepen from brown to burned in a matter of seconds. Unlike most copper cookware, caramelizing pots aren't lined with tin: copper and sugar are compatible (other foods and copper are sometimes adverse) and the high temperatures that sugar work requires can melt tin. They come in 1- and 2-quart sizes and have a hollow, rolled handle and a pouring spout.

CHICKEN FRYER

An American invention, the chicken fryer is a deep, covered frying pan well-suited for frying, browning, and braising. With its short handle and lip (to more easily pour off accumulated fat), it resembles a cast-iron skillet, and is usually made of cast iron or enameled cast iron. To help control spattering, its sides are higher than those of a skillet; and its domed lid is useful for slow, covered cooking. Both are about 12 inches in diameter. Although extremely versatile, the chicken fryer isn't as popular as it once was; those who saw their grandmothers using one to make great fried chicken do know its value.

DEEP-FAT FRYER

A deep-fat fryer should be tall enough to hold at least several inches of fat with sufficient additional room for the hot fat to bubble up without spilling over when food is dropped in; the fryer should be wide enough so that food can float freely to an evenly browned crisp. Depth is more critical than surface area, as safety is a key issue for this technique; width is a convenience that allows more food to fry at a time. French-style models are deep and wide, with a narrow base and wider surface, and ear handles. American deep-fat fryers resemble oversized saucepans, with a single long handle. Four quarts is a standard size and is appropriate for most recipes; steel, enameled steel, and aluminum are the usual materials.

Basket inserts, useful for lowering food into the fat, then lifting it out again when done, are often packaged with the pot. These baskets are also sold separately, to use with a pot you already have. The handles on some models are designed to hold the basket up out of the pan so that the fat can drain away. Other pans have a clip attached to one side for the same purpose. Helpful accessories include wire and mesh skimmers and deep-fat thermometers. Thermostatically controlled, electric deep-fat fryers are also available in large and small sizes.

DOUBLE BOILER

Foods that need some protection from direct heat—custards, chocolate, egg-based sauces—usually cook in a double boiler, which is, in effect, a pair of stacked saucepans. The lower pan holds a few inches of simmering or boiling water that gently heats food held in the upper section. The water diffuses the heat and softens its impact. Most manufacturers make double boiler inserts to fit their cookware. Double boilers are also available; 1½ and 2 quarts are basic sizes. Common materials are stainless steel, aluminum, enameled steel, clad metals, and copper with a porcelain upper pot.

Some cooks devise their own double boilers by setting a large bowl partway in a pan of smaller diameter. Or, they use a footed, cast-aluminum ring called a double boiler maker; this trivet sits on the bottom of a saucepan and keeps a bowl set within the pan about an inch above the pan bottom, away from the direct heat.

FISH POACHER

Typical dimensions for this long, narrow, covered pan are 18 inches long, 5 inches wide, and 3½ to 4 inches deep—sized to hold a medium-sized whole fish. It is used for poaching, whether fish, chicken breasts, or even pasta rolls. The rack lifts food off the pan bottom, providing gentle cooking in surrounding poaching liquid. The rack also permits the poached food to be safely removed from the pan. The most beautiful of these pans are of tin-lined copper; these are also the most costly. Stainless steel and tinned steel are acceptable alternatives. Although useful, fish poachers require a great deal of storage space.

GRIDDLE

These thick, flat pans are used for pancakes, French toast, scones, crumpets, bacon, sausage, hamburgers, thin steaks, fish, and eggs. Griddle-cooking is quick and requires little water or fat; heat is transferred by conduction directly from burner to pan to food. Unlike a skillet, which can also function as a griddle, these flat pans can have a trough or shallow rim, rather than true sides, to collect or contain excess fat or cooking oil. They are typically 12- or 14-inch squares or rounds, or 12- by 18- or 20-inch rectangles. They should be made of a material that heats evenly and quickly and holds heat well. After cooking, wipe away bits of food, rather than scrubbing the cooking surface, so a seasoning will develop; then lightly grease and store dry.

GRILL PAN (STOVE-TOP BROILER)

A hybrid, this pan functions as a combination griddle, skillet, and grill. The bottom surface is ridged, so, like a grill, food doesn't cook in its own fat—a boon to those restricting fat intake. It has raised sides, like a skillet, and is made of a heavy material such as cast iron or enameled cast iron since it is often used with high heat.

OMELET PAN

Strictly defined, an omelet pan is French, made of spun steel, and only used for this preparation. But with the development of nonstick finishes and the increasing demand for versatile cookware, there is less call for a single-purpose pan. Today, most so-called omelet pans are actually small—6-, 7-, or 8-inch—skillets. They have an open, slope-sided shape that allows eggs to slide around the pan as they cook and lets the finished omelet ease effortlessly from the pan onto a plate. Long, angled handles permit the cook to keep the pan in motion on the burner. Choose one made of heavy-gauge metal, for good heat control, and preferably with a nonstick interior.

PRESSURE COOKER

Although uncommon in American kitchens today, pressure cookers were much appreciated by our mothers and grandmothers for their ability to cut cooking time by one third to one half for foods requiring long, moist cooking, such as stews, soups, and stocks. A flavorful chicken stock is pressure-cooked in 30 minutes; artichokes are ready in 15 minutes. They are still used by a majority of European home cooks and seem to be on the verge of a comeback in the United States.

Pressure cookers work by steam action, which builds up in the tightly sealed pot. A valve system controls the amount of pressure, releasing excess steam through a series of openings in the cover. These pots scare away many cooks, who perhaps recall their mothers' dire warnings about standing near the stove when the pressure cooker was in action. Today's versions have improved safety controls, so there is little danger that the valves will blow off the pot from uncontrolled internal pressure, as they sometimes did in previous generations of these cookers. They are also much quieter than older models, emitting occasional quiet hisses instead of tooting like a steam engine. The busy cook who has embraced the microwave oven because it is quick and clean will find a pressure cooker appealing for similar reasons.

Most are manufactured in Europe; some American companies distribute these imports under their own labels. The most common size is 2 liters (about 2 quarts), perfect for small families; larger pots are 4, 6, and 8 quarts. They are made of heavy-gauge stainless steel and aluminum, and can also be used as a conventional pot.

SAUCEPAN

The versatile saucepan is best for making sauces, cooking vegetables and rice, reheating and warming, and melting solids such as chocolate, butter, and other fats, and viscous liquids such as honey and molasses. Ideally it should heat quickly and evenly, sit firmly on the burner, pour without dripping, have a snug-fitting lid, and be well balanced, easy to clean, not too heavy, and nonreactive to acid foods. Because it is moved around a great deal, the handle should be in proportion to the pan's size and weight for easy lifting.

Saucepans range in size from 2 cups to 6 quarts, and are made of copper, aluminum, stainless steel, enameled cast iron, ceramic, glass, and clad metals. They can be either tall and narrow or wide and shallow; each is useful, but a unique shape can also be the manufacturer's way of making a statement about a product as much as anything else. Saucepans with tall sides are well suited for warming and reheating; less surface area is exposed to the air, so less evaporation occurs. Low-sided saucepans, which give greater surface exposure to air, are perfect for quick cooking, mixing, and reductions. A shallow pan can also function as a water bath or double boiler; the pan is filled with several inches of gently simmering water and a bowl smaller in diameter is set in it. You will probably want to have at least two saucepans, probably more; 1-, 2-, and 3- to 4-quart capacities are basic sizes.

SAUCEPOT

These large, useful pans, with ear handles and covers, are also called Dutch ovens and casseroles. They are invaluable for cooking in large quantities: pasta, vegetables, soups, and stews. Because they are used for slow cooking, which requires holding a simmer for long periods of time, they should be made of a material that conducts and holds heat well. Sizes range from 4 to 14 quarts; 5 quarts will meet the needs of most households. Materials include aluminum, stainless steel, enameled steel, enameled cast iron, and clad metals.

Quality cookware is one of the most important purchases the home cook will make for the kitchen. Select those pots and pans that suit your cooking needs and personal cooking style. Shown clockwise from bottom left are: sauté pan, skillets, stove-top broiler, griddle, chicken fryer, deep-fat fryer, stockpot, saucepans, couscousière, steamer, pressure cooker, Chinese steamer, asparagus steamer, fish poacher, folding steamer, double boiler, wok, caramelizing pot, butter warmer.

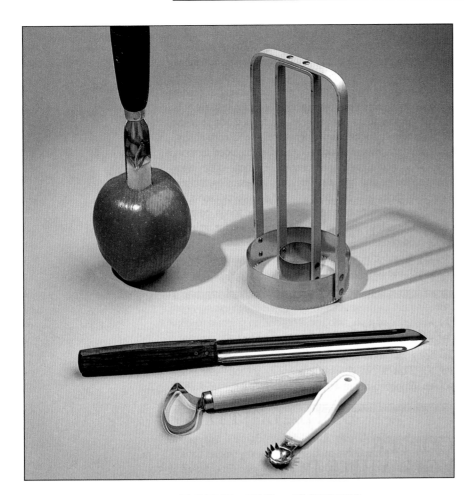

Coring tools make quick work of removing the core of a fruit or vegetable. Be sure to select a corer with a cutting edge that is sharp enough to do its job.

CORE, TO; CORER

The central seed-bearing structure of a fruit is the core; the tool with which to remove it is the corer. Apples, pears, pineapples, tomatoes, cucumbers, and zucchini have cores that may need to be removed for certain uses; special tools are available to perform this procedure on each of these foods. A knife or vegetable peeler will also do the job.

CORERS: APPLE, PEAR, PINEAPPLE, TOMATO, ZUCCHINI

These are straightforward, form-follows-function tools that do what their name suggests: remove the inedible or otherwise undesirable core from certain fruits and vegetables. When hollowed these foods are more attractive to serve, whether whole or sliced, and make versatile containers for stuffing.

Before you buy a cutting tool, check that its edge is sharp by running your finger lightly across the blade. Remember that although these machine-made corers are perfectly straight or round, chances are the fruits and vegetables aren't; even with the best technique, all the core or seeds will not come away on the first try.

APPLE CORER

Buy one that is long enough to cut all the way through an apple and has a wide enough shaft to remove all of the core and seeds in one operation. These corers usually have a hollow stainless steel shaft that traps the core. The handle is wood.

PEAR CORER

The blade is a ribbon of metal that looks like a baby pear. Cored pears are poached and served whole, or sliced or halved for use in a pastry.

PINEAPPLE CORER

This device removes peel and core at the same time. It consists of two round, serrated metal cutters, one inside the other, joined by a pair of tall, arched handles. The corer cuts down through the pineapple, whose top and bottom have been removed, with a clockwise rotating motion. The outer cutter separates peel from flesh as the inner cutter removes the core.

TOMATO CORER

Dubbed the tomato shark by manufacturers and retailers, this small stainless steel bowl has a toothy, zigzag edge. This tool also cleanly removes the ribs and seeds of cherry tomatoes to ready them for stuffing.

ZUCCHINI CORER

This tool resembles an apple corer, but the metal shaft is elongated to match the shape of a zucchini and comes to a point that better pierces the end of the squash. It works with cucumbers, apples, and pears as well.

Recipes and Related Information
Baked Pear Tart, 423; Nutty Baked Apples, 10.

CORK-PULLING DEVICES

All the devices available for pulling the cork from a bottle of wine can be divided into two categories: corkscrews and everything else. The simplest corkscrew is a coil of wire; one end is pointed and the other is attached to a handle. You screw the point of the coil into the cork and, lifting with the handle, pull out the cork.

Unfortunately, not every cork is willing to come out easily. As a result, corkscrews have been designed with every variety of leverage imaginable. In choosing a corkscrew, be sure to look for one with a helical (open-centered) screw, rather than the type that looks like an oversized wood screw. Because the latter bores a hole straight through the center of a cork, the screw will likely pull out of a stubborn cork. In general, whatever design you select, the simpler the better.

An air-pump cork puller—a long hollow needle attached to a compressed gas cylinder or hand pump—is not recommended. Once the needle is inserted through a cork, the gas pressure is activated to push out the cork. Table wine bottles, however, are not built to withstand internal pressure, as sparkling wine and soda bottles are. It may never happen, but the possibly explosive combination of a weak bottle and a stubborn cork is a frightening scene to contemplate.

DOUBLE SCREW

This corkscrew uses a second screw to pull the cork. Both the wooden model and the all-metal version rely on the same principle, but one screws a threaded tube out of the body, and the other screws a threaded handle down around a sliding tube, drawing the cork out with it. Both of these draw the cork smoothly and slowly without jostling the bottle, which is an important advantage in an older wine that has thrown a sediment.

DOUBLE-WING CORKSCREW

To operate this basic chrome and plastic device, the coiled wire is screwed into the cork until the wings are forced upward and the body rests on the rim of the bottle opening. Pressing both wings down draws the cork up and out. A reverse-thread version is available to ease the job for left-handed oenophiles.

PROFESSIONAL LEVER CORKSCREW

A commercial wine opener for serious wine tasters who think they have everything, this extravagant cork puller is more home accessory than basic kitchen equipment. Various models are made of solid copper, chrome-plated steel, or cast aluminum, often accented with wood. Extremely elaborate and in a class by itself, it is at the same time extremely simple to use: push the handle up and the cork pulls out; push down and the bottle is recorked.

SCREWPULL

One wine writer called this plastic device the first real advance in corkscrew technology in almost two centuries. Its ingeniously simple design uses a very long screw and a body to locate it on top of the bottle—nothing else. To pull the cork, the body is aligned on top of the bottle, and the tip of the teflon-coated screw is inserted, then rotated. The screw penetrates the cork until the handle stops against the body; with further turning (and very little effort), the cork climbs up the screw. A pocket version complete with a folding knife for cutting capsules allows devotees of this cork-pulling device to have it always close at hand.

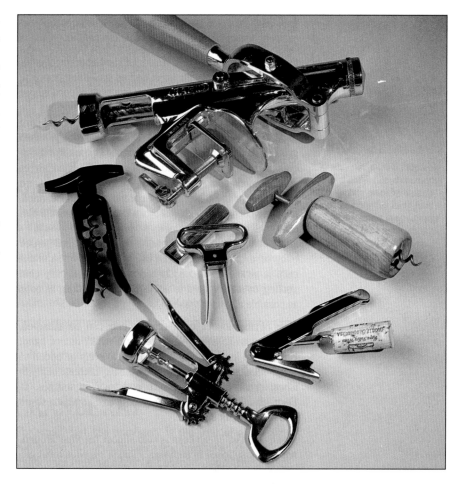

An assortment of cork-pulling devices, clockwise from top: professional lever corkscrew, simple corkscrew with wooden handle and case, waiter's knife, double-wing corkscrew, Screwpull, twin-bladed cork puller.

TWIN-BLADED CORK PULLER

This tool does not use a screw, but two flexible metal blades that slip down between the cork and the neck of the bottle. You pull the cork by simultaneously twisting and pulling up the handle. This device takes a little practice to master and a good deal of brute force, and if used incorrectly, it will neatly shove the cork back into the bottle. Once mastered, however, this tool makes pulling the cork a fairly quick operation. A minor advantage is that you can reverse the cork-pulling procedure to recork the bottle.

WAITER'S KNIFE

Although a bit harder to master than the double-wing corkscrew, the metal waiter's knife is a popular and reliable design. An arm attached to one end of the corkscrew hooks onto the top of the bottle, and the hinge forms the fulcrum. The waiter's knife also includes a small knife for cleanly cutting the capsule (lead or foil wrapping). The inexperienced user might find that the cork breaks or gets pushed into the bottle with this cork puller; novices should practice on *vin ordinaire* before attempting to open a vintage selection.

To form éclairs, pipe 5-inch strips of paste 2 inches apart on a parchment-lined baking sheet (see Chocolate Éclairs, right). To form cream puffs, pipe 2½-inch mounds of paste 2 inches apart on baking sheet (see Cream Puffs, page 163).

▉ CHOCOLATE ECLAIRS

Eclairs, fingers of cream puff pastry, are filled with flavored (chocolate, praline, or coffee) pastry cream and iced with a thin, shiny glaze. They are shaped by piping the pastry onto baking sheets with a pastry bag and plain tip (see photograph at left). Several delicious variations follow this recipe. Before using the Bittersweet Chocolate Sauce, cool to 90° F; then spread 1 to 2 tablespoons on top of each éclair or finish by dipping top of each pastry into the warm icing.

  1⅓   cups Cream Puff Pastry (see page 163)
    1   egg lightly beaten with 1 teaspoon water
  1½   cups Pastry Cream (see page 251)
    ½   cup whipping cream
    1   cup Bittersweet Chocolate Sauce (at right)

1. Preheat oven to 425° F. Place Cream Puff Pastry in a large pastry bag fitted with a ¾-inch tip. Cut a piece of parchment paper to fit a baking sheet; using a dark pen or pencil, draw along the long edges of the paper two parallel lines that are 5 inches apart; then turn paper over on baking sheet.

2. To form éclairs, pipe eight 5-inch strips of pastry, 2 inches apart, onto paper-covered baking sheet, using the lines on the paper as a guide. Brush éclairs with egg-water mixture. Run the back of a fork along top of each éclair to score top and keep it flat during baking.

3. Bake 15 minutes; reduce heat to 400° F and bake 15 minutes more. Remove éclairs from oven and make a few small slits along one side of each éclair to release steam. Turn off oven; return éclairs to oven for 10 minutes, keeping oven door slightly ajar with a wooden spoon. Cool éclairs on wire racks.

4. Prepare Pastry Cream and flavor as desired. Stir cold Pastry Cream until smooth. Beat whipping cream until it holds stiff peaks and fold into Pastry Cream.

5. Just before serving (no more than 2 hours before), place filling in a pastry bag fitted with a ¼-inch tip. Poke a hole in one end of éclair with the tip and fill with 3 to 4 tablespoons of the filling. If you don't have a pastry bag, use a serrated knife to slit each éclair along one side and then spoon filling inside.

6. To ice éclairs spread 1 to 2 tablespoons warm (90° F) Bittersweet Chocolate Sauce on top of each éclair, or dip top of each éclair in warm icing. To do as much as possible in advance (up to 4 or 5 hours before serving), ice éclairs before filling them. Store iced pastries in a cool, dry place; to keep them crisp, fill them carefully just before serving.

Makes 8 éclairs.

Caramel Eclairs   Dip éclairs in a sugar syrup that has been cooked to a medium caramel color (see SUGAR AND SYRUP); cool éclairs icing side down on a cold baking sheet. Fill with vanilla- or praline-flavored Pastry Cream.

Coffee Eclairs   Fill pastries with coffee-flavored Pastry Cream. Glaze with Glacé Icing flavored with coffee or chocolate (see page 250).

Double Chocolate Eclairs   Fill pastries with Pastry Cream flavored with chocolate. Glaze with Bittersweet Chocolate Sauce or chocolate-flavored Glacé Icing (see page 250).

Mocha Eclairs   Fill pastries with Pastry Cream flavored with chocolate and coffee (to make mocha). Glaze with Bittersweet Chocolate Sauce or Glacé Icing flavored with coffee or chocolate (see page 250).

▉ ICE CREAM–FILLED PROFITEROLES

Tiny cream puffs filled with ice cream and topped with a deep, rich chocolate sauce are the classic dessert: profiteroles. The sauce is everything a chocolate sauce should be, it flows easily and coats well.

  1⅓   cups Cream Puff Pastry (see page 163)
    1   egg lightly beaten with 1 teaspoon water
    1   pint vanilla or coffee ice cream

Bittersweet Chocolate Sauce

    3   tablespoons water
    3   tablespoons sugar
    6   ounces semisweet chocolate, broken into pieces
    2   ounces unsweetened chocolate, broken into pieces
    1   cup whipping cream

1. Preheat oven to 425° F. Line baking sheets with parchment paper. Attach parchment to baking sheet at corners with dots of Cream Puff Pastry. Place Cream Puff Pastry in a pastry bag fitted with a ½-inch tip. Pipe forty-eight 1-inch-diameter mounds of pastry onto paper-lined baking sheets (at least ½ inch apart). Brush each puff with egg-water mixture, flattening the top slightly.

2. Bake 10 minutes; reduce heat to 400° F and bake until crisp and brown (about 10 minutes). Remove from oven and poke a ⅛-inch hole in bottom of each puff with tip of knife or tiny pastry tip. Turn off oven; return puffs to oven until dried out (5 to 10 minutes); prop oven door slightly ajar with a wooden spoon. Cool cream puffs on wire racks.

3. To fill pastries: Place a baking sheet in freezer. Slice each puff in half horizontally. Form 48 tiny mounds (1 rounded teaspoon each) of ice cream on cooled baking sheet. Flash-freeze. Cover ice cream mounds and store in freezer until ready to fill profiteroles. Before serving, fill bottom half of each shell with one of the ice cream mounds, then cover mound with top half of shell. Place 6 to 8 filled profiteroles in each dessert bowl. Pour about 3 tablespoons warm Bittersweet Chocolate Sauce over puffs. Serve immediately.

Makes 4 dozen profiteroles, serves 8.

Bittersweet Chocolate Sauce

1. Combine the water and sugar in a saucepan; bring to a boil over low heat, stirring constantly until sugar dissolves. Remove from heat and cool to 120° F (test with an instant-read thermometer).

2. Combine semisweet and unsweetened chocolates in top of double boiler; place over hot (not boiling) water until chocolate is just melted. Remove from heat. Pour in sugar syrup (at 120° F) all at once. Stir until smooth.

3. Heat cream in a small saucepan over low heat to 120° F. Pour into chocolate mixture and stir until smooth and shiny.

■ GOUGERE

In the Burgundy region of France, this cheese-flavored, seasoned cream puff pastry ring is a traditional specialty. Gruyère or Swiss cheese is mixed into the dough and sprinkled on top of each dough mound. Serve it as an appetizer or salad accompaniment.

> 2⅔ cups Cream Puff Pastry (see page 163)
> Pinch *each* cayenne pepper and
>   freshly grated nutmeg
> 1 cup diced Gruyère or Swiss cheese

1. Preheat oven to 375° F. Prepare Cream Puff Pastry, stirring into mixture the cayenne and nutmeg just before adding flour. Mix in ¾ cup of the cheese after all the eggs have been added and mixture is smooth and shiny.

2. Spoon out dough to make 8 equal mounds in a circular shape on a parchment-lined or greased baking sheet. Sprinkle mounds with remaining ¼ cup cheese.

3. Bake until ring is well browned and crisp (40 to 45 minutes). Serve hot.

Makes 1 ring, serves 8.

Profiteroles are a variety of cream puff pastry petits fours. They make a stunning presentation and are sure to be the highlight of any party.

cessor or blender; for dry bread crumbs, use day-old (or older) slices and dry slowly in a 325° F oven until completely dried out (at least 15 to 20 minutes). Tear into pieces and process as for fresh crumbs. To make cracker crumbs, crush crackers with a rolling pin until of the desired coarseness or fineness (it's less messy if what is to be crushed is contained in a plastic bag or between sheets of waxed paper).

CRIMP, TO

To create a decorative pattern on the edge of a pie or pastry by using a fork or other tool such as a pastry crimper. This device resembles a pair of wide-armed tweezers, which grabs the dough between its "teeth." If a pie has two crusts or a lattice top, crimping will also join top and bottom crusts. The seal will be tighter if crusts are first bonded with water, milk, or beaten egg (egg yolk makes a stronger bond than a whole egg).

CRUMB, TO

To break up bread, crackers, or cookies into crumbs or to coat food with crumbs. Fresh, soft crumbs are made by processing pieces of bread (crusts removed) in a food pro-

CRUMBLE, TO

To break into small pieces with the fingers, as in crumbling blue cheese for use in a salad dressing.

CRUSH, TO

To reduce to crumbs (crackers or dried bread) or fine particles (peppercorns) by pounding with a mallet, rolling pin, or other device or machine (such as a food processor) or by grinding with a manual or electric mill. Garlic is crushed, typically with a garlic press or with a knife, to release as much of its flavor as possible.

CUSTARD

Beloved by children of all ages, custard is a mixture of eggs, milk, sugar, salt, and flavoring, either gently cooked on top of the stove until thickened but still pourable (stirred custard), or slowly baked until firm (baked custard). Although a seemingly simple food, custard is temperamental and must be assembled and cooked with great care and attention. It is such a classic dish, with so many applications, that all cooks should develop a level of comfort with its preparation.

Stirred custard, also known as *crème anglaise*, is used as a sauce, as a pastry filling, and as the base for many chilled and frozen desserts, including ice cream and Bavarian cream. Baked custard is wonderful simply garnished with fresh fruit or whipped cream, or bathed in caramelized sugar syrup as in the famous French dessert *crème caramel* and its Latin counterpart, flan.

Made properly, custard is creamy and tender, not the curdled or weepy mess that has frustrated most cooks at one time or another. Custards thicken because egg proteins jell (form a semisolid network that enmeshes liquid) in the presence of heat. As a general rule, 1 whole egg or 2 egg yolks will thicken 1 cup milk. Problems occur when mixture is cooked too quickly and at too high a temperature. Always cook custards slowly and with gentle heat.

Stirred custards usually take about 10 to 12 minutes to thicken. Don't rush the process by raising the temperature. The line between a thickened custard and a curdled one is often only a few degrees of heat. Protect stirred custards by using a double boiler over hot, but never boiling, water. Keep stirring throughout cooking time to break up and evenly disperse the gel as it forms; this action will develop a thick mixture that is not rigid or lumpy. A custard has thickened sufficiently when it leaves a velvety coat on the back of a spoon and if a track made by running a finger down the coated spoon stays clear. It will have the consistency of cream whipped to soft peaks. Remove finished custard from heat immediately as it will continue to thicken as it cools. Strain into a bowl to achieve a smooth texture (for the same reason, strain baked custards before pouring into baking dish). Set pan in a bowl of ice or ice water to stop cooking. If you think custard has overheated, add a few slivers of ice to lower temperature. If the custard starts to curdle while cooking, remove from heat immediately and beat.

Although baked custards aren't stirred, they still must be prepared with care. They need to cook in a moderate oven and should be insulated from the heat by being set in a pan of hot water (a bain-marie or hot water bath). They are done when the center still jiggles slightly and a knife inserted halfway between center and edge comes out clean. Another test is to touch the surface with your finger; if it comes away clean, custard is ready. When properly cooked, texture is smooth and fine. An overheated baked custard is watery.

▉ STIRRED CUSTARD
Crème anglaise

This is the basic vanilla custard sauce. It can be used right away or held in the refrigerator. For additional flavor, add 2 tablespoons orange-flavored liqueur (or liqueur of choice) to the finished sauce.

   2 cups milk
   ½ vanilla bean *or* 1 teaspoon vanilla extract
   4 egg yolks
   3 tablespoons sugar

1. If using vanilla bean, bring milk to a boil with bean in a heavy-bottomed saucepan, remove from heat, and let sit for 10 to 15 minutes to infuse milk with vanilla flavor. If using extract, it is added later; bring milk without flavoring to a boil.

2. In a medium bowl beat yolks and sugar together until thickened and lemon-colored. Add milk, stirring to combine well.

3. Turn mixture into a double boiler or return to same saucepan and cook over low heat, stirring, until it thickens and coats back of a spoon (about 10 minutes; a finger drawn across back of spoon should leave a trail). Remove custard from heat and strain through a fine sieve into a clean bowl set over ice to stop cooking; if using vanilla extract, stir in. Note that if using vanilla bean, which has now been strained out of custard, it can be put back into custard to enhance flavor further, or it can be washed, dried, and stored for later use.

4. Use custard immediately as a sauce, or refrigerate, with plastic wrap laid on surface to prevent a skin from forming, for up to 24 hours.

Makes about 2 cups.

▉ BAKED CUSTARD

This is true comfort food, enriched with the addition of extra egg yolks. For a smooth consistency, remember to strain the custard before putting into the baking dish. Baked custard may be served immediately after cooking or set in the refrigerator to chill.

   2 eggs
   2 egg yolks
   2 cups milk
   3 tablespoons sugar
   Vanilla extract or freshly grated nutmeg, to taste

1. Preheat oven to 350° F. In a medium bowl beat eggs, egg yolks, milk, sugar, and vanilla together; strain through a sieve into a 1-quart baking dish or soufflé dish.

2. Set in a larger pan and fill pan with enough hot water to reach halfway up sides of baking dish. Bake until just set (30 to 35 minutes; center will be slightly wobbly). Serve warm, or refrigerate and serve chilled.

Serves 4 to 5.

A hot water bath (bain-marie) is used for Baked Chocolate Custard to ensure very gentle cooking and to guard against overheating.

■ BAKED CHOCOLATE CUSTARD
Petit pots de crème

Little porcelain custard pots with matching lids have given their name to the rich custard dish that is served in them. The most common flavor for this custard is chocolate, although coffee and vanilla are other popular choices. The custards must chill for several hours or overnight; they will keep up to one day, covered, in the refrigerator.

> 6 ounces semisweet chocolate, chopped
> 3 cups half-and-half
> 1 vanilla bean
> 1 egg
> 8 egg yolks
> ⅓ cup sugar
> 2 teaspoons instant coffee powder
>   dissolved in 2 tablespoons hot water

1. Preheat oven to 325° F. Melt chocolate in a double boiler over hot, but not boiling, water. In a medium, heavy-bottomed saucepan, bring half-and-half to a boil with vanilla bean, remove from heat, and let sit for 10 to 15 minutes to let milk infuse with vanilla flavor.

2. In a medium bowl beat egg, yolks, and sugar until thickened and lemon-colored. Add milk, stirring to combine well. Add dissolved coffee and warm, melted chocolate. Stir well to combine into a creamy mixture. Strain mixture through a sieve into a pitcher and skim off any bubbles or foam from surface. Fill 7 individual molds (5 ounces each) or 8 *pots de crème;* set custards in

a baking dish or pan and fill with enough hot water to reach halfway up sides of molds.

3. Bake until set (35 to 40 minutes). Remove from oven and cool to room temperature; cover and refrigerate at least 3 hours, or overnight. Serve lightly chilled.

Serves 8.

■ CREME CARAMEL

The Spanish counterpart for this satiny smooth, syrup-drenched, baked French custard is flan. Note that the dish must be prepared at least six hours in advance of serving, and preferably the day before.

> ½ cup sugar
> ¼ cup water
>   Baked Custard (opposite page)

1. In a small, heavy-bottomed saucepan, dissolve sugar in the water over low heat (stir only until dissolved; do not stir while it colors). As soon as sugar is dissolved, raise heat to a boil and cook until it turns light brown (8 to 10 minutes). Remove caramel from heat and pour into a 1-quart ovenproof baking dish or soufflé dish. Set aside.

2. Prepare Baked Custard through step 1. Strain through a sieve onto reserved caramel. Bake as for Baked Custard. Cool and refrigerate for at least 6 hours, or preferably overnight (you will have more caramel syrup if you make the dish a day in advance).

Serves 4 to 5.

CREME BRULEE

This famous dessert, also known as burnt cream or Trinity cream, is a rich custard protected by a sugary crust broiled golden brown. England claims it as its own, although its lineage is often debated. It is a standard dish on the menu at celebratory dinners at Trinity College in Cambridge, where it is said to have originated.

    3 cups whipping cream
    1 vanilla bean, split
    6 egg yolks
    3 tablespoons granulated sugar
    1½ cups superfine or brown sugar, for topping

1. *To make custard:* In a medium, heavy-bottomed saucepan, bring cream to a boil with vanilla bean, remove from heat, and let sit for 10 to 15 minutes to infuse milk with vanilla flavor.

2. In a medium bowl beat yolks and granulated sugar together until thickened and lemon-colored. Add warm cream, stirring to combine well.

3. Turn mixture into a double boiler or return to same saucepan and cook over low heat, stirring, until mixture thickens and coats back of a spoon (about 10 minutes; a finger drawn across back of spoon should leave a trail). Remove custard from heat and strain through a fine sieve into a clean bowl. (Vanilla bean can be washed, dried, and stored for later use.)

4. Pour into a 3-cup shallow baking dish or 4 individual 5-ounce molds. Chill 2 to 3 hours, or overnight.

5. *To make sugar crust:* Preheat broiler. Remove custard from refrigerator; sieve superfine sugar over custard. Brown sugar under broiler until caramelized; watch carefully so that sugar doesn't burn (to keep custards cold while they broil, set them in a tray of ice, if desired). Chill until ready to serve.

Serves 4.

Variation   For a firmer custard use 2 whole eggs and 4 egg yolks instead of all yolks.

BAVARIAN CREAM

When a stirred custard is lightened with whipped cream and set with gelatin, it becomes a delightful chilled dessert called Bavarian Cream. Shape in a lightly oiled mold or use as a filling for desserts such as Charlotte Russe (at right) or Lemon Roulade Charlotte (see page 171). The filling for the Charlotte Russe is a basic vanilla Bavarian; if desired, substitute 2 tablespoons rum, orange-flavored liqueur, or other liqueur for the vanilla extract. To use by itself, spoon into a 4- to 5-cup oiled mold and chill four hours or overnight. For a fruit-flavored Bavarian cream, use the Lemon Bavarian Cream filling recipe from Lemon Roulade Charlotte and substitute an equal amount of lightly sweetened, puréed fruit for the Lemon Curd. Spoon into an oiled 4- to 5-quart mold and chill four hours, or overnight.

For a particularly effective presentation, layer two colors of Bavarian cream in one mold or marble two of contrasting colors, such as vanilla and strawberry.

CHARLOTTE RUSSE

A special tinned steel charlotte mold with flaring sides is traditional for this dish, but any ovenproof dish of the proper size will work.

    24 to 30 ladyfingers (see page 84 and Note, below)
    2 cups whipping cream
    4 egg yolks
    ⅓ cup sugar
    1 envelope unflavored gelatin
    2 tablespoons water
    1 tablespoon vanilla extract
    1 cup Chantilly Cream (see page 252),
       for decoration
       Raspberry or Strawberry Sauce
       (see page 522), for accompaniment

1. Tightly line a 6-cup charlotte mold or soufflé dish with ladyfingers, standing them on end, sides touching. Cover with plastic wrap and set aside. Whip 1 cup whipping cream to soft peaks and set aside.

2. In a medium, heavy-bottomed saucepan, bring remaining cup of cream to a boil. In a medium bowl beat yolks and sugar together until thickened and lemon-colored. Add cream to yolk mixture and stir well.

3. Turn mixture into a double boiler or return to same saucepan, and cook over low heat, stirring, until mixture thickens and coats back of a spoon (about 10 minutes; a finger drawn across back of spoon should leave a trail). Remove custard from heat and strain through a fine sieve into a clean bowl set over ice to stop cooking.

4. In a small saucepan sprinkle gelatin over the water and let stand to soften; dissolve over low heat (3 to 4 minutes). Pour into warm custard and stir to blend thoroughly. Add vanilla and keep stirring until mixture is on point of setting (it will have the consistency of cream whipped to soft peaks); fold in whipped cream.

5. Pour mixture into lined mold, smooth top, cover, and refrigerate until set (2 to 4 hours). Any leftover ladyfingers can be crumbled and sprinkled over top of custard before refrigerating.

6. To serve, unmold charlotte by carefully running a knife between ladyfingers and mold. Invert onto a serving platter. Pipe rosettes of Chantilly Cream around top edge (if desired), and spoon a pool of Raspberry or Strawberry Sauce around bottom of charlotte.

Serves 6.

Note   If using packaged ladyfingers that are a little sticky, sprinkle them with sugar before lining mold.

▪ LEMON ROULADE CHARLOTTE

This is a spectacular rolled charlotte. Although the preparation takes time, so much of it can be, or needs to be, done in advance that it's actually a good party dessert. Use lemon or any flavor Bavarian cream (see opposite page) and fill with a fruit preserve instead of the Lemon Curd.

1 Basic Sponge Cake Roll (see page 83)
1 cup Lemon Curd (see page 252)
  Basic Glaze (use apricot preserves; see page 250), for topping
  Raspberry Sauce (see page 522), for accompaniment

Lemon Bavarian Cream

1 cup whipping cream
1½ cups milk
  Grated rind of 1 lemon
4 egg yolks
⅓ cup sugar
1 envelope unflavored gelatin
½ cup fresh lemon juice
1½ cups Lemon Curd (see page 252)

1. As smoothly as possible, line a round-bottomed 1½- to 2-quart bowl or mold with aluminum foil. On flat Sponge Cake Roll, evenly spread Lemon Curd, stopping 1 inch from each edge. Gently roll up, jelly-roll fashion. Cut into ½-inch slices. Lay slices in lined mold, beginning in center and working out to make a complete, balanced shell (save any leftover slices and lay over filling). Cover and set aside.

2. Pour Lemon Bavarian Cream into cake-lined mold, cover, and refrigerate 4 hours, preferably overnight.

3. To serve, unmold by laying a serving platter on top and inverting; lift off foil-lined mold. Brush with Apricot Glaze. Serve as is or with Raspberry Sauce (if desired).

Serves 8.

Lemon Bavarian Cream

1. Whip cream to soft peaks and set aside. In a heavy-bottomed saucepan bring milk and lemon rind to a boil. In a medium bowl beat yolks and sugar together until thickened and lemon-colored; combine with milk.

2. Turn mixture into a double boiler or return to same saucepan and cook over low heat, stirring, until mixture thickens and coats back of a spoon (about 10 minutes). Remove custard from heat and strain through a fine sieve into a clean bowl set over ice to stop cooking.

3. In a small saucepan sprinkle gelatin over lemon juice and let stand to soften; dissolve over low heat (3 to 4 minutes). Pour into warm custard and stir to blend thoroughly. When custard is cool, add 1½ cups Lemon Curd, stirring continually until mixture is on point of setting (it will have the consistency of cream whipped to soft peaks); fold in whipped cream.

▪ ZABAGLIONE

Zabaglione is an Italian wine custard; sabayon is the French counterpart. Serve the frothy whipped egg custard warm or cold with crunchy *biscotti* for textural contrast, or spoon it over sliced strawberries.

6 egg yolks
½ cup sugar
½ to 1 cup Marsala, sherry, or Madeira
  Sliced strawberries, or Biscotti (see page 8), for accompaniment

1. Whisk egg yolks, sugar, and wine in a double boiler over simmering water. Whisk by hand or with electric mixer until mixture doubles in volume and is very smooth and fluffy.

2. Serve immediately with strawberries or Biscotti. Mixture is unstable and will separate if left standing. To serve it cold, set over ice and continue whisking until chilled. It will then hold for about 3 hours; serve as is, or fold in whipped cream, or gelatin and whipped cream.

Serves 4 to 6.

CUT IN, TO

To mix solid fat (butter, solid vegetable shortening, or lard, or a combination) and dry ingredients (flour, mixed with any or all of the following: salt, baking powder, baking soda, sugar) with a cutting motion. The process, used when making pastry, whittles the fat into smaller and smaller flour-coated pieces by the action of a pastry blender, two knives, a fork, the fingers, or the metal blade of a food processor, until reduced to the desired texture. *Rub in* is another recipe term that has the same meaning, but this process is done with the fingertips.

To develop flakiness, fat is left in relatively large pieces, usually described as coarse crumbs or small peas, rather than being ground so fine that it merges with the flour. As pie crust or biscuits bake, particles of fat melt and create empty spaces that fill with steam and expand. This expansion causes pie crust or biscuit to rise, and creates layers of crust or crumb called the flake. Large particles of fat leave bigger air pockets and create a lighter, more flaky pastry or biscuit; fine particles hardly leave a trace and produce a dense, sandy pastry or a biscuit that lacks characteristic texture.

Work with chilled fat and utensils (even the fingers, especially on a hot day). If fat starts to melt, briefly chill mixture; try not to heat the room with other cooking. Work quickly but gently so as not to toughen dough.

Recipes and Related Information
Biscuit, 49; Cake and Pastry Tools, 91; Pie and Tart, 431.

F

between 360° and 385° F. The squares will fall, then rise, as they puff into little pillows. Push them down and turn often until they are golden. Remove with a slotted spoon, drain on paper towels, and keep warm in oven. Sprinkle with confectioners' sugar and serve hot with honey to spoon into the cavities.

Makes 16 puffs.

▨ YEAST-RAISED DOUGHNUTS

These doughnuts are lighter and more tender than Old-fashioned Cake Doughnuts (see page 180) because they are leavened with yeast.

> 1 cup warm (105° to 115° F) milk
> 1 package active dry yeast
> ½ cup sugar
> 1½ teaspoons salt
> ¼ teaspoon *each* ground cinnamon and nutmeg
> 2 eggs
> ¼ cup butter, melted
> 3½ to 4 cups flour
>   Oil, for frying
>   Cinnamon Sugar, optional (see page 180)

1. Pour milk in a large mixing bowl, sprinkle on yeast, stir, and let stand a few minutes to dissolve.

2. Add sugar, salt, cinnamon, nutmeg, eggs, and melted butter, and beat vigorously until blended. Add 2 cups of the flour and beat until batter is heavy but smooth. Add 1 more cup of flour, beating well, then add enough of the remaining flour to make a soft but manageable dough.

3. Turn out onto a lightly floured surface and knead a few minutes, until dough is smooth and elastic, sprinkling on a little additional flour if necessary to keep it from being too sticky.

4. Place in a greased bowl, cover with plastic wrap, and let rise until doubled in bulk (or refrigerate and let rise overnight if you wish to make fresh doughnuts the next morning).

5. Turn dough out onto a floured surface, punch down, then roll and pat until dough is about ½ inch thick. Cut with a floured doughnut cutter and set aside on baking sheets covered with waxed paper, leaving about 1½ inches between doughnuts. Reroll scraps and continue until all dough is cut. Cover with a towel and let rise until doubled in bulk.

6. When you are almost ready to fry doughnuts, heat 2 to 3 inches of oil to 360° F in a Dutch oven, heavy frying skillet, or other frying kettle.

7. Gently drop 3 or 4 doughnuts and their holes into hot fat. Turn frequently until golden brown on both sides (2 to 3 minutes). Remove with a slotted spoon and drain on paper towels. Fry remaining doughnuts the same way and toss while warm in Cinnamon Sugar (if used).

Makes about 18 to 20 doughnuts and holes.

▨ MAPLE BARS

For authentic maple flavor, make the glaze with real maple syrup instead of an imitation product.

> 1 recipe Yeast-Raised Doughnuts (at left)

Maple Glaze

> 1 cup confectioners' sugar
> 4 to 5 tablespoons maple syrup

1. Prepare Yeast-Raised Doughnuts through step 4. Turn dough out onto a floured surface, punch down, then press, pat, and roll to a fairly even rectangle about ½ inch thick. With a sharp knife, trim off any uneven edges. Cut into rectangles about 2 inches wide and 4 inches long. Set aside on baking sheets covered with waxed or parchment paper, cover with a towel, and let rise until doubled in bulk.

2. Fry as in Yeast-Raised Doughnuts. While still warm, brush top of each with Maple Glaze.

Makes about 15 bars.

Maple Glaze Beat confectioners' sugar and 4 tablespoons of the syrup together until smooth. If glaze is too stiff to spread, beat in a little more syrup.

Makes about ½ cup.

▨ JELLY DOUGHNUTS

Another name for jelly doughnuts is Bismarks.

> 1 recipe Old-fashioned Cake Doughnuts (see page 180) or Buñuelos (see page 181) or Yeast-Raised Doughnuts (at left)
> 2 cups jelly or thick jam (do not use preserves; they will clog pastry bag)

1. Prepare one of these recipes, cutting cake doughnuts or raised doughnuts into rounds, not rings.

2. After pastries have cooled, use a knife point to make a small slit in the side of each pastry. Fill a pastry bag, fitted with a round tip, with about 2 cups jelly or jam. Pipe a generous tablespoon of jam or jelly into pastry.

Makes 18 to 24 doughnuts, depending upon recipe.

Recipes and Related Information
Deep-fry, 174; Fry, 254.

DRAIN, TO

To separate liquids and solids by setting both in a colander or strainer and letting the liquid pass through the holes (pasta from its cooking water), or by setting on absorbent paper (fat from fried food). This process also describes removing excess fat by pouring from the cooking pan into a receptacle, leaving only the pan juices.

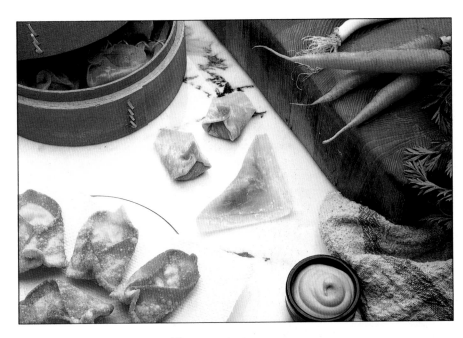

Whether steamed or fried and paired with a dipping sauce, or simmered in soup, Wontons are among the most versatile and popular of Chinese dumplings. They can be cooked immediately after assembling, or frozen uncooked for later use.

■ WONTONS

Probably the most familiar Chinese dumpling to Westerners is the wonton, a relatively large noodle skin wrapped around a small amount of stuffing. Most often served in soup, they can also be fried or steamed. Fried, they go well with tangy sweet-and-sour sauces or mustard dips; steamed, they are best with soy sauce dips. To fill the wontons, use the Pork and Cabbage Stuffing given here, the Pork and Shrimp Stuffing from Potstickers (see page 191), or 1 pound seasoned ground pork.

    1 pound wonton skins
      Oil, for deep-frying (optional)

Pork and Cabbage Stuffing

    ½ cup shredded cabbage (bok choy, Chinese,
      or any green variety)
    ½ teaspoon salt
    1 pound boneless pork
    ¼ cup *each* minced green onion and bamboo shoots
    1 tablespoon minced fresh ginger
    2 tablespoons *each* soy sauce and
      Shaoxing wine or dry sherry
    1 teaspoon sesame oil
    1 egg
    1 teaspoon cornstarch

1. Have at hand a small bowl of water with a brush for sealing edges. Peel off 2 or 3 wonton skins and place on the table, one corner "south" or toward you. Keep remaining skins covered with a towel to prevent drying.

2. Place a scant teaspoon of stuffing just south of center of skin. Brush near edges lightly with water and fold south corner over stuffing to within ½ inch of north corner. Press edges to seal. Pick up east and west corners and bring together at south end. Pinch or twist

slightly to seal corners together. Repeat with remaining skins and stuffing.

3. Keep finished Wontons covered with a towel to prevent them from drying, or freeze on a baking sheet and transfer to plastic bags when fully frozen. Boil in plain or lightly salted water before adding to soup, steam 6 to 8 minutes as a simple appetizer, or deep-fry in 375° F oil until golden brown and crisp.

Makes 60 to 70 Wontons.

Pork and Cabbage Stuffing   Toss cabbage with salt and place in a colander to drain 30 minutes. Squeeze out excess moisture. Grind pork finely in a food processor or mince by hand to a fine texture. In a large bowl, combine pork, drained and squeezed cabbage, green onions, bamboo shoots, ginger, soy sauce, wine, oil, egg, and cornstarch; blend thoroughly.

Makes 2 cups.

Variation   Substitute beef, lamb, or dark meat from chicken or turkey for pork.

Pork and Mushroom Stuffing   Add ¼ cup soaked and minced black mushrooms (about 3 caps) to Pork and Cabbage Stuffing.

■ GOLDEN CHICKEN STEW WITH CHEESE DUMPLINGS

Choose an attractive Dutch oven in which to stew this creamy chicken dish. After the fluffy, cheese-flecked dumplings have steamed atop the bubbling chicken, the stew is served directly from the pot.

    4½ to 5 pounds meaty chicken pieces
      (thighs, drumsticks, and breasts)
      Salt, white pepper, grated nutmeg, and paprika
    2 tablespoons butter or margarine
    2 shallots, finely chopped (about ¼ cup)
    ½ pound large mushrooms, quartered
    1 stalk celery, thinly sliced
    3 medium carrots, sliced about ⅛ inch thick
    ½ teaspoon dried tarragon
    ¼ teaspoon dried thyme
    2 cups water
    ½ cup *each* dry white wine and whipping cream
    3 tablespoons cornstarch, blended with
      3 tablespoons cold water
    ½ cup shelled fresh or frozen peas
    ¼ cup chopped parsley

Cheese Dumplings

    2 cups flour
    1 tablespoon baking powder
    ½ teaspoon salt
      Pinch freshly grated nutmeg
    ⅓ cup grated sharp Cheddar cheese
    ¼ cup butter or margarine
    1 cup milk

1. Sprinkle chicken pieces lightly on all sides with salt, pepper, nutmeg, and paprika. Melt butter in a 4½- to 5-quart Dutch oven over medium heat. Add chicken pieces, about half at a time, and brown lightly on all sides, removing them as they brown.

2. To the same pan add shallots and mushrooms; cook, stirring occasionally, until mushrooms brown lightly. Spoon off and discard as much fat as possible. Mix in celery and carrots. Return chicken pieces to pot. Sprinkle with tarragon and thyme. Add the water and wine. Bring to a boil, cover, reduce heat, and simmer until chicken is tender (1 to 1¼ hours).

3. Remove pot from heat. Remove and reserve chicken pieces. Skim and discard fat from cooking liquid. Blend in cream. Place over medium heat; blend in cornstarch mixture. Cook, stirring, until mixture thickens and boils. Add peas and parsley, then return chicken pieces to sauce. Reduce heat to low.

4. Using two tablespoons to shape them, drop rounded dumplings about 1 inch apart over chicken pieces. To prevent dough from sticking, dip spoons into sauce before forming next dumpling. Cover and simmer until dumplings feel firm when touched lightly (15 to 20 minutes; do not uncover until dumplings have cooked for 15 minutes). Serve directly from Dutch oven.

Serves 6 to 8.

Cheese Dumplings In a large bowl stir together flour, baking powder, salt, nutmeg, and cheese. Using two forks or a pastry blender, cut in butter until mixture resembles coarse crumbs. Add milk all at once, stirring just until ingredients are moistened and a soft dough forms.

■ **APPLE DUMPLINGS WITH NUTMEG SAUCE**
These dumplings from New England are made of whole apples wrapped in a rich biscuit dough, baked until tender and golden, and served with creamy Nutmeg Sauce. They are a perfect conclusion to a family dinner and a wonderfully homey dessert for guests. If you wish, omit the Nutmeg Sauce and serve with any remaining pan juices and a pitcher of cream or a scoop of vanilla ice cream. The amount of dough given here is generous, since it's far easier working with too much than too little.

> 6　Golden Delicious apples
> 2　tablespoons *each* sugar and butter
> 1½　cups apple juice

Biscuit Dough

> 3　cups flour
> 2　tablespoons sugar
> 4　teaspoons baking powder
> 1　teaspoon salt
> 1　cup solid vegetable shortening
> ¾　cup milk

Nutmeg Sauce

> 1　cup apple juice
> 1　cup whipping cream
> ½　teaspoon freshly grated nutmeg
> 2　tablespoons sugar
> ¼　cup butter

1. Preheat oven to 375° F. Butter a 9- by 13-inch baking dish. Peel and core apples, leaving them whole; set aside.

2. On a smooth, lightly floured surface, push, pat, and roll Biscuit Dough to a rectangle 13 by 20 inches, keeping sides as even as possible and lifting and flouring often to prevent sticking. Cut in half lengthwise, then in thirds crosswise, thus making six 6½-inch squares.

3. Place an apple in the center of each dough square. One at a time, bring the 4 corners of each square together at the top to enclose apple. Twist and pinch attached corners together to seal. If dough tears, just patch it; don't worry if it looks a little ragged.

4. Place dumplings in prepared baking dish about 1 inch apart. Sprinkle with sugar and dot with butter; pour apple juice around dumplings. Bake until dough is golden brown and apples are tender when pierced with a toothpick or skewer (about 45 minutes). If they brown too much while baking, cover loosely with foil. While apples bake, prepare Nutmeg Sauce.

5. When apples are done, remove dumplings to a platter. Pour juices remaining in baking dish into Nutmeg Sauce, reheat if necessary, and pass sauce with dumplings.

Serves 6.

Biscuit Dough In a medium bowl stir and toss together flour, sugar, baking powder, and salt. Cut in shortening until mixture resembles coarse crumbs. Pour in milk and stir with a fork just until dough holds together in a shaggy, cohesive mass. Turn onto a smooth, lightly floured surface and knead 10 times.

Nutmeg Sauce In a medium saucepan combine apple juice, whipping cream, nutmeg, and sugar. Bring to a boil and boil until reduced to about 1¼ cups (about 10 minutes). Swirl in butter and set aside.

DUST, TO

To sprinkle very lightly with a powder. Dusting implies a fine coating, as opposed to dredging, which involves covering food with a heavier layer. Greased baking pans may be dusted with flour to keep batters and doughs from sticking; cakes and pastries are often given a light dusting of confectioners' sugar, cocoa, or ground nuts as a finishing touch.

Extremely versatile, eggs are a delicious food on their own. As a recipe ingredient, they add nutrients, flavor, richness, leavening, and thickening properties.

EGG

Among the most versatile and nutritious foods available, whole eggs contain vitamins, minerals, fats, and complete protein. The white is mostly water with some proteins; the yolk contains much of the protein and all of the fat, vitamins, minerals, and cholesterol. Although the eggs of ducks, geese, and other poultry are important to some cuisines, chicken eggs are by far the most commonly used. In general, this entry pertains to chicken eggs only; see Availability for information about eggs from other types of poultry.

Use Eggs are enjoyed both as a dish in themselves and as ingredients in many other dishes.

Availability Although the commercial baker has access to dried, frozen, and liquid eggs, these products are rarely available to the home cook. Fresh whole eggs are sold in all supermarkets, reaching most markets within four or five days.

Shortly after eggs are collected, they are graded for quality and size. Quality gradings are AA, A, and B, although B-grade eggs are rarely seen in stores. Gradings do not indicate freshness, but are based on thickness of white, firmness of yolk, and size of interior air pocket. To grade eggs, they are passed in front of a light source that reveals their interior. High-grade eggs have thick whites, compact, rounded yolks, and a small air pocket.

Size classifications are based on the minimum allowable weight per dozen (see below). Size does not reflect quality or freshness. Most recipes, however, are based on large eggs; using smaller or larger eggs may require adjustment of a recipe. Some markets carry both white and brown eggs. Shell color does not affect nutrition, quality, flavor, or appearance; it is determined by the breed of the hen.

Egg Size	Minimum Weight per Dozen
Jumbo	30 ounces
Extralarge	27 ounces
Large	24 ounces
Medium	21 ounces
Small	18 ounces
Peewee	15 ounces

Duck Eggs Substitute duck eggs in any recipe calling for chicken eggs, although they are larger and impart a richer flavor and deeper yellow color. They may even be used in baking if the recipe is adjusted to account for the added volume. In China, duck eggs are used to prepare Thousand-Year Eggs (see page 195).

Quail Eggs Black-and-white-speckled quail eggs are usually no more than 1 inch long. Their flavor is similar to that of chicken eggs, but their daintiness gives them a special appeal. In Japan, raw quail eggs are served with sushi as an accompaniment. Use hard-cooked peeled quail eggs to garnish salads, or pickle them and serve as an appetizer. Fresh quail eggs are available in some Japanese and specialty markets; cooked, peeled quail eggs are available in some specialty markets in cans or jars.

Salted Duck Eggs (Preserved Eggs) To prepare salted eggs, duck eggs are soaked in brine for 30 to 40 days. The brine turns the yolk firm and bright orange and makes the white salty. Salted eggs are used in small quantities to add spark to a bland dish. Unlike Thousand-Year Eggs, they must be cooked. Hard-cooked salted eggs are eaten with steamed rice or are steamed with minced pork.

Store salted duck eggs in refrigerator for up to six months. To prepare, wash away salt covering. Cook in simmering water 1 hour, changing water several times (fresh water should be at a simmer, not cold). Cool, shell, and slice or quarter.

Thousand-Year Eggs (Preserved Eggs) These duck eggs are a Chinese delicacy available in many Chinese markets. To make them, raw duck eggs are coated with a mixture of lime, salt, ashes, and tea, then buried in earth for six to ten weeks. The claylike mixture colors, preserves, and flavors them. When peeled, the whites are amber, the yolks green; the texture is smooth and creamy, like a ripe avocado, and the flavor is strong and cheesy. Thousand-Year Eggs are quite rich and are eaten in small quantities, usually at breakfast or as one element of a cold appetizer platter. They do not require cooking and may also be made with chicken eggs.

Store eggs at room temperature for up to 10 days or wrapped in plastic and in the refrigerator for up to one month. To prepare, soak in cold water for 1 hour to soften outer black coating; scrape it away. Crack gently and shell. Slice or quarter. The eggs are sometimes served with a dipping sauce of soy, ginger, and vinegar.

Selection As a rule, buy eggs as fresh as possible. To test an egg for freshness, place it in a bowl of cold water. A fresh egg will remain on the bottom; an older egg will float to some degree. Discard any egg that rises to the surface of the water.

Storage Eggs deteriorate quickly under improper storage conditions. Refrigerate eggs immediately, small end down. Because they lose moisture and absorb odors through their thin shells, it is better to store them in their container than in an open refrigerator rack. Most commercial eggs have been coated with mineral oil to prevent loss of moisture and improve shelf life; they remain edible for up to five weeks, although the egg white gradually thins and the yolk flattens.

Keep leftover whites in a covered container in the refrigerator for one week to ten days. Cover leftover yolks with water and store in an airtight container in the refrigerator; use within two or three days. Store leftover whole eggs in an airtight container in the refrigerator and use within 24 hours.

Leftover yolks and whites freeze well. Ice-cube trays or muffin pans make ideal containers for tray-freezing separated eggs. Fill tray or pan with yolk or white and freeze; when firm, place individual cubes in plastic freezer bags. Calculate the capacity of a single ice-cube mold or muffin cup. How many whites or yolks will it hold? They can also be packaged in plastic containers, allowing ½-inch headspace for expansion. To prepare yolks for freezing, stir slightly, without producing foam (air bubbles beaten into egg will cause it to dry out during freezing). Add ½ teaspoon salt (if yolks will be used for savory dishes) or 1½ teaspoons sugar (if used for desserts) to each cup of egg yolks before freezing; this will prevent yolks from thickening and becoming gummy during freezing. Freeze egg whites without stirring or adding salt or sugar. Frozen egg whites whip just as well after thawing as when they are fresh.

EGGS AS AN INGREDIENT

As an ingredient in other dishes, eggs are used for a variety of purposes: to adhere, bind, clarify, emulsify, glaze, leaven, and thicken. In the process, they impart richness, color, and flavor to dishes.

Adhere Breaded fried foods often use eggs as glue to hold their crumb coat in place; the moisture in raw egg performs this function before cooking and the coagulated egg protein holds all together afterward.

Bind Egg acts as a binder in many cooked foods, giving structural support to ground meat mixtures, croquettes, pancakes, breads, and cakes. For baked products, the egg fulfills a variety of functions: the fat in the yolk contributes a shortening (tenderizing) effect; the moisture in the egg helps gelatinize the starch (flour); and, perhaps most importantly, the coagulation of egg proteins when heated gives the baked product much of its structure.

Clarify Egg whites are used to remove the impurities from cooked stock that cause it to become cloudy. To clarify, egg whites are added to simmering stock. As whites set with heat, they trap minute food particles; this "raft" of coagulated material floats to the top of the stockpot and, when strained off, reveals a clear stock.

Emulsify Eggs act as a stabilizing agent for emulsions—a dispersion of one liquid within another (such as oil and water)—which cannot freely mix except in the presence of an emulsifier that forces them together. In egg-based emulsions, oil, butter, wine, or stock is evenly dispersed in egg yolk to form a variety of sauces, from mayonnaise to Hollandaise to sabayon. Emulsions may be either cooked or uncooked. The principal uncooked egg emulsion is mayonnaise. Hollandaise sauce and its variations are examples of cooked egg emulsions. Whisking cooled clarified butter into warmed egg yolks produces a delicate emulsion with many uses. To make a sweet sabayon, another cooked egg emulsion, eggs and sugar are whisked over hot water until thick and warm. Then wine is whisked in and the mixture is beaten for several more minutes over heat. It doubles in volume and forms a thick, airy, fairly stable emulsion.

Emulsions, by their very nature, are unstable. Strict attention to timing and temperature is required to ensure success. Follow recipe instructions carefully.

Glaze Brushing bread or pastry before baking with an egg wash—beaten egg mixed with water, milk, or cream—imparts a shiny surface. An egg-yolk–water wash results in a golden surface; egg white with water creates a sticky surface that holds seeds in place; an egg wash containing milk or cream produces a soft crust.

Leaven The ability of egg whites to form a stable foam when beaten enables them to give volume to soufflés, angel food and sponge cakes, mousses, and meringues; air trapped in the beaten white expands in the presence of

WORKING WITH EGGS

TO CRACK AN EGG

Gently tap side of egg against an angled hard surface, such as the edge of a countertop or the side of a mixing bowl, and as close to the center of the egg as possible. If egg does not crack in half, crack it again once or twice, or use a knife to tap egg gently around its midsection. Break egg apart over a clean bowl.

TO SEPARATE YOLKS
FROM WHITES

It's easiest to separate eggs when they are cold because yolk is firmer, making it less likely to break. Egg whites beat most easily, however, when they are at room temperature. Therefore, when you need to beat whites, the best working procedure is to separate eggs as soon as you remove them from the refrigerator and then leave them at room temperature while preparing other ingredients for recipe.

Whites will not beat properly if there is a trace of egg yolk in them, so it is essential to separate eggs with care. When a recipe calls for several separated eggs, you can avoid the frustration of ruining a bowl full of whites with egg yolk by first breaking each egg over a small bowl. If white separates neatly, add it to a bowl set aside to hold all of the whites. If it picks up even a speck of yolk, try to scoop up yolk with a piece of egg shell; if this proves impossible, save white for another use.

To separate an egg, have ready two small bowls (use three bowls if separating more than one egg). Crack egg as described above. Holding half of shell in each hand, transfer yolk carefully from one half to the other, letting egg white drip into a bowl. When all of white has dripped into bowl, put yolk in second bowl. Another method is to crack egg into your clean palm; the less viscous white will drip through your fingers into a bowl set beneath your hand while the yolk stays on your palm.

heat. Whole-egg and egg-yolk foams are used as leavening agents in sponge cakes.

Thicken   Eggs are used to thicken sauces, soups, and custards. With heat, the egg proteins gel, thereby thickening or setting a liquid. Making a classic custard sauce (*crème anglaise*) by heating milk, sugar, and eggs; thickening a soup with a mixture of cream and beaten eggs; and setting a baked rice pudding with eggs are examples of the thickening power of eggs.

BEATING EGGS: WHOLE, YOLKS, AND WHITES

When eggs are beaten until they thicken and expand in volume, they form a network of air bubbles which is referred to as a foam. An egg-white foam is probably the most familiar of these, but whole-egg and egg-yolk foams also play important, although less common, culinary roles. Whole-egg foams lighten génoise, the delicate French cake; egg-yolk foams leaven the American sponge cake; a souffléed omelet uses both types.

Beaten whole eggs or egg yolks lighten in color and thicken as air bubbles are incorporated, but because of the physical properties of yolks, the resulting foam is unstable and will not set. In fact, an egg-yolk foam, unless used right away, will separate.

Often a recipe will direct you to beat eggs—whole or yolk, with or without sugar—until thick and lemon-colored, a readily discernible transformation. Another term used to describe this point is *to beat to a ribbon;* this is the stage at which the mixture falls slowly from the beater in a thin, ribbonlike band and leaves a trail in the bowl that remains for a few seconds, then disappears. When making génoise with anything but a heavy-duty stand mixer, the egg-sugar mixture is first beaten with a whisk over simmering water until mixture is lukewarm; the bowl is removed from heat and the mixture beaten to ribbon stage. This treatment both dissolves the sugar and gives the eggs greater elasticity so that further beating will develop a foam of great volume.

The process of beating causes egg whites to trap air bubbles. In the presence of heat, beaten whites expand and increase the volume of whatever mixture they are combined with—soufflés and cake batters are leavened completely or in part this way. Uncooked beaten egg whites, although they don't expand further because of the absence of heat, are used to lighten the texture of cold dishes such as mousses.

Fat, such as that found in egg yolks, hampers the ability of egg whites to develop a stable foam and results in less volume. For this reason, be sure that bowl and whisk or beaters are scrupulously clean and dry; even a speck of butter or egg yolk will inhibit the process and can decrease volume by as much as two thirds.

An unlined copper bowl and balloon whisk will develop a very stable foam with maximum volume; studies suggest that copper and the protein in egg whites form a very strong bond that results in a longer-lasting structure of air bubbles. A stainless steel bowl is next best; avoid plastic, glass, ceramic, and aluminum. Plastic, a petroleum product, can retain an oily film even with repeated washing; the slippery surface of glass, ceramic, and plastic make it harder for whites to billow up; aluminum will gray whites. Also keep in mind that properly beaten whites will increase to three times their original volume, so choose a bowl with sufficient capacity.

Recipes may suggest adding an acid, such as cream of tartar, to whites if you aren't using a copper bowl. As little as ⅛ teaspoon cream of tartar per egg white will make foam less prone to collapse; this addition will delay foam formation, however, so add it to whites after they have been beaten slightly and are just bubbly. Sugar acts as a stabilizer as well. A meringue, which contains sugar, is far more stable than sugarless whipped egg whites. Egg whites foam more slowly, however, in the presence of sugar and develop less volume. The best way to add sugar to egg whites is as follows: By hand or with an electric mixer at low speed, slowly beat whites without sugar just until frothy; then add 1 teaspoon sugar per white and whip egg whites until almost stiff (be carefully not to overbeat). Fold in remaining sugar by hand.

Remember that although eggs are easiest to separate when cold, both whites and yolks beat to greater volume when warm. Let cold yolks and whites sit at room temperature for at least 30 minutes before they are beaten.

BEATING EGG WHITES

Foamy *Egg whites are just slightly beaten; white suds begin to form in a matter of seconds. The mass is still transparent and liquid. Salt and cream of tartar (if used) are added at this stage once some foam develops. If these ingredients are added right away, the whites will need to be beaten longer before they will start to foam.*

Soft peaks *The foam in soft peaks is thicker, whiter, and finer. When beater is lifted from bowl, whites form droopy, moist-looking, but definite, peaks. Use at this stage for soufflés.*

Stiff, but not dry *Some sugar is added now. With continued beating, foam thickens and develops a glossy sheen; it should still look moist. Volume has increased. When beater is lifted from bowl, peaks stand in stiff points. When bowl is tipped, mass does not slide.*

STAGES OF BEATEN EGG WHITES

Less experienced cooks tend to overbeat rather than underbeat. If you are unsure whether whites have reached the desired stage, it's best to stop. If you continue beating until they are stiff and dry, they lose elasticity. When whites attempt to expand further in the oven, they will collapse. Dry whites are overbeaten and cannot be rescued. The structure looks dry and curdled, and liquid will separate out. See Beating Egg Whites, above, for photographs of stages of beaten egg whites.

FOLDING EGG WHITES

When beaten egg whites are to be combined with other ingredients, the recommended procedure is folding. To fold means to incorporate one mixture into another gently without deflating the air in the lighter mixture. For a complete discussion, see FOLD.

EGG DISHES

As a dish in themselves, or as the main component of a dish, eggs may be hard-cooked, soft-cooked, poached, fried, baked, scrambled, or used for omelets, frittatas, and soufflés.

HARD-COOKED EGGS

Peeled, hard-cooked eggs make a nutritious snack or addition to a lunch box. They may be mashed for egg salad; quartered and simmered in a cream sauce; pickled; sliced as a garnish for a salad or sandwich; minced for a salad or vegetable garnish. Scotch Eggs, a popular dish served in English pubs, consists of peeled, hard-cooked eggs coated with ground sausage and bread crumbs, then deep-fried. Chopped hard-cooked eggs are often added to potato salads; tuna, chicken, or shellfish salads; or giblet gravy.

The best eggs for boiling and peeling are at least one week old. Very fresh eggs are difficult to peel. Both fresh and older eggs will peel more easily if dropped immediately into cold water after boiling.

However, hard-cooked eggs are easier to peel when they are warm, so if they are to be peeled soon after cooking, remove from cold water before they cool completely. Peel by tapping all around shell with a knife to form a network of cracks. Peel shell away under cold running water. Use shelled eggs immediately or store in a bowl of cold salted water in the refrigerator up to two weeks.

After boiling and cooling, unshelled hard-cooked eggs may be refrigerated for up to one week. Mark with an *x* to distinguish from raw eggs. If you forgot to mark an egg and can't remember if it's cooked or not, spin egg on counter. A raw egg will whirl evenly; a cooked egg will falter. Peel eggs just before using.

■ NO-FAIL HARD-COOKED EGGS

Fill a pan with enough cold water to cover eggs by 1 inch. Add 2 teaspoons salt per quart of water; bring water to a boil. Using the oldest eggs in your refrigerator, lower them into boiling water with a slotted spoon. Reduce water to a simmer, with bubbles that barely break on the surface. Simmer, uncovered, 10 minutes. Immediately plunge eggs into cold water or set under cold running water (eggs will be easier to peel and won't develop a green ring around yolk). Cool 1 hour in cold water if not peeling right away.

Deviled eggs look particularly decorative when the egg-yolk filling is piped into the cooked white with a pastry bag.

DEVILED EGGS

Highly seasoned foods are sometimes referred to as "deviled." In this recipe, the spice is mustard.

> 6 hard-cooked eggs, peeled and halved
>   lengthwise
> 3 tablespoons mayonnaise
> 1 tablespoon Dijon mustard
> ⅛ teaspoon salt
>   Paprika, for sprinkling

1. With a small spoon lift egg yolks out of whites. Place yolks in small bowl.

2. Add mayonnaise, mustard, and salt to egg yolks; mix well with a fork to make a very smooth paste. Adjust seasonings, if necessary.

3. Arrange egg white halves on a serving platter. Mound some of yolk mixture into each and sprinkle with paprika. Serve immediately or store, covered, in refrigerator until ready to use.

Makes 1 dozen Deviled Eggs.

SCOTCH EGGS

An excellent picnic food, Scotch Eggs have an herbed sausage and bread crumb coat that protects the hard-cooked eggs secreted inside. When sliced in quarters or rings, they make a pretty addition to a buffet breakfast.

> 1 pound ground sausage
> 1½ teaspoons dried basil
> 1 teaspoon dried oregano
> ½ teaspoon salt
> ¼ teaspoon freshly ground pepper
> ¼ cup parsley, minced
> 1¼ cups soft bread crumbs
> 2 raw eggs
> 1 tablespoon water
> 6 hard-cooked eggs, peeled
>   Oil, for frying

1. In a large bowl combine sausage, basil, oregano, salt, pepper, parsley, ½ cup bread crumbs, and 1 raw egg.

2. In a small bowl beat remaining raw egg and the water. Place remaining bread crumbs in a small dish. Wet hands with cold water to prevent sausage mixture from sticking. Place one sixth of sausage mixture in palm of your hand; flatten slightly. Place a hard-cooked egg in center of mixture and enclose in sausage. Roll in beaten egg, then bread crumbs, and place on a plate. Repeat with remaining hard-cooked eggs. Chill 1 hour.

3. Pour oil into a wok or 2-quart heavy-bottomed saucepan to about 3 inches deep; heat to about 365° F. Carefully add eggs and fry 5 minutes. Turn and fry 4 minutes. Remove with a slotted spoon to paper towels to drain and cool briefly.

Serves 6.

PICKLED EGGS

Walk into almost any English pub and you'll spot a jar of pickled eggs on the bar. Patrons down them with pints of ale for a quick, nourishing snack, or add cheese and a chunk of bread and call it lunch. As hors d'oeuvres, they can be served sliced atop buttered dark bread, or halved as a garnish for a platter of cold meats. Exceptionally easy to make, they also keep well; store them in a covered glass jar in the refrigerator for up to one month.

> 3 cups cider vinegar
> 3 cups water
> 2 tablespoons mixed pickling spice
> 1 medium onion, sliced
> 1 teaspoon salt
> 1 dozen hard-cooked eggs, peeled

In a saucepan combine vinegar, the water, pickling spices, onion, and salt. Bring just to a boil, then remove from heat and let cool 15 minutes. Pack eggs into a large, clean glass jar and pour in warm liquid; let cool, then cover and refrigerate at least 1 day before using.

Makes 1 dozen eggs.

SOFT-COOKED AND CODDLED EGGS

Prepared in the same manner as hard-cooked eggs but in less time—usually 4 to 5 minutes—soft-cooked eggs have a firm white and a soft yolk. Soft-cooked eggs are generally set in an eggcup; the top is cracked with a knife and removed, the egg then eaten directly from the shell with a spoon.

Coddled eggs are soft-cooked eggs that are gently finished away from heat. As with soft-cooked eggs, coddled eggs start in boiling water. They are then immediately covered, removed from heat, and left to stand until set to desired firmness. Consequently, they take slightly longer to cook—6 to 8 minutes—than soft-cooked eggs. Coddling produces an especially tender white. Eggs for Caesar salads are traditionally coddled. Special ceramic egg coddlers are available; to use, the egg is broken into the cup, topped with butter and seasonings, and covered with a metal lid. The cup is immersed in boiling water, then removed and set aside until egg is done to taste. The coddled egg is served in its cup.

To avoid rapid temperature changes that might crack the shell, bring refrigerated eggs to room temperature before soft-boiling or coddling. Steeping egg in tepid water will bring it quickly to room temperature.

NO-FAIL SOFT-COOKED EGGS

Follow directions for No-Fail Hard-Cooked Eggs (see page 197) and simmer, uncovered, until eggs are done to taste (3 to 5 minutes). Serve each egg, in the shell, in an eggcup, cracking top lightly with a spoon and peeling away about ½ inch of shell so egg can be eaten from remainder of shell. Alternatively, quickly cut egg in half, then use a spoon to scoop egg out into a small, warm dish.

▦ SHRIMP-CROWNED EGGS

A simple soft-cooked egg becomes quite another story when you top it with buttery little shrimp to stir into each spoonful. Another topping you might present in the same way is a teaspoon of caviar and a dollop of sour cream seasoned with chives. Part of the charm of soft-cooked eggs is the eggcups they are served in. If this preparation is one you make often, you may want to collect a variety of eggcups to make your breakfast or brunch table even more decorative.

    2 **teaspoons butter or margarine**
    1 **green onion, finely chopped**
    ¼ **cup tiny peeled, cooked shrimp**
    6 **eggs**
        Hot, buttered toast strips, for accompaniment

1. Melt butter in a small frying pan over medium heat. Mix in green onion and stir just until limp. Add shrimp and mix lightly, just until shrimp are heated through. Remove from heat and keep warm.

2. Soft-cook eggs according to directions on page 198. Place eggs in eggcups and carefully slice off top fourth of each egg, using a serrated knife or egg scissors.

3. Scoop out and discard white from each egg top. Fill each eggshell with about 2 teaspoons of shrimp mixture. Quickly invert shrimp-filled top onto eggs and serve at once, accompanied by toast strips to dip into egg yolks.

Serves 6.

Recipes: Caesar Salad, 506.

POACHED EGGS

To poach is to cook gently in liquid. The best eggs for poaching are very fresh; a new-laid egg has a thick white and a firm yolk that tends to hold together when simmered. When poaching an egg, the goal is to produce a just-set egg with a neat, round shape. Sometimes the shape has to be helped along by trimming away trailing bits of cooked white before serving. Specially designed egg-poaching equipment makes the job easier but is not a must. Adding a little lemon juice or vinegar to the poaching liquid helps coagulate the white more quickly and preserve the shape of the egg, but also flavors the egg adversely. After cooking, poached eggs are drained and served alone or in a variety of savory preparations: nestled in artichoke bottoms and covered with Hollandaise or béarnaise sauce, dressed with brown butter, served atop toast with wine sauce, or simply accompanied with buttered toast.

▦ BASIC POACHED EGGS

If not using poached eggs right away, have a bowl of ice water ready for cooling the cooked eggs. Eggs can be poached hours ahead, even as far as two days in advance of serving, and refrigerated in a bowl of ice water.

    Bring water to a boil in a large, nonreactive saucepan (add 2 tablespoons vinegar per quart of water, if desired). Reduce heat to medium-low so that water just simmers. Break an egg into a small cup or ramekin and slide egg into bubbling water (or break directly into water). Repeat with remaining eggs. Reduce heat to low and poach eggs, uncovered, for 3 minutes. Lift each egg carefully with a slotted spoon and touch it; white should be firm and yolk still soft. Remove poached eggs from cooking water with a slotted spoon and serve at once, or transfer to a bowl of ice water. When eggs cool, remove from water and trim edges with a knife or kitchen scissors. Return to ice water.

    To reheat eggs, transfer to a bowl of water that is just hot to the touch and let stand 5 to 10 minutes. Remove carefully to paper towels to drain.

Soft-cooked eggs have a firm white and a runny yolk. They are usually served in a decorative eggcup with the top part of the shell removed, an always appealing presentation.

EGGS BENEDICT

Most restaurant breakfast or brunch menus feature this well-known open-faced poached egg sandwich. The eggs can be poached ahead of time, even up to two days in advance, and held in the refrigerator. When needed, reheat in hot water. The Hollandaise is more delicate, but it can be held briefly in a double boiler or thermos.

    16 eggs
    16 slices Canadian bacon or ham, cut in
       ¼-inch-thick rounds
     4 to 6 tablespoons butter or margarine
     8 English muffins, split
     2 cups Hollandaise Sauce (see page 516)

1. Poach eggs according to directions on page 199, and refrigerate until ready to reheat.

2. Keep Hollandaise Sauce warm over hot (not boiling) water in a double boiler.

3. In a large frying pan over moderate heat, cook Canadian bacon in a little of the butter, adding more butter as needed (1 tablespoon at a time), until meat is lightly browned on both sides. Keep warm.

4. Reheat poached eggs as directed on page 199. Broil split English muffins until crisp and golden brown.

5. For each serving, place 2 muffin halves on a warm plate and cover each with (in order) Canadian bacon, poached egg, and Hollandaise Sauce. Serve at once.

Serves 8.

FRIED EGGS

Very fresh eggs are best for frying; the thick white of a fresh egg will not spread like the thin, runny white of an older egg. Eggs may be fried in butter, bacon fat, or oil, on one side (sunny-side up) or both (over easy). They may be served as is, on buttered toast, or in a sandwich. Mexican *huevos rancheros* are fried eggs served atop fried tortillas with a spicy tomato sauce.

BASIC FRIED EGGS

Using a frying pan just large enough to hold the number of eggs to be cooked, melt enough fat over medium heat to cover bottom generously; when fat foams, break eggs gently into pan.

Reduce heat to medium-low and cook, uncovered, occasionally spooning butter over eggs, until whites are set and yolks are covered with a pale, translucent film. As an alternative, after adding eggs to pan and reducing heat, cover and cook until eggs are done to your liking as in first method. For eggs sunny-side up, cook on one side only in a covered pan until whites set (about 1 minute) and transfer eggs to warm plates. For eggs over easy, cook in an uncovered frying pan on one side until underside sets (about 1 minute), turn carefully with a spatula, and cook on other side for a few seconds just to firm white.

HUEVOS RANCHEROS

This hearty breakfast or brunch dish is perhaps the best known of all Mexican egg dishes.

       Oil, for frying
       Salt, as needed
     6 corn tortillas
     6 eggs
       Sour cream and avocado slices,
       for garnish

Salsa Frita

    ½ small white onion, minced
     1 clove garlic, minced
     1 tablespoon oil
     2 fresh or canned jalapeño chiles, seeded
       and chopped, *or* 1 can (4 oz) diced green chiles
       for a milder salsa
     2 large tomatoes, peeled and chopped
       Salt, to taste
     1 tablespoon chopped cilantro or
       pinch dried oregano

1. Heat a thin (about ⅛ inch) layer of oil in a skillet. Lightly salt tortillas and fry them one at a time. Fry briefly until golden brown but not hard or crisp. Drain on paper towels.

2. Fry eggs to suit individual taste. Eggs sunny-side up are traditional for this recipe.

3. To serve, top each tortilla with a fried egg. Spoon warm Salsa Frita over egg. Garnish with a dab of sour cream and several avocado slices.

Serves 3 to 6.

Salsa Frita Chiles can burn the skin. When handling them, keep hands away from face, especially eyes. When finished, wash hands thoroughly with soap and water. In a skillet sauté onion and garlic in oil until soft. Add chiles and tomatoes, and simmer for 15 minutes. Check seasoning and add salt to taste. Stir in cilantro.

Makes 2 cups.

Variation Eggs can be poached in Salsa Frita. To serve, spoon eggs and salsa onto fried tortillas.

CREAM-BASTED FRIED EGGS

For a delicious Sunday breakfast, pair these eggs with a chunky applesauce, seasoned sausage, and sweet rolls. A recipe for applesauce appears on page 11, one for sausage is on page 530, and one for nut-filled, cinnamon-flavored pecan rolls is on page 629.

     2 tablespoons butter or margarine
     2 tablespoons whipping cream
     4 to 6 eggs
       Salt and white pepper, to taste

To flavor Parmesan Baked Eggs, you can add such toppings as thinly sliced green onions, snipped fresh chives, salsa, crumbled bacon, or grated cheese.

1. In a large, heavy frying pan over medium-low heat, melt butter. Swirl in cream. Break eggs into pan, being careful not to break yolks.

2. Cook, uncovered, occasionally spooning cream mixture over eggs, until whites are set and yolks are covered by a pale, translucent film (3 to 5 minutes). Serve at once, seasoned with salt and pepper.

Serves 4 to 6.

BAKED EGGS, SHIRRED EGGS, AND EGGS EN COCOTTE

Also known as shirred eggs, baked eggs are oven-cooked in buttered ramekins until just set. The eggs may be baked on a bed of creamed spinach or tomato sauce, or they may be broken over asparagus spears or buttered bread, then baked until set. To keep top of eggs moist and tender, they are lightly basted with cream or butter. Some recipes call for covering eggs during baking to keep tops soft.

After baking eggs, if desired sprinkle on a topping such as snipped fresh chives or thinly sliced green onions (including some of the green tops), red or green salsa, caviar, sour cream or crème fraîche, crumbled crisp bacon, or grated Swiss or sharp Cheddar cheese.

To make eggs *en cocotte* (eggs baked in ramekins), break eggs into buttered round porcelain cups and dot with butter and cream. Place cups in a pan of barely simmering water (bain-marie or hot water bath) and bake until eggs are set (about 7 minutes in a 400° F oven).

PARMESAN BAKED EGGS

In the basic recipe, eggs are baked in buttered shallow casseroles with Parmesan cheese. For variety try Prosciutto Baked Eggs or the topping variations suggested at right.

> 2 tablespoons butter or margarine
> ¼ cup freshly grated Parmesan cheese
> 4 eggs
> Salt, freshly grated nutmeg, and freshly ground pepper, to taste
> Chopped Italian parsley, for garnish

1. Preheat oven to 325° F. Using about half the butter, grease 4 shallow individual baking dishes about 5 inches in diameter. Coat each with 1 tablespoon cheese.

2. Break one egg into each dish. Sprinkle lightly with salt, nutmeg, and pepper. Dot with remaining butter.

3. Bake, uncovered, until eggs are set to your liking (12 to 15 minutes). Garnish with Italian parsley.

Serves 4.

Prosciutto Baked Eggs Do not coat baking dishes with Parmesan cheese. Instead, cook 4 thin slices prosciutto or other ham in butter or margarine until lightly browned, and line each baking dish with a prosciutto slice. Pour in any butter from frying pan. Continue as in basic recipe with eggs, salt, nutmeg, and pepper. Then sprinkle each egg with 1 tablespoon grated Parmesan cheese before baking, instead of dotting with butter.

Hangtown Fry is a dish with roots in the gold-rush era of California history when oysters were as precious as miners' nuggets.

In a medium frying pan over moderate to low heat, melt enough butter or margarine to coat bottom generously. When butter foams, add beaten eggs. Cook, stirring constantly with a wooden spoon, until eggs are set but still shiny and moist looking. For luxuriously creamy eggs, cook in top of a double boiler set over barely simmering water. Cooking time will be about 20 minutes, but eggs will be extraordinarily soft and moist.

Other ingredients might be added to the butter in the same pan in which the eggs are to be scrambled. For example, first cook onions, chopped green bell pepper, sliced mushrooms, or bits of ham, then reduce heat before adding eggs. Eggs can be sprinkled with grated cheese when they are nearly cooked. A scattering of snipped parsley or other fresh herbs at the finish also adds flavor. Other garnishes include cooked tomatoes, cream cheese, smoked fish, salami, asparagus tips, and bacon bits.

HANGTOWN FRY

Soon after the gold rush of 1849, the town of Placerville, California, in the Sierra foothills, became a major center for transacting business and administering justice. The latter activity prompted the miners to nickname it Hangtown. As the story goes, a miner who had struck it rich came to one of the hotels in Placerville and asked for the most expensive breakfast in the house. The most precious delicacy on hand was fresh oysters, which the cook fried and combined with scrambled eggs—Hangtown Fry.

    1 pint small shucked oysters, drained
    ½ to 1 teaspoon Worcestershire sauce
    1 cup plain or seasoned bread crumbs
      Oil, for deep-frying
    2 tablespoons *each* butter and oil
   12 eggs, beaten, at room temperature
      Salt and freshly ground pepper, to taste
    1 tablespoon snipped fresh chives or
      chopped parsley, for garnish

1. Place oysters in a bowl and sprinkle with Worcestershire sauce. Roll oysters one at a time in bread crumbs; shake off excess crumbs and set aside.

2. In a saucepan or deep skillet, heat 2 inches of oil to 375° F. Fry oysters, a few at a time, until golden brown (3 to 5 minutes each). Drain on paper towels and keep warm.

3. Heat 1 tablespoon each butter and oil in a large skillet over medium heat. Add half of beaten eggs. Cook until eggs on bottom begin to set (about 1 minute), then gently stir whole mass once. Continue cooking, stirring only occasionally, until eggs are mostly set in large curds but still quite moist. Stir in half the oysters and season with salt and pepper. Transfer to a warm serving platter. Garnish with chives or parsley. Repeat with remaining eggs and oysters.

Serves 8.

SCRAMBLED EGGS

For scrambled eggs, raw eggs are first whipped with a fork to blend. Adding a little cream, milk, or water (1 tablespoon per egg) will produce a moister, softer texture; water gives a lighter flavor, milk or cream a richer one. Scrambled eggs are generally cooked in butter. Slow cooking yields soft, moist curds; cooking at high heat toughens eggs and produces dry curds.

To add interest, other ingredients such as herbs, cheese, or chopped vegetables can be blended into the eggs as they cook or can be used as garnish.

BASIC SCRAMBLED EGGS

Place eggs in a bowl large enough to allow for brisk beating. Season with salt—about ¼ teaspoon for every 3 eggs (unless you plan to add other salty ingredients)—and a pinch of pepper. Add about 1 tablespoon water, milk, or cream per egg (or less, if desired). Then beat with a fork, wire whisk, or egg beater until yolks and whites are completely blended.

JOE'S SPECIAL

San Francisco has had a number of restaurants named Joe's, all claiming to be the "original" Joe's and all featuring some variation of the following recipe. According to local legend, the dish was concocted when a hungry patron arrived at the end of a particularly busy night. About all the cook had left was eggs, spinach, and sausage (hamburger in some versions of the story)—and Joe's Special was born.

¼ pound mild Italian sausage or ground beef
2 tablespoons olive oil
1 small onion, sliced
2 cloves garlic, minced
1 bunch (about 1½ cups) spinach, washed, trimmed, and shredded
4 eggs, lightly beaten, at room temperature
Salt and freshly ground pepper, to taste

1. Remove casing from sausage and slice or crumble. In a large skillet over medium heat, sauté sausage in oil until meat loses raw color. Pour off all but 2 tablespoons of fat; gently cook onion and garlic until onion begins to brown.

2. Reduce heat to medium-low. Add spinach, eggs, salt, and pepper (season more heavily if using beef, less with sausage). Cook, stirring frequently, until eggs are nearly set. Serve on warm plates.

Serves 2.

Food Processor Version Use metal blade to mince garlic; leave in work bowl. Use slicing disk for onion; remove and cook as directed. Use thick slicing disk to shred spinach. Pack leaves in feed tube loosely and process.

OMELETS AND FRITTATAS

The classic omelet is made with three whole eggs, is cooked quickly, and is often embellished with a filling. Total cooking time should be less than one minute. The inside of a properly cooked omelet is creamy; the outside is barely browned. The simplest fillings are minced herbs or grated cheese; more elaborate fillings include sautéed mushrooms or asparagus tips, smoked salmon with cream cheese, roasted chiles with Cheddar cheese, and sautéed chicken livers.

For a puffy or souffléed omelet, whites and yolks are separated; the whites are beaten to firm peaks, then are folded into yolk mixture. The omelet is cooked over medium heat on both sides. It may be filled or not, as desired.

Frittata (the Italian word for *omelet*) is a thick, open-faced egg pancake. Like an omelet, a frittata may incorporate a wide variety of foods, such as sweet peppers, artichoke hearts, herbs, cheese, sliced potatoes, onions, or leeks. Although omelets are usually served as soon as they are cooked, a frittata may be eaten hot, lukewarm, or even cold. It is usually turned out before it has completed cooking, then is inverted and returned to the frying pan to brown on both sides.

BASIC SINGLE-SERVING OMELET WITH HERBS

Try the fillings suggested here or create your own. Allow 3 to 4 tablespoons of filling for each single-serving omelet

3 eggs
1 tablespoon water
Pinch salt and freshly ground pepper
1 tablespoon butter
1 teaspoon *each* minced fresh parsley, tarragon, and chives

1. In a small bowl mix eggs, the water, salt, and pepper with a fork until well blended but not foamy.

2. In a 7- or 8-inch omelet pan, heat about 1 tablespoon butter over medium-high heat until it begins to foam; add eggs.

3. At first, slide pan back and forth to keep omelet from sticking. As bottom begins to set, slip a thin spatula under eggs, tilting pan and lifting cooked portion to let uncooked egg mixture flow under it to the center. Repeat until most of omelet is set, but center and top are still moist and creamy.

4. Add herbs or filling of your choice (see below). For a filled omelet, spoon filling across center in a line with handle. Have a warm serving plate ready. Loosen one side of omelet with spatula and fold it over to cover about one third of the remainder. Then hold pan over serving plate so the other side begins to slide out. Flip omelet so that previously folded side flips over, producing an omelet folded into thirds with center third on top.

Serves 1.

Apple-Roquefort Omelet Sauté half a tart green apple, cored and thinly sliced, in 1 tablespoon butter. In step 4, add apple, grated Parmesan or shredded Monterey jack cheese, and ½ to 1 ounce Roquefort cheese. Garnish with watercress leaves.

Mexican Omelet Sauté 2 tablespoons chopped onions in a little butter. Add diced green (mild) or jalapeño (hot) chiles, black olives, and any shredded cheese, to make a total of ¼ cup. Add to omelet in step 4 and top with a dash of salsa or a dollop of sour cream or yogurt.

Princess Omelet Cook ½ cup asparagus tips; mix half with a little whipping cream. Add to omelet in step 4. Garnish with sliced raw mushrooms and remaining cooked asparagus tips.

Provençale Omelet Sauté ¼ cup diced tomatoes and a pinch minced garlic in olive oil. Add to omelet in step 4. Sprinkle omelet with minced parsley before serving.

Spinach Omelet Sauté ¼ cup chopped fresh spinach and 1 anchovy fillet, diced, in a little butter. Add to omelet in step 4; top with 1 tablespoon shredded cheese and a sprinkling of freshly grated Parmesan cheese. Garnish omelet with a fresh spinach leaf.

HOW TO MAKE AN OMELET

As egg mixture sets, tilt pan and gently lift cooked portions with a spatula, enabling the uncooked egg to flow underneath.

When most of the omelet is set but top is still slightly moist, spoon filling across center in a line with the handle of pan.

Loosen omelet with spatula and fold a third of it (from far side) toward the middle; tip pan over serving plate, then flip so that previously folded side turns over.

Although a baked soufflé must be served immediately, the soufflé base can be made ahead so that the only work at the last minute is beating egg whites and putting the soufflé in the oven. Soufflés make a wonderful main course for lunch or light supper, along with a salad and a fruit dessert such as the sorbet shown here.

■ CHEESE ROULADE

The word *roulade* indicates that this cheese soufflé is baked flat and rolled. Any of the variations suggested for the Blue Cheese Soufflé (see page 205) will work for the roulade. The filling is a tasty combination of sautéed mushrooms and ricotta cheese, complemented by a seasoned, uncooked tomato sauce. This roulade is delicious served warm from the oven or chilled for a festive picnic. Parchment paper makes assembly and cleanup easier.

    1 recipe Parmesan-Spinach Soufflé
       (see page 205)
    ½ cup freshly grated Parmesan cheese or
       dry bread crumbs, for dusting
    ½ pound mushrooms
    1 tablespoon butter
    ¼ pound Monterey jack cheese, grated
    1 clove garlic, minced
    ¼ cup snipped fresh chives
    2 cups ricotta cheese
    1½ teaspoons kosher salt

Tomato-Shallot Sauce

    1 large tomato, minced
    4 shallots, minced
    2 tablespoons red wine vinegar
    6 tablespoons olive oil
    1 teaspoon oregano
    ½ teaspoon kosher salt
    ¼ teaspoon freshly ground pepper

1. Preheat oven to 350° F. Line a 10- by 15-inch jelly-roll pan with parchment paper, or grease with butter and dust with ¼ cup Parmesan cheese. Spread soufflé mixture into prepared pan and bake until puffed and golden brown (10 to 15 minutes); cool in pan 5 minutes.

2. While roulade is cooling, place a piece of parchment paper or a towel on work surface. Sprinkle with remaining ¼ cup Parmesan cheese. Loosen edges of soufflé and invert onto parchment. Roll parchment and roulade together, jelly-roll fashion, and cool completely (about 1 hour).

3. Slice mushrooms about ¼ inch thick. Heat butter and sauté mushrooms until lightly browned (12 to 15 minutes). Remove to a 3-quart mixing bowl to cool for 10 minutes.

4. Place jack cheese in bowl with mushrooms. Add garlic, chives, ricotta, and salt. Mix well to combine.

5. Carefully unroll roulade and spread with filling, leaving 1 inch uncovered around edge. Roll up again and refrigerate until serving time.

6. To serve, remove and discard parchment, and cut roulade into 2-inch-thick slices. Place on individual plates. Top pieces with Tomato-Shallot Sauce.

Serves 8.

Tomato-Shallot Sauce   In a small bowl mix together tomato, shallots, vinegar, oil, oregano, salt, and pepper. Marinate for 1 hour before serving.

Food Processor Version   Use metal blade to process Parmesan cheese (about 1 minute) and remove. Slice mushrooms with slicing disk and remove. Use shredding disk to process well-chilled Monterey jack cheese with light pressure and remove. Use metal blade for garlic and chives. Use ingredients as directed in recipe.

■ HOT LEMON SOUFFLE

Dessert soufflés are often sprinkled with confectioners' sugar as soon as they come out of the oven. The most efficient way to do this is to put the sugar in a shaker (also called a dredger) made for this purpose. With a slight change in ingredients, this versatile base becomes the classic Grand Marnier version or the popular chocolate soufflé. See the variations at the end of the recipe.

    1 cup milk
    3 egg yolks
    6 tablespoons granulated sugar
    4 tablespoons flour
    2 tablespoons fresh, strained lemon juice
    4 teaspoons grated lemon rind
    5 egg whites
       Confectioners' sugar, for dusting (optional)

1. Set aside 2 tablespoons milk. Bring remaining milk to a boil in a small, heavy-bottomed saucepan.

2. In a medium bowl whisk yolks lightly. Add 4 tablespoons granulated sugar and 2 tablespoons reserved milk and whisk until thick and smooth. Stir in flour with whisk.

3. Gradually whisk in half the hot milk. Return mixture to milk in pan and whisk. Cook over low heat, whisking, until mixture comes to a boil.

4. Remove from heat and whisk in lemon juice and rind. If not using immediately, dab mixture with a small piece of butter to prevent a skin from forming. Mixture can be kept, covered, up to 8 hours in refrigerator.

5. Preheat oven to 425° F. Generously butter a 5-cup soufflé dish.

6. Transfer lemon mixture to a heavy saucepan and whisk until smooth. Heat over low heat, whisking, until just hot. Remove from heat.

7. Beat egg whites until stiff. Add remaining granulated sugar, beating at high speed. Continue beating for about 30 seconds. Stir about one quarter of whites into lemon mixture. Spoon this mixture over remaining egg whites and fold together as gently but as quickly as possible, until just blended.

8. Transfer soufflé mixture to buttered soufflé dish and quickly smooth top with spatula. Bake until puffed and browned (about 15 minutes). When you carefully move dish, soufflé should shake very gently in center.

9. Set soufflé dish on serving platter, sprinkle soufflé with confectioners' sugar (if desired), and serve immediately. Dish up with 2 spoons so that each portion includes some soft center and some firmer crust.

Serves 4.

Chocolate Soufflé   Substitute 2 teaspoons vanilla extract and 2 ounces semisweet chocolate, melted, for lemon juice and lemon rind.

Grand Marnier Soufflé   Substitute grated orange rind for lemon rind and Grand Marnier or other orange-flavored liqueur for lemon juice.

■ **CHILLED LEMON SOUFFLE**

Cold soufflés are more like mousses. Set with gelatin, they give the appearance of rising because they expand upward from their dish. Of course, this is an illusion. The sides of the mold are made taller with the use of a paper collar. Orange juice and rind can be substituted for the lemon juice, if desired.

> ¾ **cup fresh lemon juice**
> 1 **envelope unflavored gelatin**
> 3 **eggs, separated**
> ¾ **cup superfine sugar**
> 2 **teaspoons finely grated lemon rind**
> 1 **cup whipping cream**
>   **Pinch cream of tartar (optional)**
> 1 **cup Chantilly Cream (see page 252),**
>   **for decoration**

1. Wrap a 4- to 5-cup soufflé dish with a collar made from parchment paper, aluminum foil, or waxed paper. To make collar, cut a 12- by 19-inch rectangle; fold in half so that it is 6 by 19 inches. Turn folded edge up about 2 inches and tape collar around mold, with double fold hugging rim of dish. Fasten with kitchen string. Lightly oil inside of collar.

2. Place half the lemon juice in a small saucepan; sprinkle gelatin over juice and let soften (3 to 4 minutes); dissolve over low heat. Set aside.

3. In a double boiler over simmering water, whip egg yolks and sugar until thick and lemon-colored (ribbon stage); add remaining lemon juice and half the grated lemon rind.

4. Add gelatin mixture to egg-yolk–lemon mixture and continue to whip until blended. Set bowl over ice and stir until mixture is on the point of setting (it will have the consistency of cream whipped to soft peaks). In a separate bowl whip cream to soft peaks; fold into egg mixture.

5. In a copper or stainless steel bowl (add cream of tartar if not using copper bowl), whip egg whites until stiff, but not dry, peaks. Fold one third of whites into soufflé base to lighten, then fold in remaining whites and finally remaining lemon rind.

6. Pour soufflé into prepared mold and chill until set (2 to 3 hours).

7. When ready to serve, remove soufflé from refrigerator, carefully unwrap paper collar, and decorate with Chantilly Cream.

Serves 6.

> ### *Recipes and Related Information*
> *Angel Food Cake, 82; Basic Sponge Cake, 83; Bind, 49; Cake, 77; Clarify, 131; Copper Egg-White Bowl, 155; Custard, 168; Egg and Caper Salad, 98; Egg-Preparation Equipment, 210; Egg Wash, 211; Emulsion and Emulsifier, 212; Génoise, 84; Hollandaise Sauce, 516; Mayonnaise, 519; Meringue, 359.*

EGGPLANT

An ancient fruit probably native to India, the eggplant belongs to the nightshade family along with the tomato. Eggplants are cultivated in a variety of shapes, sizes, and colors. All have a thin, glossy, edible skin, a pale whitish green flesh that becomes soft and watery when cooked, and a mild flavor that combines well with oil, cheese, herbs, and other seasonings. The flesh of the large, globular Western eggplant has more moisture and is more bitter than that of the Asian varieties. To draw off some of the bitter juices, Western eggplants are often salted before cooking; Asian eggplants do not require salting.

Use Eggplants can be steamed or boiled to soften the pulp, then baked in a casserole with eggs, cheese, and bread crumbs; sliced and fried, either in flour or in batter; skewered and grilled; halved, stuffed, and baked; stewed with tomatoes and peppers or with oil and garlic; or sliced, layered with cheese and tomato sauce, and baked parmigiana. Indian cooks include eggplant in curries.

Asian cooks pickle it, braise it with pork, or fry it in tempura batter. In southern Italy, eggplant is part of pasta sauces, baked dishes, and the popular relish caponata. Greek moussaka is a baked casserole of eggplant, lamb, and cream sauce. The mild flavor of eggplant makes it a good foil for spicy sauces or highly seasoned dishes. It readily soaks up oil and seasonings.

Availability In the United States the most common variety is the large, globular, purple type, weighing about 1 pound each. The Japanese eggplant is long, slender, and deep purple; a similar Chinese variety is slightly longer, with a lavender skin. Other cultivated varieties, usually grown on farms near Asian communities, are the small, round, white Thai eggplant and the tiny, round, white Chinese variety used for pickling. Peak availability is July and August, but eggplants are available all year.

Selection Choose eggplants that feel heavy for their size. Skin should be smooth and shiny; flesh should feel firm, without bruised areas.

Storage Place eggplant in a plastic bag and refrigerate in crisper for up to four days.

Preparation Eggplants do not need to be peeled. Wash and trim stem ends. Large globe varieties may be bitter; to remove some bitterness, slice and salt eggplant liberally, then drain for one hour between sheets of paper towels weighted with a heavy plate. Pat dry.

Cooking See BRAISE, BROIL, DEEP-FRY, GRILL.

■ MEDITERRANEAN EGGPLANT SPREAD

The warm flavors of the Mediterranean come through in this coarse eggplant spread, designed to be made in a food processor. Serve it with savory crackers or wedges of pita bread before a dinner of garlicky roast lamb or chicken. It can be stored in the refrigerator for up to two weeks.

> 1   **eggplant (about 1 lb)**
> ¼   **cup olive oil**
> 2   **red bell peppers, chopped**
> 2   **large tomatoes, peeled, seeded, and chopped**
> 1   **medium zucchini, chopped**
> 2   **cloves garlic, minced**
> 1   **teaspoon paprika (preferably Hungarian)**
> 1   **teaspoon ground cumin**
>   **Juice of 1 lemon**
>   **Salt, to taste**
>   **Crackers, pita bread wedges, or Belgian endive leaves, for accompaniment**

1. Preheat oven to 450° F. Trim ends of eggplant; cut eggplant into lengthwise slices, about ¼ inch thick.

2. Brush a baking sheet with 2 tablespoons oil, then heat in oven 5 minutes. Place eggplant slices on heated baking sheet and bake 10 to 15 minutes. Remove from oven and let cool.

3. Place eggplant in food processor and purée coarsely, turning motor on and off rapidly. Set aside.

4. In remaining oil, sauté peppers over medium heat until soft (7 to 8 minutes). Add tomatoes, zucchini, garlic, paprika, cumin, lemon juice, and salt to taste and continue cooking 2 minutes. Remove from heat and cool slightly.

5. Combine pepper mixture and eggplant; process briefly. Spread should be very coarse. Pack into crocks and seal with a little olive oil.

6. At serving time, taste and adjust salt and lemon as necessary. Serve with crackers, warm pita bread, or leaves of Belgian endive.

Makes 2 cups.

■ EGGPLANT RELISH

Sicilians are renowned for their sweet-and-sour dishes, a particularly winning example of which is caponata. This eggplant relish of wonderfully complex flavors and textures is scooped up with hearts of lettuce or chunks of bread. Smooth and crunchy, hot and cool, sweet and tart—it's all there in this beguiling dish.

> 3   **large eggplants *or* 6 small Japanese eggplants**
> 1½   **cups olive oil**
> 3   **cups minced onions**
> ⅓   **cup minced garlic**
> 1   **cup diced celery**
> 2   **cups peeled, seeded, and chopped tomatoes (½-in. chunks)**
> 3   **tablespoons capers**
> ⅔   **cup minced carrot**
> ½   **cup toasted pine nuts**
> 2   **cups oil-cured black olives**
> ⅓   **cup sugar**
> ⅔   **cup red wine vinegar**
> ½   **teaspoon cayenne pepper, or more to taste**
>   **Salt, to taste**
> ⅔   **cup minced parsley**
>   **Olive oil, for garnish**
>   **Minced parsley, for garnish**

1. Preheat oven to 375° F. Peel eggplants and cut into ½-inch dice. Oil a large baking sheet or roasting pan with 3 tablespoons olive oil. Toss eggplant with ¾ cup olive oil to coat well, then transfer to baking sheet or pan. Bake, tossing eggplant frequently, until soft and lightly browned (about 20 minutes).

2. Heat remaining oil in a large skillet over moderate heat. Add onions and garlic and sauté until soft (7 to

10 minutes); do not allow garlic to brown. Add celery, tomatoes, capers, carrot, pine nuts, olives, sugar, vinegar, and cayenne. Simmer slowly 30 minutes. Add salt to taste. Add eggplant and cook an additional 10 minutes. Add the ⅔ cup parsley and let cool. Taste again and correct seasoning. To serve, transfer to a bowl, drizzle with olive oil, and garnish with minced parsley.

Serves 12.

Food Processor Version   Use metal blade to process parsley, onions, garlic, celery, tomatoes, and carrots to desired consistency. Process each vegetable individually. For best results, process parsley first.

MOUSSAKA

Plan a Greek dinner with this layered lamb and eggplant casserole as the main course. Start with a lemon and rice soup. For dessert, serve Baklava (see page 222), a sweet pastry made with tissue-thin filo dough, ground almonds, and honey.

> 1 **large eggplant (about 1½ lb)**
>   **Salt, as needed**
> ⅓ **cup (approximately) olive or vegetable oil**
> 1 **pound ground lamb, crumbled**
> 1 **large onion, finely chopped**
> 1 **clove garlic, minced**
> ¼ **teaspoon ground cinnamon**
> 1 **teaspoon salt**
> ⅛ **teaspoon *each* freshly grated nutmeg and white pepper**
> ¼ **teaspoon dried oregano**
> ¼ **cup chopped parsley**
> 2 **tablespoons tomato paste**
> ½ **cup dry red wine or Beef Stock (see page 560)**
> ½ **cup freshly grated Parmesan cheese**

Cream Sauce

> 2 **tablespoons butter or margarine**
> 2 **tablespoons flour**
> ½ **teaspoon salt**
>   **Dash *each* freshly grated nutmeg and white pepper**
> 2 **cups milk**
> 2 **eggs**
> 1 **egg yolk**

1. Preheat oven to 350° F. Cut off stem end of eggplant; cut unpeeled eggplant in half lengthwise. Cut crosswise in ½-inch slices; liberally sprinkle both sides with salt. Set in a single layer between sheets of paper towel and weight with a heavy plate; set aside for 1 hour to drain.

2. In a large frying pan, heat 1 tablespoon oil and cook lamb, stirring, until browned. Spoon off excess fat. Mix in onion and cook, stirring occasionally, until onion is tender. Mix in garlic, cinnamon, salt, nutmeg, pepper, oregano, parsley, tomato paste, and wine. Bring to a boil,

reduce heat, and simmer, covered, for 15 minutes. Uncover and continue simmering until sauce is thick (about 5 minutes).

3. Pat eggplant dry with paper towels. Arrange slices in a single layer in a large shallow pan. Brush with some of the remaining oil. Broil, about 4 inches from heat, until lightly browned (about 5 minutes). Turn, brush second sides with oil, and broil until browned (5 minutes longer).

4. To assemble, place half the eggplant slices in a single layer in an ungreased square or oval casserole of about 2-quart capacity. Top with meat sauce; sprinkle with 2 tablespoons Parmesan cheese. Cover with remaining eggplant; sprinkle with 2 more tablespoons cheese. Pour on Cream Sauce; sprinkle with remaining cheese. At this point casserole can be covered and refrigerated overnight.

5. When ready to serve, bake until top is lightly browned (45 minutes to 1 hour).

Serves 6.

Cream Sauce   Melt butter in a medium saucepan; stir in flour, salt, nutmeg, and pepper. Remove from heat and gradually stir in milk. Return to heat and cook, stirring, until thickened. In a small bowl beat eggs and egg yolk. Mix in a little of the hot sauce. Over low heat, blend egg mixture gradually into sauce and mix well.

Food Processor Version   Use metal blade to process Parmesan cheese, then parsley, onion, and finally garlic.

Moussaka, a Greek lamb and eggplant casserole, should be on everyone's list of dinner party entrées. It can be prepared up to the point of baking and then refrigerated overnight, if desired. An hour before serving, put the casserole in the oven to cook while the rest of the meal is being assembled.

EGGPLANT PARMESAN

This popular recipe is similar to lasagne, but here slices of eggplant replace the flat lasagne noodles. Eggplant has a meaty, satisfying texture. Note that the eggplant slices must drain for 1 hour to remove bitter juices before they are browned.

2 medium eggplants, peeled
Salt, as needed
Flour, as needed
Olive oil, for frying
2 cups Basic Tomato Sauce (see page 516)
½ pound mozzarella cheese, coarsely grated
½ cup freshly grated Parmesan cheese
3 tablespoons butter

1. Cut eggplants horizontally in ½-inch slices; liberally sprinkle both sides with salt. Place in a single layer between sheets of paper towel and weight with a heavy plate; set aside for 1 hour to drain. Pat dry with paper towels. Dredge with flour and fry slices in a shallow amount of olive oil in a heavy pan over medium-high heat until lightly browned, adding more oil as necessary. Salt to taste and drain on paper towels.

2. Preheat oven to 400° F. Butter a 9- by 13-inch baking dish. Place a single layer of fried eggplant in dish; cover with ⅓ of the tomato sauce, ⅓ of the mozzarella cheese, and ⅓ of the Parmesan cheese. Continue layering eggplant, sauce, and cheese for 2 more layers, ending with Parmesan. Dot with butter and bake until bubbling hot throughout (about 30 minutes).

Serves 4.

RATATOUILLE

Complement this robust red pepper and eggplant stew with grilled garlic sausages and a green salad.

¼ cup olive oil
1 small unpeeled eggplant (about 1 lb), cut in ½-inch cubes
1 medium onion, slivered
½ pound mushrooms, thinly sliced
1 sweet red or green bell pepper, cut in strips
1 clove garlic, minced
¾ teaspoon *each* dried basil and dried oregano
½ teaspoon salt
⅛ teaspoon freshly ground black pepper
Pinch cayenne pepper
1 can (1 lb) tomatoes

1. In a large frying pan over medium heat, heat olive oil and cook eggplant and onion, stirring often, until vegetables are soft (about 10 minutes). Add mushrooms and pepper; cook, stirring occasionally, until the mushrooms brown lightly. Mix in minced garlic, basil, oregano, salt, pepper, cayenne, and tomatoes (coarsely chopped) and their liquid.

2. Bring mixture to a boil, reduce heat, and simmer, stirring occasionally, until mixture is thick and reduced to about 4 cups (20 to 25 minutes). Remove from heat and let cool for about 10 minutes.

3. Serve warm or at room temperature.

Serves 8.

Recipes and Related Information
Tempura Batter, 28; Vegetable Mixed Grill, 296.

EGG-PREPARATION EQUIPMENT

These devices won't make your cooked egg more tender, but they aid preparation in some way and are quite popular according to retailers. See EGG for cooking information.

EGG CODDLER

These are servers and cooking pans in one. They are made of porcelain with a screw-on metal lid, or of heatproof glass with a plastic top. To use, one or two eggs are broken into a cup, covered with butter, cream, some chopped herbs, or other seasoning, and the lid is fastened. To cook the egg, the cup is immersed in simmering water. The finished dish is presented in the coddler. Some versions have an optional rack with handle that holds one or two cups and makes it easier to lower coddlers into hot water and draw them out when eggs are ready.

EGG POACHERS

Perfectly shaped poached eggs—cooked in the classic manner, in simmering water—can be difficult to achieve, especially if you are trying them for the first time. Help is available if you seek it out.

From England come deep, round rings; from France, egg-shaped perforated stands; from the United States, a multiple-egg poacher that fits into a skillet. All three give a poached egg a regular shape and prevent most of the white from drifting away from the yolk as egg cooks.

To use rings or individual stands, butter well or spray with a nonstick vegetable cooking spray. Place one in a pan with simmering water, break egg into it, then cook as directed in recipe. Rings can also be used for frying eggs—handy if you want to make them exactly round to match an English muffin.

The multiple-egg poacher is an aluminum plate coated with a nonstick finish. It has four separate wells—one egg goes in each—which maintain shape of the eggs as they poach. The plate has short feet that sit on the bottom of a shallow pan and holes between egg cups so that the cooking water can rise up through the plate, cover eggs, and cook them.

These tools are designed to simplify egg preparation or cookery. Shown clockwise from top right are egg poacher, egg slicer, egg wedger, egg separator, egg coddlers.

EGG SEPARATOR

This utensil is for those who lack confidence to separate yolk and white with the eggshell transfer technique or are too squeamish to crack the egg into their palm and let the white slip through their fingers. The separator is an aluminum, plastic, or ceramic saucer with slots cut around a cuplike center depression. To use, set over a receptacle of some sort. The design takes advantage of the differing viscosities of yolk and white; the thicker yolk gets trapped in the saucer while the more fluid white slides through the slots into the bowl set beneath.

EGG SLICER AND WEDGER

These devices create perfect slices or wedges of hard-cooked eggs. Both slicers and wedgers are two-part, hinged devices. The lower section holds the egg in place and is slatted or divided; the upper arm is made of stainless steel wires strung parallel for slicers, or intersecting for wedgers, across a metal frame. A shelled egg is set on the base and the wires are brought down and through white, yolk, and between the slats or sections. Slicers and wedgers also work for slicing mushrooms.

EGG WASH

This mixture of egg or egg yolk lightly beaten with water or milk has several uses. When brushed on pastry or bread, it promotes a shiny surface; it also works as a glue to join two pieces of raw pastry or to give seeds something to adhere to when sprinkled on raw dough. If milk or cream is used rather than water, a soft, rather than crusty, surface develops. The term can also refer to beaten egg combined with a splash of water or milk, a typical binding mixture for bread coatings.

Egg washes fall into three categories: whole egg, egg yolk, and egg white.

Whole-Egg Wash This mixture can be used for sweet or savory dishes. It creates a medium-brown finish and works well as a glue.

Egg-Yolk Wash This is the strongest. It promotes a rich, brown color when baked, is usually seasoned with a pinch of salt, and is used on savory dishes.

Egg-White Wash Often used on sweet dishes as a base for a dusting of sugar, this wash promotes a silvery, crispy surface and is suitable for sweet pies and pastries.

A warm, sweet-and-sour dressing softens the raw crispness of the greens in Hot Romaine and Escarole Salad. Like all wilted salads, this one should be served immediately after tossing.

EMULSION AND EMULSIFIER

When two liquids usually incapable of forming a stable mixture are in suspension, the combination is called an emulsion. What links them together is the addition of a third substance, called an emulsifier, which is compatible with both. For example, oil and water will mix when beaten, but will separate as soon as the beating stops unless stabilized with an emulsifying agent. Emulsions can be temporary (lasting a few minutes, such as an oil and vinegar salad dressing) or more permanent (lasting hours, days, or longer, such as mayonnaise).

Egg yolk is the most effective emulsifier for sauces. Other common ones are acids (lemon juice, vinegar, wine), dry and prepared (wet) mustard, and paprika, which is why these ingredients are basic to vinaigrette dressings.

Recipes and Related Information
Hollandaise Sauce, 516; Mayonnaise, 519; Vinaigrette Dressing, 520.

ENRICH, TO

To add an ingredient, known as an enrichment, to a dish to deepen its flavor and develop a luxurious finish, both visually and to the taste. Butter and cream, and sometimes egg yolks, are enrichments that are often swirled into sauces and cream soups just before serving.

ESCAROLE

A sturdy salad green of the chicory family, escarole has broad, wavy, jagged-edged green outer leaves that whiten near the core. The flavor is slightly bitter; the texture is firm and crisp.

Use An escarole salad can stand up to hot bacon dressings or assertive vinaigrettes. Wilted escarole leaves can be added to bean or vegetable soups. Just a few hearty escarole leaves contribute pleasing texture to a mixed green salad.

Availability Escarole is sporadically available throughout the year. However, it is at its best and most abundant in the winter.

Selection Leaves should be crisp and creamy inside; avoid wilted heads with browning edges.

Storage Keep escarole in a plastic bag in refrigerator crisper for up to three days.

Preparation Discard ragged or dark green outer leaves. Wash well and dry, trim core end, and tear by hand into smaller pieces.

▦ HOT ROMAINE AND ESCAROLE SALAD

This barely wilted salad combines two greens with substantial texture—romaine and escarole—in a piquant sweet-and-sour dressing with bacon and tomato.

> 2 **tablespoons fresh lemon juice**
> 1 **tablespoon catsup**
> 1 **teaspoon** *each* **sugar and Dijon mustard**
> ½ **teaspoon Worcestershire sauce**
> 1 **clove garlic, minced**
> 6 **slices bacon**
>   **Vegetable oil, as needed**
> 1 **medium onion, finely chopped**
> 6 **cups torn romaine lettuce**
> 4 **cups torn escarole**
> 1 **medium tomato, cut in thin wedges**
>   **Freshly ground pepper**

1. In a small bowl mix lemon juice, catsup, sugar, mustard, Worcestershire sauce, and garlic.

2. Cut bacon crosswise into ½-inch strips. In a large frying pan, cook bacon until crisp and brown, stirring often; remove with a slotted spoon and drain.

Measure ¼ cup bacon drippings; add oil (if needed) to make ¼ cup, or discard any drippings in excess of ¼ cup. In the same pan cook onion in drippings over medium heat, stirring, for about 1 minute. Add lemon juice mixture; bring to a boil.

3. Add romaine, escarole, and tomato; immediately remove from heat. Mix lightly to coat well with dressing. Transfer to a salad bowl and sprinkle with bacon and pepper. Serve at once.

Serves 4 to 6.

■ ESCAROLE SOUP

Try this very simple soup that can be prepared and served within one hour. Fresh spinach or other greens may be substituted for escarole.

⅓ **cup butter**
1 **small onion, minced**
1 **head escarole, well washed and coarsely chopped**
  Salt and freshly ground pepper, to taste
4 **cups homemade Chicken Stock (see page 560)**
  or regular-strength canned broth
¼ **cup crushed vermicelli**
¼ **cup freshly grated Parmesan cheese, for topping**

1. In a large saucepan melt butter and sauté onion over medium heat until browned. Add escarole and salt and pepper to taste. Sauté briefly, then add stock. Cover and cook over low heat for 15 minutes. Add vermicelli and cook an additional 15 minutes.

2. Taste and season. Serve with Parmesan cheese.

Makes about 8 cups, 4 servings.

EVAPORATE, TO

To release steam from a liquid by boiling. Cooks use this principle when boiling liquids to decrease their volume and to intensify their flavor. Sauces are often thickened or reduced this way. A shallow, wide pan promotes faster evaporation than does a deep, narrow one, because the heat reaches more of the liquid at one time and the greater surface area allows water vapor to escape more quickly.

EVISCERATE, TO

To remove the internal organs from freshly killed birds, animals, and fish. Because the viscera spoil quickly and the enzymes in the digestive tract speed deterioration, evisceration is done for sanitary reasons. Also called draw and gut, it is typically done by slitting from the base of the gullet to the bottom of the belly and trimming the entrails from where they are attached to the chest cavity.

EXTRACT AND ESSENCE

The many extracts and essences used to flavor foods are derived from aromatic plant oils, from natural, nonplant ingredients, and from synthetics combined in a laboratory.

The characteristic taste and fragrance of many fruits, flowers, spices, and other plants are contained in the essential oils of the plant. Pure extracts are made by distilling these essential oils and dissolving them in alcohol or a diluted alcohol base, which keeps the oil in suspension. Pure vanilla and almond extracts, for example, are made in this fashion. Unlike extracts, flavorings—butterscotch and rum are two examples—are neither alcohol-based nor derived from plants.

Some flavors, such as maple or banana, cannot be extracted by distillation. In place of pure extracts, scientists have developed imitation and artificial flavorings. Imitation flavorings contain all or some nonnatural ingredients; artificial flavorings such as butterscotch may contain natural or synthetic flavors but do not have a natural counterpart that they are attempting to reproduce.

Use Extracts and essences impart flavor to a given dish without adding solids or excess liquids. They are most commonly used in baking. Home cooks add vanilla, almond, lemon, and peppermint extracts and butter and rum flavorings to cakes, puddings, ice creams, custards, cookies, and candies. Rose water and orange flower water are used not only in baked goods and custards but also in savory rice dishes.

Extracts and essences are highly volatile; they dissipate rapidly in the atmosphere, even more rapidly in the presence of heat. As a result, they should be added to cool or cooling mixtures for maximum effect. When creaming butter and sugar for cakes or cookies, add extracts to the fat to slow vaporization and promote even distribution.

In general, 1 teaspoon of extract is enough to flavor 1 pint or 1 pound of food. Delicate flower waters—orange flower water and rose water—may be used more liberally.

Availability Although many extracts and flavorings widely used in commercial food manufacturing are unavailable to the consumer, dozens of extracts and essences are packaged for consumers and are sold on spice shelves in supermarkets.

Selection Pure extracts will give a truer, more concentrated flavor than imitation or artificial flavorings. For flavorings unavailable in pure form, such as banana or pistachio, an artificial extract will probably taste less harsh than the imitation product.

Storage Extracts lose potency when exposed to light and heat. Stored in a cool, dark place, they will keep indefinitely.

Solid cooking fats such as butter, margarine, and lard, along with liquid oils, play important culinary roles: They add tenderness, flavor, and color, keep foods from sticking to cooking pans, and add richness to sauces and dressings.

FAT

Fats and oils have similar chemical compositions. Both are made up of triglycerides (glycerol molecules with three fatty acids attached). However, fats are solid at room temperature and oils liquid because fats contain more saturated fatty acids. As a result of this difference, fats and oils have different cooking qualities.

The following section looks at the role of solid fats in cooking. Also see BUTTER; MARGARINE; PORK, About Pork Lard; and POULTRY, About Chicken Livers, Giblets, and Fat. For information on liquid fats, see OIL.

Use   To the cook, solid fats are especially important in baking, deep-frying, and sautéing. In addition, they are useful as flavor enhancers, emulsifiers, and sealants. The best fat for a particular dish depends on the flavor and texture desired.

Storage   Although the decomposition process is not entirely understood, it is known that saturated fats oxidize and turn rancid more slowly than unsaturated fats. Beef, for example, has a longer freezer life than chicken or pork because its fat is more saturated. Pastries made with lard stay fresh longer than those made with polyunsaturated oils. These facts probably have more implications for the commercial food processor than for the home cook who will choose a cooking or baking fat for its flavor and texture.

For specific storage instructions, see individual fats.

FAT IN BAKING

The primary role of fat in baking is as a shortening or tenderizing agent. When fat is combined with flour in a batter or dough, it limits development of gluten, an elastic protein network that gives a baked product its structure. If less strands of gluten are developed, the result is a more tender cake, cookie, pie dough, or loaf of bread; more gluten means baked goods will be tougher. Cookies without solid fat, such as meringues, are hard rather than tender.

Fat is also responsible for making pastry doughs flaky. In puff pastry and Danish pastry, for example, the fat content (usually butter) is extremely high. Butter is rolled between the layers of dough to make alternating layers of gluten and fat. When baked, the fat melts and generates steam, which leavens the dough and produces flaky sheets of pastry.

Fat imparts flavor and color to baked goods. An all-butter pie crust has a noticeably different flavor and color than an all-lard crust. The flavor of lard is important to Mexican and Chinese breads and pastries; the flavor of butter is important to French pastries. Although, technically, butter can be substituted for lard (or vice versa), the authentic, characteristic flavor of the product often depends on the fat used.

Some baked goods use fat as a leavening agent. When fat and sugar are creamed, the air trapped in the dough or batter adds volume to the baked product. For this reason, thorough creaming is essential to producing a cake with a light texture. Fats at room temperature cream more easily; they incorporate and hold air better (see CREAM).

Fat adds richness, smoothness, and sheen to the crumb of baked goods. High-fat breads such as brioche have a richer flavor and smoother, shinier crumb than fat-free breads such as a French-style baguette.

Fat improves the longevity of baked goods. By coating the starch granules, it slows moisture loss. Breads with fat last for several days, in contrast to the fat-free baguette, which goes stale in one day.

FAT IN DEEP-FRYING

Deep-frying requires a fat that does not burn or break down at high temperatures or in the presence of moisture. The temperature at which a fat or oil begins to deteriorate is called its smoke point. In general, saturated fats are more stable and have higher smoke points than unsaturated fats. The presence of free fatty acids in a fat, however, lowers its smoke point. Animal fats such as suet and butter have lower smoke points than vegetable oils because of their high proportion of free fatty acids. The best fat for deep-frying, then, would be a saturated (fully hydrogenated) vegetable shortening. These shortenings have a smoke point of about 460° F, compared to 320° to 330° F for butter and 340° to 350° F for lard.

Repeated use will lower the smoke point of a fat because of the moisture and the food particles left behind from previous use. To extend the life of a frying fat, carefully strain or filter it after each application, and store in a tightly capped container away from light and heat. Frying in a deep kettle, as opposed to a shallow, wide pan, exposes less of the fat to air and thus extends its life somewhat (and is safer). Fat that smokes or foams has broken down and should be discarded.

FAT IN SAUTEING

In panfrying and sautéing, the hot pan is coated with a thin layer of fat. The hot fat keeps the sautéed food from sticking to the pan and it aids in the formation of a crust, which helps to contain juices. It also imparts flavor and helps conduct heat from the pan to the item being cooked.

Although the mild flavor of butter may be desirable in sautéed items—especially in delicate foods such as fish and veal—butter burns easily. Clarified butter (see page 68) is preferred for high-heat sautéing because it has a higher smoke point than whole butter. Alternatively, adding oil to the butter in the sauté pan raises its smoke point.

OTHER USES FOR FAT

Apart from cooking, the most obvious use for fat is as a flavor enhancer. Adding butter to mashed potatoes or spreading goose fat on toast is the cook's way of taking advantage of the flavor of fat. Fat also adds what food scientists call mouthfeel to a dish, a palate sensation that largely determines whether we accept or reject a particular dish.

Fat also acts as an emulsifier in some sauces. To make a classic French beurre blanc, softened butter is whipped into a reduction of wine and shallots. The acid in the wine holds the butter in suspension and creates a filmy sauce. Whisking a few tablespoons of butter into a sauce enriches it, emulsifies it, and gives it sheen.

English potted meats and French *rillettes* (potted pork) and duck *confit* (preserved duck) are packed into jars or crocks and sealed with a layer of melted fat—usually fat rendered from the meat itself. The fat effectively keeps out moisture and air, and extends the storage life of the food. Potted meats sealed with fat will keep for several weeks under refrigeration.

Recipes and Related Information
Bard, 25; Beurre Blanc, 518; Cake, 77; Cream, 161; Cream Puff Pastry, 162; Deep-fry, 174; Emulsion and Emulsifier, 212; Fry, 254; Lard, 338; Panfry, 404; Puff Pastry, 480; Sauté, 531; Stir-fry, 557; Yeast Bread, 613.

FEIJOA

Also known as the pineapple guava, the feijoa is a small oval fruit with a smooth, gray-green skin, a creamy white flesh with a juicy, pearlike texture, and a sweet flavor reminiscent of pineapple, pear, and banana. It is native to South America but is now grown in California and throughout the South Pacific.

Use Enjoy feijoa "on the half shell," with lime or lemon. Peel, slice, and serve with prosciutto, or use it in fruit salads, preserves and jellies, sorbets, and mousses.

Availability The New Zealand crop is available from March through June, the California fruit from September through December.

Selection Ripe feijoas are fragrant and give slightly to gentle pressure.

Storage Place ripe fruit in a plastic bag in the refrigerator crisper. Underripe fruit will ripen if kept at room temperature. Use ripe fruit as soon as possible.

FENNEL

Also known as finocchio, fennel is a plant of Mediterranean origin, valued for its bulb, leaves, stems, flowers, and seeds. The greenish white bulb is made up of overlapping ribs like those of celery, broad at the bulbous base but narrowing to tubular stems. Feathery green leaves grow up from the middle of the bulb. Raw fennel has a licoricelike flavor and a crunchy, celerylike texture. Cooking mutes the flavor somewhat and softens the texture.

PREPARING FENNEL

Cut off and discard upper portion, including feathery leaves and ribs; remove bruised or discolored outer ribs; trim base.

Halve trimmed bulbs and remove a wedge of tough core from each.

Slice halves thinly lengthwise; bulbs can also be sliced crosswise, depending upon use.

Use　Fennel bulb is eaten raw or cooked. Slice thinly and add it to salads, or dress with lemon, olive oil, and freshly grated Parmesan cheese for a first course, or serve it raw with an assortment of vegetables and a dipping sauce. Bake it with butter and bread crumbs, add it to soups or stews, or steam it and dress with butter and lemon or cheese sauce. Fennel bulb is particularly compatible with white-fleshed fish and lobster.

French cooks stuff fish with feathery fennel leaves or add leaves to salads or fish soups. The edible flowers may also be added to salads. Young fennel branches may be eaten raw with oil and salt or with a dip. Adding dried fennel branches to a fire imparts a special fragrance to grilled fish.

The small, yellowish brown fennel seed adds a licorice-like flavor to fish soups, breads, sausages, pork roasts, stuffings, and apple pie. Indians often serve fennel seed after dinner as a digestive and breath freshener.

Availability　Fresh bulb fennel is sold in Italian markets and many supermarkets in fall and winter. Fennel seed is available on supermarket spice racks.

Selection　Fennel bulb should be smooth and whitish green without cracks and discoloration; leaves should look fresh and lively, not wilted. The bulb should be compact; spreading at the top indicates overmaturity. For fennel seed, remember that packaged seasonings lose quality after a while; try to buy from a store that restocks its spice section fairly often.

Storage　Keep fennel in a plastic bag in the refrigerator crisper; use within three to four days. Store fennel seed in an airtight container in a cool, dark place; it will keep indefinitely.

Preparation　Trim bulb base and cut away feathery stalks (save for other uses). Remove thick, tough outer ribs. Halve, core, and slice crosswise or lengthwise. See Preparing Fennel at left.

Cooking　See BOIL, BRAISE, GRILL, STEAM, STIR-FRY.

■ BRAISED FENNEL

This simple treatment brings out the subtle, sweet flavor of fennel. Although the fennel takes some time to tenderize, the preparation is easy and needs little attention other than occasional stirring. If desired, substitute chicken stock for the water or use a mixture of half stock and half water. If stock was used, taste the finished dish before adding salt; most stocks are already seasoned.

　　3　**large fennel bulbs**
　½　**cup olive oil**
　　　Salt, to taste

1. Remove and discard damaged or wilted outside parts of fennel, as well as tops, and cut a slice off bottom of bulbs. Cut bulbs into lengthwise slices and wash slices in cold water.

2. Place fennel slices, olive oil, and water to barely cover in a saucepan. Cook over medium heat, uncovered, until fork-tender (30 to 40 minutes), stirring occasionally. If fennel becomes dry, add a bit of hot water. Add salt to taste and serve on a preheated platter.

Serves 4.

■ FENNEL AND ARTICHOKE SALAD

The first spring artichokes are a delicious partner for the last of the fennel. Marinated in oil and lemon, then served with toast and Parmesan cheese, the two vegetables flatter each other and almost any main course. Grilled fish, roast lamb, or chicken are all fine choices.

　　1　**large *or* 2 small fennel bulbs**
　　3　**lemons**
　¾　**cup olive oil**
　　　Coarse salt and freshly ground pepper, to taste
　　4　**small artichokes (about 2 to 3 in. diameter)**
　12　**slices toasted baguette (see Note)**
　¼　**pound Parmesan cheese, sliced in long, thin slabs**
　　　Olive oil and freshly ground pepper, for garnish

1. Wash fennel bulbs and remove any tough outer stalks. Halve and core them, and slice thinly lengthwise. Put fennel slices in a stainless steel, glass, or ceramic bowl. Add juice of 2 lemons, olive oil, and salt and pepper to taste. Toss to blend and set aside to marinate.

2. Remove dark green outer leaves of artichokes; cut off top third of artichokes with a serrated knife. Rub all cut surfaces with lemon. Cook in boiling, salted water until just tender (12 to 15 minutes). Drain and refresh under cold running water, then drain thoroughly and pat dry. Cut artichokes in half. Add to fennel in bowl and stir to coat with oil. Marinate an additional 30 to 45 minutes. Taste and add more salt or remaining lemon if necessary.

3. To serve, spoon a little of the marinade onto individual salad plates. Arrange fennel atop marinade. Surround with slices of baguette. Top bread with artichoke hearts. Alternate Parmesan slices with bread slices on plates and drizzle salad with a little additional olive oil. Serve immediately and pass the pepper mill.

Serves 4.

Note　If desired, brush toast with garlic oil while bread is still warm.

FENUGREEK

The small, yellowish brown seeds inside the pods of the fenugreek plant are actually legumes, like peas and beans, but they are so aromatic when dried and roasted that they're used as a spice. Fenugreek is especially important to the cuisines of India and North and East Africa.

Use Fenugreek is an important ingredient in most curry powder blends. It is also, surprisingly, used to flavor imitation maple syrup. Ethiopians eat the tiny fenugreek seeds as a vegetable, cooking them as they do peas or beans; they also use fenugreek as a spice in stews. In India, fenugreek is an ingredient in chutneys and mango pickles as well as curries; in Morocco, fenugreek is added to breads.

Availability Whole fenugreek seed can be found in Indian and Middle Eastern markets and some specialty and health-food stores, usually in bulk.

Selection Packaged seasonings lose quality after a while; try to buy from a store that restocks its spice section fairly often.

Storage Keep fenugreek in an airtight container in a cool, dark place. It will last indefinitely. Ground fenugreek quickly loses its aromatic qualities; for maximum flavor, grind whole fenugreek as needed.

Preparation The full flavor of fenugreek is brought out by roasting. Toast whole seeds in a skillet over low heat, shaking skillet often, until seeds are fragrant. Soak them in water to soften, then grind in a pepper mill, clean coffee grinder, or electric minichopper, or with a mortar and pestle.

FERMENTATION

For home cooks, the most relevant application of fermentation relates to the action of yeast in breadmaking. When yeast is mixed with sugar in a moist, warm environment (around 80° F), a chemical reaction occurs, which as a by-product gives off carbon dioxide gas—the primary leavening agent for yeast bread doughs. Sugar is introduced into these doughs directly in granulated form and indirectly as the yeast converts starch present in flour into glucose, a simple sugar. Alcohol is also released during fermentation, but evaporates during baking. The appealing, yeasty aroma of making bread is in part due to products of fermentation.

Fermentation begins when the dough is mixed. Under conditions of proper temperature and the availability of fermentable sugars, it continues until the dough heats to 138° F in the oven, a temperature that kills yeast. Many bakers believe that a more flavorful yeast dough develops from slow fermentation. Most recipes more commonly refer to this process as rising or proofing.

Fermentation is also the process by which wine is made. A yeast naturally present on the skin of grapes feeds on the sugars in the fresh, crushed fruit to produce ethyl alcohol (ethanol) and carbon dioxide gas. Vintners commonly kill most of the wild yeast at the time of crushing with sulfur dioxide, because it produces inconsistent fermentation, and then add a "pure" strain of cultured yeast with known properties.

Once yeast starter is added to grapes (or juice) in the fermenting vessel, the yeast quickly multiplies, and before long millions of yeast cells are alive in the must (unfermented juice). For several days, the must ferments rapidly, and the carbon dioxide quickly bubbles out of the fermenting tank. Gradually, as the sugar is consumed and the alcohol level rises, the yeast cells begin to die and settle to the bottom of the tank.

Left alone, the wine will ferment completely dry, that is, until all the sugar is consumed. The vintner will step in, however, to control the fermentation process by monitoring temperature and adding sulfur dioxide, and, by filtering, to achieve a desired result.

Some wines undergo a second type of fermentation, known as malolactic fermentation, after the sugar fermentation is complete. Malolactic bacteria transform one of the natural grape acids, malic acid, into the less-tart-tasting lactic acid.

Ripe grapes, such as those shown here entering a stemmer/crusher, can contain as much as 25 percent sugar by weight, making them among the sweetest fruits. Fermentation by microscopic yeast cells turns the sugar to alcohol, and the juice into wine.

Recipes and Related Information
Yeast, 613; Yeast Bread, 613.

FIDDLEHEAD FERN

The ostrich fern, which grows wild in New England and Canada, puts forth tightly curled green shoots every spring. These shoots, known as fiddlehead ferns, are gathered when they are 2 to 5 inches long and very tightly curled and are a prized wild delicacy. The texture of the shoots resembles that of string beans; the flavor is akin to asparagus and spinach. The unfurled, mature shoots are poisonous.

Use Fiddlehead ferns are eaten both raw in salads and cooked. Steamed, they are delicious hot with butter or cold with vinaigrette. Stir cooked fiddleheads into scrambled eggs or toss with pasta; try them deep-fried or stir-fried with other vegetables.

Availability Fiddlehead ferns are gathered wild in the late spring in New England and Canada. They are available fresh in some markets at that time. Some specialty shops carry frozen and canned fiddlehead ferns.

Selection Choose the smallest fiddlehead ferns with solid green color and without browning. They should look tightly curled and crisp, not wilted.

Storage Wrap in damp paper towels, then place in a plastic bag in the refrigerator for no longer than one or two days.

Preparation Rub off fuzzy scales or wash under running water to remove them. Cook whole.

Cooking See DEEP-FRY, SAUTE, STIR-FRY.

FIG

The plump, soft fig is the fruit of the ficus tree, of which there are hundreds of varieties. The ficus tree probably originated in Asia Minor and is certainly one of the most ancient edible plants. When ripe, figs are one of the sweetest fruits. Depending on variety, the most common cultivated figs are purple, green, yellow, or white skinned, with flesh that ranges from gold to deep red. The skin is edible, the ripe flesh moist and intensely sweet. See DRIED FRUIT, Dried Figs, for information on the dried fruit.

Use　Fresh, ripe figs are a nutritious out of hand snack. Sliced, sugared, and drizzled with milk or cream, they make a delicious breakfast or dessert. Serve halved figs as an appetizer with thinly sliced prosciutto. Slice or halve them and add to fruit salads, or poach them briefly for fruit compotes. Baked fresh figs flavored with butter, lemon, and honey are a delicious late-summer or early-fall dessert. Sliced figs make a beautiful, softly colored topping for a fruit tart.

Availability　Fresh figs are sold sporadically from June through October, with the best supply in August and September.

Selection　Choose figs that are as soft and ripe as possible. However, overripe fruit will have a sour odor due to fermentation of juice. Avoid bruised fruit, but fruit shriveled by the sun will be especially sweet.

Storage　Leave underripe figs at room temperature until ripe. Ripe figs are highly perishable; store on a paper-towel–lined tray in the refrigerator and use as soon as possible; hold no more than one or two days.

Preparation　Remove stem ends. Fresh figs do not require peeling, although some recipes may call for it.

Cooking　See POACH.

■ FIGS WITH FLAVORED RICOTTA

This elegant dessert only takes a few minutes to assemble. The citrus-infused ricotta-cheese filling can be prepared in advance and held in the refrigerator until needed. The nuts can be chopped ahead as well. All that is left to do is slice the figs and fill them.

> 12　medium-sized ripe fresh figs
> 1　cup ricotta cheese
> 1　teaspoon *each* grated lemon rind
> 　　and orange rind
> ¾　teaspoon vanilla extract
> ¼　cup honey
> 　　Chopped pistachios, hazelnuts,
> 　　or almonds, for garnish

1. Remove stem ends from figs. Cut each into a tulip shape by slicing in quarters from stem almost to blossom end. Press on stem end to open petals.

2. In a blender or food processor, whirl ricotta, citrus rinds, vanilla, and honey. Stuff each fig with 2 tablespoons flavored ricotta. Serve garnished with chopped nuts.

Serves 6.

FILET; FILLET, TO; FILLET

Filet refers to slices cut from the narrow end of a beef tenderloin, the most well-known being filet mignon steaks.

　To fillet is to completely bone and trim a cut of meat or fish; *fillet* is the name of the long, boneless piece of meat or fish that results.

> ***Recipes and Related Information***
> *Beef, 37; Bone, 55; Fish, 223.*

FILO PASTRY

Also spelled *phyllo,* filo pastry is made from a wheat-flour dough rolled into tissue-thin sheets. It is a common ingredient in Greek and Middle Eastern cooking. Although filo resembles strudel leaves, it is generally rolled thinner. In fact, filo dough is rolled and stretched so thin that it is difficult and time-consuming to make at home. When basted liberally with butter and baked, filo makes a crisp, flaky wrapper for turnovers and other baked dishes.

Use　Traditionally filo dough is used as a wrapper for the Greek feta cheese–stuffed turnovers called *tiropita* and for the spinach-stuffed *spanakopita.* Filo is layered with walnuts and honey to make a sweet dessert called baklava. Substitute filo dough for other pastry wrappers in turnover recipes or as a replacement for strudel leaves in cabbage or apple strudel. Filo can also be substituted for *warka,* the thin pastry used in Morocco for *pastilla* (a pigeon pie) and *brik* (a large fried turnover).

Availability　Filo pastry is found frozen in most supermarkets and fresh in some Middle Eastern markets. It is generally packaged in 1-pound boxes.

Storage　Filo dough may be frozen for up to one year. Refrigerated filo dough may be frozen immediately after purchase or refrigerated unopened for up to three weeks. After opening, use within a few days. Thaw frozen dough 8 hours or overnight in the refrigerator; do not refreeze.

Preparation　Filo is fragile and dries out quickly. It must be handled rapidly and kept moist. Open package only after remaining ingredients are ready. After removing filo from its plastic bag, lay flat and cover with waxed paper weighted with a damp towel. (Do not allow towel to touch filo.) For further guidance, follow package instructions or a particular recipe.

MOROCCAN PASTILLA

Moroccan restaurants serve small portions of this dish as a first course, but it also makes a substantial main dish. In this recipe chicken has been substituted for pigeon, the traditional bird. The pastry is filo, the same thin dough as used for Baklava on page 222.

  1 frying chicken (3 to 3½ lb), cut up
  2 small onions, 1 coarsely chopped and
    1 finely chopped
  ¼ cup finely chopped parsley, plus 1 sprig
  2½ teaspoons salt
  ⅛ teaspoon dried thyme
  2 cups water
  1 cup finely chopped blanched almonds
  ¼ cup granulated sugar
  2 teaspoons ground cinnamon
  ½ teaspoon ground ginger
  ¼ teaspoon *each* freshly grated nutmeg and
    ground cardamom
  1 cup butter or margarine
  6 eggs
  2 cloves garlic, minced
  ¼ teaspoon freshly ground pepper
  ½ pound (half package) filo dough, thawed
    8 hours in refrigerator if frozen
  ¼ cup confectioners' sugar, for dusting
  ½ teaspoon (approximately) ground cinnamon,
    for dusting

1. In a large skillet or Dutch oven, combine chicken with coarsely chopped onion, parsley sprig, 1½ teaspoons salt, dried thyme, and the water. Bring to a boil, reduce heat, cover, and simmer until chicken is very tender (about 1½ hours). Strain and reserve broth for another use. Remove chicken from bones in large pieces, discarding bones and skin.

2. Preheat oven to 350° F. Place almonds in a shallow baking pan; bake, stirring occasionally, until golden brown (10 to 15 minutes). Cool. In a small bowl mix granulated sugar, 2 teaspoons cinnamon, ginger, nutmeg, and cardamom.

3. In a large frying pan, cook finely chopped onion in 3 tablespoons butter until limp but not browned. In a medium bowl beat eggs with garlic, 1 teaspoon salt, pepper, and chopped parsley. Add to onion mixture and cook over low heat, stirring occasionally, until eggs are softly set. Remove from heat.

4. Melt remaining butter. Use it to brush a 9-inch springform pan generously. Unfold sheets of filo dough so they lie flat. Cover with waxed paper, then a damp towel, to prevent them from drying out. Line pan with 1 sheet of dough, allowing dough to extend over edge of pan; brush generously with butter. Top with a second sheet of dough and brush with butter. Fold 6 more sheets of dough to fit pan and stack in pan one atop the other, brushing each with butter.

5. For filling, arrange a layer of prepared chicken, egg mixture, then toasted almonds. Sprinkle sugar and spice mixture over almonds.

6. Fold remaining sheets of filo dough to fit pan. Reserve 2 sheets for topping. Stack filo over almonds, brushing each layer with butter. Fold edges of filo that extend beyond the pan in toward center. Top with last 2 sheets, folded to fit pan; tuck any protruding edges down inside rim of pan. Brush with remaining butter. Using a razor blade or small sharp knife, cut through top layers of dough down to the almonds to mark pie in 8 wedge shapes. (At this point, you can cover and refrigerate pie for several hours or until you are ready to bake it.)

7. Bake until well browned and heated through (45 minutes to 1 hour). Remove pan sides. Sift confectioners' sugar over pie, then ½ teaspoon cinnamon. Serve immediately; cut in marked wedges.

Serves 8.

Food Processor Version Use the metal blade to process the following, setting each aside until needed: almonds, onion, parsley, and garlic. If you wish, leave parsley and garlic in work bowl. Add eggs, 1 teaspoon salt, pepper, and chopped parsley (if not already in bowl) and process 10 seconds.

Made with delicate filo dough, a common ingredient for many Middle Eastern cuisines, Moroccan Pastilla makes for an exotic Sunday brunch. This dish combines the light flavor of chicken with a nutty mixture of almonds, cinnamon, ginger, nutmeg, and cardamom in a crisp shell.

Honey-sweetened Baklava, made with layers of paper-thin filo dough and ground almonds, is a satisfying accompaniment to a cup of rich, strong coffee.

■ BAKLAVA

These aromatic Greek pastries make a nice addition to a dessert buffet. They also freeze well.

>   ½ **pound (half package) filo dough,**
>   **thawed 8 hours in refrigerator if frozen**
>   2 **cups ground blanched almonds**
>   ¾ **cup sugar**
>   1 **teaspoon grated lemon rind**
>   ¾ **teaspoon ground cinnamon**
>   1 **cup unsalted butter, melted**
>   **Sliced almonds, for garnish**

Honey and Rose Water Syrup

>   ¼ **cup *each* sugar and water**
>   1 **cup honey**
>   1 **tablespoon rose water**

1. Unfold sheets of filo dough so they lie flat. Cover with waxed paper, then a damp towel, to prevent them from drying out.

2. Preheat oven to 325° F. In a medium bowl combine almonds, sugar, lemon rind, and cinnamon. Generously butter an 8- or 9-inch-square pan.

3. Carefully fold 2 sheets of filo to fit pan; place in pan one at a time, brushing each with butter. Sprinkle about 3 tablespoons of the almond mixture over top sheet. Fold 1 sheet of filo to fit pan; brush with butter. Sprinkle evenly with another 3 tablespoons almond mixture.

4. Continue to add layers, using 1 folded sheet of filo, a generous brushing of butter, and 3 to 4 tablespoons almond mixture for each, until nut mixture is used up (there should be about 10 nut-filled layers).

5. Fold remaining 2 to 3 sheets of filo to fit pan. Place on top, brushing each with butter before adding the next. With a very sharp knife, carefully cut diagonally across pan to make small diamond shapes—about 1½ inches on a side—cutting all the way to bottom of pan. Pour on any remaining butter.

6. Bake until golden brown (about 45 minutes). Pour warm Honey and Rose Water Syrup over top. Decorate each piece with an almond slice. Cool before serving.

Makes about 2 dozen pastries.

Honey and Rose Water Syrup   Combine sugar and the water in a 1½-quart saucepan; bring to a boil, stirring. Mix in honey and cook until syrup boils again. Remove from heat; mix in rose water.

■ WALNUT-APPLE STRUDEL

Strudel is a typical Hungarian dessert, which traditionally uses homemade, paper-thin dough as the wrapper. The dough is extremely time-consuming and difficult to prepare. Using frozen filo dough streamlines the process.

>   6 **sheets filo dough, thawed 8 hours**
>   **in refrigerator if frozen**
>   ½ **cup unsalted butter**
>   1 **cup soft white bread crumbs**
>   ½ **cup coarsely chopped walnuts**
>   2 **large baking apples, cored and coarsely chopped**
>   ¼ **cup sugar**
>   ¼ **cup raisins**
>   1 **teaspoon ground cinnamon**

1. Unfold sheets of filo dough so they lie flat. Cover with waxed paper, then a damp towel, to prevent them from drying out. Preheat oven to 350° F. Butter a baking sheet.

2. In a small sauté pan over medium heat, melt ¼ cup butter. Add bread crumbs and sauté until golden brown (about 7 minutes); set aside.

3. In a medium bowl combine walnuts, apples, sugar, raisins, and cinnamon; toss to coat walnuts and apples thoroughly.

4. Melt remaining butter in a small saucepan; remove from heat. Spread a slightly damp cloth over work area. Stack 2 sheets filo dough on cloth. Brush top sheet with melted butter. Repeat twice, stacking 2 sheets of dough each time.

5. Spread sautéed bread crumbs on top sheet of dough, leaving a 3-inch border of dough uncovered. Cover bread crumbs with walnut-apple mixture.

6. With longer edge of dough facing you, fold nearest edge back over filling, then lift cloth and roll dough and filling like a jelly roll. Seal seam with water. Pinch edges to seal; tuck under.

7. Place on buttered baking sheet; brush top with melted butter. Set sheet on center rack of oven and bake until strudel is golden brown (25 to 35 minutes). Slice roll into individual servings about 1½ inches wide.

Serves 4 to 6.

Food Processor Version   Tear slices of fresh bread into pieces and put in work bowl with metal blade. Process 15 seconds and set aside. Use shredding disk for walnuts and set aside. Put cored, quartered apples in work bowl; turn motor on and off a few times to chop.

TIROPITA

Because the cheeses vary in saltiness, taste the filling first and reduce the salt, if necessary. The little triangles can be frozen up to two months and baked direct from the freezer for quick party fare.

       2 **bunches green onions, minced**
       ½ **cup parsley, minced**
       1 **clove garlic, minced**
       ¼ **pound Monterey jack cheese, shredded**
       ¼ **pound feta cheese, crumbled**
       2 **eggs**
       ¼ **teaspoon salt, or to taste**
           Freshly ground pepper, to taste
      12 **sheets filo dough, thawed 8 hours
           in refrigerator if frozen**
       ¾ **cup unsalted butter, melted**

1. In a medium bowl stir together green onions, parsley, garlic, jack cheese, feta cheese, eggs, and salt and pepper to taste.

2. Place filo dough on work surface. Cut into strips about 3 inches wide; cover strips with waxed paper and a damp cloth to keep from drying out. Working with one strip at a time, brush with melted butter. Place a rounded tablespoon of cheese mixture at bottom of strip. Fold on diagonal to create a triangular shape; bottom edge of filo dough will touch left side of strip. Bring bottom of triangle up against straight edge. Fold again on diagonal so that left edge now touches right side. Repeat folding to top of strip, forming an enclosed triangular pastry. Brush folded triangle with melted butter. Repeat with remaining dough and filling.

3. Preheat oven to 400° F. Bake triangles on a baking sheet until lightly browned and hot (about 20 minutes). Cool about 2 minutes before serving.

Makes 3 dozen triangles.

Food Processor Version   Cut green onions into 1-inch pieces. Use metal blade to chop green onion pieces, parsley, and garlic, turning motor on and off until desired consistency is obtained. Transfer to mixing bowl and add feta, eggs, salt, and pepper. Have jack cheese well chilled; process cheese with shredding disk and add to mixing bowl. Stir to blend with other ingredients. Continue with recipe.

FINISH, TO

Adding the final touches to a dish. This can include bringing food prepared ahead of time to serving temperature, arranging the food attractively on its plate, and adding garnishes to enhance visual appeal.

The term also specifically refers to the final attention paid by the cook to a sauce before serving it: to correct seasonings; to enrich with one or more of certain ingredients (butter, sour cream or crème fraîche, cream, or essences); and, when deemed appropriate, to add a splash of liquor to heighten the aroma.

FISH

How to purchase, prepare, and cook fish could be the subject of a multivolume cookbook. The world's lakes, rivers, and oceans are full of hundreds of species, many of which are unique to each region. Indeed, some cooks will argue that a bouillabaisse is authentic only when made in or near Marseilles, France, with local fish.

Modern transportation has improved that situation somewhat, bringing fresh Dover sole to Dallas and Maryland soft-shell crab to San Francisco. However, it is still true and worth acknowledging that fish is extremely perishable, that it ships successfully only under the most carefully controlled conditions, and that the most delicious fish is the one eaten within hours of capture. Anyone who has ever panfried and eaten a trout within moments of hooking it knows that even day-old fish has a markedly different flavor and texture. Freshness in fish is the first key to enjoyment. The second is selecting the proper cooking method.

This entry includes information to help the home cook select and prepare fish successfully; also see SHELLFISH.

CATEGORIZING FISH

Despite their great diversity, fish may be readily categorized in ways helpful to the cook. The three most important distinctions are: Is the fish round or flat? Is its flesh lean or oily? Is it from salt water or fresh water? The first question affects how the fish is cut for cooking. The second affects the choice of cooking method. The third has important health and safety implications.

basted generously during cooking to keep them moist, they may also be baked, broiled, or grilled.

Oily fish contain 5 to 50 percent fat. Their flesh is stronger tasting, richer, and less white than that of lean fish. Examples of oily fish are swordfish, trout, salmon, tuna, mackerel, catfish, sturgeon, smelt, sablefish, pompano, herring, anchovy, and eel. Because of their high oil content, they stay moist when cooked with little or no added liquid or fat (grilling, baking, and broiling). Only those oily fish lowest in fat, such as salmon, are appropriate choices for poaching.

SALT WATER OR FRESH WATER
As the popularity of sushi increases in the United States, it is important that cooks be aware of some dangers regarding raw fish. Freshwater fish from lakes and streams may carry parasites harmful to humans. Consequently, freshwater fish should never be eaten raw and are never used in sushi. Cooking to doneness—by any method—will kill any parasites present.

Parasites harmful to humans cannot survive in the flesh of saltwater fish. Consequently, such saltwater fish as tuna, halibut, salmon, and shellfish of all kinds are safe to eat raw if caught in nonpolluted waters.

Use   Depending on the character of the meat, fish may be poached, steamed, baked, panfried, grilled, broiled, braised, fried, smoked, or eaten raw. Fish bones can be used to make a stock for soups and sauces. Cooked cold fish can be used in salads, chowders, sandwich fillings, layered casseroles, fried cakes, or baked loaves. Whole fish can be stuffed and baked. Delicate fillets such as sole can be stuffed and rolled before baking. Firm-fleshed fish such as halibut and swordfish can be cubed and skewered for grilling.

Availability   Fish is available fresh or frozen, with the best selection usually found at specialty fish markets. Some markets keep fish in holding tanks for live purchase. For information on the most common retail market cuts, see Roundfish or Flatfish, Lean Flesh or Oily Flesh, and photograph at left.

Selection   Some people define fresh fish as fish that has never been frozen. However, a never-frozen fish can be considerably less than fresh. A truly fresh fish should not smell fishy—a sign of age or improper handling by the fishmonger. A fresh fish has a mild odor; firm, elastic flesh that springs back when pressed; clear, protruding eyes; reddish or pink gills; and scales that are shiny, bright, and tight to the skin.

As always, there are a few exceptions. Shark, skate, and ray, primitive fish with unique metabolisms, will have an ammoniated odor when freshly killed. Soaking them in milk or lightly acidulated water eliminates the smell. Without soaking, the odor will dissipate in a day or two, making shark, skate, and ray among the few fish that are better when not quite fresh.

There are two types of whole fish: flat and round, as illustrated by the top two fish in the photograph. Starting below the flatfish and moving clockwise, the most common cuts of fish include: whole pan-dressed fish (a small fish with head and tail, scaled, fins removed, and gutted); pan-dressed body (without head and tail); steak (a cross-section of a fish); butterflied fillet (both sides of fish still connected); fillets without skin; and fillets with skin.

ROUNDFISH OR FLATFISH
Based on their skeletal structure, all fish can be classified as either round or flat. Roundfish can be cooked whole or cut off the bone into two fillets. Large roundfish, salmon for example, can be cut crosswise into steaks. The fillets of some roundfish are thick enough to slice crosswise. Flatfish, such as flounder, cannot be satisfactorily cut into steaks or slices. They are either cooked whole or cut from the bone into four fillets, two top and two bottom.

LEAN FLESH OR OILY FLESH
Leaner fish have a mild flavor and firm white flesh. The oil or fat (5 percent or less of the total body substance) is concentrated in the liver, which is removed during cleaning. Sole, halibut, flounder, snapper, sea bass, burbot, turbot, and rockfish are examples of lean fish. Because their flesh dries out readily, they are well-suited to cooking with some sort of liquid or fat (poaching, steaming, sautéing); if

Some deep-water fish may have cloudy eyes from pressure changes when raised to the surface. Also, some flatfish may have dark, muddy gills, but they should be red or pink when washed.

If the fish has been frozen, ask how long it has been defrosted. Do not buy anything that has been defrosted for more than two days. It is better to purchase frozen fish and defrost it at home. For best quality, try to find fish that were individually quick-frozen on the fishing vessel.

Fillets offer fewer clues to freshness than whole fish. Look for flesh with a natural sheen; avoid fillets that are yellowing or browning around the edges. As with whole fish, the odor should be fresh and the flesh firm. If buying packaged frozen fillets, avoid packages that look as if they may have been thawed and refrozen. The telltale signs of fish that have been thawed at least once include a misshapen package and interior ice that is bloody.

When planning a meal, choose a recipe appropriate to the fish in season. When marketing, be prepared to change the recipe if the required fish is unavailable in good condition. It is wiser to buy the freshest fish available and plan the recipe around it.

Storage   The colder the storage temperature, the less rapidly fish deteriorates. To store fresh fish, pat dry, arrange in one layer in a baking dish lined with paper towels, cover with plastic wrap, and refrigerate. If possible, set the baking dish atop crushed ice in a larger pan, making sure the melting ice cannot enter the dish. Use as soon as possible.

Store frozen fish immediately in freezer, preferably at 0° F or below. Never refreeze thawed fish. One of the best ways to freeze a whole fresh fish is to ice glaze it. First set fish on a baking sheet and freeze just until firm. Dip frozen fish in ice water; a glaze will form immediately. Return fish to freezer to solidify glaze. Repeat glazing process until fish is coated with a layer of ice at least ⅛ inch thick. Wrap in heavy-duty foil, freezer paper, or a large plastic freezer bag and freeze. To freeze fillets and steaks, wrap individually or stack between sheets of freezer wrapping material. Wrap tightly, then overwrap. Always thaw frozen fish slowly in refrigerator.

Lean fish can be frozen longer than oily fish, large fish longer than small ones, whole fish longer than steaks or fillets. Freeze whole oily fish no longer than two months, whole lean fish no longer than six months. Freeze oily fillets no longer than one month, lean fillets no longer than three months.

Preparation   Both roundfish and flatfish need to be cleaned before use, but the cleaning procedures vary. Although a fishmonger can clean and cut up fish, there are advantages to buying fish whole: You will have a better idea of how fresh the fish is; you will have the bones and trimmings for stock; and on some fish, particularly salmon, you will get a better price per pound if you cut it up yourself.

Almost all fish require scaling. Some exceptions are trout, which have scales that are an integral part of the skin, and catfish, which have tough skin that must be removed altogether. If poaching the whole unboned fish, leave the dorsal and anal fins attached; they will help hold the fish together during poaching. See Scaling and Finning, page 227.

Gutting—removing the viscera or internal organs—can be done by the fishmonger or you can do it yourself. Because the entrails contain the bacteria that start decomposition, fish should be gutted as soon as possible—ideally, the moment it is caught, or immediately after being removed from the holding tank. If you plan to bone and fillet the fish, remove the entrails by gutting through the belly. If serving the fish whole, preserve the shape by gutting through the gills. The gutting techniques for roundfish are different from those used for flatfish. See Gutting, page 227.

Though many pan-sized fish have tasty skin that enhances flavor, some fish, such as largemouth bass and butterfish, have strong-tasting skin that interferes with the flavor of a dish. Leave skin on when poaching or grilling a whole fish. See Skinning, page 227.

Fillets are pieces of boneless fish. Steaks are cross sections cut from a whole fish. Roundfish and flatfish require slightly different filleting techniques. See Cutting Fillets and Steaks, page 228.

Cooking   The type of fish determines the most suitable cooking method. Select lean fish such as cod, sole, sea bass, or snapper for moist-heat or fat-based approaches. Use dry-heat methods on oily fish such as mackerel or tuna. Lean fish may be cooked by dry-heat methods if basted during cooking to prevent drying out. Frozen whole fish may be cooked from the frozen state. Fillets may have to be thawed to separate them; otherwise, cook from the frozen state.

See BRAISE, BROIL, DEEP-FRY, GRILL, PANFRY, POACH, SAUTE, STEAM, STEW, STIR-FRY.

The Common Fresh Fish chart on page 226 indicates preferred cooking methods for the major types of fish available in this country.

DRY-HEAT COOKING

Dry-heat cooking methods include baking, broiling, and grilling. Whatever the means, the goal is the same: cooking without robbing the food of moisture. Fish with a high internal fat or oil content are especially well suited for dry-heat cooking because they baste themselves. However, most fish have little internal fat to keep them moist during cooking, so to prevent them from drying out, a variety of precautions are available: wrapping with grape leaves, leafy greens, aluminum foil, or parchment paper; covering with vegetables, cream or bread crumb topping, or another coating; marinating and basting; stuffing; and leaving the head and tail attached.

TIPS

TESTING FOR DONENESS

The Canadian Department of Fisheries has developed a relatively reliable guideline for timing fish cookery. Measure the fish at its thickest point. Allow 10 minutes' cooking time for each inch of thickness (20 minutes per inch if fish is frozen).

Although the Canadian method is a good guide, it is inexact. The opacity test is the most reliable way to determine doneness. Insert a pointed knife into the thickest part of the fish to check the flesh. Properly cooked fish will be opaque and will not cling to the bones. Because both water and oil transfer heat faster than air, poached or deep-fried fish will cook faster than the same piece of fish baked in the oven. Do not overcook fish. It will continue to cook from retained heat after removing it from the heat source. Overcooked fish is hard and dry.

COMMON FRESH FISH

Improved transportation, refrigeration, and freezing methods have broadened the choice of fish species available to cooks across the country. This chart offers cooking information for the most commonly available fish.

Type of Fish	Source	Flesh	Cooking Method
Anchovy	Salt water	Oily	Bake, Deep-fry, Grill, Pickle
Angler (monkfish, goosefish, lotte)	Salt water	Lean	Bake, Braise, Broil, Grill, Poach, Steam, Stew
Bonito (bonita)	Salt water	Moderately oily	Bake, Broil, Grill
Butterfish (Pacific pompano on West Coast)	Salt water	Oily	Bake, Broil, Grill
Carp	Fresh water	Moderately oily	Bake, Braise, Panfry, Poach, Steam, Stew
Catfish	Fresh water	Moderately oily	Bake, Braise, Broil, Grill, Panfry, Poach, Steam, Stew
Cod	Salt water	Lean	Bake, Braise, Broil, Grill, Panfry, Poach, Steam, Stew
Corbina (corvina)	Salt water	Moderately oily	Bake, Broil, Grill, Poach, Steam
Drum (redfish)	Salt water	Lean	Bake, Broil, Grill, Poach, Steam
Eel	Fresh water and salt water	Oily	Bake, Braise, Grill, Stew
Flounder	Salt water	Lean	Bake, Broil, Grill, Poach, Sauté, Steam
Grouper	Salt water	Lean	Bake, Braise, Broil, Fry, Grill, Poach, Steam, Stew
Haddock	Salt water	Lean	Bake, Braise, Broil, Fry, Grill, Poach, Steam, Stew
Hake	Salt water	Lean	Bake, Braise, Broil, Grill, Panfry, Poach, Steam, Stew
Halibut	Salt water	Lean	Bake, Broil, Grill, Poach, Sauté, Steam
Herring	Salt water	Oily	Bake, Broil, Grill, Pickle
Lake trout	Fresh water	Oily	Bake, Broil, Grill, Poach, Sauté, Steam
Mackerel	Salt water	Oily	Bake, Braise, Broil, Grill, Pickle, Stew
Monkfish (see Angler)			
Perch	Fresh water	Lean	Bake, Braise, Broil, Grill, Panfry, Poach, Sauté, Steam, Stew
Pike	Fresh water	Lean	Bake, Braise, Broil, Grill, Panfry, Poach, Sauté, Steam, Stew
Pollock	Salt water	Lean	Bake, Braise, Broil, Grill, Poach, Sauté, Steam, Stew
Pompano (Florida pompano)	Salt water	Moderately oily	Bake, Broil, Grill, Panfry, Sauté
Porgy	Salt water	Lean	Bake, Broil, Grill, Panfry
Ray	Salt water	Lean	Bake, Braise, Poach, Sauté, Steam, Stew
Red snapper (many fish labeled "snapper" are actually rockfish)	Salt water	Lean	Bake, Braise, Broil, Grill, Panfry, Poach, Sauté, Steam, Stew
Rockfish	Salt water	Lean	Bake, Braise, Broil, Grill, Panfry, Poach, Sauté, Steam, Stew
Sablefish (fillets known as butterfish on West Coast)	Salt water	Oily	Bake, Braise, Broil, Grill, Stew
Salmon	Salt water and fresh water	Moderately oily	Bake, Broil, Grill, Poach, Sauté, Smoke, Steam
Sea bass	Salt water	Lean	Bake, Braise, Broil, Grill, Panfry, Poach, Steam, Stew
Sea trout (weakfish)	Salt water	Moderately oily	Bake, Braise, Broil, Grill, Panfry, Poach, Steam, Stew
Shad	Fresh water	Moderately oily	Bake, Braise, Broil, Grill, Stew
Shark	Salt water	Lean	Bake, Braise, Broil, Grill, Panfry, Poach, Steam, Stew
Skate (see Ray)			
Smelt (whitebait)	Salt water	Oily	Bake, Broil, Grill, Panfry
Sole (petrale sole, rex sole, lemon sole, Dover sole)	Salt water	Lean	Bake, Broil, Grill, Poach, Sauté, Steam
Striped bass	Salt water and fresh water	Moderately oily	Bake, Braise, Broil, Grill, Poach, Sauté, Steam, Stew
Sturgeon	Salt water and fresh water	Oily	Bake, Broil, Grill, Sauté, Smoke
Swordfish	Salt water	Moderately oily	Bake, Braise, Broil, Grill, Stew
Tilefish	Salt water	Lean	Bake, Braise, Broil, Fry, Grill, Poach, Sauté, Steam, Stew
Trout	Fresh water	Moderately oily	Bake, Broil, Grill, Poach, Sauté, Smoke, Steam
Tuna	Salt water	Oily	Bake, Braise, Broil, Grill, Sauté, Stew
Turbot	Salt water	Lean	Bake, Poach, Sauté, Steam
White	Salt water	Lean	Bake, Broil, Grill, Panfry, Poach, Sauté, Steam
Whitebait (see Smelt)			
Whitefish	Fresh water	Oily	Bake, Broil, Grill, Smoke

SCALING AND FINNING

Wet fish and salt hands for a better grip. With a knife or scaler, start at tail and scrape toward head. Rinse fish well.

The dorsal (back) fin can be clipped with kitchen scissors, although this leaves part of the fin connected to the fish. Cut against the grain, tail to head.

To remove the whole dorsal fin, cut along each side of fin with a filleting or boning knife and pull fin toward head to remove it. Use the same method to remove anal fin (closest to tail at bottom). Clip other fins with scissors.

GUTTING

Flatfish *To gut a flatfish, make a small cut behind gills and pull out viscera. Rinse.*

Roundfish *To gut through belly, cut off head behind gill opening. Cut open belly from head end to just above anal (tail) fin area. Remove membranes, blood veins, and viscera. Rinse.*

To gut through gills, open outer gill with thumb. Reach a finger into gill and snag inner gill. Pull gently to remove inner gill and viscera. Rinse.

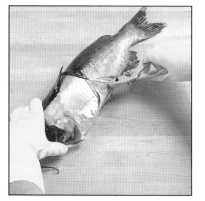

SKINNING

Catfish *Cut skin just behind head all around body. Wear gloves to protect hands from whiskerlike barbels and barbed fins. Hold head firmly and use pliers to peel skin toward tail.*

Flatfish *Place dark side of fish up, and cut across skin where tail joins body. Beginning at the cut, with knife or hand, pry up a piece of skin. Grasp skin flap with one hand while anchoring fish with other hand. Pull skin away from cut and over head. Turn fish over. Holding head, pull skin down to tail.*

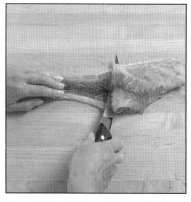

Roundfish *Make a slit across body just behind gills and another slit just above tail. Make another cut down back. Using a thin knife, separate skin from flesh, starting at tail. Pull (don't saw) knife toward head, holding skin firmly with other hand.*

CUTTING FILLETS AND STEAKS

To fillet a skinned flatfish Place skinned fish on a board with eyes up. Cut through flesh to the backbone (which is in the middle of the fish) from head to tail. Insert knife blade at a shallow angle between ribs and end of the fillet close to the head. Cut down the length of a fillet on one side of the backbone and remove it. Cut remaining fillet using the same technique. Turn fish over and remove two bottom fillets; rinse fillets in cold water.

To fillet flatfish with skin left on Cut along line that runs along skin to expose backbone. Cut around backbone to expose ribs. Insert knife between ribs and the end of fillet close to the head. Continue as for skinned flatfish. Turn fish over, cut through line on skin, and cut back away from backbone for one fillet; repeat on other side for second fillet.

To skin a flatfish fillet Place fish skin side down on a board; at tail end cut down at a 45-degree angle to the skin, but not all the way through. Pick up flesh at slit to get at skin. Holding skin taut, slide knife along skin without cutting it, wiggling skin back and forth (this motion will help the knife scrape through between flesh and skin).

To fillet a roundfish Make a very shallow cut along either side of the backbone with the tip of a paring knife, just to release ribs from backbone; don't cut into flesh. Entering fish at dorsal fin hole, slice along backbone from hole to tail; cut across tail, reverse direction, and cut up to head, stopping at gill cut. Trim half fillet from head by cutting down through backbone.

To remove backbone Slip knife under backbone about half way down from head; cut back to tail; reverse and cut back to head. Pull bone up and off to head; cut away head. To remove ribs, slip knife just under rib; cut away from you to remove ribs. Use tweezers or strawberry huller to remove any fine bones that may remain.

Cutting a steak Using a large, sharp knife, cut off the head just behind gills. Slice the fish crosswise into steaks of the desired thickness, usually between 1 and 1½ inches.

■ CLASSIC BAKED FISH

This recipe lends itself to the use of any number of sauces, which can change the flavor of the fish in a variety of interesting ways.

    1 whole fish (3 to 4 lb), cleaned
 1½ teaspoons salt
  ½ teaspoon freshly ground pepper
  ½ lemon, sliced
      Unsalted butter, for greasing
  ½ cup water

1. Preheat oven to 425° F. Rub fish with salt, pepper, and lemon slices. Generously grease a large baking dish with butter. Place fish in dish and pour in the water.

2. Grease parchment paper or foil with unsalted butter and place over fish in baking dish.

3. Bake for 20 to 35 minutes; baking time depends on thickness of fish. Serve with sauce of your choice.

Serves 4 to 6.

■ BROILED SALMON
WITH SOUFFLE TOPPING

If you substitute dried herbs for fresh, use whole leaves. Serve this salmon dish with Fried Green Tomatoes (see page 581).

  ¾ cup unsalted butter
    1 large shallot, minced
    2 tablespoons minced fresh tarragon *or*
       1 tablespoon dried tarragon
    1 tablespoon minced fresh dill *or*
       ½ tablespoon dried dill
    2 tablespoons snipped fresh chives
    6 salmon fillets or steaks

Soufflé Topping

 1½ cups Mayonnaise (see page 519)
    2 tablespoons minced fresh *or*
       1 tablespoon dried tarragon
    1 tablespoon minced fresh *or*
       ½ tablespoon dried dill
    2 tablespoons snipped fresh chives
    2 egg whites

1. Preheat broiler. In a small saucepan melt butter. Add shallot, tarragon, dill, and chives. Place salmon in a large, heat-resistant gratin dish, and brush fish with the herb butter. Broil until fish is cooked (about 10 minutes); broiling time depends on thickness of fish.

2. Cover salmon with Soufflé Topping. Broil until puffy and brown (2 to 3 minutes).

Serves 6.

Soufflé Topping In a small bowl combine Mayonnaise, tarragon, dill, and chives. Mix well. Beat egg whites until stiff but not dry; fold into mayonnaise mixture.

■ STURGEON BROCHETTE
WITH HONEY MUSTARD SAUCE

A brochette is usually served on a bed of rice. Try delicious Onion and Rice Soubise instead.

    4 sturgeon steaks (6 oz each), cut in
       6 to 8 equal pieces
    1 cup whipping cream
    3 tablespoons dry white wine
    1 tablespoon honey
    1 tablespoon coarse-grain mustard

Onion and Rice Soubise

    2 pounds white onions
    3 tablespoons unsalted butter
  ¾ cup rice
    2 cups Fish Fumet (see page 451) or
       Chicken Stock (see page 560)
    1 teaspoon salt
  ⅓ teaspoon white pepper
  ⅓ cup whipping cream
    2 tablespoons unsalted butter

1. Preheat broiler. Place fish on metal skewers.

2. In a small saucepan over medium-high heat, reduce cream by half (watch carefully to prevent cream from boiling over). When reduced add wine, honey, and mustard. Mix well, simmer 1 minute, and remove from heat.

3. Brush sturgeon with sauce. Place fish on baking sheet and broil 2 to 3 minutes, turning once. Serve with remaining sauce on a bed of Onion and Rice Soubise.

Serves 4 to 6.

Onion and Rice Soubise Peel and coarsely slice onions. Melt the 3 tablespoons butter in a saucepan, add onions and cook for 5 to 7 minutes. Add rice, mix well, then add fumet, salt, and pepper. Cover and simmer 30 minutes. Purée the mixture in a food processor, adding cream and the 2 tablespoons butter. Reheat over low heat. Adjust seasonings and serve.

■ SWORDFISH PAILLARD WITH SALSA

In this recipe, *paillard* refers to a large, thin slice of fish. Serve with tortilla chips or warm corn tortillas.

    6 swordfish steaks (each ½-inch thick)
    3 tablespoons unsalted butter, melted
    1 teaspoon salt
  ½ teaspoon freshly ground pepper
      Salsa Cruda (see page 521)

1. Preheat broiler. Brush fish with butter and sprinkle with salt and pepper.

2. Broil fish 4 inches from heat for 1½ minutes. Turning the fish is unnecessary. Serve with Salsa Cruda.

Serves 6.

COOKING IN OIL

Sautéing, stir-frying, panfrying, and deep-frying are different cooking methods that have in common their reliance on the use of fats, a term that includes oils. Sautéing uses a very small amount of fat that often becomes part of the finished dish. Deep-fried food, on the other hand, is totally immersed in fat, which is not served with the final dish. Both of these cooking processes use extremely high temperatures; this seals in the flavor and succulence of the fish. To avoid greasy fried foods, it is important to monitor the temperature of the cooking fat; if too cool, the food could absorb the fat, and if too hot, the food will burn on its surface before being done inside.

▧ PAN-FRIED CATFISH

As a bottom feeder, the "wild" catfish has an uncertain culinary reputation, but the rolling green hills of Tennessee are studded with limpid freshwater ponds where catfish are carefully bred and raised. Typically, a catfish farm includes a ramshackle roadside restaurant, from which an irresistible aroma of crisp, cornmeal-coated fried catfish wafts up and down the highway. One taste is enough to improve the catfish's reputation.

  4 to 6 small catfish (about 1 lb each) *or*
    2 to 3 pounds thick fillets from larger catfish
 ½ cup flour
  1 teaspoon salt
 ½ teaspoon coarsely ground pepper
  2 eggs
  1 tablespoon water
  1 cup white cornmeal
    Oil, for frying

1. Rinse catfish in cold water; dry with paper towels.

2. Mix flour, salt, and pepper. Dredge fish in the mixture and shake off excess. Place fish on waxed paper. Place eggs in a pie pan, add the water, and beat lightly to combine. Spread cornmeal on a large plate.

3. Heat ¼ inch oil in a large, heavy skillet (or two skillets, to cook all the fish at once). While oil is heating, dip fish in egg mixture, then roll in cornmeal to coat thoroughly, gently pressing the cornmeal onto fish. Place each coated fish on waxed paper.

4. When oil is rippling and fragrant (350° F), gently add fish to skillet(s), using long tongs to protect against spattering oil. Fry until coating is browned and fish is cooked through, turning carefully midway through cooking. Whole fish takes about 3 minutes per side, fillets 2 minutes per side. (For fillets, check doneness by inserting a knife; flesh should flake easily. For whole fish, inspect the flesh at the opening. Catfish retains a slightly pink color when cooked, but the flesh turns opaque.) Drain fish on paper towels and keep in the oven at low heat until ready to serve.

Serves 4 to 6.

▧ HOT-AND-SOUR SHARK

Shark is a wonderfully full-flavored and versatile fish that lends itself to many types of cooking. Its lean flesh makes it well-suited for cooking techniques that use fat or other liquid—here a combination of deep-frying and stir-frying. The technique of coating with egg white and partially cooking the fish is called velveting and is common in Chinese cuisine. It produces a particularly attractive, crispy finish. Serve with steamed rice. For directions on how to prepare the sticky type of rice favored by the Chinese, see About Cooking Rice, page 274.

  2 cups water
    Zest of 1 orange, julienned
  2 egg whites
  2 tablespoons dry sherry
  3 tablespoons cornstarch
  4 tablespoons peanut oil
  1 teaspoon salt
  1 pound shark, cut in 1- by ½-inch cubes
    Oil, for deep-frying
 ½ cup fresh orange juice
 ½ cup Chicken Stock (see page 560)
  4 tablespoons rice vinegar
  2 tablespoons sugar
  2 tablespoons soy sauce
 ½ cup julienned ginger (2-in. strips)
  2 dried red chiles, seeded and minced
 ½ cup slivered green onion (3-in. strips)
  1 cup seeded, julienned red bell pepper
  2 tablespoons minced green onion

1. In a medium saucepan bring the water to a boil over medium-high heat. Add julienned orange zest and boil 1 minute. Remove zest from saucepan with slotted spoon, drain, and reserve.

2. In a medium bowl combine egg whites, sherry, 2 tablespoons of the cornstarch, 2 tablespoons of the peanut oil, and salt. Add shark pieces to mixture and toss to coat well.

3. In a Dutch oven, heavy deep skillet, or other frying kettle, heat at least 2 inches of oil for deep-frying to 350° F. Add shark pieces and fry until golden brown on all sides (2 to 3 minutes). Remove shark and drain on paper towels. Keep warm.

4. In small bowl combine orange juice, Chicken Stock, vinegar, remaining 1 tablespoon cornstarch, sugar, and soy sauce. In wok heat remaining 2 tablespoons peanut oil. Add ginger and chiles; stir-fry 1 minute. Add the ½ cup slivered green onion and bell pepper; stir-fry 1 minute. Add orange juice mixture; stir until it thickens.

5. Transfer shark to wok, add zest, toss, and reheat. Garnish with the 2 tablespoons minced green onion and serve immediately.

Serves 4 to 6.

Fresh trout is at its best when prepared simply. Here it is sautéed quickly, then served with a sauce of butter, lemon juice, and parsley, and garnished with toasted sliced almonds.

TROUT WITH ALMONDS

Golden sautéed almonds are a crisp, flavorful contrast to the delicate trout. You can use almost any small whole fish in this recipe.

    4 **medium trout, cleaned**
       Fresh lemon juice
       Freshly cracked black peppercorns
    6 **tablespoons butter**
    2 **tablespoons oil**
  ½ **cup sliced almonds**
  ¼ **cup *each* fresh lemon juice or white wine and minced parsley**
       Lemon slices and dill sprigs, for garnish

1. Rub trout with lemon juice and pepper.

2. Warm serving platter for fish in 200° F oven.

3. In a wide frying pan large enough to hold the 4 trout (use two pans if necessary), melt 2 tablespoons of the butter with the oil over medium-high heat. Add trout and sauté until lightly browned on one side. Turn when edges become opaque and curl slightly (3 to 5 minutes). The fish is done when it flakes at the touch of a fork at the thickest portion near the backbone. Remove fish to warm platter. Wipe out pan.

4. Melt the remaining ¼ cup butter in pan. Add almonds and sauté until golden.

5. Combine lemon juice and parsley and add to almonds. Swirl and pour sauce over trout. Garnish with lemon slices and sprigs of dill.

Serves 4.

BLACKENED FISH

The technique of charring fish in a hot cast-iron skillet was created by Paul Prudhomme especially for Louisiana redfish. It is now prepared coast to coast in Cajun and Creole restaurants. A good exhaust fan is essential because a great deal of smoke is given off during cooking. The fish cooks rapidly, so to avoid fish that are finished on the outside but underdone within, use fillets that are not more than ½ inch thick.

  ½ **cup unsalted butter, melted**
    4 **tablespoons vegetable oil**
    1 **teaspoon salt**
    1 **teaspoon cayenne pepper**
  ½ **teaspoon freshly ground black pepper**
  ½ **teaspoon dried thyme**
  ½ **teaspoon paprika**
    4 **fish fillets (about 2 lb total), each ½ inch thick**

1. Place a cast-iron skillet over high heat until white hot (about 10 minutes).

2. Combine 4 tablespoons of the butter with oil in a shallow bowl. In another small bowl mix salt, cayenne, black pepper, thyme, and paprika. Dip each fish fillet in butter-oil mixture, then sprinkle with about 1 teaspoon seasoning mixture.

3. Place fillets in hot pan for exactly 2 minutes. Turn fillets over and cook second side for exactly 2 minutes. Remove from pan and serve immediately, drizzled with remaining butter.

Serves 4.

MOIST-HEAT COOKING

Fish requires delicate cooking. Moist heat provides a gentle means of cooking that is suitable for any type of fish. Moist-heat cooking methods—poaching, steaming, braising, and stewing—use liquid as a cooking medium. The differences among these methods lie in whether the food is cooked above the liquid (steaming) or in it (poaching, braising, and stewing), and in whether the cooking liquid is served as a part of the finished dish (braising and stewing) or not (poaching and steaming).

▨ STEAMED WHOLE FISH, CHINESE-STYLE

This presentation of steamed fish is a Chinese classic. The use of more fresh onions and herbs at the finish enhances the dish. Serve with steamed or fried rice.

  1 whole carp or sea bass, cleaned
  2 tablespoons soy sauce
  2 tablespoons dry sherry
  ¼ cup julienned peeled fresh ginger
  2 green onions, slivered (4-in. strips; use part of the green)
  8 sprigs cilantro
     Cilantro, for garnish
     Green onion, slivered, for garnish

1. Place fish on plate in steaming rack. (If you do not have a steamer large enough, put the plate on a rack in a turkey roaster.)

2. Sprinkle soy sauce, sherry, ginger, and the 2 slivered green onions over fish. Arrange the 8 sprigs of cilantro on top of fish.

3. Pour boiling water into pan until it comes within 1 inch of fish. Cover and steam about 15 minutes (cooking time depends on the size of the fish).

4. Remove plate from steamer and serve fish directly from plate. Garnish with cilantro and green onion.

Serves 6 to 8.

▨ COLD FILLET OF SOLE WITH CILANTRO, LIME, AND POMEGRANATE

This dish makes a wonderfully cool summer lunch or a fine first course to balance a heavy entrée such as lamb. To seed a pomegranate, see page 453.

  8 fillets sole
  1 teaspoon salt
  ½ teaspoon freshly ground pepper
 16 sprigs cilantro
  2 jalapeño or serrano chiles, seeded, deveined, and minced
  6 to 8 cups Wine Court Bouillon (page 450)
     Cilantro leaves
     Lime juice
  8 thin slices of lime, for garnish
  ½ cup pomegranate seeds, for garnish

1. Pat fillets dry. Place outer side of fillet down and sprinkle with salt and pepper. Place 2 sprigs of cilantro and some of the minced chiles in the center of each fillet. Fold the fillets in thirds and place folded side down in a wide, shallow saucepan.

2. Pour court bouillon over fish. The fish should be completely immersed. Cover and bring to a simmer. Poach 8 to 10 minutes. Remove from heat and cool in poaching liquid. When cool, remove from liquid.

3. To serve, sprinkle fish with the cilantro leaves and fresh lime juice. Top each fillet with a slice of lime and some pomegranate seeds.

Serves 8.

▨ PORTUGUESE FISH STEW

The distinct flavors and the herbaceous quality of the kale provide a perfect foil for the fish. The original dish used salted cod instead of fresh fish; in this version the smoked ham supplies the extra flavor.

  3 tablespoons olive oil
  2 pounds cod
  ¼ cup fruity olive oil
  3 pounds new potatoes, cooked, peeled, and cut in ½-inch dice
  8 cloves garlic, peeled and quartered
  1 pound kale, shredded in ¼-inch strips
     Salt and freshly ground black pepper
  ¼ pound smoked ham cut in slivers
  1 cup dry white wine

1. In a large Dutch oven heat the 3 tablespoons olive oil. Add fish to pan, fry 1 minute on each side, and remove from pan.

2. Add the ¼ cup olive oil to pan. Add potatoes and toss over medium heat until coated. Add garlic and sauté 1 minute. Add kale to pan, turning to coat with oil. Cover and cook until the greens begin to wilt (2 to 3 minutes).

3. Sprinkle potatoes and greens with salt, pepper, and slivered ham. Arrange fish on top and pour in wine. Add enough water to barely reach top of greens.

4. Cover and simmer 25 to 35 minutes, shaking pan occasionally. When potatoes are done, correct seasonings and serve.

Serves 6 to 8.

OTHER WAYS WITH FISH

Not all fish is cooked in the conventional way, or even cooked at all. The recipes here are for Japanese sushi (see opposite page), which is vinegared rice garnished with raw fish and served with various condiments. Scandinavian gravlax (see opposite page) consists of raw fish in a dry, sugar-based marinade; and Latin American seviche (see page 234) uses citrus juice to firm up fish protein in much the same way that heat does.

NIGIRI SUSHI

Although it takes many years to become a full-fledged sushi chef, any cook with a sharp knife can make a modest platter of *nigiri* sushi. Nigiri are thin slices of raw fish draped across "fingers" of molded sushi rice. Tuna and shrimp both lend themselves to this treatment. See the photographs at right for guidance in making sushi. Accompany sushi with warm sake (Japanese rice wine), a dry white wine, or cocktails.

> 1 tablespoon wasabi (Japanese horseradish, available powdered in Japanese markets)
> 2 tablespoons rice vinegar
> 1 cup water
> 1½ pounds fresh tuna fillet, in one piece
> 2 cups Sushi Rice (recipe follows)

Wasabi Dipping Sauce

> 2 tablespoons wasabi (see note, above)
> ¼ cup soy sauce
> 2 tablespoons minced green onion
> 1 tablespoon rice wine

1. In a small bowl mix *wasabi* with just enough cold water to form a thick paste. Set aside. In another bowl combine rice vinegar and water. Slice fish into twenty-four 1-ounce portions.

2. Using the vinegar-water solution to keep your hands damp, pick up a small portion of rice and gently form it into a small oval. Dot the top of the oval with a little wasabi paste and place a slice of tuna on top. Repeat with remaining rice and tuna. Arrange sushi on a platter, preferably a Japanese-style lacquer or porcelain tray. Serve with dipping sauce.

Makes 2 dozen sushi.

Wasabi Dipping Sauce Combine wasabi with just enough cold water to form a thick paste. Just before serving, combine wasabi paste, soy sauce, green onions, and rice wine.

SUSHI RICE

A vinegar dressing adds flavor to this rice, which has a sticky, but not mushy, consistency.

> 3⅓ cups short-grain rice
> 4 cups water
> 1 three-inch square of konbu (dried kelp, available in Japanese markets); optional

Vinegar Dressing

> 5 to 6 tablespoons rice vinegar
> 5 tablespoons sugar
> 4 teaspoons salt

1. Place rice in a large bowl; cover with cold water. Run hands through rice to remove starch, until water turns cloudy; drain. Repeat until water remains clear; drain.

2. Place rice in saucepan with the 4 cups cold water. Place *konbu* (if used) on top. Cover saucepan and bring to a boil over high heat; boil 2 minutes. Reduce heat to medium and boil, covered, for 5 minutes. Reduce heat to lowest possible setting and cook until all moisture is absorbed (about 15 minutes). Uncover; place a towel over top of pot, and cover again. Let rest 15 minutes.

3. With a thin tool like a wooden spatula held vertically, cut dressing into cooked rice, being careful not to mash rice. Mix until rice is glossy and holds together but is not mushy. Rice may be kept in a cool place, covered with a damp cloth, for up to 2 days; it should not be refrigerated.

Makes about 6 cups.

Vinegar Dressing In a small saucepan over low heat, combine all ingredients and cook until sugar and salt dissolve. Cool to room temperature. Keeps indefinitely.

GRAVLAX

Salt and sugar draw out juices, while the flavors of herbs and spices are absorbed by the fish.

> 1 salmon (4 lb), boned, head removed, skin intact
> ¼ cup kosher salt
> ¼ cup sugar
> 1 tablespoon crushed white peppercorns
> 1 cup chopped fresh dill

Mustard Sauce

> 4 tablespoons Creole mustard
> 1 teaspoon hot mustard
> 3 tablespoons sugar
> 2 tablespoons white vinegar
> ⅓ cup vegetable oil
> 2 to 3 tablespoons chopped fresh dill

1. Cut salmon into 2 pieces along the backbone. Wipe dry. In a small bowl, combine salt, sugar, and peppercorns, and rub fish on both sides with mixture. In a large, deep dish, sprinkle part of salt mixture and one third of the dill. Lay one piece of fish in dish, sprinkle with one third of the dill, and some salt mixture. Lay other piece of fish on top of the first piece. Sprinkle with remaining salt mixture and dill.

2. Cover tightly with foil, place heavy book or two bricks on top of foil to press down on fish. Refrigerate. After 4 to 6 hours some liquid will leach out; discard it. Refrigerate for 3 days, turning periodically so that the salt and seasonings penetrate evenly.

3. Before serving, drain fish on towel and scrape off the marinade. Place each fillet skin side down on serving board and cut thin diagonal slices across the grain. Serve with Mustard Sauce.

Serves 10 to 12.

Mustard Sauce In a small bowl combine all ingredients. Mix well.

HOW TO MAKE NIGIRI SUSHI

Slice boned fish fillet across the grain, approximately ¼ inch thick, to fit the shape of the rice oval (see middle photograph). To butterfly shrimp, using a sharp knife, slit the shrimp down its back, being careful not to cut all the way through. Gently flatten out the shrimp, with the cut side down.

Moisten hands with mixture of rice vinegar and water (see Nigiri Sushi recipe at left). Form a small amount of Sushi Rice (see recipe at left) into an oval.

Finished Nigiri Sushi: Rice oval is topped with a dab of wasabi paste and a slice of fish or a butterflied shrimp.

Fresh cauliflower and broccoli florets can be tray-frozen (see page 242) and then packaged airtight for later use.

■ SEVICHE

Putting limes in boiling water for one minute will yield more juice, as will warming them in a microwave oven at 50 percent power for one minute.

1½ **pounds white-fleshed fish, skinned and boned**
1½ **cups fresh lime juice**
1 **cup vegetable oil**
1 **cup fresh orange juice**
1 to 2 **hot red chiles, seeded and slivered**
1 **small onion, sliced paper-thin**
1 **clove garlic, minced**
 Kosher salt and freshly ground pepper, to taste

1. Cut fish into ½-inch cubes; place in a small glass dish and cover with lime juice. It is extremely important that lime juice covers all of the fish. Add more if necessary.

2. Cover with plastic wrap and refrigerate for 4 to 5 hours. In the meantime, combine vegetable oil, orange juice, chiles, onion, and garlic. After fish has marinated for 3 hours, add orange juice mixture. Chill at least 2 more hours. Add salt and pepper to taste.

Serves 6 to 8.

Recipes and Related Information
Alder-Grilled Salmon, 296; Bombay Tuna, 509; Cioppino, 556; Coulibiac, 377; Dry Spice Rub for Fish, 350; Fritto Misto With Caper Mayonnaise, 176; Grilled Tuna, 295; Makizushi, 392; Poached Fish Steaks With Fresh Herbs and Cream, 452; Quenelles, 241; Steamed Salmon Steaks With Black Bean Sauce, 554.

FLAMBE, TO; FLAME, TO

To ignite foods that have liquor added, done for dramatic effect and to develop a rich flavor. Cherries Jubilee (see page 315)—vanilla ice cream with a sauce of cherries, brandy, and kirsch—is finished this way. Many savory sautés are flamed to enhance the perfume of the sauce.

If using a gas burner, tip pan slightly so wafting fumes ignite. For either gas or electric burners, ignite with a long kitchen or fireplace match. Let cook until flame disappears (at this point all alcohol has burned off). To retain some alcohol for its flavor, cover flaming dish to extinguish, or snuff out by adding wine or stock.

Liquor can also be heated in a microwave oven: Set in microwave-safe dish and heat 30 to 45 seconds at 100 percent power.

Caution Never pour liquor from a bottle into a pan that is near an open flame. The flame can follow the stream of alcohol into the bottle and cause it to explode. Remove food from heat, add liquor (from a small pan or dish; if from the bottle, remember to set bottle away from cooking area after use), and return pan to burner.

FLAVOR, TO; FLAVORING

To give or enhance taste by the addition of extra ingredients. Extracts, herbs and spices, and wines and liqueurs are commonly used for this purpose.

A flavoring is any substance that adds taste.

Recipes and Related Information
Extract and Essence, 213; Herb, 299; Spice, 549; Wine in Cooking, 608.

FLORET

These bud clusters that form the head of broccoli and cauliflower are often cut from their stalks and cooked separately. They are also called flowerets. Fresh broccoli has tightly closed flower buds, without yellowing; a head of fresh cauliflower should be creamy white and free of brown spots.

FLOUR, TO; FLOUR

To coat with flour; the finely ground meal itself. Flour is often used as a covering for foods that will be sautéed or panfried. It acts as a barrier to keep the surface of food dry (moisture causes hot oil to sputter and drop in temperature; wet foods steam instead of fry and don't brown properly). A light first layer of flour also helps batters and bread crumb coatings adhere better. Bakers often dust cake pans with flour to prevent sticking and, in some cases, to give batter something to grip as it rises. Always remove excess flour; otherwise the coat will be unpleasantly thick. To do this, lightly tap the food or pan with your hand so that the coating is even, but fine.

Flour as an ingredient is a difficult word to define precisely. Although it most commonly describes the powdery meal derived from a grain (wheat flour, rye flour), some flours (soy flour, chick-pea flour) are ground from legumes or are made from potatoes and other starchy vegetables, nuts, and carob. For clarity of presentation, the following remarks apply only to wheat flour. Other flours are discussed separately at the end of the section.

FROM GRAIN TO FLOUR: MILLING, BLEACHING, AND AGING

Milling is the process that turns whole hard grain into fine flour. Historically most grains were ground into flour between rotating stones. Although stone-ground flour is still available, especially in health-food stores, most flour today is milled between two grooved rollers.

The mechanical rollers crack the grain, allowing germ and bran to be sieved off the endosperm (the heart of the grain). The endosperm is then ground to desired size. For whole grain flours, bran and germ are then added back. The mechanical rollers generate considerable heat; if the high-fat germ and bran were left in during grinding, the heat would accelerate rancidity.

Wheat flour has a light yellow color after milling. For aesthetic reasons, some wheat flour is bleached, usually with chlorine dioxide, to turn it white quickly. If allowed to age for one or two months it would turn white naturally through oxidation. Aging improves baking qualities but takes time and space. To speed the process, both bleached and unbleached flours are chemically aged with potassium bromate or iodate.

Use Wheat flour serves as a thickener; as a coating for fried foods; as the basis for noodles; as the foundation of many batters such as those for pancakes, waffles, and fritters; and as the main ingredient in an enormous variety of baked goods, from breads, muffins, and biscuits to cakes, cookies, pies, and pastries.

Wheat flour is a protein food that is highly absorbent. When mixed with a liquid and manipulated, two of the water-soluble proteins—glutenin and gliadin—combine to form gluten. As a batter or dough is stirred, beaten, or mixed, strands of gluten develop into a cellular, elastic network that traps air and other gases released by leavening agents. In the oven, heat causes these gases to expand, which in turn stretches the gluten. This expansion creates volume and lightness in breads, cakes, pastries, and all leavened baked goods. Toward the end of the baking time, the proteins firm, giving the final product its structure. The amount of gluten that can be developed in any batter or dough is directly related to the protein content of the flour (see Availability for a discussion of the types of flour, including protein content; also see About Nonwheat Flours).

Baking Flour gives structure to an endless variety of baked goods. When a firm, sturdy texture is desired, as for breads, the dough is kneaded repeatedly to help develop gluten (see KNEAD). When a tender, crumbly texture is desired, as in cakes and pie crusts, the moistened flour is handled lightly to avoid development of gluten.

Batter Flour gives structure to batters for fritters, pancakes, waffles, and crêpes. To avoid development of gluten and to ensure a tender texture, flour should be mixed in lightly; overmixing produces a tough texture.

Coating Pan-fried foods, such as fish, veal and pork scallops, and sliced eggplant, are usually dusted with flour before cooking to prevent them from sticking. Deep-fried foods, such as chicken, fish, and onion rings, are frequently given an initial light dusting with flour to promote the formation of a protective coating that will keep moisture in.

Thickening When dissolved in a hot liquid, the starch granules in flour swell, absorbing water molecules and causing the mixture to thicken. Flour is added to sauces, stews, soups, puddings, and creams for this purpose. As a rule, using 1 tablespoon flour per cup of liquid produces a thin sauce; using 2 tablespoons per cup produces a medium-thick sauce; using 3 tablespoons per cup produces a thick sauce. In general, flour-thickened liquids should be cooked for at least several minutes after flour is added to remove any raw flour taste.

Availability The flours sold to consumers are of three basic kinds: hard-wheat, soft-wheat, and all-purpose.

All-Purpose Flour A blend of hard- and soft-wheat flours, this type is a hybrid. Its medium protein and starch content makes it acceptable for most culinary purposes. All-purpose flour can successfully be used in both bread and cake recipes, although it will not produce the superior product a specialized flour will. In most recipes that call simply for flour, use all-purpose flour.

Durum Flour Ground from durum wheat, the hardest wheat grown, durum flour makes an extremely sturdy dough and is thus the choice for commercially manufactured dried pasta. Durum flour is also known as semolina. It is coarsely ground and never bleached.

Enriched Flour When bran and germ are removed from wheat flour during milling, most of the A and B vitamins and iron are removed as well. To make enriched flour, the B vitamins and iron are added back. Some manufacturers also add calcium and vitamin D. Enrichment is not mandated at the federal level; however, 38 states require enrichment of white flour to specifications determined by each state.

Gluten Flour or High-Gluten Flour This flour is derived from hard wheat that has been treated to remove some of its starch and concentrate its protein. It contains at least 70 percent pure gluten. Gluten flour is used in special diets for people who cannot otherwise tolerate wheat flour. It can be used in combination with low-gluten flours to improve the gluten-forming abilities of a dough, or it can be combined with regular wheat flour in bread doughs in the ratio of two to one. If used this way, decrease kneading time by one fourth to avoid overdeveloping gluten. The first rising will be quicker, the second rising slower than for a regular wheat dough.

Hard-Wheat Flour (Bread Flour) This type is generally packaged as bread flour. It is ground from hard wheat—wheat with a high protein and low starch content. The relatively high quantities of glutenin and gliadin make hard-wheat flour preferable for baking bread.

Self-Rising Flour The miller has preblended chemical leavenings and salt into flour to make self-rising flour, most common in southern states. Unless self-rising flour is stored under ideal conditions and turns over quickly in the store, the leavenings may lose some of their potency. It is inadvisable to use self-rising flour in recipes that don't specify it.

Soft-Wheat Flour This flour has a low protein and high starch content. When moistened, it develops weak gluten, so the products made from soft-wheat flours are tender and crumbly. Consequently, soft-wheat flour is preferred for cakes and some pastries. The product identified in supermarkets as cake flour is a soft-wheat flour. Pastry flour contains less protein than all-purpose flour and more protein than cake flour.

Whole Wheat or Graham Flour This flour is milled from the whole kernel: endosperm (the central, starchy cells), bran (the skin of the kernel), and germ (the portion containing the seed). Used alone, whole wheat flour produces a heavy, compact, dark bread. The bran and germ tend to hamper gluten formation by shearing the developing gluten strands. The resulting dough rises slowly and forms a finished bread that is denser than a comparable bread made with white flour.

Storage Refined flour should be kept in an airtight container in a cool, dry, dark place and used within six months. Whole grain flours turn rancid much faster because they contain the oil-rich germ and bran. They should be stored in an airtight container, refrigerated, and used within three months.

Preparation Measure flour by spooning it lightly into a measuring cup, then leveling off the top with the straight edge of a metal spatula or knife. For greatest accuracy, professional bakers and some home bakers use a scale to measure flour (see MEASURE). Most yeast bread and certain quick bread recipes call for a varying amount of flour (3 to 3½ cups, for example). This range is indicated because different flours absorb different amounts of liquid. Softness or hardness of the wheat from which the flour was milled affects absorbency, as does humidity in the air. Add just enough flour to produce the type of batter or dough described in your recipe.

ABOUT NONWHEAT FLOURS

Nonwheat flours have very little or no glutenin and gliadin, the two proteins that combine with water to form gluten (see Use). Rye and triticale flours have more than other nonwheat flours, but neither has enough to make a light-textured bread on its own. To yield a loaf with a pleasing texture, nonwheat flours must be combined with wheat flour. The following individual entries give recommended proportions of nonwheat flour to wheat flour to produce a satisfactory final product. Exceeding the proportion results in a heavier loaf.

Barley Flour This type is available in some health-food stores. On its own it makes a dense, heavy bread. To add its nutty, malty flavor to a loaf while retaining a light texture, use no more than 1 part barley flour to 5 parts wheat flour.

Brown Rice Flour Available in some health-food stores, brown rice flour contains rice bran and germ. It has a nuttier, richer flavor than white rice flour and produces a darker loaf. Use no more than 1 part brown rice flour to 4 parts wheat flour in a bread dough. Store brown rice flour in refrigerator to slow rancidity.

Buckwheat Flour Carried in some health-food stores, it adds a full-bodied, earthy flavor to wheat breads but on its own makes a dense, heavy bread. To make a light-textured loaf, use no more than 1 part buckwheat flour to 4 parts wheat flour. Buckwheat flour is also traditionally used in Russian blini and in French Brittany crêpes.

Corn Flour Cream-colored and slightly sweet, corn flour is more finely ground than cornmeal; some health-food stores carry it. Because of its lack of gluten-forming proteins, use no more than 1 part corn flour to 4 parts wheat flour in a bread dough. Do not confuse with cornstarch, which is used as a thickener.

Millet Flour It adds a nutlike, slightly sweet flavor to wheat breads, and is available in some health-food stores. To retain a light texture, use no more than 1 part millet flour to 4 parts wheat flour in bread doughs.

Oat Flour This flour contains a natural antioxidant and will improve the longevity of a loaf of bread. It is, however, very low in gluten-forming proteins. To add its sweet, earthy flavor to a loaf while retaining a light texture, use no more than 1 part oat flour to 3 parts wheat flour. Buy oat flour at health-food stores.

Potato Flour Also known as potato starch, potato flour is made from steamed potatoes that have been dried and ground. It is stark white and very fine. Potato flour is a useful thickening agent for some delicate sauces. Because it gelatinizes quickly and does not impart a flavor of its own, it is good for last-minute corrections. Sauces thickened with potato flour will not hold very long and should not be heated over 175° F. Potato flour is a tender starch and is desirable in some cakes and cookies; it is called for in many cakes for Jewish Passover to replace the wheat flour forbidden during the holiday. It is also a suitable flour for those on a gluten-free diet.

Rye Flour Well-stocked supermarkets and most health-food stores sell rye flour in both medium and dark varieties. Dark rye contains the bran; medium rye sometimes does. Both produce a loaf with full-bodied, bitter, slightly sour flavor; in a dark rye loaf, the flavors are simply more pronounced. Rye flour contains some gluten-forming proteins but not enough to raise loaves well. For best results, use at least 1 part wheat flour to 2 parts medium rye, or 1 part wheat flour to 1 part dark rye in bread baking. Gluten formed by rye flour is fragile; knead a rye dough gently to avoid breaking gluten strands.

Soy Flour and Soya Flour   These are both derived from soybeans: Soy flour is ground from raw beans, soya flour from lightly toasted beans. In addition to a high protein content, both varieties have a high fat content; however, it is possible to find them with the fat partially or fully extracted. Soy and soya flours add a slightly sweet, pleasantly musty flavor to breads and improve shelf life. Because they do not have gluten-forming ability, use no more than 1 part soy or soya flour to 4 parts wheat flour in a bread dough. Breads containing soy flour brown quickly; reduce oven temperature about 25° F. Some health-food stores carry these types of flour.

Triticale Flour   This flour is ground from triticale, a cross between rye and wheat. Available in most health-food stores, it has the slightly bitter flavor of rye as well as the sweetness of wheat. On its own it produces a heavy, dense loaf. For best results, use no more than 1 part triticale flour to 1 part wheat flour in a bread dough. Like rye, triticale forms delicate gluten strands; doughs containing triticale should be kneaded and shaped gently.

White Rice Flour   Available in some health-food stores, white rice flour imparts a slightly sweet flavor to a loaf of bread. It is, however, very low in gluten-forming proteins. Use no more than 1 part rice flour to 4 parts wheat flour in a bread dough. Rice flour absorbs more liquid and absorbs it more slowly than wheat flour; adjust recipe and mixing times accordingly.

FLOWER, EDIBLE

Many plant blossoms are edible and tasty. Before experimenting with edible flowers, however, learn with certainty which ones are edible and make sure they have not been treated with pesticides or other harmful sprays often used on ornamental plants. Among the more familiar varieties of edible flowers are acacia and mimosa blossoms; almond blossoms; alyssum; apple, peach, and plum blossoms; borage; chrysanthemums; daisies; daylilies; dianthus; English primroses; geraniums; hollyhock; jasmine; lavender; lilacs; lily of the valley; nasturtiums; orange and lemon blossoms; pansies; pot marigolds; roses; squash blossoms; violas; and violets.

Use   Edible flowers make a beautiful garnish for all manner of dishes. Float them on drinks, sprinkle them on soups, or use them to brighten canapés. Some, such as nasturtium blossoms, have a peppery flavor that makes them a delicious addition to salads. Others, such as rose petals, are full of aromatic oils; they may be infused in creams and syrups to extract their perfume, then removed. The scent of fresh fruit blossoms or other aromatic blossoms flatters ice creams, puddings, and liquids for poaching fruit. Squash blossoms, especially zucchini, are often large enough to stuff; Italians serve them deep-fried, filled with cheese, and coated with egg and bread crumbs. When crystallized with egg white and sugar, edible flowers are a striking adornment for ice cream and other desserts.

Availability   Large, fresh zucchini blossoms are occasionally available in Italian or specialty markets. Some supermarkets now carry zucchini blossoms, tiny purple borage flowers, and nasturtium flowers in season, packed in plastic bags. Few other edible flowers are available commercially; home gardens are the best source for most edible varieties.

Selection   You are most certain of obtaining unsprayed blossoms if you harvest them from your own garden. If buying commercially grown flowers, confirm that they are free of pesticides. In cooking, flowers are used for their appearance as much as anything else, so choose those that look fresh, not bruised or wilted.

Storage   All edible flowers are fragile, some extremely so. If possible, use shortly after picking. Store flowers loosely in an airtight plastic bag in refrigerator.

Experiment with a range of edible flowers for a salad that's interesting and beautiful as well as tasty. The salad shown above includes nasturtiums, violets, rose petals, and rosemary blossoms, plus a mixture of less common greens such as arugula, chicory, and mâche.

Preparation If possible gather flowers in the early morning when dew has just dried on them. If necessary, wash gently and pat dry. If they must be held for several hours, dip in ice water to refresh them just before using. When adding flowers to a salad, incorporate them after salad has been dressed and tossed, just before serving.

▇ DEEP-FRIED ZUCCHINI BLOSSOMS

Fried squash blossoms are an Italian specialty that has stimulated many creative American chefs to develop their own versions. This recipe uses zucchini blossoms, available at specialty produce markets or from a home vegetable garden. The filling is a rich, seasoned blend of mozzarella cheese and hot peppers; a variation made with goat cheese and sun-dried tomato is offered as well. Serve this dish as an appetizer or first course.

Batter

        2 eggs, separated
     ½ cup water
     ¼ cup white wine
        2 tablespoons vegetable oil
        1 teaspoon Worcestershire sauce
        1 cup flour
     ½ teaspoon salt

Blossoms

     ½ to ¾ pound mozzarella cheese, cut into
            ½-inch cubes
        2 to 4 jalapeño chiles, chopped, *or* 1 can (4 oz)
            diced green chiles for a milder taste
      30 squash blossoms, flowers cleaned and
            stems removed
            Oil, for frying
            Salt and freshly ground pepper

Tomato Dipping Sauce

        3 shallots, finely chopped, *or* ½ onion,
            finely chopped
        2 tablespoons olive oil
        3 cloves garlic, finely chopped
     ½ teaspoon *each* crushed dried oregano, thyme,
            and basil *or* 1 teaspoon *each* chopped fresh
            oregano and thyme, and 1 tablespoon chopped
            fresh basil
        1 teaspoon sugar
        1 can (28 oz) plum tomatoes (preferably
            peeled, crushed, and with added purée)
     ½ teaspoon *each* salt and freshly ground pepper
            Dash hot-pepper sauce, or to taste
            Dash Worcestershire sauce, or to taste

1. *For the batter:* In a blender combine egg yolks, the water, wine, oil, Worcestershire sauce, flour, and salt on high speed. Let batter stand at least 1 hour.

2. *For the blossoms:* In a medium bowl toss together mozzarella and chopped chiles (do not handle chiles with bare hands; use a wooden spoon or wear gloves). Gently fill blossoms with cheese mixture. Twist ends of petals to enclose stuffing. (Blossoms may be prepared ahead to this point, chilled on paper towels, and brought to room temperature about 30 minutes before frying.)

3. *To cook:* In a Dutch oven, deep, heavy skillet, or other frying kettle, heat 3 to 4 inches of oil to 370° F. Beat reserved egg whites to soft peaks; fold into batter.

4. Dip blossoms into batter, making sure they are completely coated. Drop into hot oil, frying several at once, but do not crowd in pan. Fry until golden, turning occasionally. Remove from pan with a slotted spoon and drain on paper towels. Sprinkle with salt and pepper, and serve immediately accompanied with Tomato Dipping Sauce.

Makes 30 appetizers or 10 first courses.

Tomato Dipping Sauce In a medium saucepan sauté shallots in olive oil over medium heat until softened and transparent. Add garlic and cook 30 seconds. Add oregano, thyme, basil, and sugar, then tomatoes, and bring to a boil, stirring. Reduce heat to simmer and cook, stirring occasionally to prevent scorching, until a rich sauce develops, thick enough to coat stirring spoon (about 30 minutes). Taste, add salt, pepper, hot-pepper sauce, and Worcestershire sauce; adjust seasonings if necessary. Serve hot, at room temperature, or cold. If a smoother, less chunky sauce is desired, purée in a blender or food processor, or strain through a sieve or food mill.

Makes 2 to 2½ cups.

Variation Combine ¾ pound softened goat cheese with 6 to 8 chopped sun-dried tomatoes. Use this mixture to fill zucchini blossoms. Twist ends of petals to enclose stuffing. Proceed with step 3 in main recipe.

▇ CRYSTALLIZED FLOWERS

These flowers make lovely edible decorations for elegant desserts. Choose white or brightly colored flowers (not sprayed or treated in any way) with simple petal arrangements, such as small orchids, roses, sweet peas, and violets. This treatment also works well with grapes.

Wash blossoms quickly and gently pat dry with paper towels. Place 1 egg white in a small bowl; beat until foamy. Dip flowers, one at a time, in egg white or apply egg white with a small artist's brush; cover all parts of petals. Remove excess egg white so that petals won't stick together.

Sprinkle or sift superfine sugar over petals. Cover all egg white, shaking to avoid clumping. Blow softly on flowers to remove excess sugar. Place flowers on an aluminum foil–lined baking sheet. Let dry in cool area or in refrigerator for 2 to 3 days.

Recipes and Related Information
Candy, 93; Salad, 506.

FLUFF, TO

To lighten texture and remove lumps by tossing with a fork. Rice is commonly fluffed before serving to separate the cooked grains.

FLUTE, TO

To make an attractive edge on a pie crust by pinching the pastry with thumb and index finger into interconnecting V shapes or scallops. Decorative grooves or channels are also cut into mushrooms and other vegetables and fruits.

FOLD, TO; FOLD IN, TO

To incorporate a light, aerated mixture (usually beaten egg whites or whipped cream) into a heavier mixture without deflating the lighter mixture. This can be done with your hand, a rubber spatula, or a spoon, and with a down-up-and-over motion. It is a technique that even many experienced cooks perform improperly, but one that can be mastered with some practice and an understanding of its purpose.

Folding in beaten egg whites can have two goals: to lighten the texture of a batter or cream, and to act as a leavening agent for batters. Whipped cream also lightens a mixture and is often gently blended into sauces, soufflés, and other sweet and savory dishes.

When folding, first carefully stir about one fourth to one third of the beaten whites or whipped cream into the heavier mixture to lighten it. The resulting lightened mixture is easier to blend with the remaining whites or cream because mixtures of similar consistency can be more readily folded together.

Pour remaining whites or cream on top of the heavier mixture. Cut down through the center of the mixture, then scrape across the bottom of the bowl and up one side with a single, fluid lifting motion. This brings the mixture pushed by the spatula or spoon up and over the surface. As you fold, give the bowl a quarter turn with the other hand. Repeat the motion several times just until all the ingredients are blended (some streakiness is acceptable). Work quickly but lightly, taking care not to deflate the lighter mixture and therefore decrease volume of final product.

FOOD COLORING

The composition of food coloring and food dyes is highly regulated. Approved colorings vary from country to country. They may be artificial (derived from oil) or natural (derived from vegetables, plants, or insects). In general the natural colors are weaker and less stable. Most com-

mercial food processors prefer artificial colors because they are stronger, are more heat resistant, and are less expensive.

Use Food colorings tint an enormous array of processed foods, from baked goods to salad dressings. The home cook may find them useful in tinting icings, cakes, and confections. They should be used sparingly. Liquid colorings are volatile and should be added at the end of cooking.

Availability Most food colorings sold to home cooks are packaged in liquid form. Some cookware stores and bakery suppliers offer highly concentrated food coloring pastes, which are particularly useful for icings because they mix better with fat than do liquids. Pastes also impart a darker color than liquids, which create pastel hues.

Storage Keep in a cool, dark place. Pastes will last indefinitely; liquid colorings will last three to four years.

Beaten egg whites are carefully folded into a chocolate cake batter to lighten it before baking. A large bowl, here a copper one for beating egg whites, makes the process easier.

FOOD PROCESSOR

The European-designed and manufactured food processor made its debut in the United States in the early 1970s. Although it is still not standard equipment in the majority of American kitchens, many cooks have come to consider this extremely versatile, multi-functional machine their most valuable kitchen appliance. It makes quick work out of many tedious and time-consuming culinary chores. With one machine, a cook can chop, slice, shred, mix, and purée almost instantaneously. The more powerful processors have the muscle to knead heavy bread dough with little effort.

The food processor is composed of a motor-driven shaft, a work bowl that fits over the shaft, and various blades and disks that attach to the shaft inside the work bowl and rotate at high speed when the machine is on. Food is either placed directly in the bowl or fed in through a tube on the cover of a bowl.

Full-size food processors are most efficient when used for several consecutive tasks. It's often faster and easier to do a single small job by hand—chop one clove of garlic or one tablespoon of parsley—than it is to set up the machine and have to face cleanup afterward. On the other hand, a recipe that calls for a variety of chopped vegetables—say, to be sauteed and then puréed for a soup—is perfect for the food processor.

Recognizing that consumers appreciate the speed and power of these machines, but are reluctant to dirty them for processing spoonfuls of food, manufacturers have introduced compact versions ranging from small-capacity electric chopper-grinders (electric minichoppers) to small-sized food processors. The latter have small work bowls and interchangeable blades plus a chute attachment that sends food through the work bowl for processing and out into a freestanding container. Ideal for small quantities and small households, electric minichoppers are easy to use, affordably priced, and sized to take up a minimum of space. They cannot slice or shred, however.

Food processors vary in capacity and power, from the very compact for households of one or two persons to machines intended for cooks who prepare food on a large scale. Which processor to buy depends on how often you will use the machine and the amount of food you will need to prepare at one time. A large work bowl obviously holds more—some as much as 16 cups of shredded food, or up to 7 cups of liquid. These maximum-capacity machines need a powerful motor for peak performance and are thus highest in price. With the introduction of special whisk or beater attachments, food processors are now competitive with electric mixers for whipping egg whites and cream to airy clouds, but they still cannot match the ability of the mixer to make acceptable whipped potatoes. Full-size models also cannot grind coffee beans, grains, or hard spices—tasks the minichoppers perform very well.

Standard features with most models are a large feed tube; a multipurpose steel blade for blending, mixing, and puréeing; a plastic dough blade for breads; a slicing disk; and a shredding disk. Standard on some models is a whole-bowl feed tube that accommodates larger items such as an entire tomato or onion, or several all at once. Options vary according to the manufacturer. Among the options offered are a range of slicers and shredders, including the previously mentioned whisk; a French fry cutter; an attachment for making pasta; and a citrus juicer, with strainer insert. The juicer is an automated reamer, and the strainer functions like a motorized fine-mesh sieve to create refined purées by trapping seeds, skins, peels, and fiber from fruits and vegetables.

The machine is so fast that control of its speed is critical to obtaining a quality final product. Proper technique makes the difference between finely ground nuts and nut butter, or chopped onions and onion purée. Many models have a pulse function that turns the motor on and off in bursts, letting the cook monitor the processing more accurately. For best results when chopping watery vegetables such as onions, bell peppers, or celery, it's best to turn the motor on and off (pulsing) rapidly. The same pulsing technique is used to incorporate dry ingredients into a cake batter or liquid into a pastry. When slicing or shredding foods, the amount of pressure you apply is important. Generally firm foods require firm pressure and softer foods require light to medium pressure. However, all shredded cheeses require light pressure only.

Buy a food processor that has a direct drive, rather than one that is belt-driven. Also, as with any small electrical appliance, check the warranty, customer service records, and repair policy of the food processor you have selected before you pay for it.

FORCEMEAT

Derived from the French *farce* (stuffing), this rich, savory mixture is made of finely minced, ground, pounded, or puréed raw meat, fish, fowl, or game, plus a good deal of fat, usually pork fat. Forcemeat is classically used as the filling for pâtés and terrines. Sometimes chopped vegetables and nuts are blended in for textural contrast, herbs and spices for flavor, and some sort of liquor—brandy, Cognac, or Armagnac—for depth and perfume. Eggs and often a flour-based panada, a firm paste made of bread or cooked flour soaked in milk or water, are added to bind all the ingredients together.

Forcemeats can be coarse or fine; for a more varied consistency, they can be a combination of fine pieces and a purée. To make forcemeat before the advent of the food processor, pieces of meat were fed through a meat grinder or minced by hand. If a smooth paste was desired, the meat was pounded in a mortar and then rubbed through a fine sieve. The food processor has automated and shortened this labor-intensive process, although even a processed purée should be further refined by sieving.

Seasonings vary, but generally cold forcemeat-based dishes require more generous amounts to overcome the deadening effect chilling has on flavor.

Mousseline forcemeats, which resemble a soufflé, have been lightened with cream and bound with egg white and a panada. The feather-light quenelle, a French dumpling, is made from a mousseline forcemeat. Another classic mixture consists of rolled fillets of fish lined with this airy mixture and gently poached.

■ QUENELLES

This classic mousseline recipe is lighter and more delicate than the flour-based panada originally used for quenelles. Without the help of a food processor, making quenelles is a laborious task. The flesh of the fish must be first pounded with a mortar and pestle, then sieved to remove the connective tissue. With the processor, the fish is easy to puree. You still need to sieve it because small amounts of invisible connective tissue may remain in the puree. Keeping the ingredients cold helps them absorb the cream and makes the quenelles light. The ramekins called for in the variation are single-serving pottery baking dishes. They are available at most cookware stores.

1 pound sole or other white, firm-fleshed fish, cut in 1-inch pieces and chilled
1 egg
1 egg white
1 teaspoon salt
½ teaspoon white pepper
2 cups whipping cream, well chilled
Boiling stock

1. In a food processor fitted with steel blade, purée sole. Then push puree through a sieve with a wooden spoon and return sieved purée to processor.

2. Add egg, egg white, salt, and pepper. Purée again. With machine running, slowly pour in cream and process until absorbed into fish mixture. Refrigerate the mousseline until ready for forming.

3. Use 2 tablespoons as a mold to form chilled mousseline into oval balls. As you work, dip spoons often in hot water. To form quenelles you can also use a large pastry bag with a plain tip.

4. Place formed quenelles in bottom of a large, well-buttered saucepan. Slowly pour boiling stock into pan to cover quenelles. Over low heat poach quenelles until they are firm (12 to 15 minutes).

Serves 6.

Variation Using ramekins saves the cook from having to mold the mousseline and, if you wish, serves as the vehicle for an oyster surprise. The bain-marie (hot water bath) is essential for even poaching. Preheat oven to 350° F. Heavily butter six 4-ounce ramekins. Fill halfway with mousseline. Place a small, well-drained oyster in the middle of each ramekin. Cover top with remaining mousseline mixture. Place ramekins in baking dish and surround with boiling water. Water should come up almost to top of ramekins. Bake until a knife inserted into middle of mousseline comes out clean (15 to 20 minutes).

Serves 6.

■ CHICKEN QUENELLES

Quenelles can be served as a main course with a sauce, as a soup dumpling, or as an accompaniment to other dishes. Using ground chicken rather than the fish of the previous recipe, this version is flecked with specks of peppery watercress and can be served with the chicken stock in which it poaches. Ask the butcher to grind the chicken for you, or you can do it yourself in a food processor.

½ cup water
½ teaspoon salt
2 tablespoons butter
⅓ cup flour
1 egg
1 egg white
1 cup ground chicken
2 tablespoons whipping cream
2 tablespoons fresh watercress leaves
Salt and white pepper, to taste
2 cups Chicken Stock (see page 560)

1. In a 2-quart, heavy-bottomed saucepan, combine the water, salt, and butter. Simmer over medium-low heat until butter melts.

2. With a wooden spoon, beat flour into butter-water mixture all at once. Cook over medium-high heat, beating continuously until mixture forms a ball and does not stick to sides of pan. Remove from heat.

3. Beat in egg, then egg white; set aside to cool completely.

4. In a medium bowl combine chicken, cream, watercress, and salt and pepper to taste. When flour mixture has completely cooled, blend with ground chicken mixture.

5. Simmer stock in a large, heavy-bottomed sauté pan or skillet over medium heat. Drop in quenelle batter, 1 tablespoon at a time, until pan is full. Simmer until quenelles puff and roll over easily (about 10 minutes). Remove with a slotted spoon. Repeat until all batter has been used.

Makes 20 quenelles.

TIMETABLE FOR FREEZING

Plan a constant turnover of the contents of a home freezer so that no food is kept too long. First in, first out is a good rule. Observe recommended storage periods listed below and in chart on opposite page.

Food	Storage Time at 0° F*
Fish and Shellfish	
Clams and scallops	3–4 months
Crab and lobster	1–2 months
Fatty fish (tuna, salmon, etc.)	1–3 months
Lean fish (haddock, sole, etc.)	4–6 months
Oysters	1–3 months
Shrimp	4–6 months
Meat	
Beef	
Roasts, steaks	6–12 months
Beef for stew	3–4 months
Ground beef	3–4 months
Beef variety meats (liver)	3–4 months
Corned beef, bologna, luncheon meats**	2 weeks
Lamb	
Roasts, chops, cubes	6–9 months
Ground lamb	3–4 months
Pork	
Roasts, chops, ribs	3–6 months
Ground pork	1–3 months
Ham***	2 months
Bacon, frankfurters***	1 month
Veal	
Roasts, chops, cutlets, cubes	6–9 months
Ground veal	3–4 months
Sausage***	1 month
Cooked meat	2–3 months
Poultry	
Chicken, capon, turkey, Cornish hens, small game	
Whole	12 months
Pieces	6–9 months
Giblets	2–3 months
Cooked poultry	
Pieces not in broth or gravy	1 month
Pieces in broth or gravy	6 months
Poultry dishes (casseroles, stews)	3–6 months
Goose, duck, game birds	
Whole	6 months

*Foods stored longer than the recommended period will suffer a loss of quality, but will still be safe to eat. Storing foods at temperatures higher than 0° F shortens the storage period considerably.
**Processed, cured, smoked, and ready-to-serve meat products do not retain their quality long.
***Do not freeze canned hams and canned picnics.

FREEZE, TO

Freezing has many advantages over other methods of food preservation. Frozen food tastes fresher, and it also retains its original color, texture, flavor, and nutritional value better than food preserved by other methods. And freezing is one of the simplest ways to put up food for later enjoyment.

If you expect to do a lot of freezing, you'll need a freezer rather than just the freezing compartment of a refrigerator. Home freezers reach and maintain the optimum temperature, 0° F, needed to preserve food quality better than refrigerator-freezer combinations. Fluctuations in temperature, common in the combination appliances, have an adverse effect on frozen food; with every 10° F above 0° F, storage life is cut by up to half.

BASIC FREEZER MANAGEMENT

To make the best use of your freezer, be sure foods are sealed airtight with wrapping material or containers designed for freezing. Use materials that are airtight, vapor-proof, and moistureproof.

Food loses quality if stored too long or at improper temperatures (although it can still be safe to eat). Keep an inventory of the foods you have in storage so that you'll know what's on hand and how long it has been there. Label each item with contents, entry date, weight, and number of servings. Periodically check the freezer temperature with a freezer thermometer (see THERMOMETER) to be sure that it is at 0° F or a little below.

FREEZING METHODS

Freeze foods only after they have cooled to room temperature. In each 24-hour period, freeze a maximum of 3 pounds of food per cubic foot of freezer space. Overloading slows down the freezing process, and foods frozen too slowly lose quality and may spoil.

QUICK-FREEZING

This is the recommended method of freezing packaged foods. To quick-freeze, place packages in a single layer close to the outside freezer walls, where freezing plates or coils are located. Allow space between packages so that air can circulate freely around them. Freeze packages 24 hours before sorting and stacking them.

TRAY-FREEZING

"Piece" foods, such as meatballs or drop cookies, keep best when tray-frozen. An advantage of this method is that pieces freeze individually and remain separate, allowing you to remove only as many as you need. Thawing is quicker, too. Another reason for tray-freezing is to firm up foods such as cakes and pies before packaging so that the packaging material will not adhere to them. To tray-freeze, spread unwrapped food on a baking sheet and freeze just until firm. Then immediately package as usual.

MEASURING QUALITY DURING STORAGE

Almost all food, whether plant or animal in origin, is subject to deterioration and eventual decay. To minimize loss of quality (and in severe cases, contamination) in frozen foods, you need to control the growth of microorganisms and enzymes to avoid oxidation.

Unlike canning, freezing does not sterilize foods by destroying the microorganisms present in them. Cold temperatures only inhibit the growth of microorganisms and slow down enzyme activity and oxidation. During thawing, spoilage organisms start to grow again; as the temperature of the food rises, so does the rate of growth of the organisms. The best protection against oxidation is to store food in airtight packages at the proper temperature for the recommended storage period.

The following clues indicate that foods may have suffered deterioration during freezing. If you discover any of these warning signs, chances are the food is still safe to eat, but the flavor will no longer be of top quality. You don't need to throw the food out unless it has developed off-odors, but plan to use it as soon as possible and take its condition into consideration when deciding on a cooking method.

Color Change   When foods are stored in the freezer too long, their colors fade. Vegetables, for example, turn a dull, drab color.

Freezer Burn   When foods are not carefully packaged, moisture is drawn out of them by the dry air of the freezer, resulting in freezer burn: a dry surface with grayish white spots. To protect against freezer burn, use proper packaging materials and be certain that packages are airtight.

Ice Buildup   Icy crystals inside the package indicate that the food has thawed, at least partially, and refrozen, or that the food didn't freeze quickly. To minimize the size of ice crystals, freeze foods as quickly as possible and maintain them at 0° F or lower.

Sauce Consistency   When food has passed its optimum storage period or has been allowed to thaw and refreeze, the consistency of the sauce may change. Starches may break down and the sauce may lose smoothness.

Texture Change   The texture of foods deteriorates when they have thawed and refrozen. Vegetables become soft and limp, meats toughen slightly, and the pasta in combination dishes may become soggy from absorbing moisture from the sauce.

THAWING FROZEN FOOD

Thawing in the refrigerator is the safest, although slowest, thawing method. Thawing foods at room temperature invites the risk of spoilage. If time is short, some foods, particularly poultry and meats, may be placed (in their

TIMETABLE FOR FREEZING

The length of time frozen food can be stored depends on the care with which the food was handled before freezing, the type of food, the quality of the packaging materials, and the maintenance of the proper storage temperature (0° F or less).

Food	Storage Time at 0° F*
Baked Goods	
Angel, chiffon, and sponge cakes	4–6 months
Biscuits	2–3 months
Butter and pound cakes	2–4 months
Cheesecake	4 months
Cookies	6–8 months
Cream puff and éclair shells	1–2 months
Fruitcakes	12 months
Muffins	6–12 months
Nut and fruit breads, coffee cakes, and steamed breads	2–4 months
Pancakes and waffles	1–2 months
Pie and tart shells	
Baked	3–4 months
Unbaked	6–8 weeks
Puff pastry	1–2 months
Yeast breads	
Baked	6–8 months
Unbaked	6 weeks
Eggs and Dairy Products	
Butter	
Salted	6 months
Unsalted	2–3 months
Buttermilk, for baking	1 month
Cheese	
Cream cheese	2 months
Hard and semihard natural cheese	2–3 months
Pasteurized process cheese	4 months
Soft cheese	2 months
Cream	
Whipped	1 month
Whipping (heavy)	2 months
Eggs: whole, yolks, or whites	9–12 months
Ice cream, ice milk, sherbets, and ices	1–2 months
Margarine	12 months
Milk	3 months
Yogurt, for baking	1 month

*Foods stored longer than the recommended period will suffer a loss of quality but will still be safe to eat. Storing foods at temperatures higher than 0° F shortens the storage period considerably.

freezer wrappings) in a plastic bag and thawed in a basin of cold water; this cuts thawing time about in half. A microwave oven is by far the fastest and easiest method of all. Your oven manual lists appropriate settings and approximate defrosting times.

Thaw most food in the freezer wrapping. However, cakes can be affected by the moisture that collects on the inside of the package as it warms to room temperature; therefore, loosen wrapping before thawing.

REFREEZING THAWED FOOD

If food feels cold, is still firm, and contains ice crystals, you may refreeze it without cooking it first. Be aware, however, that refreezing involves a loss of food quality and flavor and that refrozen food cannot be kept as long as freshly frozen food.

Once food has thawed, organisms that can cause spoilage begin to multiply. Therefore, unless you cook it first, do not refreeze food that has thawed completely. (You can, for example, cook thawed raw meat and then refreeze it.) Foods that have been held between 32° and 40° F for more than 24 hours should be used as soon as possible; they should not be refrozen. Seafood spoils quickly and should not be refrozen; cook it and use as soon as possible. Casseroles or dishes that have been precooked should not be refrozen. Discard any foods that have developed off-odors or off-colors.

To refreeze foods, label foods as refrozen, date, and use as soon as possible; spread the packages out in the freezer so that cold air circulates around them.

FRENCH FRY, TO

To fry directly in deep fat, traditionally without a protective coating of bread crumbs or batter, although batter-coated foods such as onion rings have come to be called French fried. The term most probably derives from a French preparation, *pommes frites*, fingers of deep-fried potatoes, and it has come to refer to any food so prepared.

> ***Recipes and Related Information***
> *Batter, 27; French-fried Potatoes, 468.*

FRICASSEE

This stew, usually of poultry, but also of veal (see Blanquette de Veau, page 593) or rabbit, is made with a white sauce. Sometimes the meat is first sauteed. The cooking liquid is most often white wine. After cooking, the sauce is bound with a white roux and enriched with egg yolk and cream.

FROSTING, ICING, AND FILLING

"The icing on the cake" has come to mean a detail that adds a special, delightful finale or flourish. The phrase of course comes from that magic moment when the baker turns artist. A coat of frosting transforms a basic cake or pastry into a stunning and distinctive creation. A line of filling, revealed in cross section with each slice, adds another level of visual and edible enjoyment. Decoration can be elaborate—applied in swirls and peaks or piped with a pastry bag. It can also be as simple as a coat of whipped cream, a sprinkle of confectioners' sugar, or a poured glaze made of just a few ingredients.

EQUIPMENT FOR CAKE DECORATION

Beautiful results are possible with tools you probably already have in your kitchen drawers and cabinets. However, if you bake a lot or are particularly interested in cake decoration, you may want to purchase some or all of the following equipment, which is available at better cookware shops or cake-decorating supply houses: pastry brushes (for applying glazes); flexible, narrow stainless steel icing spatulas in various sizes (both straight bladed and offset); toothpicks; skewers; a cake comb (a serrated metal triangle used to create grooves in frosting and icing); cardboard cake rounds (for supporting a cake as you apply decoration); cake-decorating turntable (raises cake closer to eye level and allows more even application of decoration); and a pastry bag and tubes. For a detailed description of specialty equipment for cake decoration, see CAKE AND PASTRY TOOLS.

FROSTING, FILLING, AND GLAZING BASICS

Any successful procedure, culinary or otherwise, is based on adequate preparation. Before you begin, have all equipment at hand and ingredients out and in the form or amount called for in the recipes. If the frosted cake or pastry must chill at any time during the decorating process, make sure that you have cleared a space for it in your refrigerator ahead of time.

Unless otherwise directed in the recipe, cakes must be completely cool before applying any decoration. If the top or sides of the cake or pastry are uneven, and if this will bother you, gently trim away the uneven area. Brush away crumbs, which, if left, will cause the frosting to roll away from the surface of the cake. An alternative is to seal the crumbs to the cake with a thin layer of melted jelly or preserves. If you don't want to see a fine line of brown crust, the characteristic golden surface of a baked cake, between cake and frosting, slice off the crust with a serrated knife. (However, if the cake or frosting is dark, the crust won't be noticeable.)

Set cake or pastry on a piece of cardboard (see Which Way Is Up?). For frosting a cake with a spatula, use a cardboard the same shape and size as cake; for frosting on a turntable or when applying a poured icing or glaze, the cardboard should be slightly smaller. Secure the cake to the cardboard with a tablespoon of frosting. Or, set on a flat plate that is several inches larger than cake or pastry and that has been covered around the rim with strips of waxed paper larger than the diameter of the plate.

APPLYING FILLING

If the filling was cooked, cool it before using. A metal spatula with a blade at least as long as the diameter of what is to be filled will give you the most control. If it is too small, its handle will continually drag against the surface of the cake or pastry. Scoop up the entire amount of filling at one time; set in center of layer. Spread from center to edges. If filling is soft, stop just short of the edge of the layer; this leaves room for the filling to spread when covered with another layer of cake or pastry.

APPLYING FROSTING OR ICING

If the cake or pastry is still rough even after you've trimmed it, coat with a very thin layer of frosting to even out the surface (it doesn't matter at this point if the cake shows through in spots); chill to set this precoat. Using a metal icing spatula, spread the sides with an even coating of frosting; be sure to carry frosting up the sides to the top of the cake, including any excess. Even the surface; it will be evened again, so this time it needn't be perfectly smooth. For the top, scoop up the entire amount of remaining frosting with the spatula and place in center of top of cake. Be sure to work with a clean spatula or crumbs may get into the frosting, creating an undesirable texture. With the spatula, smooth frosting evenly across top. For a decorative touch at the edge where top and sides meet, pipe a trim of frosting with a pastry bag. To create a smooth finish with buttercream frosting, dip knife or spatula in hot water; smooth around the sides, then across the top. This can only be done one time; repeated attempts will create lines. See photographs, page 247.

If frosting is to be textured or swirled, apply about a ¼-inch layer of frosting. Work on sides, then top. To create grooves, drag a cake comb or fork in straight or wavy lines around cake. (A cake-decorating turntable or lazy Susan is very helpful for this step; both raise the cake off the counter so your hand can maneuver around it better, and rotating produces a more uniform texture.) As a final textural touch, chopped nuts, crumbs, or flaked coconut can be pressed into the sides near the bottom. For swirls, use a knife, the back of a spoon, or metal spatula and pull frosting up in peaks; for ripples draw across frosting with knife or spatula in a wavy line. See photographs, page 247.

It is sometimes harder to get a really smooth finish when applying whipped cream. It will help if the whipped cream and the spatula or knife are chilled.

APPLYING A GLAZE

Glazes are used for European-type cakes, tube and loaf cakes of all kinds, fruit tarts, and pastries such as éclairs and cream puffs. For cakes, glazes add luster and visual appeal. Fruit tarts are glazed to impart a sheen and to make them look more appetizing, and, more practically, to keep the fruit juicy by protecting it from the drying effects of air. The temperature and consistency of a glaze are critical to its successful application; to make a glaze more fluid, it is sometimes better to loosen it by warming it slightly rather than by thinning it with more liquid (see Glacé Icing, page 250).

To glaze completely set cake on cardboard cut slightly smaller than its diameter (or glaze will pool on edges of cardboard). Set cake on wire rack resting on a baking sheet or on waxed paper to catch drips. Pour glaze over cake all at once. Tilt and rotate cake so that glaze flows and coats evenly. Never use a spatula to spread glaze or it will lose its sheen. Let cake rest on wire rack to allow excess to drip off and to allow glaze to set. Before transferring from rack to serving plate, run a thin-bladed knife around edge of cake to release it where glaze has stuck to the wires of the rack.

To glaze partially, apply glaze with a spoon in a network of random lines called drizzles, or pour on. For a drizzled effect, let the glaze run off the spoon in a thin stream as you move your hand back and forth over the surface of the cake. Some bakers prefer a thinner glaze for drizzling, but this is personal preference. Whatever the consistency, the glaze must be able to flow. To pour, put the glaze in a ladle or glass measuring cup with a lip. Let the glaze fall steadily from the ladle or cup as you move in a circular fashion around the cake. For tube cakes, apply more glaze on the outside of the cake than in the center.

To dip in glaze, a typical treatment for cream puff pastries, hold pastry in hand and dip; let excess run off and then set on tray to firm glaze. See photographs, page 247.

USING A PASTRY BAG
AND PAPER PIPING CONE

Learning to use a pastry bag and the simpler paper piping cone takes some effort and a bit of practice, but will greatly expand your decorating repertoire. See CAKE AND PASTRY TOOLS for a complete description of the pastry bag and tips.

The technique for either of these tools is not difficult; the skill is in learning how much pressure to apply and how to move the bag to create a particular effect (see photographs, page 246). To use, either a bag or piping cone is filled partway with frosting and gently squeezed. A ribbon of frosting is forced out of the bag or cone in a shape formed by the opening of the tip. Pastry bags have interchangeable metal tips that come in a variety of different sizes with openings of different shapes. With these tips, you can create stars, rosettes, ribbons, leaves, flowers, and many other designs. The paper cone is used for small

HOW TO USE A PASTRY BAG

Fold about one third of top over to form cuff. Set tip in place. To seal tip while filling bag, twist bag just above tip and push twisted portion of bag into tip.

Hold bag cuffed over one hand; fill no more than two thirds full. Hold bag by edges and shake to force filling into lower half of bag. Then twist top of bag below cuff so filling can't back up. Untwist small end of bag to open tip.

Grasp bag at neck with thumb and index finger of right hand; squeeze with fingers of right hand only. Guide bag with left hand while piping. Maintain even pressure; periodically twist bag to keep filling moving out of tip.

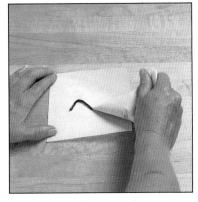

**HOW TO MAKE A
PAPER PIPING CONE**

Cut a 10-inch square of parchment paper in half to form two triangles (enough for two cones). With 90-degree-angle point facing you, fold right-hand point in toward middle so that points meet, forming a cone. Repeat with opposite point.

Fold points into cone to secure. With a spoon or spatula, fill no more than half full with frosting, gently pushing frosting into cone to eliminate air pockets.

To contain frosting and to keep cone from unraveling, fold top of cone over several times. To form opening, cut closed tip of cone with scissors. Width of strand of frosting forced out of cone depends upon how much of tip is snipped off.

---

amounts of frosting, for line work, or for writing a message. The opening is created by snipping off part of the pointed end (see How to Make a Paper Piping Cone, above). Precut parchment triangles for making these cones are available in cookware stores.

It is important to not overfill the pastry bag or piping cone, so that you can control the bag. Allow the filling to flow from the bag. Keep the tip away from the surface of the cake—a half inch at least—so that the design can take shape without being squashed or destroyed, a common frustration for beginners. Practice with mashed potatoes rather than real frosting; their textures are similar. Pipe sample designs onto a piece of waxed paper, parchment paper, or other smooth surface. Repetition will lead to perfection. Before you decorate a cake, warm up with a few practice designs on a clean surface. If you make a mistake on the cake or pastry, scrape if off with a spatula and start over. Rechill the icing if it becomes too warm.

Any frosting or icing that is thick enough to hold its form when pressed through a tip and that is soft enough to flow smoothly out of the bag can be used to decorate a cake. Buttercream Frosting (see page 248) and Chantilly Cream (see page 252) are good choices for a pastry bag. Confectioners' Decorating Icing (see page 250) and plain, melted semisweet chocolate (cooled to 86° F) are commonly used with a paper cone.

HOW TO APPLY FROSTING

If cake is uneven, trim top. Coat with a thin layer of frosting to even surface. Don't worry if some of the cake's sides show through. The next layer will cover.

Spread sides with an even coating of frosting. Carry enough frosting up to top of cake so patches of cake are not visible. Excess frosting can be used to cover top.

Scoop up enough frosting to cover top completely. Spread to cover. Trim away any excess with spatula by holding against cake and rotating cake on turntable or with hand. Smooth with flat side of blade.

DECORATIVE TECHNIQUES

Piping *Lay pastry bag at edge of cake. Squeeze gently as you slowly rotate cake. Use an open-star tip to create chains of rosettes, ribbons, or shells. Shown above is a ribbon.*

Swirls *Form waves and swirls by drawing knife or spatula along frosting. Create peaks with knife, spatula, or spoon by dipping into frosting and pulling up.*

Textures *Use a cake comb or fork. Make free-form grooves by resting comb against cake and dragging through frosting. For more uniform grooves, rotate cake slowly on turntable with comb touching.*

HOW TO APPLY GLAZES

Full glaze *Pour on glaze all at once. Tilt and rotate cake so that glaze flows to cover completely. Do not use a spatula to even glaze.*

Drizzle and partial glaze *Drizzle by letting glaze drip from spoon to form fine lines. Create a partial glaze by pouring glaze in a thin stream over cake as hand moves in circles over cake.*

Dipping *Hold pastry upside down and dip into glaze. Set on tray, glaze side up, until set.*

■ BUTTERCREAM FROSTING

This creamy, rich, versatile frosting is used, in varying amounts, in many of the cake recipes included in this book. It works well with a pastry bag used for decorating. Buttercream frosting can be refrigerated for later use; before applying bring to room temperature (see Note).

For 1 cup

     2 egg yolks
⅓ cup sugar
¼ cup water
½ cup unsalted butter, softened

For 1½ cups

     3 egg yolks
     7 tablespoons sugar
⅓ cup water
¾ cup unsalted butter, softened

For 2 cups

     4 egg yolks
½ cup sugar
⅓ cup water
     1 cup unsalted butter, softened

For 3 cups

     6 egg yolks
     1 cup sugar (scant; 14 tablespoons)
½ cup water
     1½ cups unsalted butter, softened

1. In a medium stainless steel bowl, beat yolks until light.

2. In a heavy 2½-quart saucepan, combine sugar and water; stir over medium heat until sugar dissolves and syrup comes to a boil. As sugar is dissolving, wash down any sugar crystals that cling to sides of pan with a pastry brush dipped in cold water.

3. Boil syrup gently, without stirring, until it reaches 239° F (soft-ball stage). When syrup reaches the soft-ball stage, immediately remove from heat and pour into yolks, beating constantly as you pour. Continue to beat until the mixture is light, fluffy, and cool to the touch.

4. In medium bowl of electric mixer, cream butter. Gradually beat butter into yolk mixture, 2 tablespoons at a time, until smooth, shiny, and spreadable. At this point you may fold in some stiffly whipped cream or vanilla pastry cream to lighten the buttercream, if desired. Flavor the buttercream according to the chart at left. Use buttercream immediately or refrigerate until ready to use. Store up to 3 days in the refrigerator or freeze up to 2 months.

Note If buttercream separates at any point after butter is added, the butter may be too cold. Add a little hot, melted butter, then beat until smooth. If buttercream has warmed up too much, refrigerate a few minutes, then beat until smooth. If using cold buttercream, remove from refrigerator, warm to room temperature (20 to 30 minutes), then beat frosting until smooth, shiny, and spreadable. Should the mixture separate as it loses its chill, add hot, melted butter as directed above.

■ CHOCOLATE FUDGE FROSTING

Use this dark, richly flavored frosting for layer cakes.

     6 ounces unsweetened chocolate
     1 cup butter
     2 cups confectioners' sugar
     2 eggs
¼ cup hot water
     2 teaspoons vanilla extract

1. In a double boiler melt chocolate and ½ cup butter; cool. In a medium bowl, cream remaining ½ cup butter, sugar, eggs, water, and vanilla until fluffy.

TO FLAVOR BUTTERCREAM FROSTING

Versatile Buttercream Frosting can be flavored in a multitude of ways to accompany many types of cakes. Add flavoring to the basic recipe as a last step.

Buttercream Flavor	Flavoring	Amount of Buttercream			
		1 cup	1½ cups	2 cups	3 cups
Chocolate	Semisweet chocolate (melted and cooled)	3 oz	4 oz	6 oz	8 oz
Citrus fruit	Finely grated orange or lemon rind	1 tsp	1½ tsp	2 tsp	3 tsp
Coffee	Coffee extract	To taste			
	Instant coffee dissolved in boiling water	2 tsp 1 tbsp	1 tbsp 1 tbsp	4 tsp 1½ tbsp	1½ tbsp 2 tbsp
Fruit	Fruit purée	⅓ cup	½ cup	⅔ cup	1 cup
	Fruit liqueur	To taste; see Liqueur below			
Liqueur	Liqueur or brandy	2 tsp	1 tbsp	1½ tbsp	2 tbsp
Mocha	Semisweet chocolate (melted and cooled) and coffee extract	3 oz	4 oz	6 oz	8 oz
		To semisweet chocolate add coffee extract to taste or instant coffee in amounts under Coffee			
Nuts	Finely ground toasted nuts	3 tbsp	⅓ cup	½ cup	¾ cup
Praline	Finely ground caramelized nuts	2 tbsp	¼ cup	⅓ cup	½ cup
Vanilla	Vanilla extract	1 tsp	1½ tsp	2 tsp	1 tbsp
White chocolate	White chocolate (melted and cooled)	3 oz	4 oz	6 oz	8 oz

2. Add cooled chocolate mixture and beat on high speed until smooth and creamy. Use immediately.

Makes 2½ cups.

■ CARAMEL FROSTING

Although this frosting, also known as penuche, is most commonly paired with white or yellow cakes, try it with chocolate for something different. It has a rich brown sugar flavor, which complements chocolate quite well.

> **2 cups firmly packed brown sugar**
> **½ cup granulated sugar**
> **1 cup whipping cream**
> **¼ cup butter**
> **1 tablespoon vanilla extract**

1. In a large, heavy-bottomed saucepan, cook sugars, cream, and butter over low heat until sugars and butter are dissolved. Increase heat to medium and cook until mixture is 239° F on a candy thermometer (soft-ball stage); remove from heat and cool 15 minutes.

2. Stir in vanilla and beat mixture until it loses its shine and thickens to a spreading consistency; this may take 10 minutes or more and can be done in intervals, letting the mixture cool between beatings. Use immediately.

Makes 2 cups.

■ WHITE MOUNTAIN FROSTING

Probably this classic American boiled frosting got its name because of the way it peaks when beaten. Another name for it is Italian meringue (see MERINGUE). When made with brown sugar it is called sea-foam frosting. If you won't be using the frosting immediately, wait to add the vanilla extract or the optional orange or lemon rind; refrigerate, covered, up to 24 hours.

> **1½ cups sugar**
> **½ cup water**
> **4 egg whites**
> **Pinch cream of tartar (optional)**
> **2 teaspoons vanilla extract**
> **1 teaspoon grated orange or lemon rind (optional)**

1. In a small, heavy-bottomed pan dissolve sugar in the water over low heat. Increase heat to medium and cook until 239° F on a candy thermometer (soft-ball stage).

2. As the sugar syrup approaches desired temperature, beat egg whites in a copper or stainless steel bowl until foamy; add cream of tartar if using a stainless steel bowl and beat until soft peaks form. Slowly pour hot syrup onto egg whites and beat at high speed until bowl feels cool to the touch.

3. Add vanilla and orange or lemon rind (if desired), and beat to incorporate. Use immediately.

Makes 3½ cups.

■ SEVEN-MINUTE FROSTING

Another cooked frosting, this recipe got its name because it takes approximately seven minutes to beat to the proper consistency.

> **1½ cups sugar**
> **¼ cup water**
> **2 egg whites**
> **1 tablespoon corn syrup**
> **½ teaspoon cream of tartar**
> **1 tablespoon vanilla extract**

1. In a large mixing bowl, combine sugar, the water, egg whites, corn syrup, and cream of tartar. Stand bowl over pan of simmering water and beat mixture at high speed with an electric mixer until light, fluffy, and of spreading consistency (about 7 minutes).

2. Remove from heat and continue to beat until mixture has cooled. Mix in vanilla. Use immediately.

Makes 2½ cups.

Citrus Seven-Minute Frosting   Omit vanilla extract; substitute ¼ cup fresh orange or lemon juice for the water and add 1 teaspoon grated orange or lemon rind to other ingredients.

Tropical Seven-Minute Frosting   Fold ½ to 1 cup chopped nuts, ½ to 1 cup chopped dried fruit, and 1 cup flaked coconut into cooled frosting.

Angel Food Cake and White Mountain Frosting are classics of American cooking. The cake is light, delicate, and pristine white. The pale frosting adds to the airy quality when applied in peaks and swirls. The recipe for Angel Food Cake is on page 82.

Preparation Most fruits should be washed gently just before using. Peel and slice with a stainless steel knife to avoid discoloration. Fruits that oxidize rapidly—bananas, apples, pears, feijoas—should be sprinkled with citrus juice or acidulated water to slow browning.

▥ FRUIT FONDUE

Put the chocolate sauce in a heavy ceramic pot set over a candle to keep it warm. Around it arrange bowls of fruit and cubes of pound cake for dipping. Consider these additional accompaniments: apricots, bananas, figs, melon, peaches, orange sections, seedless grapes, glacéed fruits, marshmallows, and popcorn.

    ½ **cup whipping cream**
    8 **ounces semisweet chocolate, finely chopped**
    1 **teaspoon vanilla extract**
    2 **tablespoons rum (optional)**
    1 **Pound Cake (see page 88)**
    2 **apples**
    2 **pears**
      Juice of 1 lemon
    1 **pint strawberries**

1. Place cream in fondue pot or 1-quart saucepan; slowly heat. As soon as cream begins to form bubbles around edge, turn off heat and whisk in chocolate. When chocolate is completely melted, stir in vanilla and rum (if used).

2. Cut pound cake, apples, and pears into 1-inch-square cubes. Drizzle lemon juice over apples and pears. Wash and dry strawberries. Use fondue forks or bamboo skewers to dip fruit and cake into chocolate sauce.

Makes 1½ cups sauce, 6 to 8 servings.

▥ FRUIT FOOL

Crushed raspberries, peaches, apricots, blackberries, or blueberries work equally well for this old-fashioned English dessert, although crushed gooseberries are the traditional choice. The juice released from the berries stains the whipped cream a lovely color.

    2 **pints strawberries**
    2 **cups confectioners' sugar**
    2 **cups whipping cream**
      Classic Scotch Shortbread (see page 144), for accompaniment

1. Wash strawberries and remove stems; pat dry. In a large bowl mash berries with a potato masher or fork. Sift confectioners' sugar over berries and stir to combine well. Macerate 1 hour.

2. Whip cream to soft peaks. Stir strawberries to mix berries and juices, and gently fold whipped cream into them. Some white streaks of cream may remain. Serve in stemmed goblets accompanied by shortbread cookies.

Serves 8.

FRY, TO

To cook in hot fat. Frying is part of almost every cuisine and a component of many cooking methods. Its appeal is in the wonderful flavor and crisp, browned surface of food cooked this way. Frying is particularly versatile, and when properly executed, it produces foods that are light and not at all greasy.

Within the broad category of frying, there are several subcategories, defined mainly by the amount of fat used and how much the food is moved around in the pan. Sautéing and stir-frying are the same technique, differentiated by national origin, typical ingredients, and type of pan used. Both methods require food cut to cook quickly—either in small pieces or in thin, even fillets. Sautéing, which comes from the classic French tradition, tends to use creamy sauces and few vegetables, and is done in a sauté pan, essentially a frying pan. Stir-frying, a technique most common in Asian cooking, usually involves a number of vegetables, but omits dairy products, and employs a wok. Deep-frying calls for total immersion of food in fat. Technically, there is also a fourth category of frying, panfrying, which is halfway between sautéing and deep-frying. Panfried foods are first dipped in a flour or crumb coating, then are cooked in an inch or more of hot fat.

Frying is an active, fast-moving cooking method that demands concentration and quick responses. The cook must be alert to alterations both in the food, as it changes from raw to cooked, and in the hot fat. Even a slight hesitation can make the difference between brown or burned, tender or tough meat.

WHICH METHOD TO USE?

Choice of method is often determined by what's on hand to cook with and the amount of preparation time available. Sautéed dishes are perhaps the simplest to put together. For a basic sauté, all that is needed are tender fillets of meat, poultry, or fish, a liquid to make the sauce, and seasonings. You'll want to pound poultry or veal to a uniform thickness, but further preparation is unnecessary. Deep-frying—chicken, for example—also calls for a minimum of ingredients—perhaps just a coating—and time. Stir-frying, although equally quick and simple, entails the most preparation. All ingredients must be cut to proper size; sauce ingredients should be portioned out and ready; marinades must be mixed and applied well ahead of cooking. Each of these methods is simplified with some planning and a well-stocked pantry and refrigerator.

FATS, OILS, AND TEMPERATURE

The high heat of frying rapidly cooks tender cuts of meat, sears their surface, retains moisture, and promotes browning. For all of the frying methods, fats and oils are the media by which heat is transferred to food. With a boiling point higher than water, fats and oils cook hotter, and therefore faster, than other liquids. Because heated fats caramelize sugars in the food, they encourage the characteristic browned surface on fried foods. Fat also keeps food from sticking to the pan.

HOW TO CHOOSE AN OIL

When frying, it is most important to use a fat that will stay intact at high heat. Eventually, any fat or oil will become hot enough to decompose. The point at which this breakdown occurs is called the smoke point. At this stage, smoke and an acrid gas are given off, the liquid begins to darken, and an unpleasant taste is imparted to food. Oils with high smoke points include safflower oil, grapeseed oil, corn oil, and peanut oil. Lard and solid vegetable shortening are also sometimes used for frying. Sesame and olive oils, which have lower smoke points, are less suitable for frying, and work better as seasonings.

The smoke point of an oil is lowered each time the fat is reused. After it has been cooked three or four times, it must be discarded. Bits of food afloat in the oil accelerate this breakdown; it is important to continually skim off crumbs from the hot oil and strain used oil through cheesecloth before storing. Exposure to air also lowers the smoke point. For this reason, a narrow, deep pot is preferred over a shallow, wide pan when a great deal of fat is used, as in deep-frying.

Select an oil that is appropriate to the recipe. An oil with a mild or neutral taste does not mask the flavor of the food. A stronger oil, such as peanut oil, imparts its own flavor and is used where additional taste would be desirable, such as in stir-frying.

FRYING TEMPERATURE

Not only is it critical that you choose a fat that stands up to high temperature, but you also need to maintain this high heat throughout the cooking process. Fluctuating temperature results in food that is either overdone on the outside and raw in the middle, or bland and greasy. An electric skillet or fryer with a built-in thermostat monitors temperature changes and corrects them automatically. With any other frying method, however, the cook needs to evaluate the cooking process and adjust the heat or the food as necessary. A deep-fat thermometer helps by indicating temperature variations. Experienced cooks often depend on their senses—sight, smell, and hearing—in addition to a thermometer, to judge when a fat is hot enough to use.

For deep-frying, drop a cube of bread into the hot oil and slowly count to 60. If the bread browns nicely, the oil is ready. If the bread burns, the oil is too hot. If the bread stays pale and becomes saturated with fat, the oil is not hot enough.

For sautéing with butter or a combination of butter and oil, watch for the butter to foam. Unclarified butter is quick to burn, so it must be watched carefully. With butter you can also be alert to the point of fragrance—the moment at which its characteristic aroma becomes apparent.

For all methods, the familiar sizzle when food meets hot fat is yet another indicator that proper frying temperature has been reached.

FRYING TECHNIQUE

Meat and other ingredients should generally be at room temperature at the time of cooking. Cold food immediately lowers the temperature of the fat below an optimum level. If food must be fried before it has warmed to approximately 70° F, cook only a few pieces at a time.

The surface of what is to be fried should be as dry as possible. Pat pieces of meat, poultry, and fish with a paper towel or, when appropriate, coat with flour, bread crumbs, or batter. Any surface moisture instantly converts to steam as it meets hot fat, causing fat to bubble up and possibly overflow sides of pan, and brings about an immediate drop in temperature as well. Overcrowding the pan also produces excess moisture and will steam, not brown, the food being cooked. Between batches, always allow oil to return to proper temperature.

Lightly cooked seasonal vegetables and green salads make good partners for fried fish, poultry, and meat. Deep-fried and sautéed foods are rarely served with elaborate garnishes. In this way, they keep their pure and simple character.

> **Recipes and Related Information**
> Deep-fry, 174; Fat, 216; Oil, 394; Panfry, 404; Sauté, 531; Stir-fry, 557.

FUNNEL

Narrow-necked funnels are a convenient way to channel liquids, particularly cooking oils, into bottles or other receptacles with a similar shape, to consolidate liquids from several sources, and to transfer finely milled grains and flours from their packages to your own storage  containers. Some have screen inserts that trap bits of burned food or other undesirable matter as the liquid pours through; those for canning have very wide necks that permit easy filling of canning jars. Choose a funnel made of stainless steel, for its durability and because it won't interact with acidic foods or corrode. Canning funnels are usually plastic. Size is measured in inches across the top; depending upon how it will be used, a 4- or 6-inch funnel is most versatile.

G&H

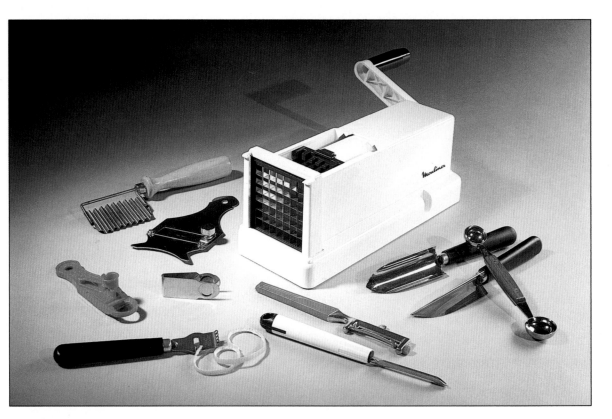

Those small kitchen tools known as gadgets can be useful if they are well made, if there is room to store them, and if the cook remembers to use them. Counterclockwise from top right are: French-fry maker, melon cutters, peelers, citrus zester and stripper, bean slicer, strawberry huller, truffle slicer, crinkle-chip cutter.

GADGETS: CUTTER, PEELER, AND ZESTER

Although dismissed by overly serious chefs as novelties or even space wasters, kitchen gadgets have a purpose and will earn their keep if they are well made and therefore perform their job well. What are gadgets? They encompass all those small devices that hang from racks or fill counter bins in housewares departments. They range from the familiar, such as citrus zesters and vegetable peelers, to the unidentifiable. Many are garnishing tools—the cutters that flute, hollow, and scallop all sorts of fruits and vegetables.

As is true of all cutting tools, unless the edges are sharp they won't work. Why mention the obvious? Unfortunately, some implements on the market are dull and therefore useless. So before you buy a tool, ask the salesperson for assurance that it will work.

ASPIC-TRUFFLE CUTTER

Usually sold in sets of 12 patterns, these tinned steel cutters are so tiny that a set will nestle in a box no bigger than 2 inches in length. These miniatures are used to punch out decorative garnishes from aspic, truffles, pastry, pimientos, olives, candied fruits, and cooked egg white. The many whimsical patterns include paisleys, circles, squares, triangles, clovers, hearts, spades, clubs, crescents, and alphabet letters. Dry the cutters immediately after washing or they will rust.

BEAN SLICER

Green beans look more delicate when cut lengthwise into thin pieces. This cutter is a combination guillotine and slicer. One blade chops off the stem and blossom ends; the other creates the narrow strips. The tool is made of molded plastic with stainless steel blades.

CITRUS STRIPPER

This tool cuts a ¼-inch-wide strip of rind from a lemon or orange. Use the resulting spirals to flavor a drink or preserve them in sugar syrup for decoration. To avoid pulling away the bitter white pith with the peel, set the cutting edge against the skin and pull it around the fruit without digging too deeply. Make short strips by cutting from stem to blossom end; cut longer ones by working around the midsection of the fruit. The tool also flutes mushrooms and cuts decorative channels in cucumbers, carrots, and other vegetables; when sliced they will have scalloped edges. Measuring about 6 inches long, the stripper has a molded plastic handle and a stamped, stainless steel blade.

CITRUS ZESTER

Five little holes at the blade end of this tool cut threads of colored rind when drawn across the skin of citrus fruit. Use the long threads as is or chop fine with a chef's knife or electric minichopper. Cooks who use this method for mincing rind love it. The alternative is rubbing the fruit against a metal grater, which always takes away some knuckle and bitter citrus pith with the rind, and is difficult to clean. Lemons and oranges with the rind removed should be saved for juicing; store them in a plastic bag in the refrigerator to prevent them from drying out. Measuring about 6 inches, the citrus zester has a molded plastic or wood handle and a stamped, stainless steel blade. If storage is tight, consider a combination zester-stripper (see photograph, opposite page).

CRINKLE-CHIP CUTTER

The wavy-edged blade of this cutter slices ruffled rounds and sticks of vegetables and cheeses. It is typically used on potatoes, carrots, squash, jicama, beets, and cucumbers. The blade is stainless steel, the handle molded plastic.

FRENCH-FRY MAKER

This device cuts a potato into the familiar, even sticks used to make French fries. A chef's knife can do this chore, but it will take longer and the results won't be as uniform. Of the two basic designs, the simplest has a sharp, stainless steel grid set in a cast aluminum frame. To use, the grid is placed on an upright end of a peeled potato and then pushed through to the bottom. The other type is larger and more mechanized. A slot in the plastic housing of the cutter holds the potato in place; a push of a lever sends the potato through the metal grid. The French-fry maker also cuts carrots and other root vegetables, and can be useful when preparing ingredients of equal size to be stir-fried.

MELON BALLER

This tool forms fruits and vegetables into little balls for fruit plates or salads. It also hollows cherry tomatoes and mushrooms for stuffing. The handle is plastic or wood and the bowl is stainless steel in graduated sizes. One- and two-scoop models are sold; round bowls are most typical, but oval and fluted ones are also available.

MELON V OR U CUTTER

This garnishing tool has a V- or U-shaped, stainless steel blade that cuts a zigzag (the V) or scalloped (the U) edge. Handles are wood or molded plastic. If garnishing is important to you, these cutters give an extra, decorative touch to foods used as containers, such as watermelon baskets and melon, lemon, and orange shells. The technique is simple and the effect attractive, although this tool is certainly not a high-priority item. To make shells, insert the tool so that successive cuts touch and are continuous around the circumference of the fruit. When the last cut reaches the first, the fruit will open. To make baskets with a handle, don't cut all the way around the fruit; instead, cut almost to the center, then up and down the other side and back around. Repeat on the opposite end to finish the handle and shape the basket.

PEELER

No matter what type of cooking you do, you always have to peel an apple, pear, potato, carrot, cucumber, eggplant, asparagus, or any of numerous other fruits and vegetables. Peelers have swivel or fixed blades; buy what feels comfortable in your hand and what works best. Choose a quality peeler. The better tools will stay sharper longer; some even have replaceable blades, or blades that reverse to accommodate both right- and left-handed cooks.

Specialty peelers, designed for particular vegetables and fruits, such as asparagus, avocado, and citrus, are also available.

STRAWBERRY HULLER

Why this small device that resembles squatty, wide tweezers works as well as it does is a mystery, but it neatly plucks the stem and leaves from a strawberry in a single motion without mashing the fruit. Also use it to pick tiny bones from fish.

TRUFFLE SLICER

This relatively simple and straightforward device is made of a sheet of stainless steel and has a shape that resembles a musical instrument you can't quite identify: long neck, pinched waist, and little legs. An adjustable blade projects from the upper surface. To use, the slicer is held at a 45-degree angle, supported by the legs, and the truffle is rubbed across the blade. It can also be employed to shave chocolate.

Recipes and Related Information
Basic Aspic, 265; French-fried Potatoes, 468; Garnish, 263; Truffle, 582.

GAME

Animals hunted for food or sport fall under the category of game. To the cook this includes both animals freshly killed by the hunter and those that are farm raised for the market. Small game animals include rabbit and hare, beaver, muskrat, raccoon, and opossum. Among the large game animals are venison (which usually refers to deer, but also includes other antlered animals such as caribou, moose, elk, and antelope), bison (American buffalo), wild boar, and bear. Duck, pheasant, and quail are some of the better-known game birds (see POULTRY). By strict definition, game also includes fish (see FISH).

Use Game furnishes some of the tastiest and most wholesome of all meat—it is rich in flavor, high in protein and minerals, and low in fat. Germans enjoy rabbit in *Hasenpfeffer,* a richly flavored stew that takes its name from the German words *Hasen,* which means hare, and *Pfeffer,* meaning pepper. Jugged hare is a Scottish rabbit

Although gumbos are most often associated with the Gulf Coast of Louisiana, these okra-thickened soups can be found throughout the Deep South. The version pictured here, featuring rabbit and oysters, is from the Georgia Sea Islands.

stew, which sometimes uses rabbit blood as a thickener. Roast saddle of venison is a classic preparation. Ground venison, when mixed with a little beef fat for moistness, makes superbly flavored patties. Buffalo steaks are delicious when grilled, particularly over a smoky fire.

Availability   Both wildlife protection and food-safety laws restrict the commercial sale of meat from the wild animals of America. The only North American game animals that can be found readily in markets are those that have been farm raised. These include rabbit, bison, some deer, and the occasional raccoon or opossum, along with numerous types of game birds. However, farm-raised American game, along with game meats from other countries (especially the wide variety of ranch-raised game of New Zealand), are becoming increasingly available.

Some of the better-stocked, upscale supermarkets are beginning to carry buffalo, venison, and boar, along with rabbit and game birds, in frozen food cases. Rabbit can be found in many butcher shops, which can also provide game by special order. The alternative to buying game is hunting it, or sharing a hunter's bounty. However, this entry addresses game that is the most widely available commercially; consult a cookbook on game for information on the special requirements of handling and preparing freshly killed game.

Selection   The game you buy will most often be frozen; as with all frozen meats, check for signs that the package

has been handled properly. Avoid those that are torn or that contain frozen liquid; a tear will expose the meat and allow it to dry out, while the latter could mean that the meat was thawed and refrozen, resulting in a considerable loss of quality. If you are fortunate enough to find fresh game, use the same criteria to judge the quality as you would for other meats and fowl—look for resilient flesh; avoid a slimy surface and an off odor.

Storage   Keep frozen game under proper conditions: in a freezer compartment able to maintain the recommended temperature of 0° F. Store fresh game in the coolest section of your refrigerator and use promptly.

Preparation   Thaw frozen game as you would other meat, then follow the recipe for specific preparation.

Cooking   Of all small game, rabbit is the easiest to find in the marketplace, and preparation methods for rabbit apply to most other small game as well; nearly any recipe for chicken, pheasant, or partridge can be adapted to rabbit, hare, or squirrel. The parts of large game, such as boar, buffalo, and venison, are similar to those of other meat animals (see BEEF, LAMB, PORK), so be guided accordingly in choosing a cooking method. Bison destined for market will have been raised similarly to beef cattle and will be as tender as fine grain-fed lean beef. Wild boar, a close relative of the domestic hog, generally tastes like the finest pork; recipes for pork are equally suitable for boar. Venison, the meat of deer and antelope, has a flavor that is faintly reminiscent of the finest, best-aged, most greaseless lamb.

■ GEORGIA RABBIT AND OYSTER GUMBO

The word *gumbo* comes from West Africa, where it means both okra and soups thickened with okra. African slaves brought the dish to America. This recipe is fairly peppery, so if hot food isn't your passion, you may want to reduce (or eliminate) the cayenne.

> 1 rabbit, cut into 6 or 8 pieces
>   (see Cutting Up a Rabbit, opposite page)
> 2 quarts Chicken Stock (see page 560) or
>   Fish Stock (see page 561)
> ¼ cup oil (preferably peanut, corn, or sunflower)
> ½ cup flour
> ½ pound okra, ends trimmed, sliced
>   into ½-inch rounds
> 1 large green bell pepper, chopped
> 1 large onion, chopped
> 1 stalk celery, chopped
> ½ teaspoon cayenne pepper
> ¼ teaspoon dried thyme
> ¼ teaspoon salt, or to taste
> ¼ teaspoon freshly ground black pepper,
>   or to taste
> 1 jar (1 pt) East Coast oysters, drained
> 2 to 3 cups cooked rice
>   Tabasco sauce (optional)

1. Trim and discard all visible fat from rabbit (see Cutting Up a Rabbit, right). Put rabbit and stock in a large pot and bring to a boil. Lower heat to medium, partially cover, and simmer for 1 hour, skimming occasionally. Remove rabbit pieces with a slotted spoon and let cool. Leave stock over low heat, covered, to keep hot. When pieces are cool enough to handle, bone and reserve meat.

2. In a large, heavy skillet, heat oil over medium-high burner until oil is quite hot. Make a roux by stirring in flour a bit at a time, whisking vigorously to break up any lumps. Cook until roux turns peanut butter brown (about 10 minutes), stirring constantly and whisking whenever necessary to break up any lumps. Do not stop stirring or roux will burn.

3. When roux is the right color, add okra, green pepper, onion, and celery, stirring in vegetables carefully, in small batches, so their moisture does not make the roux burn. Lower heat to medium and cook until vegetables are tender (about 13 minutes), stirring frequently.

4. Add contents of skillet to stockpot and raise heat to high. Add cayenne, thyme, salt, pepper, and reserved rabbit meat. Bring to a boil, lower heat, and simmer 5 minutes, skimming occasionally. Add oysters, remove from heat, cover, and let stand 10 minutes.

5. Serve in large soup bowls over rice. Tabasco may be added at the table to raise the "heat" if desired.

Serves 4 to 5.

■ **WILD BOAR MEDALLIONS OR CHOPS WITH TANGY BERRY SAUCE**
Swift and simple but luxurious, the sauce for the boar will also go with venison medallions.

   1 **pound ½-inch-thick medallions cut from loin of boar *or* 4 thick boar chops (approximately 6 oz each)**
      Salt and freshly ground pepper
   2 **tablespoons vegetable oil**

Tangy Berry Sauce

  ¼ **cup shallots**
  ¼ **cup balsamic vinegar**
  ¼ **cup dry red wine**
  ¼ **cup port**
  2 **tablespoons honey**
     Pinch cayenne
  ¼ **cup lingonberries or cranberries (fresh or frozen without juice)**
  2 **tablespoons unsalted butter, cut in small pieces**

1. Trim fat and silvery membrane from meat. Rub meat with salt and pepper and allow to stand at room temperature to develop flavor while sauce is prepared. If using boar chops, preheat oven to 300° F.

2. In a heavy skillet heat oil. Add meat and rapidly sauté on both sides until well browned. If using chops, transfer to a 300° F oven for 20 minutes to complete cooking. Place meat on a serving dish and nap with sauce.

Serves 4.

Tangy Berry Sauce   In a small nonreactive saucepan, place shallots, vinegar, wine, port, honey, and cayenne. Stir well, adding berries. Bring to a simmer and cook over moderately low heat until liquid is very thick (about 20 minutes), stirring occasionally. Swirl in butter.

Makes about 1 cup sauce.

GARLIC

An odoriferous member of the lily family, garlic (*Allium sativum*) is a single bulb that consists of several small cloves, each wrapped in a papery skin and all held together by a papery outer skin. The long, gray-green leaves of the plant are usually cut off before the garlic is sent to market.

Use   The pungent aroma and flavor of garlic make it valuable as a seasoning for savory dishes. It is generally peeled and minced to release its aromatic oils. Raw minced garlic is very strong, but cooking moderates its flavor. Long, slow cooking renders garlic very mild; even whole cloves soften and develop an almost sweet flavor.

Garlic is widely used in almost all the regions of the world, with the exception of Japan, England, and Scandinavia. Its indescribable flavor enhances numerous foods and dishes, including soup, salads, breads, sauces, meats, fish, vegetables, and eggs.

Availability   California grows about 90 percent of the domestic crop. The predominant variety, harvested in midsummer, has ivory cloves sheathed in an off-white skin. A milder variety is harvested about a month earlier. Elephant garlic, which is not actually a garlic but a different species of allium, has especially large cloves and mild flavor. Mexican red garlic, harvested in January, has very small cloves and papery reddish skin. Mexican white garlic is generally harvested and shipped in March.

Thanks to this staggered harvest, fresh garlic is available the year around. Also in the market are granulated garlic, instant minced garlic, instant garlic powder, garlic salt, and minced garlic in oil. The first three products are pure garlic; the fourth is garlic powder combined with table salt; the fifth is pure garlic in oil.

Selection   Choose fresh garlic that looks plump and feels firm. Avoid heads that are withered or have obviously bruised or darkened cloves.

Store   Keep fresh garlic in a cool, dry, dark place with some air circulation. Try to leave heads whole because individual cloves dry out rapidly. Keep dried garlic products airtight in a cool, dry, dark place; they strengthen with age; replace every six months. Store minced garlic in oil airtight in the refrigerator for up to three months.

TIPS

CUTTING UP A RABBIT

Cut a cleaned, skinned rabbit along center of breast from neck to tail end to expose central cavity. With a small, sharp knife, detach and remove all organs from the cavity. (Liver and heart may be reserved for some other use, such as meat loaf or pâté.) Trim away and discard all tallowy fat in cavity, at leg joints, and along backbone. Thin white membrane over flesh may be left in place.

Rabbit can be cut into serving pieces much like chicken. Use both hands to dislocate front and hind leg joints by snapping them sharply away from body. Carefully sever from body with a knife or poultry shears. Repeat with other front leg, then with both hind legs. If desired, separate hind legs from thighs.

With torso of rabbit held between both hands, cavity facing you, break backbone between upper and lower back by snapping backward; finish by cutting along crack in bone. If desired, cut each torso piece in half by inserting knife along one side of backbone. If you wish, remove "armature" of annoying small bones by grabbing breast piece with both hands and snapping armature away from breastbone. Use sharp yanks with fingers or needle-nose pliers to remove small bones from flesh; most of meat remaining on breastbone will be boneless.

▨ OEUFS EN GELEE

The beauty of this light luncheon dish is in the clarity of the stock used to make the aspic. Garnish with tomato slices and black olives, and serve with a crusty bread.

> 2 **cups clarified Chicken or Beef Stock (see page 560)**
> 1½ **teaspoons unflavored gelatin**
> 1 **teaspoon dried tarragon**
> ½ **teaspoon salt**
> 6 **sprigs fresh tarragon, parsley, or watercress**
> 6 **hard-cooked eggs, peeled**
> 6 **lettuce leaves, for garnish**
> 12 **thin tomato slices, for garnish**
> 12 **black olives, for garnish**

1. In a small bowl place ½ cup stock. Sprinkle gelatin over stock and stir. Place remaining stock in a medium saucepan and bring to a boil. Stir in gelatin-stock mixture, tarragon, and salt. Set aside to cool to room temperature (about 20 minutes).

2. Lightly oil a 4-cup ring mold. Line with tarragon sprigs. Place eggs horizontally in mold. Slowly pour half the cooled gelatin-stock mixture into mold. Chill 30 minutes; slowly pour remaining gelatin-stock mixture over eggs. Chill at least 5 hours.

3. To unmold, loosen edges with a knife. Fill a large pan with warm water about 1 inch deep. Lower egg mold into water and let sit 3 to 5 minutes. Remove mold and cover with a serving platter. Invert platter and mold; jelled mixture should fall onto platter. Lift platter off.

4. To serve, slice between each egg and garnish with lettuce leaves, tomato slices, and black olives.

Serves 6.

Recipes and Related Information
Bavarian Cream, 170; Charlotte Russe, 170; Lemon Roulade Charlotte, 171; Mousse, 372.

GIBLETS

The edible innards, or giblets, of birds, particularly chicken and turkey, consist of the gizzard, the heart, the liver, and often the neck. They are usually packaged by the processor in small paper bags and tucked inside the bird. Giblets are used to make gravy or are cut up and mixed into a bread stuffing.

Giblets for gravy are first simmered in water or stock to cover for about 30 minutes, then are cut up and blended with the pan drippings and stock.

Recipes and Related Information
Poultry, 468; Roast Turkey With Giblet Gravy, 474.

GINGER

A perennial herb, ginger grows from thick underground stems called rhizomes, which are the parts of the plant used in cooking. It is marketed both fresh and as a dried ground powder. Resembling a thick knobby root, fresh ginger has thin, pale brown skin and moist, pale gold flesh. It has a pungent, slightly hot flavor and a lively, fresh aroma. Young ginger, occasionally available in Asian markets, is cream-colored with pink-tipped shoots. It has a very thin, pale yellow skin, pale flesh with few fibers, and a particularly delicate flavor prized by Chinese cooks. Young ginger can be substituted for more mature ginger in all recipes, although you may want to increase the amount. Powdered ginger, which serves as a spice, has a delightful hot-sweet flavor. Sun-dried and finely ground, ginger is appreciated as a spice in many countries where fresh ginger is not used. Its flavor is only vaguely reminiscent of the fresh rhizome. The two are not interchangeable.

Use   Fresh ginger plays a prominent role in the cooking of India and most other Asian countries. Fundamental to Chinese cooking, it figures in everything from soups to sweets. Minced ginger is added to oil in a wok before stir-frying vegetables or meats. Long, fine strips of ginger are scattered on fish before steaming to subdue fishy taste. Slices of smashed ginger are used to flavor marinades and steaming mixtures. Japanese cooks add ginger to marinades, soups, and dipping sauces. Pickled ginger is always served as a condiment with sushi. Korean cooks use ginger in seasoning mixtures for grilled meats, salads, and kimchee. Fresh ginger is used throughout Southeast Asia in noodle dishes, curries, salads, stir-fries, and steamed foods. In India, ginger contributes sharp flavor to curries and chutneys.

Ginger or ginger extract also flavors a wide variety of beverages, from ginger ale and ginger beer to the traditional English wassail bowl.

Ground ginger adds fragrance and spice to cakes, cookies, puddings, and quick breads. Moroccan cooks use it to flavor chick-pea and lentil soups, to season the stews served atop couscous and the meats used in *tajine*s (earthenware-pot stews). Swedish cooks rub pork with ginger before roasting it. Ground ginger complements carrots, beets, winter squashes, and most fruits. Add the spice to baked apples or peaches or to crumb toppings for fruit crisps.

Availability   Fresh ginger is sold in all Asian markets and in most supermarkets throughout the year. Young ginger is available in some Asian markets from early summer through fall. Ground ginger is stocked on all supermarket spice racks.

Pickled Ginger   Japanese markets carry two types of pickled ginger. One kind, *hajikamishoga*, is also known as blushing or bashful ginger because it is pale pink. Made from the whole shoots of young ginger pickled in rice vinegar, it is served with grilled fish. The pink color is natural.

The second variety, *benishoga* or *gari,* is served in sushi bars as a condiment. It is made from whole fresh ginger preserved in salt and vinegar, then grated in thin, wide slivers. It may or may not be dyed a pinkish red, and is usually packed in plastic tubs or bags.

Preserved Ginger Ginger preserved in sugar is available in a variety of forms: ginger stems, crystallized ginger, and preserved red ginger. The stems are the immature knobs of young ginger. Many Asian markets carry ginger stems in syrup. This product is usually packaged in a glazed, lidded crock but is also available in a plastic container without the extra syrup. Stems can be eaten after dinner as a sweet, or minced and added to baked goods, fruit compotes, and ice cream.

Crystallized ginger—bits of ginger preserved in sugar syrup, then coated with granulated sugar—is found in the spice section of supermarkets. It is used in the same ways as ginger in syrup.

Many Chinese markets carry preserved red ginger—ginger candied in red syrup. Packaged in jars, it adds color and piquant flavor to fruit dishes and salads. Chinese markets often carry another variety of preserved ginger, seasoned with sugar, salt, and licorice rhizome. Chinese cooks use it with fish and *congee* (rice porridge).

Selection When choosing fresh ginger, look for extremely hard rhizomes that snap easily into pieces. Avoid dry, shriveled stems that feel light for their size. For ground ginger, remember that packaged seasonings lose quality after a while; try to buy from a store that restocks its spice section fairly often.

Storage Keep fresh ginger in refrigerator crisper in a plastic bag with a paper towel to absorb moisture (to prevent mold, change towel occasionally). It will last for two to three weeks. Store ground ginger in a cool, dry, dark place; replace every six months.

After opening, store Japanese pickled ginger in its brine in the refrigerator for up to six months. Properly stored, ginger stems, crystallized ginger, preserved red ginger, and preserved ginger with licorice will keep indefinitely. Refrigerate jars of ginger stems after opening. Store crystallized ginger in an airtight container in a cool, dry place. Refrigerate preserved red ginger and preserved ginger in licorice in their jars.

Preparation Peel fresh ginger with a sharp knife, vegetable peeler, or ginger grater. Young ginger does not require peeling. Slice, mince, or grate as desired. To release ginger juice from slices, smash gently with the flat side of a large knife or cleaver. To grate ginger, use a Japanese or Chinese ginger grater with a series of fine teeth that rake the flesh off the fibers. The finest side of a box-shaped grater also works, although it is harder to clean. A knife is best for chopping ginger. If ginger is

firm, it can be chopped in the food processor using the metal blade; otherwise, don't use the food processor. With soft ginger, there is the possibility that the machine will smash or tear it instead of cutting it into discrete bits.

▨ GINGERBREAD

Few recipes have so many variations. Gingerbread ranges from mildly spicy to dark and pungent, from soft as cake to hard as crackers. This recipe produces gingerbread that is firm, cakelike, and not too sweet.

> 2½ **cups flour**
> 2 **teaspoons baking soda**
> ½ **teaspoon salt**
> 1 **tablespoon ground ginger**
> ½ **cup solid vegetable shortening**
> ¼ **cup firmly packed dark brown sugar**
> 2 **eggs**
> 1 **cup *each* molasses and boiling water**

1. Preheat oven to 375° F. Generously grease and lightly flour an 8-inch-square pan. In a medium bowl stir and toss together flour, baking soda, salt, and ginger.

2. In large bowl of an electric mixer, beat shortening and sugar together until well blended. Beat in eggs, then add molasses and blend well. Stir in the water. Immediately add flour mixture and stir until batter is smooth.

3. Spread batter evenly in prepared pan. Bake until a toothpick or skewer inserted in center comes out clean (35 to 40 minutes). Remove from oven and set on a rack to cool. Serve warm or cold.

Serves 6 to 8.

In colonial New England, hard-textured gingerbread was often carried on journeys as an energy-rich snack, and slices of gingerbread were sold by food peddlers on the street. The spicy cake is still a favorite today, whether served as a snack, dessert, or even as an accompaniment to the main course.

GLACE

The French word for ice is *glace;* it can mean ice cream, the icing on a cake, or a glaze made from stock that has been reduced to the point where it is thick and syrupy. *Glacé* means iced or frozen, and usually refers to candied fruits (fruits preserved in sugar syrup), possibly because the surface has a sheen resembling ice.

Recipes and Related Information
Candied Fruit, 93; Candy, 93; Glace de Viande, 560.

GLAZE, TO

To coat a surface with a thin layer of syrup, chocolate, icing, melted jelly or preserves, egg wash, or other substance, in order to give it a shiny finish.

Recipes and Related Information
Egg Wash, 211; Frosting, Icing, and Filling, 244.

GOOSEBERRY

A small, round, thin-skinned fruit, the gooseberry looks somewhat like a grape. Its striated skin can be smooth or fuzzy. When ripe, the berry is green, pink, yellow, or white. Underripe gooseberries, best for cooking, are green. The English are probably the biggest consumers of gooseberries, although the commercial market even in England is small. In the United States, gooseberry cultivation is discouraged. In some states it is outlawed because the gooseberry, like the currant, is a carrier of white pine blight. A noninjurious hybrid strain is now grown commercially on a small scale in Oregon, Washington, and Michigan, adding to imports from New Zealand.

Use Gooseberries are eaten raw, with milk and sugar, or cooked in pies, tarts, jams, jellies, and sauces. To make a popular English dessert, a gooseberry fool, fold lightly whipped cream into a gooseberry purée made from cooked, sweetened, and sieved fruit.

Availability Fresh domestic gooseberries are sold in some specialty markets from May through August; imported New Zealand berries are on the market October through December. Canned gooseberries can be found in specialty stores and some supermarkets.

Selection Choose underripe berries for cooking, ripe berries for eating raw.

Storage Keep at room temperature or in the refrigerator crisper for up to two days.

Preparation Remove tops and tails with scissors.

GRAIN

Among the many members of the grass family, fewer than a dozen are important to the human diet. But those few are very important, providing 70 to 80 percent of the caloric intake in less developed countries. Bamboo and sugar cane aside, these valuable grasses are called cereal grains after Ceres, the Roman goddess of agriculture.

The grains themselves are the seed kernels of cereal plants. According to the botanical definition, a grain is a complete fruit, containing all the genetic equipment for reproduction. Underneath the outer layer (or bran) is the endosperm—often the only part of the grain we eat—and the embryo (or germ).

After harvesting, some grains undergo processing to make them easier to cook and to prolong their shelf life. Some grains—such as barley, oats, and rice—have a tough inedible husk that must be removed before milling. Other processing steps may include polishing to remove the bran and germ, steaming or precooking to soften the kernel, and cracking, rolling, or grinding to shorten the cooking time.

Because most of the fiber, B vitamins, and oil and 25 percent of the protein in a grain are located in the bran and germ, processing significantly reduces nutritive value. Whole grains are slower to cook and quicker to go rancid, but they are definitely more nutritious than polished grains because bran and germ are left intact.

Use Throughout the world, grains are a major part of the daily diet. In many countries, in fact, it is the rare meal that does not include grains. Where meat is scarce or where vegetarianism is widespread, some form of grain is the major dish in a meal. In contrast, in the wealthier nations of Western Europe and in the United States, grains are usually given a supporting, although appreciated, role.

Grains appear at every meal and in a multitude of guises. At breakfast, grains turn up as cooked and dry cereals, in breads, biscuits, and buns, and in pancakes and waffles. From the hominy grits of the American South to the creamy rice porridge (*congee*) of China, grains are a soothing and sustaining way to start the day.

At the midday or evening meal, grains can be the main event or a side dish. In southern China, a meal usually centers around steamed rice, with other dishes added as the market and budget permit. In Japan, rice is the foundation for every sushi variation; wheat- or rice-based noodles, simply garnished, are a popular Japanese lunch; and a large bowl of steamed rice is usually part of every main meal.

In India, rice is the staple for two thirds of the population, with wheat (in the form of bread) the predominant staple in the northern part of the country. Rice in the south and breads in the north are used to soak up the rich gravies and creamy lentil preparations typical of Indian cooking. An Indian meal may include little, if any, meat, but it always features rice or bread. Millet, also a popular grain in India, is eaten as a breakfast cereal or pilaf and is ground into flour for breads.

In Mexico, corn plays a fundamental role. It is dried and ground for use in tortillas, the principal breadstuff. Rice, usually partnered with beans, is a staple throughout Latin America. It accompanies stews or is layered with other ingredients and baked.

Grains add body and texture to soups and stews. They act as an absorbent foundation for saucy dishes and as an inexpensive and nutritious filler in casseroles. They can be ground for flour and used in breads; baked in puddings, both sweet and savory; cooked, cooled, dressed with a vinaigrette, and served as a salad, often garnished with meats, seafood, or vegetables; and cooked, seasoned, and combined with other ingredients to make a stuffing for meats, fish, poultry, and vegetables.

Grains are further processed to yield flour for breads, noodles, and breadstuff; cornstarch for thickening; and corn syrup for sweetening. In the breadth of their culinary uses and their nutritive value in the diet, grains are doubtless the most important cultivated crops.

Availability Many health-food stores offer a large variety of whole grains, either packaged or in bulk. Supermarkets stock some of the more popular grains, such as rice, barley, and cornmeal.

Selection Grains containing the bran and germ are subject to relatively rapid rancidity. When purchasing grains in bulk, try to buy from a store with a rapid turnover. Make sure the retailer takes the trouble to store the grains properly—in a covered container in a cool, dry place, and with a scoop provided for handling grains.

Storage Whole kernels of grain (groats) still contain the oil-rich germ and are thus more susceptible to rancidity than polished kernels. Cracked groats become rancid even more quickly because the oily germ is exposed. Buy whole groats or cracked groats in small quantities; they will keep in the refrigerator in an airtight container for up to six months. Polished kernels (with bran and germ removed) have a longer shelf life; they may be stored in a cool, dry place in an airtight container for up to one year.

The following section discusses the major culinary grains, their processing, availability, and traditional uses.

BARLEY

The tough outer hull on barley must be removed if it is to be used for anything but animal feed. To remove the hull, barley is pearled or polished between abrasive disks, then sifted. Three pearlings yield pot barley, which still has some of its bran intact. Most barley, however, is pearled five or six times to yield pearl barley, which is missing its hull, its bran, and most of its germ. Pearl barley may be further ground into barley grits, coarse, medium, or fine.

COOKING A VARIETY OF GRAINS

Grains add different tastes and textures, as well as important nutrients, to the diet. Grains with similar cooking times may be combined, as in Wheat Berry–Rice Pilaf (see page 276). Following steps for Measured Water Method for Brown Rice (see About Cooking Rice, page 274), prepare grains to use in various recipes.

Type of Grain	Cooking Method
Barley	*Groats:* Cook 1 cup raw in 4 cups liquid for 45 minutes to yield 3½ cups cooked. *Grits:* Cook 1 cup raw in 2½ cups liquid for 35 minutes to equal 3 cups cooked.
Buckwheat	Toasted buckwheat is known as kasha. *Groats:* Cook 1 cup raw in 2 cups liquid for 15 minutes to yield 2½ to 3 cups cooked. *Grits:* Cook 1 cup raw in 2½ cups liquid for 12 minutes to yield 2½ to 3 cups cooked.
Bulgur	*For pilaf:* Cook 1 cup raw in 2 cups liquid for 15 to 20 minutes to yield 2½ to 3 cups cooked. *For porridge:* Cook 1 cup raw in 4 cups liquid, uncovered, for 20 minutes to yield 3 cups cooked.
Cornmeal	Cook 1 cup raw in 3 to 4 cups liquid—depending on consistency—for about 25 minutes to yield 4 cups cooked.
Millet	Cook 1 cup raw in 1½ cups liquid 15 minutes; let rest, covered, 10 minutes, then fluff with a fork to yield 2½ cups cooked.
Oats	*Rolled oats:* Cook 1 cup raw in 2 cups liquid for 5 to 8 minutes to yield 1¾ cups cooked. *Groats:* Cook 1 cup raw in 2 cups liquid for 1 hour to yield 2 cups cooked. *Grits:* Cook 1 cup raw in 3 cups liquid for 25 minutes to yield 2½ cups cooked.
Quinoa	Cook 1 cup raw in 2 cups liquid for 10 to 15 minutes to yield 4 cups cooked.
Rice	See About Cooking Rice (page 274).
Rye	*Berries:* Cook 1 cup raw in 2 cups liquid for 30 to 40 minutes to yield 2¾ cups cooked. *Cracked:* Cook 1 cup raw in 2 cups liquid for 30 to 40 minutes to yield 2¾ cups cooked. *For porridge:* Cook 1 cup raw rye flakes in 4 cups liquid 25 minutes to yield 3 cups cooked. *For pilaf:* Cook as for cracked rye 15 minutes.
Semolina	Cook 1 cup raw in 3½ cups liquid for 25 minutes to yield 2¾ cups cooked.
Triticale	Cook 1 cup raw in 2 cups liquid for 30 to 40 minutes to yield 2¾ cups cooked.
Wheat	*Berries:* Cook 1 cup raw in 2 cups liquid for 40 to 60 minutes to yield 2¾ cups cooked. *Cracked:* Cook 1 cup raw in 2 cups liquid for 30 to 40 minutes to equal 2⅔ cups cooked.

About half the barley grown in this country is used for animal feed. An additional 30 percent is sprouted and ground for malt, an ingredient in beer. Barley has several culinary uses, too. It is added to soups and stews, eaten as a breakfast porridge (barley grits are especially suitable for breakfast cereal), steamed and eaten as a savory side dish, and baked with mushrooms and stock as a pilaf. Barley flour has poor gluten-forming ability, but can be blended with wheat flour in bread.

Baked in corn-shaped molds to give them their characteristic shape, corn sticks make a delicious accompaniment to hearty soups and stews.

Pearl barley is widely sold in plastic bags and in bulk. Pot barley and barley grits are sold in some health-food stores. Barley flour is also occasionally available in health-food stores.

BUCKWHEAT

Technically, buckwheat is not a cereal grain, for it is not a member of the grass family. Because it is treated as a grain in the kitchen, however, it deserves discussion here. Buckwheat has a full, nutty flavor that is even more pronounced when the grain is toasted.

Buckwheat groats add nutty flavor and texture to pilafs and stuffings; they may be mixed with rice or other grains, or with noodles. Steamed buckwheat grits make a hearty breakfast cereal. Buckwheat flour adds sturdy flavor to pancakes, Russian blini (yeast-risen pancakes), dumplings, Brittany crêpes, and breads.

Buckwheat is marketed either as whole unpolished kernels, called groats, or as ground kernels, called grits. The groats may be toasted or untoasted; the grits are usually toasted. Some supermarkets carry uncooked buckwheat groats or grits packaged as kasha (the Russian word for toasted buckwheat groats or grits). Buckwheat flour is available in health-food stores and some supermarkets.

Recipes: Blini, 602; Buckwheat Pancakes, 600.

CORN

The following section deals with dried corn and dried corn products. For information on fresh sweet corn, see CORN.

Cornmeal   Cornmeal is finely ground from dried white or yellow corn. Some health-food stores sell unbolted cornmeal, which includes both bran and germ. Most supermarket cornmeal, however, is ground from the kernel with the hull and germ removed.

Boiled cornmeal is eaten as a breakfast porridge with butter and syrup, or is molded, cooled, sliced, and fried for a breakfast dish or savory side dish. Cornmeal is used in a wide variety of puddings, muffins, corn breads, fried dumplings, and pancakes. It also serves as a coating for fried foods, such as catfish and trout. Italians cook coarsely ground cornmeal, called polenta, in water or stock to make a thick cornmeal mush, also called polenta. They serve it hot with butter, cheese, meat sauces, or roast fowl. They also chill it, slice it, and fry it, or reheat it in a baking dish, layered with cheese or meat sauce.

Cornmeal is sold in bulk or packed in boxes in the supermarket. Polenta is available in Italian markets and some supermarkets. Blue cornmeal (see opposite page) is available in specialty stores and by mail order. Store unbolted cornmeal in an airtight container in the refrigerator and use within three months. Regular cornmeal can be kept in a covered container in a cool, dry place for up to one year.

■ OLD-FASHIONED BUTTERMILK CORN STICKS

Corn sticks are quick breads made in the same way as muffins. They make a flavorful accompaniment to salads, chowders and soups, casseroles, and other savory dishes. To mold them into the traditional ear-of-corn shape, use a seasoned cast-iron corn-stick pan (see page 21). Corn sticks are best when served soon after baking; they don't keep well.

   1 cup *each* yellow cornmeal and all-purpose flour
   ¼ cup sugar
   2 teaspoons baking powder
   ¾ teaspoon salt
   ½ teaspoon baking soda
   1 egg
   1 cup buttermilk
   2 tablespoons vegetable oil

1. Preheat oven to 425° F. In a large bowl blend cornmeal, flour, sugar, baking powder, salt, and baking soda.

2. In a medium bowl beat egg with buttermilk and oil. Add egg mixture to cornmeal mixture and mix just until dry ingredients are moistened.

3. Divide batter evenly into 2 well-greased corn-stick pans (or greased standard muffin pans).

4. Bake until golden brown (15 to 20 minutes). Best when served warm.

Makes 14 to 16 corn sticks or 1 dozen muffins.

▣ TEXAS JALAPEÑO-CHEESE CORN BREAD

This moist, multiflavored bread is a substantial side dish (and some Texans use sour cream in place of buttermilk to make it even heavier). New Mexico's famed (and somewhat odd-looking) blue corn bread follows, with coarsely ground blue cornmeal replacing the yellow. Corn bread does not keep well. However, the batter can be prepared as much as a day ahead and refrigerated, then baked when needed and served fragrant and warm.

- 1½ cups yellow cornmeal
- 1½ tablespoons flour
- ½ teaspoon salt
- 2 tablespoons sugar
- 1 tablespoon baking powder
- 1 small onion, minced (about ¾ cup)
- 1¼ cups buttermilk
- 1 can (8 oz) creamed corn *or* 1 cup fresh corn scraped with its "cream" from cob
- ½ cup melted butter
- 1 cup grated Cheddar cheese
- ½ pound chorizo, fried and finely chopped (optional)
- ¼ to ½ cup minced canned jalapeño chiles *or* 1 can (4 oz) diced mild chiles

1. Preheat oven to 400° F. In a large bowl stir together cornmeal, flour, salt, sugar, and baking powder. Add onion, buttermilk, corn, and butter; mix rapidly until flour is well moistened. (Batter may be refrigerated overnight.)

2. Grease an 8-inch-square baking pan or 10-inch cast-iron skillet. Pour in half the batter. Sprinkle on half the cheese, *chorizo* (if used), chiles, and remaining cheese. Cover with remaining batter and bake until firm (45 to 50 minutes). If top is not browned, broil about 5 minutes. To serve, cut into sixteen 2-inch squares or 8 wedges.

Makes 16 squares or 8 wedges, serves 8.

Texas Jalapeño-Cheese Corn Muffins Preheat oven to 425° F. Mix cheese and chiles into batter; do not use chorizo. Pour into 12 to 16 greased muffin cups and bake 20 to 25 minutes.

Texas Jalapeño-Cheese Blue Corn Bread Preheat oven to 350° F. Substitute coarsely milled blue cornmeal for yellow cornmeal; do not use chorizo. Bake 1 hour.

Food Processor Version Use metal blade to mince onion and shredding disk to shred well-chilled cheese.

▣ BASIC POLENTA

Although polenta must be watched and stirred continuously as it cooks, diligence yields delicious results: a thick, creamy, golden pudding that has inspired cooks to create countless variations. Common throughout northern Italy, polenta can be eaten hot, with butter and cheese or shaved truffles. It can also be poured into a pan, cooled until firm, and sliced, then layered with meat sauces or with mushrooms and cheese, and baked until bubbly. Often it's reheated with a mantle of grated fontina or Gorgonzola cheese. Serve this recipe hot from the saucepan, to accompany grilled sausages, chicken, or chops.

- 4 cups water
- 1½ teaspoons coarse salt
- 1 cup polenta
- 4 tablespoons unsalted butter
- ¼ cup freshly grated Parmesan cheese

Bring the water and salt to a boil in a heavy saucepan. Gradually add polenta, whisking constantly. Stir in half of the butter. Cook over low heat, stirring constantly with a wooden spoon, 20 minutes. Mixture will become quite thick. Stir in remaining butter and Parmesan; serve hot.

Serves 4.

▣ GRILLED POLENTA

When cooled until firm, then sliced and grilled, polenta makes a great companion to dishes rich in sauce. Serve it with braised rabbit or veal stew, Ragù Bolognese (see page 412), or with plump sausages sautéed with peppers.

- 1 recipe Basic Polenta
- Oil, for greasing rack

1. Oil an 8- or 9-inch loaf pan or a 1-inch-deep cake pan and fill with hot polenta. Cool, then chill until firm.

2. Prepare a medium-hot charcoal fire. Oil grilling rack. Slice polenta ½ inch thick. Grill on both sides until hot throughout. Polenta may also be successfully cooked on an indoor griddle. Serve immediately.

Serves 4.

Recipes: Pan-fried Catfish, 230.

Dried Blue Corn This variety of field corn with blue kernels is cultivated by Pueblo and Hopi Indians in New Mexico. The dried kernels are sold whole or ground into blue cornmeal. The cornmeal is used for blue corn tortillas, corn bread, pancakes, and mush. Baked goods made with blue cornmeal have a bluish gray tinge. Dried blue corn and blue cornmeal are available in some specialty markets or from mail-order sources.

Recipes: Texas Jalapeño-Cheese Blue Corn Bread, at left.

Dried Indian Corn Multicolored Indian corn is sometimes dried on the cob and sold in supermarkets for decorative use on autumn tables.

Dried Sweet Corn Dried either on or off the cob, sweet corn is still used in Pennsylvania Dutch cookery and is available in markets that cater to a Pennsylvania Dutch clientele. It is usually reconstituted in water, then added to soups or stews or made into a side dish.

Hominy This dried field corn has been heated and soaked in a basic solution to soften its hull, then hulled and the germ removed. It is then dried and sold in bulk or plastic bags as dried whole hominy. Look for it in Latin American markets.

When heated and soaked, the hull and germ removed, and finely ground, the dried corn is known as *masa harina* and is used to make tortillas, tamales, and other basic Mexican foods. Fresh prepared *masa* (corn dough) is available in many Latin American markets.

Mexican cooks also boil whole hominy until tender, then add it to soups, such as *menudo* (tripe soup), and to stews. When fully cooked, whole hominy has a sweet flavor and a firm but creamy texture.

Whole cooked hominy, both white and yellow, is also canned and sold in supermarkets. Southern cooks add whole hominy to scrambled eggs, simmer it in cream, or bake it in puddings.

Hominy Grits When cracked, dried whole hominy is called hominy grits. Quick-cooking hominy grits are ground finer than regular grits. Instant hominy grits have been precooked and dehydrated; they can be quickly rehydrated in hot water. Hominy grits are eaten as a breakfast cereal, with butter and syrup; molded, cooled, sliced, and fried; and baked in puddings, cheese-topped casseroles, and soufflés.

■ BAKED GARLIC GRITS

Hospitable southerners who want to help their northern friends develop a taste for grits are likely to introduce them to this elaborate and delicate version, which resembles a fallen cheese soufflé. Serve baked grits for brunch (the batter can be mixed the night before) or at dinner; they are especially suited to accompany roasts and barbecues. Use Cheddar cheese if grits will be eaten with a hearty dish, Swiss cheese if with a light main course.

   ½ **cup milk**
   3 **eggs**
   ½ **pound sharp Cheddar cheese or Swiss cheese, grated**
   2 **tablespoons freshly grated Parmesan cheese**
   8 **tablespoons unsalted butter, cut in small pieces**
   2 **medium cloves garlic, minced (about 2 tsp)**
   ¼ **teaspoon freshly ground pepper**
   1 **tablespoon snipped fresh chives or minced green onion tops**
   4 **cups water**
   1 **teaspoon salt**
   1 **cup quick-cooking hominy grits**
   1 **teaspoon butter**

1. Preheat oven to 325° F. In a medium bowl beat together milk and eggs. Add cheeses, unsalted butter, garlic, pepper, and chives. Set aside.

2. Bring the water and salt to a boil. Add grits, stir, and return to a boil. Lower heat to medium and continue cooking, stirring often, until grits are thickened (about 5 minutes). Pour out any unabsorbed water. Remove from heat, immediately pour cheese mixture into grits, and stir until cheeses and butter melt. (Grits may be prepared in advance to this point; cover and refrigerate up to one day until ready to serve.)

3. Grease a 2-quart casserole or soufflé dish with the 1 teaspoon butter. Spoon grits mixture into prepared casserole and bake until a knife inserted in center comes out clean (about 1 hour). Baked grits may be left in oven, with heat turned off, for 10 minutes before serving.

Serves 8.

Recipes: Menudo, 591.

MILLET

A small round yellow seed, millet does not require processing after harvesting. It is a common ingredient in birdseed mixtures but is otherwise used infrequently in this country. It has a crunchy texture and a flavor resembling that of corn.

Millet may be steamed and eaten as a breakfast cereal with butter, maple syrup, and cream; cooked in stock like a pilaf or baked in a pudding; or when cooked added to stuffings or breads for texture and flavor.

Millet is sold in bulk in most health-food stores and in some supermarkets.

OATS

Whole oats must be hulled before they are fit for human consumption. Hulled whole oats are also known as oat groats. Steel-cut oats are groats that have been sliced with steel blades. Rolled oats (old-fashioned oats) are groats that have been steamed and flattened by rollers into flakes. Quick-cooking rolled oats are groats that have been cut into smaller pieces before rolling, yielding thinner flakes that cook more quickly. Instant oats are made from partially cooked groat pieces rolled even thinner than quick-cooking oats. Some brands of instant oatmeal are flavored with sugar and spices; most have salt added. Regular and quick-cooking oats can be used interchangeably in recipes; using flavored instant oats alters the taste of a recipe that calls for regular or quick-cooking oats.

Apart from the morning bowl of oatmeal, oats do not figure largely in the American diet. Yet they are a flavorful and nutritious grain with several culinary uses. Although most Americans make their oatmeal from rolled oats, steel-cut oats also make a delicious cereal with chewier texture and slightly more nutritive value. Cooked whole oats can be added to soups or stews. Rolled oats are used in granola, cookies, muffins, and cakes. They can also be added, either raw or cooked, to yeast bread doughs. Cooked oatmeal contributes moisture and bulk to stuffings, breads, and meat loaves. It can also be molded, cooled, sliced, and fried like cornmeal mush. Oat groats can be ground into flour for baking.

Health-food stores generally stock oat groats, steel-cut oats, and rolled oats. Most supermarkets sell rolled, quick-cooking, and instant oats. Oat flour is available in some health-food stores.

■ OATMEAL GEMS

These chewy, slightly sweet muffins are good with soups and stews. The name *gem* refers to the old-fashioned cast-iron pans that produce a first-rate muffin with a crusty exterior and rounded top. If you don't have cast-iron gem pans, use plain muffin tins; for a similar result, try to find tins made of a heavyweight material. Leftover muffins are delicious split, toasted, and buttered. Note that the recipe calls for quick-cooking oats; however, regular oats can also be used as the two types are interchangeable in recipes.

    2 cups quick-cooking oats
 1½ cups buttermilk
  ¼ cup molasses
    2 tablespoons sugar
    2 eggs
  ½ teaspoon salt
    1 cup flour
    1 teaspoon baking soda

1. Preheat oven to 400° F. Grease standard muffin pans or line with cupcake papers. Combine oats and buttermilk in a medium bowl and let stand about 15 minutes.

2. Beat in molasses, sugar, eggs, and salt. Stir together flour and baking soda, then add to oat mixture and mix just until dry ingredients are moistened.

3. Fill prepared pans two thirds full. Bake until a toothpick inserted in a muffin comes out clean (about 20 minutes). Serve warm.

Makes about 16 muffins.

QUINOA

Relatively new to the American marketplace, quinoa (pronounced keen-wa) is actually an ancient food. Native to the Andean region of South America, it was a staple of the Incan diet. Quinoa has an excellent nutritional profile, with more protein than other grains. In contrast to other grains, its protein is complete (containing all the essential amino acids).

Although, like buckwheat, quinoa isn't technically a grain, it looks, cooks, and tastes like one. It can be substituted for rice in side dishes, casseroles, salads, and stuffings. It has a notably light texture and mild flavor. Look for quinoa in health-food stores.

RICE

An extremely important food crop, rice provides basic sustenance to half the population of the world. The cuisines of Japan, China, India, Indonesia, and Southeast Asia are all rice-based; few meals there are served without rice or a rice dish.

Thousands of varieties of rice are cultivated, but the most important distinction from the cook's standpoint is the length of the grain. Long-grain rice has a decidedly different texture when cooked than short-grain rice and is thus better suited to certain types of dishes.

Store rice in an airtight container in a cool, dry place. It will keep indefinitely.

Some cooks insist on washing or soaking rice before use. Although washing removes external starch particles that might cause stickiness, it also washes away any vitamin or protein enrichment (see Enriched Rice). On the other hand, some cooks claim that rinsing gives the rice a cleaner, lighter taste. Whether the nutritional loss is worth the improved flavor, or whether indeed the flavor improvement is noticeable, is a matter of personal taste.

Rice fits comfortably into most meals, whether as a background for highly seasoned dishes, as a vehicle for sauces, or as a filling accompaniment to simply prepared roasted or broiled meats and poultry.

ABOUT COOKING RICE

For a task that appears so simple, there is much disagreement about rice cookery. Some cooks prefer to boil rice in a large quantity of water until it is tender, pouring off the excess liquid and drying the grain in a slow oven. The advantages of this technique are that it does not require precise measurement and it yields a fluffy, dry grain; however, the discarded liquid contains valuable nutrients.

Other cooks steam rice. A precise quantity of liquid is brought to a boil, the rice is added, covered, and slowly steamed until done. This method produces moister, more nutritious kernels.

A third method, preferred by some Chinese cooks, calls for adding rice to precisely measured boiling liquid and simmering, uncovered, until much of the liquid is absorbed. Then the mixture is stirred, the pot covered, and the rice steamed until done. Stirring releases the starch from the kernels' surface and produces a stickier rice.

Yet another method, the pilaf method, calls for sautéing the grains in butter or oil first, then adding hot liquid, covering, and steaming until tender. The pilaf method produces distinct, flavorful grains. It is popular among Western cooks, but less so among Asian cooks, who prefer rice plain and dry.

The method chosen depends on the results desired. Here are more precise directions for different methods.

UNLIMITED WATER METHOD

Boil rice, uncovered, in an unlimited amount of salted water for 12 to 15 minutes until softened, but still firm at the core. Drain well in a sieve. Transfer to a shallow baking dish, cover, and steam in a 300° F oven 10 to 15 minutes, or until tender and dry. Toss with butter and serve. Timing given is for white rice; brown rice and wild rice can be cooked by this method, but will take longer.

MEASURED WATER METHOD

For White Rice Bring 1½ cups lightly salted water to a boil. Add 1 cup rice and stir once with a fork. Cover, reduce heat to low, and cook 18 minutes. Remove from heat and let stand 5 minutes. Fluff with a fork.

For Brown Rice Bring 2 cups lightly salted water to a boil. Add 1 cup rice and stir once with a fork. Cover, reduce heat to low, and cook 45 to 50 minutes. Remove from heat and let stand 5 minutes. Fluff with a fork.

For Wild Rice Bring 2½ cups lightly salted water to a boil. Add 1 cup wild rice and stir once with a fork. Cover, reduce heat to low, and cook 40 to 45 minutes. Remove from heat and let stand 5 minutes. Fluff with a fork.

CHINESE METHOD

Put 1 cup rice in saucepan with 2 cups cold, salted water. Bring to a boil over high heat, cover, and cook until water has been absorbed down to level of rice. Stir rice well with a spoon, cover, and reduce heat to low; cook about 15 minutes or until grains are tender. Fluff with a fork.

PILAF METHOD

Melt 2 tablespoons oil, Clarified Butter (see page 68), or a butter-oil mixture in a heavy-bottomed saucepan over moderate heat. Add 1 cup rice and stir to coat all grains with fat. Sauté rice 2 to 3 minutes, stirring constantly. Add 1½ cups boiling, salted water (2 cups for brown rice, 2½ cups for wild rice), cover, reduce heat to low, and steam until tender (15 minutes for white rice, 30 to 45 minutes for brown and wild rice). Remove from heat, let stand 5 minutes, and fluff with a fork.

COOKING RICE IN THE MICROWAVE OVEN

Using a microwave oven to cook rice saves cleanup and keeps the kitchen cool, but it won't save time. Rice will require the same number of minutes whether cooked by microwave or on top of the stove. If you choose the microwave method, use a larger container than seems necessary to prevent overflow. Reheat cooked rice 1 minute per cup at 100 percent power. Fluff all rice with a fork after cooking.

Type of Rice	Amount	Liquid	Cooking Time
Long-grain white	1 cup	2 cups	5 minutes at 100% power 15 minutes at 50% power
Brown	1 cup	2–2½ cups	5 minutes at 100% power 45–55 minutes at 30% power

Some Japanese rice is coated with cornstarch after milling to retard rancidity. It must be rinsed to prevent the cornstarch from making the rice gummy. Imported rice, such as Indian *basmati* rice, is not always as carefully cleaned as American rice. It should be picked over carefully to remove small pebbles and bits of chaff.

Arborio Rice Grown in the Po Valley of Italy, Arborio rice is a short-grain rice. Its high starch content is responsible for the distinctive creamy texture of Italian risotto. Arborio rice is also a good choice for rice puddings and soups.

Basmati Rice A particularly aromatic variety of long-grain rice, *basmati* is grown in India and Pakistan, and, more recently, in California. It is the preferred rice for Indian cooking, but its special fragrance and nutty flavor make it a delicious rice for use with Western dishes as well. Before cooking, it should be picked over for small stones, then washed well and soaked; follow cooking directions for white rice. Basmati is available in specialty stores, Indian markets, and some health-food stores.

Glutinous Rice A short-grain rice used in Asian cooking, glutinous, or sweet, rice has a high starch content and is very sticky when cooked. It is an ingredient in a variety of Asian sweets and snacks, such as molded rice puddings and dumplings. It is the variety used to make *mochi,* the Japanese chewy rice cake. It is not used as an everyday table rice.

Long-Grain Rice These varieties produce a kernel that is four to five times as long as it is wide, with tapered ends. The cooked grains tend to be separate, dry, light, and fluffy, making long-grain rice the best choice for salads and pilafs. Most of the rice served in America and in Western Europe is long-grain rice.

Short- and Medium-Grain Rice These varieties have short, rounded kernels; when cooked, the kernels are moist and slightly sticky, and tend to cling. The Japanese favor short-grain rice, perhaps because the grains are easier to pick up with chopsticks. Short-grain rice (also called pearl rice) has a higher proportion of waxy starch molecules (amylopectin) in its starch granules than long-grain rice, which explains the tendency of short grains to adhere. This quality is desirable in such dishes as croquettes, rice puddings, molded rice rings, and sushi.

■ BAKED RICE PUDDING

Long, slow baking results in a rich, sweet, golden cream, which is equally good warm or cold.

    Butter, for greasing pan
½ **cup raw short-grain rice (see Note)**
4 **cups half-and-half**
1 **cup whipping cream**
½ **cup sugar**
1 **teaspoon vanilla extract**

1. Preheat oven to 300° F. Generously butter a 2-quart ovenproof dish. Sprinkle rice over bottom of dish. In a large bowl combine half-and-half, cream, sugar, and vanilla; pour over rice, stirring to combine.

2. Bake 1 hour, stirring every 20 minutes. Raise heat to 350° F and bake until a creamy, golden crust forms (45 minutes to 1 hour). Serve hot or warm.

Serves 6.

Cold Rice Pudding   To serve cold, reduce amount of rice to ⅓ cup; just before serving fold in 1 cup whipping cream, whipped to soft peaks.

Raisin Rice Pudding   Fold into cream mixture 1 cup golden raisins that have been soaked in rum, if desired; pour over rice.

Note   If short-grain rice is unavailable, long-grain rice can be used, but will produce a thinner pudding.

FRIED RICE WITH HAM, EGG, AND CABBAGE

What started as a way to use leftover rice has become a popular dish in its own right—fried rice. Actually the rice is not really fried, but stir-fried in a little oil. The catchall found in some restaurants, dark brown with soy sauce, cannot compare with good homemade fried rice. Most fried rice dishes are seasoned with salt, not soy sauce, to preserve the color of the rice. Cloud ears, an ingredient in this recipe, are edible fungi used for their crunchy yet gelatinous texture. You'll find them in Asian markets and some well-stocked supermarkets.

  1½ ounces trimmed Smithfield ham
  2 to 3 tablespoons vegetable oil
  1 egg, beaten
  1 teaspoon minced fresh ginger
  1 clove garlic, minced
  ⅓ pound bok choy, cut crosswise into ¼-inch slices
  2 tablespoons cloud ears, soaked until soft and drained
  2 to 3 cups cooked rice, at room temperature (see About Cooking Rice, Chinese Method, opposite page)
    Salt, to taste
  ¼ cup Chicken Stock (see page 560)

1. Soak ham in water for 30 minutes. Drain and cut in thin slices. Heat wok or skillet over medium-high heat, and add 1 tablespoon oil. Pour beaten egg into pan and swirl to make a large, flat omelet. Cook egg just until set, transfer to cutting board, and cut into thin 1-inch strips.

2. Add remaining oil to pan. Add ginger and garlic; cook until fragrant. Add bok choy, ham, and cloud ears; stir-fry until heated through (about 2 minutes).

3. Add rice to pan and stir to break up clumps. Stir-fry vigorously, scraping up any bits of rice that cling to pan. When rice begins to brown, add salt to taste (allow for saltiness of ham), then add stock and egg strips. Turn heat to high and stir-fry until liquid is nearly all evaporated. Transfer to serving platter.

Serves 2 as a one-dish meal, 4 or more with other dishes.

LEMON RISOTTO

Serve this sprightly Italian rice dish before a fish main course. Add more stock to the rice mixture only after previous quantities have been absorbed.

  2 tablespoons plus 2 teaspoons unsalted butter
  2 tablespoons olive oil
  ¼ cup minced onion
    Grated rind of 1 lemon
  1½ cups Arborio rice
  4½ cups Chicken Stock (see page 560)
  ¼ cup plus 2 teaspoons fresh lemon juice
  ½ cup freshly grated Parmesan cheese
    Salt and freshly ground pepper, to taste

1. Melt 2 tablespoons butter in a heavy saucepan over moderately low heat. Add olive oil, then onion and lemon rind, and sauté slowly for 5 minutes. Add rice and stir to coat with oil. Turn up heat to high and toast, stirring, for 30 seconds. Immediately add ½ cup stock and reduce heat to medium-low. Stir constantly until stock is absorbed. Keep adding more stock, ½ cup at a time, stirring constantly and adding more only when the previous quantity has been absorbed. When all the stock is absorbed, stir in ¼ cup lemon juice. Rice should be tender. If not, add a little warm water bit by bit until rice is tender yet firm.

2. Stir in Parmesan and remaining butter. Cook briefly to blend and melt cheese. Season to taste with salt and pepper. Add remaining lemon juice and serve immediately in warm bowls.

Serves 4.

SPECIAL PROCESSING

All rice is processed before it reaches the commercial market. At the least, it is hulled. In addition, it may be polished, parboiled, precooked, or flavored.

Brown Rice   This type has been minimally processed. The tough hull has been removed, and the outer bran remains. Because of the presence of bran, brown rice is more nutritious than polished (white) rice but does take longer to cook.

Enriched Rice   In an attempt to replace some of the vitamins and protein lost through milling, the rice is sprayed after milling with vitamins in solution, then coated with protein powder and dried.

Flavored Rice   Some seasonings and/or other ingredients have been combined with the rice, which has been milled and possibly parboiled or precooked before being packaged.

Parboiled Rice   This is also known as converted rice. The whole unhulled grain is soaked, drained, partially pressure-cooked, then dried and milled. The aim is to make converted rice more nutritious than regular white rice by diffusing the B vitamins from the bran and germ into the endosperm before the grain is milled.

Precooked Rice   This is white rice that has been fully or partially precooked, then dehydrated.

White Rice   An abrasive process mills or polishes the kernels and removes the bran and most of the germ. The result is white rice.

Recipes: Maki Zushi, 392; Nigiri Sushi, 233; Onion and Rice Soubise, 229; Red Beans and Rice, 32; Roast Chicken With Rice, Fruit, and Almond Stuffing, 470; Stuffed Green Peppers Mexicana, 426; Sushi Rice, 233.

RYE

Few Americans have ever cooked with whole rye berries, although many have made breads with rye flour. Rye grass thrives in poor soils and hard climates and is often planted where wheat would be unable to survive. The grain has a strong, distinctive flavor. It has no hull and does not require milling.

Whole cooked rye berries may be used in casseroles, soups, stuffings, or stir-fried dishes. Cracked rye is suitable for pilafs or breakfast cereals. Rye flakes may be used like rolled oats. Rye flour has poor gluten-forming ability and makes a heavy bread on its own; for that reason, rye breads usually contain some portion of wheat flour.

Whole rye berries, cracked rye, and rolled rye flakes are available in health-food stores. Rye flour is sold in most supermarkets, in bulk or packed in boxes or paper bags.

TRITICALE

A relatively new hybrid of wheat and rye, triticale is designed to be as productive as wheat, as hardy as rye, and more nutritious than either.

Cooked whole triticale may be used as any other whole grain: in pilafs, casseroles, soups, or stuffings. Triticale flour may be used, either by itself or mixed with wheat flour, in breads, cookies, pancakes, muffins, and other baked goods. The flour has a full, nutty flavor but has low gluten-forming abilities. For a lighter baked product, use 50 percent wheat flour.

Whole triticale berries and triticale flour are sold in health-food stores. Triticale flakes (rolled triticale) are available in some health-food stores.

WHEAT

In its worldwide importance, wheat is second only to rice. Although more people depend on rice than on wheat, more acreage is planted with wheat and more wheat is produced. Wheat was probably the first cereal cultivated, and it can thus be argued that wheat is responsible for changing the human race from nomads to settlers.

Although there are at least thirty thousand known varieties of wheat, the most important distinction for the cook is between hard and soft varieties. Hard wheats are relatively high in glutenin and gliadin, the two proteins that, when moistened, combine to form gluten. Gluten is the elastic substance that allows a bread dough to trap gases and hold a shape or a pasta dough to be rolled and stretched into noodles. Consequently, flours milled from hard wheats are the best choice for breads and pasta; flours milled from soft wheats are best for cakes, cookies, and quick breads.

The wheat berry, or whole kernel, may be processed to yield a variety of different products. Some of those products are described below; for further information on processed wheat products, see FLOUR.

Whole Wheat Berries   The unprocessed kernels of wheat are called whole wheat berries. Because they still contain bran and germ, berries are slow to cook, but are correspondingly high in nutrition and flavor.

Whole wheat berries may be boiled or steamed for pilafs, stuffings, breads, and porridge. Berries may also be sprouted for use in salads, breads, or stir-fried dishes.

Look for whole wheat berries in health-food stores. Store them in an airtight container in a cool place or in the refrigerator for up to six months.

WHEAT BERRY–RICE PILAF

This pilaf offers an opportunity to try a mixture of different grains that lend balance, protein, and flavor to a meal. Triticale, a hybrid of wheat and rye, is an especially nutritious substitute for wheat berries. Barley can also be exchanged for the wheat berries.

- **2 tablespoons vegetable oil**
- **1 onion, minced**
- **2 carrots, finely diced**
- **1 stalk celery, finely diced**
- **1 cup wheat berries**
- **1 cup brown rice**
- **⅓ cup wild rice**
- **4½ cups Chicken Stock (see page 560) or water**
- **½ tablespoon kosher salt**

1. Heat oil in a 2-quart saucepan over medium heat. Stir in onions, carrots, and celery, and cook until softened but not browned. Add wheat berries, brown rice, wild rice, stock, and salt. Stir to combine.

2. Cover pan and cook about 40 minutes over medium to low heat.

Serves 8.

Food Processor Version   Cut onion, carrots, and celery into 1-inch pieces. Put in work bowl with metal blade and pulse 3 or 4 times. Scrape work bowl and pulse until desired texture is reached. Use as directed.

Wheat Bran   The outer coating of the wheat berry is called the bran. Removed from the wheat berry during milling, it is often packaged and sold separately. Bran is valued principally as a source of dietary fiber, although it also contains B vitamins and protein.

Add bran to muffins, cereals, yeast breads, and quick breads for improved nutritive value. It is available in health-food stores and some supermarkets, both in bulk and in packages. Store bran in refrigerator in an airtight container; use within six months.

Recipes: Bran Muffins, 375; Refrigerator Bran Muffin Mix, 376.

Wheat Germ   When wheat is milled for white flour, the bran and germ are removed. The oil- and protein-rich germ, often packaged and sold separately, is valued for the nutty flavor and nutrition it adds to dishes. Use wheat germ in breads, muffins, cookies, granola, and cooked cereals.

Wheat germ, toasted or raw, is available in bulk in health-food stores or in vacuum-sealed jars in supermarkets. It is sold flaked or as a coarse meal. Because of its high oil content, it is the most perishable part of the wheat kernel and goes rancid quickly. If purchasing wheat germ in bulk, buy it from health-food stores that keep it under refrigeration and have a rapid turnover. If the bulk wheat germ is not refrigerated, the vacuum-packed variety may be a better choice. Store bulk wheat germ in the refrigerator in an airtight container. After opening, keep vacuum-packed wheat germ in the refrigerator in the original container. If properly stored and sealed, bulk or packaged wheat germ will keep for two to three months.

Cracked Wheat   Coarse, medium, or fine, cracked wheat is made from the whole unprocessed wheat berry cut with steel blades. When cooked, it has a nutty flavor and a slightly crunchy texture.

Eat cooked cracked wheat as a breakfast cereal, either alone or mixed with other grains. Use it for stuffings, pilafs, and cold salads. Cooked cracked wheat adds moist texture and nutty flavor to whole wheat breads.

Cracked wheat is available in health-food stores and some supermarkets, in bulk or packaged. Store it in an airtight container in a cool, dry place or in the refrigerator for up to six months.

Bulgur   Whole wheat berries that have been steamed, then dried and cracked are known as bulgur. It has a nuttier flavor than cracked wheat and when cooked has a softer texture.

Use bulgur for salads, stuffings, breakfast cereals, and pilafs, or as an addition to bread doughs or meat loaves. Bulgur in coarse and fine grinds is available in health-food stores and some supermarkets, in bulk or packaged. Store in an airtight container in a cool, dry place for up to one year.

■ TABBOULEH

To use this Middle Eastern salad as an hors d'oeuvre, provide leaves of romaine to scoop up the mixture.

    1   cup bulgur
    ⅓   cup fresh lemon juice
    1   teaspoon salt
    ⅛   teaspoon freshly ground pepper
    ⅔   cup olive oil
    ½   cup *each* thinly sliced green onions and
        finely chopped parsley
    ⅓   cup fresh mint leaves
    1   medium tomato, seeded and chopped
        Inner romaine lettuce leaves, for accompaniment

1. Rinse bulgur and drain well. Cover with cold water and let stand for 1 hour. Drain well, pressing out moisture.

2. In a large bowl mix lemon juice, salt, and pepper. Using a whisk or fork, gradually beat in oil until well combined. To oil mixture add drained bulgur, onion, parsley, and mint; mix lightly. Cover and refrigerate until ready to serve (at least 2 hours).

3. Mound Tabbouleh in a shallow serving dish; sprinkle with tomato. Surround with romaine leaves, and use them as scoops for serving and eating.

Serves 4 to 6.

Semolina   A pale ivory grain with a nutty flavor, semolina is ground from the endosperm of an especially hard wheat called durum wheat. Because durum wheat is high in glutenin and gliadin, the two proteins that form gluten when moistened, semolina dough is firm and elastic. The dough is so pliable that semolina is the flour used for most dried Italian pastas.

Generally, the coarse grind of semolina is preferred for cereals, the fine grind for pasta. (In Italy, semolina flour is used for factory-made dried pasta, not for homemade fresh pasta.) Use semolina for hot cooked cereal, puddings, and Italian *gnocchi*. Add finely ground semolina to bread dough for creamy color and nutty flavor.

Semolina is sold in Italian markets, some health-food stores, and some supermarkets, in bulk and packaged. It is available in coarse, medium, and fine grinds. Store in an airtight container in a cool, dry place for up to one year.

Couscous   A semolina product, couscous is made from moistened semolina rolled into tiny pellets and dried. It is popular in Northern Africa, especially Morocco and Tunisia, where it gives its name to a dish built around it. A Moroccan or Tunisian couscous is an elaborate dish: a spicy stew of lamb, chicken, or fish and vegetables, or a sweet stew of dried fruits and nuts, rich in broth and served atop a mound of the steaming couscous grain.

Use couscous in casseroles, pilafs, or stuffings; enjoy it as a breakfast cereal with butter, sugar, and milk, or as a savory side dish for a roast or stew; or serve it in a traditional Tunisian or Moroccan couscous.

Couscous is sold in Middle Eastern markets, health-food stores, and some supermarkets, in bulk and packaged. A convenient instant version is available but yields a less desirable texture. Store in an airtight container in a cool, dry place; it will keep indefinitely.

■ COUSCOUS

Both the grain and the dish prepared from it are referred to as *couscous*. Traditionally the main ingredients—vegetables and chicken—cook in the bottom of a special *couscousière* while the couscous grains steam over it. You may also prepare the chicken and vegetables in one pan and cook the wheat grains separately. Quick-cooking or instant couscous is available to simplify this step.

    4 cups regular or instant couscous
    ½ cup unsalted butter
    3 tablespoons salt
    4 tablespoons vegetable oil
    4 onions, diced
    2 cloves garlic, minced
    2 teaspoons freshly ground black pepper
    1 teaspoon cayenne pepper
    ¼ gram saffron threads (1 vial)
    1 teaspoon ground turmeric
    2 tablespoons fresh ginger, minced
    2 tablespoons ground cinnamon
    6 cups water
    1 whole chicken (2½ to 3 lb)
    6 small red boiling potatoes, halved or
       quartered depending on size
    6 carrots, cut in 3-inch lengths
    3 zucchini, cut in 3-inch lengths
    3 golden zucchini, cut in 3-inch lengths
   12 ounces cooked chick-peas
    1 cup golden raisins

Spicy Harissa

    ½ teaspoon cumin seed
    ¼ teaspoon coriander seed
    1 clove garlic, minced
    1 red jalapeño chile, minced
    ¼ cup Chicken Stock (see page 560)
    1 tablespoon olive oil
    1 teaspoon cilantro, minced
    ½ teaspoon parsley, minced
    ⅛ teaspoon cayenne pepper
    ¼ teaspoon salt

1. If using regular couscous, rinse grains under running water, then soak in 8 cups water for 30 minutes (this allows them to swell later while they absorb flavors of stew). Drain couscous and pat dry with paper towels. Rub grains together to remove any lumps. Line colander or deep steamer with cheesecloth, add soaked couscous, place colander or deep steamer over a 4-quart pot of boiling water, and steam, uncovered, 30 minutes. (If

colander and pan do not fit tightly you may have to wrap cheesecloth around bottom of colander to form a seal.) The goal is to have grains swell as large as possible and not become lumpy or soggy. For instant couscous follow instructions on package.

2. When couscous is cooked, place on a platter and spread out. Toss with 2 tablespoons butter and 1 teaspoon salt. Stir to remove any lumps. If preparing ahead, cover loosely with foil and reheat by steaming for 20 minutes.

3. Heat 4 tablespoons butter and oil in a large stockpot. Add onions and garlic; sauté 5 minutes. Add remaining salt, pepper, cayenne, saffron, turmeric, ginger, and cinnamon; cook 2 to 3 minutes. Add the water and bring to a boil. Reduce heat, place chicken in pan, cover, and simmer for 35 minutes. Add potatoes and carrots and simmer 15 minutes more. Add zucchini, chick-peas, and raisins; continue cooking 15 minutes.

4. To serve, put couscous into a large shallow bowl or platter and toss with remaining butter to remove any lumps. Place chicken in center of couscous. Surround with vegetables, and spoon pan juices on top. Serve Spicy Harissa as a condiment.

Serves 6 to 8.

Spicy Harissa   Toast cumin and coriander seed in a small, dry skillet over medium heat for about 4 minutes. Purée with garlic, jalapeño, Chicken Stock, olive oil, cilantro, parsley, cayenne, and salt in blender or food processor.

Makes ½ cup.

WILD RICE

The seed of an aquatic grass, rather than a variety of rice, wild rice grows wild in Minnesota lakes and is cultivated in California. The grain is dark brown, slender, and even longer than long-grain rice.

Although Californians and Minnesotans defend the superiority of their products, there is little difference in flavor between the two. California rice is generally less expensive because it is harvested by machine. Most of the Minnesota crop is harvested by traditional hand methods.

Wild rice has a nutty, earthy flavor that is particularly appealing with game and dark-meat fowl. Ground into flour, it is used in combination with white flour for pancakes, waffles, crêpes, muffins, and other baked goods. Mix the grain with brown rice or white rice for pilafs and cold salads; stir it into soups; or use it as the foundation for a poultry stuffing.

Some supermarkets carry packaged wild rice or packaged rice blends containing wild rice. Check health-food stores and specialty shops for wild rice in bulk.

Recipes: Wheat Berry–Rice Pilaf, 276.

GRAPE

A prehistoric fruit, grapes have been known to man at least since Neolithic times and have been cultivated, possibly, since then. Today they are cultivated in many temperate regions of the world. The thousands of grape varieties are very sensitive to climate. Many varieties cultivated in California would not survive a New York winter, although dozens of hardier ones thrive on the East Coast. Grapes grow in clusters on vines. Ranging from ⅓ inch to more than 1 inch in diameter, they are oval or round, with smooth green, red, purple, or purplish black skins.

Use Grapes are loosely classified as either table grapes or wine grapes, although there is considerable overlap. Because grapes grown primarily for wine—such as Cabernet Sauvignon and Riesling—rarely appear on the consumer market, they are not considered here. Most wine grapes, however, are very flavorful; if you live in a region where wine grapes are grown, seek them out.

Grapes are eaten out of hand or as part of fruit compotes, fruit salads, or chicken salad. They are the classic garnish for filet of sole or chicken breast prepared à la Veronique. Whole grapes can be pickled and used as a garnish, pressed for juice, or made into handsome preserves, conserves, and jellies.

Availability Fresh grapes can be found the year around. Imports from the southern hemisphere fill in for the domestic crop in late spring. Check Common Table Grape Varieties for specific grape seasons.

Selection Buy firm, plump grapes without signs of withering. Bunches should be well developed and fairly loose to allow for air circulation and to prevent mildew. Stem end should be green and healthy, not dry and blackened. White or green grapes are sweetest when color has a yellowish cast with a tinge of amber. Red grapes are best when red predominates.

Storage Before refrigerating, remove any spoiled grapes. Store in a plastic bag in refrigerator; they will keep for up to two weeks.

◼ FLORENTINE GRAPE COFFEE CAKE

Serve this grape-dotted cake as part of an Italian-accented brunch along with frittata (see page 204) and caffè latte.

> 1 teaspoon anise seed, coarsely crushed
> ½ cup sugar
> 1 package active dry yeast
> ¼ cup *each* warm (105° to 115° F) water and warm milk
> ⅛ teaspoon salt
> ½ teaspoon vanilla extract
> ½ cup butter or margarine, softened
> 2½ to 3 cups flour
> 1 egg
> 3 cups Concord or red seedless grapes

COMMON TABLE GRAPE VARIETIES

The consumer market offers dozens of varieties of table grapes. These are some of the best-known varieties.

Grape Variety	Color	Availability
Cardinal	Red	June
Catawba	Purple-red	September through October
Concord	Purple-black	September through October
Delaware	Pink	September through October
Emperor	Light red	September
Flame Tokay (seedless)	Red	September through November
Italia Muscat	Yellow	August through November
Perlette (seedless)	Green	Early June through July
Queen	Red	Late July through December
Red Malaga	Red	Late July through September
Ribier	Purple-black	July through February
Thompson Seedless	Green	June through November

1. In a small jar stir together crushed anise seed and sugar. Cover and let stand for 8 hours or overnight to blend flavors. Pour through a fine sieve to remove seed; discard seed.

2. Sprinkle yeast over the water in large bowl of electric mixer. Add 1 tablespoon of anise-flavored sugar. Let yeast-sugar mixture stand until yeast is soft (about 5 minutes).

3. Add 2 tablespoons anise sugar, warm milk, salt, vanilla, and butter.

4. Add 1 cup flour. Mix to blend, then beat at medium speed until smooth and elastic (about 3 minutes). Beat in egg until smooth. Stir in about 1½ cups more flour to make a soft dough.

5. Turn dough out onto a floured board or pastry cloth. Knead until smooth and satiny and small bubbles form just under surface (5 to 10 minutes), adding just enough flour to prevent dough from being sticky.

6. Turn dough in a greased bowl. Cover with plastic wrap and a towel; let rise in a warm place until doubled in bulk (1¼ to 1½ hours).

7. Punch dough down. Cover with inverted bowl. Let rest for 10 minutes.

8. Roll dough out on a floured surface to a large rectangle. Press into a greased, shallow 10- by 15-inch baking pan. Sprinkle evenly with grapes, then sprinkle grapes with remaining anise sugar.

9. Let rise until dough looks puffy (20 to 25 minutes). Preheat oven to 400° F.

10. Bake coffee cake until well browned (15 to 20 minutes). Let cool slightly in pan, then cut into generous strips. Best served warm.

Serves 8 to 10.

One of the most elegant ways to serve boneless chicken breasts is in a wine-cream sauce with seedless grapes.

CHICKEN BREASTS WITH GRAPES

Boneless chicken breasts can be cooked in an almost limitless variety of quick, elegant ways. Accompany these chicken breasts with fluffy rice and a fruity white wine such as Chenin Blanc.

  3 **whole chicken breasts (3 lb), halved, boned, and skinned**
    Salt and freshly grated nutmeg, as needed
  2 **tablespoons butter or margarine**
  1 **tablespoon orange marmalade**
  ¼ **teaspoon dried tarragon**
  1 **green onion, thinly sliced (use part of top)**
  ⅓ **cup dry white wine**
  1 **cup seedless grapes**
  ¼ **cup whipping cream**

1. Sprinkle chicken breasts with salt and nutmeg. In a large frying pan, heat butter over medium-high heat and brown chicken lightly. Add marmalade, tarragon, green onion, and wine. Cover, reduce heat, and simmer 10 minutes; add grapes, cover again, and continue cooking until chicken is cooked through (about 10 minutes longer; test in thickest part with a small, sharp knife).

2. Using a slotted spoon, remove chicken and grapes to a heated serving dish; keep warm. Add cream to liquid in pan. Bring to a boil, stirring; cook until sauce is reduced and slightly thickened. Salt to taste. Pour sauce over chicken.

Serves 4 to 6.

GRAPEFRUIT

A relatively new citrus species, grapefruit was not acknowledged as such until 1830 and was not commercially cultivated until the late nineteenth century. Today, the United States produces about 90 percent of the world crop, with Florida growing about 70 percent. The most popular variety today is the (nearly) seedless Marsh, which has a yellow rind and yellow fruit. Thompson (also called Pink Marsh) and Ruby are pink-fleshed varieties developed in Texas. Ripe grapefruit is full of juice and has an invigorating flavor that is both sweet and tart.

Use A large part of the Florida crop is processed for juice. Fresh grapefruit is generally eaten raw—by the half or peeled and sectioned. Grapefruit sections make a tangy addition to fruit salads and compotes and to green salads. Grapefruit and avocado are a particularly harmonious combination for a salad. For a hot brunch offering or as dessert, grapefruit halves can be dusted with white or brown sugar, dotted with butter and sprinkled with rum, then glazed under a broiler. Chilled grapefruit juice is enjoyed on its own in the morning, in combination with rum or vodka as a cocktail, or in fruit punches.

Availability Fresh grapefruit can be found all year, but quality is best and prices lowest in winter. Grapefruit sections are available canned. Grapefruit juice is sold canned, bottled, and frozen.

Selection Pick grapefruit that feels heavy for its size. Avoid soft, puffy fruit with pointed ends. Varieties with smooth, thin skin and good weight will be juicier than those with rough, thick skin. Surface blemishes do not affect quality.

Storage Keep grapefruit at cool room temperature for five or six days or refrigerate for several weeks.

Preparation The flesh of the grapefruit is firmly attached to the rind. A serrated grapefruit knife makes sectioning easier. Halve the grapefruit and run the knife around the perimeter of each half. Then cut around each section to separate it from interior membranes. Grapefruit spoons with serrated edges eliminate the need to section the fruit with a knife.

◼ AVOCADO, JICAMA, AND GRAPEFRUIT SALAD

Avocado and grapefruit are often paired for their contrasting, yet complementary, textures and flavors. Crisp, juicy jicama adds even more textural interest.

> 1 large *or* 2 small avocados
> 2 medium Ruby grapefruit
> ½ pound jicama
> 2 tablespoons olive oil
> Salt and freshly ground pepper, to taste

1. Peel avocado and cut into wedges. Peel grapefruit and cut fruit into sections, reserving juice. Peel jicama and slice it into thin wedges about the length of the avocado wedges.

2. Alternate pieces of avocado, grapefruit, and jicama in a circle on a round serving plate or on individual plates. Combine reserved grapefruit juice, olive oil, and salt and pepper to taste. Drizzle dressing over salad.

Serves 4.

> ***Recipes and Related Information***
> *Citrus Reamer, 131; Knife, 328.*

GRAPE LEAF

In early to mid-summer, when the grape leaves on the vine are large, green, and tender, they may be harvested for culinary use.

Use Fresh grape leaves should always be blanched or brined before using. Middle Eastern cooks blanch grape leaves, then stuff them with rice or a mixture of rice and meat, and roll them into cigar-shaped dolmas. In France, grape leaves are used to protect and flavor some small cheeses. The flavor of mushrooms is enhanced when cooked in a pot lined with grape leaves. Wrapping quail, goat cheese, and anchovies with grape leaves before grilling over coals or baking imparts a special flavor. Some cooks put grape leaves in the brine for cucumber pickles to make the pickles crisp.

Availability Fresh grape leaves are not generally sold commercially, but cooks who live near vineyards will probably find vineyard owners willing to part with some for personal use. Grape leaves bottled or canned in brine can be purchased at Middle Eastern markets and some well-stocked supermarkets.

Storage Refrigerate grape leaves in their brine in an airtight, nonmetal container; they will keep indefinitely.

Preparation Blanch or steam fresh grape leaves briefly just to soften. Rinse canned or bottled grape leaves before use to remove brine flavor. Be careful when removing grape leaves from bottle or jar; they tear easily.

◼ STUFFED GRAPE LEAVES

Fresh mint, plenty of garlic, and a little feta cheese enliven these classic Greek dolmas. These are a perfect hors d'oeuvre because, if you like, they can be prepared up to one week ahead. Refrigerate them in their cooking liquid and bring to room temperature before serving.

> 1 jar (1 lb) grape leaves preserved in brine
> ¼ cup olive oil
> 1 tablespoon butter
> ⅓ cup minced shallot
> 2 tablespoons minced garlic
> 3 cups cooked rice
> ¼ cup dried currants
> 2 tablespoons golden raisins
> ¼ cup chopped fresh mint
> ¼ cup finely minced parsley
> 1 teaspoon chopped fresh dill
> 2 ounces crumbled feta cheese
> Salt, pepper, and fresh lemon juice, to taste
> 3 to 4 cups hot Chicken Stock (see page 560)
> Cucumber-Mint Sauce (see page 294)
> Lemon wedges, for accompaniment

1. Preheat oven to 350° F. Blanch grape leaves in boiling water 45 seconds to remove briny flavor; drain and refresh under cold running water. Drain well and pat dry.

2. In a small skillet heat oil and butter. Add shallots and garlic and sauté over moderate heat until soft and slightly colored. Transfer to a large mixing bowl and add rice, currants, raisins, mint, parsley, dill, feta, and salt, pepper, and lemon juice to taste. Toss well with a fork to blend.

3. Lay a grape leaf out flat; put about 1½ tablespoons filling near base of each leaf. Roll leaf into a cigar-shaped package, tucking in sides as you roll. Repeat with remaining leaves. Transfer leaves to a roasting pan large enough to hold them snugly. Cover with stock and poach in the oven, covered, for 20 minutes. Cool in stock. To serve, mound grape leaves on a platter and accompany with Cucumber-Mint Sauce and a bowl of lemon wedges.

Serves 15 to 20.

GRATE, TO; GRATER, SHREDDER, AND MILL

To reduce food to shreds, flakes, or tiny particles by rubbing against a grater or by processing in a food processor, blender, electric minichopper, clean coffee grinder, or other similar-acting device. Also the category of specialized equipment that changes the texture of raw or cooked foods—cheeses, vegetables, fruits, meats, herbs and spices, nuts—to smaller pieces, even as fine as a powder, purée, or paste.

Greens sautéed with onions and bacon are standard southern fare, here paired with puffs of mashed potatoes and pork chops smothered with onions.

GREENS (POTHERBS)

Many of the sturdier leafy greens are also known as potherbs; although they may be eaten raw in salads when young and tender, these herbaceous plants most often end up in a pot with salt pork or a ham bone. They are delicate when young but are rarely marketed at that stage. The older, tougher leaves are too strong in flavor to eat raw, but boiling or stewing tenderizes and tames them.

Also see BEET, BROCCOLI RAAB, KALE, and SORREL. Other major potherbs are described below.

Use   In the American South, potherbs are traditionally boiled with smoked pork or fatback. In Italy, greens such as Swiss chard and broccoli raab are cooked in olive oil with garlic and served hot with pork, or seasoned with wine vinegar and eaten lukewarm as a salad. In Ethiopia, stewed collard greens are served with buttermilk curds as a traditional side dish for Ethiopian stews. Cooked kale or collard greens are traditional accompaniments to the Brazilian national dish, *feijoada completa*. Wilted greens also make a hearty addition to bean soups and minestrone. Stewed greens are particularly good with pork in any form, whether a single green cooked alone or a mixture of several. Most of these greens substitute well for each other, although they differ in the intensity of their flavor.

Availability   Many greens are sold inexpensively in supermarkets all year; peak availability is October through April.

Selection   Look for crisp greens with bright color; avoid those with woody stems or wilted, yellowed, or bruised leaves. Small leaves with thin stems are milder and more tender.

Store   Keep greens unwashed in a plastic bag in the refrigerator crisper. Greens are best and most nutritious when eaten immediately but will stay fresh for two to three days.

Preparation   Before use, wash greens well, in several changes of water if necessary. Discard any bruised or wilted leaves. If stems are woody or thick, they should be either peeled or cut away (and may be cooked separately). Cook small leaves whole; cut up large leaves.

Cooking   See BOIL, BRAISE, SAUTE, STEAM, STIR-FRY.

COLLARD GREENS

Like kale, collard greens are a member of the cabbage family. The dark green leaves strongly resemble kale, but they are flat and smooth, not crinkled.

DANDELION GREENS

Dark green, long and slender, dandelion leaves are less than 1 inch wide. When young, they are tender and delicate and are delicious in salads, especially with a hot bacon dressing. The leaves become bitter with age and must be cooked to mellow their flavor.

MUSTARD GREENS

These have a slightly fuzzy texture and may be flat or frilled at the edges. They are bright green and quite pungent, even when young. The spicy, bitter quality develops with age and only the youngest, handpicked leaves are likely to be suitable for eating raw.

SWISS CHARD

Both white- and red-ribbed varieties are available, with little discernible difference in taste. The ribs are wide, the leaves flat and deep green. Because ribs take longer to cook, they are trimmed away and cooked separately. The leaves are often cooked, then combined with the cooked stems just before serving. Chard is among the milder greens, stronger in flavor and sturdier in texture than spinach but milder than mustard, dandelion, and turnip greens. Italian cooks add it to soups; braise and serve it with oil and lemon; stuff the ribs with bread crumbs and deep-fry; and use as filling for ravioli.

TURNIP GREENS

Unless very young, strong-flavored turnip greens must be cooked to tame their taste. The dark green leaves are flat and smooth, with a narrow but often tough central rib. To mute their strong flavor, turnip greens can be cooked with other, milder greens or blanched before stewing.

▮ COUNTRY-STYLE GREENS

Contrary to rumor, greens do not need hours of boiling in a sea of liquid, as this Mississippi recipe proves. What they do need, however, is the flavor of smoked slab bacon or ham. If you must substitute ordinary bacon or ham, you'll need twice as much. Greens are the traditional southern accompaniment to pork or ham; they also pair well with corn bread or candied yams.

> 2 **bunches fresh collard, turnip, or mustard greens**
> 1 **tablespoon lard or rendered bacon fat**
> 1 **medium onion, minced**
> ¼ **pound good-quality smoked slab bacon or**
>   **smoked ham, cut in ½-inch dice** *or*
>   **½ pound ordinary sliced bacon or ham**
> 2 **cups water**
>   **Salt and freshly ground pepper, to taste**
>   **Dash of Louisiana-style hot sauce**

1. Trim away and discard tough stems of greens. To loosen grit, place leaves and remaining tender stems (you should have about 2 quarts) in a large bowl, cover with lukewarm water, and soak for 5 minutes. Rinse several times in lukewarm water to wash away any remaining sand.

2. Melt lard in a large, heavy, nonreactive pot with a lid. (Do not use an aluminum pot; if possible, use one with an enamel coating.) Add onions and bacon. Fry together over medium-high heat, stirring often, until onions wilt and bacon starts to brown (about 5 minutes).

3. Add greens and the water and bring to a boil over high heat. Cover, lower heat to medium, and cook until greens are tender, with just a little crunch (about 20 minutes).

4. Uncover, raise heat to high, and boil off some of the excess water (about 5 minutes). Season with salt, pepper, and hot sauce to taste, and serve hot (dish should be slightly soupy).

Serves 6.

GRILL, TO

To cook food on a *grill,* a grid of metal bars set over a heat source—charcoal, wood, gas, or electricity.

Grilled food is cooked by radiant heat (see RADIANT ENERGY) and direct contact. Rays of heat warm the outer surface and then, by conduction, move through the food's interior mass. Open-fire cookery may appear simple, but to be successful it requires constant attention. Starting the fire, maintaining an even temperature, achieving the correct distance from the heat, knowing when food is done, avoiding sudden flare-ups—all must be considered and understood.

GRILL VERSUS BARBECUE

The terms *grill* and *barbecue* are often used interchangeably for this cooking technique. Barbecue has, perhaps, a more informal connotation, redolent of casual entertaining and down-home cooking. Purists and the U.S. Department of Agriculture, however, consider only foods cooked by direct heat over wood or charcoal real barbecue.

Barbecue also refers to a type of food, which is an American institution, with strong roots in many different regions of the country. As varied as the different styles of barbecue are, they all share several common traits: Barbecue is the art of slowly cooking large pieces of meat over a smoky, cool (about 225° F) fire. Most barbecue is served with a tangy sauce at the table to moisten and flavor the meat. Each area has its own version, varying from a simple and pure North Carolina sauce made of cider vinegar and crushed red chiles to the spicy, vegetable-laden tomato sauces of the Southwest.

How does barbecue differ from grilled food? Barbecue has a distinctive smoky flavor and is served with a vinegar-based tangy sauce. Grilled food also has a smoky flavor, but is served plain or with one or more of a number of sauces. In general, grilled food is cooked quicker and is much more varied in style and taste.

TOOLS AND EQUIPMENT

Equipment for outdoor cooking is a matter of personal preference, available space, and frequency of use. Following are those tools that are most common.

GAS GRILL

On the market is a new generation of gas grills with sophisticated heat circulation and control. Versions with either lava rock or porcelain-coated metal bars both serve the same function, evenly emanating heat from the gas burners below and vaporizing drippings from the food above. Their primary assets are that the cook can control cooking temperature through (usually) three gas burners, which permit heat regulation to whatever temperature is required, and they are very easy to use. A major drawback of gas grills is their inability to give food a smoky flavor.

TIPS

PREPARING SKEWERS

On a single skewer combine foods that cook in the same amount of time (blanch slower-cooking elements ahead of time).

Skewers can be metal or bamboo. They should be flat sided if possible so the ingredients don't slip around when the skewer is rotated.

When you use bamboo skewers, presoak them for about 30 minutes to keep them from burning when exposed to high heat.

If all ingredients on a brochette require a relatively long cooking time, consider precooking them, then grilling or broiling as the final step to add color.

Either grilled or broiled, skewered foods usually cook in 6 to 12 minutes.

KETTLE-SHAPED GRILL

These grills are designed for cooking with the lid closed. Carefully located vents in the top and bottom provide air flow to keep the fire going while completely eliminating flare-ups. Thus, searing over a very hot fire can easily be accomplished without burning the food. If the coals are moved to each side of the kettle and a drip pan positioned in the center, food can also be cooked more slowly with the indirect-heat method of cooking. The two major drawbacks are the lack of hinged lids, which creates awkward juggling of equipment each time you open and close the grill, and the fixed grill position.

OPEN GRILL

These are not as easy to use as kettle-shaped grills, but are often less expensive. Since this type does not have a lid, the cook is likely to experience flare-ups during cooking. The best way to handle this is to use an open grill only for foods that don't have an oil-based marinade or are low in fat, such as fish or poultry. You can't use the indirect-heat method of cooking very well on an open grill because most of the heat diffuses in the air.

RECTANGULAR HINGED GRILL

Rectangular grills have the advantage of heat control because the grill can be raised or lowered. Briquettes, hardwood chips, or moistened fresh herbs can be added to the fire more easily than when using a kettle-shaped grill. A hinged lid makes opening and closing much easier. But, when it comes to heat control and evenness of cooking, kettle-shaped grills are better. The rectangular grill simply doesn't have the good heat circulation that a kettle-shaped grill does, and flare-ups are harder to control.

OTHER EQUIPMENT

Whether cooking in the kitchen or on the patio, your equipment should be close at hand and well organized. The following is considered basic for grilling.

Basting Brush   An inexpensive, twisted-wire brush works just as well as the more costly wooden-handled versions. The brush should have a long handle to keep the cook back from the fire while basting.

Charcoal Rails   Use charcoal rails to hold charcoal in even piles on each side of the drip pan for the indirect-heat method of cooking. Because the sides of the drip pan adequately perform the same function, charcoal rails are optional.

Drip Pans   These are essential for the indirect-heat method of cooking. Purchase disposable rectangular aluminum ones, 2 to 3 inches deep; because they are almost impossible to clean, they are usually used only once.

Grill Brush   There is less chance that food will stick to a clean grill. Scrub grill after each use with a special wire brush, available in hardware stores and supermarkets.

Instant-Read Thermometer   Internal temperature is an extremely accurate measure of doneness for many foods. An instant-read thermometer, well-suited for the fast pace of grill cooking, will give a very accurate reading within seconds of insertion.

Long-Handled Fork   Although long-handled forks are not recommended for turning foods (punctures will cause valuable juices to ooze out), they are very handy for removing large roasts from the fire, or for piercing food to check for doneness by looking at the color of the juices.

Mitts   Heavy-duty fireproof mitts are invaluable to protect the cook against unexpected fires. Find a pair that covers forearms as well as hands.

Roast Racks   Made of aluminum or stainless steel, V-shaped roast racks do an excellent job of holding large pieces of meat or poultry during cooking. If used with the indirect-heat method of cooking, the meat needn't be turned to cook evenly on all sides.

Skewers   Both metal and bamboo skewers are available. Metal ones can be used repeatedly; those made of bamboo are meant to be discarded after one use. Bamboo skewers need to be soaked 15 to 30 minutes so they won't flame (although even presoaked ones sometimes burn at the ends over very hot fires). If you have rosemary in your garden, strip away the needles, soak the branches for 30 minutes, and use as skewers; they imbue food with a wonderful rosemary flavor.

Spatula   Use an offset (angled-neck) stainless steel spatula with a blade that is 5 to 6 inches long. This blade will slide completely under most chops and fish fillets, preventing them from tearing and sticking to grill. Stainless steel won't rust and is easy to care for.

Spray Bottle   Always keep a spray bottle filled with water next to the grill to douse flare-ups.

Tongs   Perhaps the most useful grill tool, tongs should be at least 12 inches long and spring loaded. It's best to have two pairs—one for handling food and the other for moving hot briquettes. Tongs are preferred over long-handled forks because they don't puncture food (and allow natural juices to escape).

Wire-Hinged Baskets   These wire baskets will hold fish fillets, meat, hamburger patties, or even bread for toast between two hinged grills secured by a latch. The grills should be lightly oiled before food is set on them.

FUELS AND FRAGRANCES

Traditional hardwood briquettes now share shelf space with many other fuels. They all work well in the right situation; which fuel to use is a matter of personal preference. Many are available at well-stocked supermarkets, hardware stores, cookware stores, or can be ordered by mail through selected catalogs.

CHARCOAL BRIQUETTES

Briquettes are made from wood chips smoldered into carbon, then bound together with fillers and starch, and pressed into a uniform shape. Some brands add petroleum products to make "self-lighting" briquettes. A charcoal briquette fire is ready when the coals are completely coated with a thin layer of gray ash; at this point all of the additives have burned off. Briquettes burn evenly and consistently.

FRESH HERBS AND FRUIT RINDS

Thyme, bay, rosemary, oregano, and marjoram impart a pleasant flavor when added to the fire. Moisten fresh herbs with water (or wine or liquor) and toss them onto the coals just before the food goes on the grill. Lemon, orange, or lime rinds are other choices. Do not directly inhale the fumes of burning herbs or fruit rinds; they can be very powerful.

HARDWOOD CHARCOAL

Though not nearly as prevalent as mesquite charcoal, other hardwoods are carbonized in the same manner as mesquite into an excellent fuel. They impart a smokier flavor to food than does mesquite, but they are more costly and don't burn as hot. Using mesquite as the fuel and adding presoaked hardwood chunks as the smoke source work well.

HARDWOOD CHUNKS AND SAWDUST

Hardwood adds a unique smoky flavor to food cooked over it. Hickory, alder, mesquite, and apple wood are the most popular and available woods. For gas grills, hardwood chips work better than chunks. Use wood pieces ½ to 1 inch thick. Soak pieces in water at least 30 minutes before using. Place an old aluminum pie plate over the gas heating elements toward the back corner of the grill before turning the grill on. As the grill gets hotter, the chips will begin to smolder. With very high heat, the chips may flare up; have a spray bottle filled with water nearby.

MESQUITE CHARCOAL

Made from a Mexican hardwood, mesquite charcoal contains no additives or fillers of any kind. It burns very hot, perhaps twice as hot as charcoal briquettes and most other hardwood charcoals. This means you can use less of it and can cook at a higher temperature, which produces a tastier product. It imparts a subtle, natural flavor, which is not nearly as pronounced as fruitwoods, oak, or hickory. Mesquite coals can be used two or even three times before they need to be replaced. However, mesquite can be difficult to start, and can also emit burning embers into the air. Be careful, especially when windy outside, to avoid sending embers toward nearby trees or structures.

WOOD

You can use oak, hickory, cherry, apple wood, mesquite, or alder wood for outdoor cooking. But wood takes a very long time to burn down to usable coals and the coals are short-lived. A better use of these woods is as kindling; cut the remaining larger pieces into 1-inch chunks to add a smoky complement to your fire (see Hardwood Chunks and Sawdust, left). Never use softwood for either smoking or as a fuel. Their thick resins produce a distinctly unpleasant aftertaste. Be careful of burning any scrap wood. For instance, pressure-treated lumber (used in outdoor construction) contains chemicals that can be toxic.

The outdoor chef has many options when selecting equipment for grilling. Shown clockwise from upper left: open grill; wire-hinged basket (with hamburgers); charcoal and briquettes; charcoal chimney; kettle grill with cover; long-handled spatula, knife, and fork; aluminum drip pan; grill brush; rectangular hinged grill; basting brush; spray bottle; wire-bristle grill brush; portable gas grill; long-handled tongs.

Herbs can be kept in the freezer for up to one year. Wash them in cold water after removing any deteriorating leaves. Pat them completely dry with paper towels, then package in small, airtight bags.

mints and lemon verbena are occasionally paired with fruits, but otherwise, herbs rarely appear in sweet dishes.

As more and more Americans attempt to reduce their sodium intake, many are finding that herbs can enliven the blandness of a low-salt diet. In addition to their use in specific dishes, herbs are frequently incorporated into other ingredients such as mustards, vinegars, and salts. Herbs have also long been employed to brew tea (see below and TEA). Minced tarragon, chives, parsley, or cilantro adds a dimension of freshness and spark to storebought mustard or homemade blends. Almost any fresh herb is suitable for use in flavoring vinegars (see JAM, JELLY, PRESERVE, AND CONDIMENT). Herb-flavored salts (see HERB AND SPICE BLENDS) sprinkled on salad greens, fresh vegetables, and many cooked dishes add flavor without calories, often eliminating or greatly reducing the need for a sauce or dressing.

Teas brewed from the leaves of herbs are called tisanes. Most are made by infusion, that is, by steeping in hot water. Start with 2 to 3 teaspoons fresh or frozen leaves or 1 to 2 teaspoons dried herb per cup in a warm nonmetal teapot. Cover with the proper amount of boiling water and steep 5 to 10 minutes. Strain into cups. All herbal teas may be served iced. Just make them a little stronger to allow for the melting ice.

Availability Dried herbs are widely marketed through supermarket spice racks, health-food stores, and specialty stores. For years parsley was one of the only fresh herbs regularly available in supermarkets; today hothouse cultivation brings a wide variety of fresh herbs to supermarkets throughout the year.

Selection Purchase or gather fresh herbs only as they are needed. It is wise to buy dried herbs in small quantities. Some supermarkets and many health-food stores offer herbs in bulk. Try to buy them from a market with rapid turnover.

Storage Fresh herbs are highly perishable. To preserve them in their fresh state, see individual herb entries. For longer storage, herbs may be dried, frozen, salt-cured, or packed in vinegar. Store dried herb leaves as whole as possible in airtight jars in a cool, dark place. Pulverize between the fingers or with a mortar and pestle just before use to release oils. When kept in a cool, ventilated place, home-dried herbs should retain freshness for one year. Commercially available herbs should last six months or slightly longer before beginning to lose flavor. Discard any that smell musty or dusty or that have lost their original punch. Frozen herbs are best used within one year. Once thawed, they cannot be refrozen. Salt-cured herbs and herbs packed in vinegar will keep indefinitely if properly stored in a cool, dark place.

Drying For most herb leaves, drying is the time-honored method of preserving. Herbs to be used in cooking should be dried as whole as possible to retain flavor. See Drying Herbs, opposite page, for more information.

Some herbs are used extensively in one cuisine and hardly at all in another. Cilantro, for example, plays a major role in Latin American and Chinese cooking and a somewhat lesser role in Indian and Southeast Asian cooking. It is not used at all, however, in the cooking of Western or northern Europe.

Herbs are primarily used to accent and enhance the flavor of foods. An Italian tomato sauce without oregano is hard to imagine, although the dominant flavor of tomato sauce is always tomato. In a few dishes, however, the herb is the main or a major ingredient: basil in Italian pesto, parsley in Iranian *gormeh sabzi* (parsley and lamb stew), and watercress in a watercress soup.

As a flavor accent, herbs may be added to just about every dish in the cook's repertoire: soups, salads, stuffings, roasts, stews, sauces, marinades, breads, dressings and mayonnaise, pickles and jellies. As a garnish, herb-flavored butter (see BUTTER, Compound Butters) makes a simple, flavorful finish to grilled meats, fish, and poultry (use 1 tablespoon minced fresh herb to each ¼ cup softened butter). Herbs complement all types of meats, fish, fowl, vegetables, beans, grains, eggs, and cheese. The

Freezing This method is recommended for a few of the tender herbs, including basil, burnet, fennel, tarragon, chives, dill, and parsley. Tie a small bundle of the herb together and dip headfirst into boiling water for a few seconds. Immediately plunge into ice water and let cool in the water for a couple of minutes. (Blanching isn't necessary for basil, chives, and dill.) Remove leaves from stems and pack in small batches in plastic bags, label, and freeze. When ready to use, remove only the amount needed from the freezer. Add frozen herbs to foods to be cooked; let herbs thaw before adding to cold foods.

Packing in Vinegar The French tightly pack tarragon leaves in little jars, then completely fill the jar with vinegar. They keep indefinitely in a cool, dark place.

Salt-curing Some of the tender herbs such as basil, burnet, dill, fennel, and parsley can be packed in salt. Wash and drain, remove leaves from their stems, and place them in alternate layers with plain table salt in a container, beginning and ending with a salt layer. Fill completely and cover container with an airtight lid. Label and store in a cool, dark place. Remove salt from leaves just before using. They will keep indefinitely.

Preparation Mince or chop herbs only just before using. Flavors are quickly lost as volatile oils are released by heat or oxidation. Add herbs to hot dishes at the last minute, unless it's a simmering stock. Steeping dried herbs brings out their flavor; steep for 15 minutes in a small amount of warm liquid—such as stock, butter, or water. If desired, add liquid as well as herbs to recipe.

SUBSTITUTING FRESH HERBS FOR DRIED

Because oils become concentrated in the drying process, dried herbs are generally more pungent than an equal quantity of fresh. The strength of the dried herb, however, depends on how it was harvested and preserved, how it has been stored, and how old it is. Follow this rule of thumb: ¼ teaspoon dried, finely powdered herb equals ¾ to 1 teaspoon dried, loosely crumbled herb equals 1½ to 2 teaspoons chopped fresh herb.

HERB AND SPICE BLENDS

The spice racks in supermarkets are filled with dozens of herb and spice blends. Many seem designed for specific uses, such as pizza spice and pumpkin-pie spice, although the packagers would contend that these blends have multiple functions. Others, the creations of well-known chefs or restaurants, are meant to provide home cooks with the unique blends needed to reproduce particular dishes.

Herb and spice blends are convenience products. Most are composed of spices and herbs found beside them on

---

DRYING HERBS

Fresh herbs are one of the easiest foods to dry. Very low temperature and good air circulation are important to ensure that herbs dry properly to preserve flavor.

To dry in an oven To dry herbs in a hurry, set oven at the lowest temperature. Wash leaves only if necessary to rinse away insects or dust; shake off water and drain well. Spread leaves on a cheesecloth-lined rack in the oven. Leave oven door open and stir leaves until they are crisp. They'll be ready in a few minutes.

To dry in a microwave oven Place four or five stems of herbs on a double thickness of paper towels; cover with a single layer of towels. Turn on microwave at full power (high) until leaves are brittle (about 2 minutes for small leaves, 3 minutes for large). If leaves are not yet brittle, leave in microwave an additional 30 seconds.

To dry at room temperature Hang herbs by their stems in bunches from the ceiling (called bunch-drying), or lay herbs flat on trays. Dry away from direct sunlight. An attic, covered porch, or kitchen that stays at 65° to 90° F is a good location. If you dry herbs in a covered area outdoors where dew collects, bring them indoors overnight.

Bunch-drying is ideally suited for herbs with long stems, such as marjoram, rosemary, and sage. Tie bunches at the stem ends, and hang upside down to dry. Bunches can be dried in small brown paper bags to keep dust from collecting on them and to catch seeds. Gather bag opening around steams and tie so that herbs hang freely inside bag. Cut several ½-inch holes in bags and suspend from the ceiling at varying heights to increase air circulation. Leaves and seeds will be thoroughly dry in one or two weeks.

Tray-drying works well for herbs with large leaves, such as basil, and herbs with short stems. Use stackable drying trays with mesh screens. Make one layer in each tray. If stacking trays, leave plenty of air circulation between them. Spread leaves or stems in a single layer. To protect against insects and dust, cover with cheesecloth. Turn leaves or stems each day or two. Most herbs dry crisp within one week to 10 days, depending on the weather. The crisper they are, the better they will keep. Remove from trays and package in airtight jars when crisp (see DRY).

STORING DRIED HERBS
When herbs are crumbly and feel dry, remove leaves from stems. Whole leaves keep their flavor longer than those that are crumbled before storage. Package in small glass jars. Inspect during the first week for moisture. If condensation appears, redry. Label and date containers. Store in a cool, dry, dark place. Properly stored, dried herbs retain their flavor and color for up to one year.

---

the supermarket shelf. Pumpkin-pie spice, for example, usually contains cinnamon, allspice, ginger, and nutmeg, all readily available in supermarkets. Garlic salt is often simply garlic and salt. Comparison shoppers quickly see that they can make many herb and spice blends at home for less than the cost of most commercial products.

If you maintain a large range of herbs and spices, properly stored and replaced every few months, you may find that your own blends are more satisfying than the commercial ones. Spice blends made from whole spices ground to order are far more pungent than storebought, preground blends. You can control the salt level and the balance of ingredients, eliminating a particular herb or spice or adding one to suit your palate.

Nevertheless, many recipes call for specific herb or spice blends and there is no denying their convenience. The major blends are described on the next two pages.

Use Herb blends should be rubbed between the fingers to release their aromatic oils before adding to a dish. Spices can impart a raw taste if not given sufficient time to cook. Sautéing spices in oil or butter, if a recipe permits, will remove the raw flavor.

Availability   Most of the following blends are found in the spice section of any well-stocked supermarket. Other sources are suggested in the individual entries below.

Selection   Packaged seasonings lose quality after a while; try to buy from a store that restocks its spice shelves fairly often.

Storage   Store spice and herb blends in a cool, dark, dry place. Herb blends will keep for up to one year. Spice blends made of ground spices should stay pungent for up to six months. Those made of whole spices, for example, pickling spice, may be kept for one to two years.

HERB BLENDS

Some herb blends are proprietary and unique to the company that produces them; others are blended by almost all manufacturers. Theoretically, any herbs may be combined to make a blend, but only a few commercial blends enjoy widespread use. The following are among the most popular.

Bouquet Garni   The traditional bouquet garni consists of fresh parsley, fresh thyme, and a bay leaf tied together in a bundle and used to flavor stocks and soups. It is removed before serving. Some manufacturers pack a blend of dried herbs labeled bouquet garni that may include oregano, summer savory, marjoram, rosemary, basil, sage, thyme, dill, and sometimes tarragon. Herbs should be rubbed between the fingers when added to a dish. They can be used to flavor stuffings, soups, sauces, stews, and vegetable dishes. See BOUQUET GARNI.

Fines Herbes   This combination of fresh herbs is used often in French cooking. The traditional blend includes chervil, parsley, tarragon, and chives. Some manufacturers pack this combination of herbs, or a similar one, in dried form. Others pack fines herbes blends that do not bear a resemblance to the classic combination. One major brand consists of such pungent dried herbs as thyme, oregano, sage, rosemary, marjoram, and basil. Obviously, this blend is not a substitute for the fines herbes called for in French cookbooks, usually in combination with eggs, fish, and salads. More pungent fines herbes blends should be reserved for meats, tomato sauces, and eggplant preparations.

Herbes de Provence   Dried herbs typical of southern France—such as thyme, lavender, summer savory, basil, and rosemary—make up this aromatic blend. Use it to season lamb, chicken, tomato sauces, and other tomato-based dishes.

Italian Seasoning   This blend of dried herbs is intended to give a characteristic Italian flavor to dishes. Common components include oregano, marjoram, red pepper, basil, rosemary, thyme, and sage. Italian seasoning can be used with chicken and meats, with tomato-based dishes, squash and eggplant, pizza, and bean soups.

Poultry Seasoning   Usually a blend of sage, thyme, marjoram, savory, onion, black pepper, celery seed, or other herbs, poultry seasoning is always in powdered form. It can be used to season chicken, veal or pork dishes, stuffings, and biscuits.

SPICE BLENDS

Packers use different spices and proportions of spices in their blends. One major packer, for example, puts cinnamon, allspice, ginger, and nutmeg in pumpkin-pie spice. Another packer adds mace and cloves to the blend. The following descriptions are based on commonly available brands. Check the package label for a specific list of ingredients.

Apple-Pie Spice   This mixture usually contains such sweet baking spices as cinnamon, nutmeg, allspice, and cardamom. Use it in other fruit desserts or in spice cakes and cookies as well as in apple pie.

Beau Monde Seasoning   The components of this blend are salt, dextrose, onion, celery seed, and an anticaking agent. It is used to season meats, poultry, fish, sauces, stuffings, soups, and vegetable dishes.

Celery Salt   A mixture of salt and celery seed, celery salt is used to flavor soups, stuffings, meat loaves, Bloody Marys, baked fish, and dishes in which the flavor of celery is desired.

Chili Powder   Don't confuse this blend with ground red chile, which is made exclusively from ground dried chile pepper. Chili powder varies greatly from packer to packer. One major brand includes chili pepper, cumin, salt, allspice, garlic, oregano, cloves, and coriander. Chili powder adds characteristic hotness to such southwestern specialties as chili con carne, enchiladas with *salsa ranchera,* and barbecue sauce. It adds a lift to hamburgers, meat loaves, and tomato-based cocktail sauces. Sprinkle it over corn on the cob and baked fish for a touch of heat.

Crab Boil   Also known as shrimp spice, crab boil is popular among southern and New England cooks. It is a mixture of herbs and spices added to the water in which crab, lobster, shrimp, and crayfish are cooked. A typical version contains mustard seed, coriander seed, cayenne, bay leaf, dill seed, allspice, and cloves. Generally the mixture is added to boiling water and allowed to boil for 5 minutes before shellfish is added. Detailed directions for use appear on the package.

Curry Powder   A blend of cumin, coriander, turmeric, fenugreek, ginger, chiles, fennel, garlic, cinnamon, salt, mustard, cloves, black pepper, and more, curry powder imparts what Westerners perceive as a typical curry flavor to dishes. In fact, few Indian cooks would ever use a commercial curry powder, preferring instead to toast whole spices and grind their own blend to order. Curry powder can also be used to flavor stuffed eggs, mayonnaise, cabbage salad, chicken and seafood salads, and chowders.

Five-Spice Powder Star anise, anise seed, clove, cinnamon or cassia, and Szechuan peppercorns ground to a powder are the typical spices in five-spice powder. Brands vary in pungency and balance; some even include cardamom or orange peel. Five-spice powder is used in Chinese cooking to flavor red-cooked meats—pork, chicken, duck, or beef simmered in soy sauce with ginger and spices—to marinate pork before barbecuing, and to season dipping sauces. It is available in plastic pouches in Chinese and other Asian markets.

Garam Masala Translating as *warm spice blend, garam masala* is an Indian blend that usually contains such elements as cardamom, black peppercorns, cloves, coriander, and cinnamon. The blend varies from region to region and from cook to cook. It is usually added to dishes near the end of their cooking time; occasionally, it is sprinkled atop a finished dish as a garnish. Garam masala may be purchased in Indian markets, but most Indian cooks blend and grind their own spices. This spice blend is added to countless Indian dishes in much the same way Americans use salt and pepper.

Garlic Salt This is a simple blend of salt and garlic. Some blends also contain parsley, modified food starch, sugar, and monosodium glutamate. Garlic salt can be used to make garlic bread or to add garlic flavor to soups, stuffings, tomato juice cocktails, roasts, and grilled meats and poultry.

Onion Salt A mixture of salt and onion, this blend can be used wherever the flavor of onion is desired, as in hamburgers and meat loaves, roast meats, stuffings, soups, Bloody Marys, and other tomato juice cocktails.

Pickling Spice This pungent mixture is used to flavor vegetable and fruit pickles. It generally contains such ingredients as mustard seed, cinnamon, allspice, bay leaf, black pepper, ginger, red pepper, cardamom, turmeric, and mace.

Pizza Spice In addition to garlic, sugar, onion, and salt, pizza spice can contain unidentified ground spices. It is sprinkled atop pizza before or after baking.

Pumpkin-Pie Spice This powdered blend can contain cinnamon, ginger, nutmeg, allspice, mace, and sometimes cloves. It may be also used in custards, spice cakes, and cookies.

Quatre Epices *Four spices,* the translation of the French term, is a powdered mixture of white pepper, cloves, nutmeg, and ground ginger. French cooks use it primarily to flavor pâtés. *Quatre épices* is available in some supermarkets and in specialty stores.

Ras el Hanout Containing 50 or more exotic ingredients, this Moroccan spice is probably the most complex described here. Common flavorings include turmeric, ginger, allspice, cinnamon, cardamom, clove, nutmeg, peppercorns, and orrisroot as well as flowers such as rosebuds and lavender. *Ras el hanout* is used to flavor game, stewed lamb, stuffings, and other Moroccan dishes. It is available in Middle Eastern markets.

Seasoned Salt Formulas for this mixture vary from manufacturer to manufacturer. One popular brand includes salt, dextrin, sugar, garlic, monosodium glutamate, cornstarch, black pepper, celery seed, oleoresin paprika, cardamom, cumin, fenugreek, red pepper, sage, thyme, and turmeric. Seasoned salt can be sprinkled on salads, added to stuffings, and sprinkled on meats and fish before broiling.

Premixed seasonings are a convenience. Buy commercial blends or prepare your own from herbs and spices you use often. Freshly ground seasonings are always more pungent than packaged ones.

RECIPE MODIFICATION FOR HIGH-ALTITUDE BAKING

Baking at altitude (above 3,000 feet) can affect ingredients, proportions, and cooking times.

Feet Above Sea Level	Reduce Each Teaspoon Baking Powder by	Reduce Each Cup Sugar by	Increase Each Cup Liquid by
3,000–5,000	⅛ teaspoon	1 tablespoon	2 tablespoons
5,000–7,000	⅛–¼ teaspoon	2 tablespoons	2–3 tablespoons
7,000–10,000	¼ teaspoon	2–3 tablespoons	3–4 tablespoons
Above 10,000	¼–½ teaspoon	2–3 tablespoons	3–4 tablespoons
Over 3,000 feet:	Increase oven temperature by 25° F. Underbeat eggs (beat whites to soft peak stage).		
Over 10,000 feet:	Add one extra egg and increase each cup flour by 1–2 tablespoons.		

HIGH-ALTITUDE COOKING

At altitudes over 3,000 feet, foods cook differently than at sea level because of lower air pressure. Water boils at a lower temperature and food takes longer to heat; liquids evaporate more quickly; leavenings expand more; sugar becomes more concentrated; and batters have a greater tendency to stick to pans.

To compensate for these differences, increase cooking time for foods that are boiled, and raise oven temperature for baked goods by 25° F. Increase liquids, decrease leavenings, underbeat eggs and egg-based batters, decrease sugar, and butter and flour pans well or line with nonstick parchment paper. For baked goods, consult the chart above for exact recipe changes. Specific information about the effect of altitude on cooking in your area is available from cooperative extension agents of the U.S. Department of Agriculture or newspaper food editors.

EFFECT OF ALTITUDE ON BOILING WATER

Above 2,000 feet, the boiling temperature of water drops, as demonstrated in this chart.

Altitude	Water Boils at
Sea level	212° F
2,000 feet	208° F
5,000 feet	203° F
7,500 feet	198° F
10,000 feet	194° F
15,000 feet	185° F
30,000 feet	158° F

HONEY

Flower nectar gathered by bees and deposited in the waxy network of cells known as a honeycomb is the source of honey. Depending on the flower from which it is derived, honey can be quite strong and dark like buckwheat honey, or pale and delicate like clover honey. Among the best-loved honeys in the world are those made from thyme, orange, heather, rosemary, acacia, sage, and tupelo.

Use The sweetness and spreadable texture of honey make it popular as a topping for breads, toast, biscuits, and corn muffins. As an ingredient in baked goods, it adds sweetness and moisture. Cakes, cookies, and breads with honey stay moist longer than those sweetened with sugar. Honey is traditional in Greek baklava (walnut-filled pastry), Israeli honey cake, Italian *panforte,* and in many Moroccan pastries. Moroccans also use honey to glaze poultry in several savory preparations. Honey is the principal sweetener in many confections, such as Turkish halvah and nougat.

Availability Dozens of varieties of honey are marketed in the United States, but all are of three basic kinds: comb or straight from the hive; chunk, which contains bits of honeycomb; and extracted, the most common form. Extracted honey is removed from the comb with a centrifuge, heated to destroy yeasts, strained to remove wax and debris, then filtered for clarity. Honey is generally packed in jars or plastic squeeze bottles.

Selection As honeys vary in flavor (see introduction), select one whose character will best complement its intended use.

Storage Honey will keep indefinitely in a cool, dark place. Store it in an airtight container to prevent the absorption of moisture from the air.

Preparation If honey becomes crystallized on standing, reliquefy by setting jar in a pan of hot water and warming gently over low heat.

■ SPICED FRENCH HONEY BREAD

Classic French *pain d'épice* does not contain eggs or shortening, but gets its moist richness from the inclusion of honey and cream.

½ teaspoon anise seed
1 teaspoon *each* baking soda and ground cinnamon
½ teaspoon *each* ground ginger and cloves
¼ teaspoon salt
3 cups flour
2 tablespoons dried currants
¼ cup firmly packed brown sugar
¾ cup honey
⅔ cup whipping cream
⅓ cup milk
1 teaspoon grated orange rind

1. Preheat oven to 325° F. Lightly grease and flour a 4½- by 8½-inch loaf pan. Whirl anise seed in a clean coffee grinder or electric minichopper until powdery.

2. In a large bowl combine ground anise seed, baking soda, cinnamon, ginger, cloves, salt, flour, currants, and brown sugar.

3. In a small bowl blend honey, cream, milk, and orange rind. Add honey mixture to flour mixture, stirring just until dry ingredients are moistened. Spread in prepared loaf pan.

4. Bake until a skewer inserted in center comes out clean (1 hour and 20 minutes to 1 hour and 30 minutes). Let cool in pan 5 minutes, then turn out onto a rack to cool completely. Wrap and let stand for at least 1 day before slicing thinly to serve.

Serves 8.

Recipes and Related Information
Baklava, 222; Honeyed Chicken With Apricots, 557; Panforte, 186; Sopaipillas, 182.

HORSERADISH

Native to Eastern Europe but cultivated today in the United States, horseradish is a pungent cylindrical root in the cabbage family. It has a rough, thin, light brown skin and a white flesh that, when sliced or grated, releases an acrid oil. Its origins are unknown, but today it grows in cool regions of the United States and Europe. The plant known as Japanese horseradish (see WASABI) is botanically unrelated, although it too is valued for its pungent root.

Use Because the pungent character of horseradish is highly volatile, the root is rarely cooked. Instead it is used raw as a condiment or as an ingredient in other condiments. Grated horseradish is part of most tomato-based cocktail sauces for shellfish. Mixed with whipped cream and/or sour cream, it becomes a favorite sauce for prime rib, boiled meats, and smoked fish. It adds a lively hotness to cream dressings for beets and coleslaw. Grated horseradish is the standard accompaniment to gefilte fish, fish cakes traditional on Jewish holiday tables.

Availability Grated horseradish bottled in vinegar is sold in most supermarkets. Some varieties are colored red with beet juice. Most supermarkets also carry bottled imitation horseradish flavored with oil of horseradish. Fresh horseradish root can be found in some markets fall through spring. It is most widely available in the spring, around the time of the Jewish Passover celebration, because it has a traditional function at the holiday table. Some European specialty markets also carry dried powdered horseradish.

Selection Choose a root of fresh horseradish that is smooth and unblemished.

Storage Keep horseradish in a paper bag inside a plastic bag in the refrigerator crisper for up to one week. Freeze whole fresh horseradish up to six months (see Preparation). Bottled horseradish should be refrigerated, tightly capped, in its original container. Because it quickly loses pungency, it should be used within one month. Store dried horseradish in an airtight container in a cool, dry place; it will gradually lose pungency but should stay vigorous for up to one year.

Preparation Scrub fresh horseradish and scrape away outer skin; halve and cut out center core.

■ HORSERADISH CREAM SAUCE
The sharpness of horseradish livens up cool sour cream and makes a wonderful sauce for roasted meats.

> 1 **cup sour cream**
> 3 **tablespoons freshly grated horseradish**
> ½ **teaspoon salt**
> ⅛ **teaspoon white pepper**

Combine sour cream, horseradish, salt, and pepper. Serve chilled with hot or cold roast beef or other roasted, broiled, or grilled meats.

Makes about 1 cup.

HUCKLEBERRY

Although huckleberries resemble blueberries, they are unrelated. The huckleberry is the fruit of a native American plant of the genus *Gaylussacia*. Huckleberries are not cultivated; they grow wild, generally on low, spreading bushes, and they are generally smaller and darker than blueberries. Whereas blueberries have many tiny unnoticeable seeds, huckleberries have ten hard, rather large ones. They are also tarter than blueberries.

Use Many cooks prefer the huckleberry over the blueberry for pies because it is a tarter berry. Huckleberries can also be added to muffin and quick bread batters, or eaten fresh for breakfast with sugar and milk.

Availability Because huckleberries are not cultivated, they are generally available only to foragers.

Storage See BLUEBERRY.

Preparation Wash gently and dry quickly.

HUSK; HUSK, TO

The dry outer covering, as in the corn husk; also the act of removing the husk. Dried corn husks are the traditional wrapper for Mexican tamales.

I-L

Ice cream bombes are layered desserts formed in a special melon-shaped mold. Frozen Watermelon Bombe features a vanilla ice cream "rind" with raspberry sherbet "flesh" and chocolate chip "seeds." A wash of food coloring tints the outside surface an appropriate green hue.

LEMON SHERBET

When fruits that provide a lot of juice but very little pulp—such as lemon, orange, grapefruit, and other citrus—are used in sherbet, the texture may become grainy because of the greater proportion of liquids to solids. The same is true of sherbets made from Champagne, wines, and liqueurs. Adding stiffly beaten egg whites to the sugar syrup base smooths the texture. The syrup base in such sherbets is called an Italian meringue (see Note).

> 2   large egg whites
> 2¼   cups sugar
> 1   cup water
> 1½   cups fresh lemon juice

1. In a large bowl beat egg whites until very stiff; set aside. In a medium saucepan over high heat, cook sugar and the water, stirring constantly until sugar dissolves and the mixture reaches a full, rolling boil. Remove from heat and slowly drizzle hot syrup into egg whites, whisking constantly until all the syrup is incorporated. Continue whisking and slowly add lemon juice. Stir over an ice-water bath or cover and refrigerate until cold.

2. Transfer to an ice cream machine and freeze according to manufacturer's instructions.

Makes about 1 quart.

Note Another technique for improving the texture of such sherbets is to increase the proportion of sugar syrup to 50 percent of the total volume of the mixture. The extra sugar helps to keep the ice crystals, which form during freezing, small.

WHITE ZINFANDEL GRANITA

Any dry white wine will work in this refreshing *granita,* which does not need an ice cream machine; it freezes in the freezer compartment of the refrigerator.

> 1½   cups water
> ¾   cup sugar
> 1½   cups white Zinfandel

1. In a medium saucepan bring the water, sugar, and half the wine to a boil, stirring constantly until sugar dissolves. Reduce heat and simmer 3 minutes without stirring.

2. Allow syrup to cool to room temperature, or cool in refrigerator. Add remaining wine to cooled syrup. Place in a shallow metal pan and freeze in freezer compartment of refrigerator.

3. Stir well every 30 minutes until firm, 3 to 4 times. Let warm slightly, and stir one final time before serving.

Makes about 1 quart.

SOME WELL-KNOWN FROZEN DESSERTS

Frozen desserts are favorite treats all over the world. Italians love *tortoni,* the French love profiteroles, and Americans love mud pie, among many others. The following recipes capture some of the distinctive flavors of a number of countries. Additional frozen desserts can be found in other entries in this book (consult Recipes and Related Information).

TORTONI

Your guests will never guess how simple this Italian treat is to prepare. Note that the mixture with almond-flavored liqueur must freeze at least six hours.

> 1   cup whipping cream
> ¼   cup confectioners' sugar
> ½   cup crushed amaretti cookies or chopped, toasted almonds
> 3   tablespoons almond-flavored liqueur
> 1   large egg white, at room temperature
>   Crushed amaretti cookies, toasted almonds, or maraschino cherries, for garnish (optional)

1. In a medium bowl whip the cream and sugar to soft peaks. Fold in crushed cookies and liqueur.

2. In a separate bowl beat egg white until stiff but still shiny and moist. Fold into whipped cream mixture.

3. Spoon into a 1-quart bowl, parfait glasses, or paper-lined muffin cups. Garnish (if desired). Cover tightly and freeze at least 6 hours.

Serves 8.

MUD PIE

This is a favorite among coffee and chocolate lovers.

> 1 recipe Hot Fudge Sauce (see page 522)
> 1 Chocolate Crumb Crust (see page 436)
> 1 quart Coffee Ice Cream (see page 312), softened
> ¾ cup whipping cream
> 1 teaspoon vanilla extract
> 1 tablespoon confectioners' sugar
> ⅓ cup toasted almonds, for decoration

1. Pour a thin layer of fudge sauce into the cooled Chocolate Crumb Crust and freeze until firm.

2. Spoon ice cream into the frozen crust and level the top. Press plastic wrap over ice cream and freeze at least 1½ hours.

3. Spread a generous layer of fudge sauce over ice cream. Freeze at least 30 minutes. Meanwhile, whip the cream with vanilla and sugar. Spread over the frozen pie. Decorate with almonds and freeze another 2 hours or longer.

Serves 8 to 10.

FROZEN WATERMELON BOMBE

This ice cream bombe looks like a watermelon. It's a treat for the eyes as well as the palate. The bombe must freeze in stages, so preparation must begin early the day it will be served, or the day before.

> 1 quart French Vanilla Ice Cream (see page 312), slightly softened
> ¼ cup miniature semisweet chocolate chips
> 1 quart Raspberry Sherbet (see page 313), slightly softened
> Green food coloring

1. Place an 8-cup melon-shaped mold in the freezer for at least 1 hour.

2. Line inside of mold with an even layer of Vanilla Ice Cream. Cover with plastic wrap, pressing against the ice cream to seal it tightly and fill any air pockets. Return mold to freezer for at least 4 hours.

3. Stir chocolate chips into Raspberry Sherbet to simulate watermelon seeds; remove plastic wrap from mold and fill cavity with sherbet. Top with plastic wrap and freeze until firm.

4. To unmold, dip quickly in lukewarm water and invert onto a chilled platter. Return to freezer to set exterior.

5. Paint outside of molded ice cream with green food coloring, varying shades to resemble stripes on a real watermelon. Cover well and keep frozen. Slice to serve.

Serves 8 to 10.

PEACH MELBA

The great French chef Escoffier created this dessert in honor of a popular opera singer, Nellie Melba.

> 3 cups water
> 2 cups sugar
> 4 large peaches, peeled, halved, and pitted
> 1 tablespoon vanilla extract
> 1 cup fresh raspberries
> 1 quart French Vanilla Ice Cream (see page 312)

1. In a medium saucepan combine the water and sugar; bring to a boil. Add peach halves. Lower the heat and simmer, covered, for 10 to 15 minutes. Remove from heat; let cool. Stir in vanilla, then chill.

2. In a small saucepan heat raspberries to boiling, stirring and mashing berries with a spoon; cool, then chill.

3. To serve, place prepared peach halves on chilled dessert plates. Top each half with a scoop of ice cream. Drizzle raspberry topping all over each serving.

Serves 8.

CHERRIES JUBILEE

This well-known flambéed dessert provides a colorful, dramatic ending to any dinner party.

> 2 tablespoons sugar
> 1 can (16 oz) pitted sweet or sour red cherries, with juice
> 2 tablespoons kirsch
> 1 tablespoon cornstarch
> 1 pint French Vanilla Ice Cream (see page 312)
> ½ cup brandy

1. In a small saucepan over moderate heat, warm sugar and cherries with their juice until hot but not boiling. Make a paste of kirsch and cornstarch. Whisk into cherry mixture; heat, stirring, until thickened (do not boil).

2. Scoop ice cream into dessert dishes. Pour brandy into a ladle and hold it over a medium burner or candle for a minute to warm it slightly. To serve, light a match, ignite the warmed brandy, and pour it over cherry sauce. Stir until the flame dies down. Spoon cherry sauce over ice cream and serve at once.

Serves 4 to 6.

Recipes and Related Information
Ice Cream–Filled Profiteroles, 164; Papaya Ice Cream, 405; Prickly Pear Snow, 479; Rosé Pears and Ice Cream, 612; Sauce, 522; Watermelon Sherbet, 359.

Always a favorite, Classic Orange Marmalade is chunky with fruit and peel and permeated with a rich citrus flavor. To best show off its warm, golden color, present it at the table in a clear serving bowl.

CLASSIC ORANGE MARMALADE

Traditionally, the finest orange marmalade is made from slightly bitter Seville oranges. They are hard to come by in this country, but if you can find them, by all means use them in this recipe. If you can't find bitter oranges, substitute sweet Valencia or navel oranges. Note that the fruit must sit for two 24-hour periods to soften the peel and release the natural pectin before cooking and processing.

> 6   bitter oranges (if available) or sweet oranges
> 2   sweet oranges
> 1   lemon
> 9½   cups water
>   Sugar, as needed
> 1½   tablespoons fresh lemon juice

1. Slice oranges and lemon very thinly. Remove seeds and place slices in a small bowl with ½ cup of the water; set aside.

2. Place lemon and orange slices in a large pot and cover with the remaining water. Soak 24 hours.

3. Place pot containing orange and lemon slices over medium heat and simmer until peel is tender (about 35 minutes). Remove from heat and let stand another 24 hours.

4. Measure fruits and their liquid and return them to pot, adding an equal amount of sugar. Bring to a boil, reduce heat to medium, and cook, stirring frequently, until jell point is reached (45 to 60 minutes).

5. Combine lemon juice and water strained from seeds, add to pot, and cook marmalade 10 minutes more, stirring constantly.

6. Quickly ladle into clean, hot, sterilized jars, leaving ¼-inch headspace; fasten lids.

7. Process in boiling water bath 15 minutes.

Makes 6 half-pints.

CRANBERRY CONSERVE

Modify tradition a bit this year with this cranberry conserve. It's one less thing you'll have to prepare for busy holidays, and it tastes terrific with turkey, chicken, and wild game.

> 1   unpeeled orange, very finely chopped
> 2   cups water
> 3   cups sugar
> 1   quart fresh or frozen cranberries
> 1   cup raisins
> ½   cup chopped walnuts or other nuts

1. Combine orange and the water in a 6-quart or larger pot; cook rapidly until peel is tender (about 20 minutes).

2. Add sugar, cranberries, and raisins. Bring slowly to boiling, stirring occasionally until sugar dissolves.

3. Cook rapidly until mixture starts to thicken (about 8 minutes). As mixture thickens, stir frequently to prevent sticking. Stir in nuts the last 5 minutes of cooking.

4. Quickly ladle into clean, hot, sterilized jars, leaving ¼-inch headspace; fasten lids.

5. Process in boiling water bath 15 minutes.

Makes 4 half-pints.

APPLE BUTTER

Old-fashioned apple butter is difficult to find in stores and very easy to make. It is delicious on toast and waffles, or eaten as a fruit dessert with cream.

> 6   pounds apples
>   Sugar, as needed
> ½   teaspoon ground cinnamon
> ½   teaspoon ground allspice

1. Slice, peel, and core apples. Put in a large kettle and add water to halfway up amount of apples. Cook over medium heat until softened (15 to 20 minutes); cool.

2. Preheat oven to 300° F. Purée apples in a blender or food processor. Measure purée. Add ½ cup sugar for each 1 cup purée. Put sweetened purée into a shallow glass baking dish. Stir in cinnamon and allspice.

3. Bake until butter is thick but not dry (2 to 2½ hours), stirring every 15 minutes.

4. Quickly ladle into clean, hot, sterilized jars, leaving ¼-inch headspace. Process in boiling water bath 10 minutes.

Makes 6 pints.

■ MINT JELLY

Traditionalists insist that the best accompaniment to roast lamb is a dollop of mint jelly. There is no comparison between artificially flavored commercial jellies and your own version, made with fresh mint leaves and stems.

> 1 **cup chopped, solidly packed mint leaves and tender stems**
> 1 **cup water**
> ½ **cup apple cider vinegar**
> 3½ **cups sugar**
> 5 **drops green food coloring (optional)**
> 1 **pouch (3 oz) liquid fruit pectin**

1. Put chopped mint into a 6-quart pot. Add the water, vinegar, and sugar; stir well.

2. Over high heat, stirring constantly, bring quickly to a full, rolling boil that cannot be stirred down.

3. Add food coloring (if desired) and pectin.

4. Return to a full, rolling boil. Boil rapidly 30 seconds.

5. Remove from heat. Skim off foam with slotted spoon. Strain immediately through two thicknesses of damp cheesecloth.

6. Ladle jelly quickly into hot, sterilized jars, leaving ½-inch headspace; seal with paraffin.

Makes 3 to 4 half-pints.

■ SPICY BLUEBERRY FREEZER JAM

Freezer jams glisten with the natural color and flavor of fresh fruit. Thinner than traditional cooked jams, they are simple, fast, and fresh tasting.

> 2½ **pints blueberries**
> 1 **tablespoon fresh lemon juice**
> ½ **teaspoon ground cinnamon**
> ⅛ **teaspoon freshly grated nutmeg**
> 5 **cups sugar**
> ¾ **cup water**
> 1 **package (1¾ oz) powdered fruit pectin**

1. In a large bowl crush blueberries one layer at a time (crushing too many at a time inhibits free flow of juice).

2. Measure 3 cups crushed blueberries and place in a large bowl. Stir in lemon juice, cinnamon, and nutmeg. Thoroughly mix sugar into fruit. Let stand 10 minutes.

3. Combine the water and pectin in a saucepan. Bring to a full boil and boil 1 minute, stirring constantly.

4. Stir hot pectin liquid into fruit and continue to stir vigorously for 3 minutes to distribute pectin.

5. Ladle into freezer containers, leaving ½-inch headspace. Cover with lids and let stand at room temperature until set. (It may take up to 24 hours.) Store jam in freezer up to 8 months.

Makes about 6 half-pints.

PICKLES AND RELISHES

Making pickles and relishes is as easy as preserving, and many of the same principles apply. You will use water-bath canner, mason jars, and fresh, crisp produce. Pungent spices that have not lost their zest are important. You may want to grow your own herbs for the best quality possible. Kosher salt is used for brining because it does not have additives that would cloud the brine.

Follow the directions at the beginning of the chapter for using a water-bath canner. Store pickles and relishes in a cool, dark spot. Before using, let them age at least one month to mellow their sharp flavor.

■ BREAD AND BUTTER PICKLES

Most collections of early American pickled foods will include a recipe for Bread and Butter Pickles. These are sliced cucumbers, packed with onions, green peppers, and spices in a sweet-and-sour brine.

> 8 **cups sliced pickling cucumbers**
> **Salt**
> 2 **cups sliced onions**
> 4 **green bell peppers (with red on them if possible)**
> 2 **cups distilled white vinegar**
> 2 **cups sugar**
> 1 **tablespoon salt**
> 2 **teaspoons dry mustard**
> 2 **teaspoons turmeric**
> 2 **teaspoons celery seed**
> 1 **cinnamon stick, broken**

1. Sprinkle cucumber slices with salt and let soak 1 hour. Rinse with cold water and drain.

2. Cut onion slices crosswise and cut peppers (remove seeds) in about 1½-inch lengths.

3. Combine vinegar, sugar, the 1 tablespoon salt, mustard, turmeric, celery seed, and cinnamon stick in large kettle; add cucumbers, onions, and peppers. Bring to a boil; cook until cucumbers start to look glassy (3 to 5 minutes).

4. Pack pickles into clean, hot, sterilized jars, leaving ½-inch headspace; fasten lids.

5. Process in boiling water bath 5 minutes.

Makes 5 to 6 pints.

With the addition of vinegar, these cucumbers and flavorings will become delicious Dill Spears.

■ DILL SPEARS

Most pickling spices use dill as a major flavoring element. Dill weed (the feathery leaves) has a refreshing, cool quality; the small, hard, dried seeds are pungently warm and slightly bitter.

    4 pounds pickling cucumbers, washed, blossom
       ends removed, and cut into spears
    3 cups distilled white or apple cider vinegar
    3 cups water
    ⅓ cup salt
    3 peppercorns per quart
    2 dill heads *or* 2 tablespoons dill seed per quart
    1 clove garlic per quart

1. Combine vinegar, the water, and salt in a small saucepan and bring to a boil.

2. Add peppercorns, dill (or dill seed), and garlic to each clean, hot 1-quart jar.

3. Pack cucumber spears in jars. Fill jars with boiling pickling mixture, leaving ½-inch headspace; fasten lids.

4. Process in boiling water bath 20 minutes.

Makes about 3 quarts.

■ GINGERED PEACH PICKLES

These pickles are delicious over ice cream or served with crème fraîche.

    8 pounds (about 3½ qt) small peaches
    3 pounds light brown sugar
    1 quart cider vinegar
       Fresh ginger (1-in. piece), peeled and crushed
    2 tablespoons whole cloves, crushed
    3 cinnamon sticks, broken up
    1 whole clove per peach
       Additional whole cinnamon sticks, for each jar
    3 to 4 tablespoons brandy (optional)

1. Peel peaches and treat to prevent darkening. Halve and pit or leave whole.

2. Combine sugar and vinegar in a large pot; bring to a boil over medium heat and boil 5 minutes. Tie ginger, crushed cloves, and broken cinnamon sticks loosely in cheesecloth. Add to syrup and simmer 5 minutes.

3. Stick a whole clove in each peach. Add only enough peaches to boiling syrup to fill one 1-quart jar; cook until peaches are hot but not soft (about 2 minutes). Do not overcook. Remove peaches with slotted spoon and pack tightly in a clean, hot, sterilized jar along with a small stick of cinnamon. Repeat process until all peaches are packed in jars.

4. Bring syrup to a boil; remove spice bag. Pour hot syrup over peaches in jars, leaving ½-inch headspace. Add 1 tablespoon brandy (if desired). Fasten lids.

5. Process in boiling water bath 15 minutes.

Makes 3 to 4 quarts.

■ CORN RELISH

Corn relish tastes good with country-style cooking such as fried chicken, baked ham, and sausages of all kinds.

    22 medium ears of corn (enough to make
        10 cups kernels)
     1 cup chopped red bell pepper (1 large pepper)
    1¼ cups chopped celery
     ¾ cup chopped onion
    1½ cups sugar
    2½ cups distilled white vinegar
     2 cups water
     1 tablespoon salt
     1 teaspoon celery seed
    2½ tablespoons mustard seed
     ½ teaspoon turmeric

1. Cook ears of corn in boiling salted water 3 to 5 minutes. Plunge into cold water.

2. Drain corn. Cut kernels from cob with knife or corn kernel remover. Kernels should measure 10 cups.

3. In a large pot, combine kernels with remaining ingredients in large pot and simmer 15 minutes.

4. Immediately pack into clean, hot, sterilized jars, leaving ½-inch headspace; fasten lids.

5. Process in boiling water bath 15 minutes.

Makes 5 to 6 pints.

APRICOT AND CURRY CHUTNEY

Mention chutney, and mouths water for spicy East Indian dishes. Chutney is equally delicious with barbecued meats, roasts, poultry, chops, or cold cuts. In India, chutney is served fresh, but here it's more often preserved.

> 1½ **pounds dried apricots, chopped (4 cups chopped)**
> 1 **quart water**
> 1½ **cups chopped onion**
> ½ **cup sugar**
> 3 **cups golden raisins**
> 3 **cups distilled white vinegar**
> 1½ **tablespoons grated fresh ginger**
> 1½ **to 2 teaspoons curry powder**
> 2 **cinnamon sticks (2 in. each)**
> ¾ **teaspoon salt**

1. Combine apricots, the water, onion, and sugar in a 6-quart pot and simmer 5 minutes, stirring occasionally. Add remaining ingredients and cook 10 minutes more.

2. Remove cinnamon sticks and ladle chutney into clean, hot, sterilized jars, leaving ½-inch headspace; fasten lids.

3. Process in boiling water bath 10 minutes.

Makes about 4 pints.

HERB AND FRUIT VINEGARS AND MUSTARDS

Flavored vinegars are effective in salads and stir-fries or as pan glazes. They add zest to food and are satisfying to make. Collect different vinegars to flavor and see which ones you enjoy. Try Chinese and Japanese rice vinegars, wine vinegars, and apple cider vinegar. Wash and store empty wine bottles for vinegars. New corks are sold at hardware stores. The simple mustard recipe always works and is a great way to start to learn about this condiment.

HERB VINEGAR

The following is a basic method that can be used with any herb. Use about 4 ounces of fresh herbs or 2 ounces of dried herbs per quart of vinegar. Let the flavored vinegar sit for five or six weeks to deepen its flavor before using.

> **Tarragon sprigs (or other fresh herb)**
> **White wine vinegar or rice vinegar**

1. Wash fresh tarragon and pat dry with paper towels. Place a few sprigs in each sterilized bottle.

2. Pour vinegar into bottles and cap tightly.

3. Allow herbs to steep in vinegar for 5 to 6 weeks before using.

FRAN'S RASPBERRY VINEGAR

Use this raspberry vinegar in salad dressings, when poaching pears or apples, or to deglaze the sauté pan in which chicken or veal has been browned. This vinegar mellows as it ages. It keeps indefinitely, improving with time. Store in a cool, dark, dry place and refrigerate after opening.

> 12 **pints raspberries (6 oz each)**
> 1 **cup sugar**
> 2 **quarts or more good-quality red or white wine vinegar**

1. Rinse berries and place in large, clean, sterilized glass jars.

2. In a saucepan, combine sugar and vinegar, and bring to a boil, stirring until sugar dissolves.

3. Pour hot vinegar over berries. Berries must be completely covered with vinegar. Cover loosely and let stand in a cool place 3 to 4 weeks.

4. Strain mixture through a fine sieve into a saucepan, pressing gently to extract juice from berries. Bring to a boil, reduce heat, and simmer 10 minutes; skim off foam.

5. In the meantime, boil canning jars or glass bottles, completely immersed in water, for 15 minutes to sterilize. (Any type of bottle that can withstand the boiling temperature may be used.)

6. Ladle hot vinegar into hot, sterilized jars or bottles, leaving ¼-inch headspace; cap tightly.

Makes 2 quarts.

HOMEMADE MUSTARD

This recipe is basically foolproof. It makes the French-style wine mustard.

> ¼ **cup dry mustard**
> ¼ **cup white wine vinegar**
> ⅓ **cup dry white wine**
> 1 **tablespoon sugar**
> ½ **teaspoon salt**
> 3 **egg yolks**

1. Mix together all ingredients except egg yolks and allow to stand 2 hours.

2. Whisk yolks into mixture; transfer to top of a double boiler. Cook, stirring constantly, over hot, not boiling, water until mustard thickens (about 5 minutes).

3. Cool mustard. Cover and refrigerate up to 1 month.

Makes 1 cup.

Tarragon Mustard Mix in ½ teaspoon crushed dried tarragon when adding egg yolks.

Lemon or Lime Mustard Mix in ¾ teaspoon grated lemon or lime rind and 1½ teaspoons fresh lemon or lime juice when adding egg yolks.

JELLY-ROLL STYLE

This term takes its name from the dessert made from a sheet of sponge cake that is spread with jelly, rolled, and baked. When sliced, the cross section shows a spiral design of cake and filling. The term has come to mean a thin, flat piece of meat, fish, cake, bread, pastry, or other food rolled around a filling.

JERUSALEM ARTICHOKE

Also known as the sunchoke, the Jerusalem artichoke is a native American vegetable. Samuel de Champlain discovered it growing in Indian gardens in Cape Cod in 1604. Despite its name, it is not an artichoke but a tuber of a species of sunflower. The word *Jerusalem* may be derived from *girasole*, Italian for sunflower.

The fresh tubers have ivory flesh and a thin, light brown skin that may have a reddish hue. Ranging from 2 to 6 inches in length, they may be either rounded with fairly smooth skins or elongated with knobby protuberances. The tubers closely resemble fresh ginger.

When raw, the Jerusalem artichoke has a crisp texture like that of a potato and a delicate, somewhat nutty flavor. When cooked, the tuber has a texture resembling boiled turnips and a flavor reminiscent of artichoke. Most consumers are surprised to discover that the Jerusalem artichoke contains no starch.

Use   Slice or grate raw Jerusalem artichokes and add to salads, or marinate in vinaigrette and serve as a salad. Bake tubers in their skins as you would potatoes; slice and sauté or deep-fry; boil or steam, then sauté in butter, or peel and purée. Substitute for water chestnut in stir-fries. Purée for soup or preserve as relish or pickles.

Availability   Fresh Jerusalem artichokes are sold fall through winter.

Selection   Pick firm tubers without soft spots. For easy cleaning and preparation, choose those with smooth, regular shapes. Jerusalem artichokes are sold in bulk in some supermarkets; in other markets, they are scrubbed and packed in plastic bags.

Storage   If packaged in a plastic bag and kept in the refrigerator crisper, Jerusalem artichokes should remain crisp and firm for at least one week.

Preparation   Scrub well, using a stiff brush if necessary to remove dirt from knobs and crevices. Leave on skin or peel, as desired. Peeled raw Jerusalem artichokes oxidize rapidly; drop in acidulated water immediately to prevent browning. Drain just before using. The tubers are easier to peel if cooked first.

Cooking   See BOIL, DEEP-FRY, PUREE, SAUTE, STEAM.

JICAMA

The tuber of a tropical vine, jicama (pronounced *hee-ka-ma*) has long been important to Mexican cooks but only recently has been widely found in American supermarkets. It looks like a large, squat, knobby turnip with a rough earth-colored brown skin. The stark white flesh inside is as cool and crunchy as an apple and almost as sweet. Jicama is a member of the legume family and is also known as yam bean.

Use   Jicama can be eaten raw or cooked. In Mexico it is cut into slivers and served with ground chiles and lime as an appetizer. Cut into spears, it is perfect for dipping, and when dressed with citrus juice, chiles, and oil becomes a refreshing savory salad. Raw jicama adds crunchy texture and sweetness to fruit salads. Its natural sweetness and low calorie count make it an appealing dieter's snack. Substitute jicama for water chestnut in stir-fries, or prepare like a potato—boiled and mashed, or baked.

Availability   Fresh jicama appears all year in Mexican markets and some supermarkets, but peak availability is October through May. Some markets cut up large jicama and sell portions wrapped in plastic.

Selection   Jicama should be firm, without blemishes. It should feel heavy for its size.

Storage   Keep in a plastic bag in the refrigerator crisper for up to two weeks. Store small cut pieces in cold water to prevent drying out.

Preparation   Wash and peel, removing the fibrous white layer just underneath the skin.

■ JICAMA WITH CHILE AND LIME
Jicama con chile y limon is commonly sold from little carts on the streets of Mexico. The mild flavor of jicama is an excellent foil for the bite of the ground chile and salt, and the tang of the lime juice. It is a delicious, simple to prepare snack or hors d'oeuvre.

> 1 **small jicama, peeled and cut into bite-sized wedges**
> **Salt, to taste**
> **Ground red chile, mild or hot, to taste**
> 2 **limes, cut into wedges**

1. Place jicama wedges on toothpicks and arrange on a platter. Sprinkle with salt and ground chile.

2. Serve with lime wedges. Each person squeezes a little lime juice over jicama before eating.

Serves 6 to 8 as an appetizer.

Recipes and Related Information
Avocado, Jicama, and Grapefruit Salad, 281; Nopalito Salad, 391.

JUICE EXTRACTOR

If you want to squeeze a pitcherful of fresh orange or grapefruit juice, you would use a reamer (see CITRUS REAMER). To press out the healthful juices from hard, raw fruits and vegetables such as carrots, apples, and cabbage, juice-bar style, you need this machine. All models function essentially the same: Pulp is finely grated so that its liquid is released, and as a result of centrifugal action, the juice is passed through a strainer that traps the pulp. More expensive models have a larger capacity and are probably able to extract more juice. Some heavy-duty electric mixers and food processors have extractor attachments.

JULIENNE, TO

To cut into fine, even-sized sticks, which are also called matchsticks. These strips are used to garnish soups, stews, and salads; or, they can be steamed and served as a side dish. See KNIFE, Cutting Techniques, for information on how to julienne.

JUNIPER BERRY

A small, round, blue-black berry of an evergreen shrub native to Europe, the juniper berry is the principal flavoring in gin. It is about the size of a large pea and is extremely aromatic.

Use Apart from its importance in making gin, juniper is employed to flavor marinades for game of all kinds, for lamb, and for the German braised meat dish, sauerbraten. It is also traditionally added to Alsatian sauerkraut.

Availability Whole juniper berries are sold on most supermarket spice racks.

Selection Packaged seasonings lose quality after a while; try to buy from a store that restocks its spice section fairly often.

Storage Keep in an airtight container in a cool, dark, dry place for up to two years.

Preparation Toasting berries briefly in a warm skillet will bring out their fragrance. Crush berries gently with a mortar and pestle for use in marinades; crush finely for stuffings or sauces. They are pungent and should be used in moderation.

KALE

The leafy green vegetable known as kale, borecole, or cow cabbage is a non-head-forming member of the cabbage family and one of the first cabbages to be cultivated. Its dark green, ruffled leaves are high in vitamin C and calcium and very low in calories. It thrives in cold climates; indeed it is said that frost increases its sweetness. Collards belong to the same family but have smooth, flat leaves. Some markets now carry an ornamental kale, also known as salad savoy, which has handsome crinkly leaves bearing shades of rose, cream, purple, and green.

Use Because it thrives throughout cold Scottish winters, kale has long been an almost daily staple in the Scottish diet. Scotch cooks use it in colcannon (mashed potatoes with kale) and in lamb and barley soup. Portuguese cooks make a simple potato and kale soup called *caldo verde*. In the southern United States, kale is boiled with ham bone or salt pork, sometimes in conjunction with collards. Ornamental kale is edible but not choice; its best use is decorative.

Availability Fresh kale is sold fall through spring. Frozen kale is carried by many supermarkets.

Selection The best kale has crisp, dark leaves. Avoid bunches with limp, wilted, or yellowed leaves.

Storage It will stay fresh for several days in a plastic bag in the refrigerator crisper.

Preparation Wash well. Discard any limp or discolored leaves. Cut away tough stems. Shred, chop, or cook whole (cut large leaves in half).

Cooking See BOIL, STEAM.

■ STEAMED KALE AND PEARL ONIONS
If you've never tried kale, this simple steamed side dish would be a good introduction.

> ¼ **pound pearl onions, peeled**
> 1 **bunch kale, coarsely chopped**
> **Lemon wedges, for garnish**

Place onions and then kale in steamer over boiling water and cook until kale is wilted (8 to 10 minutes). Serve immediately with lemon wedges.

Serves 4.

KAMPYO

Also spelled *kanpyo,* these long, buff-colored, ribbonlike strips are made from dried gourd shavings.

Use *Kampyo* is employed in Japanese cuisine both as an edible string—to tie neat food packages—and as an ingredient in fillings for rolled sushi.

Availability Look for kampyo in Japanese markets in 1-ounce plastic packets.

Storage Leftover kampyo should be kept in a plastic bag in a cool, dry place. It will keep indefinitely.

Preparation Kampyo must be softened before use. Wash first, then massage with a generous amount of salt to break down the fibers and increase absorbency. Wash again, then boil until soft. Drain.

KATSUOBUSHI

Along with kelp, *katsuobushi* (dried bonito) is the main flavoring agent in the basic Japanese stock called *dashi* (see Miso Soup, page 562). It is almost as hard as wood and must be shaved into flakes before using. The best dashi is made from katsuobushi that is shaved with a special utensil just before use. For convenience, many Japanese cooks purchase dried bonito flakes (*hanagatsuo* or *kezuribushi*).

Use Dried bonito flakes are primarily used in dashi. They are also employed to flavor a soy-based dipping sauce for sashimi and as a garnish for some vegetable dishes such as chilled, boiled spinach.

Availability Whole dried bonito is not generally sold in this country. Pale pink, dried bonito flakes are available in Japanese markets and some supermarkets, packed in boxes or plastic bags.

Storage Leftover bonito flakes should be stored in an airtight container in a cool, dry place. Replace every six months because they lose flavor.

KIMCHEE

Almost every meal in Korea is accompanied by at least one kind of kimchee (also spelled *kimchi*), a fermented, pickled vegetable. The best-known kimchee, at least in this country, is made from cabbage, but in Korea it is also made from carrots, radishes, and other vegetables. Generally, the vegetables are grated or shredded, seasoned with salt, garlic, and red pepper, and left to stand for several days. Kimchee has a pungent fermented flavor and may be quite spicy and have a strong smell.

Use For some families in Korea, kimchee is a winter replacement for fresh vegetables that are hard to find. It is served the year around, however, in much the same way pickles are served in this country. Its crunchy texture and pungent character are refreshing and revivifying.

Availability Bottled cabbage kimchee is sold in many supermarkets; most Asian markets carry a larger variety of kimchee.

Storage Refrigerate kimchee in a covered container; it will keep indefinitely.

KIWIFRUIT

Underneath the fuzzy brown skin of the kiwifruit is a lime green flesh studded with tiny black seeds. Its texture is moist and melonlike, its flavor refreshingly tart and sweet. Kiwifruit was practically unknown in this country until the late 1950s, when it began to be exported from New Zealand. Today it is also cultivated in California. Originally known as Chinese gooseberry, the fruit was renamed by exporters to avoid confusion with the green gooseberry (to which it is not related) and to identify it more strongly with their country.

Use The delicate flavor of kiwifruit is best appreciated raw. Halve lengthwise and eat with a spoon, or peel, slice in rounds, and add to fruit salads. Sliced kiwifruit makes a striking garnish for fruit tarts and frozen desserts. It may also be puréed for sorbets or sauces. Like the papaya, the kiwifruit acts as a meat tenderizer. A halved kiwifruit can be rubbed over steaks or chops before grilling or broiling to tenderize them.

Availability Fresh kiwifruits are sold all year in most supermarkets. The California crop is marketed from November through April; New Zealand imports take their place May through October.

Selection Look for kiwifruits that are firm but not hard, with no soft spots. They should give slightly to pressure. Hard kiwifruits will ripen at room temperature if stored in a plastic bag.

Storage Refrigerate ripe kiwifruit in a plastic bag for up to two weeks.

KNEAD, TO

When making bread, to work dough with hands into a smooth and malleable mass by pressing and folding. Kneading also forms and arranges gluten (a protein substance found in wheat-flour doughs) into an elastic network that gives structure to the finished product. A heavy-duty mixer with dough hook or a food processor using the steel blade will perform this task for you, but many bakers find kneading the most enjoyable part of the whole bread-making process and are reluctant to turn this step over to a machine.

Pastry and biscuit doughs are also kneaded. Unlike bread doughs, these mixtures are worked with a light touch just until all ingredients are combined. For flaky pastry, the kneading is even briefer—just until ingredients hold together.

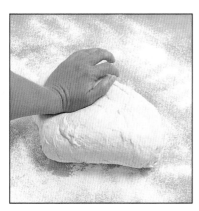

HAND-KNEADING BREAD DOUGH

With heel of hand, push dough away from you.

Bring end of dough back over with your fingers and give it a slight turn.

Repeat process until dough feels smooth, satiny, and elastic, and small bubbles appear just under surface of dough.

HAND-KNEADING PASTRY DOUGH

With fingertips, push the dough away from you and gently fold the top over; continue this motion just until the mass looks smooth and homogeneous.

Fraiser: Gather dough into a mound. Work small portions at a time, pushing away from you with heel of hand to smear dough across work surface.

To hand-knead rich, sticky bread doughs: For brioche, pick up, flip over, and throw back down; or pick up and slam down on surface without flipping. For very liquid doughs (baba, savarin, Kugelhopf), with the flat of your hand or a flat wooden spatula, slap the dough against the side of the bowl.

KNEADING BREAD DOUGH

Set dough on a lightly floured board; flour prevents dough from sticking. Using heel of your hand, push dough away from you; bring far end of dough back over with your fingers and give it a slight turn. Repeat the pushing, folding, and turning in a continuous, rhythmic, fluid motion until dough feels smooth, satiny, and springy, and small bubbles form just under surface. Depending on amount of flour you are working and how firmly you knead, this process can take anywhere from 8 to 15 minutes. Many bread recipes give a range for the amount of flour; use the lesser amount when mixing ingredients and add more flour as you knead if it seems appropriate. In the early stages of kneading, when dough is still sticky, you may want to sprinkle work surface occasionally with flour (taken from what is as yet unused from recipe). You also may want to scrape away any wet dough with a dough scraper before reflouring.

To knead with a heavy-duty mixer with dough hook, follow manufacturer's instructions.

KNEADING BREAD DOUGH IN A FOOD PROCESSOR

The food processor makes quick work of kneading any yeast dough. The plastic dough-kneading blade works best with more than 3 cups of dry ingredients; use the metal blade for less than 3 cups. Put all dry ingredients, including solid shortening, into work bowl. Mix all liquid ingredients together in a measuring cup. Start the motor and slowly add liquid in a stream only as fast as flour absorbs it (about 20 seconds). It is better to add more slowly than too quickly. Dough should gather into a ball and clean sides and bottom of work bowl. If dough is too dry, add more liquid by tablespoons through feed tube; if dough is too wet, add flour by tablespoons. Knead 60 to 90 seconds.

A food processor makes quick work of the usually time-consuming task of mixing and kneading yeast doughs. Use the metal blade for smaller batches, the plastic blade for larger ones.

Processor kneading not only saves time but also allows you to make moist, elastic doughs with the minimum amounts of flour. You can adapt any bread recipe to the processor without altering amounts of ingredients. Just remember to add liquid to dry ingredients as described above, and follow manufacturer's recommendations for maximum amounts.

KNEADING PASTRY, BISCUIT, AND RICH YEAST DOUGHS

For pastry such as pie and tart crusts, both the work surface and dough should be cool. With just the tips of your fingers, push dough away from you and fold top over gently. Continue this motion just until mass looks smooth and homogeneous. Biscuits require a minimum of handling—maybe only 12 to 15 turns.

Fraisage is a French term for working tart dough until pliable and blended but not tough by smearing it with the heel of the hand. To perform this technique, gather dough into a rough mound on a floured work surface. Work small portions at a time, pushing away from you. When pieces of dough are smooth, elastic, and peel away from surface in one piece, press all into a ball and shape crust as directed in recipe.

Rich yeast doughs such as brioche, *Kugelhopf,* baba, and savarin can be kneaded in a heavy-duty mixer which has both dough hook and flat paddle. For brioche, knead 5 minutes using a dough hook; for very wet and sticky baba and savarin, use the flat beater and knead 5 minutes. To hand-knead sticky doughs such as brioche, lay dough on a floured surface and pick up, flip over, and throw back down; or pick up and slam down on surface without flipping. Continue until pliable and smooth (about 10 minutes). Baba, savarin, and Kugelhopf, which have such a high proportion of liquid that they are almost like a batter, must be worked in a bowl. With the flat part of your hand or a flat wooden spatula, slap dough against side of bowl until smooth and elastic (about 5 minutes).

KNEADING PASTRY DOUGH IN A FOOD PROCESSOR

The metal blade makes pie doughs in seconds. Just follow these steps: Put flour and salt (and sugar, if called for) in work bowl. Add chilled fat cut into tablespoon-sized pieces. (Butter can be straight from the refrigerator. Vegetable shortening should be frozen.) Pulse 3 or 4 times. Add liquid through feed tube while pulsing very rapidly 20 to 30 times until just short of when dough looks like it will gather into a ball. Remove dough from work bowl and press together. Use as recipe directs.

Recipes and Related Information
Biscuit, 49; Flour, 234; Pie and Tart, 431; Yeast Bread, 613.

KNIFE

Good cooking begins with good cutting. A basic set of fine knives is probably the first purchase student chefs make. Although quality cutlery is costly, properly handled and well-maintained knives are a lifetime investment invaluable to their work. Fine knives can be sharpened to a keen, durable edge, feel better in the hand because they are well balanced, and are sturdily constructed to last for years. Professional chefs depend upon their personal collection of knives to such a degree that they rarely travel without them when they cook or teach away from their own kitchens.

Home cooks should select knives with the same discerning eye as the professional, and for the same reasons—ease of use, comfort, and value. Safety is another reason; a properly sharpened knife actually prevents accidents. Forcing a cut with a dull knife is one of the easiest ways to injure yourself.

SELECTING KNIVES

Top-quality knives are made of either carbon steel or an alloy—high-carbon stainless steel—that combines the softness of carbon steel and the rust-resistant attributes of stainless steel to produce a blade that can be honed to razor sharpness and won't discolor. Prior to the introduction of high-carbon stainless steel, carbon steel knives were long the favorite of chefs and serious home cooks because they take an edge so well, but were prone to stains and rust unless thoroughly dried immediately after washing.

The best blades are forged, or beaten into shape, by hand with anvil and hammer. Forging develops desirable characteristics in the metal impossible to obtain when shaped by machine. A handcrafted tool is also more aesthetically appealing than a machine-made product. Blades can be stamped or cut, processes that are automated and therefore less costly. Knives made by either of these methods are predictably less expensive than those that are hand-forged.

To be effective, the sharp edge of a blade must be thin enough to cut yet strong enough not to bend or ripple. It must, of course, be able to be resharpened when necessary. Grinding, the final step in the process of making a knife, imparts this strength to a very thin piece of metal. As with forging, grinding by hand produces a knife of superior quality. Hollow grinding, a machine process, produces an edge that can't be reground and is therefore best suited for serrated knives, which keep their factory-shaped edge indefinitely.

The part of the blade that extends into the handle is called the tang. A full tang extends completely into the handle and assumes the shape of the handle, adding balance and weight to a knife. This is an important feature for most tasks except some butchering and slicing procedures; knives for these tasks have partial tangs. Very heavy knives may have a rattail tang. Narrow and thin, and extending the length of the handle, this shape imparts strength but reduces heft. Better knives use metal rivets embedded in the handle on both sides rather than glue to hold the tang in place. On a riveted handle, the tang is a visible line of metal around the center of the edge of the handle. Choose a knife with a full or rattail tang, and with full rivets, not merely inlays.

A good handle is made of resin-impregnated wood so that it is smooth and waterproof. Polypropylene is another material commonly used for handles. Some companies use dense-grained natural hardwood handles that should not be cleaned in a dishwasher, but a good knife in any case should never be washed by machine because the heat will ruin its edge, as will harsh detergents and being knocked around in the utensil basket. Whatever the handle material, it should display a refined surface without crevices or recesses where food can hide and bacteria can grow. It should not have rough edges that can irritate your hand.

Before buying a knife, don't forget to pick it up to see how it feels in your hand. Due to slight differences in handle design, width, and material, knives of comparable quality may not be of comparable comfort. If you don't like to hold it, no matter how well made it may be, you won't use it and you'll have wasted your money.

As with cookware, don't feel compelled to purchase your knives in sets. While the price of a set may seem appealing, in reality there is better value in buying knives individually. That way you know you are getting only those you will use. Consider which you need based on your cooking style and storage space, then investigate what's available. Ask retailers for specific information regarding construction and quality for the brands they carry.

CARING FOR KNIVES

If you have invested in quality cutlery, take the time to care for it properly. Hard surfaces dull even the best of edges. Always cut on a surface that has some resilience. Wood is an excellent choice, as is polycarbonate, which gives much like wood. Avoid glass, metal, hard plastic, and ceramic tile (see CHOPPING AND CUTTING BOARD).

Fine knives should be washed immediately after use—don't soak—and dried thoroughly. Even if the handle is waterproof, good cutlery lasts longer and retains its appearance better when washed by hand.

Store knives in a slotted rack or drawer, or on a magnetic bar; never throw them bare-bladed into a drawer. Not only is this a safety hazard, but such cavalier treatment also damages the edges. If you want to store knives in a drawer, protect them with plastic sheaths, available at better cookware and cutlery stores.

SHARPENING KNIVES

A sharp edge is a necessity for good cutting and, again, for safety. For proper care, knives should be honed fre-quently, sharpened occasionally, and reground every one or two years, depending upon use.

SHARPENING STEEL

The easiest and best way to maintain a sharp edge on any knife is with a sharpening steel, if it is used correctly. If you don't already own a steel, buy one and learn to handle it; it will save you time, money, and frustration. The ideal steel is at least 12 inches long, not counting the handle, with a smooth or very finely ridged surface. The steel does not remove metal from the edge of a knife, as a whetstone does; rather, it realigns the cutting edge to keep it razor-sharp. If you use the steel every time you bring out your knife, it will hardly ever need to be sharpened on a stone or reground. Frequent, regular employment of a steel will maintain a good edge for up to two years.

To use a steel, hold steel in left hand, either out in front of you at chest level or vertically with tip resting on cutting board. Place heel of blade against steel near top, with blade making a 15- to 20-degree angle with steel. (Too wide an angle dulls the edge; too narrow an angle produces a brittle, fragile edge that dulls easily with use.) Maintaining gentle sideways pressure against steel, swing blade downward, drawing length of cutting edge across steel. Repeat on other side of knife. Alternate sides, making 10 or 12 strokes in all.

WHETSTONE

Eventually, even knives sharpened daily will need regrinding. The wedge-shaped edge will have worn down to such a degree that it must be re-created. A whetstone, made of an abrasive known as Carborundum, realigns the edge so that it will respond to the sharpening steel. If you haven't made a habit of using a steel regularly, a stone will bring a dull knife back to life. To use, draw the knife across the stone at the same 20-degree angle as with the steel, alternating sides, making 5 or 6 strokes on each side.

RODS

Other alternatives to the sharpening steel are ceramic or steel rods, which are available in three forms: a free rod that you use like a steel; a fixed rod on a stand that is already angled properly—to use, hold the knife perpendicular to the floor and draw across the rod; and a pair of crossed rods preset to a 20-degree angle.

AUTOMATIC HONER-SHARPENER

Until recently, electric knife sharpeners have done little more than grind away at the blade. A new machine, which uses a grinding wheel and two grinding pads studded with diamond particles, allows you to attain a sharper edge than previously possible with a home device. Magnets keep the knife at the proper angle in each slot; all you do is pull the knife through. The grinding wheel resets the edge, the coarse diamond pad sharpens, and the fine diamond pad hones. The machine uses household current.

A well-chosen selection of quality knives should last a lifetime. Shown clockwise from upper right: whetstone, automatic honer-sharpener, Asian knife, cleaver, utility and paring knives, poultry shears, kitchen scissors, chef's fork, shrimp deveiner, oyster knife, clam knife, tomato knife, avocado pitter, bread knife, ham slicer, boning knife, sandwich knife, fillet knife, chef's knife, sharpening steel.

A GUIDE TO BUYING KNIVES

Every kitchen should have at least four basic knives: a large chopping knife, a medium-sized slicing knife, a small paring knife, and a thin boning knife for delicate operations. A pair of good quality kitchen scissors will also prove invaluable. After that choose among the specialty knives as you see fit. Because good knives will last for years if well cared for, the most economical strategy in the long run is to invest in fewer knives of top quality rather than to accumulate a slew of cheaper slicers and choppers. Size is the blade measurement, excluding the handle.

Asian Knives Because of their large, rectangular blades, which look vaguely like those of Western meat cleavers, all Chinese knives, from lightweight vegetable knives to extraheavy, bone-chopping cleavers tend to be lumped together under the name Chinese cleaver. The name is misleading, however; only the heaviest of these knives are cleavers in the Western sense, that is, knives meant to chop through bones. At first you may find these large knives unwieldy, but with practice you will soon find them indispensable because they perform with such efficiency and are so versatile. These knives are numbered on the blade—the higher the number, the smaller and lighter the knife. Number 1, the heaviest, most

closely corresponds to a true cleaver. The lighter versions are strictly for vegetables and boneless meats.

A medium-weight number 3 or 4 Chinese knife and the similar Japanese type with a narrower blade are called vegetable knives. Used like French chef's knives, they are good for slicing, dicing, and mincing; crushing garlic and ginger; and carrying chopped foods from cutting surface to cooking pan. They have wooden handles that some cooks use as pestles for grinding peppercorns and other spices.

Avocado Pitter Certainly not a necessary item, but if you typically have difficulty removing the pit from an avocado, this tool will make the process go more smoothly.

Boning Knife The extra-narrow, flexible, tapered blade of a boning knife affords maximum maneuverability when separating chicken breast from bone, the most common boning procedure for home cooks. These knives are typically 5 or 6 inches long.

Chef's Fork This two-pronged heavyweight fork performs many functions: transfers whole birds and roasts from pan to carving board or platter, holds meat and fowl in place during carving, and protects fingers from hot food by doing the lifting and moving.

Chef's Knife Serious cooks consider this knife with its wide, slightly curving blade to be the most versatile and important of all cutting tools. Although its large size and deep blade may feel unwieldy at first, you will soon find it indispensable. Its primary function is chopping, done with a rocking motion that follows the arc of the blade or with rapid up and down movements. Not only is it good for slicing, dicing, and mincing, but its broad side can be used to smash garlic cloves or to flatten chicken breasts. The blade is also handy for scooping whatever you have just cut, from a bit of minced parsley to a pile of sliced celery, and transferring it to sauté pan or mixing bowl. The best of these knives has a thickening of the blade, called the bolster, between the blade and the handle, and sometimes a metal collar that extends past the bolster to the handle. The bolster improves balance by adding weight and also serves as a barrier to keep your hand from slipping into the cutting edge. These knives range in length from 6 to 13 inches; a 6- or 8-inch blade is probably the most popular size for home cooks. Some manufacturers call this knife a cook's knife.

Clam Knife This knife tends to have a blunt, rather than a sharp edge, because clams have a different muscle structure than other bivalves. You can use an oyster knife for clams if you want to buy only one specialty tool. The technique for opening both bivalves is basically the same (see Oyster Knife).

Filleting Knife Don't consider this knife part of your basic set, but if you like to fillet fish yourself, then it will earn its price tag. It has a paper-thin, extremely flexible blade that maneuvers superbly between flesh and super-delicate bones and skin. Two popular sizes are 6 and 10 inches; you will also find them well suited to slicing fragile cakes and pastries.

Grapefruit Knife Some grapefruit lovers can't imagine life without this serrated cutter. The curved blade neatly separates flesh from membrane and from outer peel. A sharp paring knife does this job almost as well.

Kitchen Scissors A pair of durable kitchen scissors is a necessity. Use them to snip fresh herbs, cut parchment paper to fit cake pans, trim poached eggs into neat ovals, groom houseplants and trim blossoms, prepare wrapping paper, double as poultry shears for halving game hens, and perform hundreds of other jobs. Some have many functions; they open cans and bottles, as well as cut. Scissors that come apart are easier to clean.

Meat Cleaver These are meant to chop through bone. While the blades of chopping knives have a constant taper from the top to the cutting edge, the cleaver blade tapers slowly from the top to within an inch or so of the edge, then tapers quickly to the cutting edge. The result, technically known as a roll grind, is an edge that is not as fine as that of the chef's knife, but is capable of hacking through bones without denting or cracking. A cleaver can be used for coarsely chopping meats and vegetables, but its bulkier blade makes precise work, and especially thin slicing, more difficult. Choose a large knife; with practice you will find its extra size and weight working for you.

Oyster Knife Opening oysters takes strength. Using this specially designed knife with its short, strong blade and hand guard makes the job easier. There are as many versions of bivalve knives as there are varieties of bivalves to open. To use, top of knife is inserted into hinge of oyster shell and twisted to pry shell apart.

Paring/Utility Knife Use this knife as an extension of your index finger to make small cuts; used with a twisting motion of your hand and wrist, it is perfect for peeling and slicing fruits and vegetables, carving out the eyes of a potato, chopping or cutting up small amounts of herbs, and sculpting garnishes. Its shape resembles that of a chef's knife, but has less of an arc; a variation has an upwardly curved blade. Midsize paring knives are also called utility knives or sandwich knives. A 3- to 4-inch blade is typical for paring knives; utility knives have blades that are 6 to 8 inches long.

Poultry Shears Made of heavy stainless steel or chrome-plated steel, poultry shears should have a spring-lever action for extra cutting power to work through bone and cartilage. Use them to disjoint all kinds of fowl or to divide little Rock Cornish game hens. A locking hinge at the handle secures blades for safe storage. Look for shears that come apart; they are easier to clean.

Serrated Knife A serrated edge makes a clean cut through a firm crust or skin without crushing the delicate interior crumb or flesh. Serrated slicers do an excellent job cutting bread, and halving génoise, sponge, or butter cake layers for multitiered pastries (for an even cut, use a knife longer than the diameter of the cake; see photograph, page 85). Bread knives are 8 inches. Shorter serrated blades, around 5½ inches long, breeze through tomatoes—whose skin is notoriously resistant to all but the sharpest blades—with ease. They are also better suited than the longer bread knife for slicing a thin baguette loaf and for slicing fruits without forcing out the juice in the process. Use a back-and-forth sawing motion when cutting with a serrated knife.

Shrimp Deveiner The arc of the blade, which duplicates the curved back of the shrimp, permits you to slice the shell and remove the black vein in one operation.

Slicing/Carving Knives Designed to cut through cooked meats of all kinds, these knives have a pointed or round tip and long blades that are either flexible or rigid, depending on the piece to be cut. Rigid, more sturdy knives work better for slicing ham and roasts; poultry requires a thinner blade that can conform somewhat to its bone structure.

CUTTING TECHNIQUES

In the following descriptions of techniques, the right hand refers to the hand holding the knife, and the left hand to the one holding the food to be cut (with an apology to left-handed cooks). A French chef's knife and an Asian vegetable knife (Chinese or Japanese) are interchangeable in this discussion.

Work slowly at first until you get the hang of each technique; speed will come naturally. It is important to learn safe and efficient cutting habits. Give yourself plenty of room to work, stand in a comfortable position, relax, and focus entirely on the task at hand; you will find yourself cutting quickly and with minimum effort. Don't try to cut too much at one time. Work with a manageable amount so that you are aware of and can control what you are doing. The following techniques are illustrated in the photographs on the opposite page.

HAND POSITION

Holding food for safe and precise cutting is mostly a matter of keeping your fingers out of the way of the blade. For most cutting tasks, this means holding food against board with the fingertips of the left hand curled back away from blade. The blade then rides against the curved knuckles to guide the cut. As long as you do not lift the blade above the level of the knuckles and do not straighten out the fingers, you can avoid cutting yourself in this position.

The position of your hand depends upon the task. For precise cutting, grip handle close to blade, with thumb and forefinger grasping blade itself. Let the knife work with you by gripping it near its balance point. To find that point, lay the knife flat across the index finger. There are two basic blade positions: resting tip of knife on board and slicing with a rocking motion, or lifting entire blade, holding edge parallel to board, and slicing with a downward and forward motion. The former method allows more control, the latter more speed. For other grips, see Chopping, Paring, and Cleaver Chopping (following).

SLICING

Hold ingredient with fingers curled back and knuckles away from blade at a distance that equals one slice. Slice with a French chef's knife or Asian vegetable knife, using knuckles to guide blade, then move fingers back along food (or push food forward with thumb) to get into position for next slice.

SHREDDING AND JULIENNE CUTTING

To cut food into fine shreds, larger pieces, or julienne (matchsticks), first cut ingredient into slices of the desired length and thickness. Carrots and other slender vegetables may have to be sliced on a slant to achieve the right length. Stack slices, overlapping them slightly like shingles, and slice down through stack lengthwise, forming squared-off sticks. Shreds are very fine julienne pieces, less than ⅛ inch thick; matchsticks are twice as thick.

To shred green onions for garnish or stir-fries, first slice them into desired length. Slit white and pale green sections lengthwise, but do not cut all the way through. Open halves like a book and cut lengthwise into thin shreds. To shred hollow green tops, bundle them together under fingertips of left hand and carefully slice bundle into fine shreds.

DICING AND MINCING

These terms describe the same process, but differ in the size of the cut: Diced means cubes of ¼ to ½ inch, minced less than ⅛ inch, and finely diced somewhere in between. First cut (using a French chef's knife or an Asian vegetable knife) ingredient into shreds or matchsticks of the desired thickness, as described at left. Then gather sticks into a bundle and cut across into uniform cubes. Always try to keep food you are cutting in a shape that works with you. Cut round objects into sections, so that they lie flat.

Garlic, onion, and shallot are diced or minced by a slightly different method. First peel, leaving root end intact, then split in half lengthwise. Place cut side down on board and, positioning knife blade horizontally, make one or more cuts parallel to cutting board, almost to root end. Make a series of vertical, lengthwise cuts almost to root end, of the desired thickness. Slice across cuts toward root end to produce cubes. Discard root end.

SMASHING AND BRUISING

When an aromatic ingredient such as garlic, ginger, or green onion is used in large pieces to flavor a food, smashing or bruising it first helps release its flavor into the food. Cut to desired size, place pieces on board, and smack them smartly with broad side of blade. Another method is to place knife flat on top of food, then pound it with your fist. Watch out for cutting edge if using this technique.

To peel garlic, lay clove on a board. Hold flat side of a chef's knife just above it. Lightly pound knife, hitting garlic and loosening its skin. Pull skin off, cutting if necessary.

CHOPPING

Although uniform cubes (dice or mince) are sometimes unnecessary, cooking or processing will be faster if hard ingredients are cut into smaller pieces. You may also need to finely chop fresh parsley or other herbs. If the foods are very large, such as carrots or onions, first roughly cut up. For herbs, remove leaves from stems. Then place these pieces or leaves on cutting board. Grip knife a little farther out on handle than for slicing. Use left hand to press tip of knife down against board and chop with a rocking motion, pivoting knife back and forth across food. Chop to desired size with a rolling, downward and forward motion (not an up-and-down chop), scraping pile together.

If you hear your knife hitting cutting board along with vegetable, half your effort isn't reaching its target. Keep pile of food high and in a neat rectangle, if possible; remember not to chop too much at one time.

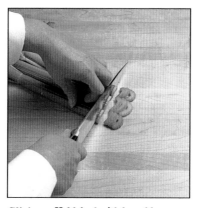

CUTTING TECHNIQUES

Hand position   For safety and to keep the food anchored while cutting, hold food against cutting board with fingertips curled back away from blade.

Slicing   Hold food with knuckles away from blade at a distance that equals one slice. Slice, then move fingers back the width of another slice or push food forward that distance.

Shredding and julienne cutting   Cut ingredient into slices of desired length and thickness. Stack slices, overlapping slightly, and slice lengthwise. The result will be squared-off sticks.

Dicing and mincing   Cut food into shreds or matchsticks (see Shredding and Julienne Cutting). Gather pieces into a bundle and slice across into uniform cubes.

Dicing/mincing garlic, onion, shallot   Place peeled, halved ingredient cut side down on cutting board. Position knife horizontally and make cuts parallel to board, almost to root end. Cut vertical, lengthwise cuts of desired thickness. Slice across cuts to root end.

Smashing and bruising   Lay ingredient on cutting board and smack with broad side of knife blade or lay blade on food and pound it with fist. Use the latter technique to loosen garlic peel.

Chopping   Arrange pieces of food on board in a high, neat pile. Grip knife handle with one hand and use other to press tip of knife down against board; chop with a rocking motion across food.

Paring   Lay blade on food, angled diagonally away from you. Cut in just the thickness of peel and draw knife toward you as you rotate food in opposite direction.

Cleaver chopping   Hold cleaver with right hand well back on handle, thumb on top or on side. Swing down from wrist. Let gravity move the cleaver; lift knife and let fall.

PARING

A paring knife is used like an extension of your index finger to make small precise cuts. The action centers more on the tip and end of the knife than with other knives. Hold a paring knife so that it moves with ease—index finger resting on top of blade and thumb gripping handle and serving as a balance. To peel away skin of a fruit or vegetable, grip paring knife as follows: grasp handle so that thumb rests against one side of blade and index finger lies along other side; handle should nestle in palm between fleshy pad and base of first finger. To peel, lay blade on fruit or vegetable, angled diagonally away from you. Make a cut just the thickness of the peel and draw the knife toward you as you rotate ingredient in the opposite direction. Skin should pull away in long strips.

CLEAVER CHOPPING

With a cleaver or heavier Asian vegetable knife, it is easy to chop meats to any texture, from rough cubes to a fine paste. Start by dicing meat, then change to a chopping grip (right hand well back on handle, thumb on top or on side). Swing from wrist for maximum chopping efficiency. With a good, heavy cleaver, little downward force is required; knife is simply lifted and allowed to fall. The left hand is not involved in this type of chopping. Stop every once in a while to scrape pile of pieces back together.

To chop through bones, as in cutting a chicken into braising pieces, hold knife as above. It may be unnecessary to hold food with other hand. For safety's sake, hold food as far away from where you will cut as possible. When you get to the last couple of inches, place food on board, get your left hand out of the way, take aim, and chop.

KOHLRABI

A member of the cabbage family, kohlrabi has a flavor reminiscent of both cabbage and turnip. It is moist and crunchy when raw; when cooked, its texture is like that of broccoli. Unlike the turnip, which it resembles, it is not a root, but a swollen, bulbous stem that grows above ground. The bulb may be pale green or purple outside; both varieties are white inside. Leaf stalks with leaves like those of turnips protrude from all sides (these stalks are generally trimmed away in the supermarket).

Use   Serve kohlrabi raw, or blanched and chilled, with a dip or marinated in vinaigrette. Steam or boil and dress with butter; add to soups or stews; purée with butter and cream; or use in any recipe in place of turnip. In Italy, raw or steamed kohlrabi is sometimes served with *bagna cauda* (a hot dip of butter, oil, garlic, and anchovies).

Availability   Fresh kohlrabi is sold in many supermarkets from May through November, with peak supply in June and July.

Selection   Choose small bulbs, about the size of a large egg; larger ones may be woody. If leaves are still attached, they should look fresh and perky. Avoid bulbs with cracks or blemishes.

Storage   Keep kohlrabi in a plastic bag in the refrigerator crisper for up to one week.

Preparation   Very young bulbs do not need to be peeled, but larger bulbs should be. If leaves are still attached, cut them off and boil or steam separately like spinach.

Cooking   See BLANCH, BOIL, PUREE, STEAM.

KONBU

Sun-dried kelp, called *konbu* (also spelled *kombu*) by both Japanese and Americans, appears in the market as a stiff, gray green sheet with a powdery finish. It must be rehydrated by soaking for use in the kitchen.

Use   Konbu imparts a delicate, fresh ocean taste to foods. Its primary function is as a flavoring for dashi, the basic Japanese stock (see page 563). Softened konbu is also wrapped around raw fish for several hours as a form of marinade; it is removed before serving. Pickled konbu is sometimes offered as a relish. Shredded konbu may be deep-fried or sautéed and used as a vegetable. Save steeped konbu sheets after making dashi, store in a plastic bag in the refrigerator, and use sheets as edible wrappers for other foods.

Availability   Dried konbu sheets are sold in Japanese markets and some health-food stores, packaged in plastic. One ounce is sufficient for four servings of dashi.

Storage   Unopened konbu will keep indefinitely in a cool, dry place. After opening, store in an airtight container in a cool place; it will keep for several months.

Preparation   Do not wash konbu. Wipe clean with a damp towel. Some Japanese cooks score surface lightly to release glutamic acid; others look down on this procedure. Steep sheets according to dashi recipe.

> ***Recipes and Related Information***
> *Miso Soup, 562; Sushi Rice, 233.*

KUMQUAT

Resembling a miniature egg-shaped orange, the kumquat is rarely more than an inch long. Part of the citrus family, it is native to China but is now cultivated in Florida and California. Unlike other citrus, the skin of the kumquat is sweeter than its flesh.

Use Massage kumquat between fingers to mingle sweet skin and tart flesh, then eat the whole fruit raw. It can also be sliced and added to fruit salads. Kumquats make excellent preserves, marmalades, and relishes. Cooked or preserved kumquats can be used in a sauce for roast duck, pork, and turkey. Mince preserved kumquats and add to desserts or roll in sugar and serve as a sweetmeat.

Availability Fresh kumquats are sold in many supermarkets. They are stocked November through June, with peak availability from November through February. Whole kumquats preserved in syrup and bottled are carried by supermarkets and specialty stores. Preserved and sugared kumquats are found in Chinese markets during the Chinese New Year.

Selection Choose plump, firm kumquats; avoid those that look shriveled or dull.

Storage Fresh kumquats will keep in the refrigerator for up to one month. Kumquats preserved in syrup may be stored indefinitely at room temperature in the original jar; preserved and sugared kumquats will keep up to six months in a covered jar in a cool place.

LAMB

Humans learned to domesticate sheep tens of thousands of years ago. Indeed, for ancient civilizations, sheep were animals of incomparable value. Their wool provided clothing, their meat and milk sustenance. Furthermore, they were rugged animals capable of surviving extreme conditions.

The early importance of sheep and their offspring is evident in the role they played, and still play, in many religions. Lamb was the traditional sacrificial offering in early religious rites and is still part of many religious observances. Celebratory tables at the Christian Easter, the Jewish Passover, and the Muslim New Year are all traditionally graced with symbolic roast lamb.

The sheep that sustained earlier cultures was much different from modern lamb. Sheep were raised as much for their wool as for their meat and were often herded long distances in search of pasturage. By the time they were slaughtered, the meat was generally tough and had a strong flavor. Cooks developed ways to combat these two qualities. They might marinate it in acidic ingredients to tenderize it and mask its flavor; or they might stew it for several hours, often with fruits; or they might grind it and season it lightly.

Today's lamb, the result of sophisticated crossbreeding, is butchered at an early age and is mild and tender. Most lamb is slaughtered at 6 to 9 months; lamb older than 12 months cannot legally be sold as genuine lamb. If the animal were 12 to 24 months old at slaughter, the meat may be identified as yearling lamb and will be stronger in flavor. Some diners appreciate the rich, full flavor

of older lamb (known as mutton if older than 24 months), but most Americans prefer the more delicate flavor of young lamb. Some specialty markets offer baby lamb, also identified as milk-fed lamb, butchered at 3 to 5 months, or hothouse lamb, butchered at 6 to 10 weeks. It is extremely tender, pale in color, and delicate in flavor.

The term *spring lamb* has no legal definition and no longer has any practical meaning. In the past, sheep gave birth in September or October and the six-month-old spring lamb was a treat looked forward to by many diners for their Easter and springtime tables. Today's modern breeding and flock management enable sheep to give birth throughout the year.

Use Lamb is most appreciated today in the regions where it was first consumed: the Middle East, North Africa, and Greece. In these areas, it is safe to say that lamb is the preferred meat. Lamb is also widely eaten in India, France, Italy, Spain, England, China, and New Zealand, the world's chief sheep-raising country. It is much less popular in the United States, Latin America, Central and Eastern Europe, and is practically unknown in Japan and Southeast Asia.

Rack of Lamb With Herbs, an international favorite, makes a perfect combination with Zinfandel, strictly an American wine. The recipe is on page 338.

CUTS OF LAMB

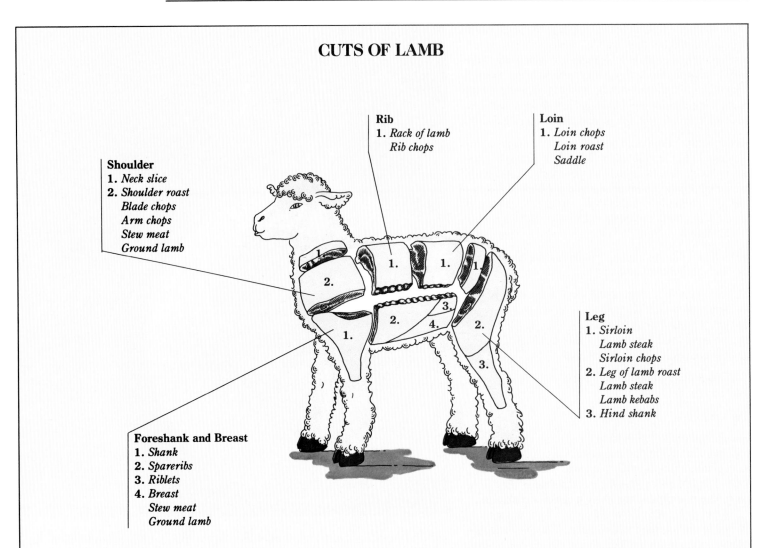

Rib
1. *Rack of lamb*
   Rib chops

Loin
1. *Loin chops*
   Loin roast
   Saddle

Shoulder
1. *Neck slice*
2. *Shoulder roast*
   Blade chops
   Arm chops
   Stew meat
   Ground lamb

Leg
1. *Sirloin*
   Lamb steak
   Sirloin chops
2. *Leg of lamb roast*
   Lamb steak
   Lamb kebabs
3. *Hind shank*

Foreshank and Breast
1. *Shank*
2. *Spareribs*
3. *Riblets*
4. *Breast*
   Stew meat
   Ground lamb

Lamb has fewer retail cuts than beef, but many of the same rules apply: The parts that do the least work are the tenderest. However, a lamb is a smaller, younger animal than a steer, and even the "tough parts" are usually more tender than the corresponding section of beef.

Shoulder This is the hardest-working muscle of the lamb, with the most fat, and plentiful bone. It is best suited for braising or stewing. The neck section of lamb is a stewing cut taken from the front of the shoulder. Boneless shoulder is sometimes sold as a roasting cut (although it is probably better braised). Chops cut from the shoulder (including both the blade chop with a long bone down the center, and the arm chop, with a round bone near the end) are fattier than the higher-priced rib and loin chops, but can be treated much the same way (baked, broiled, or panfried).

Foreshank and Breast Boneless rolled breast and bone-in breast are sometimes roasted (often with a stuffing inserted in a "pocket" cut in the center) but are more often braised, since they're rather fatty and not especially tender. Shank is always cooked in liquid, at length, until the meat starts falling off the bone. Economical lamb spareribs and riblets can be barbecued or braised, and are sometimes even roasted, but they are not entirely a bargain since the buyer is paying for a great deal of bone and a very little meat. Supermarket lamb stew meat, kebabs, and ground lamb are usually cut from the shoulder; the kebabs are from leaner shoulder meat than the stew or the ground lamb. Kebabs cut from the leg are far superior in leanness and tenderness.

Loin The whole loin roast (and the even less common whole saddle of lamb) are found at the butcher's only occasionally. Chops cut from the loin are found more frequently. These extremely tender chops can be broiled or panfried, and luxuriously sauced.

Rib The fine rib roast is sold as rack of lamb or, when bent into a circle, as crown roast. Chops from the rib are tender and juicy, whether left whole or, as in the case of the French chop, trimmed of the fatty meat from the end of the rib. Rib chops can be broiled or panfried, and double rib chops can be rapidly baked with a pocket cut for stuffing if desired. Like the loin, the rib portions of lamb are compatible with luxurious sauces.

Leg The back leg of the lamb is significantly more tender than the back leg of a steer. It may be cut into a whole leg (with the sirloin attached), a short cut leg (with sirloin trimmed off), a shank portion of the leg, and a center leg roast. These cuts are used primarily for roasting and grilling, but can be butterflied for barbecuing or cut off the bone for top-quality kebabs. Lamb steaks (to broil, panfry, or barbecue) are usually cut from either the center of the leg, or from the more tender sirloin just above the leg. Occasionally, lamb sirloin roast and sirloin chops can be found; these are both lean and tender. The hind shank, like the foreshank, is braised.

Spit-roasted suckling lamb is an Easter specialty in Greece. At other times, Greek cooks roast whole legs with oregano and white wine, or cook skewered lamb with herbs and serve it with yogurt. In the Middle East, ground lamb is massaged with cracked wheat to make kibbe, served raw or cooked. Ground lamb is used to stuff eggplants or grape leaves. In Iran lamb is marinated, grilled on skewers, and served with aromatic rice.

North African cooks braise lamb shoulder with vegetables for Couscous (see page 278) or stew it in a special covered clay pot called a *tajine*, often with fruits such as quince or prunes. In India lamb is curried, braised with spinach, or rubbed with spices and roasted in a *tandoor* (clay oven).

Milk-fed Spanish lamb is cooked in hot wood-burning ovens and served with potatoes. The French rub leg of lamb with thyme and lavender, stud it with garlic, and roast it, serving it with white beans or the green beans called *flageolets*. Italian cooks roast lamb with rosemary, or coat thin young chops with egg, bread crumbs, and Parmesan, and deep-fry them.

Irish lamb stew with potatoes and carrots; shepherd's pie from England, ground lamb topped with mashed potatoes; Finnish sauna-cured leg of lamb; and Mongolian hot pot are other ways that lamb is cooked around the world.

Availability   See Cuts of Lamb (opposite page).

Selection   All lamb sold retail is inspected by state or federal authorities for wholesomeness. About two thirds of lamb sold to consumers is also graded for quality. Lamb may be graded prime, choice, or good, depending primarily on the degree of marbling (intramuscular fat). Generous marbling contributes flavor and succulence. Most lamb sold at retail is graded choice.

In general, the paler the meat, the younger the lamb. Look for lamb with dry white fat, firm meat, and moist bones. Avoid buying lamb with yellowing fat or dark, mushy meat.

Storage   The larger the cut, the longer it may be refrigerated or frozen. Whole roasts, for example, may be stored longer than ground lamb. Large cuts may be refrigerated, well wrapped, for up to four days or frozen for up to nine months. Use ground meat within two days or freeze for up to four months. Defrost frozen meat slowly in refrigerator to promote reabsorption of melting ice crystals.

Preparation   Some cuts of lamb, such as the rack and the leg, are sold with part of the fat covering intact. Lamb fat has a strong flavor and should be trimmed away. However, be careful not to remove the fell, the papery outer membrane that holds the meat in shape. Cubed lamb for stew should be carefully trimmed of excess fat.

Cooking   See BRAISE, BROIL, GRILL, PANFRY, ROAST, STEW.

▇ LEG OF LAMB WITH GARLIC, POTATOES, AND ONIONS

Garlic slivers inserted into the lamb flavor the meat, and additional chopped garlic and roasting juices from the lamb give zest to the potatoes. Use a heavy roasting pan to prevent the vegetables from burning. Accompany this dish with green beans cooked until tender-crisp.

> 1   **leg of lamb (6 lb)**
> 4   **medium cloves garlic, peeled**
> 6   **tablespoons butter, softened**
> ½   **teaspoon dried thyme**
>   **Salt and freshly ground pepper, to taste**
> 2½ **pounds large, all-purpose white potatoes**
> 2   **tablespoons vegetable oil**
> 2   **large onions, thinly sliced**

1. Preheat oven to 450° F. Trim skin from lamb and remove as much excess fat as possible.

2. Cut 2 garlic cloves lengthwise into thin slices, then in thin slivers. Make slits in lamb about 1 inch deep with a small, sharp knife, spacing them fairly evenly. Insert garlic slivers in slits.

3. Chop remaining cloves with any remaining garlic slivers. Mix with butter, thyme, and salt and pepper to taste. Let stand at room temperature.

4. Peel potatoes, halve them lengthwise, and cut each half crosswise into slices about ¼ inch thick.

5. Set lamb on a rack in a large, heavy roasting pan. Spoon oil over lamb and sprinkle with salt and pepper. Roast 15 minutes. Reduce oven to 350° F and roast, basting lamb occasionally with juices, for 20 minutes.

6. Remove lamb and rack from pan. Put potato and onion slices in lamb juices in pan and mix well. Sprinkle with salt and pepper. Scatter garlic and butter mixture over potatoes. Replace lamb on rack in pan over vegetables.

7. Continue roasting, stirring vegetables occasionally, until lamb is done to taste (about 1 hour). To check, insert a meat thermometer into thickest part of lamb; lamb is rare at 130° to 140° F, medium at 145° F, and well-done at 160° F.

8. Transfer lamb to a carving board, cover loosely with aluminum foil, and let stand 10 minutes. Taste a relatively thick potato slice; if it is not tender, continue baking vegetables for a few minutes. Taste vegetables and add more salt and pepper, if needed.

9. Carve lamb; drain carving juices into a small saucepan and heat gently.

10. To serve, arrange lamb slices on a platter. Using a slotted spoon, transfer potato slices to platter or to separate serving dish. Pour juices remaining in roasting pan (mainly melted butter) into a small serving dish and heated carving juices into another.

Serves 10.

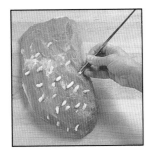

Meats that lack natural moisture benefit from larding, inserting strips of fat into the muscle with a special larding needle.

▇ RACK OF LAMB WITH HERBS

Rosemary, oregano, thyme, and bay leaf, either alone or in combination, are delicious with lamb. Fresh herbs have more flavor, but dried herbs can also be used. The garlic- and herb-flavored salt rub in this recipe could easily be adapted to other cuts of lamb, such as a roast leg of lamb or a boned and rolled shoulder.

> 1 **rack of lamb, 2 to 2½ pounds (see Note)**
> 2 **or 3 cloves garlic, peeled, and thinly sliced**
> 2 **tablespoons fresh herbs (see list above)** *or*
>   **1 teaspoon dried**
> 1 **teaspoon kosher salt**
> ¼ **teaspoon freshly ground pepper**

1. Preheat oven to 450° F. Remove excess fat from lamb. With tip of a knife, make several shallow incisions in meat and remaining fat, and push a slice of garlic into each cut (the garlic will infuse the meat with its flavor as the lamb roasts). If you are using fresh herbs, chop them finely together with any remaining garlic. If you are using dried herbs, crumble them finely.

2. Combine herbs, salt, and pepper; rub on lamb. Place lamb, fat side up, on a rack in a roasting pan.

3. Place lamb in oven, reduce heat to 400° F, and roast (without basting) to desired degree of doneness (about 25 minutes for medium rare; internal temperature should be about 140° F). Allow lamb to rest, loosely covered with aluminum foil, at least 10 minutes before serving. To serve, carve into chops.

Serves 2 to 4 (2 or 3 chops each).

Note For easier carving, ask the butcher to cut through backbone between ribs. After roasting, rack can then be neatly carved into chops with single ribs.

> ***Recipes and Related Information***
> *Butterflied Leg of Lamb With Cucumber-Mint Sauce, 294; Cassoulet, 556; Couscous, 278; Dry Spice Rub for Lamb, 350; Moussaka, 209; Russian Marinated Lamb on Skewers, 453; Spring Lamb Stew With Fresh Peas, 420.*

LARD, TO

To add fat to lean meats by running strips of pork fat, known as lardoons, through the muscles with a larding needle (see NEEDLE AND FASTENER, Larding Needles), or by piercing the flesh with a thin knife and forcing the strips of fat through. This process adds flavor and moistness by increasing fat content. As the meat cooks, the fat melts, keeping the interior from drying out. Barding is another method of basting with fat; when you bard, the fat is wrapped around the outside of a piece of meat, rather than through its mass (see BARD). Seasonings, such as fresh herbs and garlic, are also used for internal flavoring, but not as a baste as they have no fat content. To add flavor,

make shallow slits evenly around the roast and fill each slit with a sliver of garlic or piece of herb.

LEAVEN, TO

To lighten the texture and increase the volume of a batter or dough by the action of a natural agent such as air beaten into egg whites or the fermentation of yeast, or by using a chemical substance such as baking powder or baking soda, or by a combination. Each leavening agent contributes gases that expand and cause the dough or batter to rise.

> ***Recipes and Related Information***
> *Baking Powder, 23; Baking Soda, 23; Yeast, 613.*

LEEK

A mild member of the onion family much appreciated in Europe, the leek resembles a giant scallion, with overlapping green leaves and a blanched white base.

Use Very young, pencil-thin leeks are tender enough to be sliced and eaten raw in salads. Older leeks should be poached or steamed and served hot or cold in the same way as asparagus: with vinaigrette, mayonnaise, or garnish of hard-cooked egg. Leeks add a mild onion flavor to soups, stuffings, and stews. Green leek tops add onion flavor to stocks. Whole leeks can be grilled, braised in stock, or baked and served as a side dish.

Availability Fresh leeks are sold all year, but supplies peak in fall and spring. Although some specialty markets now carry baby leeks as thin as young asparagus, most markets offer leeks an inch or more in diameter.

Selection Large leeks can be woody inside. Select small to medium leeks, without ragged or wilted leaves.

Storage Refrigerate in a plastic bag and use within three to five days.

Preparation To keep the base of the leeks white, dirt is piled up around the stalk. Although leeks are cleaned for market, dirt is often still trapped between the leaves. Wash well and remove any tough, ragged outer leaves. Trim roots from base. If cooking leeks whole, slit them lengthwise at least halfway down the stalk and run cold water between the leaves to wash away any dirt. If slicing leeks, slit them lengthwise through the base and wash well before slicing.

Cooking See BOIL, BRAISE, GRATIN, STEAM, STIR-FRY.

> ***Recipes and Related Information***
> *Leeks Braised With Tasso, 59; Vichyssoise, 566.*

LEGUME

Technically, legumes are plants that carry their seeds in a pod. Beans of every shape and color, peas, and peanuts are all legumes. An exceptionally nutritious component in the human diet, they have, on average twice the protein of grains and a good dose of iron and B vitamins. With some legumes, such as peanuts and mature English peas, we eat only the seeds and discard the pods. Other legumes, such as sugar snap peas or Kentucky Wonder beans, are edible in their entirety. For more information on individual legumes, see BEAN, PEA, PEANUT.

LEMON

Although lemons are too tart to eat on their own, they are probably used more than any other fruit. Their lively tartness sharpens other flavors and gives a lift to all manner of foods.

Use Lemon is the principal flavor in a variety of desserts, from lemon ice cream and sherbet to lemon curd, lemon mousse, lemon meringue pie, and lemon cake. In addition, lemon juice and grated rind are used in many other desserts—especially fruit desserts—as a subsidiary flavor.

In the savory realm, lemon adds zest to sautéed or roasted chicken and is almost always served with fish and shellfish to heighten their flavor. A squirt of lemon juice in melted butter makes a lively dressing for cooked asparagus, broccoli, spinach, potherbs, green beans, and carrots. Italians serve the best young vegetables, such as celery hearts and baby artichokes, with nothing but lemon, salt, and olive oil. Moroccan cooks preserve lemons in salt, then use them to flavor stews and salads. Avocado is unthinkable without lemon alongside. Many melons and tropical fruits are also often served with a wedge of lemon. Lemon juice takes the place of vinegar in salad dressings and marinades. The acid juice of a lemon or lime is sometimes used to "cook" fish and shellfish. Seviche is an example.

Lemon juice enlivens such beverages as lemonade, iced tea, tomato juice, fruit punches, and cocktails. It is also valuable as an antioxidant: Rubbing lemon juice on cut bananas, apples, or pears inhibits browning; soaking some of these foods in acidulated water, an acidic mixture of lemon juice or vinegar and water, has the same effect.

Availability Fresh lemons are sold all year. Bottled lemon juice is also widely available in supermarkets.

Selection Choose firm lemons that feel heavy for their size. Generally, rough-textured ones have thicker skin and less juice than fine-skinned varieties.

Storage Refrigerated, lemons should keep for up to one month.

Preparation The desirable lemon oils are stored in the yellow peel. Be sure to grate only the yellow peel; the white pith is unpleasantly bitter. For directions on removing the rind, see GADGETS. To extract more juice from a lemon, press down on it as you roll it on a countertop or table. Lemons also yield more juice when slightly warm or at room temperature. If chilled, warm in a microwave on 50 percent power 1 minute. A citrus reamer is an effective way to juice and seed a lemon (see CITRUS REAMER).

◼ LEMON CHICKEN BREASTS

This is a speedy interpretation of a popular Chinese chicken dish.

> 3 whole chicken breasts (2½ to 3 lb), halved, boned, and skinned
> 2 lemons
> 1 tablespoon *each* butter or margarine and vegetable oil
> 1 clove garlic, minced
> ⅓ cup Rich Chicken Stock (see page 560)
> 2 teaspoons *each* cornstarch and sugar
> 1 tablespoon *each* soy sauce and water
> Salt, to taste

1. Cut chicken crosswise into ½-inch-wide strips. Grate rind from 1 lemon and squeeze juice; reserve both. Halve other lemon; squeeze juice from one half and add to reserved juice. Slice remaining half lemon thinly and reserve for garnish.

2. In a large, heavy-bottomed frying pan or wok, brown chicken breast strips (about half at a time) on both sides in butter and oil over medium-high heat, removing them as they brown. When all chicken is browned, return to pan and mix in garlic.

3. Add stock and reserved lemon juice. Bring to a boil, cover, reduce heat, and simmer until chicken is just firm and opaque (5 to 6 minutes; do not overcook). In a small bowl blend cornstarch, sugar, soy sauce, and the water.

4. Add lemon rind and soy sauce mixture, bring to a boil over medium-high heat, and stir until thickened and smooth. Add salt if needed. Garnish with lemon slices.

Serves 4 to 6.

Recipes and Related Information
Asparagus With Lemon, Tomato, and Onions, 14; Chilled Lemon Soufflé, 207; Fresh Lemon Bars, 143; Hot Lemon Soufflé, 206; Lemon Chiffon Cake, 85; Lemon Chiffon Pie, 440; Lemon Crème Fraîche, 107; Lemon Curd, 252; Lemon Custard Glaze, 117; Lemon Fondant, 251; Lemon Frozen Yogurt, 313; Lemon Meringue Pie, 439; Lemon Mustard, 323; Lemon Pasta, 412; Lemon Risotto, 275; Lemon Roof-Tile Cookies, 142; Lemon Roulade Charlotte, 171; Lemon Scones, 50; Lemon Sherbet, 314; Lemon Tart, 443; Seviche, 234; Tangy Lemon Loaf, 492; Zest, 631.

LEMON BALM

This perennial herb is appreciated for its lemon-scented, toothed leaves. The leaves add a minty lemon flavor to fruit salads, compotes, and stuffings. The leaves can be infused in hot water to make lemon tisane, a refreshing beverage that some say has medicinal properties. They are also used in cosmetics and fragrances. Fresh lemon balm is sporadically available in specialty markets; look for fragrant, sprightly leaves.

LEMONGRASS

Also known as citronella, lemongrass is a stiff, tropical grass that resembles a large fibrous green onion. It has yellowish white stems, gray-green blades and a delightful lemony aroma. An essential herb in Southeast Asian cooking, it adds a lemony flavor to many Vietnamese, Burmese, Thai, and Malaysian dishes.

Use   Lemongrass imparts a characteristic sourness to many Southeast Asian dishes, especially to soups and fish preparations. The gray-green blades are cut away and the stalks sliced crosswise very thinly. Generally, the large slices of lemongrass used in soup or sautés are considered flavoring agents and are not eaten. In Thailand, lemongrass is used in curry pastes and in hot and spicy shrimp soup; in Vietnam, it is part of meat stir-fries.

Availability   Now widely grown by Asian farmers in warmer areas of the United States, fresh lemongrass is sold in most Asian markets throughout the year. It is also available as dried blades, which must be soaked, and as a ground powder. Some health-food stores and herb shops carry ground lemongrass for use in teas.

Selection   Choose firm, unblemished stalks.

Storage   Keep in the refrigerator crisper for up to two months. Store dried and powdered lemongrass in a cool, dark, dry place; use within two months.

Preparation   Trim away the gray-green blades; wash stalks and slice thinly crosswise. Dried blades must be soaked for two hours in warm water before using. Most recipes call for the slices to be minced or pounded to a paste with other ingredients. Ground lemongrass can be added directly to a dish; substitute 1 teaspoon powder for each fresh stalk.

LEMON VERBENA

A woody deciduous shrub, lemon verbena has sharply lemon-scented leaves.

Use   The leaves of the lemon verbena shrub are employed to flavor beverages, cakes, puddings, and fruit compotes. Both fresh and dried leaves are infused in hot water to make tisane, a relaxing drink that some claim has medicinal value.

Availability   Fresh lemon verbena may occasionally be found in specialty markets. Dried lemon verbena is sold in herb stores and some health-food stores.

Selection   Look for fresh and fragrant leaves.

Storage   Keep fresh lemon verbena in a plastic bag in the refrigerator crisper and use within one or two days. Store dried lemon verbena in a cool, dark, dry place and use within a few months.

LETTUCE

Cultivated at least since 800 B.C., lettuce is today one of the most widely eaten vegetables in the Western world. In America and Western Europe, it is undoubtedly the major salad vegetable.

There are dozens of lettuce varieties but only four general types. Cos or romaine lettuce forms an elongated head with dark green, thickly ribbed outer leaves and a pale green inner heart. It is a sturdy lettuce that can take heavy or full-flavored dressings. Cabbagehead lettuce may be either crisphead, such as iceberg, or butterhead, such as Bibb, Boston, and limestone. Crisphead lettuces have tightly packed, solid heads with crisp, light green leaves; butterhead lettuces have soft leaves and loose, spreading heads. Looseleaf lettuce (also known as cutting lettuce or salad bowl lettuce) grows loosely from a central stem and does not form a heart. Oakleaf lettuce is a good example. The fourth type is stem lettuce, also known as celtuce or asparagus lettuce. Like romaine, it has a long edible stem and leaves; it is not commonly available commercially.

Use   Lettuces appear primarily in the salad bowl. Their refreshing flavor and crisp texture are best appreciated raw; because they are mostly water, cooking greatly alters their texture. French cooks, however, make lettuce soup and often cook shredded lettuce with steamed peas.

Frilly or colorful lettuces are often used to garnish serving platters. The outer leaves of cabbagehead lettuce are used as wrappers for some Chinese dishes, such as minced squab. Lettuce adds a crisp, crunchy texture to sandwiches and tacos.

Lettuce is the main or supporting ingredient in a virtually endless collection of salads, from a simple tossed green salad to the elaborate Cobb salad with diced bacon and chicken. It is almost always served with an oil- or cream-based dressing.

Availability   Stem lettuce is occasionally sold in Asian markets, but in general is not readily available commercially. The other lettuce varieties are carried in most supermarkets throughout the year.

Selection Crisphead lettuces should be firm and round, with green outer leaves that look fresh. Avoid heads with brown-tinged leaves. Heads that are especially hard, heavy, and white are probably overgrown and will have a large bitter core. Butterhead lettuces should have firm green leaves without brown edges; avoid heads with wilting or slimy leaves. Romaine lettuces should be full and compact. Avoid overly large heads, because outer leaves and ribs will be tough; reject heads with wilting leaves or rusty-looking ribs.

Storage Wash lettuce before storing. Dry thoroughly in a salad spinner or with paper towels, then wrap in paper towels, overwrap with a plastic bag, and store in refrigerator crisper. Leaf and butterhead lettuces will keep one or two days. Sturdier romaine and crisphead lettuces will keep three or four days.

Preparation Before washing lettuces, discard any wilted or bruised outer leaves. Twist out the central core, if any, or trim away base. Lettuce should be hand torn, not cut with a knife. Unless the recipe specifies otherwise, never dress a salad until just before serving; dressing makes leaves go limp and soggy.

▓ CURRIED LETTUCE AND PEA SOUP

When fresh peas are in season, it's worth the effort of shelling them to make this piquantly seasoned soup. Otherwise, use about 2½ cups of frozen peas. When the soup is served hot, the curry flavor is assertive; chilled, the soup tastes more lemony.

   2 **pounds fresh peas in shells**
   2 **medium onions, finely chopped**
   1 **large clove garlic, minced**
   ¼ **cup butter or margarine**
   2 **tablespoons vegetable oil**
   2 **tablespoons curry powder**
   1 **teaspoon ground turmeric**
   2 **tablespoons flour**
   1 **small head butterhead-type lettuce, shredded (about 4 cups, lightly packed)**
     Grated rind and juice of 1 lemon
   2 **teaspoons sugar**
   4 **cups Rich Chicken Stock (see page 560) or canned chicken broth**
   1 **cup half-and-half**
     Salt, to taste

1. Shell peas (you should have about 2½ cups). Reserve about 2 tablespoons small peas to use as garnish.

2. In a 3½- to 4-quart saucepan, cook onions and garlic in butter and oil over medium heat, stirring often, until soft but not browned. Blend in curry powder and turmeric, then flour. Add shredded lettuce, lemon rind (reserve a few threads for garnish, if desired) and juice, sugar, and peas. Remove from heat and gradually blend in stock.

3. Bring to a boil, stirring, over medium heat; then cover, reduce heat, and simmer until peas are just tender (8 to 10 minutes). Blend in half-and-half. Taste, and add salt if needed.

4. Transfer mixture, about a third at a time, to food processor or blender, and process or whirl until smooth.

5. To serve cold, cover and refrigerate until thoroughly chilled. To serve hot, return to cooking pan and heat, stirring often, until steaming hot. Serve garnished with reserved uncooked peas and reserved lemon rind (if used).

Makes about 9 cups, 6 to 8 servings.

Peas are cooked with tender lettuce and piquant seasonings to make creamy Curried Lettuce and Pea Soup, which can be enjoyed either hot or cold. Lemon zest or small peas make an appropriate garnish.

> ***Recipes and Related Information***
> *Caesar Salad, 506; Cream of Lettuce Soup, 563.*

LIAISON

A mixture—such as a butter and flour roux, beurre manié, or beaten eggs and cream—used to thicken and enrich (add a luxurious finish to) soups, sauces, and stews is called a liaison. Other thickeners include flour, cornstarch, and even vegetable purées. Delicate egg-based thickeners must be warmed slightly before adding to hot liquid. To do this, pour a little of the hot sauce or soup into the mixture and whisk to blend. Pour back into the hot liquid and gently heat. Do not allow to boil or mixture will curdle.

LILY BUD

Also known as golden lilies or golden needles, lily buds are the dried, unopened buds of tiger lilies. They generally measure 2 to 4 inches long and are golden brown, very slender, and wrinkled. They have a chewy texture and a mild, slightly musky flavor.

Use Chinese cooks use lily buds for texture in such dishes as Mu Shu Pork and hot and sour soup.

Availability Dried lily buds are sold in Asian markets packed in plastic.

Storage Dried lily buds may be kept indefinitely in an airtight container in a cool, dark, dry place.

Preparation Soak lily buds in cool water for 20 minutes, then drain and snip off any hard stems. Use whole or halve lengthwise.

LIME

Like lemons, limes are too tart to eat on their own, but they add a refreshing tang to many sweet and savory dishes. Florida, California, and Mexico are the major regions where limes are grown for the American market, with the Persian lime the most common variety. Florida also grows a small, round variety called the Key lime, which produces the juice used in the popular Key lime pie.

Use Limes are valued for the refreshing tartness of their juice and the aromatic oils in their skin. Lime wedges are often served with melons, and with tropical fruits such as papaya and mango. Lime juice gives a lift to a variety of cocktails, including the vodka gimlet and the daiquiri. Lime juice is added to marinades for chicken, pork, and fish. It is used extensively in Mexican cooking, in soups, salads, and fish dishes, the acidic juice "cooks" fish and shellfish, as in the popular Latin seviche. Juice and rind figure in a variety of desserts, including Key lime pie, lime curd, lime sherbet, and chiffon pie. Limes also make an excellent marmalade.

Availability Fresh limes come to market all year. When domestic supplies are low in the spring, they are supplemented with imports from Mexico and the West Indies. Bottled lime juice is also usually available in most supermarkets.

Selection Choose limes that are heavy for their size and that have a solid green color. Brown spots will not affect flavor, but avoid limes that are yellowish (they lack acidity) or hard and blackened (they are grainy).

Storage Refrigerated, limes should keep for approximately one month.

Preparation See LEMON.

■ **KEY LIME PIE**

This traditional recipe from Key West, Florida, takes less than 30 minutes to prepare.

> ½ cup (scant) fresh lime juice (from about 6 Key limes *or* 3 large, ripe regular limes)
> 2 to 3 teaspoons grated lime rind
> 1 can (14 oz) sweetened condensed milk
> 4 eggs, separated
> 1 prepared Graham Cracker Crumb Crust (see page 118) or homemade baked pastry crust
> 5 tablespoons sugar, or to taste

1. Preheat oven to 400° F. Stir together lime juice, lime rind, and condensed milk until mixture thickens to the consistency of heavy pastry cream (the acid of the lime juice thickens the milk). Beat egg yolks until thick and lemon colored; add to milk mixture to make a light custard. Turn custard into pie crust.

2. Beat egg whites until soft, droopy peaks form. Add sugar, 1 tablespoon at a time. (If a very sweet meringue is desired, use additional sugar.) Continue beating until meringue is shiny and forms stiff peaks.

3. Mound meringue over top of pie. Bake just until meringue is browned but still tender (about 10 minutes). Cool, then chill before serving.

Serves 8.

Recipes and Related Information
Cold Fillet of Sole With Cilantro, Lime, and Pomegranate, 232; Elotes, 158; Jicama With Chile and Lime, 324; Lime Chiffon Pie, 440; Lime Mustard, 323; Seviche, 234.

LITCHI

Also spelled litchee, lychee, and leechee, this tropical fruit is grown in China, Mexico, and the United States. The litchi tree produces a small oval fruit with a rough-textured, strawberry red hull. Underneath the hull, milky white pulp with a grapelike texture surrounds a hard brown seed. The flesh is sweet and moist. Dried litchis, also known as litchi nuts, are brown and shriveled with a prunelike flesh and a sweet, smoky flavor.

Use Peeled and chilled fresh litchis are eaten in fruit compotes and fruit salads. They can garnish chicken, duck, ham, or turkey salad. They are also sometimes added to stir-fried sweet-and-sour chicken or pork. Dried litchis are eaten out of hand as a snack.

Availability Fresh litchis are sold in Asian markets in June and July. Dried litchis and peeled, pitted litchis canned in syrup are also available in Asian markets.

Selection Select fresh litchis that look plump and firm; they should not be withered.

Storage   Refrigerate fresh litchis for up to 1 month or freeze indefinitely. Keep leftover canned litchis in their syrup in an airtight, nonmetal container in the refrigerator for one week. Refrigerated or frozen, dried litchis will keep indefinitely.

Preparation   Fresh litchis must be peeled and seeded; the leathery hull easily pulls away.

LOGANBERRY

A cross between the raspberry and the blackberry, the loganberry is red with a slightly elongated shape.

Use   It may be used in any way that blackberries or raspberries are. See BLACKBERRY and RASPBERRY.

Availability   Loganberries are found fresh in some markets in midsummer; canned loganberries are sold in some supermarkets.

Selection   See BLACKBERRY.

Storage   See BLACKBERRY.

LOQUAT

The fruit of a large evergreen shrub or tree often grown as an ornamental, the loquat is similar in texture and shape to the apricot and is usually 1 to 2 inches in diameter. The skin is yellowish gold; the flesh may be orange, yellow, or white, depending on variety. The loquat has large black seeds and a sweet-tart flesh that becomes sweeter as the fruit ripens. It is also known as the Japanese medlar.

Use   In China and Japan, peeled loquats are eaten as dessert or cooked with chicken. They can be made into jams, jellies, and preserves or can be dried for later use. Peeled and sliced or diced, loquats are added to fruit salads or compotes or cooked with roast pork.

Availability   Loquats must ripen on the tree and are too delicate to ship well. They are rarely available fresh, although some Asian markets carry them in the spring. Dried and canned loquats are sold in Asian markets.

Selection   Choose firm, unblemished loquats that give slightly to pressure.

Storage   In the refrigerator, loquats will last for up to two weeks. Dried loquats will keep indefinitely in the refrigerator or freezer. Leftover canned loquats may be stored in their syrup in a covered nonmetal container in the refrigerator for up to four days.

Preparation   Peel before using.

LOTUS ROOT

This thick, smooth-stalked vegetable has a thin, light brown skin and grows in six-inch increments resembling a string of fat sausages that may reach up to 4 feet long. The crisp ivory flesh is perforated with large holes. When the root is peeled and sliced crosswise, the slices exhibit a lacy snowflake pattern. The flavor is somewhat sweet and starchy.

Use   Lotus root may be thinly sliced, blanched, dressed, and served raw as a cold salad. Slices may also be deep-fried in tempura batter. Indian cooks incorporate lotus root in chutneys; Chinese cooks use the lacy slices to garnish platters. Because lotus root has the texture of potato, it may be substituted for potatoes in soups and stews. Lotus root starch, made from the ground root, is used as a thickener for Chinese soups and sauces and as a coating for fried foods.

Availability   Fresh lotus root is sold in Asian markets from July to February. It is also marketed as dried slices, sugared slices, or canned slices.

Selection   Choose firm, unblemished roots.

Storage   Refrigerated lotus roots will keep two to three weeks. Dried or sugared slices will keep indefinitely in a cool, dark, dry place. Leftover canned lotus root may be stored in water in a covered nonmetal container in the refrigerator for up to one week; change the water every other day.

Preparation   Lotus root discolors quickly; put peeled slices immediately in acidulated water to prevent browning. To soften dried lotus root, soak in acidulated water for one hour or until soft.

LOVAGE

The bright green leaves of this perennial herb look and taste a lot like celery. The flavor of the seeds is also celerylike.

Use   Lovage adds its pungent flavor to soups, stuffings, salads, and vegetable dishes. The ground seeds may be used to season breads, soups, roasts, and cheese dishes.

Availability   Fresh lovage is occasionally sold in some specialty markets. Lovage seed is carried in some specialty markets and herb stores.

Selection   Look for bright green leaves with no signs of wilting.

Storage   Place fresh lovage in a plastic bag and keep in the crisper; use immediately.

M

An assortment of fresh seasonal fruits macerated in sweet Muscat wine is a refreshing finish to a summer meal.

MACADAMIA NUT

Although the macadamia nut is native to Australia, most of the commercial crop now comes from Hawaii. Small and round, with a hard brown shell, the nut is almost always shelled and roasted in coconut oil before being marketed. The meat is cream colored, smooth and round, and very rich in flavor.

Use   Roasted and salted macadamia nuts are enjoyed as a cocktail snack. They can be minced and sprinkled on fish or sautéed vegetables. They are also used in desserts, including cream pies, cakes, and cookies.

Availability   Outside of their place of origin, macadamia nuts are almost always sold shelled and roasted. They are found in vacuum-packed tins or jars in most supermarkets.

Storage   Unopened tins and jars will keep indefinitely in a cool place. Once opened, the nuts should be used within one month or frozen for longer storage.

Preparation   For use in sweet dishes, salted nuts are often blanched first.

■ MACADAMIA CRISPS

Nuts of all sorts are a favorite ingredient for many kinds of cookies. These thin, crisp, buttery rounds are the perfect showcase for the rich flavor of elegant macadamia nuts. Fresh sweet cherries would be a juicy counterpoint to the crunchy texture of the cookies.

>   1 **cup flour**
>   ¼ **teaspoon baking soda**
>   ½ **cup butter or margarine, softened**
>   1¼ **cups firmly packed brown sugar**
>   1 **egg**
>   1 **teaspoon vanilla extract**
>   1 **cup chopped macadamia nuts**

1. In a small bowl stir together flour and baking soda to combine thoroughly; set aside.

2. Preheat oven to 375° F. In mixer bowl combine butter and brown sugar, and beat until well blended. Beat in egg until fluffy. Add vanilla and mix to blend.

3. Gradually add flour mixture until just blended. Stir in macadamia nuts.

4. Drop by rounded teaspoonfuls, placed about 1½ inches apart, onto lightly greased baking sheets. Bake until cookies are golden brown (8 to 10 minutes). Let stand briefly on baking sheets, then remove to wire racks to cool completely.

Makes about 5 dozen 2½-inch cookies.

MACE

Surrounding the shell of the nutmeg is a fragile, lacy, red skin called mace. The mace is separated from the nutmeg at harvest and then ground separately or broken into flakes called blades. The flavor of mace is related to that of nutmeg but is more pungent and less sweet.

Use   Mace contributes pungent flavor to sweet breads, pound cake, cherry pie, and puddings. It is an ingredient in Indian and Moroccan spice blends and is added to many Indonesian curries. Blade mace is often used whole in pickles and clear soups.

Availability   Ground mace is found on most supermarket spice racks. Whole dried blade mace is sold in some Asian and Caribbean markets.

Selection   Packaged seasonings lose quality after a while; try to buy from a store that restocks its spice section fairly often.

Storage   Keep ground mace in a cool, dry, dark place; it is highly perishable and should be replaced every three to four months. For longer storage keep mace in the refrigerator. Blade mace will keep for one year in a cool, dry, dark place.

N&O

NAP, TO

To barely coat with one thin sheet, usually when covering a food with its companion sauce. *To nap* implies to add sauce with a light hand, applying in such a way that it covers the food completely.

NECTARINE

As is obvious from its appearance, the nectarine is a smooth-skinned relative of the peach. When ripe, the skin is a deep yellow-gold with a red blush. The flesh is similarly colored, and is very fragrant and juicy when ripe. Some nectarine varieties are clingstone, others freestone.

Use The nectarine is commonly eaten out of hand, as a snack or dessert. It can also be sliced and enjoyed in pies, tarts, and cobblers, in compotes or fruit salads, and on breakfast cereal. Nectarine purée can be used in sherbets and ice creams, mousses, puddings, and whips.

Availability The season for domestic nectarines runs from late March through September, with peak supplies in July and August. Imports from the southern hemisphere are available in some markets during the domestic off-season.

Selection Look for nectarines with good fragrance and color; they should have a deep gold skin with a red blush. Avoid hard green fruit, although a hint of green is natural in some varieties. A ripe nectarine will give slightly to pressure but should not be overly soft. To ripen mature fruit, leave at room temperature for a few days.

Storage Refrigerate ripe nectarines and use promptly.

Preparation Nectarines do not require peeling but may be peeled for use in more elegant desserts. Sprinkle cut fruit with lemon juice to prevent browning.

▧ FROZEN NECTARINE TORTE

Peaches or plums also work well in this quick summer dessert, which would be a wonderful finish to a brunch.

>   2 **pounds ripe nectarines, peeled, seeded, and chopped**
>   1 **cup sugar**
>   1 **tablespoon fresh lemon juice**
>   1 **cup whipping cream**
>   1 **cup macaroon crumbs**

In a large bowl mash nectarines with sugar and lemon juice, mixing well. Whip cream to soft peaks and fold into nectarine mixture. Sprinkle ½ cup crumbs on the bottom of a 1-quart mold. Pour in nectarine mixture and top with remaining crumbs. Freeze until firm.

Serves 8.

NEEDLE AND FASTENER

These implements perform related functions: closing a cavity or pocket to hold in a stuffing or to improve appearance (lacing pins); drawing extremities (legs, wings) of a bird close to its body to form an attractive, compact shape (trussing needle, kitchen twine); holding meats, fish, fowl, and vegetables in place as they cook on a grill or under a broiler (skewers); or inserting strips of fat into lean meats to increase flavor and moistness (larding needle).

KITCHEN TWINE

For trussing or tying up poultry and meats, with or without a needle, or tying up cheesecloth bags of herbs for bouquet garni, use a heavy-gauge, natural-fiber string that can withstand high oven heat (linen is best because it won't burn under normal usage). Coated household sewing thread will impart a waxy taste to food, and nylon thread can melt. Uncoated cotton thread is satisfactory but is thin and may cut fingers when pulled tight.

LARDING NEEDLES

Of the two types of larding needles, one has a long, slender trough (about 10 inches) attached to a wooden handle. To use, strips of pork fat are set in the trough, then the needle is inserted into the roast with the grain of the meat and is rotated as it proceeds through from one end to the other. The needle is withdrawn slowly so that the fat is not pulled out. This process is repeated at regular intervals. A shorter version (about 6 inches long) has an eye, rather than a trough, and is designed for larding a shallow surface. Both needles are stainless steel. For an illustration of larding, see photograph on page 338.

POULTRY LACERS

These short, narrow shafts, with points at one end and loops or angled heads at the other, are used for closing poultry cavities, for securing pockets of stuffed meats, and for maintaining the shape of rolled meats. Widely available, they are made of stainless steel and come in sets of six pins with twine. The pins are set in place, then the twine is crisscrossed between skewers and pulled tight like the laces on a pair of boots. The loops or bent ends make it easier to remove the pins after roasting.

SKEWERS

Flat skewers are preferable because food won't slip when skewers are turned on the grill or under the broiler. Those made of stainless steel all have a loop or decorative head at one end so chunks of food won't slide off. Always soak bamboo skewers in water for at least 15 minutes before using on a grill or under a broiler so they won't burn. These picks make good cake testers as well. Sizes range from 8 to 14 inches.

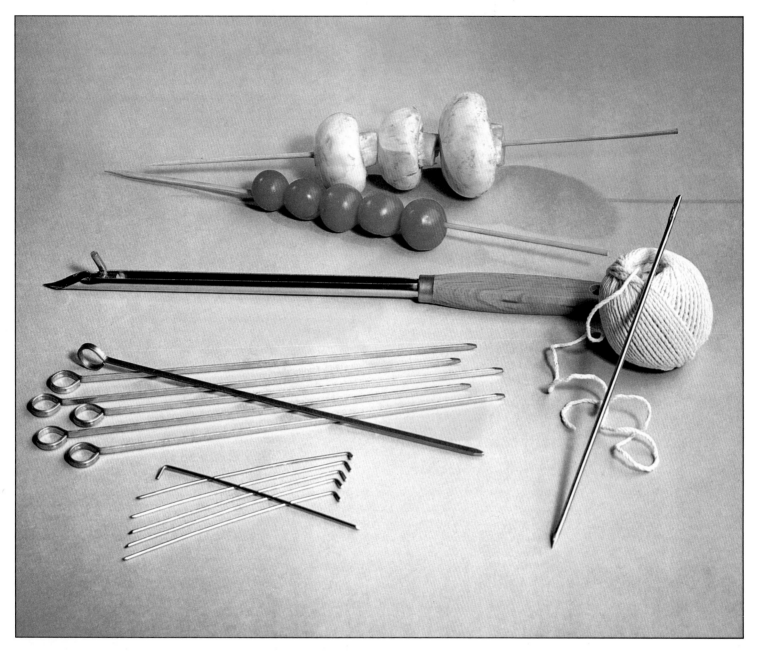

TRUSSING NEEDLE

Trussing holds the appendages of a bird together during roasting, makes a boned roast more compact so that it has a neater appearance and a more uniform shape that allows even cooking, and closes off the cavity of a bird or a pocket of stuffed meat. Trussing needles are made of stainless steel and are most commonly 8 inches long. They are used with uncoated heavyweight string made of a natural fiber (see Kitchen Twine, opposite page).

Recipes and Related Information
Bouquet Garni, 56; Lard, 338; Truss, 584.

NONREACTIVE

In the presence of an acidic food, certain metals—aluminum, cast iron, and unlined copper—produce a chemical reaction. The result is an off color or taste. When one of these foods—such as tomatoes, vinegar, lemon juice, or wine—is an ingredient in a recipe, most often you will be directed to mix or cook in a "nonreactive" or "nonaluminum" pan to avoid this undesirable reaction. Cookware made of stainless steel, enameled steel or cast iron, anodized aluminum, or a cladded metal doesn't interact with acids and is safe to use with acidic ingredients (see MATERIALS FOR COOKWARE).

Implements used by the cook to secure cavities or hold food in place include (top to bottom): bamboo skewers, larding needle, trussing needle, kitchen twine, metal skewers, poultry lacers.

An assortment of Chinese noodles of various shapes; clockwise from upper right: bean threads, two sizes of dried wheat-flour noodles, precooked rice noodles, and fresh wrappers—square for wontons and round for siu mai or potstickers.

NOODLE, ASIAN

Although many Westerners think of rice as the primary starch in Asian cuisine, noodles also play a major role. Unlike Western noodles, which are always made with wheat flour, those from Asia may have as their base wheat flour, rice flour, or vegetable starches such as yam, soybean, and potato. The best-known Asian noodle types are discussed on the following pages by country.

Due to the intertwined histories of Asian countries, noodle varieties overlap considerably throughout that part of the world. Wheat noodles (both with egg and without), rice noodles, and bean-starch or potato-starch noodles are employed in almost all these cuisines, as are small wrappers often made of rice flour. Although size and texture may vary slightly from country to country, substitutions are certainly possible and not problematic. Chinese egg noodles, for example, are widely available in supermarkets and are a fine substitute for Japanese *ramen,* Thai *bà mee,* Korean *gougsou,* or Philippine *pancit canton.*

Use   The Asian cook uses noodles in a great variety of ways. Noodles give body to soup, as in the Vietnamese *phở bo* (beef noodle soup) or the chilled Korean beef and noodle soup called *naeng myun.* Noodles are boiled and then eaten both hot and cold, with toppings or with dipping sauces. Examples include spicy *dan dan mein* (egg noodles tossed with peanut sauce, a specialty of the

Szechuan province of China) and Japanese *zaru soba* (cold buckwheat noodles accompanied with a soy-based dipping sauce). Noodles can be steamed, then stir-fried, as in the popular Thai dish called *pad Thai* (rice noodles tossed with bean sprouts, cooked egg, peanuts, and dried shrimp). Chinese cooks coil steamed vermicelli into thick pancakes, fry them on both sides until crisp, and top them with a stew or stir-fry.

Almost every Asian cuisine can boast a variety of noodle dumplings or stuffed noodle dishes. Examples include Chinese wonton and *fun* (sheets of steamed rice noodles, stuffed with shrimp and green onion), Japanese *gyoza* (pan-fried dumplings), and the Korean beef dumplings called *mandu.* In addition, noodles are used in stuffings, as in the Vietnamese *cha gio,* fried spring rolls filled with softened cellophane noodles, pork, and crab.

Availability   If you live near an Asian neighborhood, you should be able to find all sorts of fresh Asian-style noodles and wrappers. Most well-stocked supermarkets carry some varieties.

Selection   Buy fresh noodles from a market with a rapid turnover or from a store that receives fresh supplies daily.

Storage   Fresh wheat noodles should be refrigerated and used within two or three days. If truly fresh when purchased, these noodles may be wrapped with plastic wrap overwrapped with aluminum foil, and frozen for up to three months. Rice-flour noodles are often stored at room temperature in markets because they stiffen when chilled; they may be stored at room temperature for two days or kept in the refrigerator for up to one week. To soften noodles stiffened by refrigeration, steam briefly in a covered steamer just until softened, then gently run hot water over noodles and drain. If very fresh, they may also be frozen for up to two months. Dried noodles of all kinds will keep indefinitely in a cool, dry place.

Preparation Many recipes using Asian noodles call for the noodles to be boiled prior to further treatment, whether combining with a sauce, stir-frying, or braising. If you are using homemade or packaged fresh egg noodles, fluff them a little first to loosen the clumps, then drop them into a large pot of rapidly boiling, lightly salted water. Stir immediately with long chopsticks or a spoon to separate the noodles, and begin testing them as soon as the water returns to a boil. Most will be done within a few seconds. Dried noodles take longer; follow package directions. Rice noodles generally do not need preliminary boiling if they are to be cooked in a sauce. Toss the noodles under running water by hand so you can feel when they are thoroughly cooled. Drain well and toss with a little oil to keep them from sticking. If sufficiently oiled and tightly wrapped, noodles can be kept for several hours or even overnight, covered, in the refrigerator.

CHINA

Noodles have been an important part of the Chinese diet since the Han Dynasty period (206 B.C. to A.D. 220), when the Chinese learned the technology of milling flour from an unknown neighbor to the west. Before this time, most grains were simply boiled whole, as rice is today; but finely milled flour could be combined with water, kneaded, and worked into various shapes, and cooked by various methods to produce noodles, dumplings, and breads.

Bean-Starch Noodles Also known as bean threads, glass noodles, cellophane noodles, silver noodles, Chinese vermicelli, transparent noodles, and long rice, these threadlike noodles are made from mung bean starch. Folded into skeins about 6 inches long, they are packaged in plastic or net bags. They may be soaked in hot water until soft (about 30 seconds), then used in stir-fries, soups, and salads. The soaked noodles have a slippery texture and a glassy look. Like dried rice noodles (see below), they may also be deep-fried without presoaking.

Dried Rice Noodles Also known as rice stick or rice vermicelli, these noodles made from rice flour are as thin as string. They are usually coiled into nests and packaged in plastic bags. Dried noodles may be deep-fried quickly in 400° F oil. They will puff dramatically into crisp, brittle white noodles, which provide the crunchy base for Chinese Chicken Salad. Dried noodles may also be soaked

in warm water until soft and slippery, then stir-fried or added to soups.

Egg Noodles Chinese markets offer both fresh and dried egg noodles in several widths. Some supermarkets also carry fresh Chinese egg noodles. These wheat-based noodles cut in shoelace lengths are very popular in northern China, where wheat is the predominant starch. The noodles are added to soups for a quick lunch. They may also be boiled and served with meat or peanut sauce, or boiled, then fried into a crisp pancake and topped with a stew or sauce. Boiled noodles are also eaten cold dressed with oil, soy sauce, vinegar, and green onions.

Fresh Rice Noodles Many Asian markets carry cooked fresh noodles made from rice flour, which are sold in wide sheets or cut into ¾-inch widths. Soft, smooth, flimsy, and very bland, they absorb other flavors well. These slippery noodles are used in many dim sum dishes; served both cold and hot, they may be stuffed with ground pork or simply garnished with soy sauce, shrimp, and minced green onions. Narrow rice noodles are frequently used in soups or topped with stew for a quick, nourishing lunch.

Nonegg Noodles Chinese markets also offer both fresh and dried wheat noodles containing little or no egg. They are used in the same way as egg noodles.

Shrimp- and Crab-Flavored Noodles These dried noodles have been flavored with the roe of shrimp or crab. They are particularly good in soup but may be used as any other dried Chinese noodle.

Wonton or Egg Roll Wrappers The same dough in egg noodles is used for wonton skins and egg roll wrappers. These thin, square wrappers are available fresh in many supermarkets, packaged in plastic.

JAPAN

Noodles are among the most popular foods eaten in Japan, with buckwheat noodles (*soba*) more common in the north and wheat noodles (*udon*) in the south. At lunchtime, shoppers and workers throughout Japan stop for a quick bowl of noodles in one of that country's countless noodle shops. Also supplying the never-ending Japanese passion for noodles, street vendors can be found dishing up their wares at all hours of the day and late into the night. In the summer, many diners opt for chilled noodles served with a soy-based dipping sauce; in cold weather, the preference is for the warmth of noodles in steaming broth.

Harusame Also called *saifun, harusame* are long thin noodles made of potato and cornstarch. They are used in soups and salads or deep-fried for a garnish.

Hiyamugi These dried wheat noodles, about as long as spaghetti but slightly thicker, are packaged in bunches and tied with a cloth ribbon. They are usually eaten cold, served with garnishes and a dipping sauce.

Rice is an indispensable food in Asia. It may be cooked as a grain or ground and made into noodles or paperlike sheets.

Mai Fun This is the Japanese name for Chinese-style rice vermicelli. It is deep-fried and used as a salad base or garnish.

Ramen This is the Japanese name for Chinese-style egg noodles. Popular among the Japanese, they are often packaged with concentrated or dehydrated soup.

Soba Long, thin, and brownish gray, *soba* contains buckwheat flour. It may be eaten both cold with a dipping sauce or hot in broth. Variations include *cha soba* (a green-tinged buckwheat noodle containing powdered green tea) and *nama soba* (fresh soba made with egg and dusted with potato flour).

Somen These fine white wheat-flour noodles are similar to *hiyamugi*, but thinner. They are usually eaten cold. Variations include *cha somen* (containing powdered green tea) and *tomago somen* (containing egg yolk).

Udon Usually eaten in soup, with various garnishes, *udon* is a long, thick, wheat noodle with square edges. It is available both fresh and dried; fresh udon freezes well.

KOREA

Koreans are great noodle lovers and enjoy Chinese and Japanese noodles in addition to their own varieties. *Dang myun*, one specifically Korean variety, is a skinny, grayish tan noodle that resembles a cellophane noodle. It is made from potato and sweet potato starch and is cut in very long lengths. Like cellophane noodles, it is soaked in boiling water before use in soups and stir-fries. *Gougsou* is the long, thin, wheat flour noodle of Korea. It is widely used in hot and cold soups, garnished with vegetables and fish cake,

and in stir-fries with fiery chili sauces. *Naeng myun* is a long, very thin noodle made from buckwheat flour and potato starch or cornstarch. It is boiled briefly and usually served cold in an icy broth with a variety of garnishes.

MALAYSIA, SINGAPORE, AND INDONESIA

The noodles available in these three countries are very similar to those found in China and elsewhere in Asia. *Laksa* is a thick rice vermicelli used in soups and curried dishes with coconut-milk sauces. *Beehoon* (or *bihun*), a thinner rice vermicelli, is used in curried dishes, stir-fries, and soups.

Bà mee (or *bakmie*) and *hokkien mee* are Chinese-style egg noodles used in curries and stir-fries. These countries also cook with a bean-starch noodle known as *sohoon* or *tunghoon* in Malaysia and Singapore and *sotanghoon* in Indonesia.

PHILIPPINES

Pancit is the Filipino word for noodle. As in China, the many varieties of pancit may be made with wheat, rice, or bean starch. *Pancit canton* is a long, round (as opposed to flat), Chinese-style wheat noodle; it is precooked and dried for use in soups and stir-fries. *Pancit mami* is a flat Chinese-style egg noodle used in soups; *pancit miki* is similar but contains less egg. *Miswa* is an extremely fine wheat noodle that cooks in seconds; it is an ingredient in soups. *Pancit luglug* is a thick, dried, rice vermicelli incorporated in soups. *Pancit sotanghon* is a bean-starch noodle used in stir-fries and stuffings. In addition to the many pancit dishes, Philippine cooks make a type of egg roll called *lumpia*. Lumpia wrappers are very delicate, thin, crêpelike rounds made with cornstarch. Stuffed with a variety of fillings, they may be eaten as is or deep-fried.

THAILAND AND BURMA

Most of the noodles used in Thailand and Burma have equivalents or close cousins among the Chinese noodles. Thai egg noodles, called *bà mee*, are made from wheat flour and are about the size of Chinese egg noodles or Japanese ramen. Available fresh and frozen in Asian markets, they are used in soups and stir-fries and in Burmese curries. In Burma they are known as *kyet-oo kaukswe*. A dried version called *kaukswe* is also used in Burmese curries.

Fresh wide rice noodles are known as *gwaytio* in Thailand and *kyasangi* in Burma. They may be purchased in either wide sheets or precut ribbons. A dried version called *hsan kwkse* is used by Burmese cooks. Thai cooks also use thin dried rice noodles, *jantaboon*, which are not as thin as Chinese rice vermicelli and must be soaked and boiled. The Thai version of dried rice vermicelli is known as *sen mee;* in Burma, it is *hsan kyasan.* Sen mee are used in the famous Thai noodle dish *mee krob* and in soups.

The Thai version of bean-starch noodles is called *wun sen*. In Burma, these noodles are known as *pekyasan*. They are used in soups and curries and in Thai salads, in combination with cool crisp greens and warm grilled meat.

VIETNAM

Some of the most widely used Vietnamese noodles are very similar to Chinese noodles. *Bánh phở* are flat rice noodles, available both fresh and dried. They resemble spaghetti but are slightly thinner and are primarily used in soups. *Bánh ướt* are uncut rice-noodle sheets similar to fresh Chinese rice noodles. They are cut into widths for soups and stir-fries. *Bún* is a dried rice vermicelli similar to the Chinese product. When soaked, it is used in soups, grilled-meat salads, and stuffings for rice-paper rolls. *Bánh canh* are clear short noodles, slightly thicker than spaghetti, made from rice, wheat, corn, or other starches. The dried noodles are reconstituted quickly in boiling water, then used in stir-fries and soups. *Bún tau,* resembling Chinese bean-starch noodles, are an ingredient in stuffings and steamed meat loaves. *Bánh tráng* are translucent, round rice-paper wrappers used to make Vietnamese spring rolls and as a fresh wrapper for cooked meats.

■ STIR-FRIED NOODLES WITH SHREDDED PORK
Lo mein

This style of stir-frying noodles along with their toppings is sometimes called chow mein, but *lo mein* (mixed noodles) is more descriptive.

> ½ **pound thin Chinese-style egg noodles, boiled and drained**
> 4 to 5 **tablespoons oil**
> ¼ **cup Rich Chicken Stock (see page 561)**
> 1 **tablespoon soy sauce**
> 1 **teaspoon salt**
> 1 **tablespoon shredded fresh ginger**
> 2 **green onions, cut into 1-inch lengths**
> ½ **cup shredded pork**
> 2 or 3 **large leaves bok choy, cut into 2-inch slices**

1. Toss noodles with 2 tablespoons oil to coat evenly; set aside. (This may be done several hours ahead.) Combine stock, soy sauce, and salt; set aside.

2. Heat wok over medium-high heat, and add 1 tablespoon oil. Add ginger and green onions; cook until fragrant. Add pork and stir-fry until meat starts to lose its raw color. Add bok choy and stir-fry 1 minute longer, then transfer mixture to a warm plate.

3. Wipe wok clean with a paper towel and add 1 or 2 tablespoons oil. Reduce heat to medium. Swirl wok to cover sides with oil, then add noodles. Cook without stirring for 1 minute, then begin stirring and tossing noodles to brown them in places. Add a little more oil, if necessary, to keep noodles from sticking.

4. When noodles are heated through and lightly browned, add stock mixture and stir to loosen noodles from pan. Return pork mixture to pan and toss with noodles. Turn heat to high and continue cooking and stirring until liquid is nearly gone, then transfer to serving plate.

Serves 4 with other dishes.

■ SHANGHAI SPRING ROLLS

Manufacturers of Chinese noodles make very thin wrappers, 7 to 8 inches square, for spring rolls. If packaged spring-roll skins are too thick, roll them through the thinnest setting of a pasta machine to yield a rectangle twice the original size, then cut them in half.

> 16 **square spring-roll wrappers**
> **Pork and Shrimp Stuffing (see page 191)**
> ¼ **cup bean sprouts, cut into 2-inch lengths, or finely shredded bamboo shoots**
> 1 **egg white (optional)**
> **Oil, for deep-frying**

1. Place a wrapper with one edge toward you. Spread 1 tablespoon stuffing along edge to within ½ inch of end. Lay a few bean sprouts alongside stuffing. Roll up slightly to cover stuffing, fold in sides to seal ends, and roll up in remaining wrapper. Moisten edge with a little egg white or water to seal. Repeat with remaining wrappers.

2. Heat oil in a frying pan to 375° F. Fry rolls, a few at a time, until golden brown. Check a roll to make sure stuffing has thoroughly cooked, and adjust temperature or cooking time as necessary. Serve whole, or cut into bite-sized pieces.

Makes 16 rolls.

Crisp, fried Shanghai Spring Rolls are delicious dipped in either a sweet-and-sour sauce or hot Chinese mustard. When made with an egg-noodle wrapper, these rolls are known as egg rolls.

■ BEEF SOUP WITH NOODLES
Phở bo

Restaurants specializing in *phở*, a sort of soup-plus-salad served in a single bowl, are found in many Vietnamese cities, and they are an increasingly common sight in Vietnamese neighborhoods in this country as well. Phở (pronounced more or less *far*) is traditionally served for breakfast, but it is equally good to eat for lunch or a light supper. You will need to shop at an Asian market for many of the ingredients. Rice sticks are dried rice flour noodles.

> 5 pounds meaty beef bones (ribs, neck, or shank)
> 1 pound boneless stewing beef
>   (chuck or short ribs; see Note)
> 1 cinnamon stick
> 3 pods star anise
> 1 medium onion, sliced (include skin if clean)
> 10 to 12 slices fresh ginger
>   Salt or fish sauce, to taste
> ½ pound tender beef (sirloin or flatiron; see Note),
>   thinly sliced
> 2 cups bean sprouts
> 2 or 3 fresh chiles, sliced
> 2 medium tomatoes, cut into wedges (optional)
>   Lemon or lime wedges
>   Sprigs of fresh coriander, mint, or basil
> ½ pound rice sticks, cooked, boiled,
>   drained, and cooled
> 1 medium onion, sliced as thinly as possible
>   Chile sauce

1. Rinse bones and place in a large stockpot. Cover amply with cold water. Bring to a boil and cook 15 minutes, skimming off foam that rises to surface. When foaming stops, add stewing beef, cinnamon, star anise, onion, and ginger. Reduce heat so stock barely simmers and cook from 6 to 12 hours. Begin checking stewing beef after an hour or so and remove when quite tender but not yet falling apart.

2. Strain stock, and skim off and discard fat from surface. Season to taste with salt or fish sauce. Stock may be prepared up to 3 days ahead and stored uncovered in the refrigerator.

3. Bring stock to a boil. Slice stewed and raw beef thinly across grain. Arrange bean sprouts, chiles, tomatoes (if used), lemon wedges, and herbs on a platter or individual plates. Warm deep soup bowls with hot water. Place some rice sticks in each bowl and top with cooked and raw beef and sliced onion. Ladle hot stock over all (heat of stock will cook raw beef). Serve immediately, each person adding sprouts, herbs, chiles, tomatoes, lemon wedges, fish sauce, and chile sauce to taste. Serve with both chopsticks and a soup spoon.

Serves 6 to 8.

Note Blade chuck roast or steak is often a good buy, and if you bone it yourself, it can provide both the stewing and the tender cuts for this dish. Look for a 3-pound roast or several steaks with a long, slender blade bone. The flatiron muscle on top of the blade bone (the opposite side from ribs and backbone) is tender enough for quick cooking, but the remaining muscles require longer cooking. The rib eye, the large round muscle alongside the ribs, falls somewhere between in tenderness, and is best reserved for another use, such as a Thai curry. Add the bones to the stockpot.

Variation Other cuts of beef, including organ meats, can be used in place of the stewing beef. Tripe is especially good to use this way. If shanks are used for the stock, the shank meat can be sliced and included in the soup. One of the most popular items in phở restaurants is beef tendons, which become tender and gelatinous when simmered in the stock for many hours. A similar soup may be made from chicken, in which case it is called *phở ga.* Use a 4- to 5-pound stewing fowl with giblets (but omit liver) and half the amount of spices and ginger. Simmer for only 2 to 3 hours. Remove cooked meat and shred it by hand, then assemble soup as directed above, with some sliced giblets in each bowl.

> *Recipes and Related Information*
> *Chinese Chicken Salad, 508; Potstickers, 191;*
> *Wontons, 192.*

NOPALES

The "leaves" or pads of the prickly pear cactus are nopales. The tear-shaped pads are pale green to dark green, with small sharp spines that are usually removed before the cactus reaches the market. Cooked nopales have a taste and texture comparable to green beans, with a subtle tartness that is quite special.

Use Nopales are frequently eaten in Mexico and the southwestern United States. They are steamed, diced, and added to scrambled eggs or tossed with tomato, onion, and vinaigrette to make a salad.

Availability Canned or bottled nopales and *nopalitos* (sliced or diced cactus) packed in vinegar or water are available in Latin markets and in well-stocked supermarkets in some parts of the country. Fresh nopales are occasionally found in Latin and southwestern markets.

Selection Select pale, thin nopales. The thicker, darker ones are less tender.

Storage Store fresh nopales in the refrigerator and use within a few days. Once opened, canned nopales should be transferred to a nonmetal container and refrigerated. Water-packed nopales will keep for one week in the original liquid; pickled nopales will keep indefinitely in their brine.

Preparation Some species are spineless. If you get the thorny kind, you'll have to scrape the spines from the sides and edges (use tongs to handle; the spines are nasty). Leave as much of the green skin as possible. Cut nopales into small pieces and cook until tender in well-salted water.

Cooked nopales may have a slippery quality somewhat like okra, but there are several ways to minimize this. One method is to rinse the cooked nopales, drain them in a colander, cover with a damp towel to keep them from drying out, and let them stand for about 30 minutes. Another way is to cook diced nopales in an ungreased pan with several chunks of onion and one or two cloves of garlic until nopales are no longer slippery (about 5 minutes). Rinse in a colander, then proceed with recipe.

■ NOPALITO SALAD

This lively salad from the southwestern United States is based on poached strips of nopales, dark-green cactus pads, and jicama, a large, root vegetable with white flesh and a slightly sweet, crunchy flavor.

  ½ **small red onion**
  1 **jar (12 to 14 oz) nopalitos tiernos en rajas**
    (young nopal in strips)
  1 **or 2 canned or pickled jalapeño chiles,**
    seeded and sliced (optional)
  1 **small or ½ large jicama**
  2 **medium cucumbers, peeled**
  2 **small green bell peppers, trimmed and seeded**
  2 **small red bell peppers, trimmed and seeded**
  3 **thick green onions**
  1 **can (4 oz) sliced black olives**
  ¼ **cup minced parsley**
  2 **heaping teaspoons minced cilantro**
  ½ **cup grated Monterey jack cheese or**
    crumbled farmer cheese
  2 **ripe, firm avocados**
  1 **jar (2 oz) sliced pimientos, drained and rinsed,**
    for garnish

Lime Dressing

  ½ **cup peanut or olive oil**
  ⅓ **cup fresh lime juice**
    (about 4 small limes)
  3 **medium cloves garlic, crushed**
  ½ **teaspoon sugar**
  ¼ **teaspoon ground cumin seed**
    Salt and freshly ground pepper, to taste

1. Prepare dressing and chill for about 1 hour.

2. Slice onion into thin rings and place in a bowl of ice water. (This will take bite out of onion.)

3. Drain *nopalitos* and place in a large bowl. Nopalitos are usually packed with at least one jalapeño chile, along with other items such as onion slices and garlic. If a spicy salad is desired, halve jalapeño, remove seeds, cut

in strips, and mix with nopalitos. Remove other elements. If you prefer an extremely spicy salad, add one or both jalapeños.

4. Peel jicama with a small sharp knife by inserting knife tip just under beige skin and pulling off peel in strips. Discard tough flesh from root end and top. Julienne jicama into matchstick strips (about ¼ inch by ¼ inch by 1½ inches) and add to nopalitos. Julienne cucumbers, green peppers, and red peppers in matchsticks, and add to nopal mixture. Finely mince green onions, including crisp parts of green tops, and add to salad. Add olives, parsley, cilantro, and grated cheese.

5. Remove garlic from dressing and discard. At the last moment, slice avocados and add to salad. Immediately dress and toss salad to keep avocado from darkening. Let salad chill in refrigerator, marinating in dressing.

6. To serve, decorate top of salad with pimiento slices. Drain onions and scatter on top.

Serves 8.

Lime Dressing Whisk together oil and lime juice; stir in garlic, sugar, cumin, and salt and pepper, to taste.

Makes ¾ cup.

Nopales, the pads of the prickly pear cactus, make a stunning salad with a special southwestern flavor.

When rolled and sliced, the multiple ingredients in Makizushi form a beautiful mosaic. The sushi can be prepared a few hours ahead and stored in the refrigerator.

NORI

The Japanese word *nori* means paper-thin sheets of dried seaweed. It is consumed in great quantity by the Japanese, primarily in sushi and rice dishes. The sheets are dark green or dark brown and resemble carbon paper.

Use Japanese chefs use nori to wrap sushi and rice balls. Besides holding fish or rice in place, the dark nori adds a visual contrast to the white rice and a pleasantly crunchy, faintly marine flavor.

Availability Sheets of nori are usually found 10 to a package. They may be sold flat or folded in half, usually packaged in plastic. Some varieties are sold in tin canisters but they are more expensive. Some nori, identified as *yakinori,* is pretoasted by the manufacturer. *Ajitsuke-nori* has been brushed with soy sauce. Some manufacturers market nori in prepackaged bundles of short toasted strips; each package is an individual serving, to be crumbled on breakfast rice or wrapped around hot rice. Look for nori in Japanese markets.

Storage Store leftover nori in an airtight container with the moisture-absorbing granules from the package or canister. Freeze nori if not using within a few weeks.

Preparation Toasting brings out the full flavor and best texture in nori. Using tongs, wave one side only of a sheet of nori over a gas flame until the nori is crisp (a few seconds).

▉ MAKIZUSHI

This rolled sushi is a favorite take-out food in Japan. You can make it a few hours ahead of time, but the seaweed, or *nori,* will not be as crisp. You need a mat to roll the sushi ingredients. Buy a special bamboo mat at an Asian market, or use an undyed, flexible straw place mat.

> 4 sheets nori, toasted
>   Sushi Rice (see page 233)
> 1 cucumber
> 1 pickled daikon (Japanese radish)
>   Wasabi, to taste
> ½ pound fish or shellfish, thinly sliced

1. Lay a sheet of nori on a bamboo or undyed, flexible straw mat. Spread one fourth of the Sushi Rice on nori, leaving a 1-inch margin along far edge of nori and a ½-inch margin along either side. Flatten rice with back of a wooden spoon.

2. Cut a strip of cucumber to equal width of nori. Repeat with pickled daikon. Place cucumber and daikon down center of nori (parallel to long end). Spread with thin layer of *wasabi.* Place slices of fish down center and gently press down to firm ingredients.

3. Lift bamboo mat with thumbs, holding ingredients with fingers, and roll so that nori wraps around filling. Roll tightly, and remove mat. Slice each roll into 6 to 8 pieces.

Makes 24 to 32 pieces.

NUT

Although the botanical definition is slightly different, the word *nut* commonly refers to a seed or fruit with an edible kernel surrounded by a hard or brittle shell. By this definition, nuts commonly used in the kitchen include almond, brazil nut, cashew, chestnut, hazelnut, macadamia nut, peanut, pecan, pine nut, pistachio nut, and walnut (see individual entries).

Use Nuts play a great variety of roles in the kitchen. In their shells, nuts are often served as is, either as an appetizer with cocktails or as a dessert with a glass of port. Shelled nuts, either alone or in combination, can be roasted, salted or unsalted, and served with cocktails. Nut and dried fruit combinations are marketed as trail mix for hikers because of their long storage life.

Nuts add texture to almost every category of dish, from breakfast foods to desserts. At breakfast, nuts appear in dry cereals such as granola. They may be added to breakfast muffins or sprinkled on top of a fruit compote.

When toasted, nuts make a pleasing addition to salads and sautéed vegetables. Toasted walnuts with raw Belgian endive or sautéed almonds with green beans are just two among countless examples.

Because of their texture and oily richness, nuts are widely used in main courses. Buttery sautéed almonds or toasted pine nuts may be spooned on top of pan-fried sole. Chestnuts may be braised with chicken or game. Peanuts are the unusual ingredient in chicken and groundnut (peanut) stew (from western Africa). Iranian cooks braise duck in a walnut and pomegranate sauce.

Many types of breads and grains are especially complemented by nuts. Chopped walnuts add nutty richness to yeast breads and quick breads; chestnuts or toasted pecans are an ingredient in bread stuffings. Almonds or pine nuts are often added to rice pilaf for contrast.

As an enrichment or thickener, nuts may be used in soups and sauces, as in the Spanish *romesco* or the Mexican *chiles en nogada*. Nuts are even used in beverages: Ground almonds, for example, yield "almond milk" used to make orgeat, a syrup used as the base of a refreshing almond drink.

Nuts appear in many desserts: ice cream, cakes, pies, tarts, cookies, candies, soufflés, puddings, and dessert sauces. Pecan pie is a traditional Thanksgiving dessert in the southern United States; pecan pralines are another popular southern sweet. Almonds are used in nougat, nut brittle, and candy bars. Toasted ground walnuts or almonds can take the place of flour in a cake. Toasted nuts are sprinkled on top of sundaes and banana splits and are folded into cookie doughs and cake batters. Whole nuts can be candied in syrup and enjoyed as a sweetmeat.

Nuts are also valued for their edible oils. Hazelnut, walnut, almond, and peanut oils are widely used in the kitchen. See OIL for information on the various properties and uses of these nut oils.

Because of their high oil content, most nuts may also be ground into a thick spreadable paste. Peanut butter is probably the most popular example; its many uses and virtues are well known. Other nuts, such as almonds and hazelnuts, may be toasted or fried to develop more flavor, then ground into butter, seasoned with salt and/or sugar, and used as a spread.

Availability   See individual nut entries.

Selection   Unshelled nuts should feel heavy for their size. Shelled nuts turn rancid quickly; buy them from a market with a rapid turnover.

Storage   Their high fat content subjects nuts to rapid rancidity. Heat, light, and moisture promote fat oxidation; to retard rancidity, nuts should be kept in a cool, dark, dry place. Shelled nuts deteriorate faster than nuts in their shells. Freezing shelled nuts will effectively slow their decline. For specific storage instructions, see individual entries.

Preparation   *About skinning nuts:* Many nuts have thin papery skins that are often bitter or tannic. To remove these skins, nuts may be either blanched or toasted. After blanching briefly in boiling water, nuts are wrapped in a towel to steam, then rubbed with the towel to remove the skins. Skinned nuts should then be heated briefly in a 325°F oven to dry them out. This is an excellent method for almonds and pistachios. Hazelnuts and Brazil nuts may be toasted in a 325°F oven for about 10 minutes, then wrapped in a towel to steam. Skins may then be rubbed off easily.

About toasting nuts: Toasting nuts brings out their full flavor and crisps their texture. Nuts used in pastries, cakes, cookies, salads, sautés, and stuffings are almost always improved by a brief toasting in a 325°F oven. Use a rimmed baking sheet, shake sheet occasionally, and remove nuts when fragrant; they will crisp as they cool. When a recipe requires only 1 to 2 tablespoons toasted nuts, the preferred method is to place whole or ground nuts in a dry skillet over low heat. Stir constantly until aromatic oils are released and nuts color slightly (about 2 to 4 minutes depending upon size). Remove from pan to cool.

About grinding nuts: Because they are so rich in oil, nuts quickly turn to paste if grinding is not monitored. A nut mill (often preferred by serious bakers) will keep ground nuts dry and light. *To grind nuts in a food processor:* It's best to mix the nuts with some of the flour or sugar called for in the recipe. Even so, be careful not to overprocess (check every 10 seconds), or else you might get nut paste.

Recipes and Related Information
Food Processor, 240; Grate, Grater, 281.

NUTMEG

The seed of the apricotlike fruit of the nutmeg tree, nutmeg is encased in a hard shell that in turn is covered with a fragile webbed membrane called mace (see MACE). The mace is removed and the seed dried until the kernel rattles in the shell. The shell is then broken open and the nutmeg kernel removed. The kernel, the part used in the kitchen, is ovoid, dark brown, and about 1 inch in length. When grated it releases a slightly sweet and spicy aroma. Today, most nutmeg comes from Indonesia, Grenada, and Ceylon.

Use   Nutmeg is an excellent baking spice, used in pumpkin pie and custard pie, sweet breads, spice cakes, and cookies. It flatters all custard dishes and is traditionally sprinkled over eggnog. Nutmeg is often added to cheese sauce and other cheese dishes. Nutmeg complements spinach, potatoes, and winter squashes.

Freshly grated nutmeg is much more pungent and appealing than the storebought ground spice. With an inexpensive hand grater, home cooks can easily grate their own whole nutmeg.

Availability   Both whole and ground nutmeg are found on supermarket spice racks.

Selection Packaged seasonings lose quality after a while; try to buy from a store that restocks its spice section fairly often.

Storage Keep both whole and ground nutmeg in a cool, dark, dry place. Whole nutmeg will stay pungent for two years; replace ground nutmeg every six months.

Preparation Grate whole nutmeg just before using; add ground nutmeg directly to dish.

■ BAKED NUTMEG DOUGHNUTS

Although these doughnut-shaped rolls are baked, not fried, they resemble a doughnut in flavor. The dough does not require kneading and is light and puffy in texture.

>   2 **packages active dry yeast**
>   ¼ **cup warm (105° to 115° F) water**
> 1⅓ **cups warm (105° to 115° F) milk**
>   ¼ **cup sugar**
>   2 **teaspoons freshly grated nutmeg**
>   1 **teaspoon salt**
>   ¼ **teaspoon ground cinnamon**
>   ⅔ **cup butter**
> 4½ **to 5 cups flour**
>   2 **eggs**
>   ½ **cup Vanilla Granulated Sugar (see page 585)**

1. Sprinkle yeast over the water in large bowl of electric mixer. Let stand until soft (about 5 minutes). Stir in milk, sugar, nutmeg, salt, cinnamon, and ⅓ cup butter.

2. Add 3 cups flour. Mix to blend, then beat at medium speed until smooth and elastic (about 5 minutes). Beat in eggs, then gradually stir in about 1½ cups flour to make a soft dough.

3. Transfer to a greased bowl, cover with plastic wrap, and let rise in a warm place until doubled (about 1 hour). Stir down dough.

4. Turn dough out on a well-floured surface (use some of remaining flour), and shape with floured hands into a flattened ball. Coat well with flour. Lightly roll out about ½ inch thick. Cut with a floured 2½-inch doughnut cutter. Place doughnuts about 2 inches apart on greased baking sheets.

5. Brush lightly with some of remaining butter, melted, and let rise until nearly doubled (about 30 minutes).

6. Preheat oven to 425° F. Bake until doughnuts are golden brown (about 10 minutes). Brush warm doughnuts with remaining melted butter and roll lightly in Vanilla Granulated Sugar.

Makes 3 dozen doughnuts.

> *Recipes and Related Information*
> *Apple Dumplings With Nutmeg Sauce, 193; Grate, Grater, 281; Herb and Spice Blends, 301.*

OIL

The edible oils used in the kitchen are expressed from a variety of sources: seeds (such as sesame); legumes (such as peanuts and soybeans); plants (such as safflower and corn); fruits (such as olives); and nuts (such as coconuts, walnuts, and almonds).

Oils differ in both flavor and cooking qualities. Some are well suited to high-heat frying; others should be used only for salads. Selecting the right oil for the job and understanding the special requirements of an oil are an important part of even the most basic cooking.

The most common edible oils are outlined under Availability, along with specific recommendations for use and handling. The Use section below applies generally to all edible oils.

Use Oils function in the kitchen as a lubricant, an ingredient, and a cooking medium. As a lubricant, oil keeps food from sticking to a pan or baking dish. Bread pans and cake pans are often brushed with oil (or butter) to make the finished loaf or cake easy to remove. Oil is an essential ingredient in many preparations. It provides the body for salad dressings and mayonnaise, which in turn provide lubrication for lettuces, cold vegetables, and sandwiches. It is the foundation of Italian pesto, yielding a cold sauce that spreads easily over hot pasta. Other oil-based sauces such as the French aioli (garlic mayonnaise) and rouille (garlicky red pepper sauce), the Spanish *romesco* (mayonnaise with red pepper and ground almonds), and the Italian *salsa verde* (parsley, onion, and garlic sauce) are spooned on top of soups for enrichment, spread on sandwiches, and served with boiled meats or seafood.

Oil also provides the required fat in some cakes, especially moist loaf cakes such as carrot cake. It is used to enrich bread doughs and batters. Some stronger tasting oils, such as Asian sesame oil, are used as flavorings; they are rubbed over steamed chicken and drizzled over stir-fried vegetables in the same way that a Western cook would add butter to a bowl of peas.

As a cooking medium, oils are essential to frying, whether sautéing, stir-frying, or deep-frying. In sautéing and stir-frying, a thin film of oil both keeps food from sticking to the pan and transfers heat to the food being cooked. Oil also imparts flavor. Foods sautéed in olive oil have a flavor quite different from those fried in peanut oil or vegetable oil. In sautéed dishes where the flavor of butter is important, oil is often added to the butter to raise the smoke point of the butter.

Availability The following are the most often used edible oils.

Almond Oil When imported from France, almond oil has a toasty almond flavor that is pleasing in salads and cold dishes. Its flavor is destroyed by heat. Use almond oil in mayonnaise, salad dressings, and cold poultry dishes.

The domestic product is considerably paler in flavor. Refrigerated, almond oil will keep for up to one year. Look for it in specialty stores and well-stocked supermarkets.

Avocado Oil   Derived from California avocados, this mild, buttery oil has a delicate flavor suitable for mayonnaise, salad dressings, and baked goods. Because it has a high smoke point, it can be used for sautéing, stir-frying, and deep-frying.

Coconut Oil   Used as a cooking oil in India and Malaysia, coconut oil imparts a coconut flavor to foods and can be heated to high frying temperatures. It is highly saturated and is solid when cool. Coconut oil is available in markets that carry Indian or Indonesian products. Refrigerated, it will keep for up to one year.

Corn Oil   This is a bland, unsaturated oil that is excellent for frying. It is also a major component in most margarine. Because it does not contain cholesterol, it is an oil of choice for many on low-cholesterol diets. Store in a cool, dark place for up to six months or refrigerate for up to one year. It is widely available in supermarkets.

Hazelnut Oil   This very expensive French import imparts a delicious toasted hazelnut flavor to cold dishes. Heating destroys its special flavor. It is strong and should be used with restraint. Use hazelnut oil in conjunction with a milder oil in salad dressings and mayonnaise, or drizzle it over green beans, artichokes, and asparagus. Refrigerated, it will keep for up to one year. It is available in specialty stores and well-stocked supermarkets.

Olive Oil   Pressed from the fruit of the olive tree, olive oil is a prized salad and cooking oil in the Western world. Indeed, 90 percent of the world's olive crop goes to oil. It is fundamental to the cooking of the Mediterranean: Spain, Italy, southern France, Greece, and Turkey. It is not well suited to deep-frying, for it smokes at moderate temperatures. However, it is excellent for sautéing and is an ingredient used for that purpose by almost all Mediterranean cooks. Olive oil is an ingredient in salad dressings, mayonnaise, sauces, soups, marinades, and even pastries in Mediterranean countries. Italians celebrate the new crop of olive oil by drizzling it on toasted bread; they also serve olive oil as a dip for raw vegetables, along with coarse salt and lemon.

Commercial olive oil is available in several different grades according to the degree of acidity. Although oils can be deacidified chemically, the best olive oil is naturally low in acidity because it is cold-pressed. These cold-pressed, low-acid oils are termed extravirgin olive oil (although chemically deacidified oils will also qualify for this term). In increasing level of acidity, olive oil is classified as extravirgin, superfine, fine, and virgin or pure.

The first, cold pressing of the olive gives the finest, fruitiest oil. Subsequent pressings in the presence of heat yield oil of lesser quality. Because the terms on olive oil labels do not necessarily indicate quality, it is important to experiment widely and find a brand that you like. The best oils have a clear, deep green appearance, a fruity aroma, and a flavor that is clean, light, often slightly peppery, and distinctly of the olive. Avoid heavy or bitter oils. Price is also not a good indication of quality.

The best extravirgin olive oils lose their character when cooked. They should be used in cold dishes or added to hot dishes at the end of cooking. For sautéing, select a mild olive oil.

Store olive oil in a cool, dark place for up to six months or in the refrigerator for up to one year. It will cloud in the refrigerator but will clear at room temperature. Olive oils in a wide range of quality are available in supermarkets and specialty markets. France, Italy, and Spain are the major exporters.

Peanut Oil   Among Chinese cooks, peanut oil is the most popular cooking oil. It imparts a faint peanut flavor to stir-fried foods, and it may be heated to high frying temperatures. Western cooks also find it suitable for salad dressings and sautéing. It is available in all supermarkets and in Asian markets. Some health-food stores also carry a cold-pressed peanut oil that is more perishable. Peanut oil will keep for up to one year in a cool, dark place. It will cloud at refrigerator temperature but will clear again when brought to room temperature.

Safflower Oil   This flavorless cooking oil can be heated to high frying temperatures. It is excellent for deep-frying but its bland, heavy character makes it less suitable for a salad oil. It is available in many supermarkets. Store in a cool, dark place, where it will keep for up to one year.

Sesame Oil   Pressed from sesame seeds, this oil is an important adjunct to Chinese cooking. Its toasty, nutty flavor adds an intriguing note to noodle dishes, soups, stir-fries, and dipping sauces. It is often rubbed over poultry or drizzled on fish after steaming. The Chinese rarely use it for cooking as heat would alter its flavor. Chinese sesame oil is available in some supermarkets and in Asian markets, packaged in a plastic squeeze bottle. It has a deep gold color and an arresting fragrance. A Japanese version of sesame oil is slightly lighter in color and flavor. Japanese cooks add it to the cooking oil used to make tempura. A cold-pressed sesame oil, available in health-food stores, has a much more pallid flavor and is not a substitute. Store Asian sesame oil in a cool, dry place for up to six months or in the refrigerator for up to one year. Cold-pressed sesame oil is more perishable; refrigerated, it will keep for up to six months.

Soybean Oil   A major cooking oil in America, it heats to high frying temperatures and has a bland flavor. Because of its lack of flavor, it is not a superior salad oil, but it does not contain cholesterol and is thus an oil of choice for many on special diets. Soybean oil is also used in margarine. It is available in supermarkets; store in a cool, dark place for up to one year.

Oils are used in the kitchen for lubrication and cooking, and as an ingredient. Depending on their source, they can range from pale colors to deeper hues.

The season's freshest produce is paired with a fine, seasoned olive oil for a light and brightly colored first course. For a more elaborate antipasto, add a selection of cured meats and a loaf of country-style bread.

at room temperature. However, most oils are considerably cheaper when bought in large containers. For convenience, pour off small amounts into airtight bottles to keep on the kitchen counter, storing the remainder airtight in a cool, dark place.

■ VEGETABLES WITH TUSCAN OLIVE OIL DIP

Italians living in Tuscany, the region that surrounds Florence, show off their finest oil and their freshest vegetables by serving them dipped in olive oil. You're offered a basket or a platter of crisp, colorful raw vegetables, along with a bowl of the best-quality oil seasoned with nothing but salt and pepper. You pinch (*pinzare*) the vegetables and join them in marriage (*matrimonio*) with the oil. If the oil is top-notch, there is no finer dip.

> 2 **cups fruity olive oil**
> **Coarse salt and freshly ground pepper, to taste**
> **Vegetables for dipping: Sliced bulb fennel, cherry tomatoes, carrot sticks, innermost celery stalks, endive leaves, cucumber spears (seeded), innermost hearts of baby artichokes, hearts of small lettuces, spears of young, tender zucchini**
> **Lemon wedges, for garnish**

Season olive oil to taste with salt and pepper. Divide oil among small dipping bowls, one to a person. Arrange vegetables for dipping on a large, rustic platter. Offer each guest a dipping bowl, lemon wedges, and a small salad plate. You can also pour a little seasoned oil on each salad plate, arrange a bouquet of raw vegetables on top, and garnish the plate with a lemon wedge.

Serves 8.

Walnut Oil Imported from France, walnut oil has an appealing, fragrant, nutty quality. It is generally expensive, but a little goes a long way. It adds a rich, characteristic flavor to salad dressings and sauces. It may also be drizzled over cooked vegetables, such as asparagus and green beans, or used in the mayonnaise for a chicken salad. Heating destroys its special flavor. It is available in many supermarkets and in specialty stores. Refrigerate for up to one year.

Selection The cook should choose the oil that best corresponds to the character of the finished dish. Mediterranean dishes, for example, call preferentially for olive oil to convey an authentic Mediterranean flavor; most Chinese stir-frying is done with peanut oil. When deep-frying, it is important to choose an oil that can be heated to a desired high temperature without breaking down and smoking. Safflower, soybean, and corn oils have higher smoke points than peanut, olive, or sesame oils, and are therefore preferable for deep-frying (see FRY).

Storage Oils oxidize when exposed to light and heat. To extend their shelf life, store oils in a cool, dark place. The fragile nut oils are usually refrigerated. Other oils may be stored in the refrigerator to extend their useful life, but they may thicken and become cloudy at refrigerator temperature and be problematic for making salad. Some cooks prefer to buy small quantities and keep them

OKRA

An ancient native of Africa, okra was carried to America on the earliest slave ships. It was a staple of plantation cooking and important to Creole cooks. Gumbo, the Creole soup thickened with okra, is a contraction of the African name for the vegetable.

Okra grows in long slender pods; it may grow up to 9 inches in length but is usually 1½ to 3 inches when marketed. The fuzzy green pods may be ribbed or nonribbed. Inside are many small white seeds. When cooked, okra develops a mucilaginous quality, a characteristic that makes it a good thickener for soups and stews. The flavor of okra is mild, somewhat similar to that of green beans.

Use Okra can be blanched, cooled, dressed, and served as a salad, but it is generally served hot—braised, fried, or sautéed. It is a popular ingredient in the American South, particularly Louisiana. Southern cooks fry okra in cornmeal, stew it with bacon and rice, or pickle it. Louisiana cooks add it to gumbo or braise it with tomatoes.

Indian cooks fry sliced okra with onions and spices. Caribbean cooks stir it into cornmeal mush. Small whole pods may be cooked whole; large pods are usually sliced.

Availability Okra is sold the year around in southern states. Elsewhere, it is most plentiful in the summer months. Most supermarkets carry frozen okra; some stock canned okra as well.

Selection Small pods are generally more tender and sweeter than large pods. Choose small, bright green, crisp pods. Avoid any that are overlarge, stiff, shriveled, or blackened.

Storage Wrap fresh okra in a plastic bag. Transfer left-over canned okra to a covered container. Keep both types in the refrigerator crisper up to four days.

Preparation Wash just before cooking; trim stem ends. If slicing, slice just before cooking.

Cooking See BOIL, BRAISE, DEEP-FRY, SAUTE, STEAM.

▦ OKRA AND TOMATO STEW

Okra is related to both hibiscus and cotton. The sticky fuzz (removed long before the okra reaches the grocery store) makes it as nasty to pick as cotton. It is one vegetable that must be excluded from the current tendency to cook vegetables as briefly as possible (unless it is deep-fried). During cooking okra goes from crisp to slimy and finally to tender-crisp; it must be cooked long enough to recover from the slimy phase. The variations, native to the Georgia Sea Islands and the coastal lowlands, reflect the origin of okra, as they closely resemble West African dishes.

   3 **strips bacon**
   1 **medium onion, finely chopped**
   1 **small green bell pepper, finely chopped**
   1 **pound fresh okra, trimmed and sliced into rounds,**
      ***or* 1 package (12 oz) sliced frozen okra**
   1 **teaspoon flour**
   1 **pound fresh tomatoes, peeled and coarsely**
      chopped, *or* 1 can (14 oz) tomatoes,
      coarsely chopped
   1 **tablespoon light brown sugar**
      Salt and freshly ground pepper, to taste

1. Cook bacon in a large skillet until crisp. Drain on paper towels, crumble, and reserve.

2. In bacon fat remaining in the skillet (about 3 table-spoons), sauté onion and green pepper over high heat, stirring until wilted (about 5 minutes). Add okra and cook over low heat for 10 minutes, stirring frequently.

3. Sprinkle flour over skillet and cook, stirring, until flour loses its raw aroma (about 1 minute). Add tomatoes, sugar, and salt and pepper, to taste. Stir in bacon. Continue to cook over low heat until okra is tender and mixture is slightly thickened (about 10 minutes longer).

Serves 4 to 6 as a side dish.

Lowlands Okra Pilau Complete steps 1 and 2. Meanwhile, place 1 cup long-grain rice in 1½-quart saucepan with cover and add 2 cups cold water. Bring to a boil, stir once, cover, and cook over the lowest heat for exactly 12 minutes. Drain rice and add to okra along with tomatoes, salt, pepper, and bacon (flour and sugar are omitted). Cover skillet and continue to cook over low heat until rice is tender (about 15 minutes longer).

Serves 6 to 8 as a side dish.

Shrimp Okra Pilau For a main dish, prepare Lowlands Okra Pilau and add 1 pound shelled medium shrimp and a dash of cayenne pepper during the last 7 minutes of cooking.

Serves 4 as a main course.

The sensuous texture and exotic flavor of well-cooked okra are set off perfectly by tart, fresh tomatoes in Shrimp Okra Pilau (recipe at left)—the mid-South's delicate version of Spanish paella or Louisiana jambalaya.

A glaze is being applied to this luscious Orange Custard Tart. The thin slices of candied orange resemble the petals of an opening flower.

ORANGE

Because the orange tree cannot withstand frost, it is cultivated in a circumscribed area that includes Southeast Asia (where it originated), the Near East, North Africa, southern Spain and Portugal, Florida, southern California, Texas, and Arizona. The fruit is valued both for its juice and for its aromatic peel.

Both bitter and sweet varieties of oranges exist. Sweet oranges may be further divided into blood oranges, common oranges, and navel oranges. The blood orange develops pink or red flesh, juice, and rind. Many people think the distinctive flavor, usually described as resembling that of berries, is the most delicious of all the oranges. One of the best-known common oranges is the Valencia, valued for the quality and quantity of its juice. Navel oranges are known by the navellike appearance of the blossom end.

Excellent eating oranges, they peel easily, separate easily into segments, and are seedless. For information on the loose-skinned citrus fruits known as mandarin oranges, see MANDARIN ORANGE.

The best-known bitter oranges are grown in Spain and are known as Seville oranges. They are too bitter to eat but provide excellent peel and juice for marmalade and orange liqueur.

Use Sweet oranges are often eaten out of hand as a breakfast fruit, snack, or dessert. Orange sections or slices may be added to fruit salads or compotes and used to garnish chicken or turkey salad. Oranges and orange juice are used in such savory dishes as duck á l'orange, orange and red onion salad, and Mexican pork roast with orange juice. In America whole oranges are ground fine with cranberries and sugar to make a relish for holiday turkey. In Brazil sliced oranges are part of the national dish, *feijoada,* a bountiful spread of smoked and fresh meats, black beans, steamed rice, and cooked greens. The oranges are said to perk up the appetite for even more feijoada. In China, where oranges symbolize good fortune and prosperity, they are frequently offered at the end of a meal and are exchanged at the start of the new year. Oranges figure in an innumerable variety of desserts, including sherbet, cakes, curds, tarts, gelatin molds, and puddings. In France and Italy orange sherbet is often served in a hollow orange shell. Orange juice is enjoyed as a breakfast beverage, as an ingredient in cocktails and punches, and as a marinade for meats. Juice from blood oranges is particularly striking in a clear juice glass. *Maltaise* sauce, a variation on Hollandaise, is made with the juice and rind of blood oranges. Grated orange rind flavors custards, creams, doughs, stews, pastries, and cookies. Both sweet and bitter oranges can be used for marmalades, candies, and preserves.

Availability Fresh oranges are found the year around, with peak supplies December through April. Domestic navel oranges are marketed from mid-November through mid-May. Valencias are available in every month but December and January. Orange juice is sold in all supermarkets, either frozen or bottled.

Selection Look for firmness, heaviness, and bright-looking skin. Rich orange skin color is not a reliable indication of quality because the skin is frequently treated with vegetable dye. Fully mature oranges, particularly Valencias, will often regreen, turning greenish late in the season. Russeting, a brownish roughened area over the skin, often found on Florida and Texas oranges, does not affect eating quality and often occurs on oranges with thin skin and superior eating quality. Avoid lightweight oranges; those with very rough skin texture (indicates abnormally thick skin and less flesh); dull, dry skin with spongy texture (indicates aging and deteriorated quality); cuts or punctures; soft spots on the surface; and discolored, weakened areas of skin around stem end.

Storage   Keep oranges in a cool place or refrigerate. They will store well for several weeks.

Preparation   The desirable oils of the fruit are stored in the orange peel. When grating orange rind for all uses, be sure to grate only the orange rind; the white pith is unpleasantly bitter. Because vitamin C oxidizes rapidly, freshly squeezed orange juice contains considerably more than bottled or frozen juice; when serving as a breakfast beverage, squeeze juice just before serving for maximum nutrition.

ORANGE CUSTARD TART

This is a tart for orange marmalade fans. The thinly sliced, candied orange decorating the top has a taste that recalls the bitter orange flavor of orange marmalade. Note that the candied orange slices must stand in the sugar syrup overnight before using.

>   2 to 3 small seedless oranges
>   1 cup water
>   ¾ cup sugar
>   1 Sweet Tart Pastry (9½-inch; see page 441)
>   3 eggs
>   ⅔ cup sugar
>   ¼ cup fresh orange juice
>   1 teaspoon finely grated orange rind
>   6 tablespoons unsalted butter, melted and cooled
>   ½ cup apricot preserves
>   1 tablespoon orange-flavored liqueur

1. Thinly slice orange (⅛ inch or less) with very sharp knife. In a wide saucepan combine the water and the ¾ cup sugar; bring to a boil to dissolve sugar. Add orange slices and simmer over very low heat until translucent (about 45 minutes). Remove from heat and let stand in syrup overnight.

2. Roll out tart pastry and use it to line a 9½-inch tart tin with removable bottom. Blind bake until partially baked.

3. Preheat oven to 350° F. Combine eggs, the ⅔ cup sugar, orange juice, and orange rind in a mixing bowl; whisk until well mixed. Whisk in melted butter. Pour into partially baked tart shell and bake until custard is set and knife inserted in center comes out clean (20 to 25 minutes). Cool to room temperature.

4. Decorate tart just before serving, if possible. Remove orange slices from syrup; drain well. Cut half of the slices in half. Cut remaining slices in quarters. Arrange a row of overlapping quartered slices along outer edge of tart on top of custard, with rounded edges of slices touching outer edge of tart. Then place a row of overlapping halved slices so they just overlap tips of first row. Continue with this pattern, alternating rows of overlapping quarters and halves, to center of tart. Form a very thin half slice into a cone shape for the center decoration. The tart top should now resemble the opening petals of a flower.

5. Heat preserves until melted; strain to remove solid pieces of fruit. Mix in liqueur. Brush glaze lightly over orange slices. Reserve leftover glaze for another tart.

6. Remove sides of tart tin and serve at room temperature. Tart should be stored in the refrigerator if not consumed within a few hours.

Serves 6 to 8.

Recipes and Related Information
Citrus Reamer, 131; Classic Orange Marmalade, 320; Cranberry-Orange-Nut Loaf, 492; Gadgets, 258; Mandarin Orange, 348; Orange Butter, 69; Orange Buttermilk Biscuits, 50; Orange Chantilly Cream, 605; Orange Chiffon Cake, 85; Orange Fondant, 251; Orange Loaf, 492; Orange Scones, 50.

OREGANO

A member of the mint family, oregano is also known as wild marjoram. This assertive herb has small green leaves and a fragrance identified with both Mediterranean and Mexican cooking.

Use   Oregano is strongly associated by many Americans with Italian cooking; certainly it is important to many tomato sauces, pizzas, bean soups, and southern Italian stews. It is also frequently used by Greek cooks to flavor lamb, shrimp, baked fish, and stewed chicken. It flatters zucchini, tomatoes, eggplant, onions, green beans, and dried beans. Mexican cooks use a different variety of oregano to flavor tomato sauces, fish, seviche, soups, and roast pork. Dried oregano is offered as a garnish for some Mexican soups, including the tripe soup known as *menudo*.

Availability   Two main varieties of oregano are sold in the United States today: European and Mexican. The European variety is milder and is occasionally found fresh in some specialty markets. It is readily available dried, either whole or ground, on supermarket spice racks. The more pungent Mexican oregano is dried and sold in Latin American markets.

Selection   Choose bunches of lively looking, aromatic fresh herbs without signs of wilting or decay. Packaged seasonings lose quality after a while; try to buy from a store that restocks its spice section fairly often.

Storage   Store fresh herb in a plastic bag in the refrigerator and use within three days. Store dried herb in a cool, dark, dry place. Whole dried leaves will keep for one year, ground leaves for six months.

Recipes and Related Information
Menudo, 591; Stuffed Vegetarian Pizza, 448.

P

Luscious golden papaya and the zest of fresh lime combine to create an exotic ice cream with a touch of the tropic.

PAN-BROIL, TO

A quick-cooking, dry-heat method performed on the stove top by cooking in a frying pan, using little or no fat, over moderately hot heat. The food sears on the surface and pulls away from the pan; any fat given off by the food is poured away during cooking. A special pan, called a grill pan or stove-top broiler, is specifically designed for pan-broiling. On the inside it has a ridged bottom so that food is raised up and fat drips below (see COOKWARE, Grill Pan). A heavy grill pan made of a material that conducts heat well, such as cast iron, does the best job.

PANFRY, TO

A dry-heat cooking method that cooks food in a small amount of hot fat. The terms *panfry* and *sauté* are often used interchangeably, but strictly speaking, less fat is used to sauté food than to panfry food.

> ***Recipes and Related Information***
> *Fry, 254; Sauté, 531.*

PAPAYA

The papaya is a tropical fruit native to the New World, possibly to Mexico or the West Indies. Today it is cultivated in tropical or semitropical areas around the world, including Florida, Hawaii, India, Malaysia, China, Japan, and the Philippines.

The commercial variety common in the United States is the Solo papaya, a pear-shaped, smooth-skinned fruit that is usually about 6 inches long, about 3 to 4 inches wide at the widest part, and 1 inch wide at the neck. The Solo papaya weighs between 1 and 2 pounds. The skin is generally green when picked but it turns a vivid yellow-orange when ripe; the moist, melonlike flesh ranges from pastel orange to a deep salmon color. The papaya has a large seed cavity with numerous shiny black seeds that resemble caviar; although they are edible, they are usually discarded.

Use   Chilled ripe papaya makes a refreshing breakfast fruit; it is seeded and usually served on the half shell with a wedge of lime. The seed cavity can be filled with ice cream or yogurt, if desired. Skinned and sliced or cubed, it can be added to a fruit salad or compote. Sliced papaya makes a handsome topping for a fruit tart. Puréed ripe papaya can be used in sherbets and ice creams, in quick breads, and in beverages. Green (unripe) papaya is made into pickles and chutneys, sliced and stewed with meats, and sautéed or baked with butter and brown sugar. For centuries, cooks have also taken advantage of an enzyme that is found in both the fruit and its leaves. Papain, the enzyme, is a natural tenderizer. Baking meat in papaya leaves or stewing meat with papaya, especially green papaya, will tenderize the meat. (Papain is the active ingredient in many commercial meat tenderizers.) Because papain inhibits jelling, raw papaya cannot be used in gelatin desserts; however, cooked papaya presents no jelling problems. Papaya seeds have a peppery flavor and may be used as a garnish or ground for use in salad dressings and marinades.

Availability   Papayas are found sporadically all year but supplies peak in summer months. Bottled papaya juice is sold in some health-food stores.

Selection   Choose papayas with good yellow color and an enticing fragrance. Slightly green papayas that are yellow over at least one third of the fruit will ripen in three to five days at room temperature. Ripe papayas are highly aromatic and give slightly to gentle pressure. Avoid fruit with dark spots or ones with softness at the stem end; this softness is the first sign of decay.

Storage   Keep at room temperature until ripe, then refrigerate in a plastic bag and use within one week.

Preparation   To eat on the half shell, cut in half and scoop out black seeds. Alternatively, peel with a vegetable peeler, halve, and seed.

PAPAYA ICE CREAM

Before mixing with the other ingredients that make up the base for this fruity ice cream, the papayas must be heated to deactivate papain, an enzyme that would otherwise break down the protein in milk and cream and impart a slightly bitter taste.

    2 large papayas
    2 cups milk
    2 cups whipping cream
    ½ cup sugar
    4 large egg yolks
    2 tablespoons fresh lime juice

1. Scoop papaya out of its skin and scrape out seeds. Finely chop fruit; place fruit in a small, heavy-bottomed saucepan and cook over very low heat until softened into a purée, stirring occasionally (about 15 minutes). Remove from heat and let cool.

2. In a medium, heavy-bottomed saucepan over medium heat, cook milk, cream, and sugar, stirring occasionally, until sugar is dissolved and mixture is hot, but not boiling. In a medium bowl whisk egg yolks to blend. Continue to whisk while very slowly pouring in approximately 1 cup of cream mixture.

3. When mixture is smooth, pour back into pan of hot liquid, whisking continuously, and cook until mixture thickens slightly and coats the back of a spoon (about 5 minutes; do not let mixture boil or it will curdle). Strain into a clean bowl and let cool.

4. Add papaya purée and lime juice to custard. Transfer to an ice cream machine and freeze according to manufacturer's instructions.

Makes about 1 quart.

Recipes and Related Information
Ice Cream and Frozen Dessert, 308; Papaya With Prosciutto, 358.

PAPRIKA

A ground spice derived from capsicum peppers, paprika varies in color and pungency according to the peppers used to make it. Most paprikas are relatively mild, range from orange-red to red, and contain the flesh only (not the seeds or veins) of dried capsicum peppers.

Use In America mild paprika is often used more for color than flavor. Bright red paprika adds visual appeal to stuffed eggs, baked fish, and a variety of cheese or vegetable casseroles. It is widely used in sausages, salad dressings, and condiments. In Hungary paprika is appreciated for its pungency, whether sweet, half-sweet, or hot. Paprika is virtually the country's national spice; it is the predominant flavor in many hearty soups and stews.

Gulyás (goulash) and *paprikás* are two categories of Hungarian dishes that are always liberally seasoned with paprika. Spanish paprika is used in Spain to flavor shellfish dishes, rice dishes, and sausages. In Morocco Spanish paprika seasons tomato and green pepper salads, carrot salad, and most dishes containing tomato.

Availability Ground paprika is widely available on supermarket spice racks. The best paprika is Hungarian, which may be sweet (mild), half-sweet, or hot. Spanish paprika is generally of lesser quality but is suitable for most dishes; it is always mild. Some specialty shops carry concentrated paprika paste in tubes.

Selection Paprika rapidly loses pungency. Try to buy from a store that restocks its spice section fairly often.

Storage To maintain its flavor and intensity, keep paprika in a cool, dark, dry place or refrigerate; replace every six months.

POUSSIN PAPRIKASH

Hungarian cooking is a lively blend of spicy and sweet. This recipe, a paprika-spiced fricassee, substitutes quick-cooking young poussins (under 6 weeks old) for the usual older and less tender chicken. Serve with buttered noodles with poppy seeds, creamed peas, and a tossed beet salad.

    2 poussins (1 lb each), halved
      Salt and freshly ground pepper
    3 tablespoons butter
    1 tablespoon vegetable oil
    1 large onion, thinly sliced
    ⅓ to ½ cup Chicken Stock (see page 560)
    1 tablespoon sweet or hot Hungarian paprika
    1 cup sour cream
    1 tablespoon flour

1. Wash poussins and pat dry. Season with salt and pepper; set aside.

2. In a medium, heavy-bottomed skillet over medium-high heat, heat butter and oil. Add poussins and sauté, starting skin side down, until golden brown (about 10 minutes per side).

3. Add onion and sauté until translucent. Add stock and paprika, stirring and scraping with a wooden spoon to loosen any browned bits that may have stuck to bottom of pan. Cook, covered, for 15 to 20 minutes. Remove poussins to serving platter.

4. In a small bowl combine sour cream and flour. Mix into sauce, stirring until well blended (about 1 minute). Pour over poussins and serve.

Serves 4.

Recipes and Related Information
Bohemian Pork Goulash, 459; Budapest Borscht, 76.

PARBOIL, TO

To cook foods partway in boiling water. This treatment is particularly helpful for stir-fries and sautés. By partially tenderizing longer-cooking ingredients such as carrots or broccoli, for example, their final cooking time will be faster and they can be combined with ingredients that finish quickly. Parboiling can be done in advance, which adds to its appeal as a time-saving preparation technique. Blanching is identical to parboiling except that foods are cooked only for a brief time (see BLANCH).

PARE, TO

In general, to remove the outer skin of a food, usually vegetables or fruits. A short-bladed paring knife or vegetable peeler is used. A narrower definition would be to trim away the irregular outer surface in order to produce pieces of uniform size that will cook at the same rate and have a more symmetrical final appearance. An example would be the classic garnish of pared nugget-shaped carrots or potatoes for roasted meats and poultry.

> ### Recipes and Related Information
> Gadgets, 258; Knife, 328.

PARSLEY

One of the most widely used culinary herbs, parsley is important to almost all the world's cuisines. With its fragile stems and sturdy, bright green leaves, parsley imparts a clean, fresh, slightly peppery flavor to dishes. The two main varieties are the curly-leaf type, widely available in supermarkets, and the flat-leaf Italian parsley, less common in American markets but quite common in Europe. Flat-leaf parsley is more pungent.

Use   The mild, fresh flavor of parsley harmonizes with almost all savory dishes. It is frequently mixed with other, more pungent herbs. Fines herbes (see HERB AND SPICE BLENDS) always include parsley, as does the classic bouquet garni (see BOUQUET GARNI). Minced parsley is a visually appealing garnish for soups, stews, sautés, meat loaves, and casseroles. Mixed with lemon rind and minced garlic, it becomes Gremolata, an Italian garnish for braised veal shanks (Osso Buco). Mixed with bread crumbs and minced shallots or garlic, it becomes *persillade*, which is spread on rack of lamb before roasting. It is a major component of the Italian *salsa verde* (green sauce) for boiled meats and of Middle Eastern Tabbouleh (cracked wheat, tomato, and parsley salad). Parsley sprigs can be deep-fried as a garnish for fried foods. They can be added to green salads or even lightly dressed and served as a salad on their own.

Availability   Fresh curly-leaf parsley is widely found all year in supermarkets. Flat-leaf Italian parsley is available in specialty markets and some well-stocked supermarkets. Dried parsley is sold on most supermarket spice racks. Given the ready availability and affordability of fresh parsley, there is little if any reason to use dried.

Selection   Whether curly-leaf or flat-leaf, look for bright green, vigorous bunches with a fresh, clean aroma. Avoid limp bunches with dull-looking leaves.

Storage   Wash well, shake off excess water, and wrap parsley in paper towels, then in a plastic bag. Store in refrigerator and use within three or four days.

Preparation   To mince parsley, separate leaves from stems. Finely mince leaves. Save stems to flavor stocks.

■ WARM PARSLEY SAUCE FOR SHELLFISH
Keep this sauce warm in a chafing dish and serve with chilled scallops, crab legs, or shrimp.

>   4 **cups parsley, leaves only**
>   2 **cups whipping cream**
>   2 **shallots, minced**
>   ½ **cup dry white wine**
>   ¼ **cup cold butter, cut into 4 pieces**
>   **Salt and freshly ground pepper, to taste**

1. Blanch parsley in boiling water 20 seconds; drain and transfer to a bowl of ice water to stop cooking and set color. Drain and dry thoroughly on paper towels. Chop by hand or in a food processor until almost puréed; set aside.

2. In a medium saucepan over high heat, reduce cream by half. In a medium skillet over high heat, cook shallots and wine until wine has almost evaporated. Whisk in hot reduced cream. Remove from heat and whisk in butter, one piece at a time, until incorporated. Add parsley and salt and pepper to taste.

Makes 1¾ cups.

> ### Recipes and Related Information
> Gremolata, 58; Osso Buco, 58; Piquant Parsley Dipping Sauce, 46; Tabbouleh, 277.

PARSNIP

It is easy to tell by sight that the parsnip is a member of the carrot family. This sweet-flavored root vegetable looks like an ivory-colored or pale yellow carrot. It is usually less uniform in thickness, however, being wider at the top and tapering to a very narrow root. Unlike carrots, parsnips are always eaten cooked; they are starchy and tough when raw. Cooked parsnips have a texture and flavor somewhere between carrots and sweet potatoes, although they remain pale yellow when cooked.

Use Parsnips are a delicious winter root vegetable. They may be peeled, sliced, and steamed like carrots, or boiled, then mashed with butter and cream. They may be cut into chunks and added to soups or stews, or baked in the oven with meat stock and butter.

Availability Parsnips are found in many supermarkets during winter months. They are sold with their tops clipped, either in bulk or in plastic bags.

Selection Look for small parsnips; larger ones may have woody cores. Avoid parsnips that are limp or shriveled or have splits or brown spots. Choose those that are reasonably uniform; misshapen ones that have to be severely trimmed are uneconomical.

Storage Keep in a plastic bag in the refrigerator crisper and use within three or four days.

Preparation Peel and trim ends.

Cooking See BOIL, BRAISE, PUREE, STEAM.

■ **PARSLEYED PARSNIPS**
If you've only used parsnips to flavor soups and stocks, you may be surprised to learn that they are also delicious on their own as a side dish to a winter meal. If you prefer small parsnips, they may be used whole. Larger ones are more appealing and will cook faster if cut in pieces.

    8 to 10 medium (1½ lb) parsnips, peeled,
        trimmed, and quartered
    2 tablespoons butter
    ¼ cup minced parsley
    ½ teaspoon dried basil

In a large, covered skillet cook parsnips in boiling water to cover until tender-crisp (about 15 minutes); drain. Add butter, parsley, and basil. Toss to coat parsnips.

Serves 4.

PASSION FRUIT

Also known by its Spanish name, *granadilla,* the passion fruit supposedly owes its English name to its flowers: Their markings, some say, resemble the instruments used in the Crucifixion. The fruit itself is small and egg-shaped, with a brittle, wrinkled skin. Both skin and flesh color vary by variety, but the most commonly available variety has a dark purple skin and a deep gold flesh with small black seeds. Some Latin markets carry a Mexican variety with yellow skin and grayish flesh. All have a soft, juicy pulp that is highly aromatic.

Use Passion fruit can be halved and eaten from the shell, seeds and all. The fruit can also be squeezed for its juice and the juice strained through a sieve to remove the seeds. Seeded passion fruit pulp, puréed in a blender, is a

Parsnips are a flavorful winter root vegetable that makes a tasty side dish when simply cooked and tossed with herbs and butter.

delicious flavor base for sorbets and ice creams, mousses, pies, and dessert sauces. Passion fruit juice adds an exotic accent to punches, cocktails, or fruit juice blends.

Availability Passion fruit is native to Brazil, but is now grown in California, Hawaii, New Zealand, and Australia. Fresh passion fruit is sold in Latin markets and some supermarkets between late February and early October. Bottled or canned passion fruit juice is sold in specialty markets, Latin markets, and some health-food stores.

Selection The skin of ripe passion fruit will be shriveled. The fruit will ripen if left at room temperature for several days.

Storage Refrigerate ripe fruit in a plastic bag and use within two or three days.

Preparation Halve and eat from the shell (the shell is not eaten); or scoop out the pulp and press it through a sieve to remove the seeds; or purée with seeds for use in ice creams, sorbets, and mousses.

Recipes and Related Information
Ice Cream and Frozen Dessert, 308; Mousse, 372.

Pasta comes in all shapes and sizes, from shells to strands to corkscrews.

PASTA

The word *pasta* is so closely associated with Italian cooking it is easy to forget that other cuisines use noodles, too. The huge realm of Oriental noodles is discussed in NOODLE, ASIAN. This section applies to Western noodles, which will hereafter be referred to as pasta, whether Italian or not.

Pasta is based on grain—usually wheat—which is combined with a liquid and kneaded to make a smooth dough or paste (hence the word *pasta*). The dough is then rolled out and cut or formed into the appropriate shape.

Today's markets offer dozens of pasta shapes and flavors. To make sense of the multitude, it helps to divide pasta into two categories: fresh and dried.

FRESH AND DRIED PASTA

Wheat flour and whole eggs are the basic ingredients of fresh pasta. Some cooks add a little olive oil to make the dough easier to work, and some add salt for flavor. However, neither oil nor salt is necessary for good results.

After the dough is blended and kneaded, fresh pasta is rolled out—by hand or by machine—and cut into the desired widths. Flat sheets can be cut into wide lasagne noodles or into superfine *capelli d'angelo* (angel's hair). Fresh pasta is also sometimes cut into little soup squares (*quadrucci*) or into large squares for ravioli or rectangles for cannelloni. See Guide to Fresh Pasta, opposite page.

Commercial dried pasta is made with water and durum wheat, a particularly hard (high-protein) wheat. Ground durum wheat, known as semolina, is preferred for dried pasta because it contributes to firm, elastic dough that is sturdy enough to be shaped by machine and to maintain a form. To shape the dough, it is pushed through dies or molds and then oven-dried. Semolina is sometimes used to strengthen homemade pasta, but it makes a dough that is difficult to work by hand.

Use   Italian cooks use fresh pasta with certain types of sauces and dried pasta with others. The two are not always interchangeable. In general, soft fresh pasta is used with butter-based and cream-based sauces, which coat the noodles nicely. Dried pasta is usually the choice for oil-based and shellfish sauces. Because it holds its shape so well, dried pasta is a better choice for heavy, chunky vegetable sauces. Ridged and shell-shaped pastas are more appropriate for meat sauces because they trap the bits of meat in their ridges and hollows. Dried pasta, such as elbow macaroni and small shells (*conchigliette*), is good in soup because it holds its shape. *Pasta e fagioli*, the Tuscan soup made of pasta and white beans, shows how a sturdy dried pasta can stand up to a thick bean soup.

Pasta may be used in every course of a meal, from first course to dessert. You can add body to a simple broth with angel-hair pasta or tortellini; thicker vegetable- or bean-based soups such as minestrone often incorporate short, stubby dried pasta. In the United States cold pasta salads are eaten as a first course or luncheon main course.

In Italy pasta is generally served as a first course, rarely as a main course. The variety of possible sauces is literally endless, incorporating butter or oil, cream, meats, vegetables, fish and shellfish, poultry, and eggs.

Besides being tossed in sauce, some pasta shapes—such as lasagne and ziti—may be layered with sauce(s) and cheese and then baked. Non-Italian baked pasta dishes include American macaroni and cheese, and *pastitsio,* a Greek dish consisting of layers of macaroni, cinnamon-spiced meat sauce, béchamel sauce, and cheese.

In Spain thin vermicelli noodles are fried in oil, then steamed to doneness in gradually added stock. Egg noodles can also be fried in butter until crisp. Chinese cooks coil cooked vermicelli into pillows and fry on both sides, then top the noodle pillows with a saucy stir-fry, which softens the noodles and partially coats them.

Pasta is almost always served as a separate course in Italy. In other countries, however, noodles are often an accompaniment to a main course. In France buttered noodles are frequently paired with roast chicken or a creamy veal stew. In America, too, buttered noodles are a common side dish with pot roasts, stews, and creamed chicken.

Pasta also turns up in sweet dishes. Sweet noodle *kugel*—noodles baked with cottage cheese, eggs, sugar, raisins, and cinnamon—is a popular dish among Jews of Middle-European descent. In France vermicelli is simmered in cream with sugar, spices, and lemon peel, then baked like a soufflé with egg yolks and beaten egg whites.

Availability Fresh pasta is sold in many specialty stores and Italian markets around the country and is found increasingly in supermarkets. Some brands include preservatives; check the package label. Many supermarkets also stock fresh (not dried) frozen pasta, such as ravioli, fettuccine, and tortellini. All supermarkets carry a few basic dried shapes, such as spaghetti, lasagne, and macaroni. For the more unusual shapes, look for imported dried pasta in specialty stores, Italian markets, and well-stocked supermarkets.

In addition to flour-and-water dried pasta and flour-and-egg fresh pasta, flavored pastas are increasingly available in the United States. Cooked, minced spinach or cooked and puréed beets can add color and subtle flavor to a pasta dough. Herbs, beets, tomatoes, carrots, squid ink, and saffron are some of the more common additions. There is even an Italian recipe for chocolate pasta. Flavored pastas are available both fresh and dried; look for them in specialty stores. They do not require special handling, although care should be taken to choose a compatible sauce.

GUIDE TO FRESH PASTA

Because different regions of Italy apply different names to the same cut, pasta nomenclature is confusing. Some of the more commonly used names for fresh pasta are:

Agnolotti Crescent-shaped dumplings, usually stuffed with meat or pesto.

Cannelloni Rectangles of pasta, usually about 3 inches by 4 inches, stuffed, rolled into tubes, sauced, and baked.

Fettuccine The favorite flat noodle of Rome, cut about ⅛ inch wide. Particularly good with cream sauces, as in fettuccine Alfredo (with butter, cream, and Parmesan).

Lasagne The broadest fresh noodle (also available dried), lasagne are cut about 2 inches wide. The cooked noodle is layered with vegetables, cheeses, béchamel and/or meat sauce, and baked in a casserole.

Pappardelle One of the widest fresh noodles, cut about ⅝ inch wide with a fluted pastry cutter to give it a frilly edge. Traditionally served with rich meat sauces, such as hare sauce (*pappardelle con la lepre*) or chicken-liver sauce.

Ravioli Two face-to-face squares of flat pasta stuffed with a filling of meat, cheese, or vegetables.

Tagliatelle The favorite flat noodle of Bologna. Very similar to fettuccine, although slightly thinner and wider. *Tagliatelle* are cut slightly less than ¼ inch wide. They are often tossed with *Ragù Bolognese,* a rich meat sauce.

Tagliolini and Tagliarini Similar names for the same shape: a long flat ribbon, rolled paper-thin, and cut less than ⅛ inch wide. Often used in broth.

Tortellini A small square topped with meat, vegetables, or cheese, then folded and twisted into a ring-shaped dumpling.

GUIDE TO DRIED PASTA

Manufacturers have created hundreds of dried pasta shapes. The most commonly available are the following.

Acini di Pepe Tiny "peppercorns" most often used in soups.

Bucatini Like spaghetti, but thicker and hollow. Often served *all'Amatriciana:* with tomatoes, *pancetta,* and hot-pepper flakes.

Capelli d'Angelo Angel-hair pasta, similar to fine spaghetti. Often served in broth.

Conchiglie Shell-shaped pasta; good with meat sauce since it captures bits of sauce in its hollows.

Ditali Thimbles; short ridged tubes, about ½ inch long; good with meat sauce. Shorter versions known as *ditalini* are used in soups.

Farfalle Butterflies; a flat noodle about 2 inches long and ¾ inch wide, pinched together in the middle to form a bow-tie shape. Good with tomato sauce or meat sauce.

Fusilli Long, spaghetti-length corkscrew noodles; good with thick, clinging, creamy sauces with bits of meat or vegetables.

Linguine A flat ribbon noodle similar to fettuccine; also available fresh. Often served with clam sauce or with pesto.

Lumache Shells larger than conchiglie (see above) and intended for stuffing. They are frequently filled with seasoned ricotta and topped with tomato sauce.

Macaroni Short, elbow-shaped, hollow noodles; good with meat sauce or cheese sauce, or baked American-style with cheese sauce and eggs. *Macaroni* is also a generic Italian word for dried pasta, usually spelled *maccheroni.*

Manicotti Large hollow tubes, usually stuffed with cheese or meat mixtures, then sauced and baked.

Penne Also known as *mostaccioli* (little mustaches), *penne* (quills) are tubes about 2 inches long, cut diagonally on the ends. They are generally paired with a tomato sauce.

Rigatoni Ridged, hollow tubes about 2 inches long and ½ inch wide. Rigatoni are delicious tossed with meat sauces, bits of which get trapped inside. They hold their shape well and may be baked in sauce.

Rotelle Short, 2-inch-long, corkscrew-shaped pasta; good with chunky sauces.

Ruote Cartwheels; *ruote* resemble little wagon wheels and are often served in soups.

Semi di Melone Melon seeds; tiny pasta shapes used in soups.

Spaghetti The familiar long rodlike pasta. Used with oil-based sauces, shellfish sauces, and tomato sauces. Thin spaghetti is known as spaghettini or vermicelli.

Ziti Long hollow rods, about the length of spaghetti. When cut into shorter lengths (about 2 inches long), they are known as ziti *tagliati,* although some manufacturers call these ziti, too. Use with hearty meat or mushroom sauces, or bake as for rigatoni.

PATCH, TO

To repair cracks or tears in pie dough after it has been rolled out by sealing with a thin piece of leftover dough. Sometimes the patch is made stronger by gluing with water. It is better to patch pastry dough than to reroll it because rerolling will toughen it.

PATE AND TERRINE

A pâté is a spreadable paste of ground meats, livers, and seasonings. Its consistency can be airy and smooth like a mousse or more coarsely textured and country style. Ingredients for pâtés can be precooked and then combined, or the mixture can be processed and then baked in a crust, or in a mold that is often lined with pork fat. Special containers called terrine molds are traditionally used for pâtés, but any loaf pan of equal volume will work just as well (see MOLD). A terrine is made in a mold of the same name and was traditionally served in its mold. The pâté was freestanding. These definitions are, however, no longer rigidly followed. You will find the terms *pâté* and *terrine* used interchangeably.

Mixtures for pâtés are called forcemeats. These are made of fish, pork, lean veal, duck, game, or fowl, plus fat and flavorings, and are bound together with a bread or flour paste (see FORCEMEAT). Multicolored vegetable pâtés are increasingly popular.

Pâtés and terrines are served as appetizers or first courses. They are much like the American meat loaf, but have a richer, more luxurious texture and flavor. They are easy to prepare, especially with a food processor, although they may require costly or hard-to-find ingredients. Pâtés and terrines are wonderful for entertaining because they can be prepared well ahead; in fact, they improve when aged for several days.

◼ CURRIED CHICKEN OR DUCK LIVER PATE IN ASPIC

The glistening aspic decoration belies the easy assembly of this curried liver pâté. Be sure to use a mold that is attractive enough to bring to the table.

    1 pound chicken or duck livers
    1 tart apple, diced
    1 small onion, diced
    4 tablespoons unsalted butter
    1 tablespoon curry powder
    ¼ cup Chicken Stock (see page 560) or apple brandy
    1½ tablespoons flour
    ½ teaspoon salt
    ¼ teaspoon freshly ground pepper
    1 egg
    1 baguette, sliced, for accompaniment

Aspic Glaze (see Note)

1. Preheat oven to 350° F. In a large skillet sauté livers, apple, and onion in butter over medium-high heat until livers are brown on outside but remain pink on inside (about 12 minutes). Stir in curry powder and cook 3 to 4 minutes.

2. Remove to a blender or food processor. Pour stock into pan, scraping cooked bits to loosen. Add pan juices to liver, and purée until smooth. Add flour, salt, pepper, and egg, and purée again until smooth.

3. Pour into a 3½- to 4-cup mold. Cover with aluminum foil, and place in a baking dish filled with about 1 inch warm water. Bake until knife inserted in center comes out clean (about 45 minutes). Remove from oven and cool. Chill for 1 hour and decorate with Aspic Glaze. Serve with baguette slices.

Serves 12 to 20 as an appetizer.

Note   See Aspic Glaze, page 372; use one half recipe Basic Aspic.

◼ PATE MAISON

Set out this flavorful pâté with tiny French *cornichons* (pickles), a crock of Dijon mustard, and sliced baguettes. Cold and thinly sliced on French bread, it makes a splendid sandwich the next day.

    ½ medium onion, minced
    2 tablespoons butter
    ½ cup plus 2 tablespoons Cognac or Armagnac
    1 pound ground pork
    1 pound ground veal
    1 clove garlic, minced
    2 eggs, slightly beaten
    1 teaspoon salt
    ⅛ teaspoon freshly ground pepper
    1 teaspoon dried thyme
    1 chicken breast, boned and skinned
    1 pound pork fat, cut into ⅛-inch slices
    2 ounces pistachio nuts, shelled

1. Preheat oven to 350° F. In a small skillet sauté onion in butter over medium-high heat until translucent. Pour in ½ cup of the Cognac. Cook until Cognac is absorbed into onion (mixture will measure about ⅓ cup). Remove from heat and place in a large mixing bowl.

2. Add pork, veal, garlic, eggs, salt, pepper, and thyme. Mix with hands until thoroughly blended, or blend in food processor until light in texture and well blended.

3. Cut chicken breast into ½- by 3-inch slices. Put slices in a small bowl and add the remaining 2 tablespoons Cognac.

4. Line a 2-quart terrine or loaf pan with slices of pork fat. Press one half of ground meat mixture into pan. Cover with Cognac-soaked chicken, then pistachios. Press remaining ground meat mixture on top. Cover with another layer of pork fat.

5. Cover terrine with aluminum foil. Set in a pan of boiling water. Place on rack in center of oven. Bake until juices run clear yellow and pâté has shrunk from sides of pan.

6. When pâté is done, remove terrine and set on cooling rack. Place another loaf pan on top of pâté; fill with 3 to 4 pounds of weight (canned goods or bricks work well). Let pâté cool at room temperature for several hours, then refrigerate 2 to 3 days before slicing. To serve, unmold and slice.

Serves 10 as a first course.

■ HOT PORK AND HAM PATE IN BRIOCHE

French through and through, this hot pâté is baked inside a buttery brioche dough. The flavor of the pâté will intensify if the mixture is allowed to cure overnight in the refrigerator.

  2 tablespoons butter
  1 large onion, finely chopped
  1 clove garlic, minced
  ¼ cup brandy
  1 egg
  ½ cup soft bread crumbs
  1 pound ground pork
  2 cups ground baked ham
  ¼ cup finely chopped parsley
  ½ teaspoon *each* salt and dried thyme
  ¼ teaspoon ground allspice
  ⅛ teaspoon white pepper
  1 egg beaten with 1 teaspoon water

Brioche Dough

  1 package active dry yeast
  ¼ cup warm (105° to 115° F) water
  1 tablespoon sugar
  ½ teaspoon salt
  2 cups flour
  2 eggs
  ½ cup butter, softened

1. Prepare Brioche Dough and, while it is rising, make filling.

2. In a medium frying pan, melt butter and cook onion until soft but not browned. Mix in garlic and brandy; cook, stirring, until most of the liquid cooks away.

3. Beat the 1 egg in a large bowl. Mix in bread crumbs, then ground meats, onion mixture, parsley, salt, thyme, allspice, and white pepper. Cover and refrigerate until ready to enclose in dough.

4. Roll dough out on a generously floured board or pastry cloth to make a rectangle about 10 by 20 inches. Shape filling with your hands into a loaf about 4 by 8 inches. Place filling at one end of dough. Pinch dough to seal ends. With long sealed edge at bottom, place in a well-greased 5- by 9-inch loaf pan.

5. Cover lightly with waxed paper and let rise in a warm place until dough looks puffy (about 30 minutes); or cover and refrigerate for several hours or overnight, and let stand at room temperature until puffy looking (about 1 hour).

6. Preheat oven to 350° F. Brush dough lightly with beaten egg mixture. Bake until dough is well browned and juice runs clear when a long skewer is inserted in center (about 1½ hours).

7. Place pâté (still in pan) on a rack and let stand for about 15 minutes; then carefully remove loaf from pan and cut into 1-inch-thick slices. Serve warm.

Serves 6 to 8.

Brioche Dough Sprinkle yeast over the water in large bowl of electric mixer; let stand for 5 minutes to soften. Mix in sugar and salt, then ½ cup flour. Beat at medium speed until elastic (about 3 minutes). Beat in eggs, one at a time, until smooth, then gradually beat in remaining flour. Add butter, 1 tablespoon at a time, beating well after each addition. Transfer to a greased bowl, cover, and let rise in a warm place until doubled (about 1½ hours). Stir dough down.

Pâtés, such as Pâté Maison, probably developed as a Gallic solution to the universal problem of what to do with leftovers.

Hoppin' John, a richly flavorful dish of black-eyed peas, is traditionally served in the Deep South on New Year's Day.

PEA

All peas are members of the legume family, plants whose seeds are borne in pods. Some varieties, such as English peas and the French *petits pois,* are valued for their seeds only and are known as shelling peas. Some of the shelling peas—English peas, for example—are usually eaten fresh; others, such as pigeon peas, field peas (which, when split, are the common green or yellow split pea), and chick-peas, are usually dried.

The other major type of pea is the edible-podded pea, eaten in its entirety before the seeds develop. The Chinese snow pea is the best-known example.

Use Depending upon their variety, peas may be used as a side dish or added to soups, salads, stews, rice and pasta dishes, and casseroles.

Availability Fresh and dried peas are found in supermarkets and specialty produce stores; some health-food stores carry a selection of dried peas. This entry discusses the most common types of fresh and dried peas.

Selection See specific peas.

Storage Keep both shelling peas (in their pods) and edible-podded peas in a plastic bag in the refrigerator crisper and use within one or two days. Dried peas will keep for up to one year in an airtight container in a cool, dry place.

Preparation Shelling peas should be shelled just before using. Open pod by removing string. Remove peas. Snow peas and sugar snap peas should be strung as well, although the pods should be left unopened. *About soaking and quick-soaking dried peas:* Most dried peas require presoaking to soften them before cooking. Cover with cold water and soak at least 8 hours or overnight. To quick-soak, cover with cold water, bring to a boil, and boil for 1 minute; cover, remove from heat, and let stand for 1 hour. Discard soaking liquid.

Cooking *Fresh Peas:* See ʙᴏɪʟ, sᴀᴜᴛᴇ, sᴛᴇᴀᴍ, sᴛɪʀ-ꜰʀʏ. *Dried Peas:* See ʙᴏɪʟ. Also see specific peas.

BLACK-EYED PEA

See Cowpea.

CECI BEAN

See Chick-pea.

CHICK-PEA

Also known as garbanzo beans or ceci beans, chick-peas are a staple in India and figure prominently in the cuisines of North Africa and the Middle East. Use chick-peas in salads, soups, and stews or as a side dish. They may be roasted and served as a snack; ground for flour for use in breads and fritters; puréed and seasoned for a dip; or added to the North African stew known as Couscous. Chick-peas are occasionally available fresh in the summer; the pod is a small, fuzzy, green oval with one or two seeds inside. Dried chick-peas are packaged in plastic bags or sold in bulk. For fresh peas, select full, light green pods without signs of drying.

To prepare fresh chick-peas, open the pod and remove the beans. Simmer beans, covered, in boiling water until tender. To prepare dried chick-peas, soak overnight or quick-soak (see Preparation); then simmer, covered, in 3 parts water to 1 part peas until tender (1½ to 2 hours).

◼ HUMMUS

Serve this Middle Eastern dip with fresh raw vegetables, cracker bread, or toasted pita bread. Sesame tahini has the consistency of peanut butter. It's available in many supermarkets and specialty food stores. If it has separated, stir well before using.

> **2 cans (15 oz each) chick-peas**
> **3 cloves garlic**
> **2 tablespoons fresh lemon juice, or more, to taste**
> **6 tablespoons sesame tahini** *or*
>   **2 to 3 tablespoons peanut butter**
> **¼ teaspoon ground cumin, or to taste (optional)**
>   **Salt, to taste**
>   **Finely chopped parsley, for garnish**

1. Drain liquid from 1 can chick-peas and put beans in a food processor or blender. Add peas from remaining can with their liquid, and garlic, lemon juice, and tahini; purée until smooth.

2. Add cumin (if used) and salt to taste, and purée a few seconds more. Serve garnished with parsley.

Makes 3 cups.

CHINESE SNOW PEA

Edible-podded Chinese snow peas are delicious when stir-fried quickly in oil by themselves or with other ingredients. They should be cooked only until hot throughout (one or two minutes). They may be stir-fried with Chinese black mushrooms, water chestnuts, and bean curd, or lightly glazed with oyster sauce. Snow peas can be added to soups or stews or served as a stir-fry side dish for all manner of Western dishes—from baked fish to roast pork, chicken, or beef.

Chinese snow peas are available the year around in Asian markets and in some supermarkets, with peak supplies in spring and fall. They should be bright green, and firm. Choose ones that are small and flat, with immature seeds. Avoid those with drying along the seam.

■ STILTON SNOW PEAS

A quick blanching highlights the color and flavor of snow peas while retaining their crispness. The filled snow peas will hold in the refrigerator for several hours if loosely covered with plastic wrap to prevent drying out.

    40 snow peas
     3 ounces Stilton cheese, at room temperature
     3 ounces cream cheese, softened
     1 teaspoon chopped parsley

1. Remove stems from snow peas. Bring 3 quarts of water to a boil. Drop in snow peas and blanch for 30 seconds. Remove with slotted spoon and immediately place in ice-cold water to stop cooking. Remove from water and pat dry with paper towels. Carefully cut a 1- to 1½-inch slit in center of curved side of each snow pea with a sharp paring knife.

2. In a small mixing bowl, mix Stilton cheese, cream cheese, and parsley. Fill each snow pea through slit, using two spoons or a pastry bag fitted with a small star tip. Chill until serving time on paper-towel–lined baking sheets covered loosely with plastic wrap. To serve, arrange in a fan shape on an attractive plate.

Makes 40 appetizers.

Recipe: Shrimp With Snow Peas and Water Chestnuts, 606.

COWPEA

Also known as crowder peas, cowpeas are widely eaten in the American South and in Africa. They have a mealy texture and an earthy flavor that is complemented by pork, especially ham. The black-eyed pea is a type of cowpea. Use cowpeas in soups, stews, and salads or as a side dish. In the summer, cowpeas are occasionally available fresh, either shelled or unshelled. If you are buying unshelled fresh peas, select those with full, moist pods. Dried black-eyed peas and cowpeas are available packaged in plastic bags or sold in bulk; they should be used within one year of purchase. Black-eyed peas may also be purchased canned and frozen.

To prepare fresh cowpeas, open pod and remove beans. Cook fresh cowpeas in boiling water, covered, until tender. To prepare dried cowpeas, soak overnight or quick-soak (see Preparation); simmer, covered, in 3 parts water to 1 part peas until tender (about one hour).

■ HOPPIN' JOHN

In the Deep South black-eyed peas eaten on New Year's Day are supposed to bring good luck in the coming year. In some areas residents insist that the peas bestow good luck only if they're prepared in Hoppin' John and served with cooked greens, which symbolize money. This recipe uses dried black-eyed peas. Note that the peas must stand for at least one hour or as long as overnight. Accompany Hoppin' John with Country-Style Greens. That recipe appears on page 287.

    1½ cups (about ½ lb) dried black-eyed peas
    1½ teaspoons salt, plus salt to taste
     6 strips bacon, diced
     1 medium onion, chopped
     ¾ cup long-grain white rice
     2 tablespoons butter (optional)
       Salt and freshly ground pepper, to taste
       Dash of Louisiana-style hot sauce, to taste
     ½ cup minced green onions, including
       green tops, for garnish
     3 tablespoons minced parsley, for garnish

1. Rinse peas and pick them over. Cover with 3 cups cold water, add 1 teaspoon of the salt, and let stand overnight. (For a quicker soak, to serve peas the same day, see Preparation.)

2. Drain peas, discarding water, and place in a large pot. In a separate pan, sauté bacon until crisp; add it to peas, reserving rendered drippings. Add onion, remaining ½ teaspoon salt, and 2 cups water. Bring just to a boil, lower heat, and simmer until peas are tender (about 30 minutes). A small amount of cooking liquid should remain; if liquid is absorbed too quickly during cooking, add fresh water by ¼ cups.

3. In separate pot, cover rice with cold water. Bring to a boil, stir once, cover, and lower heat to the barest simmer. Simmer rice for 20 minutes.

4. When peas are tender, add cooked rice to pot. Stir in 2 tablespoons reserved bacon fat or 2 tablespoons butter (if preferred), salt, pepper, and hot sauce to taste. Cover and simmer about 15 minutes longer so flavors mingle and rice absorbs some of the remaining cooking liquid. To serve, garnish with green onions and parsley.

Serves 6 to 7.

CROWDER PEA

See Cowpea.

ENGLISH PEA

Fresh shelled peas are best when steamed briefly in a covered saucepan in a small amount of boiling water. Steamed peas are usually buttered and occasionally creamed as well. French cooks add shredded lettuce to the steaming peas; other cooks add onion or green onion. Indian cooks braise peas with spices and cubes of firm homemade cheese. Italian cooks braise peas with prosciutto. Steamed peas can be cooled, then tossed with diced ham and mayonnaise for a summer salad. They can be mixed with other vegetables, such as carrots or corn, and served hot. They can be added to soups or stews and are particularly delicious with delicate meats such as veal or veal sweetbreads.

Fresh English peas are available in supermarkets the year around, with the domestic summer crop being supplemented by imports from Mexico. The domestic crop peaks in quantity and quality in the summer months. Both English peas and the tiny French *petits pois* are available frozen and canned. Fresh shelling peas are full of sugar at harvest but begin to convert their natural sugar into starch the moment they're picked. For that reason, the sooner the pea is cooked after harvest, the better. Buy English peas from a market with rapid turnover or, better yet, buy peas at local farm stands or farmers' markets, if possible. When selecting English peas, break a pod open and taste a pea; it should be sweet, not starchy. The pods should be well filled but the seeds should not be overlarge. Look for bright green pods; avoid those that have dry seams.

■ SPRING LAMB STEW WITH FRESH PEAS

Fresh mint seasons the lamb in this glistening stew. Serve with butter-fried potatoes and a leafy green salad tossed with your favorite dressing, crusty bread and butter, and fresh strawberries for dessert.

>   3 pounds boneless lamb leg or shoulder,
>   fat trimmed and cut in 1-inch cubes
>   Salt and white pepper, to taste
>   3 tablespoons butter
>   3 tablespoons vegetable oil
>   3 shallots, finely chopped
>   1 clove garlic, minced
>   1 large carrot, cut in ¼-inch-thick slices
>   3 or 4 sprigs fresh mint
>   1 cup Rich Chicken Stock (see page 560) or
>   canned chicken broth
>   1½ cups dry white wine
>   1½ to 2 cups shelled fresh peas

1. Sprinkle lamb lightly with salt and pepper. In a large, deep frying pan or Dutch oven, melt 2 tablespoons butter with oil. Add lamb, about a third at a time. Brown well, removing lamb as it browns. When all lamb is removed from pan, add shallots, cooking and stirring until they are soft and lightly browned. Mix in garlic and carrot.

2. Return lamb to pan. Add mint, broth, and wine. Bring to a boil, cover, reduce heat, and simmer until tender (45 minutes to 1 hour).

3. Remove lamb and keep it warm. Strain cooking liquid, discarding carrot and mint. Skim and discard surface fat. Return liquid to pan and bring to a boil over high heat. Cook, stirring, until slightly reduced and syrupy. Taste, and add salt if needed. Mix in peas and cook, stirring, for 1 to 2 minutes.

4. Cut remaining butter in pieces. Off heat, stir in butter, one piece at a time, until melted.

5. Return lamb to sauce, stirring to coat well. Spoon lamb into center of each warm plate. Surround with sauce and peas and serve at once.

Serves 6 to 8.

FIELD PEA

Small round peas grown especially for drying are known as field peas; they may be green or yellow. When split, they are called split peas. Whole field peas and split peas are boiled in about 4 parts water to 1 part peas until soft (about one hour). They can be boiled further to reduce them to a purée, then seasoned with butter or spices or made into soup. Bacon, sausage, or smoked pork make a pleasing addition to dried peas and dried pea soups. Whole field peas are available in plastic packages in some supermarkets and in bulk in some health-food stores. Split peas are available in plastic packages in most supermarkets and in bulk in most health-food stores.

Recipes: Curried Lettuce and Pea Soup, 341; Split Pea Soup, Black Forest Style, 565.

GARBANZO BEAN

See Chick-pea.

PETITS POIS

See English Pea.

PIGEON PEA

Also known as *gunga, goongoo,* or congo peas, pigeon peas are native to Africa and are widely eaten today in the Caribbean, Africa, and India. The dried peas are beige or pale yellow with red mottling; they are not widely available fresh. In the Caribbean cooks make pigeon peas into soup or dumplings or serve them with rice. Look for dried pigeon peas in health-food stores and markets catering to an Indian, African, or Caribbean clientele.

SPLIT PEA

See Field Pea.

SUGAR SNAP PEA

The sugar snap pea, a relatively new variety, is a cross between a shelling pea and an edible-podded pea. Its pod is still sweet and tender when the seeds are developed. Sugar snap peas are available in spring and fall in some supermarkets and specialty markets. Sugar snap peas should be bright green and firm, not limp. They should be plump, but not filled to bursting; avoid pods that are dried around the seam. Sugar snap peas need only brief blanching—a couple of minutes in a large quantity of boiling salted water, then draining, drying, and reheating in oil or butter. They should still be crunchy when served. Sautéed sugar snap peas make an excellent side dish for fish, poultry, pork, beef, or veal.

PEACH

The sweet, juicy peaches grown today probably bear little resemblance to the earliest peaches, native to China. Until modern horticulturists developed the strains we enjoy today, most peaches were small, fairly sour, and certainly more fuzzy than modern varieties. Today, there are thousands of named peaches. Some have stones that cling to the flesh (clingstone varieties); others are freestone. Some have white or pale pink flesh; others have yellow flesh. Some have white skins with a pink blush; others have a deep yellow skin with a reddish blush. Some are firm-fleshed varieties designed for canning; others are for eating out of hand. In any case, the peach is one of America's favorite fruits and one of the country's most important fruit crops.

Use A ripe peach eaten out of hand is a delicious breakfast food or snack. Sliced peaches can be added to fruit salads and gelatin salads; they also may be poached for compotes. Sliced and sugared peaches are often spooned on top of shortcake or soaked in wine or Champagne for an easy summer dessert. They can be baked with butter and sugar and macaroon crumbs, or with a cobbler dough or a fruit-crisp topping. Peaches can be puréed for sherbet and ice cream or made into jam or preserves. They can be pickled, home-canned in sugar syrup, or made into chutney. Peach juice makes a pleasing ingredient in fruit punches or cocktails.

Availability Domestic peaches are sold from early May to mid-September. Imports from the southern hemisphere may supplement the domestic crop in some supermarkets in the winter. Frozen peaches, canned peaches, and canned peach nectar are sold in most supermarkets.

Selection An appealing fragrance is the best clue to a ripe peach. Look also for fruit that gives slightly to pressure and has a yellow or creamy background color between its blushed areas. Avoid fruit with greenish undertones and fruit that is bruised or very soft.

Storage Peaches will keep in the refrigerator crisper for up to two weeks.

Preparation Peaches eaten out of hand do not require peeling. Most peaches are peeled for use in cooked dishes, however. Very ripe peaches are usually easy to peel; others may need to be blanched first. To blanch, cut a small x in the rounded end opposite the stem; dip fruit in boiling water for about 30 seconds, then plunge into ice water. Skin will peel away readily. Peaches oxidize and brown when exposed to air; rub or sprinkle with lemon juice to prevent browning.

■ NUTTY PEACH PIE

For a variation, omit the nut topping and bake as a double-crust or lattice-top pie. Serve warm or at room temperature, topped with Chantilly Cream (see page 252) or with ice cream.

    1   9-inch single-crust Nut Egg Pastry (see page 435)
    5   cups peeled, sliced freestone peaches
        (5 to 6 large peaches)
    ½ to ¾ cup granulated sugar
    2½ to 3 tablespoons cornstarch
        Dash freshly grated nutmeg
    1   tablespoon fresh lemon juice
    ⅛   teaspoon almond extract
    1   egg white, lightly beaten (optional)
    ⅓   cup firmly packed light brown sugar
    ½   cup flour
    6   tablespoons unsalted butter
    1   cup chopped nuts (mixture of almonds
        and pecans)

1. Preheat oven to 425° F. Line a 9-inch pie plate with Nut Egg Pastry. In a large bowl combine sliced peaches, ½ to ¾ cup granulated sugar (depending upon ripeness of peaches), cornstarch, and nutmeg. Allow to stand 15 minutes.

2. Stir in lemon juice and almond extract.

3. Lightly brush uncooked pie shell with a thin layer of egg white (if used) to make pie crust moistureproof. Pour filling into pie shell.

4. Mix brown sugar with flour; cut in butter until crumbly. Stir in nuts. Sprinkle mixture over peaches.

5. Bake for 15 minutes. Reduce oven to 400° F and continue baking for 35 to 40 minutes. Cover edges of crust with strips of aluminum foil, if necessary, to prevent excessive browning.

Makes one 9-inch pie.

Recipes and Related Information
Ginger-Peach Upside-Down Cake, 87; Gingered Peach Pickles, 322; Peach Filling, 627; Peach Melba, 315; Summer Peach Jam, 319.

This Nutty Peach Pie is baked in an almond pie crust and topped with an almond-pecan crumble. It's a perfect dessert for summer, when peaches are in season.

PEANUT

Actually a legume rather than a nut, the peanut has seeds that are encased in a fragile, dry pod. Like other legumes, the oval seeds may be split into two parts. The seeds are ivory-colored and covered with a papery brown skin. Peanuts have a buttery, nutty flavor that is intensified by roasting or frying.

Use In this country half the peanut crop is made into peanut butter. Some portion of the remainder is sold in the shell; probably most of the unshelled peanuts marketed in this country are sold at sporting events. Shelled peanuts may be roasted or unroasted, salted or unsalted. They are used in candy bars and snack foods such as caramel corn, in nut mixes marketed as cocktail snacks, and in cookies. Chopped peanuts are added to salads and slaws, and to muffins and quick breads, and serve as a garnish for ice cream sundaes and sautéed vegetables. Peanuts are pressed for their oil, which is excellent for sautéing and frying and for salad dressings. Peanuts are popular in Africa, where they are known as groundnuts. African groundnut stew is a spicy chicken and tomato dish made with ground peanuts. Nigerian cooks grind peanuts into flour for bread. The Chinese eat seasoned and roasted peanuts as an hors d'oeuvre or grind them to make a sauce for noodles. Indonesian cooks make a spicy dipping sauce for skewered meats with ground peanuts, chiles, and coconut milk.

Availability Most supermarkets carry peanuts both shelled and in the shell. Shelled peanuts are usually packed in vacuum-sealed jars or cans. Peanut butter, both smooth and chunky, is sold in all supermarkets. It may contain added sugar or preservatives. Natural peanut butter is available in most health-food stores. Chinese markets are a good source for raw peanuts.

Storage Peanuts turn rancid quickly, shelled peanuts faster than unshelled. Store unshelled peanuts in the refrigerator or in a cool, dry, dark place for up to six months. Refrigerate shelled peanuts in an airtight container for up to three months, or freeze for up to six months. Natural peanut butter should be refrigerated after opening; it will keep for up to six months. Peanut butter containing preservatives will keep indefinitely in a cool, dry place.

Preparation To toast peanuts, shell them, then arrange them on a baking tray and bake at 325° F until fragrant and lightly browned (8 to 10 minutes). Rub between towels to remove skins.

Recipes and Related Information
Choco–Peanut Butter Cookies, 145; Peanut Brittle, 96; Peanut Butter–Chocolate Chip Cookies, 141.

PEAR

Of unknown origin, pears today are cultivated in temperate zones all over the world. Among tree fruits grown in these zones, only the apple is more heavily planted. Of the 5,000 varieties of pears, only a few are of commercial importance in this country. Commercial varieties vary considerably in skin color, texture, and flavor. See Availability for a description of major types.

Use Pears are probably most often eaten out of hand, as a breakfast food, dessert, or snack. Ripe pears are particularly delicious with a blue cheese such as Gorgonzola, Roquefort, or Stilton. Sliced pears are used in fruit salads and compotes. Pears may be poached, either whole or in halves, in a light wine syrup, raspberry syrup, or sugar syrup. They can be baked with butter and sugar or poached, sliced, and arranged on top of a fruit tart.

Availability In addition to fresh pears, supermarkets also carry canned pears and canned pear nectar. The major commercial pear varieties include the following.

Anjou This winter pear with greenish yellow skin and yellowish white flesh is globular in shape with a short neck. The Anjou is a hardy pear that ships and stores well; it holds its shape when cooked. It is available from October through May.

Bartlett Also known as the Williams' pear, it is a popular summer pear with yellow skin and ivory flesh. There is also a variety with red flesh. It is very aromatic, very tender when ripe, with flesh that is sweet, juicy, and buttery. It is available from mid-July through November.

Bosc This winter pear with an elongated shape and a russet brown skin has white flesh that is firm when ripe and quite sweet. Bosc pears hold their shape well when cooked and are excellent for poaching or baking.

Comice Having perhaps the finest flavor and smoothest texture of generally available pears, this winter pear has a squat, almost neckless shape, a brownish green skin, and a white flesh. Ripe Comice are highly aromatic and fairly firm; they should not be allowed to get soft. A choice pear for eating out of hand, it has a buttery texture and a winy flavor. It also bakes well and makes fragrant sherbet. Look for Comice from October through January.

French Butter Pear Also known as Beurre Hardy, this delicate pear does not cook well. However, it is exceptional for eating out of hand or with cheese. It has a brownish skin with a creamy flesh and a buttery texture that explains its name. It is available late summer through fall.

Seckel This very small, brownish pear is often poached for a ham or turkey garnish or canned in a spiced syrup. It has a grainy texture and is available in some markets in late fall and winter.

Winter Nellis This firm, spicy pear (also spelled Nelis) has a squat shape and a dull green skin with russet dots. Because it is firm, it holds its shape well when baked. It is available from late fall through spring.

Selection Pears are one of the few fruits that won't ripen properly on the tree; for that reason, they are picked mature but hard and must be allowed to soften slightly before eating. Choose pears that are fragrant, free of blemishes, and beginning to color and soften.

Storage Hold pears at room temperature in a warm place until they give slightly to pressure. Refrigerate and use within a few days. Pears intended for cooking should be cooked when still fairly firm.

Preparation Pears do not require peeling for eating out of hand, although some have coarse or tannic skins that may be unpleasant. Peel as desired. Peeled pears oxidize rapidly; rub or sprinkle with lemon juice or store in acidulated water until ready to use.

■ BAKED PEAR TART

This tart looks especially pretty when baked in a scalloped tart band. Thinly sliced pear halves radiate from the center to form the petals of a flower.

This custard-filled pear tart is baked in a scallop-edged tart band. The top is dusted with confectioners' sugar to create a delicate flower pattern.

  1   10-inch Sweet Tart Pastry for scalloped tart tin (see page 441)
  6   tablespoons unsalted butter
1½   large eggs (beat second egg and use half)
 ½   cup plus 1 tablespoon granulated sugar
  3   tablespoons sifted flour
  4   ripe pears (Anjou or Bartlett)
  2   tablespoons fresh lemon juice
 ½   cup apricot preserves
  1   tablespoon pear liqueur or water
 ¼   cup confectioners' sugar

1. Position a 10-inch scalloped tart band on a flat baking sheet. (You may substitute a 10-inch tart tin with removable bottom or 10-inch circular tart band.) Roll out tart pastry and line tart band or tin. Trim dough even with top of tart band. Wrap and refrigerate 1 hour, or freeze for later use.

2. To make custard filling, cook butter over medium heat until butter browns. Immediately remove from heat and cool in pan 5 minutes. Place eggs in a mixing bowl and gradually whisk in granulated sugar. Whisk in flour. Whisk in melted butter and all of the browned bits that cling to bottom of pan (these give tart a delicious nutty flavor and aroma). Set aside until tart is assembled.

3. Preheat oven to 375° F. Peel pears. Cut each in half lengthwise, remove core and seeds, and place into a large bowl of cold water with lemon juice (this keeps pears white). Remove pear halves from water; dry well on paper towels. Using a sharp, thin knife held at a 45-degree angle to cutting board, slice each pear half

crosswise in ⅛-inch slices, beginning at the narrow tip. Slide a narrow spatula under each sliced pear half, and transfer it to pastry-lined tart band. Center each pear half in a "petal" of the tart band, with narrow end of pear pointing toward center. Then push pear slices from narrow to wide end to fan them slightly. Trim tip off last pear half, slice, and place in center of tart. Pour custard filling in empty spaces around, but not on top of, pears. Custard should come only halfway up sides of tart.

4. Bake for 20 minutes at 375° F. Reduce oven to 350° F and bake until custard looks fully cooked (40 to 50 minutes longer). If edges of crust begin to brown too much, cover them with strips of aluminum foil. Cool completely.

5. To make glaze: Melt preserves over low heat. Strain to remove pieces of fruit; stir in pear liqueur. When tart is cool, brush pear halves with a thin coat of preserves. Then cover each pear half with an upside-down boat-shaped tartlet tin (or a cardboard pattern of the same shape). Cover center pear with an upside-down, small, round brioche tin, tartlet tin, or cardboard pattern. Sift a light layer of confectioners' sugar over tart. Carefully lift off tins.

6. Lift off tart band, slide tart onto a serving plate, and serve at room temperature.

Serves 10.

Recipes and Related Information
Pear With Prosciutto, 358; Rosé Pears in Chocolate Bath, 612.

Pralines (say praw-leens), usually associated with New Orleans, are traditionally served with strong, hot, black coffee with chicory.

PECAN

The pecan is a native American nut that is still not widely cultivated elsewhere. Most pecans today are grown in the South and Southwest, with Georgia the leading producer. Like the walnut, the pecan is a species of hickory. Its smooth, pale brown, oval shell often has black markings and is usually about an inch long. Some pecans are also dyed red to hide blemishes. The kernel is a rich, golden brown with an ivory interior; its flavor is rich and buttery, especially when toasted.

Use   Pecans are widely used in the South and Southwest in pies, cakes, ice cream, pralines, and cookies. Pecans may be shelled, buttered, and roasted for a cocktail snack, or toasted, chopped, and added to salads and sautéed vegetables.

Availability   Pecans are harvested in the fall and are available in their shells in some markets at that time. Most supermarkets and health-food stores carry shelled pecans, either in bulk or packaged, whole or chopped.

Selection   Unshelled nuts should feel heavy for their size. Shelled nuts turn rancid quickly; buy them from a market with a rapid turnover.

Storage   Because of their high oil content, pecans turn rancid quickly. Store unshelled pecans in a cool, dark, dry place and use within six months. Shelled pecans may be frozen for up to six months or refrigerated for up to three months.

Preparation   To bring out their flavor, toast pecans on a baking sheet in a preheated 350° F oven until fragrant (six to eight minutes).

▦ PRALINES

A mixture of caramelized sugar and nuts, pralines are usually crisp, but this recipe produces a softer candy. The use of buttermilk gives this version of the Louisiana classic a delicious tang. Traditionally these candies are eaten after a meal with strong black coffee.

>   2 cups buttermilk
>   2 cups sugar
>   1 teaspoon baking soda
>   ½ cup unsalted butter
>   1½ cups coarsely chopped pecans

1. In a heavy-bottomed, 4- to 6-quart saucepan, combine buttermilk, sugar, baking soda, and butter. Cook over medium heat, stirring frequently with a wooden spoon and monitoring temperature with a candy thermometer. First the mixture will foam, then darken as it thickens. It is done when it reaches 238° F (soft-ball stage).

2. Remove mixture from heat and stir in pecans with a wire whisk. Beat mixture until it cools to about 220° F (on a candy thermometer). While it is still soft, spoon nut mixture onto waxed paper in 1- to 2-tablespoon mounds.

As pralines cool, they will become firm and can be removed from waxed paper.

Makes 2 to 3 dozen pralines.

Recipes and Related Information
Butter Pecan Ice Cream, 312; Chocolate-Pecan Waffles, 599; Pecan Applesauce Cake, 87; Pecan Buttermilk Waffles, 599; Pecan Lace Cookies, 142; Southern Pecan Pie, 439; The Stickiest Pecan Rolls, 629.

PEEL; PEEL, TO

The skin of a fruit or vegetable, also called the rind. To remove this skin.

Peeling tools include the fingers, a sharp paring knife, and a vegetable peeler. Sometimes heating facilitates peeling. Blanching some thin-skinned fruits and vegetables, such as peaches, plums, and tomatoes, splits the skin, which then pulls away in strips. Peppers can be peeled by scorching them over a flame or under a broiler or by roasting them in a hot oven until blistered, then sweating them in a paper or plastic bag 10 to 20 minutes. The moisture causes the skin to loosen. The easiest way to peel a clove of garlic is to cut off its root end and crush the clove with the side of a chef's knife; the skin will slip off. To skin nuts, toast in the oven until fragrant, then rub in a towel.

PEPINO

Like the potato, tomato, and eggplant, the pepino is a member of the nightshade family. The heart-shaped fruit is yellow with purple markings; the yellow flesh is aromatic, with a flavor reminiscent of cantaloupe, honeydew melon, and pear. It has a small seed cavity that contains inedible seeds.

Use   Eat on the half shell with lemon or lime wedges. Add sliced, peeled pepino to fruit salads, compotes, and chutneys. Puree for sorbets. Sauté in butter to garnish duck or chicken.

Availability   Fresh California-grown pepino is available in some supermarkets from August to December. Imports from New Zealand appear in the markets from February to June.

Selection   Choose aromatic pepinos with good yellow skin color; a ripe fruit will give slightly to pressure.

Storage   If fruit is slightly underripe, store at room temperature until it colors and softens. Refrigerate up to three days in a plastic bag in the refrigerator crisper.

Preparation   Halve and remove seeds.

PEPPER

All peppers, whether sweet or hot, are members of the capsicum family and are native to the New World. The plant that produces peppercorns, *Piper nigrum,* is native to Asia and is not related.

Peppers are a rich source of vitamin C, superior even to citrus, and they contain as much vitamin A as carrots. For centuries, chiles (hot peppers) have been put to medicinal use, particularly as a topical healing agent. Even today, many commercial liniments contain oleoresin of capsicum. Ground hot peppers are said to be effective in homemade insecticides, and at least one commercial manufacturer exploits the irritative quality of hot peppers in a product designed to discourage thumb sucking. The color extracted from red pepper is used as a natural coloring agent in a variety of foodstuffs, including sausage and cheese. Similarly, some processors add pimiento to chicken feed to impart a deep yellow color to the birds' skin and fat.

Capsicum peppers range in flavor from mild and sweet to blisteringly hot. The heat comes from capsaicin, a compound found in the veins and seeds of hot peppers, but not in their walls.

Pepper nomenclature is confusing, as it varies from country to country. In the United States the mild peppers are known as sweet peppers; hot peppers are known either as hot peppers or chiles. In England all peppers are known as chiles, but hot ones are referred to as hot chiles. In Latin America hot peppers are chiles and mild peppers are pimientos. In the United States pimientos are just one variety of sweet red pepper. To add to the confusion, some varieties have several different common names.

The following discussion divides peppers into two types: sweet and hot. Although it is sometimes difficult to distinguish a sweet pepper from a hot one by sight, it is generally true that the smaller the pepper, the hotter. However, weather, soil, and degree of maturity can affect capsaicin content, making one pepper hotter than another of the same variety; even peppers on the same plant can vary in pungency. The following glossary should at least help you to distinguish mild, hot, and hotter.

SWEET PEPPERS

The most widely available sweet pepper is the bell pepper, named for its bell-like shape. Green bell peppers are the most common, but red, yellow, and even purple bells are increasingly available in specialty markets. Most green bells become red with age; red bell peppers are simply green bells that have been allowed to ripen on the vine. Consequently, red bells are sweeter than greens and are available later in the season. All bell peppers have a mild flavor and a crisp, crunchy texture.

Use   Raw bell peppers add color and crunchy texture to salads and to raw vegetable assortments served with dips. Mediterranean cooks sauté strips of sweet peppers and serve them as a side dish or a garnish for braised salt cod or lamb. In Spain, Italy, and southern France, cooks roast and peel sweet peppers and serve them cool, as a salad, with lemon and oil. Middle European cooks stuff bell peppers with meat and/or seasoned rice or stew them with veal or chicken. In Japan strips of bell peppers are dipped in tempura batter and fried. Chinese cooks add bell pepper strips to stir-fries of all kinds.

Availability   Green bell peppers are found in most markets the year around; peak season is August and September. The domestic red, yellow, and purple bells are harvested in late summer and fall, with some markets stocking imports from Mexico and Holland at other times of the year. Dehydrated bell pepper flakes are available on some supermarket spice racks.

Other sweet peppers include the following.

Bull's Horn   A long, narrow, sickle-shaped green pepper with a pointed tip. Roast and peel it, then serve it whole with olive oil, garlic, and lemon. It is available in late summer and fall in some specialty markets. Select and store as for bell peppers.

Cubanelle   A long (about 4 inches), tapered pepper that may be yellow or red. It has thick, meaty walls and is generally more flavorful than the bell pepper. Also known as the Cuban pepper, it is available sporadically in specialty markets. Select and store as for bell peppers.

Lamuyo   Also known as European sweet pepper or rouge royal; a very sweet bell-shaped pepper, longer, larger, and more slender than the standard bell. Thick-fleshed and flavorful, it comes in a range of colors. Look for it in specialty markets in late summer and fall; select, store, and use as for bell peppers.

Pimiento   A large, heart-shaped red pepper sold in some markets in late summer and fall. It has thicker, meatier flesh than the bell. Because of their thick walls, they are excellent for roasting and peeling. Bottled or canned peeled pimientos are available in most supermarkets. Select, store, and use as for bell peppers.

Sweet Banana   A long banana-shaped yellow pepper that also comes in a hot variety (see Yellow Wax Pepper). It may be stuffed or pickled.

Selection   Choose bell peppers that feel heavy for their size; they will have thick, meaty walls. Avoid any with soft spots or shriveled areas. Bell peppers should be firm and shiny.

Storage   Keep peppers in a plastic bag in the refrigerator for up to one week.

Preparation   If stuffing or slicing, ribs and seeds should be removed. To keep peppers whole for stuffing, cut about ¼ to ½ inch off top and scoop out or trim away seeds and white ribs. If peppers will be sliced, cut them in half, then trim away stem, seeds, and ribs.

TIPS

ROASTING AND PEELING PEPPERS

The directions for roasting and peeling sweet and hot peppers are the same. When handling hot peppers, use caution to prevent irritation of skin or eyes. Wear gloves and wash hands well afterwards.

Hold peppers over open gas flame or charcoal fire, or place under a broiler. Turn often until blackened on all sides. Transfer peppers into a paper or plastic bag; close and set aside until cool (15 to 20 minutes).

Peel peppers; halve; remove stem and seeds. Lay halves flat and use dull side of a small knife to scrape away any black bits of skin and stray seeds. Slice into ¼-inch strips.

Roasted Red Peppers
Roast 2 red bell peppers as directed above. Put sliced peppers in a medium bowl; add 1 clove finely minced garlic, 2 tablespoons extravirgin olive oil, and 1 teaspoon minced fresh oregano. Salt to taste. Toss to blend and let marinate at room temperature for 1 hour before using.

Mixed sweet peppers make tricolored Peperonata, a lively late-summer antipasto. For a more substantial first course, pair the peppers with sliced mozzarella.

■ PEPERONATA
Mixed marinated peppers

Sweet peppers stewed slowly with tomatoes, herbs, and garlic are a popular summer first course in southern Italy. Serve them with crusty bread to mop up the aromatic juices, or offer Peperonata as part of a larger antipasto platter. Select meaty peppers that feel heavy for their size.

>   ½ **cup olive oil**
>   2 **tablespoons minced garlic**
>   ½ **yellow onion, minced**
>   2 **red bell peppers**
>   2 **green bell peppers**
>   1 **yellow bell pepper (if unavailable, substitute another red or green pepper)**
>   2 **tomatoes, peeled, seeded, and coarsely chopped**
>   2 **teaspoons salt**
>   ¼ **cup fresh oregano leaves**
>   ½ **red onion, in paper-thin slices, for garnish**
>   2 **tablespoons minced parsley, for garnish**
>   2 **tablespoons fruity olive oil (optional)**

1. In a large skillet over medium heat, heat the ½ cup olive oil until it is hot but not smoking. Add garlic and onion and sauté, stirring until lightly colored (about 3 minutes).

2. Halve peppers; remove seeds and trim away white ribs. Cut lengthwise into strips ½ inch wide. Add all peppers to skillet at one time and stir to blend with garlic-onion mixture. Add tomatoes and salt and mix gently. Scatter oregano leaves across top. Cover and simmer slowly until peppers are soft (12 to 15 minutes). Remove from heat and transfer to serving bowl to cool.

3. Serve peppers at room temperature, garnishing the top with the sliced red onion and minced parsley. If desired, drizzle with the 2 tablespoons fruity olive oil just before serving.

Makes about 3½ cups.

■ STUFFED GREEN PEPPERS MEXICANA

These stuffed peppers have a sweetly spicy, south-of-the-border flavor. The peppers and filling can be cooked and the peppers stuffed ahead of time; store in refrigerator overnight, if desired, and let dish warm to room temperature before baking.

>   6 **medium-sized green bell peppers (about 2 lb)**
>   2 **tablespoons butter or margarine**
>   ½ **cup slivered almonds**
>   1 **pound ground beef, crumbled**
>   1 **large onion, finely chopped**
>   1 **clove garlic, mashed**
>   ⅓ **cup raisins**
>   1 **tablespoon cider vinegar**
>   1 **teaspoon *each* sugar and ground cinnamon**
>   ¾ **teaspoon salt**
>   ¼ **teaspoon *each* ground cumin and cloves**
>   1 **can (15 oz) tomato sauce**
>   1½ **cups cooked short-grain rice**

1. Preheat oven to 350° F. Cut a thin slice from stem end of each pepper; carefully cut out seeds. Cook peppers, uncovered, in boiling salted water to cover, for 5 minutes; turn upside down to drain.

2. In a large, heavy-bottomed frying pan, heat butter over medium heat; add almonds and cook until lightly browned. Remove from pan with a slotted spoon; reserve. In the same pan cook ground beef and onion until lightly browned. Mix in garlic, raisins, vinegar, sugar, cinnamon, salt, cumin, cloves, and half of the tomato sauce. Simmer, uncovered, about 10 minutes. Mix in cooked rice and almonds.

3. Fill peppers with ground beef mixture. Arrange in an ungreased, deep, covered baking dish just large enough to hold the 6 peppers. Pour on remaining tomato sauce. (At this point peppers can be covered and refrigerated for several hours or overnight; if chilled, let dish sit out at room temperature for 30 minutes before baking.)

4. Bake, covered, for 45 minutes; uncover, spoon sauce over, and continue baking for 15 minutes.

Serves 6.

HOT PEPPERS (CHILES)

Capsaicin, a compound found in the seeds and veins but not the walls of hot peppers, gives these peppers their heat. They range from the mildly spicy *pepperoncini* to the incendiary tabasco pepper. The jalapeño pepper, a pepper most diners consider very hot, usually measures 2,500 to 4,000 in Scoville Heat Units, the accepted measurement for heat in peppers. By comparison, the tiny tabasco may weigh in at 60,000 to 80,000 units!

Use Hot peppers are one of the world's most common seasonings. They add zest to all manner of dishes and are especially appreciated in hot climates, where their consumption has a cooling effect. Minced raw hot peppers are used in Mexican *salsa cruda* (fresh salsa), the ubiquitous table relish, or in guacamole. In fact few savory dishes in Mexico are prepared without chiles in some form, either fresh or dried; egg dishes, soups, stews, and appetizers are almost always enlivened with chiles. In the Hunan and Szechuan regions of China, hot red chiles give a lift to stir-fries and dipping sauces. Southeast Asian cooks use sliced green chiles in dipping sauces and soups; Thai curries are always liberally seasoned with green or red chiles. In this country, dried tabasco peppers are used to make one of America's most famous condiments, Tabasco Sauce. The well-known Texas specialty chili takes its name from its principal incendiary seasoning.

Availability Many supermarkets today stock at least a few fresh chiles, such as jalapeño and *serrano* varieties. Dried whole red chiles are often available in jars on the spice rack. In addition, many supermarkets carry canned or bottled chiles. For a wider selection of fresh, dried, and canned or bottled chiles, seek out a Latin or Asian market or a well-stocked specialty produce market. Most fresh hot chiles are available the year around, although supply of some varieties may be sporadic.

Recognizing the various chiles takes some practice and experimentation because there are dozens of varieties of similar shape and size. Many are sold in both fresh and dried states. The following are among the most common hot peppers.

Anaheim Also known as the New Mexico pepper, Rio Grande pepper, long green chile, or California pepper. This long (6 to 8 inches), slender green pepper is one of the mildest of the hot peppers. It is the pepper used for making *chiles rellenos* (fried cheese-stuffed chiles) in the southwestern United States. The mature Anaheim, a red pepper, is dried and ground for chili powder and paprika.

Ancho The correct name for the ripened and dried *poblano* (see Poblano; some markets incorrectly identify the fresh poblano as the Ancho, too). The dried ancho is perhaps the mostly commonly used chile in Mexico. It is about 5 inches long and dark brick red. Like the poblano, it may be slightly hot to hot. It is often ground for use in cooked sauces, such as mole.

Cayenne, Chile de Arbol, Thai Pepper Although not the same, they are similar: All are small, thin peppers marketed green, red, and dried. In Asian markets, they may be identified as bird peppers. The fresh red peppers are generally hotter than the green, but all are quite hot. The dried cayenne pepper can be soaked in vinegar and salt for a few days to make a pungent, liquid hot red-pepper sauce. Thai cooks use both fresh and dried bird peppers in dipping sauces, soups, and stir-fries.

Cherry Pepper A small round pepper that is pickled and bottled. Pickled red and green cherry peppers are available in many supermarkets. Slightly piquant, they make a colorful addition to a salad, an antipasto platter, or a sandwich plate.

Jalapeño A small (about 2 inches long), smooth-skinned green chile that is popular in Mexico and the southwestern United States. It is often pickled with carrots and onions and served as a table relish. Jalapeños are minced raw and used in salsas or split, deveined, stuffed with cheese or fish, and served as an appetizer. They are frequently canned, either whole, sliced, or in seeded strips. Jalapeño slices add zest to tacos, hamburgers, cheese dishes, and pizza. When ripened and smoked, jalapeños are known as *chiles chipotles.*

Pasilla A long (about 6 inches), narrow pepper with wide shoulders. When fresh, it is dark green to near black and may be identified in Latin markets as *chile chilaca;* when dried, it is chocolate brown. It has a deep, rich flavor and is moderately hot. Fresh ones are toasted and skinned before using in recipes; often they are cut into strips for use in soups, stews, and casseroles. Dried pasilla chiles are often ground for use in table sauces or seafood dishes.

Pepperoncini The small green pepper that is packed in vinegar, bottled, and sold in Italian markets and supermarkets. It is often used to garnish green salads or antipasto platters. A yellow variety, also pickled in vinegar and bottled, is imported from Greece and is available in some markets. Both are only slightly piquant.

Poblano Also known as the *chile ancho* (see Ancho). Ranging from 2½ to 6 inches in length and from dark green to near black, Ancho chiles are wide at the shoulder but taper to a point at the bottom. Flavor ranges from slightly hot to hot. They are usually roasted and peeled before using in recipes. Widely used in Mexico, they are stuffed with cheese, coated with batter and fried to make *chiles rellenos,* or are cut into strips for use in casseroles, soups, and sauces.

Whole chiles, mild or hot, will dry in several weeks at room temperature. When they are dry, crumble or grind them for use in chili recipes and other spicy-hot dishes.

Serrano A slender, very hot green chile, usually about 2 inches long. In Mexico it is used raw in guacamole and some salsas crudas and is cooked in other salsas. Serrano chiles are also commercially pickled.

Yellow Wax Pepper Also known as the Hungarian wax pepper or *chile guero*, it is pale yellow and usually about 5 inches long. It may be used raw in salsas; toasted, seeded, and used in salads; pickled and canned; and cooked in stews. It is extremely pungent.

Selection Fresh hot chiles should have a smooth skin without dry cracks. They should feel firm and look shiny.

Storage Wrap fresh chiles in paper towels and refrigerate for up to three weeks (they will sweat and deteriorate rapidly in plastic bags). Dried red chiles are perishable. Store them in an airtight container in a cool, dark, dry place for up to three or four months; for longer storage, refrigerate.

Preparation Hot peppers require caution in handling. Some people are extremely sensitive to the capsaicin in the pepper seeds and veins. The capsaicin irritates their skin and, if hands touch tongue or eyes, the discomfort can be severe. Wear rubber gloves when handling hot peppers until you can gauge your sensitivity. Always wash hands well after handling peppers.

Fresh hot chiles are often charred and peeled before use (see Roasting and Peeling Peppers, page 425).

Because the capsaicin in peppers is in the seeds and ribs, removing these parts significantly reduces a pepper's kick. If a recipe calls for whole hot peppers, you can reduce the heat by halving the peppers and cutting away seeds and ribs.

Dried red chiles can be ground in a pepper mill, clean coffee grinder, or electric minichopper, or with a mortar and pestle. When removing lid from appliance, keep head well out of the way because escaping fumes can burn.

Dried chiles are sometimes soaked in warm water to soften before using. Follow recipe instructions.

NACHOS

This popular translation of a traditional Mexican snack offers a balance of flavors and textures.. Beer is the perfect beverage to cool the heat of the peppers. Another way to tame their spiciness is to remove the ribs and seeds.

> 1 package (12 oz) corn tortilla chips
> ½ cup green jalapeños, minced
> ½ cup green onions, chopped
> 2¼ cups shredded Monterey jack or
>   sharp Cheddar cheese

Preheat oven to 400° F. Place tortilla chips in a single layer on 2 baking sheets. Sprinkle with jalapeños and green onions. Cover with shredded cheese. Bake until cheese melts (about 5 minutes). Serve warm from oven.

Serves 8 as an appetizer or 4 as a light lunch.

CHILES RELLENOS

A classic Mexican dish, *chile relleno* is certainly a favorite in the United States. The chile relleno is a large, mild, green cooking chile that has been roasted, cleaned, and peeled; filled and dipped in batter; and fried until puffed and golden. In Mexico the chile relleno is always served in a sauce. There are three distinct schools of thought on the egg batter in which the chile is dipped: The batter may be flat, fluffy, or extra fluffy. The recipe that follows is right in the middle and the easiest to manage. If you want flatter chiles rellenos, just beat the eggs without separating them. For fluffier chiles rellenos, fold in one tablespoon flour for each egg in the recipe.

Although in Mexico the chile relleno is most often filled with a spiced shredded meat mixture, in the United States it is usually filled with cheese, as in this version. In Mexico the cheese-filled chile relleno is identified on menus as *Chile relleno con queso*. The chile relleno is usually served as a main dish but it can also be served as a vegetable side dish or as a brunch dish. For directions on how to roast chiles, see page 425.

A variation of chile relleno is *chile en nogada,* a classic in its own right that features a meat-and-fruit filling and a walnut cream sauce. The dish originated in Puebla, the walnut capital of Mexico, and is served traditionally on Mexico's two independence days.

> 6 large, mild, green chiles, roasted and peeled,
>   leaving on stems (or canned whole green chiles)
> ½ pound jack or Colby cheese, cut into strips
>   approximately ½ inch wide, 2 inches long,
>   and ¼ inch thick
>   Flour
> 4 eggs, separated
>   Oil 1 inch deep, for frying
>   Sour cream and cilantro, for garnish

Tomato Sauce

> 1 tablespoon vegetable oil
> ½ cup chopped onion
> 2 cloves garlic, crushed
> 1 can (28 oz) solid-pack tomatoes, puréed
>   briefly in blender
> 3½ cups Chicken Stock (see page 560)

1. Carefully slit each chile lengthwise along one side; remove seeds and veins. Fill each chile with several strips of cheese, roll in flour, and set aside.

2. Beat egg whites until stiff; slightly beat yolks and fold into whites. Heat oil in a large skillet to 400° F. Drop a large spoonful of egg mixture into oil; lay a chile in the middle, top with another spoonful of egg, and smooth the egg to enclose all sides. Carefully baste the top with hot oil, to set. Cook until golden on the underside (about 1 minute); turn and cook again until golden on the underside. Drain on paper towels while preparing Tomato Sauce.

3. Carefully place the rellenos into the tomato sauce and simmer gently to heat thoroughly (about 15 minutes). Do not cook too long or batter will begin to break away.

4. Serve with some of the sauce, and garnish with a dab of sour cream and a few cilantro leaves.

Serves 3 to 6.

Tomato Sauce   Heat oil in a large saucepan. Add onion and garlic and cook only until onion is soft. Add puréed tomatoes and stock, bring to a boil, reduce heat, and simmer 5 minutes.

Makes about 6 cups.

■ PINTO BEAN CHILI

This beef and pinto bean chili may strike you as the most traditional version.

>   1   **cup dried pinto beans, rinsed and drained**
>   3   **cups water**
>   2   **pounds boneless beef chuck, fat trimmed, cut in 1-inch cubes**
>   2   **tablespoons butter or margarine**
>   1   **large onion, finely chopped**
>   1   **clove garlic, minced**
>   2   **teaspoons salt**
>   1   **teaspoon ground cumin**
>   1   **tablespoon chili powder**
>   1   **can (1 lb) tomatoes**
>   1   **can (4 oz) diced green chiles**
>   1   **can (8 oz) tomato sauce**
>   **Shredded Cheddar cheese (optional)**

1. In a large, heavy saucepan, bring beans and the water to a boil. Boil briskly for 2 minutes; then remove from heat, cover, and let stand for 1 hour.

2. In a large, deep frying pan or Dutch oven, brown beef cubes well on all sides, about half at a time, in butter over medium-high heat, removing and reserving meat as it browns. When all the beef is removed from pan, add onion to pan and cook, stirring often, until soft and lightly browned. Return beef to pan. Mix in garlic, beans and their liquid, salt, cumin, chili powder, tomatoes (coarsely chopped) and their liquid, and green chiles.

3. Bring to a boil, cover, reduce heat, and simmer until beef and beans are tender (2 to 2½ hours).

4. Mix in tomato sauce and cook, uncovered, stirring occasionally, until chili is thickened to your taste (about 15 minutes).

5. Serve bowls of hot chili with cheese for sprinkling, if desired.

Serves 6 to 8.

Recipes and Related Information
Guacamole, 15; Salsa Cruda, 521; Salsa Verde, 580.

PEPPERCORN

The *Piper nigrum* vine, native to Asia, produces the world's most-used spice. Pepper berries grow in clusters around a stem, like grapes. As they ripen, the tiny berries change from green to yellow to red. The familiar black peppercorn is picked when slightly underripe, then sun-dried until it blackens and shrivels. The white peppercorn is the same peppercorn harvested ripe and hulled; it is less pungent than the black. Green peppercorns are soft, undried, underripe *Piper nigrum* berries. Pink peppercorns are pungent pink berries unrelated to *Piper nigrum.*

Use   The importance of pepper to the world's cuisines and to world history cannot be underestimated. When Columbus and other explorers set off to search for trade routes to the Far East, they were hoping to find a shortcut to pepper. The pungent spice breathes life into dishes all over the world. Peppercorns are added to brines and marinades. Meats and fish are often seasoned with pepper before cooking; vegetables, soups, and salads with freshly ground black pepper. Cracked peppercorns are rubbed into the surface of a steak to make Steak au Poivre. Pepper is even used to heighten the flavor of strawberries and sweets. The milder and less visible white peppercorns are generally used with fish dishes. Green and pink peppercorns are a pungent seasoning for meats and fish.

Availability   Black and white peppercorns, whole and ground, are found in most supermarkets. Some specialty markets carry a variety of peppercorns in bulk. The best black varieties are Tellicherry, Lampong, and Allepeppy; the best white varieties are Muntok, Brazilian, and Sarawak. Green and pink peppercorns may be packed in water or vinegar or freeze-dried; they are available in some supermarkets and most specialty markets.

Selection   Packaged seasonings lose quality after a while; try to buy from a store that restocks its spice section fairly often.

Storage   Keep ground pepper in a cool, dark, dry place and replace every three months. Whole peppercorns will keep indefinitely in a cool, dark, dry place. Once opened, green peppercorns in water will last for one week refrigerated airtight; green peppercorns in brine will last for a month in their brine in an airtight container in the refrigerator. Discard green or pink peppercorns when they turn dark. Store freeze-dried green or pink peppercorns in a cool, dry, dark place for up to six months.

Preparation   Black and white peppers are most pungent when ground just before use. Keep a pepper mill on hand for easy last-minute grinding.

Recipes and Related Information
Steak au Poivre, 41; Tartar Sauce With Green Peppercorns, 520.

an oil; the resulting pastry is crumbly, rather than flaky, because an oil has more coating power than a solid fat and so covers many more of the flour particles (rather than making layers). You can produce a good pie crust by using all shortening, all lard, all butter, or a combination of these in any of the basic pie crust recipes in this entry. Keep in mind the effect that the type of fat will have on the crust.

Liquid   Some liquid, usually water, is needed in a pie or tart dough so that the flour particles can form a dough; the liquid also acts as a leavening when it converts to steam during baking. However, the minimum amount of water should be used; too much liquid will make a tough crust. It is always better to begin by adding the smaller amount of liquid suggested in the recipe. If more liquid is needed, add a few teaspoons or 1 tablespoon at a time until the desired consistency is reached. For flakiness, use ice water or ice-cold liquids so as not to melt the fat.

Acid   Sometimes acidic lemon juice, vinegar, sour cream, or even crème fraîche is added to the dough to relax the gluten and tenderize the crust.

Salt   When added, salt improves the flavor and color of the baked crust.

Sugar   Although not all doughs contain sugar, those that do include it for the flavor and color it imparts when it caramelizes.

EQUIPMENT FOR MAKING PIES AND TARTS

It is entirely possible to make a pie crust with the fingertips and to roll it out on the countertop with a wine bottle. However, if you have some basic pastry-making equipment in your kitchen, the process will be faster and simpler. Unless you make many pies at a time, you really only need one pie plate, preferably heat-resistant glass or heavyweight aluminum; 9 inches is the standard size. For tarts, choose a fluted pan of tinned steel with a removable bottom. Miniature tinned steel tart pans are available for tartlets.

Also helpful are a pastry blender, a rolling pin (15 inches is a versatile length), a sharp knife and other cutters, a fluted pastry-cutting wheel, a ruler, aluminum foil or parchment paper, and metal or ceramic pie weights (or dried beans). Some recipes recommend that juicy pies or delicate tarts bake on a baking sheet; a heavyweight aluminum one is best. Some cooks like to use a cloth rolling pin sleeve and a pastry cloth on which to roll dough. The same results can be achieved by keeping the work surface and rolling pin lightly dusted with flour at all times when rolling out pastry.

Other equipment useful for pastry making includes kitchen staples such as wooden spoons, spatulas, measuring spoons and cups, mixing bowls, cooking racks, a quality portable or electric stand mixer with a strong motor, and a food processor with metal blade.

MAKING THE DOUGH

Pie crusts can be mixed with the fingertips, a wire pastry blender, two knives, the paddle attachment of a heavy-duty mixer, or a food processor. The process—called cutting in or rubbing in—literally whittles the fat into smaller and smaller flour-coated pieces (see CUT IN); the fineness of texture depends on the type of pastry you are making. For flaky pie crusts, the fat should be in discrete pieces that will then layer with the dough. For tarts, the fat is mixed in more uniformly.

Chill fat; when using more than one type, soften the fats, mix them together, and then chill this mixture. When using a food processor to make pastry that contains solid vegetable shortening, first measure and freeze the fat before cutting it into the flour. By doing this, the pastry will resist the heat produced by the action of the machine. If butter, margarine, or lard is used, the fat need only be chilled rather than frozen. Cut fats in quickly; overmixing results in oily pastry.

ROLLING OUT PIE AND TART PASTRY

Let chilled dough soften slightly before rolling. Place dough on lightly floured surface; sprinkle a little flour on top of dough or rub some on rolling pin. Roll out dough from center toward edge (easing pressure near edge of dough) ⅛ inch thick and 2 inches larger than the pie plate or 1½ inches larger than the tart tin. Carefully lift dough and give a quarter turn after each rolling, reflouring surfaces as needed to prevent sticking and tearing. Cupping hands slightly, occasionally reshape dough into a circle. If dough cracks or tears, brush a small flat piece of dough with water and apply as a patch (patching is preferred to rerolling, which toughens dough; see PATCH).

To Transfer Dough to Pie Plate or Tart Tin   Place rolling pin just to one side of center of dough. Lightly and gently drape half of dough over rolling pin, rest dough across pie plate, and unfold dough onto pie plate. Fit dough into plate with fingertips or a small ball of dough. For tart, trim dough even with top of tart tin or band. Do not stretch dough or crust will shrink as it bakes. Pie or tart shell may be frozen at this point.

For a Single-Crust Pie   Trim edge so it extends ½ inch to 1 inch beyond edge of pie plate. Fold edges of dough under. Finish edges (see opposite page). Blind bake or fill and bake.

For a Double-Crust Pie   Trim lower crust even with rim of pie plate. Roll out second piece of dough (for top) slightly thinner than bottom crust. Fill pie; brush rim of bottom crust with cold water. Place top crust on pie; press edges to seal; trim edge to ½ inch from rim and finish edges (see opposite page). Cut steam vents (slits or designs) in top crust before or after crust is on pie. Bake according to recipe directions.

DECORATIVE FINISHES

The top crust of a double-crust pie can be left plain or enhanced with applied cutouts made from dough scraps. Roll out scraps as thin as possible; use cookie cutters or a knife to cut out shapes that relate to the filling—little apples and leaves or berries and vines—or design your own: stars, flowers, even initials (see Apple Pie, page 437). Brush cutouts with water and press into place on the top crust. You may brush the top crust with one of the following glazes: milk and a sprinkling of sugar, cream, or, for a shiny brown glaze, egg or egg yolks lightly beaten with a pinch of salt and 1 teaspoon of water.

A woven lattice top allows the filling to show through and is extremely attractive (see Strawberry-Rhubarb Pie, page 498). To form a lattice, line pie plate with pastry and trim bottom crust to ½ inch beyond rim. Roll out a circle of dough 2 inches larger than rim of pie plate for lattice top; with a knife or fluted pastry wheel and a ruler, cut strips of dough ½ inch wide. Fill pie. Lay half of the strips of pastry, ¾ inches apart, across pie. Fold back every other strip at center. Lay a strip across the unfolded strips; unfold other strips over this. Fold back the alternating strips (ones that were flat the last time) and lay the next strip ¾ inch from the last. Continue until half of pie is covered with lattice pattern. Repeat this procedure on other side of pie. Trim lattice strips to match edge of bottom crust; lift lattice strips at edge and moisten rim of crust underneath; press lattice strips onto bottom crust at edge of pie. Flute edges.

To make attractive edges (see below for instructions for a variety of pastry crust edges) for single- or double-crust pies, allow pastry to extend ½ inch to 1 inch beyond rim of pie plate. Fold edge of dough under so it is even with the edge of the pie plate to create a raised, even rim.

Fork-fluted edge *Trim pastry even with rim of pie plate. Firmly press tines of fork into pastry around entire rim of pie plate.*

Fluted edge *Place left index finger on inside of rim, pointing toward outside of shell. Pinch pastry into V shape between right index finger and thumb; repeat along entire edge. Pinch again to sharpen points.*

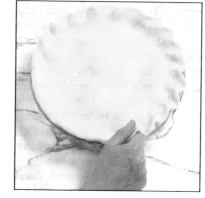

Rope edge *Press thumb at an angle into pastry and pinch pastry toward thumb with bent index finger; repeat along entire edge.*

Ruffle edge *Place left thumb and index finger 1 inch apart on edge of pastry, pointing toward outside of shell. Gently pull pastry between them toward outside of shell with right index finger; repeat along entire edge.*

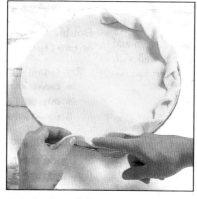

Spiral edge *Trim pastry even with edge of pie plate. Brush rim with water. Cut long, straight, ¾-inch strips of pastry. Press one end of strip to rim, twist strip, and press into rim with index finger after each twist.*

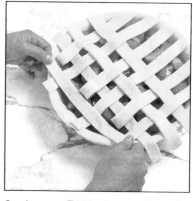

Lattice top *Fold back every other strip. Lay a strip across unfolded strips; unfold strips to cover pie and fold back the strips that were at first left lying flat. Lay next strip and repeat folding and unfolding procedure.*

One of the simplest and finest ways to cook salmon (or almost any fish) is to poach it in a court bouillon made with dry white wine.

■ POACHED FISH STEAKS WITH FRESH HERBS AND CREAM

Poached fish may be served plain, but it is usually better with a sauce. Often the poaching liquid itself can be the basis for the sauce. This recipe can serve as a model for countless dishes; it can be made with different varieties of fish, for example, or with mushrooms, tomatoes, or shellfish added to the sauce. The variations are limited only by your imagination.

    4 halibut, salmon, or turbot steaks (1 in. thick)
    ½ cup whipping cream
    4 cups Wine Court Bouillon (see page 450) or
       Fish Fumet (see page 451)
    2 tablespoons chopped fresh herbs, such as
       chives, parsley, basil, or chervil
       Salt and freshly ground pepper, to taste
       Rind of ½ lemon

1. Take fish and cream out of refrigerator at least 15 minutes ahead of cooking to let them come to room temperature.

2. Choose a deep skillet just large enough to hold fish steaks in one layer. Heat Wine Court Bouillon over moderate heat until it just reaches simmering point. Slide fish steaks into simmering stock. Adjust heat so stock simmers slowly, being careful not to let it boil.

3. Cook fish to the slightly underdone stage—about 7 minutes for salmon and 8 to 9 minutes for halibut or turbot. (To test for doneness, insert a thin skewer or toothpick into thickest part of fish. There should be some resistance in center.) Transfer almost-cooked steaks to a warm platter; cover loosely with aluminum foil to keep them warm.

4. Pour out half the liquid, reserving it for another use. Turn heat to high and boil stock until it is reduced by two thirds. Add cream and reduce sauce until it is slightly thickened. Turn down heat, stir in herbs, and season to taste with salt and pepper.

5. Return fish steaks to skillet to reheat slightly in sauce. Serve steaks topped with sauce and sprinkle a little lemon rind over top of each.

Serves 4.

Recipes and Related Information
Basic Poached Eggs, 199; Cold Fillet of Sole With Cilantro, Lime, and Pomegranate, 232; Rosé Pears in Chocolate Bath, 612.

POMEGRANATE

The pomegranate is an autumn fruit, about the size of a large orange. Most of the varieties produced in the United States have a red skin, but at least one variety, the Paper-Shell, has a yellow skin with a pink blush. Inside the thin hard skin are hundreds of small seeds, each one surrounded by juicy red pulp. The seeds are clustered in cells separated from each other by a bitter white membrane. Along with their surrounding pulp, the seeds can be eaten whole, or the juice may be expressed from them. Pomegranate juice is refreshingly both tart and sweet; however, it is a vivid reddish pink and it stains viciously.

Use Pomegranates are a refreshing snack or dessert eaten out of hand, although it requires some know-how to eat them (see Preparation). Pomegranate seeds make a bright red garnish for salads, fruit cups, desserts, and main courses. Turkish cooks sprinkle them on sweet custards; Arab cooks stuff baked fish with walnuts and pomegranate seeds. Pomegranate juice is used in punches and cocktails; although historically this juice was the basis for grenadine, a sweet pomegranate-flavored syrup used in many cocktails, many grenadine syrups today contain none. Pomegranate juice adds a sweet-tart flavor to marinades and basting sauces.

Availability Fresh pomegranates are sold from September through December, with peak supplies in October. Bottled pomegranate juice and syrup are available in Middle Eastern markets and some specialty stores.

Selection Choose fresh pomegranates that aren't rock hard, with plenty of color and without cracks or splits.

Storage They will keep in a plastic bag in the refrigerator for several weeks. Refrigerate pomegranate juice and syrup after opening. The syrup will keep indefinitely, but the juice should be used within a few days.

Preparation　Perhaps the easiest way to eat a pomegranate out of hand is to roll it repeatedly over a hard surface to reduce pulp to juice; keep rolling until fruit feels soft and full of juice. Then carefully pierce fruit in one place with a skewer and suck out juice. Alternatively, slit fruit with a knife and pull it apart into sections. Use a small spoon or your fingers to dig seed clusters away from bitter membranes. To juice a fresh pomegranate, use a fruit juicer or a reamer, but wear an apron to protect yourself from spattering juice.

■ RUSSIAN MARINATED LAMB ON SKEWERS

Many Russian recipes call for the piquant, magenta juice of autumn pomegranates for marinating lamb. Serve the skewered lamb with a rice pilaf and lightly sautéed zucchini.

- ½ **cup fresh pomegranate juice**
- 2 **tablespoons fresh lemon juice**
- 1 **small onion, finely chopped**
- 2 **tablespoons vegetable oil**
- 1 **clove garlic, minced**
- ½ **teaspoon salt**
  Dash freshly ground pepper
- 2 **pounds cubed boneless lean lamb shoulder or leg**
- 2 **green onions, thinly sliced (with part of tops), for garnish**
  Lemon wedges and parsley sprigs, for garnish

1. In a shallow glass, ceramic, or stainless steel bowl, mix pomegranate and lemon juice, chopped onion, oil, garlic, salt, and pepper. Stir in cubed lamb. Cover and refrigerate for 4 to 5 hours or overnight.

2. Preheat broiler. Drain meat and divide it among six skewers. Broil, about 4 inches from heat, turning once, until well browned on both sides (8 to 10 minutes). Serve immediately, sprinkled with green onions and garnished with lemon and parsley.

Serves 6.

Recipes and Related Information
Cold Fillet of Sole With Cilantro, Lime, and Pomegranate, 232.

POPCORN

Some food historians and archaeologists believe that popcorn is the world's oldest form of corn (see GRAIN, Corn). It is at least 7,000 years old. Native Americans brought popcorn to the first Thanksgiving in 1621. The early settlers must have been surprised at the kernels' transformation: The hard dried corn, when heated in oil, bursts into a snowy white, fluffy ball. As millions of moviegoers know, its bland, faintly cornlike flavor makes it an excellent vehicle for melted butter and salt.

Use　Popcorn is a snack food that has become a fixture at sporting events and in movie theaters. It is also coated with molasses and butter and mixed with peanuts to make caramel corn.

Availability　Unpopped popcorn is sold in all supermarkets. Although a variety of home popcorn machines are available, it is easy to pop popcorn with only a heavy lidded saucepan (see Preparation). Special popcorn for making in a microwave oven is also widely available. Popped and flavored popcorn can be purchased from some mail-order sources and specialty stores.

Storage　Unpopped popcorn should be stored in a tightly covered jar in a cool, dry place or in the refrigerator. It will keep for up to one year.

Preparation　Add 1 tablespoon of oil to a 4-quart saucepan; set over high heat. When oil is hot, add ½ cup corn kernels. Cover pan and shake continuously over heat until popping ceases. Add melted butter and salt to taste. One-half cup unpopped popcorn makes about 1 quart popped corn. To make popcorn with a hot-air popcorn maker, follow manufacturer's directions.

The piquant, reddish pink juice of pomegranates is an ingredient in many Russian recipes for marinating lamb. Squeeze this fresh fall fruit to make a tasty marinade for broiling boneless cubes of lamb on skewers. Take the precaution of wearing rubber gloves while handling the pomegranate to protect your hands from vibrantly colored stains.

dry place. Once prosciutto is cut, keep exposed surface covered and use within a few weeks.

Smithfield, Virginia, and Other Country Hams These hams are usually made from corn- or peanut-fed hogs. In a typical procedure (which varies from producer to producer), the legs are salted for about four weeks, then washed, coated with peppercorns, refrigerated for about two weeks, then smoked for about 10 days. After smoking the meat is aged for 6 to 12 months. The resulting ham may be served raw like prosciutto (see page 461), in very thin slices because it is quite salty. In the South, however, it is often cooked. To cook a Smithfield ham (or similar country ham), soak the ham for 12 to 24 hours in several changes of cold water. Using a stiff brush, scrub off any surface mold. Then cover with cold water, bring to a boil, and simmer until the small bone near the shank moves easily (15 to 20 minutes per pound). Save the cooking water for cooking greens. Slice away ham rind with a sharp knife. If desired, coat fat with brown sugar and bread crumbs and bake in a hot (400° F) oven until glazed (about 20 minutes). Let cool to room temperature before slicing thinly. Country ham can be sliced, covered with gravy, and served with grits; added to bean or vegetable dishes; or served cold with hot biscuits. Smithfield hams are available from some specialty markets and mail-order sources. See Prosciutto (page 461) for storage directions.

▦ CIDER-BAKED COUNTRY HAM

In this treatment the ham is baked with cider so that simmering on the stovetop is unnecessary.

> 1 **Smithfield ham or country-style ham (12 to 14 lb)**
> 4 **cups apple cider**
> ½ **cup bourbon**
>   **Brown sugar, for glaze**

1. Soak ham in several changes of cold water for at least 24 hours. Scrub under cold running water with a stiff brush and wipe dry.

2. Preheat oven to 350° F. Place a long sheet of heavy aluminum foil across the bottom of a shallow roasting pan with ends of sheet extending from each side of pan (foil should be long enough to make a tent for ham). Place ham on foil, pour on cider, and seal foil around ham. Bake until ham is cooked through and tender (about 4 hours).

3. Remove ham from oven and allow to cool until it can be handled. Discard aluminum foil. Remove drippings (save fat if desired). Gently and carefully remove skin, leaving a thick layer of fat. Score fat in a diamond pattern with a sharp knife, and return ham to oven for 15 minutes to heat surface. Slide out oven shelf so that ham is fully exposed. Heat bourbon in a small saucepan and pour it over ham. Be sure that nothing flammable is near oven opening. Using a long match and exercising great caution, light bourbon. When flames die

down, spread brown sugar over fat, and slide oven shelf back in. Continue baking until sugar forms a dark melted glaze (about 15 minutes).

Serves 8 to 10.

▦ COUNTRY HAM SLICES WITH RED-EYE GRAVY

All ham slices will be enlivened by this surprising sauce. The secret is black coffee.

> 4 **slices (½ in. thick) country or old-fashioned ham, cooked or uncooked (see Note)**
> 4 **tablespoons rendered drippings from baked ham or vegetable oil**
> ¼ **cup firmly packed light brown sugar**
> ½ **cup strong black brewed coffee**

1. Score through fat at edges of ham slices to keep them from curling. Heat drippings in a large, heavy skillet. Add ham and sauté over medium heat, turning several times, until lightly browned on both sides (20 to 25 minutes if using uncooked slices, about 10 minutes if cooked).

2. Remove ham and keep warm. Stir sugar into pan juices and cook at low heat, stirring constantly, until sugar dissolves. Add coffee and simmer until gravy turns rich brown (about 5 minutes); do not boil. Pour gravy over ham and serve.

Serves 4.

Note If you are using uncooked slices of a salty, dry-cured ham, add 1 cup of water to skillet along with ham. Ham will absorb all the water by the time it is cooked through; add more water if original amount is absorbed too quickly.

SALT PORK

Cut from the pork belly, salt pork is white fat streaked with lean meat. It is salted like bacon but not smoked. Most salt pork is extremely salty and should be blanched before use. Cover with cold water, bring to a boil, simmer 3 minutes, and drain. Fry a small amount and taste; if too salty, blanch again. After blanching, it can be diced, rendered (see RENDER), and used to add flavor to green beans, cabbage, or bean soups. Rendered salt pork can be added to cornbread or dumplings. It is a traditional flavoring in clam chowder and baked beans. In the American South, it is often cooked with potherbs such as collards or mustard greens.

Many supermarkets carry packaged salt pork in 6- to 8-ounce chunks. It is also available from most meat markets. Salt pork can be refrigerated, tightly wrapped, for up to a month or frozen for several months.

Recipes: Boston Baked Beans, 34; New England Clam Chowder, 539.

POTATO

Although they were introduced late, potatoes are a significant part of the American diet today and are now common on all continents. Native to Central and South America, the potato was unknown in Europe until the late sixteenth century and didn't arrive in North America until the early eighteenth century. Because it is hardy and easy to grow, it is always one of the least expensive vegetables in the market. Widespread cultivation of the potato has made it one of the world's most important food crops.

Use Because potatoes are so important to the diets of people all around the world, it is difficult to give a meaningful overview of the ways they are used. In the United States potatoes are typically boiled, mashed, baked, sautéed, or fried. Mashed potatoes may be combined with another puréed vegetable, such as celeriac, chestnuts, or parsnips. Baked potatoes are served whole, with butter and/or sour cream. Raw potatoes may be sliced thin and sautéed, or grated and sautéed to make hash browns. Cooked, cubed, and sautéed potatoes are often flavored with onion and green pepper and served with breakfast eggs. When potatoes are cut into finger-length strips and deep-fried, they are known as French fries and are a staple of the American fast-food industry, especially as the accepted companion to hamburgers.

The French slice potatoes thinly and bake them with butter and cream to make a gratin Dauphinois; when meat stock is used instead of cream and when a topping of grated Gruyère cheese is added, the dish becomes gratin Savoyard. Vichyssoise, a cold potato and leek soup, is now a classic. Italian cooks make dumplings called *gnocchi* from potatoes. Germans and Hungarians add mashed potatoes to bread for improved flavor and texture. Swedish cooks bake potato strips with cream and anchovies to make Jansson's temptation and, like the Germans, fry thin pancakes of grated potatoes. *Lefser* is a Norwegian flatbread based on potatoes and cooked on a griddle. Russian cooks add boiled potatoes to herring salad and bake grated potatoes into pudding with onions and egg. Potatoes are also distilled into vodka in the Soviet Union. In Peru, where potatoes have long been a staple, they are boiled and garnished with a spicy chile and cheese sauce. Indian cooks deep-fry potato slices in chick-pea batter, sauté them with aromatic spices, or curry them. Potatoes are not widely used in Asia, but are known there. Almost everywhere in the world, potatoes are a major food source.

Apart from their use as a food, potatoes are a good salt absorber. An oversalted soup can occasionally be salvaged by adding potato slices and simmering until the salt is sufficiently absorbed. The potatoes are discarded before serving.

Availability Potatoes are sold in supermarkets the year around. There is no peak season because crops in different areas mature at different times and potatoes

store well. Potatoes are also available in the freezer case, in the form of frozen French fries, hash browns, and other precooked shapes. Canned boiled potatoes are also found in supermarkets, as are dried potato flakes and instant mashed potatoes.

The main potato varieties, and their suitability to various cooking tasks, are as follows.

Red Skinned (New) This type has a thin red skin and a crisp white flesh. It is a waxy potato, excellent for boiling in the skin and serving whole. Because it cubes neatly after boiling and absorbs dressing readily, it is good for potato salad. Red-skinned potatoes may also be rubbed with olive oil and baked whole; they will maintain their firm, waxy texture. There are several varieties of red-skinned potatoes, but they are rarely identified by variety in the supermarket.

Russet or Idaho This standard baking potato is generally 4 to 6 inches long, about 2 inches in diameter, with a rough brown skin. The ivory flesh is dry and fluffy when baked. It is a good potato for mashing and for deep-frying, as it does not readily absorb the frying oil.

French fries are the most popular of all potato dishes. Serve them with a thick grilled steak or with fried fish in the English tradition of fish and chips. The recipe is on page 468.

White Rose A waxy potato, the White Rose is a long, white potato with a thin ivory-colored skin. It is best for boiling but may be baked or deep-fried. Like the russet, it is recommended for French fries because it does not readily absorb the frying oil.

Other potatoes that are becoming increasingly available include:

Blue Included in this category are such varieties as Blue Carib and All Blue. They have grayish blue skin and inky blue flesh. Delicate in flavor, they should simply be boiled and buttered.

Finnish Yellow Wax As its name suggest, this light-skinned variety has yellow meat and a waxy texture. Boil in the skin and dress with butter or use in potato salads.

German Fingerling This is a small, light-skinned potato with a lumpy shape and yellow flesh. It has a waxy flesh and should be boiled whole and buttered, or coated with olive oil and baked in a covered casserole until tender when pierced with a knife.

Rose Fir Small and waxy-fleshed, the Rose Fir has thin pink to red skin. It has a creamy texture and delicate flavor and is best when simply boiled and buttered.

Selection The most important distinction to draw between potato varieties is between the starchy or mealy types (best for baking) and the waxy types (best for boiling). A starchy type falls apart when boiled; a waxy type does not develop the desired dry, fluffy texture when baked. See Availability.

When selecting potatoes, look for firm specimens. New potatoes should be of a fairly uniform size to make cooking easier. Mature baking potatoes should be dry and well shaped, without sprouting. Avoid potatoes with a greenish cast. They have been exposed to too much light, either sunlight or artificial light, and may be bitter.

Storage Potatoes keep best in a cool, dark, dry place. Do not refrigerate. They should keep for two to three weeks without sprouting.

Preparation Peel if desired; otherwise, scrub skin well. Potatoes oxidize quickly; drop peeled potatoes into water immediately to slow browning.

Cooking See BAKE, BOIL, DEEP-FRY, PANFRY, PUREE, STEAM.

■ BASIC BAKED POTATO

Use russet potatoes for baking. Remember to pierce the potatoes just after removing them from the oven. Potatoes cook much faster in a microwave oven, even when you are cooking a number of them (see chart, at right). They need to be pierced before they cook.

> **3 large baking potatoes (1½ to 2 lb total)**
> **Oil or melted butter, for coating**
> **Butter, sour cream, snipped fresh chives,**
> **crumbled cooked bacon, for garnish (optional)**

1. Preheat oven to 400° F. Rub potatoes all over with oil. Set on baking sheet or directly on oven rack.

2. Bake until tender (about 45 minutes). Immediately pierce with a fork. Slit lengthwise or slice in half, and top with a pat of butter, sour cream, snipped fresh chives, or crumbled cooked bacon (if desired).

Serves 3 to 6.

POTATOES IN THE MICROWAVE OVEN

Choose whole potatoes of even size; pierce in several places with fork. Cook at 100 percent power the following times (for 6- to 8-ounce potatoes). Touch potatoes at end of cooking time. If they are very hard, cook another one or two minutes, then let them stand. They will finish cooking in the standing time.

Amount	Approximate Cooking Time	Standing Time
1	4–6 minutes	5 minutes
2	6–8 minutes	5 minutes
4	8–12 minutes	5 minutes

■ DUCHESSE POTATOES

An old-fashioned potato ricer makes quick work of mashing potatoes and eliminates offending lumps. Duchesse Potatoes are an embellished version of simple American fare.

> **4 large russet or other baking potatoes**
> **(about 2½ lb)**
> **½ teaspoon salt**
> **¼ teaspoon white pepper**
> **6 tablespoons unsalted butter**
> **2 egg yolks**
> **1 egg beaten with 1 tablespoon water, for coating**

1. Peel and coarsely dice potatoes; place in a 4-quart saucepan and cover with water. Bring to a boil, reduce heat, and simmer until tender (25 to 30 minutes); drain. Force potatoes through a ricer or mash with a potato masher. Stir in salt, pepper, 5 tablespoons butter, and egg yolks. Cool briefly.

2. Preheat oven to 400° F. Butter a baking sheet with remaining butter or line with parchment paper. Place potato mixture into a pastry bag fitted with a 1-inch open-star tip (to give a fluted design) and pipe mounds 2 inches by 2 inches in diameter onto prepared baking sheet. Alternatively, form into egg-shaped mounds with two tablespoons and place on prepared baking sheet. Brush potatoes with egg wash. Bake until golden brown and crusty (about 20 minutes).

Serves 8.

POTATO PANCAKES

Homemade applesauce and sour cream can turn this simple side dish into a satisfying meal. Shred potatoes with a grater or in a food processor fitted with a shredding disk.

   3 large baking potatoes, peeled and shredded
   1 small onion, minced
   1 teaspoon salt
   ½ teaspoon freshly ground pepper
   1 egg
   4 tablespoons dry bread crumbs
   ½ cup vegetable oil, for frying
      Sour cream and applesauce, for garnish

In a large bowl, stir together shredded potatoes, onion, salt, pepper, egg, and bread crumbs. In a medium, heavy-bottomed skillet, heat oil over medium heat. For each pancake, use 2 to 3 tablespoons potato mixture; flatten in skillet to about ½ inch thick. Sauté pancakes until crisp and golden brown (12 to 15 minutes); turn and cook second side 6 minutes. Remove from pan and serve with a dollop of sour cream and a scoop of applesauce (if desired).

Serves 6.

POMMES SOUFFLES

Twice-fried Pommes Soufflés are thinly sliced potatoes that puff into little pillows during the second dip in hot oil. For a perfect result use mature, starch-filled potatoes. Be sure to keep the oil at a constant temperature. There are always some failures, which are edible, so be prepared to make extra if presentation is important. The recipe can be made partially ahead and finished just before serving.

   2 large russet potatoes (about 1½ lb)
      Oil, for frying

1. Peel potatoes and cut each into a perfectly symmetrical rectangular block. Slicing along length (which is with the grain), cut perfectly uniform, ⅛-inch slices. Cut each slice in half. Trim corners, if desired, to form hexagonal shapes. Reserve in ice water for at least 15 minutes.

2. In a heavy-bottomed saucepan or wok, heat 4 inches of oil to 250° F. Remove potatoes from ice water and dry thoroughly. Immerse potato slices, one at a time, in hot oil. When slices rise, spoon hot oil over them and continute cooking until edges start to look translucent (about 6 minutes). Remove with a wire skimmer and drain on paper towels. Potatoes may be prepared ahead to this point and reserved; reserve oil in pan as well.

3. Just before serving, heat same oil to 375° F. Carefully lower partially fried potato slices into hot oil; they should puff immediately. Cook until golden brown and crisp (3 to 4 minutes). If some have not puffed, return to hot oil one more time. Remove with a wire skimmer and drain on paper towels. Serve immediately.

Serves 8.

POTATO NESTS

The nests are dramatic edible containers that can be filled with sautéed cherry tomatoes, sautéed leeks and peas, caramelized pearl onions, or even Pommes Soufflés. The nests can be prepared ahead and reheated in the oven. To shape the nests, you must use a special two-piece wire basket designed just for this preparation (see photograph, at right). Before using the potato-nest basket for the first time, it is important to season the baskets so the potatoes won't stick to them. To season, heat oil to 375° F in a heavy-bottomed kettle. Place basket in hot oil and let sit for about 5 minutes. Turn off heat and leave basket in oil about 1 hour. Remove basket from oil and wipe dry.

   2 large russet potatoes (about 1½ lb)
      Oil, for frying

1. Peel potatoes, julienne, and set in bowl of cold water to keep from turning brown. In a heavy-bottomed kettle or wok, heat 4 inches of oil to 380° F. Remove one eighth of potatoes from water and thoroughly pat dry (or they won't brown properly). Place in larger basket of seasoned potato-nest fryer in a ¼-inch thick layer. Fit smaller basket over potato layer and secure tightly.

2. Hold fryer basket handle with a hot pad (wire will get too hot to hold safely in bare hand). Immerse in hot oil and deep-fry for about 4 minutes. Still protecting hand, lift fryer from oil and carefully remove small inner basket. Return potato-lined outer basket to hot oil and fry until golden brown (about 1 minute more).

3. Remove and loosen potato nest from wire basket and drain on paper towels. These may be prepared several hours ahead and reheated in a 300° F oven 5 to 8 minutes. Fill with your choice of filling and serve.

Serves 8.

SCALLOPED POTATOES

This traditional American dish is a perennial favorite accompaniment to roasts—meat or fowl. It is rich with a garlic-flavored cream sauce.

   2 tablespoons unsalted butter
  2½ pounds russet potatoes, peeled
   2 cups whipping cream
   1 cup milk
   1 clove garlic, minced (optional)
  1½ teaspoons salt
   ½ teaspoon freshly ground pepper

1. Preheat oven to 350° F. Grease a 3-quart baking dish with butter. Slice potatoes ⅛ inch thick; layer in baking dish.

2. In a medium bowl stir together cream, milk, garlic (if used), salt, and pepper. Pour over potatoes and bake until potatoes are tender when pierced with a knife (1 hour and 10 minutes). Serve hot.

Serves 8.

A basket fryer gives shape to foods such as shredded potatoes as they cook in deep fat. The resulting edible nest makes an attractive container for a variety of vegetables. See Potato Nests, at left.

POMMES ANNA

This rich potato "cake" is one of the classic dishes of French cuisine. A well-buttered, 8-inch cast-iron skillet is the perfect size and shape for this dish.

> 8   large baking potatoes
> 8   tablespoons butter, melted
> 1   tablespoon vegetable oil
> 1   tablespoon salt
> ½   teaspoon freshly ground pepper

1. Preheat oven to 475° F. Slice potatoes ⅛ inch thick; soak slices in ice water to prevent browning. At baking time, drain and pat dry.

2. In a heavy, 8-inch skillet, arrange one fourth of the potato slices in overlapping circles to fill pan. Shake pan gently while filling to keep potatoes from sticking. Season with ¼ teaspoon salt and ⅛ teaspoon pepper and drizzle with 2 tablespoons of the butter. Repeat layers with remaining ingredients.

3. Sauté on top of stove over medium heat 10 minutes, then bake for 1 hour. To serve, loosen potatoes by running a knife around edge of pan. Place a flat serving dish over pan, invert serving dish and skillet together, and lift skillet from potatoes. Serve immediately.

Serves 8.

Garlicky Pommes Anna   Add 4 cloves minced garlic to melted butter before pouring over potato layers.

Parmesan Pommes Anna   Mince 5 shallots and stir into melted butter with ¼ cup freshly grated good-quality Parmesan cheese.

DOWN-HOME MASHED POTATOES

Mashed potatoes need not be uniformly smooth; in fact, a few small lumps improve the texture. Nor should the milk be premeasured and heated; the quantity needed will depend on the type and age of the potatoes. (Mealy baking potatoes that have been stored for a long time take more milk than new potatoes.) Simply pour milk in gradually, beating after every addition, until potatoes are just right. A few minutes in the oven before serving will reheat and puff up the potatoes. If you have a potato ricer, use it to mash the potatoes.

> 1   medium-large (about 11 oz) potato per person
> 1   tablespoon butter for each potato
>   Milk, as needed (¼ to ½ cup per potato)
>   Salt and white pepper, to taste
>   Paprika, for garnish

1. Bring a large pot of salted water to a boil. Meanwhile, peel potatoes and quarter or halve them (depending on size). Drop potatoes into pot as they are peeled, even if water is not quite boiling. Cook potatoes over high heat until fork-tender (about 25 minutes after water comes to a boil). Some pieces can be left a little underdone. Drain well.

2. Place potatoes and butter in a large bowl. Using a potato masher or fork, coarsely mash them together. Make a well in center and pour in a small amount of milk.

3. With an electric mixer (*not* a blender or food processor, which will turn potatoes into a starchy goo), beat potatoes, adding more milk a little at a time as needed, until desired texture is obtained. Tasting carefully, add salt and pepper. At this point, potatoes can be set aside, uncovered, until the rest of dinner is nearly ready. A half hour before serving time, preheat oven to 350° F.

4. Mound potatoes in an ovenproof casserole, sprinkle with paprika, and bake uncovered 20 minutes.

TWICE-BAKED POTATOES WITH WISCONSIN CHEDDAR CHEESE

For special occasions, potatoes put on company manners—here halved, their flesh scooped from their shells, mixed with seasonings, and returned to the shell to bake. This dish is convenient because it can be prepared ahead, then baked to serve with a sumptuous beef roast.

> 3   large baking potatoes (1½ to 2 lb total)
> 3   tablespoons butter or margarine
> ¼   teaspoon salt
> ⅛   teaspoon ground white pepper
> 1   egg yolk, beaten with 3 tablespoons milk
> 2   tablespoons snipped fresh chives
> 1½   cups (6 oz) grated sharp Cheddar cheese (Wisconsin, if possible)

1. Preheat oven to 400° F. Scrub potatoes and pierce each in several places with a fork. Rub all over with butter, using about 1 tablespoon. Bake potatoes until tender in the center when tested with a fork (about 45 minutes).

2. Remove potatoes from oven and cut each in half lengthwise. Reduce oven temperature to 350° F. When potatoes are cool enough to handle, scoop out centers, leaving a shell about ¼ inch thick. Place shells in a shallow baking pan.

3. In a medium bowl combine hot scooped-out potato, remaining butter, salt, and pepper; add egg yolk mixture. Using an electric mixer, beat until fluffy and well combined. Stir in chives and 1 cup cheese.

4. Mound potato mixture into hollowed-out shells, dividing it evenly. Sprinkle with remaining cheese. (Potatoes can be prepared ahead to this point. Cover and refrigerate for up to one day; let stand at room temperature for about 30 minutes before baking.)

5. Bake until potatoes are heated through (15 to 20 minutes).

Serves 6.

BAKED POTATO SKINS

These crisp shells are delicious served as is. To serve as part of a brunch menu, fill with scrambled or poached eggs or Cheddar cheese.

6 small baking potatoes (4 to 5 in. long)
¼ cup butter or margarine
¼ teaspoon paprika
Pinch white pepper

1. Preheat oven to 400° F. Scrub potatoes, pat dry, and rub skins lightly with a little of the butter. Pierce potatoes in several places with a fork.

2. Bake potatoes until tender when pierced (45 minutes to 1 hour). When cool enough to handle, cut in halves lengthwise and scoop out potato, leaving a thin shell about ⅛ inch thick. Reserve potato for other dishes.

3. Place skins on a baking sheet. Melt butter in a small pan with paprika and white pepper. Stir. Brush insides of potato skins with butter mixture.

4. Bake potato skins until crisp and golden (18 to 20 minutes). (For variety, try adding grated Cheddar cheese, crumbled bacon, green onion, or chives.)

Serves 6.

COTTAGE FRIED POTATOES

Give Cottage Fried Potatoes a down-home appeal by cooking, slicing, and frying them with the skins on.

5 medium potatoes
2 tablespoons *each* butter or margarine
and vegetable oil
⅛ teaspoon paprika
Salt and coarsely ground pepper

1. Scrub potatoes well. Cook, in their skins, in boiling salted water until about half cooked (15 to 20 minutes). Without peeling, slice potatoes about ⅛ inch thick.

2. In a large, heavy frying pan over medium-low heat, melt butter with oil and paprika. Add potatoes. Sprinkle lightly with salt and pepper.

3. Cook, using a wide spatula to lift and turn potatoes occasionally, until they are brown and crusty on all sides (20 to 25 minutes). Turn carefully to keep slices from breaking.

Serves 4 to 6.

HASH BROWN POTATOES

This is actually a seasoned potato cake made of shredded cooked potatoes crisply fried with a touch of onion.

5 medium potatoes
¼ cup finely chopped onion
½ teaspoon salt
Pinch white pepper
2 tablespoons *each* butter or margarine
and vegetable oil

1. Cook potatoes, in their skins, in boiling salted water until about half cooked (15 to 20 minutes). When cool enough to handle, slip off skins. Shred potatoes coarsely into a bowl. Mix lightly with onion, salt, and white pepper.

2. In a heavy, well-seasoned or nonstick 9- to 10-inch frying pan over medium heat, melt butter with 1 tablespoon oil. Add potatoes, pressing down with a spatula. Cook over low heat (without stirring) until potatoes are brown and crusty on bottom (12 to 15 minutes).

3. Loosen edges with a spatula. Cover pan with a plate, invert potatoes onto it, and add remaining tablespoon oil to pan. Swirl to coat pan well. Slide potatoes back into pan and cook until bottom is well browned and crusty (12 to 15 minutes).

4. Serve from pan or invert onto a warm serving plate.

Serves 6.

A trio of delicious potato dishes—cottage fries, potato skins, and hash browns—makes delicious breakfast fare. Serve with eggs and sausage, ham, or bacon.

FRENCH-FRIED POTATOES

Most types of potatoes can be fried, but russets or other baking potatoes are especially suitable because they absorb less oil. Putting the raw potatoes in cold water removes excess starch so they do not stick to one another during frying. Because French fries are best when fried twice, this recipe calls for a first frying at a relatively low temperature, followed by a second frying at a high temperature. This method makes meal preparation easy because after the first frying the potatoes can stand at room temperature until just before serving.

> 2 pounds large baking potatoes, peeled
> 8 cups (at least) vegetable oil, for deep-frying
> Salt

1. For the best results, read DEEP-FRY and SAUTE before beginning if these are techniques you don't use often.

2. If potatoes are over 4 inches long, halve them crosswise. Cut in lengthwise slices about ⅜ inch wide, then cut each slice in lengthwise strips about ⅜ inch wide. Trim irregular edges. As they are cut, drop potato sticks into a large bowl of cold water.

3. Rinse potatoes and drain well in a colander. Using paper towels, thoroughly pat them dry in small batches. This step is very important because fat will bubble up violently if potatoes are even slightly wet.

4. Line trays with two layers of paper towels. Heat oil in deep fryer or deep, heavy saucepan to about 340° F on a deep-fat thermometer, or test oil with a piece of potato (oil should foam up around it).

5. Dip a frying basket or a large skimmer into hot oil, then put about one third to one half of the potatoes in basket or skimmer and carefully lower into hot oil. Do not overfill because fat that bubbles up vigorously when potatoes are added can be dangerous. If using a basket, leave it in oil during frying; remove skimmer.

6. Fry potatoes until tender but pale (about 5 minutes). Check by pressing one; it should crush easily. Use slotted skimmer to remove potatoes to towel-lined trays. Reheat oil before adding next batch. Potatoes can be left for a few hours at room temperature.

7. About 10 minutes before serving, heat oil in deep fryer or deep, heavy saucepan to about 375° F on a deep-fat thermometer. Line more trays with two layers of paper towels.

8. Carefully put about half of the potatoes in frying basket or large skimmer. Carefully lower into hot oil. Fry until golden brown (about 2 minutes). Lift out basket or remove potatoes with skimmer and let drain briefly over pan. Transfer to towel-lined trays. Repeat with remaining potato slices.

9. Sprinkle potatoes with salt and toss gently. Serve immediately.

Serves 4.

HOMEMADE POTATO CHIPS

Better than any store-bought chip, this homemade version is fried twice for extra crispness. As a welcome bonus, the potato skins can be buttered and baked until golden and crisp. For best results leave a little potato flesh on the skins when you peel them.

> 3 large russet potatoes
> Peanut or corn oil, for deep-frying
> Coarse salt

1. Peel potatoes. Slice potatoes ¼ inch thick and place in a bowl of ice water until ready to fry.

2. In a heavy skillet or deep fryer, heat at least 3 inches of oil to 375° F. Dry potatoes well between kitchen towels. Add potatoes to hot oil and fry until lightly golden. Drain on paper towels.

3. Raise temperature of oil to 400° F and refry potatoes until very crisp and golden. (If doubling or tripling recipe, do second frying with fresh oil.) Drain on paper towels, salt lightly, and serve immediately.

Makes about 5 dozen chips.

Recipes and Related Information
Chive Potato Salad, 123; Church-Social Potato Salad, 506; Leg of Lamb With Garlic, Potatoes, and Onions, 337; New Potatoes With Caviar, 107; Thyme-Scented Chicken With Potatoes, Bacon, and Baby Onions, 578; Vichyssoise, 566.

POULTRY

Domesticated birds fattened for the table are referred to as *poultry*. Chicken, duck, turkey, squab, Rock Cornish game hen, and goose are the best-known examples of poultry in this country, although pheasant, partridge, and other game birds are now being raised on a small scale in some regions.

Twentieth-century scientific breeding has changed the shape of the birds we eat, giving us poultry with broad, meaty breasts and little fat. Improved efficiency in poultry raising has changed the shape of the poultry business: Most chickens today are raised in confinement to keep their muscles from toughening, and they are fed a specially formulated diet to bring them quickly to market weight. Increased efficiency in poultry processing has kept the price of chicken low, making it probably the most popular meat on the American table. However, many claim that today's supermarket chicken tastes bland compared with chicken that has been allowed to range freely for its feed. For those interested in tasting the difference, free-range chickens are being raised for specialty markets in some parts of the country; they are more expensive and usually tougher than supermarket chicken, but some consumers may find that their flavor outweighs the other drawbacks.

Use Poultry appears on the table as an appetizer, in soups, salads, and sandwiches, and as a main course. Jewish chicken soup with matzo balls, southern fried chicken, Peking duck, German roast goose with apples, and roast turkey with stuffing and giblet gravy are among the many ways that cooks around the world use poultry.

POULTRY PRIMER

At the market, poultry is grouped by species (such as chicken, turkey, and duck), and by class (for example, broilers, fryers, and roasters). Within each class, birds may be grouped by physical characteristics, primarily age, which in turn determine the cooking method (see Which Bird To Buy?, at right).

Type	Age	Size	Cooking Method
Chicken			
Poussin	Under 6 weeks	1 lb	Broil, Grill, Roast, Sauté
Rock Cornish game hen	4–5 weeks	1–1½ lbs	Broil, Grill, Roast, Sauté
Broiler	7–9 weeks	1½–2 lbs	Broil, Grill, Roast, Sauté
Fryer	9–12 weeks	3–4 lbs	Broil, Grill, Fry, Roast
Roaster	10–20 weeks	Over 5 lbs	Braise, Fry, Roast, Stew
Capon	16–20 weeks	6–9 lbs	Roast
Stewing chicken	Over 10 months	4–6 lbs	Braise, Stew, Make stock
Turkey			
Fryer-roaster	Under 16 weeks	4–8 lbs	Roast
Young turkey			
Hen	14–22 weeks	7–15 lbs	Roast
Tom	14–22 weeks	15–25+ lbs	Roast
Mature turkey	Over 15 months	12–25 lbs	Stew, Make stock
Other			
Duckling	8–16 weeks	3–5½ lbs	Broil, Roast
Young goose	Over 6 months	4–14 lbs	Roast
Pheasant	6 weeks	2–3 lbs	Bake, Roast
Quail	Under 6 weeks	¼–½ lb	Broil, Grill, Roast, Sauté
Squab	Under 6 weeks	¾ lb	Broil, Grill, Roast, Sauté

Availability Poultry is sold in many forms: fresh and frozen, whole, ready-to-cook parts, and processed meat products such as rolls, delicatessen meats, and hot dogs. Most supermarkets carry fresh chicken and fresh turkey parts all year. Chinese markets are a good source for fresh duck and quail. Most specialty butchers can order fresh goose, duck, quail, squab, or poussin with sufficient notice. See specific poultry entries.

Selection Fresh poultry is very perishable. When purchased, it should not have an off-odor or off-color and should be quite dry. If poultry is packaged, there should not be any accumulated liquid on the tray or in the bag. Prepackaged fresh poultry often has a "sell by" date stamped on the label. This date, seven days after the bird was processed, is the recommended final day for store sale. Refrigerated at a cold temperature, the bird will keep several more days. For unwrapped poultry, ask the butcher how fresh it is and how soon it should be cooked.

When buying frozen poultry, avoid torn packages or birds with signs of freezer burn. Pink-tinged ice indicates the bird thawed and was refrozen; it will likely be dry.

Storage Fresh poultry should be used within one or two days of purchase, or frozen immediately. Refrigerating fresh poultry does not kill organisms that cause food spoilage; it only slows their growth. Spoiled meat will have a definite off odor and a slimy surface. Discard any meat that is of questionable freshness.

Prepackaged poultry can be left in its package, with transparent wrapping intact, for refrigerator storage. If the wrapping is torn, or if chicken is wrapped in butcher paper, unwrap, set the poultry on a plate, and cover loosely with aluminum foil or waxed paper.

Cooked poultry can be refrigerated for three or four days, well wrapped to keep it from drying out. Freeze for longer storage. Cooked poultry in broth or gravy should be refrigerated for only one or two days. Raw or cooked poultry should not be left at room temperature for more than one or two hours.

To freeze fresh poultry, wrap tightly in plastic wrap and overwrap with freezer paper; freeze for up to one year. Frozen poultry, if not to be used right away, should be placed immediately in home freezer. Remove store wrap; rewrap in fresh plastic and overwrap with freezer paper. Freeze for up to one year. See FREEZE, Timetable for Freezing.

For best quality, thaw frozen poultry slowly in refrigerator in its wrapping, allowing three to four hours defrosting time per pound. A large turkey may take up to three days; small birds should take one to two days. Frozen parts will thaw in one day.

For quicker thawing, thaw in waterproof, completely sealed wrapping under cold running water, or in cold water that is changed frequently to maintain a consistent temperature. A 5- to 9-pound bird will thaw this way in 4 to 6 hours. A bird over 9 pounds needs 8 to 12 hours.

TIPS

WHICH BIRD TO BUY?

Younger birds are more tender and are best suited for roasting, baking, grilling, sautéing, and frying. The terms to look for are the following.

- *For chicken: Rock Cornish game hen, broiler, fryer, roaster, and capon*
- *For turkey: young turkey, fryer roaster, young hen, and young tom*
- *For duck: duckling, young duckling, broiler duckling, fryer duckling, and roaster duckling*
- *For goose: young goose*
- *For pigeon: squab*

   Older birds need long, slow cooking with moist heat to break down tough connective tissue; they should be used in stews, braises, and fricassees, or for stock.

- *For chicken: mature chicken, hen, fowl, and baking and stewing chicken*
- *For turkey: mature turkey, yearling turkey, and old turkey (hen or tom)*
- *For duck and goose: mature and old.*

Thaw poultry at room temperature only if you are able to monitor the process carefully, because bacteria that can cause food poisoning grow rapidly at this temperature. To thaw a turkey, place the unwrapped frozen bird in a double-walled brown bag or several thicknesses of newspaper. The paper keeps the surface of the bird cold while the interior thaws. Frozen small birds and frozen parts can be thawed in their wrappings. Refrigerate or cook thawed poultry as soon as possible.

Preparation All raw poultry should be cleaned and washed before cooking. Remove any clumps of visible fat around neck and tail. Remove innards (neck and giblets) from cavity. Use tweezers or fingernails to pull out any stray feathers or hairs. Wash quickly inside and out, pulling out any bloody bits from inside the bird. Pat dry with paper towels. Some whole birds are trussed, or tied together, before roasting for a more attractive appearance (see TRUSS). For a discussion about specific poultry techniques, see also BONE, CARVE, DISJOINT.

Cooking See BROIL, BRAISE, DEEP-FRY, GRILL, POACH, SAUTE, STEW, STIR-FRY, STOCK AND SOUP.

CHICKEN

As a mild-flavored meat, chicken lends itself readily to variation; in fact chicken is compatible with almost every herb, spice, and vegetable in the marketplace. When you consider the hundreds of ways that Americans prepare chicken and add to that the thousands of chicken dishes common to the rest of the world, it is clear that the options for the curious cook are virtually unlimited. As a lean, low-cholesterol meat, it is welcome in the diets of the many Americans trying to reduce their intake of fat and cholesterol.

Chicken figures in the cuisine of almost every country in the world. In this country fried chicken, roast chicken, and some form of baked chicken are in almost every cook's repertoire. Chicken is made into pot pies, stewed with dumplings, poached to make a flavorful broth that is the basis of countless soups, and chopped or sliced for a cold salad or sandwich filling.

In Mexico chicken is shredded to make fillings for tacos, enchiladas, and tamales. French cooks are famous for coq au vin (chicken in red wine). Italians roast chicken with rosemary or sauté it alla cacciatore. Spanish cooks pair chicken with rice, tomatoes, sausage, and shellfish to make paella. Chicken Kiev, deep-fried boneless breasts rolled around seasoned butter, is a Russian specialty. In Japan chicken is marinated in soy sauce, rice wine, and ginger and grilled, or steamed with cooked rice and egg to make the popular lunch dish called *donburi*. Chinese cooks stir-fry chicken with all manner of vegetables and seasonings; they also braise a whole chicken in soy sauce or smoke it over tea leaves.

In India chicken is highly spiced and braised in curries, or marinated in yogurt and spices and roasted in the tandoor (clay oven). In West Africa chicken is simmered with tomatoes and peanuts to make groundnut stew.

Both fresh and frozen chickens are widely available in supermarkets, either whole or cut into parts. Whole chickens are almost always less expensive, but some cooks prefer the convenience of precut, packaged parts. It is easy to cut up a chicken, and the method is well worth learning (see BONE, DISJOINT). The cook who buys whole chickens not only saves money but also gets the useful fat, the tasty giblets, and the bony parts for stock. Chickens may be cooked whole or cut into parts. The legs, thighs, breasts, and wings are the choice parts, with the bony wing tips, neck, and back often reserved for making stock.

Chickens are marketed in several different sizes, each with particular cooking requirements. See Which Bird to Buy? on page 469 for more information.

◼ ROAST CHICKEN WITH RICE, FRUIT, AND ALMOND STUFFING

Although roasting chickens are slightly more flavorful than frying chickens, both can be roasted. The stuffing for this chicken is a variation of rice pilaf. If you like, serve the rice as a side dish with any roast, instead of as a stuffing. In this case, cook the rice for a total of 18 minutes.

   ½ **cup slivered almonds**
   ¼ **cup vegetable oil**
   1 **small onion, finely chopped**
   1 **cup long-grain rice**
1½ **cups hot water**
   ½ **cup strained, fresh orange juice**
     Salt and freshly ground pepper, to taste
   1 **small apple, peeled, halved, and cored**
   ½ **cup raisins**
   ¼ **teaspoon ground cinnamon**
   1 **roasting chicken (3½ to 4 lb)**

1. Preheat oven to 400° F. Toast almonds in a baking dish in oven, stirring occasionally, until lightly browned (about 5 minutes). Transfer to a bowl and let cool.

2. In a deep frying pan, heat 3 tablespoons of the oil over low heat. Add onion and cook, stirring often, until tender (about 5 minutes). Increase heat to medium, add rice, and sauté for 2 minutes. Add the hot water, orange juice, salt, and pepper; bring to a boil. Reduce heat to low, cover, and cook for 10 minutes.

3. Dice apple. After rice has cooked 10 minutes, add apple and raisins to rice and stir very lightly with a fork. Cover and cook for 5 minutes; rice will be nearly tender. Stir in cinnamon and reserved almonds. Taste and add more salt and pepper, if needed.

4. Sprinkle chicken with salt and pepper on all sides. Spoon enough rice stuffing into chicken to fill it, but do not pack it too tightly; reserve extra stuffing at room temperature.

5. Set chicken on a rack in a roasting pan and roast until juices run clear when a skewer is inserted into thickest part of leg (about 1 hour). If juices are pink, continue roasting chicken a few more minutes. Transfer chicken to a carving board. Let stand 5 to 10 minutes before carving and serving.

6. Heat the remaining 1 tablespoon oil in a frying pan over low heat. Add remaining stuffing and cook, stirring often with a fork, until rice is tender and hot (about 3 minutes). Spoon into a serving dish.

7. Serve chicken and its stuffing on a platter. Serve remaining rice separately.

Serves 4.

■ CHICKEN KIEV

Unlike other coated foods, Chicken Kiev must be fried cold so that the butter trapped inside the chicken roll stays frozen. If allowed to thaw, the butter would leak out during frying. The herbed butter must be frozen one hour before you prepare the chicken rolls, and then the chicken rolls must chill one to two hours before they are cooked. If the rolls seem to be browning too quickly, remove them when they are golden and finish cooking in a 325° F oven 10 to 12 minutes.

    ½ cup butter, softened
    2 tablespoons chopped parsley
    1 clove garlic, crushed
    1 tablespoon snipped fresh chives
    ½ teaspoon salt
      Freshly ground pepper, to taste
    4 small whole chicken breasts, halved,
      boned, and skinned
    1 egg, lightly beaten
    2 cups dry bread crumbs
    4 cups vegetable oil, for frying
      Watercress sprigs, for garnish

Sauce Gruyère

    3 tablespoons butter
    3 tablespoons flour
    1 cup half-and-half
    ½ cup grated Gruyère cheese
      Salt and freshly ground pepper, to taste

1. In a medium bowl, using a wooden spoon, blend butter with parsley, garlic, chives, salt, and pepper (or blend mixture in food processor). Shape into a rectangular block, wrap in waxed paper, and freeze until solid (about 1 hour).

2. Wash chicken breast halves and pat dry. Pound breast halves between two pieces of waxed paper to ¼ inch thick. Cut frozen butter into eight sticks. Place one stick in the center of each half breast. Fold edges of breasts over butter and roll up tightly, completely enveloping butter with meat.

3. Brush each chicken roll with beaten egg. Put bread crumbs on a large square of waxed paper or on a plate, and coat rolls thoroughly with crumbs.

4. Transfer chicken rolls to a baking sheet, cover lightly with waxed paper, and refrigerate 1 to 2 hours to set coating.

5. In a heavy-bottomed, 3-quart saucepan, heat oil to 365° F as registered on a frying thermometer. Deep-fry rolls until golden brown all around (about 8 minutes per roll).

6. Gently remove with a slotted spoon to a baking sheet lined with paper towels. To hold, keep warm in a 200° F oven.

7. Serve Chicken Kiev with Sauce Gruyère and garnish with watercress.

Serves 8.

Sauce Gruyère In a small saucepan over medium heat, melt butter. Whisk in flour and cook briefly. Pour in half-and-half and cook until thickened. Stir in grated cheese and season with salt and pepper.

Makes about 1½ cups.

Diners delight in the burst of herbed butter released as they cut into Chicken Kiev. In the recipe at left, parsley, chives, and garlic flavor the butter; in classic versions, tarragon is the frequently used herb.

ABOUT CHICKEN LIVERS, GIBLETS, AND FAT

Chicken livers are enjoyed by many diners as a dish in themselves. Some supermarkets and all specialty poultry markets carry chicken livers, either fresh or frozen. Fresh livers and thawed frozen livers are perishable and should be used within one or two days; they may be tightly wrapped and frozen for up to three months (do not refreeze thawed livers). Pat them dry, flour them lightly, and sauté them in bacon fat with onions, bacon, and mushrooms; or sauté them in butter with Marsala; or sauté them with onions and chop them with hard-cooked eggs to make chopped chicken livers. Cooked livers may be added to stuffings or served with pasta, rice, or toast. After trim-

ming away tough outer skin and connective tissue, chicken giblets (heart and gizzard) may be chopped, sautéed, and added to stuffings or gravy.

Save any fat you pull from the neck or tail cavity. Render it slowly in a skillet over low heat with a little water, and store it in a tightly covered jar in the refrigerator (see RENDER). It will keep for one month; freeze for longer storage. Use chicken fat in place of butter for sautéing or spreading on bread. In Germany it is known as *schmaltz* and is important to the Jewish kitchen. Schmaltz is used in chopped chicken liver, in Matzo Balls, and wherever a flavorful cooking fat is desired.

■ DEEP-DISH CHICKEN PIE

Let this homey American dinner pie warm a cold winter evening. To speed up preparation, cook the filling a day or two ahead and refrigerate it, covered. To serve, bring it to room temperature and proceed with step 3.

>   1¼ cups flour
>   ¼ teaspoon salt
>   ¼ cup butter, cut in pieces
>   2 tablespoons lard, cut in pieces
>   1 egg
>   2 tablespoons cold water

Chicken Filling

>   1¼ cup butter
>   1 small onion, chopped
>   ¼ cup finely chopped celery
>   3 tablespoons flour
>   Pinch *each* freshly ground pepper and
>   freshly grated nutmeg
>   2 cups Chicken Stock (see page 560)
>   6 cups cubed cooked chicken
>   ½ cup fresh or frozen peas
>   ¼ pound mushrooms, quartered
>   2 small carrots, peeled and sliced
>   Salt and freshly ground pepper, to taste

1. Sift flour and salt into a bowl. Cut butter and lard into flour with a pastry blender until mixture is crumbly.

2. Separate egg and reserve white. Beat yolk with 1 tablespoon of the water and pour liquid into flour mixture. Stir with a wooden spoon until mixture begins to form a ball. With floured hands, lightly shape into a ball. Cover dough with waxed paper and refrigerate 1 hour.

3. Preheat oven to 425° F. Make filling and while it cools, roll out cold pastry on a floured surface into

a 12-inch circle. Mix reserved egg white with remaining tablespoon of the water; brush onto one side of pastry.

4. Pour cooled chicken mixture into a straight-sided, 9-inch-diameter baking dish about 2 inches deep. Place pastry, glazed side down, over filling. Trim pastry, flute edge, and cut slits in crust to allow steam to escape. Brush top with egg wash.

5. Bake until pastry is golden brown (30 to 40 minutes). Serve immediately.

Serves 8

Chicken Filling   In a saucepan over medium heat, melt butter; add onion and celery and cook until soft. Stir in flour; cook until thickened. Add pepper and nutmeg. Gradually stir in stock, stirring constantly, until mixture bubbles and thickens. Mix in chicken, peas, mushrooms, and carrots. Season with salt and pepper to taste. Set filling aside to cool.

■ CHICKEN CURRY WITH CONDIMENTS

Curry is not one spice but several, commonly consisting of cumin, coriander, black mustard seed, fenugreek, and turmeric (for the yellow color). The spiciness can be enhanced with the addition of chile pepper, although commercial curry powders are fiery enough for many palates. The condiments associated with traditional curry are both spicy and soothing: cilantro *raita*, cucumbers in yogurt, tomato chutney, mango chutney, minced green onion, coarsely chopped peanuts, shredded coconut, deep-fried garlic chips, diced green bell pepper, dried currants, and always lots of steamed *basmati* rice.

>   6 boneless, skinless chicken breasts
>   2 tablespoons vegetable oil
>   3 tablespoons unsalted butter
>   1 medium onion, diced
>   2 cloves garlic, minced
>   1 apple, diced
>   1 green bell pepper, diced
>   1 jalapeño chile, minced
>   2 tablespoons curry powder
>   ¼ cup flour
>   1½ to 2 cups Chicken Stock (see page 560)
>   ½ teaspoon salt

1. Cut chicken breasts into 2-inch cubes. Heat oil in a 14-inch skillet and sauté the chicken pieces over medium heat until lightly browned (about 12 minutes). Remove and reserve.

2. Melt butter in the same 14-inch skillet over medium heat. Stir in onion and garlic, and sauté until lightly browned (6 to 8 minutes). Stir in chicken pieces, apple, bell pepper, chile, curry powder, and flour. Cook for 5 minutes. Stir in Chicken Stock and simmer for 20 minutes to meld the flavors. Season with salt.

Serves 8.

■ CHICKEN MARENGO

Napoleon's chef created this dish for his commander-in-chief in 1800 after the Battle of Marengo. It was said to have been made from locally available ingredients—chicken, tomatoes, and garlic. This version also includes mushrooms, green pepper, and olives. It is a very flavorful poultry stew, and like all stews it improves if made ahead and gently reheated just before serving. Serve with rice pilaf.

12	pearl onions
1	roasting chicken (3 to 3½ lb), cut in pieces
2	teaspoons salt
½	teaspoon freshly ground pepper
¼	cup olive oil
4	tablespoons unsalted butter
1	clove garlic, minced
1	small onion, sliced
1	green bell pepper, sliced
5	small plum tomatoes, cut in large dice
1	teaspoon dried oregano
1	teaspoon dried basil
1	cup dry white wine
1	cup Chicken Stock (see page 560)
½	pound mushrooms, halved
½	cup pitted black olives, halved
2	tablespoons parsley, minced

1. In a large saucepan bring 1 quart of water to a boil. Blanch pearl onions for 1 minute. Trim root end, slip off skins, and cut an *x* in root end of each onion; reserve.

2. Season chicken pieces with salt and pepper. In a 4- to 5-quart Dutch oven, sauté chicken legs in oil and butter over medium-high heat 5 minutes; add breasts and brown another 5 minutes. Add garlic, onion, bell pepper, tomatoes, oregano, basil, wine, stock, and reserved onions to chicken. Reduce heat and simmer 20 minutes.

3. Add mushrooms and black olives to chicken and cook 10 more minutes. To serve, sprinkle with parsley.

Serves 6.

Recipes: Barbecued Chicken With Two Sauces, 294; Chicken Breasts With Grapes, 280; Chicken Breasts With Sherry, Cream, and Mushrooms, 611; Chicken in Half-Mourning, 583; Chicken or Duck Liver Mousse, 372; Chicken Quenelles, 241; Chicken Soup With Dumplings, 189; Chicken Stock, 560; Chicken With Forty Cloves of Garlic, 262; Chinese Chicken Salad, 508; Country Fried Chicken, 176; Curried Chicken or Duck Liver Pâté in Aspic, 416; Golden Chicken Stew With Cheese Dumplings, 192; Honeyed Chicken With Apricots, 557; Lemon Chicken Breasts, 339; Paper-Wrapped Chicken, 175; Perfectly Poached Chicken for Salads and Sandwiches, 451; Rich Chicken Stock, 561; Tandoori Chicken, 351; Three-Mushroom Chicken, 380; Thyme-Scented Chicken With Potatoes, Bacon, and Baby Onions, 578.

ROCK CORNISH GAME HEN AND POUSSIN

The Rock Cornish game hen is a hybrid bird with a dressed weight of about 1¼ pounds. The hens have a delicate flavor and all-white meat; they make attractive, if large, single servings.

The poussin is a young chicken slaughtered at less than six weeks. Its dressed weight is about 1 pound. It makes a large single serving or a small serving for two. Its flavor is delicate.

Rock Cornish hens and poussins can be used in similar fashion. Whole birds may be roasted, braised, or sautéed; roasted birds may be stuffed. Because of their small size, they are usually served either whole or halved. They may also be split down the backbone, flattened, and grilled or broiled. Their delicate flavor is complemented by butter and herbs. Almost any preparation for whole chicken may be adapted to Cornish hens and poussins.

Most supermarkets carry frozen Cornish hens the year around. A specialty butcher may be able to obtain fresh Cornish hens by special order. Fresh poussins are increasingly available in specialty markets; they may require special order.

See Selection, Storage, and Preparation for more information.

Recipes: Game Hens Coq au Vin, 58; Poussin Paprikash, 405.

TURKEY

This big-breasted, mild-flavored bird, native to the New World, was probably served at the first Thanksgiving. Today's domesticated turkey is not only a fixture on most Thanksgiving tables but is now increasingly appreciated the year around. As an inexpensive, low-calorie meat, it is suitable for dozens of preparations.

Despite the increased availability of turkey, it is still closely associated in most American minds with Thanksgiving and Christmas. The brown-breasted turkey, surrounded by cranberry sauce and sweet potatoes, is a modern reminder of the turkeys eaten by the Pilgrims at the first Thanksgiving. The turkey giblets (heart and gizzard) are minced and added to the gravy.

In this country turkey is also used in soups, casseroles, sandwiches, and salads. Sliced turkey breast, smoked or unsmoked, is popular fare for buffets and parties. Turkey may be creamed and served over spaghetti or rice. Thinly sliced raw turkey breast may be used in any preparation calling for veal scaloppine.

In Italy turkey breasts are breaded and fried, then baked with mozzarella and prosciutto. In Hungary turkey parts are wrapped in bacon, panfried, then braised in stock and sour cream. Greek cooks stuff turkey with a mixture of ground lamb, chestnuts, pine nuts, apples, rice, and bread crumbs. In Mexico turkey is braised with *mole poblano,* a dark chile sauce enriched with chocolate.

TIPS

COOKING CHICKEN AND TURKEY IN THE MICROWAVE OVEN

Chicken pieces cook quickly and are tender and juicy when cooked in a microwave oven. Because they cook so quickly, pieces get neither brown nor crisp. Before cooking brush chicken with a mixture of gravy browner and oil to add color, or coat with seasoned crumbs. Cover dish with waxed paper during cooking and rotate dish a half turn halfway through cooking. Microwave at 100 percent power: 2 chicken pieces, 4 to 6 minutes; 4 pieces, 6 to 10 minutes; 6 pieces, 8 to 12 minutes. Let chicken stand 5 minutes to finish cooking.

Small turkeys (6 to 12 pounds) can be microwaved successfully. Before cooking brush turkey with a mixture of gravy browner and oil to add color. Cook turkey (breast side down for half the cooking time; turn breast side up to finish) at 100 percent power, 6 to 7 minutes per pound, or at 50 percent power, 11 to 13 minutes per pound. Let turkey stand 20 minutes before carving to finish cooking.

Moist and tender, a beautifully roasted turkey is the festive focus of any celebration, whether for the holidays or for another special occasion.

The efforts of turkey farmers and marketers to make turkey more than a one-season food are visible in the supermarket. Fresh whole turkeys, as well as turkey parts and processed turkey products, are now widely available the year around. The forms in which turkey, fresh or frozen, are available include: whole birds; halves and quarters; boneless roasts; bone-in and boneless whole, halved, and sliced breasts; fillets; drumsticks; wings; drummettes; thighs; and ground turkey.

Convenience options include prebasted birds, injected with natural ingredients intended to keep the bird moist (properly roasted, a bird will be moist and juicy without prebasting, however); frozen stuffed birds; and pop-up or retractable thermometers that activate when the bird has reached an internal preset temperature determined by the manufacturer.

Most turkeys are marketed as young turkeys, which means they are 14 to 22 weeks old, either female or male (see Poultry Primer, page 469). Despite a long-held belief to the contrary, there is no difference in quality between a hen and a tom; hens are merely smaller.

See Selection, Storage, and Preparation for more information.

■ ROAST TURKEY WITH GIBLET GRAVY

There are many ways to roast a turkey: plain (without a cover), in a foil tent, in a paper bag, and, according to one probably tall story, in a sleeping bag. This basic recipe recommends roasting the turkey unstuffed for an optimally moist bird. Garlic butter is rubbed under the skin to flavor the breast, and chopped onion, parsnip, and carrot are added to the pan to flavor the drippings. The recipe prepares a small turkey that will serve 10 to 15 persons. For a larger bird, cook according to the timetable on page 500; use a meat thermometer as the most accurate means of determining when the turkey is done. It is unnecessary to increase the amounts of the other ingredients when cooking a larger bird.

> 1 turkey (10 to 12 lb)
> 1 clove garlic, crushed
> 1 cup butter, softened
> Salt
> 2 onions, cut in large chunks
> 2 parsnips, cut in large chunks
> 2 carrots, cut in large chunks

Giblet Gravy

> Giblets and neck from turkey
> ¼ cup butter
> ¼ cup flour
> Salt and freshly ground pepper

1. Preheat oven to 450° F. Remove innards from turkey and save for Giblet Gravy. Wash turkey and pat dry.

2. Gently free skin from breast meat, starting at neck end and continuing to tail.

3. Mix garlic with butter. Stuff garlic butter under breast skin. For a crisper skin, also butter outside surface. Salt turkey inside and out.

4. Truss turkey (see page 584) and set on a rack in a roasting pan. Surround with chunks of onion, parsnip, and carrot.

5. Set pan on middle rack of oven. Roast at 450° F for 30 minutes. Reduce oven to 325° F and continue to roast for another 1½ hours, or until done to suit, basting every 15 minutes.

6. When turkey is done, remove from pan and allow to rest for 20 to 30 minutes before carving. Set aside pan with drippings to make gravy.

Serves 10 to 15.

Giblet Gravy

1. Place giblets and neck from turkey in a saucepan and cover with water. Bring to a boil, then reduce heat and simmer 20 to 30 minutes. Drain giblet stock and reserve.

2. Cut giblets in small cubes and reserve.

3. When turkey is done, remove it from pan and set aside to rest while the gravy is being made. Add at least 1 cup water to roasting pan. Blend water with drippings, stirring and scraping with a wooden spoon to loosen any browned bits that may have stuck to bottom of pan. The water and pan drippings together should equal 2 cups. Reserve this liquid.

4. In a saucepan, melt butter. Whisk in flour and cook over medium heat until golden brown. Stir in reserved giblet stock and liquid from pan drippings. Stir constantly until thickened.

5. Season with salt and pepper. Stir in giblet cubes and serve with roast turkey.

Makes 2 cups.

DUCK

In its domesticated form, the dark-meated duck usually weighs about 4½ pounds. Because it is fattier and bonier than chicken or turkey, a 4½-pound duck will only feed two. Most of the meat is in the breasts, although the legs also offer enjoyable eating.

The rich meat of duck is complemented by fruit. The roasted bird is often partnered with cherries, oranges (as in duck à l'orange), figs, apples, or other fruit. Duck is almost always roasted or grilled because of its considerable fat content. Because the legs take longer to cook than the breast, some cooks remove the breast first and serve it separately; when the legs have finished cooking, they are served as a separate course, often with a green salad. Raw boneless duck breasts may be sautéed or grilled. They have a richness comparable to beef and may be served in similar fashion—with green peppercorns or red wine sauce, for example. Cold roast duck may be used in salads or sliced and served with chutney. In France duckling is considered a spring treat and is often served with spring vegetables such as peas or turnips. In China duck is a favored bird, prepared in dozens of ways. Among the many possibilities: It may be steamed, rubbed with soy sauce, and deep-fried; smoked over tea leaves; or air-dried, roasted, and served in the elaborate series of dishes that constitute Peking duck.

Inventive cooks have created uses for almost all parts of the duck. Chinese cooks braise the gelatinous duck feet. Duck fat is particularly flavorful, good for frying potatoes or omelets. Duck skin may be cut into small pieces and rendered for cracklings to sprinkle over salads. French cooks stuff the duck neck with a sausage mixture, sew it closed, and roast it. Duck liver makes a delicious pâté or may be sautéed in butter and served on toast. Duck foie gras, an expensive delicacy, is the buttery liver from specially fattened ducks. Cooked foie gras is served hot or cold, usually with toast.

Frozen duck is sold in many supermarkets. Fresh duck is available increasingly in specialty markets and is almost always available in Asian poultry markets. Imported duck foie gras is marketed in tins in specialty stores. Recently, domestic fresh duck foie gras has appeared on the market. As of this writing, it is available from specialty wholesalers catering primarily to the restaurant trade.

See Selection, Storage, and Preparation for more information.

▓ BROILED DUCK BREASTS WITH APRICOT-MUSTARD GLAZE

Usher in the first cool night of autumn with elegant broiled duck glazed with mustard and apricot jam. To complete the menu, serve Pommes Anna (see page 466), Sautéed Cherry Tomatoes (see page 582), and Baked Pear Tart (see page 423).

> 2 whole ducks (about 4½ lb each)
>   Salt and freshly ground pepper
> 1 clove garlic, slivered

Apricot-Mustard Glaze

> ½ cup apricot jam
> 3 tablespoons Dijon mustard
> 3 tablespoons soy sauce
> 3 tablespoons honey
> 1 clove garlic, minced

1. Wash ducks and pat dry. Remove innards. Bone ducks so that breasts are removed with skin attached. Reserve duck carcasses for stock and duck legs for another recipe (they can be used for Chinese Duck Salad, page 476).

2. Split duck breasts to make 4 half breasts. Remove visible fat from underside of skin. Season lightly with salt and pepper. Prick holes in skin covering breasts and insert garlic slivers.

3. Prepare Apricot-Mustard Glaze. Brush glaze on both sides of breast halves.

4. Preheat broiler. Broil breast halves, skin side down, about 6 inches from heat for 6 minutes. Turn and broil 2 to 3 minutes more. Be careful not to burn duck (if necessary, lower rack to slow cooking).

5. To serve, slice breasts on the bias and serve with remaining Apricot-Mustard Glaze.

Serves 4.

Apricot-Mustard Glaze   In a small bowl or jar with a lid, thoroughly combine jam, mustard, soy sauce, honey, and minced garlic.

Makes about 1 cup.

Leftovers can be glamorous, as demonstrated by Chinese Duck Salad, served cold on a bed of shredded lettuce and puffy rice vermicelli.

1. In a large, heavy-bottomed skillet, bring stock to a boil. Add duck legs, cover, and return to a boil. Reduce heat to medium-low and simmer, covered, until cooked (about 25 minutes). Remove duck legs and cool completely. When cool, remove skin and discard. Tear meat off bones and cut into small cubes.

2. In a medium bowl combine soy sauce, ginger, and garlic. Add duck meat and toss to coat. Cover and refrigerate 8 to 24 hours.

3. When ready to assemble salad, heat oil in wok to 365° F (measure with a deep-fat thermometer). Fry rice vermicelli, a handful at a time, until it puffs (30 to 60 seconds). Be careful not to let it brown. Remove with slotted spoon and drain on paper towel. Set aside.

4. Place lettuce in a large bowl. Remove duck from marinade with slotted spoon, drain, and pat dry. Toss with lettuce, green onions, and almonds, then with Soy Dressing. Serve surrounded with rice vermicelli.

Serves 4.

Soy Dressing In a small bowl or jar with a lid, combine oil, vinegar, sugar, and soy sauce.

Makes about 2¼ cups.

Recipes: Chicken or Duck Liver Mousse, 372; Curried Chicken or Duck Liver Pâté in Aspic, 416.

GOOSE

Like the duck, the goose is a dark-meat bird with a high proportion of bone and fat. Most of the meat is in the breast. In England, France, Scandinavia, and Germany, goose is the traditional choice for the Christmas feast. Its rich meat is flattered by the flavors of fruit such as apples, prunes, and pears. Because of its high fat content, it is almost always roasted. Some cooks prefer to put onions, apples, and bread in the cavity to flavor the bird and absorb fat; they then cook the stuffing separately to keep it from absorbing all the fat.

A whole goose offers other attractions for the cook. The long neck may be used like a sausage casing, stuffed, tied, and roasted. The fat is very flavorful, excellent for frying potatoes or eggs or for chilling and spreading on toast. In France some geese are force-fed to encourage the development of large livers; this foie gras, an expensive delicacy, resembles an extremely rich, smooth, and buttery pâté. After cooking it may be served hot or cold, usually accompanied by warm toast.

Frozen geese are available in some well-stocked supermarkets the year around. More supermarkets stock frozen geese at Christmas time. Look for fresh geese in specialty markets at Christmas time; most markets require advance ordering.

See Selection, Storage, and Preparation for more information.

■ CHINESE DUCK SALAD

Make this salad to use up the duck legs left over from Broiled Duck Breasts (see page 475). To toast almonds, cook in a small dry skillet over medium-high heat, stirring with a spoon, until golden brown (about 5 minutes).

   4 cups duck or Chicken Stock (see page 560)
   4 duck legs, washed and patted dry
   ½ cup soy sauce
   1 tablespoon minced fresh ginger
   1 clove garlic, minced
   2 cups vegetable oil
   3 ounces rice vermicelli
   1 head iceberg lettuce, washed and shredded
   2 green onions, thinly sliced
   ½ cup toasted slivered almonds

Soy Dressing

   1 cup oil
   ¾ cup rice wine vinegar
   ½ cup sugar
   2 tablespoons soy sauce

■ BRAISED GOOSE IN HARD CIDER

The hard cider in the pan juices infuses the goose with a wonderful apple flavor.

- 2 stalks celery, coarsely chopped
- 1 carrot, peeled and coarsely chopped
- 1 parsnip, peeled and coarsely chopped
- 1 medium onion, quartered
- 1 goose (about 14 lb)
  Salt and freshly ground pepper
- 4 cups hard cider

Pan Gravy

- ¼ cup flour
- 2 cups goose or Chicken Stock (see page 560)
  Salt and freshly ground pepper

1. Preheat oven to 450° F. In a large roasting pan, place celery, carrot, parsnip, and onion.

2. Remove giblets from goose. Wash goose and pat dry; remove excess fat. Pierce skin of goose several times with the tip of a knife. Sprinkle inside and out with salt and pepper. Tie legs together and set goose on vegetables in roasting pan.

3. Roast in center of middle rack of oven for 30 minutes. Reduce heat to 325° F. After roasting for an additional 1½ hours, pour hard cider into bottom of pan. Roast 1½ more hours (a total of 3½ hours), or until done to suit. Periodically skim fat from pan with a bulb baster.

4. When goose is done, remove it from oven; allow it to rest 30 minutes before carving. Serve with Pan Gravy.

Serves 10 to 12.

Pan Gravy Skim off all but ¼ cup fat from pan juices. Place roasting pan with juices over medium-high heat. Add flour and cook until golden brown, stirring constantly. Add stock, stirring and scraping with a wooden spoon to loosen any browned bits that may have stuck to bottom of pan. Cook and stir until texture of gravy is smooth and velvety. Season with salt and pepper.

Makes 3 cups.

SQUAB

The squab is a pigeon bred for the table. The dressed bird usually weighs under 1 pound and has dark meaty breasts with a rich flavor. Squabs are generally roasted or braised, with or without a stuffing. In China squab meat is minced, stir-fried, and served with lettuce wrappers; or is fried whole, carved, and served with a fragrant pepper salt. French cooks serve braised squab with spring peas.

Frozen squabs are available from some specialty markets. Fresh squab may be ordered from some butchers; some Asian poultry markets also carry fresh squab.

See Selection, Storage, and Preparation for more information.

■ SMOKED, STUFFED SQUABS WITH CALVADOS

Smoking the squabs is easy. You will need a kettle grill with cover for this recipe, as the birds smoke while they grill. Soak apple cuttings in water mixed with apple juice for two to four hours. When the fire is hot, put the cuttings on top of the coals, place the squabs on the grill, and set the cover in place.

- ⅓ cup apple juice
- ⅓ cup Calvados or applejack
- ⅓ cup vegetable oil
- 2 squabs (about ¾ lb each)

Stuffing

- ¼ cup Calvados or applejack
- ½ pippin apple, cubed
- 1 shallot, minced

Calvados Sauce

- ½ cup apple juice
- ¼ cup Calvados or applejack
- 1 tablespoon cornstarch mixed with
  2 tablespoons water

1. Make Stuffing. Set aside.

2. In a medium bowl combine apple juice, Calvados, and vegetable oil to make marinade.

3. Wash squabs and pat dry. Set in a pan just big enough to hold both birds. Pour marinade over squabs and marinate in refrigerator for 4 hours.

4. Remove squabs from marinade, reserving marinade for basting, and pat squab dry.

5. Insert Stuffing into squabs and tie legs together with kitchen string; tuck wings under.

6. Prepare fire. When coals are ready, grill squabs 5 inches from heat, breast side down, with cover on grill so that smoke can penetrate meat.

7. After 15 minutes turn squabs breast side up. Continue grilling, basting frequently with marinade, until breast meat springs back slightly when touched (about 10 minutes).

8. To serve, snip kitchen string and remove. Spoon out Stuffing and serve on the side. Smother squabs with Calvados Sauce.

Serves 2.

Stuffing In a small bowl mix together Calvados, apple, and shallot.

Makes about ½ cup.

Calvados Sauce In a small saucepan stir together apple juice, Calvados, and cornstarch paste. Simmer until thickened.

Makes ¾ cup.

QUAIL

Small, dark-meat birds, quail weigh about ½ pound each. Most recipes call for at least two per person. The legs and wings are inconsequential; most of the meat is in the breast. Quail are almost always cooked whole, roasted, braised, panfried, or deep-fried. They may be wrapped with bacon before roasting for added flavor and moisture. They may be stuffed with fresh herbs and then roasted; deep-fried and served with Chinese roasted pepper salt; or panfried in bacon fat and served for breakfast.

Frozen quail are available from some specialty butchers, who can also provide fresh quail by special order. Some Chinese markets also carry fresh quail.

See Selection, Storage, and Preparation for more information.

■ SAUTEED QUAIL WITH RED CURRANT SAUCE

The delicate quail, in their deep red sauce, would make a romantic Valentine's Day menu. Carry out the holiday motif by serving red caviar on toast hearts as a first course.

    4 quail
    Salt
    2 tablespoons butter
    1 tablespoon vegetable oil

Red Currant Sauce

    ¼ cup red currant jelly
    ¼ cup canned gooseberries with juice
    1 tablespoon red wine vinegar
    ⅛ teaspoon *each* ground cinnamon, ground nutmeg, and ground ginger

1. Wash quail and pat dry; truss. Sprinkle with salt. Heat butter and oil in a medium, heavy-bottomed sauté pan or skillet over medium-high heat.

2. Add quail and sauté until golden brown on all sides (about 4 minutes). Reduce heat to medium-low, cover, and cook until tender (12 to 15 minutes). Remove quail and set aside. Leave drippings in pan for sauce.

3. To serve, discard trussing strings. Return quail to sauté pan; pour sauce over quail and warm gently over medium heat for 2 minutes. Arrange birds on serving platter and spoon sauce over.

Serves 2.

Red Currant Sauce   In a small bowl combine jelly, gooseberries with juice, vinegar, and spices. Transfer to a small saucepan and cook over medium heat until jelly melts (about 3 minutes). Pour mixture into sauté pan, stirring and scraping with a wooden spoon to loosen any browned bits that may have stuck to the bottom of the pan. Cook over medium heat until heated through.

Makes about ½ cup.

POUND, TO

To flatten meat to a uniform thickness, usually about ¼ inch, for even cooking and an attractive appearance. Veal scallops are often compressed to ⅛ inch, which enables them to cook in mere seconds. Pounding also tenderizes tougher cuts by breaking down connective tissue that is difficult to chew. To prevent meat from tearing, place it between two sheets of plastic wrap. With the flat bottom of a meat pounder (not the edge, which will shred meat), pound with a downward stroke until meat is evenly flattened.

PREHEAT, TO

To warm an oven or broiler to a specified temperature before food is set in it. Heating oil or another fat in a skillet before adding food serves the same preparatory purpose as does preheating an oven, although it isn't called preheating. Foods that cook in dry heat—baked goods and roasts particularly—need that burst of hot air provided by a preheated oven before cooking or to create a crisp outer coat. Deep-fried foods will be soggy and greasy if cooked at too low a temperature. Preheating is less important for foods that use moist heat, such as stews and casseroles, or for oven-cooked foods that take several hours or more to finish. Most recipes will specify preheating, but some don't, so use your own judgment as to when the step will make a difference in the final product.

PREPARING PAN FOR BAKING

To release cooked food more easily and cleanly, baking pans, casseroles, and baking sheets are often coated with a thin layer of butter, oil, or shortening, or a light film of vegetable cooking spray as a first step. Some pans are also dusted with flour, sugar, crumbs, or grated cheeses. These coatings give batters, including sweet and savory soufflés, something to cling to as they rise. The layer of sugar, crumbs, or cheese adds a crisp coating or sandy texture as well as more flavor to the finished product.

Personal preference most often dictates which fat to use, and whether you want it to be neutral or flavored. Butter imparts a rich, distinctive taste; vegetable shortening, oils, and vegetable cooking spray do not have a flavor of their own. Applying the fat in a thin, even layer is really more important than which fat you choose. If the coating is unevenly applied, there is a chance the food will stick in the bare areas. If the layer is too thick, the food will be greasy. Liquid fats can be wiped on with a pastry brush, with your fingers, or with paper towels. Use your fingers or paper towels for solid fats.

Lining pans with parchment paper, aluminum foil, or waxed paper is another way to prevent sticking. It also facilitates cleanup. Cookies baked on parchment-lined baking sheets can be transferred to cooling racks simply by sliding the paper onto the rack. Sugar-rich meringues are easier to remove after baking if piped onto paper-covered baking sheets.

Nonstick pans should always be coated. Most recipes give instructions for preparing pans for baking. If not, experiment with different methods and use the one that works the best for you.

Recipes and Related Information
Baking Pans, for Batter and Dough, 18; Cake, 77.

PRICKLY PEAR

Also known as tuna, cactus pear, Indian fig, and barbary fig, the prickly pear is the fruit of the prickly pear cactus. It is an egg-shaped fruit, slightly larger than an egg, with skin that ranges from yellow to red. The skin has sharp spikes that are usually removed before it is sent to market. The sweet, moist flesh ranges from salmon or pink to magenta and contains small, hard seeds.

Use Peel and eat raw with lemon or lime (discard seeds). Purée for sorbet, ice cream, and dessert sauce.

Availability Fresh prickly pear can be purchased from September through December in Latin markets and some supermarkets.

Selection Choose firm but not rock-hard fruit with a shiny appearance. Hard ones will soften at room temperature in a few days.

Storage Refrigerate ripe prickly pears in a plastic bag and used within two or three days.

Preparation Remove any remaining sharp spines with pliers. Cut off ends, then peel fruit back from top to bottom with a sharp knife. To remove seeds, press fruit through a sieve or pass through a food mill.

▉ PRICKLY PEAR SNOW
Prickly pear tastes like a seedy watermelon. Prickly pear syrup is delicious as a topping on ice cream, in milk shakes, and in this light, refreshing, "southwestern nouvelle cuisine" sorbet. The sorbet will keep packaged airtight in the freezer two to three weeks.

½ cup sugar
1 cup water
6 prickly pears
1 tablespoon fresh lime or lemon juice
2 egg whites
  Pinch cream of tartar
½ teaspoon orange-peel liqueur

1. Heat sugar and the water together in a heavy, 2-quart saucepan over low heat, stirring occasionally until sugar dissolves. Simmer mixture for 10 minutes until it has reduced slightly and thickened but has not yet started to color.

2. Meanwhile, wearing thick rubber or leather gloves, halve prickly pears and spoon out pulp. (Handle prickly pears with care. Even storebought ones may have a few tiny spines that will stick to fingers. Discard shells before removing gloves.) Add prickly pear pulp and lime juice to reduced sugar mixture, and simmer until fruit is mushy (about 20 minutes).

3. Briefly purée prickly pear mixture in a food processor or blender. With a wooden spoon, push purée through a strainer into a bowl. Discard seeds left in strainer. Pour syrupy purée into two pie pans and freeze until partly solid (2½ hours), stirring purée after 1 hour and again 30 minutes later.

4. Beat egg whites with cream of tartar until they are stiff but not dry. Remove frozen purée from freezer and stir again (or purée again in food processor if it has become too firm to stir). Blend in orange liqueur, then fold purée into egg whites. Place sorbet in a serving bowl, cover with plastic wrap, and return to freezer until it chills to the consistency of ice cream (3 to 4 hours). Before serving, place in refrigerator for 30 minutes to soften slightly.

Serves 6 to 8.

Variation Use the syrup yielded at the end of step 3 as a sauce for vanilla ice cream or fresh fruit salad, or to lend a brilliant beet-red color to any fruit dessert.

PROOF, TO

A bread-baking term, *proof* is used two ways. The first meaning refers to the test for the potency of yeast: In a small bowl put ½ cup warm (about 110° F) water. Sprinkle in a pinch of sugar and 1 tablespoon active dry yeast (1 package) or 1 crumbled, compressed, small yeast cake. Stir and let sit 5 to 10 minutes to soften. If the yeast is alive, the surface of the liquid will form a thick foam. There's the proof. A lack of foam indicates that the yeast is most likely dead; discard that batch and begin again with a fresher package.

Proofing also describes the second rising of a yeast dough after it has risen, been punched down, and shaped. The dough sits in a warm spot (75° to 80° F) until it has doubled in bulk and retains the mark of your finger if pressed into it.

Recipes and Related Information
Yeast, 613; Yeast Bread, 613.

PREPARING BAKING PANS

To grease pan, use fingers, paper towel, or brush if using liquid fat. Apply a thin, even layer of butter, margarine, vegetable shortening, or oil, or spray with a fine mist of vegetable cooking spray. Use a light touch or surface of baked good will be gummy.

If lining pan with parchment paper, use pan as a template. Set pan on paper and trace around it with a pencil. Cut out just inside of pencil line. Set in pan and smooth to fit; remove and trim if too large.

If called for, dust pan lightly with flour, crumbs, or sugar. Hold pan at an angle over paper or sink, and tap gently to loosen excess coating. Let excess fall from pan.

PUFF PASTRY

Also called *pâte feuilletée*, puff pastry holds the distinction of being the most versatile, intriguing, and delicious of all the pastry doughs. Like conventional pie and tart pastry, puff pastry is made from very basic ingredients—flour, salt, water, and butter. The dough is much richer in butter than the others, however, and the butter is worked into the dough in a unique manner—not in one step, but re-peatedly, through a series of rollings and foldings. What results are paper-thin sheets of dough separated by equal-ly fine layers of fat. During baking the fat melts and re-leases steam that causes the dough to rise up to ten times its original height.

The dough is leavened solely by steam and hot air, rather than by yeast or chemical leaveners. Folding traps air within the dough. During baking the air fills the many spaces left by the butter when it melts. The air expands from the heat and puffs the pastry. Moisture from water in the dough and from the many layers of butter convert to steam when heated during baking, which also causes the dough to rise.

Close inspection of the airy, golden brown pastry re-veals hundreds of separate, crispy layers, one upon the other. The estimate is that more than 700 layers are cre-ated by the time the dough and butter have been rolled and folded the traditionally recommended six turns. The flavor and aroma of puff pastry are rich and buttery.

Volumes could be written on the attributes of puff pastry and its many sweet and savory applications. It can be made into pastry cases for all sorts of fillings in many shapes and sizes, freestanding pastry decorations, applied pastry decorations, hors d'oeuvres, cookies, and wrappers for meat, fish, cheese, and fruit *en croûte*.

PUFF PASTRY BASICS

The reputation of puff pastry for being temperamental and time-consuming causes many novice bakers to shy away from attempting to make it. Admittedly, making puff pastry is not a one-step procedure. But the process is nei-ther difficult nor time-consuming. Each step actually takes only 5 to 10 minutes to accomplish. Between steps, the dough rests in the refrigerator for about one hour. If you subtract the resting time from the total amount of time needed to make the dough, you will see that actual work-ing time is only 30 to 40 minutes.

Puff pastry dough is made from two basic elements: (1) a smooth, elastic dough called the *détrempe* and (2) a block of butter beaten until pliable. When dough and block of butter are the same temperature and consistency, the butter is wrapped up in the dough, and this lump of dough-wrapped butter is given six turns. To give the dough a turn, it is rolled out into a rectangle, folded into thirds like a business letter, and rotated a quarter turn (90 degrees) on the work surface. Each turn is an exact repetition of this rolling, folding, and turning process.

The end product of this turning is virgin puff pastry: puff pastry that has been given six turns and has not been rolled out, cut out, or shaped in any way. Some pastries require virgin puff pastry and some pastries can be made with puff pastry trimmings and scraps.

Don't throw away the trimmings left over after virgin puff pastry is cut. Layer scraps, wrap, and refrigerate for at least one hour. (They can be stored up to two days in the refrigerator or can be frozen for up to one month.) The scraps can then be rolled out into a sheet and used. All pastries can be made with virgin puff pastry, but in some cases—where a high, puffy rising is unnecessary—the scraps will suffice. They can be used quite successfully for the following: as the base for a dessert or as one of the layers of a dessert; for *mille-feuilles* or napoleons; as pastry cases for pies (blind baked without filling) to be used as a first course, an entrée, or a dessert.

INGREDIENTS FOR PUFF PASTRY

Use the ingredients recommended in the recipe. A com-bination of pastry flour and all-purpose flour yields a dough that will roll out easily and has enough strength to be rolled out without tearing and baked without breaking. The resulting dough can hold its shape when baked, but remains tender. You can use 50 percent pastry flour (soft flour) and 50 percent all-purpose flour (a combination of hard and soft flours) or 75 percent pastry flour and 25 percent hard flour (bread flour high in gluten). Fresh, cold, unsalted butter and ice water are essential.

PREPARING PUFF PASTRY

To produce the characteristic layers of dough and but-ter, the butter should be neither too soft nor too hard. Ideally, the dough and butter should be of equal tempera-ture and consistency, which is why the détrempe is chilled before the first rolling. Very soft butter will blend too thoroughly with the dough. The result will be crumbly rather than multilayered and flaky, much like a short pie crust. Butter that is too hard will shear through the dough, leaving holes that will allow steam and air, which leaven the dough, to escape.

The butter also should be plastic, which means that it can be manipulated. Usually, a recipe recommends that you beat the cold butter with a rolling pin to make it pli-able, although not work it so much that it loses its chill.

Temperature is critical, not only for butter but for all the ingredients, the equipment, and the room you are working in. The goal is to keep everything cool enough so the layers of butter stay separate from the layers of dough. Try to make puff pastry during the coolest part of the day, and on a day when you plan to be home for several hours. On warm days, chill the work surface and rolling pin for 30 minutes. If you have room, you can chill a portable marble slab or cutting board in the refrigerator. Other-wise, place on the work surface a rimmed baking sheet filled with ice cubes.

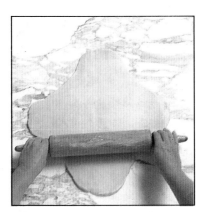

WORKING WITH PUFF PASTRY

Roll chilled détrempe (dough) into a rounded cross shape. Work surface and rolling pin should be chilled and lightly floured. When rolling, do not press down hard on dough; use even pressure. Roll dough thinner at edges.

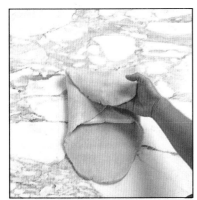

Place square of cold butter in center of dough cross. Wrap butter in dough as shown. If dough seems warm, return to refrigerator 10 minutes before rolling.

Complete wrap as if forming an envelope. Then for each turn, roll dough into a rectangle. Fold in thirds as if you were folding a business letter. Rotate a quarter turn clockwise (90 degrees), square edges, and either roll again or refrigerate, as directed in recipe. Remove any excess flour by brushing dough with a pastry brush before and after folding.

The dough also should chill between every two turns. This firms up the butter and relaxes the dough, making it easier to roll out without compressing the layers. The dough should also be allowed to rest in the refrigerator again just before it's baked so the baked puff pastry will maintain its original shape and size.

A marble work surface is best for puff pastry, as it is for other pastry doughs. It naturally maintains a temperature 20° F cooler than the air, and because it is nonporous, pastry won't stick to it. However, marble is expensive and quite heavy. An alternative is a cutting board made of white polycarbonate if you can find one of sufficiently large size. If you have one of these portable boards, make a lot of pastry, and have room in your refrigerator, store board on a refrigerator shelf to keep it at the proper cold temperature. Countertops made of plastic laminate are also suitable for making puff pastry. Chill when necessary with ice cubes and tray as described in Preparing Puff Pastry (see opposite page).

**CUTTING PUFF PASTRY:
UNBAKED AND BAKED**

Always cut puff pastry dough when cold and use a sharp knife. Cut straight down into dough with a clean, sharp movement. Do not drag knife through warm dough or you will seal layers of dough together, making it difficult for them to separate and rise to their fullest volume. Always trim away folded edge of puff pastry; if left, folded edge won't rise. Large pastries like vol-au-vents (see page 483) sometimes shrink out of shape in the oven. To help them rise straight, cut them at a slight angle: Slant the knife so that the edge of the pastry is slightly wider at the bottom. Flip pastry so top is wider. As it bakes, the pastry will rise evenly.

To make rectangular puff pastry cases out of baked pastry dough, slice puff pastry horizontally with a serrated knife. This will create a case, with a top and bottom, like a box, which can be filled with your choice of filling.

To serve pastry, cut with a serrated knife held at a 45-degree angle to the pastry. Use a gentle sawing motion. Cut carefully because puff pastry is very fragile and flaky. Using a nonserrated knife may crush pastry and cause it to splinter.

**REFRIGERATING OR FREEZING
PUFF PASTRY**

After four turns, unbaked dough may be wrapped in plastic wrap and refrigerated for two to three days, or it may be wrapped well and frozen for one month. Thaw, wrapped, in refrigerator (several hours or overnight). Before using, give pastry one more turn. It is best not to freeze pastry in a self-defrosting freezer for more than one week.

After dough is cut and shaped, let it rest for up to one hour in the refrigerator. Then it should be either baked immediately or frozen as follows: Place pastry on a tray, freeze, remove from tray, wrap well, and freeze for up to one month. Frozen puff pastry shells and other puff pastries may be blind baked without thawing; brush with egg wash and bake.

Baked pastries don't refrigerate well. To freeze, cool completely, freeze on a tray until firm, wrap well or place in freezer containers, and freeze for six to eight weeks. Loosen wrapping and thaw at room temperature. Crisp pastry in 350° F oven 5 to 10 minutes.

◼ CLASSIC PUFF PASTRY
Pâte feuilletée

To keep the pastry light and puffy, don't apply too much pressure to the dough when rolling or give the dough an excessive number of turns.

>   1 cup plus 1 tablespoon unbleached
>   all-purpose flour
>   1 cup plus 1 tablespoon unbleached
>   white pastry flour
>   1 teaspoon salt
>   3½ tablespoons cold unsalted butter,
>   cut into small pieces
>   ½ cup plus 1 tablespoon ice water
>   1 cup cold unsalted butter

1. *In a food processor:* Place flours, salt, and the 3½ tablespoons butter in bowl of food processor fitted with metal blade. Process with 1-second pulses until butter is cut into flour and resembles coarse meal. *To make by hand:* Combine flours and salt. Cut in butter with pastry blender or two knives.

2. Put flour mixture in a medium bowl and sprinkle with a scant ½ cup ice water; toss with fingertips to moisten. Add more water, a few drops at a time, until mixture is just moist enough to be gathered into a ball. Knead two or three times to form a soft, smooth ball of dough.

3. Cut an *x* into top of dough, ½ inch deep, with a knife; wrap well. Refrigerate until firm (2 to 3 hours). Can be refrigerated overnight.

To Wrap Butter in Détrempe and Give Dough Six Turns

1. Remove *détrempe* from refrigerator. Let sit out to warm slightly (10 minutes).

2. Place butter between two pieces of waxed paper on work surface and beat with rolling pin to soften. Beat until butter is pliable and smooth but still cold. Pat butter into a 6-inch square.

3. When détrempe and butter are the same temperature and consistency (test by inserting a finger into each), roll out détrempe into a rounded cross shape (see photographs, page 481) 12 inches in diameter on an ice-cold, lightly floured surface (marble is best). Roll edges of dough thinner than center.

4. Place square of butter in center of dough and wrap dough around it as shown (see photographs, page 481).

5. Return dough to refrigerator for 10 minutes if it has warmed up too much in wrapping process.

6. Place cool dough on a cold, lightly floured surface with vertical seam pointing toward you. Press dough down with rolling pin to flatten slightly. Begin rolling dough at end farthest from you, always rolling away from you, never sideways or toward you. Ease up on rolling pin when you come to ends of dough to avoid pushing butter

out of the dough. As you roll out dough and fold it, keep sides and ends parallel and thickness even. If butter breaks through dough at any time during rolling process, dust problem areas generously with flour and then continue rolling dough.

Turn 1   Roll dough into an 8- by 18-inch rectangle, with the short side facing you. Brush dough with soft pastry brush to remove flour. Fold bottom third of rectangle up (brush away any flour with pastry brush), then fold top third down, as if it were a business letter. Dust off excess flour and rotate dough a quarter turn clockwise (90 degrees) so seam is on your left. Square up edges by tapping them with rolling pin.

Turn 2   Roll out dough as before. Fold in thirds as before (like a business letter). Square up edges of dough. Mark dough with two finger indentations to indicate number of turns. Wrap and refrigerate for 1 hour. After 1 hour proceed to turns 3 and 4. Do not store dough longer than 1 hour.

Turn 3   Remove dough from refrigerator and allow to warm slightly if very stiff and cold. Place seam on your left, and roll and fold as if for turns 1 and 2.

Turn 4   Turn dough a quarter turn clockwise (90 degrees) and roll and fold again. Mark dough with four finger indentations, wrap, and refrigerate at least 1 hour, or until ready to use. Dough can be frozen at this point or refrigerated 2 to 3 days.

Turns 5 and 6   Give dough two more turns and roll out to thickness specified in recipe. Cut or shape as directed. Rest 1 hour. Bake at 450° F unless otherwise indicated. After dough has been given six turns, it is best to roll out, shape it, and either bake it or freeze shaped dough. The best time to store unshaped puff pastry dough is after four turns.

Makes 21 ounces puff pastry.

◼ QUICK AND EASY PUFF PASTRY

This quick method is like the one for Classic Puff Pastry in that it calls for repeated rolling, folding, and turning. The difference is in how the butter is incorporated into the dough. (Note that the butter must be frozen 30 minutes before using.) With this method, you can achieve very similar results with half the effort. The finished product is exceptionally light and flaky, suitable for tarts, twists, and turnovers. The dough may be frozen, well wrapped, for several months, or refrigerated for up to three days. If it is frozen, thaw in refrigerator overnight before using.

>   1⅓ cups all-purpose flour
>   ⅔ cup cake or pastry flour
>   1 teaspoon salt
>   14 tablespoons unsalted butter, cut in pieces
>   and frozen 30 minutes
>   ½ to ¾ cup very cold whipping cream

1. Combine flours and salt in a bowl or on a marble work surface. Cut in butter coarsely until it is reduced to ¼-inch bits. Add ½ cup cream and mix gently, adding additional cream if necessary, until mixture just forms a ball. Amount of cream will vary depending on humidity and type of flour.

2. Roll dough out on a lightly floured surface into a rectangle measuring approximately 8 by 20 inches. Fold the two 8-inch ends toward center until they meet in middle. Then fold one half over the other. Wrap in plastic and refrigerate dough 1 hour. Repeat rolling and folding process twice, refrigerating dough 1 hour after each time. Repeat rolling and folding one more time. Puff pastry is now ready to use.

Makes about 1 pound puff pastry.

■ VOL-AU-VENT

One of the classic French pastry cases for either savory or sweet fillings, a vol-au-vent looks lovely as a centerpiece for a first course or as the featured dish on a buffet table. The pastry is shaped and trimmed so that a lid is formed from the upper pastry layer. A *bouchée* is a miniature vol-au-vent. *Bouchée* is the French word for *little mouthful*, which is just what they are: little mouthfuls of flaky, filled pastry. Bouchées are a useful part of an hors d'oeuvres repertoire, for they can be partnered with just about any type of filling, including mushrooms and chopped chicken livers sautéed in wine, creamed chicken or sweetbreads, spicy curried crab or shrimp, or creamed asparagus.

Classic Puff Pastry (opposite page)
2 egg yolks, beaten with a pinch of salt

1. Roll out pastry ¼ inch thick. Using a plate as a guide, or your own pattern made of cardboard, cut out two 8-inch circles. Cover and refrigerate dough circles 30 minutes. Gather pastry scraps and reroll ⅛ inch thick; cover and refrigerate.

2. Place one circle of pastry on a parchment-lined baking sheet. With a 5-inch-diameter plate or cardboard pattern as a guide, cut a circle in center of other round of chilled dough, but do not cut through. Brush egg wash around outer 3 inches of full circle, making sure that egg does not drip down sides of dough. Cover with second circle, pressing dough just gently enough to seal two pieces together. Freeze 10 minutes. Remove rolled scraps from refrigerator and cut into fancy shapes for decorating lid of pastry.

3. When dough is chilled but not frozen, mark a chevron pattern with a very sharp knife on surface of outer rim of upper circle. Use egg wash to glue on decorative cutouts made from scraps. Freeze 20 minutes (if freezing longer, wrap well with plastic wrap).

4. Preheat oven to 425° F. Remove pastry from freezer and brush surface with beaten egg, making sure that egg does not drip down sides. Bake until golden brown and

puffy (25 to 35 minutes). If dough starts to brown too much before pastry is ready, lower temperature after about 20 minutes to 400° F.

5. Remove from oven and carefully cut around inner circle of dough with a very sharp knife and a gentle, sawing motion. Remove this lid and, with a fork or spoon, scoop out any soft, uncooked dough from inside. Cool completely and fill with desired filling.

Makes 1 Vol-au-Vent.

Bouchées Follow Vol-au-Vent recipe, but cut out rounds with a 2-inch biscuit cutter. Use a small sharp knife or a 1-inch biscuit cutter to make small lids on half of the 2-inch rounds. Brush unmarked 2-inch rounds lightly with egg. Position marked rounds directly on top. Transfer to parchment-lined baking sheets and chill or freeze 10 minutes, if desired; brush again with egg wash and bake in a preheated 475° F oven 5 minutes; reduce heat to 400° F and bake an additional 5 to 8 minutes or until done. Cool Bouchées on a rack. When cool, remove lid and scoop out the soft centers.

Makes about 12 Bouchées.

This fresh fruit tart band is filled with pastry cream, topped with peach halves and blueberries, and then glazed with apricot jam. This dessert can be made with almost any fruits in season. The recipe is on page 485.

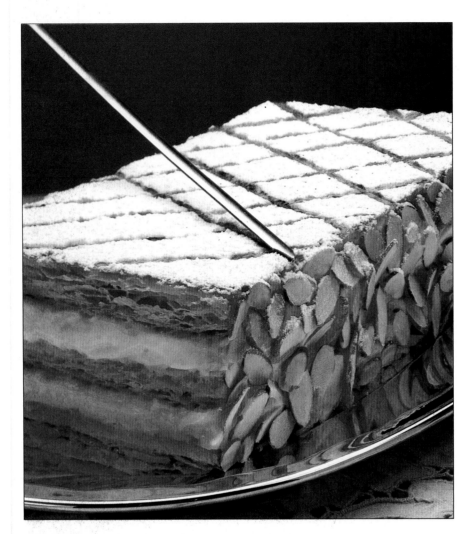

A red-hot metal skewer burns caramelized lines into the sugar on top of Mille-Feuilles. The Mille-Feuilles features three layers of puff pastry filled with vanilla pastry cream.

■ MILLE-FEUILLES

In French *mille feuilles* means *a thousand leaves,* and that is what you get—many thin, delicate leaves of puff pastry. Here they are layered with rum pastry cream to form the base for Mille-Feuilles and for napoleons. Both preparations begin with a long, narrow pastry that is either dusted with confectioners' sugar (for Mille-Feuilles) or iced with marbled glaze (napoleons). Assembled as a large pastry, it is then cut into small servings. Puff pastry is very flaky and should be cut with a serrated knife and a sawing motion. It is best when assembled just before serving. Puff pastry trimmings can be used instead of virgin puff pastry.

> 2½   cups Pastry Cream (see page 251)
>   Classic Puff Pastry with 6 turns (see page 482)
>   1   cup apricot jam, melted and sieved
>   2   teaspoons rum
> ¼   cup whipping cream
>   1   cup toasted sliced almonds, coarsely chopped
> ⅓   cup confectioners' sugar

1. Prepare Pastry Cream and chill.

2. Roll out Classic Puff Pastry into a 12- by 18-inch rectangle, ⅛ inch thick; chill until firm (about 20 minutes). Cut into three equal rectangles that measure 6 inches by 12 inches each. Prick each rectangle all over. Place on parchment-lined baking sheets, cover, and refrigerate 30 minutes. If you have an oven and baking sheets that will accommodate the 12- by 18-inch sheet of puff pastry, this large sheet can be pricked all over and baked whole. Then, after baking, it can be cut into three equal strips with a serrated knife.

3. Preheat oven to 425° F. Cover pastry strips or whole sheet with parchment paper. Set another baking sheet on top of each pastry layer to weight dough. Bake 10 minutes. Lift up baking sheet and parchment paper, prick dough again, replace top baking sheet and parchment, and bake 5 minutes more. Reprick dough. When pastry is browning and appears to be set, remove baking pan and parchment paper from top of pastry. When pastry is crisp, golden brown, and thoroughly baked, remove from oven. Transfer to wire racks and set aside to cool.

4. Trim pastry rectangles with a serrated knife so they are all the same size. Reserve flattest layer for top. Cut out a cardboard rectangle slightly smaller than puff pastry rectangles to use as a base for the cake. Wrap cardboard with aluminum foil.

5. Place one of the three pieces of puff pastry on the foil-wrapped cardboard. Brush this pastry with a thin layer of warm apricot jam. Stir rum into Pastry Cream. Whip cream until stiff and fold into Pastry Cream (see Note).

6. Spread half of Pastry Cream on first layer of pastry. Place second layer on top. Brush with a thin layer of jam. Spread all but ¼ cup of remaining cream on second layer. Place third layer of pastry on top with smoothest side up. Ice long sides of cake with remaining cream and press toasted almonds on sides.

7. Sift a fine layer of confectioners' sugar evenly over top of cake. Heat a long metal skewer over stove burner (gas burners work best) until red-hot. Hold skewer at a 45-degree angle to long sides of cake with point angled toward top left corner of cake. Burn lines in the confectioners' sugar 1½ inches apart on top of cake. Reheat skewer as necessary to create dark caramelized lines in the sugar. To create a crosshatch pattern, burn another set of lines beginning with skewer angled toward upper right corner of cake.

Serves 6.

Note If you must assemble cake several hours before serving, you can add a small amount of gelatin to Pastry Cream. Sprinkle 2 teaspoons gelatin over 2 tablespoons water or rum. When gelatin is spongy, place bowl over hot water (double boiler) and stir to dissolve gelatin. Cool over ice until syrupy. Stir into Pastry Cream just before folding in whipped cream.

PUFF PASTRY TART BAND

Showcase fresh seasonal fruits in a puff pastry tart band. Create colorful combinations of flavors and textures by using more than one kind of fruit on a tart. Raspberries can be combined with sliced figs or fresh poached peaches. Or arrange peach halves down the center of the band and edge with fresh blueberries. Let each peach half equal one serving. Kiwi slices look pretty with strawberries. Puff pastry scraps may be used in place of virgin puff pastry to make tart band.

> 1¼ cups Pastry Cream (see page 251)
> ½ recipe Classic Puff Pastry with 6 turns (see page 482)
> 1 egg yolk lightly beaten with 1 teaspoon water
> 1 tablespoon fruit liqueur or brandy
> ¼ cup whipping cream or Crème Fraîche (see page 161)
> 3 cups fresh raspberries, hulled, halved strawberries, or sliced fruit
> ¼ cup apricot preserves, sieved (for light-colored fruits) or currant jelly (for dark fruits)
> 1 tablespoon liqueur or brandy

1. Prepare Pastry Cream and chill.

2. To prepare tart band: Roll out Classic Puff Pastry into an 8- by 16-inch rectangle that is ⅛ thick. Cover and refrigerate until firm.

3. Cut out three cardboard templates with the following dimensions: 5 inches by 15½ inches, ⅞ inch by 15½ inches, and ⅞ inch by 3¼ inches .

4. When dough is well chilled, use cardboard templates and a long, sharp knife to cut out one 15½- by 5-inch rectangle of dough for tart base, two 15½- by ⅞-inch strips of dough for side walls of tart, and two 3¼- by ⅞-inch strips of dough for ends of tart.

5. Place large rectangle of puff pastry (base) on a parchment-lined baking sheet. Prick all over with a fork. Brush 1-inch border at edge of dough with cold water. Place thin strips of dough on moistened border to form tart walls and lightly press into place. Score edges of tart with back of a small knife, making ⅛-inch-deep marks every ¼ inch along border. Cover and refrigerate 30 minutes.

6. Preheat oven to 425° F. Brush top only of narrow strips (walls) with egg wash. Bake 20 minutes, or until tart is puffed and light brown. Lower oven to 400° F and bake until golden brown and done. Cool completely on wire rack before filling.

7. To assemble tart: Stir fruit liqueur into Pastry Cream with a wooden spoon. Stiffly whip cream into Pastry Cream. Spread a ¼-inch layer of cream on bottom of tart. Arrange fresh fruit on top of cream. Melt preserves or jelly in small saucepan until bubbly; stir in liqueur to make glaze. Brush glaze over fruit.

Serves 6 to 8.

CHEESE PALMIERS

Rolled in sugar, dainty *palmiers* (palm leaves) can be eaten with dessert; rolled in salt or grated cheese, they become a savory to enjoy with cocktails or wine.

> **Quick and Easy Puff Pastry (see page 482)**
> 1½ cups freshly grated Parmesan cheese

1. On a surface covered with grated Parmesan, roll out puff pastry dough into a rectangle 8 inches wide by 12 inches long by ⅛ inch thick.

2. Fold two 8-inch sides toward center, meeting in middle. Dust surface lightly with cheese. Then fold top half of dough down over bottom half. Dust dough with any remaining Parmesan. Chill dough, wrapped in plastic, for 1 hour.

3. Preheat oven to 350° F. Cut roll into ¼-inch widths. Place on ungreased baking sheets, widely separated. Bake until golden brown (20 to 25 minutes). Serve warm, or cool on a rack and store in an airtight container for up to 2 weeks.

Makes about 50 palmiers.

Quick puff pastry dusted with Parmesan can be turned into buttery Cheese Palmiers, to serve warm or cool with cocktails or red wine. Provide plates or large napkins: The palmiers are deliciously flaky.

To make Raspberry Feuillantines, a puff pastry rectangle is baked, then split horizontally and filled with vanilla pastry cream, raspberries, and Chantilly Cream. Use a large open-star tip to pipe the cream.

■ RASPBERRY FEUILLANTINES

Feuillantines are rectangles of puff pastry that are decorated and baked to form pastry cases. These elegant containers are a perfect pastry to follow any dinner party. Here they hold kirsch-flavored pastry cream, fresh raspberries or strawberries, and Chantilly Cream.

1¼	cups Pastry Cream (see page 251)
	Classic Puff Pastry with 6 turns (see page 482)
1	egg yolk lightly beaten with 1 teaspoon water
1	tablespoon kirsch or other liqueur
4½	cups fresh raspberries, or halved or quartered fresh strawberries
2½	cups Chantilly Cream (see page 252)

1. Prepare Pastry Cream and chill.

2. To prepare feuillantines: Roll out Classic Puff Pastry into a 12- by 14-inch rectangle that is ¼ inch thick. Place on a parchment-lined baking sheet and refrigerate until very firm (about 20 minutes).

3. Meanwhile cut out a cardboard rectangle that is 2¾ inches by 5 inches to use as a pattern. Using this pattern, cut out eight rectangles of puff pastry from chilled dough with a sharp knife. Turn each rectangle of dough over and place on parchment-lined baking sheet. Cover and refrigerate 1 hour.

4. Gather scraps into a ball; chill. When scraps are firm, roll out very thin. Place on a baking sheet and freeze briefly to chill dough. Cut out small leaves, flowers, stems, and other designs from dough to decorate tops of

rectangles. Brush tops of rectangles with egg wash. Arrange cutouts decoratively on top of each rectangle. Chill 20 minutes. Rectangles may be frozen at this point. The frozen puff pastry dough may be baked unfilled and without thawing.

5. Preheat oven to 425° F. Brush top of each rectangle with egg wash. Bake 20 minutes. Lower oven to 400° F and continue baking until golden brown and puffy. Cool on wire racks. Store in dry place at room temperature until ready to fill.

6. To assemble: Split each rectangle in half horizontally with a serrated knife, creating a bottom and a top. Remove any uncooked dough from center. Place bottoms on dessert plates.

7. Stir kirsch into Pastry Cream. Spoon 2 tablespoons Pastry Cream into each bottom. Sprinkle fresh berries on top of cream.

8. Prepare Chantilly Cream. Place Chantilly Cream in a pastry bag fitted with a large, open-star tip. Pipe a layer of rosettes on top of berries. Place puff pastry tops on filled bottoms. Decorate plate with a few berries. Serve immediately while pastry is still warm.

Makes 8 pastries.

Recipes and Related Information
Brie or Camembert in Puff Pastry, 112; Cake and Pastry Tools, 89.

PUNCH DOWN, TO

A bread-making term that means to put your fist gently into risen yeast dough to deflate it. At this point the dough has lightened from a heavy mass into an inflated foam due to the action of the gases given off by yeast during fermentation. These gases are trapped by strands of gluten formed when the dough was mixed and cause this gluten network to expand.

Yeast doughs are punched down to avoid overstretching and breaking the gluten strands. This step also creates more gas bubbles, which means a wider distribution of carbon dioxide in the dough and a more even grain when the bread is baked.

Actually, you don't really have to punch the dough; if you lift it gently, it will collapse in the same way.

> **Recipes and Related Information**
> *Yeast, 613; Yeast Bread, 613.*

PUREE, TO; PUREE

To blend, sieve, or process food into a soft, smooth consistency; the food that results from this process. A purée is a thick liquid made from finely ground, cooked vegetables, fruits, grains, or legumes. Familiar purées include applesauce, mashed potatoes, and pumpkin pie filling. Purées are the primary flavor base for many ice creams, mousses, pâtés, soups, and sauces. Purées add more nutrition when thickening a soup or sauce than do flour, fat, or dairy products.

Prepare food for puréeing by washing, trimming blemishes, and removing seeds. Skins should be scrubbed but do not always have to be removed. Hard-skinned vegetables, however, such as pumpkins and winter squash, should be peeled; peeling most other foods is a matter of personal taste. Cook food until tender in stock or water, then purée with some of the cooking liquid (for soups) or a few tablespoons of butter (for vegetables). Most fruits and vegetables puree best while still warm. Mash food with a potato masher, if desired, then purée by pressing through a fine strainer; or cut into uniform pieces and purée in a food processor or blender, or with a food mill. Although unnecessary, using a blender or food processor is the easiest method. A food mill is useful for puréeing fibrous vegetables such as celery and watercress.

Different foods can be cooked separately or combined for purées. Nonstarch foods such as beans and tomatoes produce very liquid purées, which are good for sauces. Starchy vegetables such as carrots, potatoes, and parsnips produce thicker purées.

Serve purees immediately, or store in the refrigerator for up to four days or in the freezer for up to one month. Reheat in a double boiler or in a heavy-bottomed saucepan over low heat.

In general, 1 pound of trimmed and cleaned raw fruits and vegetables makes about 2 cups of purée. Thick-skinned vegetables and pitted fruits are an exception. For these foods, about 1 pound of raw food yields 1 cup of purée. One-half pound of beans makes 2½ cups of purée. When using purée as a thickener, 1 cup of puréed potato or a similar starchy vegetable is enough to thicken 2 quarts of vegetable soup.

▮ VEGETABLE PUREES

A delicious variation for serving vegetables, purées are good with broiled, baked, or sautéed meats. Almost any vegetable is suitable; the list below gives some suggestions. If you wish to serve more than one, prepare them separately and serve them side by side or swirled together on the plate. Purées can also be made into soup (see instructions at end of recipe).

> 1 **pound fresh vegetables, trimmed**
> 1 **tablespoon butter or margarine**
> ¼ **to ½ cup half-and-half**
>   **Salt and freshly ground pepper, to taste**

1. Cut vegetables into pieces of even size. Steam until tender in a small amount of water. Drain, reserving any liquid for soups, if desired.

2. Place vegetables and butter in food processor or blender. Process until smooth.

3. With machine running, slowly add half-and-half to make a smooth, creamy purée. Season to taste with salt and pepper.

Serves 4 to 6.

Variation Herbs and spices add another dimension to vegetable purées. Here are a few suggestions.

Broccoli Add a pinch of cayenne pepper.

Carrots Add fresh or dried dill to taste.

Cauliflower Add curry powder or ½ cup shredded Swiss or Cheddar cheese. Dust with paprika or serve with a purée of contrasting color.

Parsnips Add ground allspice or ground nutmeg to taste.

Spinach Add ground nutmeg to taste.

Zucchini, pattypan, or crookneck squash Add a few sprigs of dill.

Puréed Vegetable Soup Blend vegetable purée with enough chicken or beef stock to make a soupy mixture. Gently heat in saucepan until warmed throughout.

> **Recipes and Related Information**
> *Ice Cream and Frozen Dessert, 308; Mousse, 372; Pâté and Terrine, 416; Persimmon Pudding, 430; Pumpkin Purée Filling, 438; Sauce, 512; Stock and Soup, 558.*

Q&R

S

Paella, a Spanish casserole of poultry, sausage, shellfish, and vegetables, uses a saffron-infused chicken stock to tint the rice a warm golden yellow.

SAFFRON

It isn't hard to understand why saffron is the most expensive spice in the world. Made from the dried yellow-orange stigmas of a species of crocus, saffron must be picked by hand. Each crocus blossom yields three stigmas; about 225,000 stigmas make 1 pound.

Fortunately, a little saffron goes a long way. Just a few threads dissolved in hot liquid can add a rich golden color to a pot of soup or rice. Its distinctive flavor and aroma are indescribable but immediately recognizable; if overused, saffron can have an unpleasant medicinal taste.

Use   Saffron imparts color and flavor to many Mediterranean, North African, and Middle Eastern dishes. Paella and many other Spanish rice recipes are seasoned with saffron. It can be found in Italian *risotto alla Milanese* and Mediterranean fish soups such as bouillabaisse, and is present in most Moroccan versions of couscous, in Iranian rice dishes, and in Indian curries, tandoori dishes, and pilafs. In Sweden, Spain, and Italy, saffron is added to buns, breads, and cakes. The Pennsylvania Dutch are also great consumers of saffron, adding it to chicken and noodle dishes and soups.

Availability   Saffron is packed both in thread form and as a powder. It is widely carried in supermarkets; some store it on the spice rack and others require customers to request it.

Selection   Because powdered saffron quickly loses its pungency, threads are preferred. Powdered saffron is sometimes adulterated with turmeric or other powders that are less expensive.

Storage   Keep saffron, whether powder or threads, in a cool, dark place and use within six months.

Preparation   Saffron must be heated to release its color and flavor. To dissolve powdered saffron or saffron threads, steep for 2 minutes in a small amount of hot water or other liquid used in the recipe; add infusion directly to dish, straining out threads if desired (it is not necessary). For fullest flavor, add saffron near the end of the cooking process.

■ PAELLA

Traditionally, this rice-based Spanish dish is cooked in a shallow, wide-bottomed pan known as a paella pan.

1 chicken (3½ lb), cut into 8 pieces
1 teaspoon salt
½ teaspoon freshly ground black pepper
1 teaspoon dried oregano
4 cups Chicken Stock (see page 560)
¼ gram (1 vial) saffron threads
4 tablespoons olive oil
½ pound spicy Italian or Spanish sausage
2 onions, diced
3 cloves garlic, diced
4 tomatoes, diced
1 bell pepper, diced
2 cups uncooked long-grain rice
1 pound fresh peas *or*
  1 package (10 oz) frozen tiny peas
1 pound prawns, shelled
½ pound clams in the shell, scrubbed
½ pound mussels in the shell, scrubbed

1. Wash chicken pieces and pat dry. Season with salt, black pepper, and oregano. Let rest for 30 minutes. Meanwhile, in a medium saucepan, heat stock; add saffron, turn off heat, and let steep.

2. In a 6- to 8-quart Dutch oven, sauté chicken in oil over medium heat until golden brown (about 7 minutes). Turn and brown 5 minutes. Remove to paper-towel–lined plate and reserve. Add sausage and brown, turning to cook all sides, for about 5 minutes. Remove sausage to a paper-towel–lined plate and reserve. Cut sausage in half. Add onion and garlic to Dutch oven and sauté 5 minutes. Add tomatoes, bell pepper, rice, reserved chicken, and saffron stock to cover and simmer 20 minutes. Add halved sausages, peas, and prawns. Stir to mix well. Cover and cook 10 minutes. Add clams and mussels. Cover and cook 15 minutes. Fluff the rice and serve in casserole dish.

Serves 8.

SAGE

A member of the mint family native to the southern Mediterranean, sage is one of the more pungent herbs in the cook's pantry. Sage leaves are long, narrow, grayish green ovals with a coarse texture. They are aggressive in aroma and flavor, slightly musty or camphorlike, especially when subjected to heat.

Use Sage is especially appreciated in Italian and English cuisines. Italians use it to flavor dried-bean dishes and pork. To make the famous saltimbocca, a whole sage leaf is sandwiched between a veal scallop and a slice of prosciutto; the "package" is skewered with toothpicks

and sautéed in butter with wine. English cooks use sage in stuffings and blend it with cream cheese or cottage cheese to make a sandwich spread. They also layer Derby cheese with the juice of fresh sage leaves to make the green-streaked Sage Derby. In America minced sage is popular as a sausage seasoning; it is also a virtual fixture in turkey stuffings. Because of its pungent character, it should be used with restraint.

Availability Some well-stocked supermarkets and specialty markets now carry fresh sage the year around. Dried, rubbed (crumbled) sage and ground sage are sold on supermarket spice racks.

Selection Choose fresh sage with a strong aroma and no signs of wilting. Packaged seasonings lose quality after a while; try to buy from a store that restocks its spice shelf fairly often.

Storage Fresh sage can be stored for a few days in the refrigerator if wrapped in a paper towel and placed inside a plastic bag. It can also be preserved in salt: Wash and dry the leaves, then layer them with salt in a jar or freezer container. Cover and refrigerate or freeze indefinitely; wash salt off leaves before using. Dried, rubbed, and ground sage quickly go musty; keep in a cool, dark, dry place and replace every three months.

■ SALTIMBOCCA

This Roman dish is a good example of the Italian penchant for whimsical food names; it is so succulent it almost leaps into your mouth (*salta in bocca*). The success of the dish depends on tender, milk-fed veal and fresh sage. Serve with a light red wine or a rich Italian Chardonnay.

1¼ pounds leg of veal, cut into 12 scallops
  Salt and freshly ground pepper
12 fresh sage leaves
12 paper-thin slices prosciutto
2 tablespoons unsalted butter
3 tablespoons dry white wine
1½ tablespoons minced parsley, for garnish

1. Place each scallop between pieces of plastic wrap and, using a mallet or the bottom of a skillet, pound to a uniform ⅛-inch thickness. Salt and pepper scallops lightly. Put a sage leaf on each and cover with a slice of prosciutto. Secure prosciutto to scallop with toothpicks.

2. Melt 1 tablespoon of the butter in each of two large skillets. Add scallops and brown quickly on both sides. When scallops are just barely cooked, transfer them to a warmed serving platter; remove toothpicks.

3. Scrape juices and browned bits from one skillet to the other. Add wine to skillet with juices and reduce slightly over high heat. Pour sauce over scallops; garnish with parsley.

Serves 4.

Red Fruit Plate is a spectrum of reds, oranges, and pinks. Each bite-sized piece can be dipped in the tasty Cream Cheese Dressing, which is flavored with plum jam.

2. Arrange lettuce leaves on a large salad plate. Place tuna in center of lettuce-lined plate. Arrange beans, quartered beets, green pepper strips, hard-cooked eggs, and tomatoes around tuna. Decorate vegetables with anchovy fillets and olives.

3. Drizzle dressing over ingredients after they have been set on plate, or marinate each ingredient in a little dressing and then arrange.

Serves 4.

■ RED FRUIT PLATE WITH CREAM CHEESE DRESSING

A jewel box of summer fruits, ranging in color from pink through crimson to burgundy, makes an eye-catching summer salad arrangement.

> **Red-leaf lettuce**
> 1 **cup sweet cherries with stems**
> 1 **basket (2 to 3 cups) strawberries**
> 8 **figs, sliced crosswise**
> 4 **wedges (about 1½ in. thick) watermelon**
> 2 **nectarines, pitted and cut in wedges**
> 4 **red plums, halved and pitted**
> 1 **bunch (about 1 lb) red seedless grapes**

Cream Cheese Dressing

> 1 **package (3 oz) cream cheese**
> 1 **tablespoon fresh lemon juice**
> 2 **tablespoons plum jam**
> ¾ **cup whipping cream**

Line 4 plates with lettuce. Divide fruits among the 4 plates, arranging them with red surfaces up. Serve with Cream Cheese Dressing to spoon over each serving.

Serves 4.

Cream Cheese Dressing   Soften cream cheese; beat until creamy. Gradually add lemon juice, jam, and cream, beating until thick. Refrigerate for about 1 hour to blend flavors.

Makes about 1½ cups.

■ SALADE NICOISE

Traditionally, this showcase salad from the south of France near Nice consists of tuna, anchovies, capers, beans, and tomatoes, but any seasonal favorites may be successfully included.

> ½ **pound thin green beans (haricots verts, if possible)**
> 1 **bunch small beets**
> 1 **small head lettuce, torn into bite-sized pieces**
> 1 **can (6½ oz) tuna, packed in olive oil, drained**
> 1 **green bell pepper, cut in thin strips**
> 2 **hard-cooked eggs, quartered**
> 2 **tomatoes, quartered**
> 1 **can (2 oz) anchovy fillets**
> 16 **black Niçoise olives or oil-packed olives from Italy or Greece Mustard Vinaigrette (see page 520)**

1. Trim ends from green beans; in a large pot bring 3 quarts water to a boil. Boil beans until tender-crisp and bright green (about 7 minutes). Using a slotted spoon, remove to a bowl of ice water to stop cooking and to chill. Trim leaves from beets (do not peel beets). Boil beets in the same 3 quarts water until tender (15 to 20 minutes depending on size). Slip skins from beets while still warm, then quarter.

Recipes and Related Information

SALAMANDER

In mythology the salamander is a beast able to endure fire without being burned. Over the centuries, some literary chef gave this name to a tool used to brown foods. This special oven, found in professional kitchens, has an overhead heat source de-

signed to glaze gratins (see GRATIN) or caramelize the sugar topping of desserts such as Crème Brûlée. For glazing and browning, the home cook can use the broiler set to high heat or a portable salamander. This utensil, also sometimes called a crème brûlée iron, is a small, heavy, iron disk attached to a long rod ending in a wooden handle. To use, heat the disk to red-hot over the stove burner; for caramelizing sugar, press the head into the sugar until it reaches the desired state; for browning savory dishes, hold the head close to the surface and move across from one side to the other.

The salamander is easier to control than a broiler, which is important for cold custards; the sugar will melt with the concentrated infusion of heat, but the custard won't heat up as well.

SALT

This is the most common culinary seasoning in the world. Available in unlimited quantities from the sea and rocks, it also is naturally present in the human body and is in many foods. Although excessive salt consumption is believed to promote hypertension, some salt intake is essential to the human diet.

WHEN TO SALT

There is considerable disagreement among cooks about the proper moment in the cooking process to add salt. Because salt draws out moisture, many cooks claim that salting roasts after cooking results in a juicier roast. However, other cooks claim that moisture loss is immaterial for roasts cooked immediately after salting; they claim that salting before cooking results in better flavor than merely salting the surface of the food after cooking. Most cooks agree that salt sprinkled on meats or vegetables prior to cooking in a microwave oven will toughen the foods.

Some cooks insist that dried beans should be salted after cooking since salt toughens them otherwise. The same cooks, however, will add a salty ham bone or salt pork to the bean cooking liquid. There seems to be no agreement; experiment and decide for yourself.

Many cookbooks and recipes suggest adding a pinch of salt to egg whites while beating them. In fact the salt destabilizes the foam. If salt is desirable for flavor, add it at the end of the beating process.

Use   The most prominent function of salt is as a seasoning. When used in moderation, it heightens the flavor of food. Dishes prepared without salt often seem bland and flat. Starchy foods—potatoes, rice, beans, and bread—seem to beg loudest for the flavor-enhancing quality of salt, but even sweet baked goods benefit from a pinch.

Salt also functions as a preservative. For thousands of years salt has been employed to withdraw moisture from bacteria and mold cells in food, slowing cell growth considerably. In the presence of a lot of salt, the cells may even dry up. This inability of bacteria and mold cells to survive in a salty medium is what preserves such items as salt cod. (In the past, it preserved bacon and salt pork, although neither is salted enough today to be preserved by salt alone.) Processors add salt to butter and cheese to flavor them and to prolong their refrigerated life.

Salt contributes to the pickling process by establishing a high-acid, low-pH, anaerobic (oxygen-free) environment in which bacteria are unable to live. Salting cabbage, for example, generates a brine which, if allowed to ferment, produces an environment inhospitable to bacteria. The result is sauerkraut, which can be preserved for long periods without refrigeration if kept submerged in brine.

Withdrawing moisture from foods with salt can also improve flavor. Salting cucumber and eggplant, for example, removes the bitter juices.

Added to the water in which vegetables are boiled, salt improves flavor and raises the boiling point of the water slightly, enabling the vegetables to cook more quickly and therefore better retain color and nutritive value.

Salt can also lower the freezing point of water, which is why it is added to the ice packed around ice cream freezers. Without salt the surrounding brine pack would never get cold enough to freeze the ice cream.

Cooking foods in hot salt is a popular technique in some cuisines, and surprisingly, these foods do not taste particularly salty. Chinese cooks bake whole chickens in salt; Spanish cooks similarly bake whole fish. The salt is heated in the oven, then the food is completely buried in it and returned to the oven. Because salt is a more even conductor of heat than air, the food cooks evenly and quickly and the finished product is especially moist despite salt's proclivity to draw moisture out.

Availability   Most supermarkets carry the following salt varieties. Sea salt is also found in most health-food stores and in specialty markets.

Common or Table Salt   Most table salt, which is fine grained, contains additives to keep it from clumping. Iodized salt is supplemented with iodine to reduce the incidence of goiter.

Kosher Salt   This coarse-grained salt has no additives and is about half as salty as table salt. Some cooks prefer

TIPS

SEASONING WITH SALT

Always add salt in small increments, tasting as you go. An oversalted dish is difficult to salvage. To correct an oversalted soup or stew, stretch it with water if feasible or add more vegetables or bland starches. A peeled, quartered potato simmered in a salty soup for 15 minutes will absorb some of the excess salt. When making foods ahead, always recheck seasoning just before serving. Often the balance of flavors shifts and more salt is required. Perceptions are dulled when food is very hot or very cold. If you're seasoning the dish when it's warm, taste it again once it's chilled or reheated. The salt level will probably need adjusting.

it for salads and uncooked dishes because they like its texture. Others object to the texture and use it only where it will dissolve, such as in soups or water used to boil pasta or vegetables.

Pickling or Canning Salt More finely ground than table salt, pickling or canning salt has no additives that might cloud pickles.

Rock Salt Coarse-grained rock salt is crystallized salt found in rocks. It is less refined than table salt. Because it is used, along with ice, to pack around the outside of ice cream freezers to speed the rate of freezing, it is sometimes referred to as ice cream salt.

Sea Salt As its name suggests, sea salt is obtained from sea water; its texture can be coarse or fine. The best varieties come from England, France, and the United States and have a fresh, light taste.

Storage Store salt in a closed container; it will keep indefinitely.

Recipes and Related Information
Gravlax, 233; Ice Cream and Frozen Dessert, 308.

SANDWICH GRILLING IRON

The French version of a grilled cheese sandwich, *croque-monsieur* has a filling of a slice of ham topped with Swiss, Emmentaler, or Gruyère cheese; *croque-madame* uses chicken as the meat. To cook, the sandwich is sautéed in butter in a skillet or browned in  a cast-aluminum grilling iron that impresses the bread with a decorative shell pattern. The iron, which sits directly on the burner unit of a stove, consists of two plates joined with a hinge at the back. Each plate has two shell-shaped impressions. Heatproof handles allow safe movement of the iron. A version without the shell design is also available and is slightly smaller in size.

Aside from the classic sandwiches, consider these combinations, all on buttered bread: fresh peaches or other fruit; whipped cream cheese and jam; asparagus tips with basil butter; or thin slices of red onion with romaine lettuce and mayonnaise.

To use, butter the grilling-iron plates or spray them with vegetable cooking spray. Clean by washing gently and wiping dry.

SAUCE

Broadly defined, a sauce is any fluid dressing, including relishes and condiments. An exquisite sauce has always been the hallmark of fine cuisine and the test of a cook's expertise. A well-made sauce is impressive even when it may actually be easily and quickly prepared. It implies luxury and competence and mastery of a revered culinary art. Most of all, however, sauces are a treat to the palate, in both flavor and texture.

A sauce is basically a thickened liquid—usually stock, milk, cream, melted butter, or wine, but other liquids are sometimes used. The most common thickeners are flour, or other starches, and egg yolks. Some sauces contain no thickeners but gain body by being reduced or boiled until they are concentrated. Once a liquid has been thickened, it needs only seasonings to give it flavor. The preparation of a sauce usually involves the following steps: gently simmering the ingredients, skimming away any impurities that may rise to the surface, and reducing to add body and ripen the flavor.

Sauces can be thought of as belonging to groups. They are categorized according to their major ingredients and their thickening agent. The major sauce families are white and brown sauces, which are thickened with flour and made with milk or stock; tomato sauces; butter sauces; flourless cream sauces, which are thickened by reduction; and dressings.

Each family of sauces has a different use. In general the white sauces, butter sauces, and flourless cream sauces are served with seafood, light meats, and vegetables, and the brown sauces are served with dark meats. Tomato sauces are served with pasta, fish, fowl, and some light meats. Dressings, of course, are for salads. However, because saucing is such a question of taste, there are many exceptions to these guidelines.

Once you master the techniques of preparation, you can vary any sauce to suit your own preference or particular need. Remember, however, that sauces are meant to enhance, not to disguise, the flavor of food. Add new seasonings gradually and taste the sauce before adding any additional flavor.

Use heavy saucepans of good quality so that flour-thickened sauces will not stick or burn and egg yolks will not curdle. A small whisk, which can quickly and easily reach all parts of the saucepan, is also essential. A food processor or blender is an invaluable aid in making some sauces, especially those in the mayonnaise family, which otherwise require prolonged whisking.

WHITE SAUCES

The simplest of the hot sauces, white sauces are quickly made with ingredients usually at hand. This group can be subdivided: the milk-based white sauces and the stock-based, cream-colored *velouté* sauces.

The techniques for making both types are similar. Both are thickened with a light roux—a mixture of butter and flour that is cooked until bubbling and until the starchy taste of the flour has dispersed. The liquid is added only after the roux cooks long enough to toast the flour lightly. If the roux is not properly cooked, or if too much flour is used for the amount of liquid, the sauce becomes unpleasantly pasty and sticky.

Flour tends to cause lumps if not combined properly with the liquid. To avoid lumps, the liquid should be whisked into the roux rather than mixed in with a spoon. Whisking, which blends the mixture more thoroughly, should be constant while the liquid is being added and until the sauce comes to a boil.

A roux gives a creamy texture to these sauces, which are often further enriched with cream and egg yolks. With or without added enrichment, white sauces can be quite rich, although they are lower in calories than butter sauces and flourless cream sauces.

Almost all vegetables, light-meat chicken and turkey, fish, and shellfish can be served with a white sauce. For poultry and seafood, velouté is generally preferred because then the stock is related to the dish. Fish stock reinforces the fish flavor and poultry stock enhances the flavor of a chicken or turkey dish.

Almost any flavoring can be added to these basic sauces. Cheeses—from the mild Swiss cheeses to the sharper Parmesan or tangy blue cheeses—are popular additions to milk-based sauces. Fresh herbs, Dijon mustard, and spices such as curry powder and paprika also excite the palate.

White sauces can be made up to two days ahead and then refrigerated or frozen. If sauces are to be enriched with egg yolks, however, it is best to add the yolks after the sauce has been reheated. Reheat white sauces in a medium saucepan over low heat, whisking often.

▧ BASIC WHITE SAUCE

Also known as béchamel, this is a classic French sauce usually made with milk (but sometimes enriched with cream) and a white roux. Sauces derived from Basic White Sauce are often served with vegetables but also accompany eggs, fish, pasta, and sometimes poultry. White sauce can also be mixed with cooked vegetables to make creamed vegetables or poured over vegetables, sprinkled with grated cheese, and baked as a gratin. Béchamel is sometimes layered in baked lasagne and is the secret to making macaroni and cheese creamy. A thicker version of the sauce, made with more flour, is the base for soufflés; a thinner version, made with less flour, is the foundation for cream soups.

     1 cup milk
     1½ tablespoons butter
     1½ tablespoons flour
        Salt and white pepper, to taste
        Freshly grated nutmeg

1. In a small, heavy-bottomed saucepan, bring milk to a boil. Remove from heat. Melt butter in a small, heavy-bottomed saucepan over low heat. Whisk in flour. Cook, whisking constantly, until mixture is well blended and bubbly (about 2 minutes). Let cool slightly.

2. Gradually pour milk into flour mixture, whisking. Return pan to heat and bring to a boil over medium-high heat, whisking constantly. Add pinch of salt, pepper, and nutmeg. Reduce heat to medium-low and simmer, uncovered, whisking often, for 5 minutes.

3. Taste and add more salt, pepper, and nutmeg, if needed. If not using sauce at once, dab top with butter to prevent a skin from forming. Sauce can be refrigerated, covered, for up to 2 days or frozen. To reheat, whisk over medium heat. Serve hot.

Makes 1 cup.

Cheese Sauce Bring 1 cup Basic White Sauce to a simmer in a small, heavy-bottomed saucepan over medium heat, whisking often. Remove from heat and whisk in ¼ cup freshly grated Parmesan, Gruyère, or sharp Cheddar cheese until melted. Quickly whisk in 1 egg yolk (if sauce is to be part of a baked dish, but do not reheat sauce with yolk, which may curdle) or 2 tablespoons butter (if sauce is to be used as an accompaniment). Taste and add salt and pepper.

Cream Sauce Bring 1 cup Basic White Sauce to a simmer in a small, heavy-bottomed saucepan over medium heat, whisking often. Whisk in ¼ cup whipping cream. Simmer sauce, whisking often, until slightly thickened (about 2 minutes). Taste and add salt, pepper, and nutmeg, if needed. If desired, stir in 1 tablespoon chopped fresh chives, tarragon, parsley, or basil. Serve hot.

One of the classics of French cuisine, béchamel is the base of many sauces. Made with milk or cream, it is white, smooth, and rich enough to be pleasurable in itself—over fish, poultry, or vegetables—yet adaptable enough to accept other flavorings.

Madeira Sauce dresses up any roast, poultry, or meat. If you keep brown sauce in the freezer, it can be prepared in just a few minutes.

flour into butter. Cook, whisking constantly, until mixture turns a light beige color (about 3 minutes). Remove from heat and let cool slightly.

2. Gradually pour stock into flour mixture, whisking. Bring to a boil over medium-high heat, whisking constantly. Add pinch of salt and pepper. Reduce heat to medium-low and simmer, uncovered, whisking often, for 5 minutes.

3. Taste and add more salt and pepper, if needed. If not using sauce at once, dab top with butter to prevent a skin from forming. Sauce can be refrigerated, covered, up to 1 day or frozen.

Makes 1 cup.

Creamy Velouté Sauce   Bring Velouté Sauce to a simmer in a medium, heavy-bottomed saucepan, whisking often. Whisk in ¼ cup whipping cream and bring to a boil. Simmer, whisking occasionally, until sauce thickens slightly (about 2 minutes). If desired, stir in 1 tablespoon chopped fresh chives, tarragon, parsley, basil, or dill. Taste and add salt and white pepper, if needed.

BROWN SAUCES

Like white sauces, brown sauces are thickened with a roux of butter and flour cooked together, although the roux for brown sauces is cooked until it has just taken on some color. This roux gives color to the sauce. The liquid used in the sauce, usually beef or veal stock, also adds a warm brown appearance. Even darker is the roux used as a thickener and flavoring agent in Louisiana cooking; it deepens to a rich red-brown.

Brown sauces are served mainly with dark meats, especially beef and lamb, and with duck; they are good with roast poultry and poached eggs as well. They reinforce the taste of meat and enhance it with additional flavorings. Brown sauces are not served with seafood or vegetables, although vegetables can accompany the meats served with these sauces.

These sauces are often served on the side as an accompaniment to a beautifully browned roast or steak, so as not to hide the color of the food. Not usually thick, they moisten food without coating it or clinging to it.

A favorite flavoring for brown sauce is wine, especially a fortified wine such as port or Madeira. The flavor and color of tomatoes also complement these sauces. Fresh herbs are another popular addition. A small amount of butter can be stirred into the sauces, but often this enrichment is not necessary because the meat they accompany is rich enough.

Brown sauces can be made up to three days ahead and refrigerated or frozen. Reheat them in a heavy saucepan over medium heat, whisking often. If they contain fresh herbs or fortified wines, add more of these flavorings after reheating to compensate for flavor lost during the process of chilling and reheating.

VELOUTE SAUCE

Like Basic White Sauce, Velouté Sauce is generally used as a base for other sauces served with fish, chicken, turkey, veal, and eggs. Often the fish, poultry, or meat is poached in stock, which gains more flavor and is then used to prepare the *velouté*. To vary the sauce, consider combining white wine with the stock.

> 1 **cup Chicken Stock (see page 560) or**
> **Fish Stock (see page 561)**
> 1½ **tablespoons butter**
> 1½ **tablespoons flour**
> **Salt and white pepper, to taste**

1. Bring stock to a boil in a small, heavy-bottomed saucepan. Remove from heat. Melt butter in a small, heavy-bottomed saucepan over low heat. Whisk

▣ BASIC BROWN SAUCE

This rich, meat-flavored sauce is the basis for all brown sauces. It is generally not used as is, but is flavored with Madeira, mushrooms, or other ingredients. These sauces are served mainly with beef and lamb, as well as some poultry and egg dishes. Brown sauce freezes well and can be used as needed to turn any broiled, roasted, or sautéed meat into a festive dish.

- 2 tablespoons vegetable oil
- 2½ tablespoons flour
- 2 cups Beef Stock or Brown Veal Stock (see page 560)
- 1 onion, coarsely chopped
- 1 carrot, diced
- 1 tomato, diced
- 1 bay leaf
- 1 sprig fresh thyme *or* a pinch of dried thyme
- 5 parsley stems
- 2 teaspoons tomato paste
  Salt and freshly ground pepper, to taste

1. In a medium, heavy-bottomed saucepan, heat oil over low heat; add flour and cook, whisking constantly, until mixture is golden brown. Be careful to keep it from burning. Remove from heat.

2. Gradually whisk stock into flour mixture. Add onion, carrot, tomato, bay leaf, thyme, and parsley. Bring to a boil, stirring constantly. Reduce heat to low and simmer, uncovered, stirring frequently, for 1 hour.

3. Stir tomato paste into sauce, season lightly with salt and pepper, and simmer 1 minute. Strain through a fine sieve. If not using sauce at once, dab top with butter to prevent a skin from forming. Sauce can be refrigerated, covered, up to 3 days, or frozen.

Makes about 1½ cups.

▣ MADEIRA SAUCE

Serve with grilled or sautéed steaks or with roast beef, veal, chicken, or turkey.

- 1½ cups Basic Brown Sauce (above) or Quick Brown Sauce (at right)
- 4 tablespoons Madeira
  Salt and freshly ground pepper, to taste
- 1 tablespoon butter (optional)

1. In a medium, heavy-bottomed saucepan, bring brown sauce to a boil over medium heat, whisking often.

2. Whisk in 2 tablespoons of the Madeira, add salt and pepper, and simmer, uncovered, over medium-low heat for 10 minutes.

3. Add remaining 2 tablespoons Madeira and bring just to a simmer. Remove from heat and stir in butter, if desired. Taste and add more salt and pepper, if needed. Serve hot.

Makes about 1½ cups.

▣ QUICK BROWN SAUCE

This version of brown sauce provides a quick substitute for Basic Brown Sauce (at left), although this recipe produces a sauce that is lighter in color and texture and not quite as rich; it also includes tomatoes and tomato paste for additional flavor.

- 1 tablespoon vegetable oil
- 1 onion, diced
- 1 carrot, diced
- 2 cups Beef Stock, Brown Veal Stock, or Chicken Stock (see page 560)
- 2 ripe, medium fresh tomatoes *or* 4 drained canned plum tomatoes, diced
- 4 tablespoons cold water
- 1 tablespoon tomato paste
- 1 tablespoon potato starch or cornstarch
  Salt and freshly ground pepper, to taste

1. In a medium, heavy-bottomed saucepan, heat oil over medium-high heat. Add onion and carrot and sauté, stirring often, until well browned. Be careful not to let vegetables burn.

2. Add stock and tomatoes to saucepan. Bring to a boil, stirring constantly. Reduce heat to very low, cover, and simmer 30 minutes.

3. In a small bowl whisk the cold water into tomato paste. Add potato starch and whisk to form a smooth paste. Gradually pour into simmering sauce, whisking constantly. Bring sauce back to a boil, whisking. Season very lightly with salt and pepper. Strain sauce, pressing on vegetables.

4. If not using sauce immediately, dab surface with a small piece of butter to prevent a skin from forming. Sauce can be refrigerated, covered, up to 3 days, or frozen.

Makes about 1½ cups.

Brown Sauce With Herbs Bring 1 cup Quick Brown Sauce or Basic Brown Sauce (at left) to a simmer in a small, heavy-bottomed saucepan over low heat. Remove from heat and stir in 1 to 2 tablespoons chopped fresh tarragon, chives, basil, or parsley. If desired, stir in 1 tablespoon butter.

TOMATO SAUCE

Favorites in many cuisines, tomato sauces are good with almost every food, from meats to fish and pasta. The best tomato sauces are those made with fresh tomatoes, although canned ones can be used as well. In fact, when tomatoes are not plentiful, canned tomatoes may be a better choice; they will often have more flavor than what is offered fresh in the market off-season. Because tomatoes are the star ingredient and determine the final flavor of the sauce, they must be ripe. Sometimes the appearance of

---

TIPS

HOW TO MAKE PERFECT GRAVY

For many people, a beef roast or a turkey just isn't a meal without rich brown gravy. Here are some ideas for making your gravy smooth and flavorful.

- *Think of gravy as a thickened sauce. First remove the meat from the roasting pan, then pour or spoon off the fat and measure it. For each cup of gravy, measure 1 to 2 tablespoons of fat into a saucepan. Discard the rest.*

- *Loosen the drippings in the pan with liquid—beef or chicken broth, water, or red or white wine (or a combination of these). Heat and stir to loosen brown bits, and pour the liquid into a measuring cup; if there are large undissolved bits, pour liquid through a sieve. Don't add too much liquid, or the flavor will be weak.*

- *For each cup of liquid, measure 1 to 2 tablespoons flour. Stir the flour into the fat in the saucepan and heat until bubbly. Remove from heat. Using a wire whisk, gradually stir in the liquid. Return to heat and cook, stirring constantly, until mixture is thickened. Boil 3 to 5 minutes more. Salt to taste.*

- *If you prefer a creamy gravy for pork or chicken, use a liquid of about half milk, and half broth or water.*

tomatoes is misleading because they are red on the outside but turn out to have disappointingly pale flesh. To avoid these, choose tomatoes that are not too firm and that have a strong aroma of tomatoes. No extra thickening is required for most tomato sauces because the tomato pulp thickens the sauce as it cooks.

Herbs and tomatoes are natural partners. Besides the familiar tomato-loving herbs—basil, thyme, and oregano—almost any fresh herb or good-quality dried herb can flavor a tomato sauce. Members of the onion family, especially yellow onions, leeks, shallots, and garlic, can be chopped, sautéed, and cooked with the tomatoes to increase depth of flavor.

Although tomato sauce is delicious alone, it is so versatile that it can also be mixed with most other sauces. Add a few tablespoons to Basic White Sauce (see page 513) or Velouté Sauce (see page 514) to make an orange-colored sauce that is good with fish. Combine tomato sauce with a brown sauce and serve with roast tenderloin of beef, or mix with one of the butter sauces, such as Béarnaise (see page 518) and use with steaks, veal, and eggs.

▨ BASIC TOMATO SAUCE

The flavor of this chunky sauce is fresh because the tomatoes cook only briefly. This sauce is good with pasta, fish, chicken, meat, eggs, and vegetables. There are many ways to vary the flavor of the sauce: Butter or olive oil can replace the vegetable oil; thyme and bay leaves as well as a variety of fresh herbs can be added to the finished sauce (basil is especially good, but tarragon, oregano, and cilantro also add an interesting change of flavor). Adding a tablespoon of tomato paste brightens the sauce. When tomatoes are out of season, use 2½ pounds (undrained weight) of canned whole plum tomatoes; drain them well and chop them. For a very smooth sauce, purée Basic Tomato Sauce in a food processor or blender.

>   2 tablespoons vegetable oil
>   ½ onion, chopped
>   1 clove garlic, finely chopped
> 2½ pounds ripe tomatoes, peeled, seeded,
>   and chopped
>   Pinch dried thyme
>   1 bay leaf
>   Salt and freshly ground pepper, to taste

1. In a medium, heavy-bottomed skillet, heat oil over low heat. Add onion and cook, stirring occasionally, until soft but not browned (about 7 minutes). Stir in garlic and cook 30 seconds.

2. Add tomatoes, thyme, bay leaf, and salt and pepper. Cook over medium heat, stirring often, until tomatoes are soft and mixture is thick and smooth (about 20 minutes).

3. Discard bay leaf. Taste and add more salt and pepper, if needed. Sauce can be refrigerated, covered, up to 2 days, or frozen. Serve hot.

Makes about 1½ cups.

BUTTER SAUCES

Probably the most popular group of sauces, these are rich and silky in texture because their main ingredient, butter, not only enriches but also constitutes the body of the sauce. Butter sauces are reserved for special occasions and for the most festive foods, such as lobster, scallops, fresh salmon, and asparagus.

Although butter sauces can be made quickly, they also demand the most care and can separate if not prepared properly. They are emulsions, or fragile combinations of fat (in this case heated butter) and liquid. If the butter separates from the liquid, the sauce loses its lovely texture and becomes watery and unattractive. Hollandaise and béarnaise sauces, which contain egg yolks in addition to the butter, lose their smoothness if the egg yolks curdle, or cook into small bits resembling scrambled eggs. To avoid both problems, whisk the sauce constantly and do not cook it too long or over too high a flame. They should be served warm, not boiling hot.

Because these sauces are so sensitive to heat, it is best not to serve them on heated plates. Often they are served separately, in sauceboats. A small amount of the rich sauce is all that is needed: 3 tablespoons per person is usually enough with most foods.

Butter sauces should not be prepared ahead. If some sauce is left, however, do not discard it; store it in the refrigerator or freezer. Leftover sauce cannot be reheated to its former smoothness, but it can be whisked in small pieces into another sauce, especially a velouté or tomato sauce, or stirred into dishes such as hot cooked rice, pasta, or vegetables for a special flavor.

▨ HOLLANDAISE SAUCE

One of the most delicate of sauces, Hollandaise is a favorite with poached fish, shellfish, and vegetables. Also try it with poultry: Enrich the basic sauce with whipping cream, or mix chopped fresh tomatoes into room-temperature Hollandaise and serve over cold poached chicken breasts. The predominant flavor in the sauce is butter. A small amount of lemon juice is added as a seasoning. Many cooks increase the amount of lemon juice, especially when serving the sauce with fish. Hollandaise can be held up to 45 minutes in a double boiler set on a warming tray.

>   3 egg yolks
>   3 tablespoons water
>   Salt
>   ¾ cup unsalted butter, clarified (see page 68)
>   Pinch cayenne pepper
>   ¼ teaspoon strained fresh lemon juice, or to taste

1. In a small, heavy-bottomed nonreactive saucepan, combine egg yolks, the water, and salt; whisk briefly. Cook over low heat, whisking vigorously and constantly, until mixture is creamy and thick enough that whisk leaves a visible trail on bottom of pan. (Be careful not to let mixture overheat or egg yolks will curdle. Remove pan from heat occasionally so that it does not become too hot; sides of pan should be cool enough to touch.) When yolk mixture becomes thick enough, remove it immediately from heat and whisk for another 30 seconds.

2. With saucepan off heat gradually whisk in clarified butter drop by drop. After sauce has absorbed about 2 or 3 tablespoons butter, add remaining butter in a very thin stream, whisking vigorously and constantly. Stir in cayenne and lemon juice. Taste and add more salt, cayenne, and lemon juice, if needed.

3. Serve sauce as soon as possible. It can be kept warm in saucepan for about 15 minutes if set on a rack above warm water, but it must be whisked frequently. It can also be kept warm in a thermos.

Makes about 1 cup.

■ QUICK HOLLANDAISE SAUCE

Using a blender or food processor to prepare Hollandaise sauce makes a more stable emulsion, but the sauce will lack some of the body and flavor of the traditional preparation. This quick version can be served with the same foods as the traditional Hollandaise sauce. There is no need to heat the egg yolks in a saucepan; the butter, heated until bubbling, cooks the egg yolks slightly. A quick version of Béarnaise sauce (see page 518 for the traditional recipe), is offered at the end of the recipe.

> **3 egg yolks, at room temperature**
> **1 tablespoon water**
>   **Salt**
> **¾ cup unsalted butter, clarified (see page 68)**
>   **Pinch cayenne pepper**
> **½ teaspoon strained fresh lemon juice, or to taste**

1. In a blender or food processor, process egg yolks with the water and salt until the color lightens and they are very well blended. Heat butter to just bubbling. With machine running, gradually incorporate hot butter drop by drop into yolk mixture. After 2 or 3 tablespoons butter have been added, pour remaining butter through in a fine stream, with machine still running.

2. Add cayenne and lemon juice and process briefly to mix. Taste and add more salt, cayenne, and lemon juice, if needed.

3. Serve sauce as soon as possible. To keep it warm for about 15 minutes, transfer to a saucepan placed in a pan of warm water, and whisk sauce frequently. It can also be kept warm in a thermos.

Makes about 1 cup.

Quick Béarnaise Sauce Prepare the liquid flavoring for Béarnaise Sauce, page 518, step 2, and substitute it for the water in Quick Hollandaise Sauce. In step 2 of Quick Hollandaise Sauce, omit lemon juice. Stir 1 tablespoon chopped tarragon and 1 tablespoon chopped parsley into finished sauce.

THICKENERS FOR SAUCES AND SOUPS

The same thickeners are employed for both sauces and soups. Listed below are the most commonly used thickening agents and enrichments. Where appropriate, guidelines are offered.

Beurre manié An uncooked paste of equal amounts of butter and flour, beurre manié is used to build up sauces that are too thin. To make beurre manié, knead flour and butter together with fingers, or mash with a fork or spoon. For a soup use 1 tablespoon flour and 1 tablespoon butter to thicken 1 cup of liquid. For a sauce use 2 tablespoons flour and 2 tablespoons butter to thicken 1 cup of liquid. Extra beurre manié can be stored, wrapped in waxed paper, in the refrigerator for about 10 days.

Butter swirls Although used mostly as a finish, butter swirls will thicken sauce and soup slightly. Add bits of butter to the sauce or soup at the end of cooking and swirl in the pan to create a spiral; do not stir; 1 or 2 tablespoons will be enough to finish most sauces and soups.

Cornstarch A sauce thickened with cornstarch is glossy and translucent. Cornstarch is a familiar ingredient in Asian cuisines. To avoid lumping, always add cornstarch mixed with liquid, in paste form. To thicken 1 cup of liquid, mix 1 tablespoon cornstarch with 2 tablespoons water.

Egg yolks and cream When combined, egg yolks and cream act as both thickener and enrichment. For a prepared sauce that is already somewhat thick, mix 1 egg yolk with 2 to 3 tablespoons whipping cream for 1 cup of sauce. If the sauce is quite thin, 2 to 3 yolks may be needed to thicken sufficiently. Pour a little of the hot sauce into the combined yolk and cream and whisk to blend. Pour this mixture back into the sauce and gently heat. Do not allow it to boil or it will curdle. To thicken 6 cups of soup, use 2 egg yolks and ¼ cup of whipping cream. Proceed as for a sauce.

Flour One of the most familiar thickeners, flour contains insoluble proteins that make the sauce opaque (cornstarch is close to a pure starch). Flour should be added as a paste, and then the sauce should be allowed to simmer a few minutes; uncooked flour imparts a strong, undesirable cereal taste. Or, add flour as a roux (see Roux at right).

Reduction This process slowly simmers sauce over low heat until the volume of the sauce decreases and the flavor is greatly concentrated. Cooks in a hurry should avoid reduced sauces, although the patient sauce maker will be rewarded with a bonus of extra flavor. Straining is necessary at times to produce a smooth sauce. Because flavor will intensify as the sauce cooks down, seasoning should be added after reduction. The reduction process is also applied to vegetable purées; the purée alone is cooked down to produce an intense yet lightly flavored sauce.

Roux The most common thickener, roux is equal parts of flour and butter cooked over medium heat to form a paste. One of the secrets of successful sauce making is a properly cooked roux. The combination of butter and flour adds body and flavor to sauces and soups. The paste can be used immediately, or stored in the refrigerator up to 2 weeks. There are three kinds of roux: white, blond, and brown. White roux is barely cooked, just enough to remove the taste of the flour; it is used in cream sauces. Blond roux is cooked to a pale golden color and is used in sauces where a white color is not as essential. Brown roux is cooked until it gives off a nutty aroma; it is used for brown and flavorful sauces. In making roux, heat the butter carefully, or use clarified butter (see page 68). Do not let the butter brown or burn. When adding the flour, whisk vigorously to blend. It will take 2 to 3 minutes over medium heat to cook out the flour taste. For a soup use 1 tablespoon butter and 1 tablespoon flour to thicken 1 cup of liquid. For a sauce use 2 tablespoons butter and 2 tablespoons flour to thicken 1 cup of liquid.

Vegetable purées Used with soups in place of roux, these purées provide a unique taste. Vegetable purées add bulk so that another thickener is usually not required. However, cream is often added to a vegetable-purée–based soup for richness. Vegetables suitable for puréeing and adding to soups include beans (such as lentil, black bean, and split pea), tomato, carrot, cucumber, zucchini, potato, and leek. The quantity of purée needed to thicken a soup varies with the vegetable; add it in small amounts until the desired consistency is achieved.

Whipping cream By itself, whipping cream is considered a thickener and an enrichment. Reduced, cream is one of the preferred thickening agents for sauces in nouvelle cuisine. For soups add cream at the end of cooking, in whatever amount produces the desired flavor and consistency.

A Mexican table setting is incomplete without a bowl of salsa. The ingredients common to most red salsas are onions, garlic, tomatoes, fresh cilantro, and, of course, chiles.

■ TARTAR SAUCE WITH GREEN PEPPERCORNS

Green peppercorns give extra zip to tartar sauce, a traditional accompaniment to fried fish. The sauce is also delicious with fried vegetables, especially cauliflower, and with cold chicken or turkey. For added interest, use green peppercorn mustard or herb mustard instead of Dijon mustard.

> 1 cup Mayonnaise (see page 519)
> 1 tablespoon Dijon mustard
> 2 tablespoons chopped parsley
> 1 tablespoon chopped green onion, preferably green part
> 1 hard-cooked egg, chopped
> 1 tablespoon drained capers, rinsed and chopped
> 2 teaspoons drained green peppercorns
> 1 tablespoon chopped dill pickle
> 1 teaspoon strained fresh lemon juice (optional)
> Salt and pepper, to taste

1. In a bowl mix mayonnaise and mustard until thoroughly blended. Stir in parsley, green onion, egg, capers, peppercorns, and pickle.

2. Taste and add lemon juice (if desired) and salt and pepper, if needed. Sauce can be refrigerated, covered, up to 2 days.

Makes about 1¼ cups.

■ VINAIGRETTE DRESSING

This popular salad dressing is perfect for green salad because it coats the greens lightly. It is also good with almost any salad ingredient, from raw or cooked vegetables to meats, fish, and pasta. Herb vinaigrette is especially good with seafood salads. Although vinaigrette is usually associated with cold dishes, it also makes a quick and pleasant sauce for hot food, especially fish, poultry, and meat.

There are many ways to vary the basic dressing. Replace the vegetable oil with olive, walnut, or other oil. Use white wine vinegar or red wine vinegar for dressings used every day; or try Champagne vinegar, sherry vinegar, or tarragon vinegar for special occasions.

> 2 tablespoons wine vinegar or strained fresh lemon juice
> Salt and pepper, to taste
> 6 tablespoons vegetable or olive oil

1. In a small bowl whisk vinegar and salt and pepper until salt dissolves.

2. Whisk in oil. Taste, and add more salt and pepper, if needed. Dressing can be refrigerated, covered, up to 1 week. Whisk before using.

Makes about ½ cup.

Caper Vinaigrette   With the oil, whisk in 1 tablespoon chopped capers and 2 tablespoons chopped parsley. As capers are salty, add salt to the dressing with a light touch. This dressing flatters grilled fish and fish salads.

Herb Vinaigrette   Just before using, add 1 tablespoon chopped parsley, chives, basil, or tarragon. For a more intense tarragon flavor, make the dressing with tarragon vinegar and add chopped fresh tarragon.

■ MUSTARD VINAIGRETTE

This dressing is thicker than most vinaigrettes because the oil is whisked in gradually. In addition the mustard helps to thicken it. Instead of plain Dijon mustard, you can use a grainy type or a flavored version such as herb mustard or green peppercorn mustard. If desired, add capers for more texture and flavor.

> 1 teaspoon Dijon mustard
> 3 tablespoons red wine vinegar
> 1 clove garlic, minced
> Salt and pepper, to taste
> 9 tablespoons olive oil
> 1 tablespoon capers (optional)

1. Whisk mustard, vinegar, garlic, and salt and pepper together in a small bowl. Gradually pour in oil in a fine stream, whisking constantly.

2. Mix in capers, if used. Adjust seasoning, if needed. Dressing can be refrigerated, covered, up to 1 week. Whisk before using.

Makes about ¾ cup.

RASPBERRY VINEGAR AND SHALLOT DRESSING

This pink dressing has a wonderful aroma of raspberries. Use it to flavor poultry salads and to add unexpected zip to simple green salads. The dressing is made quickly in a food processor, but it can be prepared in a blender or bowl instead if the shallot is finely chopped by hand. If you are using a blender, combine the chopped shallot with the other ingredients in step 1 and continue with the rest of the recipe. If you prefer to prepare the dressing by hand, follow the procedure for Vinaigrette Dressing (opposite page), adding the chopped shallot at the beginning.

  ½ **small shallot, peeled and halved**
  3 **tablespoons raspberry vinegar**
     Salt and pepper, to taste
  ½ **cup plus 1 tablespoon vegetable oil**

1. Chop shallot until fine by dropping pieces one by one down feed tube of a food processor while blade is turning. Add vinegar and salt and pepper; process until combined.

2. As blade is turning, gradually pour in oil. Dressing will thicken slightly. Taste and add more salt and pepper, if needed. Dressing can be refrigerated, covered, up to 2 days. Whisk before using.

Makes about ¾ cup.

OTHER SAUCES

In addition to the classic sauces, we enjoy many other types throughout a meal, as dipping sauces for hors d'oeuvres, as accompaniments to the main course, and as toppings for all kinds of desserts.

CURRY SAUCE

A smooth and silky curry dip works magic on hard-cooked eggs, boiled shrimp and crab, or a basket of snow peas and hearts of bok choy. Or, serve it with thinly sliced cold chicken, smoked turkey, roast pork, or ham. The sauce keeps up to two weeks in the refrigerator.

  ¼ **cup honey**
  1 **cup Chicken Stock (see page 560)**
  2 **tablespoons hot curry powder**
  1 **tablespoon ground coriander**
  ½ **teaspoon cayenne pepper**
  ½ **teaspoon white pepper**
  ⅓ **cup Dijon mustard**
3⅓ **cups Mayonnaise (see page 519)**

1. In a small saucepan combine honey and stock. Heat and stir until honey dissolves. Add curry powder, coriander, cayenne, and white pepper. Continue cooking over moderate heat until mixture is reduced to ¾ cup.

2. Remove from heat and cool completely. Add mustard and Mayonnaise. Mix well.

Makes about 4 cups.

WATERCRESS DIP WITH GREEN ONIONS AND BASIL

This dip is a showstopper—a nutty, coarse-textured creation fragrant with basil and brilliantly green. Beside it arrange a basket of crudités: cherry tomatoes, cauliflower and broccoli florets, snow peas, endive leaves, zucchini and carrot spears, artichoke hearts, and radishes or fennel. The dip keeps up to 10 days in the refrigerator. To stem the watercress easily, hold the base of the watercress in one hand. With the other hand, pull along the stem. All the leaves on one stem will come off with this one movement.

  3 **cups watercress, stems trimmed**
  ¾ **cup fresh small basil leaves**
  ¼ **cup minced garlic**
  ½ **cup good-quality olive oil**
  1 **cup freshly grated Parmesan cheese**
  ¾ **cup whipping cream**
  ½ **cup finely ground walnuts**
  ¼ **cup minced green onions**
     Salt and freshly ground pepper, to taste
  1 **tablespoon milk or water (optional)**

1. In a blender combine watercress, basil, garlic, olive oil, and grated Parmesan cheese. Blend until pasty. Add cream and blend only until ingredients are mixed (do not overblend).

2. Transfer mixture to a bowl and stir in walnuts and green onion. Add salt and pepper. Mixture will thicken as it stands; if desired, add milk or water to thin it out before serving.

Makes 2 cups.

SALSA CRUDA

This basic uncooked salsa is found on the tables of practically every restaurant in Mexico. It is an indispensable presence at a Mexican meal and should be a part of any repast with a Mexican theme. Set it out as a dip for fried tortilla chips or as a sauce for grilled or broiled seafood. It is delightful spooned onto raw oysters or steamed mussels on the half shell; or try it wrapped up in a warm soft tortilla with crispy *carnitas* or pork in green chile.

  1 **yellow onion, peeled and minced**
  3 **fresh ripe tomatoes, peeled, seeded, and coarsely chopped**
  2 **tablespoons minced cilantro**
  1 **clove garlic, minced**
  1 **small green chile, minced, or more to taste**
  1 **tablespoon fresh lime juice**
     Salt, to taste

In a small bowl combine all ingredients except salt no more than 1 hour before serving. Do not add salt until the last minute. Salsa is best when freshly made.

Makes about ¾ cup.

ORANGE FLOWER WATER

A highly perfumed, clear liquid, orange flower water is distilled from fresh orange blossoms. In Morocco orange flower water is sometimes used to scent the water poured over hands before dining. Middle Eastern cooks use it to scent rice dishes, puddings, cookies, cakes, and pastries. It is an ingredient in some cocktails, such as the Ramos gin fizz. The fragrance of orange flower water dissipates with air and heat; for maximum effect, add it to cooked dishes when they are cool or cooling. Orange flower water is available in liquor stores and some supermarkets. Store in a cool, dark place; it will keep for several months but will gradually lose strength.

OYSTER SAUCE

This thick, pourable brown liquid is made by fermenting dried oysters with soy sauce and brine. The best oyster sauces are fermented for several years before bottling. They are widely used in Cantonese cooking as a flavor enhancer. Chinese cooks use oyster sauce to impart richness and body to many dishes. It is added to stir-fried meats and vegetables and is offered as a table condiment for roast pork and cold chicken. Oyster sauce in bottles, jars, and cans is readily available in Asian markets. It will keep indefinitely in the refrigerator. Some brands contain cornstarch and will thicken a sauce slightly; adjust ingredients accordingly. Because oyster sauce is salty, most recipes calling for it do not require salt.

PLUM SAUCE

Made from plums, apricots, chiles, vinegar, and sugar, this thick Chinese condiment is dark amber in color, with a sweet-tart, slightly hot flavor. Also known as duck sauce, it accompanies roast duck, pork, spareribs, and egg rolls. Plum sauce is sometimes used as a basting sauce for roast duck and as a sauce enrichment in stir-fried dishes. Plum sauce, bottled or canned, is widely available in Chinese markets. Once opened, canned plum sauce should be transferred to an airtight nonreactive container; it may be refrigerated for up to one year.

ROSE WATER

A highly perfumed, clear liquid, rose water is distilled from fragrant rose petals. A more concentrated form is known as rose essence. Rose water is a popular flavoring in Middle Eastern cooking, added to orange salads, rice pudding, and custard-filled pastries. In India, where rose flavoring is also appreciated, rose essence is preferred and used in a version of ice cream, in the yogurt drink called *lassi,* in sweet carrot pudding, and in the syrup served with fried dessert dumplings. Iranian cooks make a sherbet of rose water, sugar, and water. Rose water is also required in some exotic cocktails. The essence is much stronger than the water and should be added drop by drop.

Bottled rose water is available in some supermarkets, liquor stores, and specialty markets. Rose water and rose essence are sold in Middle Eastern and Indian markets. Store rose water and rose essence in tightly closed bottles in a cool, dark place. They will keep for at least one year but lose strength with age. Because these fragrances are alcohol based, they are volatile (dissipating with heat). Add them to cooled or cooling mixtures for maximum effect.

SOY SAUCE

Essential to Chinese and Japanese cooking, soy sauce is a fermented product based on soy beans. Most brands also contain wheat. Tamari is essentially the same as soy sauce but is made without wheat (see Tamari). Although brands and styles vary in color and flavor, most soy sauce is dark brown. Japanese soy sauce has a relatively sweet flavor and is less salty than either Chinese or American varieties. Chinese soy sauce is extremely salty. Black soy sauce, specified in some recipes, has molasses added; it is richer and saltier in flavor than regular soy sauce. Most American-made soy sauce falls between the two styles. The most widely distributed brand, Kikkoman, is light bodied, light flavored, and lacks the sweetness of the Japanese brands and the saltiness of the Chinese. Synthetic soy sauces made from hydrolized soy protein, which are also manufactured in this country and have wide distribution, are a poor substitute for the real thing.

Soy sauce is used by Chinese and Japanese cooks in much the same way that Westerners use salt—as a flavor enhancer. In China it is not considered a table condiment; rather, it is added to foods before or during cooking. Soy sauce adds a distinctive fermented flavor to almost all stir-fried dishes, whether of meat, chicken, fish, or vegetables; it adds a brown gloss to steamed chicken and roast duck; it flavors noodle dishes, both hot and cold. In Japan soy sauce is on the table to be used as a dipping sauce for sushi, sashimi, and tempura; it is used in soups such as *shabu-shabu* and provides the base for dozens of basting sauces brushed on pork, seafood, or chicken while grilling.

All supermarkets stock American-made soy sauce in bottles or cans. Many also stock synthetic soy sauce and low-sodium soy sauce. Asian markets stock imported soy sauces from China and Japan. Because of its high salt content, soy sauce does not require refrigeration. It will keep indefinitely in a cool, dark place. Low-sodium soy sauce must be refrigerated.

STEAK SAUCE

Although steak sauces vary from manufacturer to manufacturer, most are liquid to semiliquid condiments with a sweet-sour-salty balance of flavors. The most popular brand in this country, A-1 Sauce, contains tomato paste, vinegar, corn syrup, raisins, orange peel, and other herbs, spices, and seasonings. Other popular brands contain chile peppers, molasses, or soy sauce.

Sprinkle steak sauce on steaks, chops, or hamburgers before or after grilling or add to barbecue sauces and marinades. Most supermarkets carry a variety of bottled steak sauces, which should be stored in the refrigerator after opening; steak sauce will keep indefinitely.

SWEET-AND-SOUR SAUCE

The contrast of sweet-and-sour flavors is important to Chinese cooking but bottled sweet-and-sour sauce was created for the American palate. Most commercial versions of this sauce are thick with cornstarch and may contain food coloring. The texture and flavor they impart are far removed from the texture and flavor of authentic Chinese sweet-and-sour dishes. In the American kitchen, the sauce can be used to glaze ham or spareribs. Bottled sweet-and-sour sauce is available in most supermarkets and some Asian markets. After opening, store lidded jar in the refrigerator; it will keep indefinitely.

TABASCO SAUCE

See Hot-Pepper Sauce.

TAMARI

A cultured and fermented liquid soybean product, tamari resembles soy sauce, but is thicker and stronger in flavor than soy. It is used in Japan as a dipping sauce and a base for basting sauces. Tamari is available in many health-food stores and Japanese markets. A salt-free tamari is also available in some markets. Refrigerate tamari after opening; it will keep indefinitely.

THAI CURRY PASTE

In Thai cooking, many dishes seasoned with a paste of herbs and spices are known as curries. The major types of curry paste in Thailand are red (based on red chile peppers), green (based on green chiles and coriander), and yellow (based on yellow chiles and turmeric). Many cooks make their own curry pastes regularly, altering them with herbs and spices to suit individual tastes. However, bottled curry pastes are widely available and are acceptable to many Thai cooks.

Check Asian markets for bottled Thai curry paste. After opening, store lidded jars in refrigerator; they will keep for several weeks.

WORCESTERSHIRE SAUCE

A liquid condiment reputedly devised by two British chemists in the nineteenth century, Worcestershire sauce today is a fixture in most American refrigerators. The exact formula is a secret, but the label lists vinegar, molasses, tamarind, anchovies, and spices. It is dark brown, with a distinctive flavor that incorporates sweet, sour, salty, and spicy elements. It can be sprinkled on hamburgers or

steaks before or after cooking; some cooks add it to barbecue sauce, marinades, and basting sauces. It is used in most renditions of Caesar salad, in cocktail dips and cheese spreads, in English steak and kidney pie, in steak tartare, Welsh rarebit, and Bloody Marys.

Bottled Worcestershire sauce is available in supermarkets. Refrigerate after opening; it will keep indefinitely.

Grilled Italian sausages and sautéed bell peppers and onions are robust accompaniments to omelets. Cook the meat outdoors on a grill or indoors in a skillet.

SAUSAGE

Highly seasoned ground pork is the basis for most of the world's sausages, although some delicious sausages are made using chicken, turkey, game birds, and even seafood. Perhaps the best definition is that sausage is made from ground meat, usually stuffed in a casing (but not necessarily), usually highly seasoned with herbs and/or spices, and frequently laced with such flavorful additions as cubes of fat, truffles, pistachios, peppercorns, wine, or chiles.

A piquant green sauce unites all elements in Boiled Dinner Bolognese (recipe is on page 530). If you wish, serve the cooking broth as a first course. Or, strain and freeze it to use later as the base for your next bollito misto.

Use   Sausage is used in sandwiches, stuffings, pasta sauces, savory pies and pastries, soups, casseroles, and stews. From breakfast links to the midday hot dog to a dinner of grilled wurst and potatoes, sausage satisfies American appetites all day long.

Availability   Most of the sausage available in the United States is made there or in Canada. Imported pork products must conform to extremely strict federal regulations and are, at this writing, essentially unavailable in the United States.

     The major types of sausages sold in America are described in the following pages. Although supermarkets carry a variety of fresh and cured sausage, the best sausages are generally found in ethnic markets and specialty stores. Italian, German, and French markets are good sources for sausages made by traditional European methods.

Selection   An off odor is the first clue to deterioration in sausage; avoid any that smell strong or sour. Fresh sausage is especially perishable and should be bought from a market with a rapid turnover.

Storage   Because it is so perishable, sausage should be refrigerated and used within two or three days or it can be frozen for up to two months. If the meat has been lightly smoked, it can be refrigerated for up to one week. Cooked sausages can be kept for up to one week in the refrigerator or two months in the freezer; if vacuum-packed and unopened, they can be refrigerated longer. Semidry sausages may be kept at room temperature for two or three days; for longer keeping, refrigerate for up to three weeks. Dry sausages may be stored unsliced at cool room temperature for six weeks; after slicing, refrigerate and use within three weeks. Both semidry and dry sausages may be frozen for up to three months, but with some loss of flavor and texture.

FRESH SAUSAGE

Made from raw ground and seasoned meat, fresh sausage is often bound with eggs, bread crumbs, or cereals. It may or may not be stuffed in a casing and may or may not be smoked. It must be cooked before it is served. Some of the better-known types of fresh sausage are described below.

Bockwurst   A German-style veal sausage, occasionally with pork added, *bockwurst* is usually first boiled, then grilled or panfried. It is traditionally served with potatoes, mustard, and German beer.

Chaurice   See Chorizo.

Chorizo   Both Mexican- and Spanish-style *chorizos* are available. The Mexican type is made from fresh pork and is highly seasoned with vinegar, chiles, garlic, and cumin. It is stuffed into casings and made into links, but most recipes call for removing the casings and crumbling and frying the chorizo. Spanish-style chorizo is usually made from smoked pork and is firmer than the Mexican version; it can be grilled in its casing and sliced for use in soups and bean dishes. *Chaurice* is the Cajun version, made of ground pork highly seasoned with garlic and hot red pepper.

Cotechino   This large, Italian-style pork sausage is usually seasoned with garlic, pepper, fennel seed, and wine. The sausage is poached whole and served hot, with potato salad, lentils, or other boiled meats and vegetables as part of a *bollito misto* (mixed boil).

Crépinette   A French-style sausage that is shaped into a patty and wrapped in caul fat, most *crépinettes* are made of ground pork and seasoned with herbs, although ground chicken, cooked spinach, and nuts such as pistachios and chestnuts are other common additions. They may be panfried without any fat, or brushed with butter, coated with bread crumbs, and grilled.

Italian Link Sausage   Most Italian markets carry hot and sweet versions of this link sausage. Both are pork sausages seasoned with garlic, wine, and fennel, but the hot version has red pepper, too. To cook, the sausages are poached briefly, then panfried or grilled. The meat can be removed from the casings and used on pizzas or in sauces or stuffings.

Saucisson à l'Ail This French garlic sausage is comparable to Italian *cotechino* without fennel. It is usually served with lentils, potato salad, mashed potatoes, or white beans.

Weisswurst This white German sausage is made from veal. After steaming it can be eaten in a bun with mustard or cut up and added to stews and soups.

COOKED SAUSAGE

Although the following sausages are generally sold fully cooked and ready to eat, many taste better when hot; they are usually reheated before serving.

Andouille Usually salted and smoked, *andouille* is a large French-style tripe sausage that is most often eaten cold in thin slices. *Andouillette* is a similar but smaller sausage, made of tripe and spices stuffed in a sausage casing; it is not usually smoked. Andouillettes are usually grilled and served hot with mashed potatoes, potato salad, or French fries.

Blood Sausage The British call this sausage *black pudding;* the French, *boudin noir;* Cajuns, *boudin rouge;* and the Germans, *blutwurst.* It is made from pork blood, pork fat, and seasonings. French varieties usually contain bread crumbs and cream; English varieties may include barley or oatmeal; Cajun blood sausage commonly contains cayenne pepper and garlic. They are generally grilled or sautéed in butter or bacon fat and served hot with French fries, potato salad, mashed potatoes, or sauerkraut.

Bologna Spelled baloney in American markets, *bologna* is the term applied to a large variety of lightly smoked sausages that are sliced thin and eaten cold. Bologna may be made of pork, beef, turkey, veal, ham, or a combination. It may be fine or coarse textured and lightly or richly spiced. Bologna is usually served in thin slices as an appetizer or sandwich filling.

Boudin Blanc This smooth-textured French-style white sausage is made of pork, veal, and/or chicken, usually bound with cream, onions, and bread crumbs. *Boudin blanc* is usually panfried or grilled before serving and is often accompanied by mashed potatoes.

Bratwurst A German-style pork or pork and veal sausage, bratwurst may be fresh or cooked. If fresh, it must be boiled first. Fresh bratwurst is often simmered in beer, then panfried or grilled, and served with sauerkraut. Cooked bratwurst is reheated—either steamed, panfried, or grilled—before serving.

Braunschweiger See Liverwurst.

Frankfurter Today, *frankfurter* is a generic name for a huge variety of sausages, also known as wieners or hot dogs. Frankfurters may be made of pork, beef, turkey, chicken, or a combination; kosher franks are all beef. Frankfurters range from the tiny cocktail size (24 to a pound) to foot-long dogs (4 to a pound), but most are about 4 inches long and 8 or 10 to a pound. Frankfurters are usually steamed or grilled before being served in buns with such optional accompaniments as mustard, relish, chili, and sauerkraut. Frankfurters may also be cut into chunks and added to stews or soups, such as old-fashioned split pea soup.

Head Cheese Composed of small pieces of hog's head bound in gelatin, head cheese is usually seasoned with white wine and spices. It is sliceable and commonly served cold with vinaigrette and a salad.

Knockwurst Similar to frankfurters, but usually thicker and more highly seasoned, knockwurst (or knackwurst) are German-style sausages that may be cooked whole and served like hot dogs or may be sliced and added to potato salad.

Liverwurst and Braunschweiger Both variations on the same theme, these two sausages are smooth textured, spreadable, and usually made of pork liver (sometimes beef or goose liver). American-style liverwurst is usually not smoked, but German-style braunschweiger usually is. Both are served as an appetizer with crackers or as a sandwich filling.

Thuringer Several types of German-style sausage are called Thuringer. It may be fresh, in which case it must be poached before serving, then panfried or grilled. Or it may be semidry, smoked, and ready-to-eat. The semidry type is often served as an appetizer, thinly sliced, or cut up and added to split pea or bean soups.

SEMIDRY AND DRY SAUSAGE

Semidry sausages have been smoked to remove some of the moisture. They are often called summer sausages, a legacy from prerefrigeration days. Because they were partially dried, they could be kept for some time without spoiling, even in warm weather.

Fully dry sausages may be smoked or unsmoked but have been dried from one to six months for preservation. They usually have a slightly shriveled exterior and are firm enough to slice thinly.

Cervelas A semidry French-style pork sausage, *cervelas* is usually seasoned with garlic. To serve, it is poached, then sliced and accompanied with mustard and potato salad. It is also occasionally poached, then wrapped in brioche dough and baked.

Cervelat The name *cervelat* is applied to a variety of Middle European–style summer sausages. Most are made of pork or beef and are smoked. They may be thinly sliced as an appetizer or diced and added to salads, soups, or bean dishes.

Kielbasa This is the Polish word for sausage, usually applied in this country to a smoked, semidry sausage seasoned highly with garlic, pepper, paprika, and herbs. Most American-made *kielbasa* is shaped into long, thick links that may weigh a pound or more. They are usually made of pork but some contain beef or veal as well. Kielbasa can be sliced and eaten cold, but it is usually poached and served with potatoes, lentils, or sauerkraut. It may also be sliced and added to soups and stews or used in recipes that call for garlic sausage.

Linguiça A Portuguese-style pork sausage seasoned with red pepper and garlic, *linguiça* is similar to chorizo but generally thinner, firmer, and milder. It is diced and scrambled with eggs or added to omelets. It may be added to soups, or cut into chunks, skewered, and grilled.

Mortadella Smooth-textured mortadella is an Italian-style pork sausage larded with cubes of fat and black peppercorns. Most domestic mortadella is about 6 inches in diameter; in Italy it can be much wider. Mortadella is thinly sliced and eaten cold as an appetizer; it may also be diced and added to stuffings.

Pepperoni Another dried type of Italian-style sausage, pepperoni is made of beef or pork, usually 1 to 1½ inches in diameter, and highly seasoned with red and black pepper. It is thinly sliced and served as an appetizer or a pizza garnish.

Salami Including a variety of dried, sliceable sausages made throughout Europe, most salami is made of raw pork or beef that is highly seasoned, stuffed into casings, and air-dried. It is usually not smoked. Popular salami made in the United States include Genoa and French Lyonnaise types, the latter identified as *saucisson sec.* Salami is usually sliced thin and served as an appetizer or sandwich filling. Jewish delicatessens often scramble eggs with sliced kosher all-beef salami.

▨ HOMEMADE PORK SAUSAGE

Pork butt often contains a generous proportion of fat. Trim off some of it if you prefer a leaner sausage—but not all of it. Fat makes the sausage juicy and carries the flavors of the seasonings. Grind the meat, using a meat grinder or a food processor, then mix in savory seasonings.

> 2 pounds boneless pork butt, cut in 1-inch cubes
> 1 clove garlic, minced or pressed
> 1½ teaspoons dried sage
> 1 teaspoon salt
> ½ teaspoon *each* coarsely ground black pepper and dried summer savory or marjoram
> ¼ teaspoon *each* ground allspice and dried thyme
> ⅛ teaspoon cayenne pepper

1. *To make in a meat grinder:* Using coarse blade, grind pork cubes twice. *To make in a food processor:* Spread pork cubes in a single layer on a baking sheet and place in freezer until meat is firm but not frozen (about 20 minutes). Then process, using short on-off bursts, until meat is coarsely ground.

2. Using mortar and pestle or blender, combine garlic, sage, salt, black pepper, summer savory, allspice, thyme, and cayenne thoroughly. Add to ground meat and mix well until seasonings are evenly distributed. (Use your hands, if desired.)

3. Wrap well and refrigerate for 8 hours or overnight to blend flavors.

4. Form into patties and cook in a frying pan over medium-low heat until well browned and crusty, or use in recipes as directed.

Makes 2 pounds.

▨ BOILED DINNER BOLOGNESE

A dazzling array of meats and vegetables, each added at just the right stage to achieve tenderness, makes up the Italian simmered dinner known as *bollito misto.* Look for the distinctive, plump *cotechino* sausage in Italian delicatessens; if it isn't stocked regularly, perhaps the dealer can order it for you. It contributes a lot of flavor to the dish.

> 1 beef rump roast (3½ to 4 lb)
> 12 cups water or Beef Stock (see page 560)
> 1 fresh beef tongue (2½ to 3 lb)
> 1 veal shank (1 to 1½ lb), cut through bone into 3 sections
> 1 large onion, finely chopped
> 4 large carrots
> 2 stalks celery, sliced
> 5 sprigs parsley
> 1 tablespoon salt
> ¼ teaspoon *each* whole allspice and black peppercorns
> 1 cotechino sausage (1 to 1½ lb)
> 4 to 6 leeks, well rinsed, with coarse outer leaves discarded and leafy tops trimmed to about 5 inches
> 10 to 12 small red potatoes, scrubbed (unpeeled)
> 1 small savoy cabbage (about 1 lb), cut into 8 wedges

Green Sauce

> ½ cup olive oil
> ¼ cup white wine vinegar
> 3 green onions, coarsely chopped
> 1 cup lightly packed parsley sprigs
> 2 tablespoons capers
> 1 clove garlic, minced
> 1 tablespoon anchovy paste
> Pinch freshly ground pepper
> ¼ cup lightly packed fresh basil leaves *or* 1 tablespoon dried basil
> Salt (optional)

1. Preheat oven to 500° F. Place rump roast in a shallow, heavy roasting pan. Bake, uncovered, turning once, until meat is well browned (20 to 25 minutes). Transfer roast to a 10- to 12-quart, heavy-bottomed kettle with cover. Add a little of the water to juices left in bottom of roasting pan, stirring to loosen any brown drippings that may be stuck to pan bottom and to blend water, juices, and drippings; pour water-drippings mixture over roast in kettle.

2. To kettle add tongue, the 3 pieces of veal shank, and chopped onion. Slice one of the carrots and add it to meats with celery, parsley sprigs, salt, allspice, peppercorns, and remaining water. Bring to a boil over medium heat, cover, reduce heat, and simmer for 2 hours. Add sausage, cover again, and cook for 1 hour more until meats are tender.

3. Meanwhile, cut remaining carrots lengthwise into quarters; cut quarters crosswise into halves. Add carrot pieces to kettle with trimmed whole leeks and whole unpeeled potatoes; cook until meats and potatoes are tender (about 45 minutes).

4. With a slotted spoon remove tongue and set it aside. Remove rump roast, veal shank, and sausage to a large, heated platter. Surround with leeks, potatoes, and carrots. Cover lightly with foil and keep warm while preparing cooked tongue.

5. Cut off and discard bones and gristle at thick end of tongue. Slit the skin on the underside, and starting at the thick end, peel it off. Add tongue to meats and vegetables on platter.

6. Add cabbage wedges to gently boiling broth and cook, uncovered, until cabbage is tender when pierced with a knife and bright green (8 to 10 minutes). While cabbage cooks, prepare Green Sauce. Add cooked cabbage to meats and vegetables on platter.

7. If you wish to serve broth as a first course, strain through a wire sieve, taste and salt if needed, and serve it hot. Then carve meats and serve with vegetables and Green Sauce.

Serves 10 to 12.

Green Sauce In a food processor fitted with a metal blade or a blender, combine olive oil, wine vinegar, green onions, parsley sprigs, capers, garlic, anchovy paste, pepper, and basil. Process or whirl until smooth. Taste and add salt if needed. Serve at room temperature.

Makes about 1¼ cups.

Recipes and Related Information

Barbecued Pork Ribs and Sausages, 292;
Cassoulet, 556; Choucroute Garni, 75; Red Beans
and Rice, 32; Split Pea Soup, Black Forest Style, 565;
Stuffed Mirliton, 110.

SAUTE, TO

Sautéing has been done for centuries, with the French and Chinese its most accomplished practitioners. In fact sautéing and stir-frying are the same technique (see STIR-FRY). In its strictest culinary application, sauté, from the French *sauter* (to jump), means to rapidly cook small, uniformly sized pieces of food over high heat in oil or fat in a specially designed straight-sided, shallow pan with an extralong handle. To keep the food from sticking, the pan is kept in constant motion, so the food "jumps" in the pan. More typically, sautéed food is turned, rather than tossed. Any skillet made of a material that conducts heat well can be substituted for a sauté pan.

When the food is browned on all sides, it is removed from the pan, set aside, and kept warm while the juices are made into an accompanying sauce. Deglazing removes caramelized bits of food from the bottom of the pan and incorporates them into the liquid that is the base for the sauce (see DEGLAZE).

Sautéed Beef Steaks Marchand de Vin is a beef- and red-wine-lover's dream dish—tender, aged beef and a deglazing sauce of good red wine, enriched at the last minute with a bit of butter. The recipe is on page 533.

The tastes of toasted nuts and sweet raisins offer an interesting contrast to the mild-flavored fish in Sole With Almonds, Pine Nuts, and White Raisins. Sauté the nuts in clarified butter to bring out their flavor.

WHAT FOODS CAN BE SAUTEED?

Meats of the highest quality are most suitable for sautéing. Among the dark meats, thin beef steaks and relatively small lamb chops are ideal because they cook through in the time it takes to brown them. Sautéing is also a favorite way to cook chicken livers or thin slices of beef or calf's liver. It is a perfect technique for cooking slim pieces of tender light meats, such as veal chops, and slices of veal scallop, chicken breast, or turkey breast. Food should be uniform in size so the pieces cook quickly and evenly; for this reason slices of meat or poultry are often pounded before being sautéed.

Any fish fillet can be sautéed. Try to choose fillets that are relatively firm fleshed and do not appear to be falling apart. Short fish fillets are easiest to sauté because there is less chance of breakage during turning or transferring to the serving platter. Cut fillets in half before cooking them if they are too long to be handled easily. Very thin fillets such as sole require only about 2 minutes of sautéing on each side. Fish steaks up to 1 inch thick and small whole fish are suitable for sautéing, too, as are shrimp and scallops.

Almost any vegetable can be sautéed. Those that are naturally tender, such as peppers, mushrooms, and zucchini, can be cut into small pieces and sautéed. Others, such as broccoli and cauliflower, should first be blanched to soften them slightly. The blanching process is actually a timesaver: Cut vegetables in appropriately sized pieces, blanch in boiling water and refresh in cold water to stop cooking; then just before serving, sauté vegetables briefly in butter to heat and flavor them.

GETTING STARTED

A successful sauté depends upon three factors. First, the fat must be hot. If it is not hot enough, the food will stick to the pan, the outside won't be seared, and the juices will escape. Second, the food must be absolutely dry. Moisture on the food forms a layer of steam between the food and the fat that prevents searing and browning. Third—and many cooks overlook this factor—the pan must not be too crowded. Space between pieces of food is a prerequisite for thorough browning. Crowding causes steaming, rather than searing, and results in the juices escaping from the food into the pan. It is equally important not to allow too much space between pieces of food in too large of a pan (the more the food covers the fat, the less likely the fat will burn).

Oil alone, or a combination of butter and oil, is used for sautéing. Oil can withstand higher temperatures without burning than butter and is often the choice for searing meats. Butter gives a lovely flavor, but burns easily at higher temperatures; restaurant chefs often add 1 or 2 tablespoons of cooking oil to the butter to raise the temperature at which it will begin to smoke. Or, they use clarified butter (see page 68), which can heat to a higher temperature without deteriorating than unclarified butter.

To protect the delicate flesh of white meats, poultry, and fish from sticking to the pan, cooks often flour these foods lightly before sautéing. Floured meat browns more easily than uncoated meat and has an appetizing appearance. If a nonstick pan is used, these foods can be sautéed without being floured but they will not brown as well. Red meat does not require flouring because the higher fat content helps to keep it from adhering to the pan.

Although the coating has a protective function, it too should be treated with care. Floured food should not be allowed to sit for more than a few minutes because moisture from the food will make the coating gummy. For the same reason, the coated pieces of food should never be piled one on top of the other.

THE SAUTE PANTRY

If the simplicity and speed of sautéing appeal to you, consider having the following on hand as staples in the refrigerator and pantry.

In the refrigerator Butter (including clarified butter), cream or half-and-half, eggs, sauce bases, and stock. Freeze stock and sauce bases that will be held longer than a few days.

On the shelf Bread crumbs, flour, herbs and spices, oils, canned tomatoes and tomato purée, red and white wine, sherry, and brandy.

Equipment Sauté pan or skillet, wooden spoons, slotted spoons, spatula, meat pounder, and paper towels.

SOLE WITH ALMONDS, PINE NUTS, AND WHITE RAISINS

This is a variation of a Venetian dish called *sfogi in saòr*, which means savory soles.

¼ cup white raisins
2 cups dry white wine
5 tablespoons Clarified Butter (see page 68)
¼ cup slivered almonds
6 sole fillets
1 teaspoon salt
½ teaspoon freshly ground pepper
4 tablespoons flour
3 tablespoons unsalted butter
2 tablespoons minced shallot
   Salt and freshly ground pepper, to taste
2 tablespoons pine nuts

1. Soak raisins in white wine for 30 minutes. Remove raisins and reserve both wine and raisins.

2. In sauté pan heat the 5 tablespoons clarified butter. Add almonds to pan and sauté until they begin to color. Remove almonds with slotted spoon and drain on paper towels.

3. Sprinkle fish with the 1 teaspoon salt, ½ teaspoon pepper, and flour. Add fish to pan and sauté each side to a golden brown. Remove fish to a warm platter. Add the 3 tablespoons butter to pan. When butter has melted, add shallot and cook until soft. Add reserved wine and raisins. Cook for 2 to 3 minutes and season to taste with salt and pepper. Add pine nuts to sauce and pour over fish.

Serves 6.

SAUTEED VEGETABLE MEDLEY

This quick side dish pairs well with most roasted meats.

¾ pound small new potatoes, quartered
1 large carrot, cut in sticks
4 small white onions, peeled and halved
2 tablespoons butter
½ pound (20 medium) mushrooms, halved
1 teaspoon dried basil
   Grated Parmesan, Romano, or Sapsago cheese, for garnish (optional)

1. In a large saucepan cook potatoes in boiling salted water to cover for 10 minutes; drain and set aside. Blanch carrot and onions briefly and refresh in cold water to stop cooking.

2. Meanwhile, in a large skillet melt butter; then add mushrooms to skillet and sauté.

3. Add potatoes, carrot, and onions to skillet, and sauté briefly with mushrooms.

4. Add basil; toss vegetables to mix. Garnish with cheese, if desired.

Serves 4.

SAUTEED BEEF STEAKS MARCHAND DE VIN

This simple dish, "wine merchant style," relies on two basic ingredients: good beef and good red wine.

1½ to 2 pounds tender beef steaks (filet mignon, strip, sirloin), ¾ to 1 inch thick
   Salt and freshly ground pepper, to taste
2 tablespoons minced shallot
4 tablespoons butter
½ cup red wine

1. In a heavy skillet over medium-high heat, rub a piece of fat trimmed from steak. Cook steaks, turning once and season after turning with salt and pepper. Test for doneness by pushing on steak with finger: A rare steak offers slight resistance; when medium-rare, it springs back lightly; when medium or beyond, it gets increasingly stiff and resistant. Remove steaks to warm plates.

2. Cook shallot in meat juices until translucent. Add a little of the butter if the pan is nearly dry. Add wine, bring to a boil, and reduce by two thirds. Remove pan from heat, swirl in butter, check seasoning, and spoon the sauce over the steaks.

Serves 4.

Recipes and Related Information
Broccoli Sautéed With Garlic, 60; Chicken Breasts With Grapes, 280; Chicken Breasts With Sherry, Cream, and Mushrooms, 611; Sautéed Cherry Tomatoes, 582; Sautéed Quail With Red Currant Sauce, 478; Trout With Almonds, 231.

Sautéing is a fast-moving process in which food is cooked quickly in a shallow pan and turned frequently with a spatula.

SAVORY

An herb native to the Mediterranean region, savory is of two types: summer savory, an annual, and winter savory, a hardy perennial. The two have a related peppery flavor, but summer savory is milder.

Use Summer savory flatters egg dishes, fish soups, and summer vegetables. Winter savory complements dried bean dishes, meats, sausages, and stuffings.

Availability Look for dried summer and winter savory, both whole and ground, in well-stocked supermarkets. Fresh savory is carried sporadically by specialty markets.

Selection Fresh savory should be crisp and green, with no signs of wilting or decay. Packaged seasonings lose quality after a while; try to buy them from a store that restocks its spice section fairly often.

Storage Dried savory will keep one year in a cool, dark, dry place. Refrigerate fresh savory wrapped in paper towels and plastic wrap.

SCALD, TO

To heat milk so that tiny bubbles form around the inside edge of the pan, although milk should not boil. To dip foods in boiling water or to pour boiling water over them (the same as blanching).

Before milk was pasteurized, scalding was a sanitary measure. Although unnecessary for sanitation today, some recipes specify scalding in order to improve flavor and shorten cooking time. Yeast bread recipes suggest scalding for outmoded reasons. Most custards use heated milk, although it's wisest to let scalded milk cool slightly before mixing with eggs to avoid curdling.

SCORE, TO

To cut shallow lines partway through the top layer of a dough to create a decorative pattern, or into meats to tenderize and allow a marinade to penetrate more fully. The lines are usually in a crisscross, diamond pattern.

SCUM

Impurities that float to the top of a stock, sauce, or other liquid are called scum. They often form a gray, filmy covering on the surface of the liquid. This layer is removed by skimming with a special long-handled spoon with a wire or perforated bowl (see SKIM).

SEAR, TO

To brown meat with intense heat in order to seal in the juices and to impart color and more flavor; this is done in a skillet or in the oven. Searing is often the first step when preparing a stew or braise.

SEED, TO; SEED

To remove, from a fruit or vegetable, the seeds, which are the portion normally capable of germination. The method of seeding depends on the size of the seed and how easy it is to access. Some seeds, such as those in watermelons and cherimoyas, are large enough to be removed by hand when you encounter them while eating or preparing fruit. Seeds that run in the core of a vegetable, such as a cucumber or zucchini, can be removed by scraping with a spoon or with a special coring tool (see CORE). Apple and pear seeds are removed through coring. Tomatoes are seeded by squeezing cut pieces gently or by being puréed and then strained. Berries can be seeded only by being puréed and then strained through a fine-mesh sieve. Citrus seeds revealed in slices and wedges get picked out with the point of a knife; when citrus fruits are juiced through a reamer with a strainer basket, the seeds are trapped by the strainer.

SEPARATE, TO

To divide a whole egg into yolk and white. Also, to become divided into two distinct parts, as when a custard curdles into liquid and gel or when the ingredients in an emulsion cease to be in suspension.

Recipes and Related Information
Curdling, 167; Custard, 168; Egg, 194; Emulsion and Emulsifier, 212.

SESAME SEED

The tiny sesame seed is the seed of an herbaceous plant native to Indonesia and East Africa. The creamy white variety is the most common, but a black variety is used in southern Indian cooking. Sesame seeds have a mildly sweet, nutty flavor that is enhanced by toasting.

Use Sesame seeds are pressed for oil, which may be made in several different styles (see OIL). The seeds themselves are a valued cooking ingredient in the Middle East, India, China, Japan, and Korea. Middle Eastern cooks blend sesame seeds into a paste called tahini, which they use to season dressings and dipping sauces (see TAHINI). In India sesame seeds are added to pilafs, stuffings, sauces, chutneys, and candies. Chinese cooks use both black and white sesame seeds as a garnish, in candies, and as part of a coating for fried foods. In addition the Chinese use toasted white sesame seeds to make a paste that is used in salad dressings and noodle dishes. In Japan white sesame seeds are ground and added to salad dressings; black sesame seeds garnish grilled squid and hand-shaped rice balls wrapped in seaweed. Cooks in Korea use great quantities of sesame seed, sprinkling it over braised beef ribs and grilled chicken and adding it to chicken salad, meatballs, noodle dishes, and mixed vegetables.

Sesame seed is also found in confections all over the world. In the United States, for example, it is sprinkled on breads for a nutty garnish; in the south, where it is known as benne seed, it is baked into crackers.

Availability White sesame seeds are found commonly in jars or tins on supermarket spice racks. Health-food stores often stock them in bulk. Asian, Middle Eastern, and Indian markets also carry sesame seeds, often including black as well as white varieties.

Storage Because of their high oil content, sesame seeds go rancid quickly at room temperature. However, they will keep in the refrigerator or freezer indefinitely.

Preparation Toasting brings out the full flavor of sesame seeds. To toast, cook them in a dry skillet over moderately low heat, shaking pan constantly, until they are lightly browned and fragrant (about 3 minutes).

SESAME FRIED FISH FILLETS

This Chinese version of the familiar three-step batter uses sesame seeds rather than bread crumbs. If black sesame seeds are available, mix them with the white variety for an attractive and textured coating reminiscent of multicolored beach pebbles.

> 1 pound fillet of catfish or other lean white fish
> 2 teaspoons minced fresh ginger
> 2 green onions, minced
> 2 tablespoons Shaoxing wine or dry sherry
> Pinch of salt
> Oil, for deep-frying
> ¼ cup cornstarch
> 1 egg, lightly beaten
> ¾ cup white sesame seed
> ¼ cup black sesame seed
> Soy and Mustard Dipping Sauce
> (see page 522), for dipping

1. Slice fish crosswise into two-bite-sized slices, about ¼ inch thick. Place in a shallow bowl, sprinkle with ginger, green onion, wine, and salt, and marinate in refrigerator for 30 minutes to several hours.

2. In a wok or other deep pan, preheat oil to 375° F. Drain fish and pat dry with paper towels. Have cornstarch in one shallow bowl, beaten egg in another, and combined sesame seeds in a third. Dip a piece of fish in cornstarch and shake off excess; dip into egg (use a wire skimmer or tongs to avoid getting egg on hands; coating will stick to hands, rather than fish); then roll in sesame seeds until coated.

3. Fry until white sesame seeds are light tan (3 to 4 minutes). Drain on paper towels and serve with Soy and Mustard Dipping Sauce.

Serves 4 to 6 with other dishes.

SET, TO

To firm up or to solidify. Gelatin in the presence of cold, and egg protein when heated, cause foods to congeal. Also, as melted chocolate hardens, it sets.

> ### Recipes and Related Information
> *Chocolate, 124; Custard, 168; Egg, 194; Gelatin, 264; Mousse, 372.*

Two colors of sesame seeds— white and black—add visual interest to the coating of Sesame Fried Fish Fillets.

SHALLOT

A mild member of the onion family, shallots grow in clusters of several small bulbs, each of which is rarely larger than a walnut and may be much smaller. They are sheathed in a papery reddish brown or yellowish brown skin that is easily removed. The white flesh is tinged with red or purple.

Use Shallots are valued for their gentle onion flavor. Favored by French cooks for sauces, salad dressings, and some soups, shallots are also essential to the classic French butter sauces such as beurre blanc and its variations. They may be pickled and used as a garnish for cold meats or braised whole as part of a vegetable stew.

Availability Shallots are found in most supermarkets. In some stores they are packaged in netting or in cellophane-wrapped boxes. Many supermarkets also stock freeze-dried shallots.

Selection Select firm shallots that are not sprouting.

Storage Keep shallots in a cool, dry place with some air circulation, such as a basket. Under proper conditions, they will keep for up to one month. Store freeze-dried shallots in a cool, dark, dry place for up to six months; they lose flavor with time.

Preparation Remove papery outer skin; trim away root end. Reconstitute freeze-dried shallots according to package directions. See KNIFE, Cutting Techniques, for a description of how to mince shallots.

OPENING BIVALVES

Oysters Wearing work gloves or using a heavy cloth, hold oyster with deep cup of oyster down. Insert tip of oyster knife into hinge and twist to open shell. Slide knife along inside of upper shell to sever muscle; slide knife under flesh to sever bottom muscle.

Clams Refrigerate bivalves for a few hours or freeze 30 minutes; they will be easier to open. Slide blade of clam knife between the two shells. Work knife between shells toward hinge until you can pry shells apart. To sever muscles, slide blade along inside of one shell and under clam.

Mussels Debeard by pulling out threads of tissue that protrude from the shell. Mussels die soon after debearding; prepare immediately. Open as you would a clam.

SHELL, TO

To remove the natural outer covering, or shell, of a food. Typically the term refers to nuts; eggs; seafood such as crab, mussels, and oysters; and to vegetables such as peas and beans.

SHELLFISH

All shellfish fall into one of three categories: crustaceans (crabs, shrimp, prawns, lobsters, crayfish); mollusks (including univalves such as abalone and conch, and bivalves such as mussels, clams, oysters, and scallops); and cephalopods (such as squid and octopus), which, despite being classed as shellfish, do not have shells. Even within these categories, flavors and textures vary greatly. To discuss the best ways to select, store, and prepare shellfish, it is helpful to consider the major varieties separately.

Use Shellfish preparations are among the world's best-loved dishes. Favorites include Louisiana boiled crayfish, French steamed mussels with white wine and onion, baked clams on the half shell with buttered bread crumbs and bacon, Chinese stir-fried crab with black bean sauce, grilled lobster with drawn butter, and fried shrimp.

Availability Shellfish are marketed fresh and frozen. The best quality and selection are usually found at a specialty fish market. Some merchants keep crabs and lobsters in holding tanks for live purchase.

Selection Shellfish deteriorate rapidly after harvesting. Buy from a reputable dealer with a rapid turnover. Carefully frozen shellfish are preferable to "fresh" shellfish that have been out of the water too long.

Periodically during the summer months, local fish-and-game departments declare some sections of coastal waters temporarily unsafe due to the presence of toxic organisms that could be taken up by bivalves. Before harvesting bivalves from coastal waters, check with local fish-and-game authorities to make sure warnings are not in effect.

Storage Refrigerate fresh shellfish immediately after purchase. If possible, store on a bed of ice in the refrigerator, loosely covered with a clean towel.

Preparation See individual shellfish entries for specific preparation tips.

Cooking See BAKE, BOIL, BRAISE, BROIL, DEEP-FRY, GRILL, SAUTE, STEAM, STIR-FRY.

ABALONE

The abalone is a univalve, its mushroom-shaped flesh hiding underneath a large, one-sided shell. The highest concentrations of abalone are found along the coasts of California, Mexico, Japan, and Australia. The flesh is very chewy and must be tenderized by pounding. The texture is silky, the flavor briny and mild.

Scaloppine-like abalone steaks are usually floured lightly and fried quickly in butter. To prepare, remove shell the same way you would shuck a clam (see Opening Bivalves, at left), then scrub off or carefully cut away the outer black skin. Cut thin steaks across the muscle or cut thin strips with the grain. Pound with a mallet or the side of a cleaver to about ¼-inch thickness. Slash meat with a sharp knife to prevent it from curling during cooking. The meat may also be finely minced or ground for use in shellfish cakes or croquettes; small tenderized (pounded) strips may be deep-fried.

The harvesting of fresh abalone in California is highly regulated. Abalone is sporadically available in the shell in the spring and autumn and is easiest to find in Asian fish markets. Some markets sell tenderized steaks. Abalone is also sold canned, dried, and frozen.

Fresh abalone should be alive when purchased; if live, the exposed muscle will react when touched. Abalone flesh should smell sweet, not fishy. Refrigerate and cook within one day. Frozen abalone may be stored in the freezer for up to three months; thaw in the refrigerator. Once opened, canned abalone should be kept covered with water in a covered container; change water every two days. Keep dried abalone tightly wrapped in a cool, dry place; it will keep indefinitely.

ABALONE STEW

The classic use for abalone is as a steak quickly sautéed in butter for less than one minute on each side. This stew gives another savory use for these univalves. Fresh abalone needs to be pounded to tenderize it, but if purchased frozen or canned, that has been done.

- 1 **pound abalone steaks**
- ⅓ **cup unsalted butter**
- 1 **cup finely chopped onion**
- 1 **large clove garlic, peeled and minced**
- ⅓ **cup finely chopped red or green bell pepper**
- 1 **bay leaf**
- 1 **can (8 oz) tomato sauce**
- 2 **cups water**
- 3 **potatoes, peeled and cut in ½-inch cubes**
- ½ **teaspoon salt**
- ⅓ **teaspoon cayenne pepper**

1. Cut abalone in ½-inch cubes; reserve. In a large saucepan over medium heat, melt butter and sauté onion, garlic, and bell pepper until onion is soft and pale gold in color (about 5 minutes). Add bay leaf, tomato sauce, the water, potatoes, salt, and cayenne.

2. Cover and simmer until potatoes are almost tender (about 15 minutes). Add abalone cubes and simmer until abalone is tender (4 to 5 minutes).

Serves 8.

PREPARING SQUID

Rinse squid in cold water. Cut off tentacles just above eye. Squeeze the thick center part of tentacles, which pushes out the hard beak. Discard beak.

Squeeze the entrails from the body by running your fingers from the closed to the cut end. Pull out the transparent quill that protrudes from the body.

Slip a finger under the skin and peel it off. Pull off edible fins from either side and skin them.

PREPARING AMERICAN LOBSTER

Hold lobster right side up on a firm surface. With a sharp knife, pierce the shell and flesh at the center of the cross-shaped mark behind the head.

Cut in half lengthwise. Remove and discard gravel sac near the head and intestinal vein in tail. Remove the gray-green tomalley (liver) and any roe from body; reserve for flavoring sauces.

Twist off and save claws. With sharp knife, separate each of the two halves between tail and body. Slice tail between every other shell segment, leaving shell intact. Crack claws and joints, leaving shell in place.

PREPARING SHRIMP AND CRAYFISH

Shrimp *Remove legs. Peel a bit of shell from head end of body. Holding the peeled section with hand, pull tail with other hand and shell will come off.*

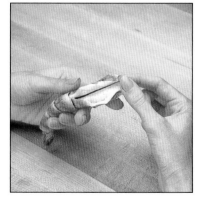

Slit shrimp down outside curve and remove the intestinal vein. On larger shrimp the intestinal vein contains grit that would interfere with the taste of the recipe. Often on medium shrimp grit is not present and the intestinal vein need not be removed before serving.

Crayfish *To remove tail, hold crayfish securely on firm surface, right side up. Lift center tail flap and twist carefully to free it from body. Holding crayfish firmly with one hand, pull tail flap away from crayfish to remove intestinal vein.*

PREPARING HARD-SHELL CRABS

Hold crab firmly against work surface. Kill it instantly by stabbing crab just behind the eyes with the point of a sharp knife. Turn crab over. Gently fold back and then twist or pull off apron or tail flap. The attached intestinal vein will pull out along with apron; discard both. Turn crab right side up.

With one hand, hold on to crab body where apron was removed and use other hand to pry up and tear off top shell. Discard shell. Remove gills from each side of crab and take out grayish, saclike sand bag. Pull out and discard mandibles from front of crab.

Holding body where legs are attached, apply pressure so that crab splits in half along center of body. Fold back halves and twist apart. Twist off claws and legs where they join the body. Crack them with a nutcracker and remove the meat.

PREPARING SOFT-SHELL CRABS

Cut across the eyes with kitchen shears or a sharp knife. Reach into the cut and pull out the gray saclike stomach, called the sand bag. Discard the stomach.

Turn crab over, lift up flap or apron, and fold it down away from body. Gently pull out the apron and attached intestinal vein. Discard apron and vein.

Turn crab right side up. Lift flaps at each side near the legs, then scrape off and discard the spongy gills.

CLAMS

A bivalve, the clam has edible flesh inside two hinged shells. Atlantic clams include the small soft-shell steamers and the hard-shell quahogs, which range in size from littlenecks to cherrystones to large chowder clams that must be ground or minced. Pacific clams include the hard-shell littleneck, the soft-shell razor clam, and the large geoduck, which has an elephantlike trunk protruding from its shell.

With the exception of the chowder clam, Atlantic clams are often shucked and eaten on the half shell or in raw clam cocktails. Most West Coast clams are too tough to eat raw. Clams may be steamed open with wine and garlic, then eaten as is or added to chowders or pasta sauces. Clams on the half shell are often topped with a seasoned bread mixture or herb butter and baked until hot.

Fresh clams are sold in the shell or shucked. Both East and West Coast varieties are available the year around but are better in the colder months. Clams are also canned and smoked. Fresh unshelled clams should be alive when purchased; if live, the shells will be tightly closed or will close when touched. Reject any that refuse to close tightly. Store live clams in the refrigerator, covered with a damp cloth. Cook and eat within one or two days. Scrub clam shells well. To shuck, see Opening Bivalves, page 536.

NEW ENGLAND CLAM CHOWDER

As with any traditional clam chowder, the amount of salt you add depends on the saltiness of the clam broth and salt pork; be sure to taste before seasoning.

20 medium-sized clams, scrubbed, *or*
    1 quart shucked clams
2 tablespoons butter
¼ pound salt pork, rinsed in cold water
    and diced finely
1½ cups diced onion
8 cups clam broth, reserved from steaming clams,
    or bottled clam juice
3 cups peeled, cubed potatoes, cooked in
    salted water
3 cups half-and-half
    Salt and freshly ground white pepper, to taste
    Butter, for garnish
    Oyster crackers or pilot crackers,
    for accompaniment

1. If necessary, steam clams and remove and discard shells. Strain clam broth and reserve.

2. In a large kettle place the 2 tablespoons butter with salt pork. Cook over low heat to render fat and brown pork. Remove pork pieces (cracklings) with slotted spoon and reserve.

3. Add diced onions to fat and cook until they begin to soften. Add clam broth or clam juice to kettle and bring to a boil. Reduce heat and simmer for 5 minutes. Chop clams into small pieces and add to kettle along with cooked potatoes.

4. Cover and simmer for 10 minutes. Add half-and-half to kettle and heat gently. Return pork cracklings to kettle and season with salt and pepper.

5. Serve in warm bowls with a pat of butter in each bowl and plenty of freshly ground pepper. Pass the crackers.

Serves 8.

MANHATTAN CLAM CHOWDER

This is the red version of the well-known New England Clam Chowder, which is white. The saltiness of the clams, salt pork, and clam broth affects the amount of additional salt and pepper required.

¼ cup salt pork, finely diced
1 green bell pepper, diced
1 onion, minced
3 medium boiling potatoes, peeled and diced
2 cups ripe tomatoes
    (about 3 large tomatoes), diced
½ teaspoon dried thyme
    Salt and freshly ground black pepper, to taste
⅛ teaspoon cayenne pepper
3 cups Fish Stock (see page 561) or
    bottled clam juice
2 cups shucked steamed clams
    Crusty bread, for accompaniment

1. In a 4-quart saucepan sauté salt pork over medium heat. Add bell pepper and onion, and cook until softened (3 to 5 minutes). Stir in potatoes, tomatoes, thyme, salt, pepper, cayenne, and Fish Stock.

2. Cover and simmer 25 minutes. Add clams, and cook 10 minutes more. Serve steaming hot with crusty bread.

Serves 6 to 8.

Recipes: Cioppino, 556; Steamed Clams, 611; White Clam or Mussel Sauce, 413.

CONCH

Also known as whelk, the conch is a univalve, its sweet flesh almost completely encased in a beautiful rose-tinged, whorled shell. The flesh is tough but may be tenderized by long, slow cooking or by pounding and parboiling. In the Caribbean, conch is eaten raw in a cold cocktail with lemon, onion, and minced tomato, or minced and made into conch chowder.

The meat may be ground, bound with a fritter batter, and deep-fried. It may be sliced thin, pounded, floured, and sautéed in butter like abalone or slowly stewed with wine and herbs. Italians call it *scungilli* and braise it with marinara sauce.

Conch is harvested the year around off the coast of Florida. It is sold in the shell or shucked. A Pacific coast variety is occasionally available in Asian markets on the West Coast. Conch is also marketed frozen (both cooked and raw) and canned, especially along the Atlantic coast and in the Gulf states.

Fresh conch should smell sweet, not fishy. Refrigerate and cook within one day. After opening, canned conch should be covered with water and stored in an airtight container; refrigerate and use within three days. Store frozen conch for up to three months; thaw in the refrigerator before using.

Conch meat is difficult to extract from the convoluted conch shell. Use a hammer to knock a hole in the shell about 1 inch below the crown. With a small, sharp knife, sever the muscle where it attaches to the crown. Grasp the portion of the conch meat that protrudes from the shell and pull to extract it. Trim away the soft parts from the crown end of the meat and cut out the intestinal vein. Peel off the skin, using a knife to cut away any parts that cling. Cut away the hard, flat operculum at the foot of the meat.

CRABS

The Atlantic and Pacific coasts harbor a variety of different crabs, all of which yield sweet white meat. Crabs are eaten both cold and hot, in the shell and shelled. The Dungeness crab and blue crab have edible body and claw meat. In the Alaskan king crab and spider crab, the edible meat is concentrated in the legs and claws; in the southern Atlantic stone crab, the edible meat is only in the claws.

Crabs are often boiled or steamed and served whole. Hot, steamed crabs in the shell are usually accompanied by lemon butter. Cold crab in the shell is usually accompanied by mayonnaise or a tomato-based cocktail sauce. Crab in the shell is added to a variety of hearty soups from gumbo to Cioppino. Chinese cooks stir-fry crabs with ginger and green onion or black bean sauce. Soft-shell blue crabs—crabs that have just molted their hard shells—are entirely edible; they are generally panfried in butter and eaten shell and all.

Crabmeat is often sold cold as a first-course cocktail, with lemon, mayonnaise, or cocktail sauce. Shelled crabmeat may be baked with seasoned cracker crumbs and butter; mixed with mayonnaise and bread crumbs, formed into cakes and fried; made into stuffings for trout; creamed and served in pastry shells; added to soups; or made into cold or hot mousses. Caribbean cooks season the meat highly, stuff it back into the shell, and bake it. Crabmeat may also be used as a filling for enchiladas, tacos, quiche, or crêpes.

Pacific Dungeness crab is available fresh from Washington state to Baja, California, from October through May; it is sold either live or precooked. Fresh Dungeness crabmeat is available locally and is shipped canned or frozen to other parts of the country.

Soft-shell blue crabs from the Atlantic and Gulf coasts are available from April through September; they are airfreighted fresh to some urban markets and are widely sold frozen. Hard-shell blue crabs are available all year, with local seasons depending on water temperature. The she-crab is a female blue crab with orange roe; she-crab soup, containing both meat and roe, is popular in the southern Atlantic states. Florida stone crab claws are enjoyed fresh locally and are frozen for shipment. The legs and claws of Alaskan spider and king crabs are frozen and sold the year around. Frozen Alaskan king crab legs are available in most fish markets.

Canned crabmeat is widely available in supermarkets; most of it is from spider crabs (sometimes identified as "snow crab"), although some markets carry Alaskan king crabmeat or Dungeness crabmeat.

Fresh uncooked crabs should be alive when purchased; if they are alive, they will be active and kicking. Avoid any sluggish or still ones. Refrigerate fresh crab immediately and cook that day. Cooked crabs and crabmeat should smell sweet when they are purchased. Refrigerate and use within three days. Once opened, canned crabmeat should be stored in an airtight nonreactive container in the refrigerator and used within two days. Fresh meat may be frozen for up to three months, although there will be some loss of flavor and texture. Thaw frozen crabmeat slowly in the refrigerator. Blot dry before using to keep it from watering down the dish in which it will be used. The liquid from canned crabmeat is usually used in recipes. All crabmeat should be picked over carefully to remove any bits of shell or cartilage.

■ MARYLAND CRAB CAKES

Nothing can match the sweetness of Chesapeake Bay crab, but this dish is worth making with other types as well. The homemade Tartar Sauce that accompanies it is wholly different from the commercially bottled product.

    1 pound crabmeat (preferably from
       Maryland blue crabs)
    1 cup soft bread crumbs
    1 large egg, lightly beaten
    ¼ cup mayonnaise
    1 tablespoon mustard
    1 teaspoon Worcestershire sauce
    2 tablespoons minced parsley
    ¼ teaspoon white pepper
       Dash Tabasco Sauce
       Oil, for frying
       Lemon wedges, for accompaniment
       Tartar Sauce With Green Peppercorns
       (see page 520), for accompaniment

1. If you are using something other than Maryland blue crab, taste a pinch of it; if it is too salty, rinse briefly under cold running water.

2. Carefully pick over crabmeat, removing any shell and other inedible bits; leave crab in large lumps. Gently mix in bread crumbs.

3. Combine egg, mayonnaise, mustard, Worcestershire, parsley, pepper, and Tabasco. Gently blend this mixture with crabmeat.

4. Form crab mixture into six thick patties. Wrap individually in plastic wrap and refrigerate for 30 minutes to firm the mixture.

5. Pour ¼ inch of oil into a large skillet; heat until aromatic and rippling (about 350° F). Add crab cakes and fry, turning once, until golden on both sides (about 3 minutes per side). Serve immediately with lemon wedges and Tartar Sauce With Green Peppercorns.

Serves 6.

Recipes: Chilled Savory Mousse, 372; Cioppino, 556; Crab Salad Louis, 509.

CRAYFISH

The crayfish (also known as crawfish or crawdad) is a freshwater crustacean harvested from rivers and ponds. It resembles a tiny lobster and is usually about 4 inches long. The prized parts are the sweet white tail meat and the fat in the head, which adds richness to crayfish dishes.

Important to Louisiana Cajun and Creole cooking, crayfish are steamed and served in the shell, cold or hot. They are added to gumbos and jambalaya and made into stews, bisques, salads, and pies.

Crayfish are available, either live or cooked, in some markets from spring through fall. They are farmed in Louisiana in flooded fields and are airfreighted around the country and to Europe. Frozen whole crayfish or frozen tail meat is available in some markets or by mail. Uncooked crayfish should be alive when purchased; avoid any that are sluggish or still. Refrigerate immediately and cook within one day. Cooked crayfish should smell sweet when purchased. Refrigerate and use within two days. Frozen crayfish will keep for up to three months. Thaw frozen crayfish slowly in the refrigerator; do not refreeze. See Preparing Shrimp and Crayfish, page 537.

Fresh crayfish are sometimes muddy; soak in cold water for 10 minutes. Crayfish are cooked in their shells, then shelled to retrieve the tail meat.

■ BOILED SEAFOOD DINNER

The liquid prepared in step 2 constitutes a homemade crab boil. It can be reused three or four times. Refrigerate and use within a week, or freeze. If you can't find blue crabs or live crayfish, use just shrimp (about 6 pounds should be enough for 12 people).

5	pounds live crayfish
2	gallons water
2	cups salt
1	cup fresh lemon juice
½	cup cayenne pepper
¼	cup black peppercorns
2	teaspoons whole allspice
1	tablespoon whole cloves
1	tablespoon thyme
12	bay leaves
2	teaspoons whole celery seed
2	tablespoons coriander
3	heads garlic
6	onions, halved
24	small red potatoes
12	blue crabs
3	pounds shrimp
12	ears corn, cut in half widthwise

1. Purge crayfish by soaking in cold salted water. Drain and rinse; repeat this process until the soaking water is no longer muddy. Set crayfish aside.

2. In a 4- to 5-gallon pot, bring the 2 gallons water and salt to a boil over high heat. Add lemon juice, cayenne, black peppercorns, allspice, cloves, thyme, bay leaves, celery seed, and coriander; continue boiling for 20 minutes.

3. Add garlic, onions, and potatoes; boil another 10 minutes. Add crabs and boil 5 minutes. Add crayfish and continue boiling for 5 minutes. Add shrimp and corn and boil until shrimp are pink and firm (5 to 7 minutes). Drain boiled food through a colander suspended over a large pot.

4. Serve seafood and vegetables in large, shallow bowls or on platters.

Serves 12.

LOBSTER

Two varieties of lobster are taken in American waters. The spiny lobster, a warm-water crustacean found along the coasts of Florida and California and in the Gulf of Mexico, contains meat in its tail only; the American lobster, found in the Atlantic from New England to southern Canada, has edible meat in both tail and claws. The spiny lobster has a rough, reddish brown shell and no claws; the bluish black American lobster has large claws with sharp pincers. Both types turn bright red when cooked.

Lobster is usually poached, steamed, baked, or grilled and may be eaten cold or hot. Cold lobster is generally served as a first-course cocktail or in a salad with mayonnaise or vinaigrette. Hot lobster is often served in the shell with melted butter and lemon. Lobster shells are used to flavor bisques and aromatic sauces and butters. The meat is used in soups, casseroles, soufflés, and sautés, or it may be creamed and served in a pastry shell. Split lobsters are topped with buttered bread crumbs and baked. Chinese cooks stir-fry lobster meat with black bean sauce or with ginger and green onion.

This spicy boiled dinner uses three crustaceans found fresh in Louisiana: blue crabs, crayfish, and shrimp. Or, if you prefer, any of these can be used alone.

Moules Mariniere is an adaptation of a classic French dish that never fails to please even the most discriminating palate. Easily prepared and economical, this recipe may well become a mainstay in your seafood repertoire.

Spiny lobsters are available live or cooked the year around in some markets. Frozen spiny lobster tails (often identified as rock lobster or *langouste*) are widely available. American lobster, also known as Maine lobster, is usually sold live from tanks and is available all year; some markets sell whole cooked American lobsters.

Live lobster should be active when taken from the tank; avoid sluggish ones. Cooked lobsters should smell sweet; their tails should be tightly curled underneath the body, a sign that they were alive when cooked. Refrigerate live lobsters and cook within one day. Cooked lobster should be eaten within two days. Frozen lobster may be stored up to three months; thaw slowly in the refrigerator.

Live lobsters are usually cooked whole. However, some recipes call for splitting and cleaning the lobster before cooking; see Preparing American Lobster, page 537. Prepare a live spiny lobster by setting it on its back on a firm surface; with a heavy, sharp knife, stab point into mouth to sever spinal cord. Turn lobster over and split in half lengthwise; use a rubber mallet, if necessary, to force knife through body. If starting with a cooked spiny lobster, begin preparation by splitting in half. With both cooked and uncooked lobsters, rinse viscera from body and intestinal vein from tail under cold running water.

LOBSTER SALAD

This salad is best with your own mayonnaise, made with lemon juice instead of vinegar. Prawns and crab can be added to the salad for variety. Note that the salad should chill for two hours before serving; chilled plates keep the salad cool longer.

> 3 cups cooked lobster meat
> (2 live lobsters, approximately 1½ lb each;
> see Basic Poached Shellfish, page 451)
> 2 stalks celery, diced
> 1 red bell pepper, diced
> 1 small bunch chives, snipped
> 1 shallot, minced
> 1 cup Mayonnaise (see page 519; use fresh lemon
> juice instead of vinegar)
> 1 head Bibb lettuce, separated into leaves
> 1 lemon, cut into 8 wedges, for garnish (optional)
> 8 parsley sprigs, for garnish

1. Cube the cooked lobster into large pieces (about ¾ inch each). In a 2-quart mixing bowl, place lobster, celery, bell pepper, chives, and shallot. Add mayonnaise and stir well to combine. For best flavor chill at least 2 hours before serving.

2. To serve, wash the lettuce leaves, then pat dry. Place one leaf on each chilled salad plate. Serve about ½ cup salad on each lettuce leaf. Garnish each plate with lemon wedge and parsley sprig, if desired.

Serves 8.

Recipes: Basic Poached Shellfish, 451.

MUSSELS

Bivalves with a smooth, bluish black shell, mussels have flesh that ranges from deep yellow to orange. They are found clinging to rocks along both Atlantic and Pacific coasts and are successfully produced by aquaculture in New England. Most of the commercial harvest is from the East Coast; due to toxic substances in the water, Pacific coast mussels are usually quarantined during the summer.

Fresh mussels are steamed in the shells, usually with white wine, oil, and garlic, until they open; they are then eaten from the shell with melted butter or tossed with pasta. They may be shelled, chilled, and used in salads or shellfish cocktails. Mussels may also be grilled over coals until they open. Steamed mussels and their liquid may be made into soups or added to shellfish stews. They may also be steamed open, then dressed with butter and bread crumbs and baked on the half shell. In most recipes, mussels can be substituted for clams.

Fresh East Coast mussels are sold the year around. West Coast mussels are available from November through April. They are generally marketed live, in the shell, although some East Coast markets sell shucked mussels. Canned smoked mussels are also available in most markets. Mussels in the shell should be alive when purchased. Their shells will be tightly closed or will close when touched; discard any that refuse to close. Refrigerate, covered with a damp cloth; cook within one day. Store cooked, shucked mussels in a tightly closed container in the refrigerator; use within two days. Scrub mussel shells well with a stiff brush. See Opening Bivalves, page 536.

▦ MOULES MARINIERE

This version of a classic French dish features a richly flavored cream sauce. Fennel adds a hint of licorice to the cooking stock. For directions on how to debeard a mussel, see photograph on page 536.

  6 **dozen mussels**
  4 **shallots, chopped**
  1 **bay leaf**
  ½ **teaspoon fennel seed**
  1 **cup dry white wine**
  1 **cup whipping cream**
  3 **egg yolks**
    Juice of 1 lemon
  2 **tablespoons unsalted butter**
    Salt and pepper, to taste
    Chopped parsley, for garnish

1. Scrub and debeard mussels. Soak them in a bowl of cold water or in sink for 30 minutes. Any sand will leach out and sink to bottom of bowl.

2. In a large stockpot simmer shallots, bay leaf, fennel seed, and wine for 5 minutes. Add mussels and steam for 5 minutes; all mussels should open in that time. If doubling recipe, it will take longer for mussels to open. Transfer mussels to a large bowl and keep them warm.

3. To make sauce, strain mussel stock and boil until reduced to about 1½ cups. In a medium bowl beat together cream, egg yolks, and lemon juice. Add 1 cup of mussel stock to cream mixture in a thin stream, then pour the mixture back into the remaining stock. Heat very gently, stirring constantly so that egg yolks do not scramble. Turn off the heat and stir in butter. Season with salt and pepper, if necessary.

4. Divide mussels among 6 large, shallow soup bowls. Ladle sauce over each bowl and sprinkle each with chopped parsley. Place a large bowl on the table for mussel shells.

Serves 6.

Recipes: Cioppino, 556; White Clam or Mussel Sauce, 413.

OYSTER

The oyster is a bivalve that lives in shallow, temperate, and tropical waters. Inside its rough, hard, gray shell is the soft, briny flesh that is appreciated both raw and cooked. Today, several varieties of oysters are commercially farmed on both Atlantic and Pacific coasts of the United States.

Most of the oysters of the world are probably eaten raw on the half shell, with lemon, vinegar, or cocktail sauce. However, there are also dozens of delicious ways to cook them. They may be grilled over coals until their shells open. They may be shelled, poached, and served in a cream sauce or simmered in milk or cream with butter for an oyster stew. Oysters on the half shell may be topped with herb butter or buttered bread crumbs and baked. Whole oysters may be wrapped in bacon and broiled or simmered in butter with hot-pepper sauce and served atop toast. Oysters are added to bread stuffings for turkey or fish and are baked in double-crust pies. Deep-fried cornmeal-coated oysters may be eaten hot with lemon or tucked into a loaf of French bread to make an Oyster Loaf (see page 544). Smoked oysters are usually eaten as an appetizer with crackers or mixed into cream cheese–based dipping sauces.

Most varieties of oysters are available fresh the year around but are better in the colder months. They spawn during the summer and their flesh gets fatty, making them less appealing on the half shell. Oysters are usually sold live in the shell; some varieties are also available shucked in jars or smoked and packed in tins.

Today's commercial oysters are carefully monitored for the toxin that shellfish can ingest in the summer months, and thus present no danger to diners. Unshelled oysters should be alive when purchased; if live, their shells will be tightly closed. Discard any with open shells. Store them in the refrigerator cup side down, covered with a damp towel; use within three days. Shucked oysters should be refrigerated in their liquor and used as soon as possible. See Opening Bivalves, page 536.

■ OYSTER LOAF

Food has always played a prominent role in San Francisco. During the rowdy days of the city in the late 1800s, carousing husbands often carried home an oyster loaf—not candy or flowers—after a late night out as a peace offering to their annoyed spouses. This makes an excellent first course for up to six people or dinner for two.

    1   loaf French bread (about 1 lb)
    8   tablespoons unsalted butter
    ¼   teaspoon freshly grated nutmeg
    ¼   teaspoon cayenne pepper
    ½   teaspoon freshly ground black pepper
    1   teaspoon salt
    ½   cup flour
    ½   cup milk
    1   egg
    16 medium oysters, shucked, or
        2 jars (10 oz each) oysters
    ¾   cup dry bread crumbs (see step 1)
    3   tablespoons vegetable oil, for frying
        Juice of 1 lemon
        Tartar Sauce With Green Peppercorns,
        for accompaniment (see page 520), optional

1. Preheat oven to 400° F. Slice top off loaf of bread. Scoop out soft center, leaving a ½-inch-thick crusty shell. Break soft bread into crumbs and place on a baking sheet. Toast 10 minutes; reserve. Coat inside of bread shell with 3 tablespoons of the butter. Place shell on baking sheet and toast in oven until golden brown (about 10 minutes); reserve.

2. In a small bowl stir together nutmeg, cayenne, pepper, salt, and flour. In another small bowl beat together milk and egg. Dip oysters in seasoned flour, then in egg-milk mixture, and finally in bread crumbs. Place on a plate and chill 1 hour.

3. In a medium skillet sauté oysters in oil and remaining butter over medium heat until golden and crusty on first side (about 4 minutes). Turn; sauté second side 2 minutes. Place cooked oysters in bread shell and pour pan juices over. Serve drizzled with lemon juice and accompanied with Tartar Sauce With Green Peppercorns (if desired).

Serves 4 to 6 as a first course, 2 as a main course.

Recipes: Hangtown Fry, 202.

SCALLOPS

The scallop is a bivalve found on the Atlantic and Gulf coasts. The edible part is the sweet white muscle that holds together the two fan-shaped, hinged shells. The larger sea scallop is about 5 inches across, with a muscle that may be 1 inch wide and ½ inch thick; it is found in water from the mid-Atlantic to the New England coast. The smaller bay scallop is about 2 inches across, with a muscle considerably smaller than that of the sea scallop. Bay scallops are found in Atlantic estuaries. The Florida calico scallop is about the same size as the bay scallop, but the calico is a deep-sea scallop.

Scallops may be baked with buttered bread crumbs or herb butter; sautéed with butter, herbs, and wine or cream sauce; added to soups, shellfish stews, and pasta sauces; floured and deep-fried; poached and eaten cold in salads; or skewered and grilled. They may be marinated for seviche or eaten raw in sushi.

Fresh sea scallops are available all year but supplies are more plentiful in summer. They are almost always sold shucked; they die quickly out of the water. However, live sea scallops are occasionally available in some markets. Bay scallops are available fresh in fall and winter on the East Coast, where they are most prevalent; they, too, are almost always sold shucked. Frozen bay and sea scallops are widely available in fish markets.

Fresh shucked scallops should smell sweet, not fishy. Refrigerate immediately and use within one or two days. Scallops may be frozen for up to three months; thaw slowly in the refrigerator.

■ COQUILLES ST. JACQUES

Scallops come in two sizes, tiny bay scallops (about 100 to the pound) and the larger and more variably sized sea scallops (from 20 to 40 per pound). The larger scallops take slightly longer to cook; if they are cut in thirds or quarters, their cooking time will match that of the smaller bay scallops.

    3   shallots, minced
    ¼   cup parsley, minced
    1   clove garlic, minced
    4   tablespoons unsalted butter
    ¾   cup dry white wine
        Bouquet garni (see page 56)
    1   pound bay scallops
    ½   cup soft bread crumbs
    2   tablespoons freshly grated Parmesan cheese
    2   tablespoons butter, melted
    ½   teaspoon salt
    ⅛   teaspoon freshly ground pepper

1. Preheat broiler. In a large, heavy-bottomed sauté pan, sauté shallots, 2 tablespoons of the parsley, and garlic in the 4 tablespoons butter over medium-low heat until soft but not browned (about 10 minutes). Add wine and bouquet garni and simmer 10 minutes.

2. Cut scallops so that all are approximately the same size. Add to pan and cook 4 to 6 minutes (scallops will appear opaque but slightly resilient when done). Remove bouquet garni and divide scallops among 4 shallow gratin dishes or shells.

3. In a small bowl stir together bread crumbs, Parmesan, melted butter, remaining parsley, salt, and pepper. Sprinkle about ¼ cup over each dish of scallops. Place on op rack of oven and broil until golden brown and slightly crisp (2 to 3 minutes).

Serves 4.

SHRIMP AND PRAWNS

Shrimp are saltwater crustaceans and prawns are found in fresh water. However, most consumers and fish markets use the word *prawn* to designate a large shrimp. Shrimp are found on all coasts: From the southern Atlantic and the Gulf of Mexico come brown, white, and pink varieties; from the California coast come spot shrimp known as Monterey prawns. The flesh is firm and white and, when cooked, has coral striations. The flavor is sweet and slightly briny.

Fresh shrimp and prawns may be cooked and served in the shell, either hot or cold. Hot shrimp in the shell are often accompanied by melted lemon butter, cold shrimp by mayonnaise or tartar sauce. Cooked peeled shrimp are used cold in salads and shellfish cocktails and hot in casseroles, crêpe fillings, curries, and fish stuffings. Shrimp may be sautéed, stir-fried, poached, grilled, or braised, either peeled or in the shell. Peeled shrimp may be battered and fried. Shrimp are an important part of Louisiana Cajun and Creole cooking, turning up in bisques, jambalaya, gumbo, and *étouffée* (stew). Crushed shrimp shells may be used to flavor sauces and butters for shellfish dishes.

Monterey prawns (spot shrimp) are available from spring through fall, either whole or with heads removed. Gulf shrimp are available the year around and are almost always sold with heads removed. Almost all shrimp have been frozen at some point in the shipping process, although they may be thawed for retail sale. Most fish markets carry cooked and peeled shrimp as well as raw shrimp in the shell. Canned and frozen shrimp are also available in most markets.

Shrimp, both raw and cooked, should feel firm and smell sweet; avoid any with an ammoniated odor. If buying thawed frozen shrimp, be sure they have not been thawed more than one or two days. Uncooked shrimp should be refrigerated immediately and cooked as soon as possible. Cooked shrimp may be refrigerated for up to three days. Shrimp may be frozen for up to three months; thaw slowly in the refrigerator.

Deveining is optional with small shrimp; with large shrimp, the black intestinal vein may be gritty and therefore should be removed. See Preparing Shrimp and Crayfish, page 537.

▢ SHRIMP CREOLE

In French and in the culinary vernacular of New Orleans, *creole* means to cook with tomatoes and sweet bell peppers, and usually to accompany with rice.

    4 **tablespoons butter**
    1 **large onion, diced**
    1 **large stalk celery, diced**
    1 **large green bell pepper, diced**
    2 **cloves garlic, minced**
    ½ **teaspoon dried thyme**
    ½ **teaspoon salt**
    ½ **teaspoon white pepper**
    ½ **teaspoon cayenne pepper**
    ½ **teaspoon freshly ground black pepper**
    1 **tablespoon flour**
    ¼ **cup dry white wine**
    1 **cup peeled and diced tomatoes**
    1 **cup Chicken Stock (see page 560)**
    2 **bay leaves**
       Hot-pepper sauce, to taste (optional)
    2 **pounds shrimp (24 to 30 per lb in shells), shelled and deveined**
    6 **to 8 cups cooked rice, for accompaniment**

1. In butter in a large skillet, sauté onion, celery, bell pepper, and garlic over medium heat until lightly browned (about 6 minutes).

2. In a small bowl mix thyme, salt, white pepper, cayenne, black pepper, and flour; stir into onion mixture and cook 2 minutes. Stir in wine, tomatoes, stock, bay leaves, and hot-pepper sauce (if used). Reduce heat and simmer 20 to 25 minutes.

3. Remove bay leaves. Stir in shrimp and simmer until bright pink (3 to 4 minutes). Serve with hot rice.

Serves 6.

Recipes: Boiled Seafood Dinner, 541; Cioppino, 556; Fritto Misto With Caper Mayonnaise, 176; Pork and Shrimp Stuffing, 191; Potstickers, 191; Shellfish Bisque, 564; Shrimp-Crowned Eggs, 199; Shrimp Okra Pilau, 397; Shrimp With Snow Peas and Water Chestnuts, 606; Spinach-Shrimp Soufflé, 205; Stuffed Mirliton, 110; Tempura Batter, 28.

SQUID AND OCTOPUS

Squid and octopus are cephalopods, mollusks with a distinct head, eyes, a beak, and muscular tentacles. Both have mottled skin overlaying smooth white flesh; when cooked, both are chewy and firm. In general the octopus is tougher and requires longer, slower cooking. Both squid and octopus have a somewhat off-putting appearance, but they are inexpensive and highly versatile.

Both squid and octopus are served in Japanese sushi bars; the octopus is always boiled first. Squid may be cut into rings and sautéed, deep-fried, or added to shellfish

If you've been hesitant about trying squid, tomato-based Squid Marinara just might change your mind. Serve with a crusty bread to mop up the wonderful sauce.

soups; the rings may also be poached and served cold in a seafood salad. Whole squid bodies may be skewered and grilled teriyaki-style or stuffed and baked. Italian cooks typically use squid in pasta sauce. The black squid "ink" is used in Italy to color and flavor rice and pasta dishes. Octopus takes well to slow-cooking methods, such as braising in red wine or in tomato-based sauces. If tenderized first, it may be grilled.

Squid is found on both coasts the year around and is sold fresh and frozen, either whole or cleaned bodies (tentacles removed) only. Octopus is also sold fresh or frozen, whole or in pieces, raw or cooked. It is readily available in fish markets that cater to a Japanese clientele. Fresh squid and octopus should smell sweet, not fishy. Refrigerate and cook within one or two days. Cooked squid and octopus should be refrigerated and eaten within three days. Frozen squid or octopus may be stored for up to three months; thaw slowly in the refrigerator.

See Preparing Squid, page 537. Octopus requires tenderizing before use; simmer for 20 to 25 minutes in salted water before adding to a soup, stew, or sauce.

■ SQUID MARINARA

This flavorful, peppery squid dish may be eaten hot or cold. It also makes a wonderful sauce for pasta. Spaghetti would be a good choice.

  4 **pounds squid**
  ⅓ **cup fruity olive oil**
  4 **cloves garlic, minced**
  4 **cups crushed tomatoes in purée**
  1 **teaspoon dried oregano oregano leaves
     (not powdered), crumbled**
  1 **teaspoon dried basil *or* 6 fresh basil leaves
     Salt and freshly ground black pepper, to taste**
  ¼ **cup chopped Italian parsley**
  1 **teaspoon red pepper flakes**

1. Clean squid (see Preparing Squid, page 537). Cut the bodies crosswise into ¾-inch-wide pieces. Also cut the tentacles if they are large.

2. In a heavy casserole or Dutch oven, heat oil. Add squid and sauté for 5 to 6 minutes. Add garlic and stir for 1 minute.

3. Add tomato, oregano, basil, salt, and pepper. Cover and cook until squid are tender (about 20 minutes). Stir in parsley and red pepper flakes. Adjust seasonings to taste.

Serves 8.

Recipes: Cioppino, 556; Fritto Misto With Caper Mayonnaise, 176.

SHORT

Dough with a high proportion of fat to flour. Short pastry and cookie doughs are tender and crumbly. By waterproofing the flour particles, fat limits the development of gluten, a structure-building offshoot of flour proteins created when flour mixes with liquid. Without this structure, the dough is more brittle, but it tastes so rich and wonderful you hardly mind the crumbs.

> ***Recipes and Related Information***
> *Classic Scotch Shortbread, 144; Sand Pastry, 442.*

SHUCK, TO

To remove the outer covering of clams, oysters, and mussels; nuts; the husk of corn; the same as *to shell* and *to husk*. For information on opening bivalves, see SHELLFISH.

SKIM, TO

To remove surface fat or other impurities from a soup, stock, stew, or sauce with a skimmer, a spoon, or a ladle.

> ***Recipes and Related Information***
> *Degrease, 177; Spoon, Ladle, and Scoop, 551.*

SKIN, TO

To remove the skin of poultry, fish, or game. Particular preparations, such as boned chicken breasts and fish fillets, are traditionally served skinless for reasons of taste, digestion, or aesthetics.

SLASH, TO

To notch the fat of a steak at even intervals all the way around or to make shallow cuts in the surface of a thin piece of veal. By doing this the meat will stay flat as it cooks; otherwise it will curl as it shrinks to its final size.

SLIVER, TO; SLIVER

To cut a thin and usually short stick of food, as fine as a splinter. The term is most often used to describe garlic cut this way; the garlic pieces are inserted into slits cut into roasts, particularly lamb, in order to flavor the meat internally as it cooks.

SMOKE POINT

The temperature at which a fat decomposes and gives off smoke and an acrid gas. Different fats break down at different temperatures; it is worthwhile knowing the smoke point of common fats since it is this characteristic that determines a fat's suitability for frying. For example, cooks appreciate the delicious flavor butter imparts to food, but know that it can't reach frying temperature without burning; vegetable oils (such as safflower, corn, peanut, and grapeseed oils) stay intact at higher temperatures and are often combined with butter in order to raise the smoke point of butter. See FRY for more information about the smoke points of different fats and about frying.

SORREL

Also known as sour grass and dock, sorrel is a leafy, deep-green member of the buckwheat family. Sorrel leaves, with their slender stems, somewhat resemble spinach, but the flavor is markedly different. Cooked sorrel has a pronounced lemonlike tang that is especially appealing in cream sauces, stuffings, and soups.

Use   Very young sorrel leaves may be added to salads with other greens. Otherwise, sorrel is almost always cooked. When simmered in butter and cream, it makes a delicious partner to salmon and trout. French cooks stuff whole shad with sorrel purée and make a sorrel soup thickened with eggs and cream; Eastern European Jews make a cold sorrel and sour cream soup called *schav*.

Availability   Sorrel grows wild throughout North America and is cultivated commercially. Fresh sorrel is marketed sporadically in supermarkets the year around, although it is most easily found in the spring. Specialty markets also carry cooked sorrel in jars.

Selection   Look for green leaves with no sign of yellowing. Sorrel wilts readily after harvesting but flavor is not compromised.

Storage   Wash and dry leaves; wrap in paper towels, then enclose in a plastic bag and refrigerate for up to four days. Bottled sorrel should be refrigerated after opening and used within one week.

Preparation   Remove leaves from stems.

T-Z

TAHINI

Common to Middle Eastern cooking, tahini (also spelled tahina) is an oily paste made of ground raw (untoasted) sesame seeds. A similar Chinese paste, much darker and nuttier in flavor, is made with toasted sesame seeds.

Use   Tahini seasons many well-known Middle Eastern dishes. Combined with lemon juice, garlic, minced parsley, and salt, it makes a dip known as *taratoor*. This sauce is particularly delicious with wedges of pita bread, grilled fish, or cold steamed vegetables. It may also be used as a dressing for green salads. Lebanese cooks add it to eggplant purée to make *baba ganoosh* and to chick-pea purée to make hummus. Falafel, the fried balls of cracked wheat and chick-peas popular in the Middle East, are served in pita bread with sliced tomato and a spoonful of tahini dipping sauce.

Availability   Bottled and canned tahini are sold in Middle Eastern markets, health-food stores, and some supermarkets.

Storage   Because of its high oil content, tahini turns rancid quickly. It should be refrigerated after opening and used within one or two months.

Preparation   Stir tahini well before using to reincorporate the oil floating on top.

TAMARIND

Also known as the Indian date, tamarind is the fruit of a large evergreen tree that grows in India, the East and West Indies, the Pacific islands, and the American tropics. The tree produces a brown pod in the shape of a flat snap bean, 3 to 7 inches long. As the fruit inside matures, the pod becomes very brittle. Inside the pod is a dark brown pulp surrounding firm white seeds. The pulp—the edible part of the fruit—is very sticky and both tart and sweet at the same time, resembling the taste of a sour prune.

Use   Tamarind imparts an intriguing flavor, both sweet and tart, to beverages, candies, condiments (it is an ingredient in Worcestershire sauce), marinades, and chutneys. Indian cooks make a sweet and spicy chutney from tamarind pulp. Filipino cooks add tamarind to soup broth to give it a cool, sour taste. In Indonesia chicken is marinated in tamarind-flavored water and spices before frying. In Vietnam tamarind flavors a peanut dipping sauce for grilled shrimp paste wrapped around sugarcane.

Availability   Whole tamarind pods are found in Latin American, Indonesian, Indian, and Southeast Asian markets. Most of these markets also carry tamarind pulp in firm bricks, concentrated pulp in jars, and instant powder. Dutch or Indonesian markets also offer tamarind syrup for use in beverages.

Storage   Tamarind pods, dried pulp, and instant powder can be stored indefinitely in a cool, dark, dry place. Fresh pulp or reconstituted dried pulp will keep one to two weeks in the refrigerator; freeze for longer storage. Tamarind syrup should be refrigerated after opening.

Preparation   With the exception of the instant powder, tamarind must be softened before use. To prepare whole pods, crack brittle shell and put fruit (pulp and seeds) in a bowl. Cover with water, break fruits up with fingers, and let stand overnight. Squeeze fruit with fingers to separate seeds from pulp. When pulp is very soft, press it through a sieve and discard seeds. If using tamarind pulp in blocks or tamarind concentrate, simply put a small piece in a bowl and cover with boiling water. When it is soft (30 minutes or more), press it through a sieve to separate it from seeds. Some recipes call only for the tamarind soaking liquid, not the pulp.

TAPIOCA

The starchy food known as tapioca derives from the root of the cassava, a South American and African plant.

Use   Tapioca serves both as a thickener and as a dessert in itself. Tapioca starch (also known as tapioca flour) is an excellent thickener for sauces and fruit fillings that must be frozen because it does not break down when thawed. It is also used to thicken glazes for fruit tarts because it does not cloud the glaze. Pearl tapioca, dried barley-sized balls of tapioca starch, can be made into a creamy cooked custard or baked pudding, akin to rice pudding. Pearl tapioca is occasionally used to thicken soups.

Availability   Tapioca starch is found in Latin American markets, Asian markets, and health-food stores. Pearl tapioca and instant pearl tapioca are available in most supermarkets.

Storage   Both tapioca starch and pearl tapioca will keep indefinitely in a cool, dark, dry place.

Preparation   Tapioca starch can be used as a thickener in the same manner as cornstarch. After adding it to a liquid, do not boil or tapioca may turn stringy.

▮ TAPIOCA PUDDING

The tapioca pearls glisten in this soothing childhood favorite. Note that the pudding cooks slowly.

> 2 cups half-and-half
> 2 cups milk
> ⅓ cup sugar
> 1 tablespoon vanilla extract
> ½ cup pearl tapioca

1. Preheat oven to 300° F. Generously butter a 1½-quart ovenproof dish.

2. In a medium bowl stir together half-and-half, milk, sugar, and vanilla. Add tapioca and stir well. Pour in prepared dish and bake until a creamy, golden skin has formed on the surface (2 to 2½ hours).

3. Serve hot or warm.

Serves 4 to 6.

Recipes and Related Information
Cornstarch, 159; Pie and Tart, 436.

TARRAGON

A perennial herb, tarragon has slender, spiky green leaves rarely more than an inch long. The leaves have a pungent aroma and flavor, reminiscent of anise.

Use Tarragon is used often in French cooking, where it is considered one of the four fines herbes (sweet herbs—chervil, parsley, chives, and tarragon) added to eggs and many other dishes. It is the principal flavoring in béarnaise sauce, a relative of Hollandaise. It is particularly compatible with fish and shellfish, tomatoes, chicken, eggs, and salad greens. Tarragon is an ingredient in many recipes for green goddess dressing and tartar sauce. The whole herb is also used to flavor vinegar; tarragon vinegar is delicious in salad dressings.

Availability Fresh tarragon can be found in well-stocked supermarkets and specialty markets; it is most plentiful in the summer. Dried tarragon is found on all supermarket spice racks.

Selection Choose fresh tarragon with rich green leaves that show no signs of wilting or drying. Packaged seasonings lose quality after a while; try to buy from a store that restocks its spice section fairly often.

Storage Refrigerate fresh tarragon wrapped in damp paper towels and overwrapped in plastic; it will keep for one week. The leaves can be removed from the stems, packed tightly in a clean jar, then covered with white wine vinegar and refrigerated for up to one year. Store dried tarragon in a cool, dark, dry place, and use within one year.

Preparation Mince fresh tarragon. Tarragon packed in vinegar should be squeezed lightly to remove as much vinegar as possible before using. Dried tarragon should be crumbled between the fingers to release its essential oils when adding it to a dish.

Recipes and Related Information
Basic Single-Serving Omelet With Herbs, 203; Béarnaise Sauce, 518; Herb, 299; Herb Vinegar, 323; Tarragon Mustard, 323; Veal Chops With Tarragon, 593.

TEA

Although the term *tea* traditionally refers to the leaves of the oriental shrub *Camellia sinensis*, it has come to apply to all drinks made from leaves, flowers, seeds, roots, or bark steeped in hot water. In a broad sense all teas are herbal teas since they are made from edible plant parts. Current usage, however, classifies Asian teas separately from caffeine-free herbal teas.

Use Teas may be brewed for consuming either hot or cold. They are frequently served with such optional additions as lemon, sugar, honey, or milk.

Availability Asian tea is widely sold in American supermarkets. Most supermarket tea is blended tea, packed in disposable tea bags for convenience, although some markets now stock loose tea in airtight canisters. Instant iced tea is also widely available. For a large selection of premium-quality loose teas, it may be necessary to visit a specialty store, a health-food store, or an Asian market. Many supermarkets and health-food stores now also sell a wide variety of caffeine-free herbal teas.

Selection Some of the world's most popular teas—such as English breakfast, Irish breakfast, and Earl Grey—are blends of tea leaves from various sources. Individual teas

Although paraphernalia for making coffee abounds, the preparation of tea has remained a fairly simple and straightforward process that requires little equipment. Shown clockwise from top right: teapot, sugar bowl and cream pitcher, ceramic tea infuser, tea-bag rest, metal tea infuser, cup with strainer, teapot with strainer, tin of loose tea leaves, cup with infuser.

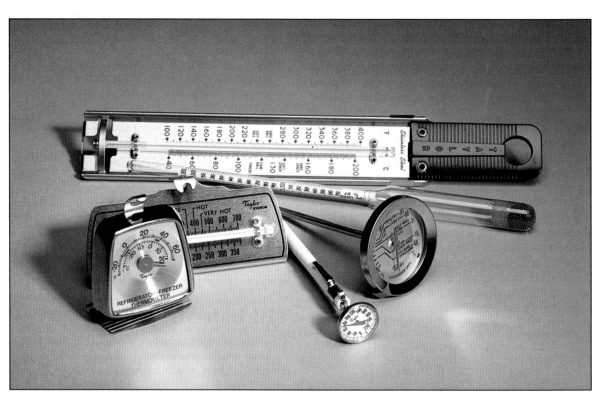

Specialized thermometers are designed for use with appliances and food. Shown top to bottom: candy and deep-fat, hydrometer, meat, instant-read, oven, refrigerator-freezer.

Instant-read thermometers are stem-type bimetal devices designed for quick response when inserted into meat, poultry, yeast doughs, and hot liquids. They have slender stainless steel shafts and a face with large numbers that register from 0° to 220° F. Unlike traditional meat thermometers that remain inserted in food throughout cooking, instant-read devices are inserted periodically, read, and removed. They will respond very quickly—in about 20 to 30 seconds. They are very versatile and highly recommended.

Glass-tube models register temperature by the expansion or contraction of a fluid—mercury or a colored liquid—trapped in a thin column of glass. The tube rests against a scale typically marked in 2°, 5°, or 10° F increments. The temperature graduations are occasionally marked on the tube itself. Glass-tube thermometers are very accurate and responsive, but are fragile and more difficult to read than a dial type. Magnifying lenses are an advantage, as are scales with dark numbers marked on a white or light background.

TO TEST FOR ACCURACY

It only makes sense that a thermometer be as accurate as possible, or why bother to use it. Use the boiling point of water, 212° F, as a reference point for probe and glass-tube stand models. Bring water to a boil, immerse either stem or entire unit (whichever is appropriate), and note the reading. If the reading is off and the model is adjustable, set it to 212° F; if you cannot reset it, note the difference, and adjust for it when you use the thermometer. For stand thermometers with dials, set in oven, refrigerator, or freezer alongside one that you know is accurate; compare readings.

Some thermometers have a narrow temperature range that stops below the boiling point. To verify accuracy, compare with one you know to be accurate or against a laboratory model, sold at scientific equipment stores.

SPECIALTY THERMOMETERS

Some thermometers are designed for multiple uses. They usually have a wide temperature range; certain probe models are suitable for roasting, testing yeast doughs, and determining the internal temperature of foods cooked in a microwave oven. Single-application models are marked to suit their purpose. Oven thermometers begin at around 100° F and climb to about 600° F. Freezer thermometers register from -40° F to 80° F. Candy and deep-fat thermometers, often one dual-purpose device, usually start at 100° F and stop at 400° F, a range that covers all the stages of working with sugar, plus the usual frying temperature range of 365° to 390° F. Meat thermometers mark from 100° F to 220° F.

What are the benefits of specialty thermometers? Their narrow temperature range means greater accuracy. Because fewer numbers need to be indicated on the dial or scale, the markings are larger and thus clearer. Some have special adaptations, such as hooks or stands, for ease of use. As with any equipment, select the thermometers that suit your needs. A well-known brand, backed by the retailer, is always a sensible choice.

CANDY AND DEEP-FAT THERMOMETERS

When working with sugar syrups, it's critical to know the concentrations. Concentration of a sugar syrup can be measured by its appearance—threads, soft-ball stage, rigid strands, or deep brown color—or by its temperature reading on a candy thermometer. These devices are preferably glass-tube types (although bimetal ones are available and do work), and the most practical are set on a stainless steel frame with a plastic extension at the top for easy handling. They usually have a clip so that, once the sugar syrup comes to a boil, the thermometer can be attached to the side of the pan, partially immersed in the liquid, to register the temperature without the cook having to hold the device in place.

For fried foods that are neither soggy and pale from cooking at too low a temperature nor burned on the outside and underdone within from an overly high temperature, hot oil must be kept at the recommended level—usually between 350° and 400° F. Deep-fat thermometers resemble those for candy making, although the upper register is usually slightly higher.

Combination candy and deep-fat thermometers are commonly available and are a practical choice for most households. Make sure that the markings accommodate both procedures.

FREEZER THERMOMETER

Foods keep best in the freezer at 0° F. Although they are still safe to eat if stored at higher temperatures, color, flavor, and texture begin to deteriorate above 5° F. For each 10 degrees above zero, the storage life of food is cut up to half. It's a good idea to monitor the temperature of the freezer section with a freezer thermometer. Place the thermometer toward the top and front of the freezer. Leave it overnight without opening freezer door. If the temperature is above 0° F the next day, adjust the temperature control and take another reading. Freezer thermometers have hooks to hang on the front of a loaded freezer shelf.

HYDROMETER

A candy thermometer measures the concentration of sugar syrup by noting its heat. When making ice cream and sorbets, you may also want to measure density, which affects both texture and flavor—smooth and sweet, grainy and intense. The lightness or heaviness (the density or specific gravity) of a syrup, the result of how much water evaporates from cooking, is expressed in degrees Baumé (named after the French chemist who developed the scale). Taking this measure requires a hydrometer, a glass tube roughly the shape of an ordinary fever thermometer and about one third larger in size, and which is marked from 0° to 40° Baumé. To use, a solution is poured into a tall container and the hydrometer dropped in and allowed to float. The measure of density is taken at the point where the stem rises above the surface of the liquid. Hydrometers are not a usual part of a well-equipped kitchen, although they are used extensively in restaurants and commercial food preparation. You may want one if you make a lot of frozen desserts or fruit syrups. However, most recipes are designed to work without such a precise measure.

MEAT THERMOMETER

A meat thermometer measures the inside temperature of a turkey, chicken, or roast while it is in the oven. Roasting charts should be regarded as very general guidelines because there are many variables to consider—how an oven heats, the shape of the food being cooked, how often the oven door is opened, the cook's definition of doneness. Internal temperature as measured by a thermometer gives a better indication than time alone whether or not food has reached a particular stage. Meat thermometers are of two types: one that stays in food throughout cooking or the instant-read type. Cooks today tend to prefer the latter as it has a thinner shaft that won't puncture as big a hole in the food as well as a larger dial that is easier to read. Instant-read thermometers are meant for quick use so you can take a range of readings.

OVEN THERMOMETER

A variation of plus or minus 25° F from the set temperature is considered normal for even the best-quality home ovens. If you regularly use an oven thermometer, you can adjust the oven setting to match the actual heat produced and avoid guesswork and failed recipes (directions for this adjustment are in the owner's manual of your oven). Both bimetal and glass-tube stand models with hook are available. Because internal temperature can vary, place the thermometer where you will be cooking, generally on the center rack. Heat the oven to the desired temperature and check thermometer (preferably through the oven window) when oven indicates it has reached the preset temperature. If necessary, adjust oven dial, wait until the new temperature has been reached, and read thermometer again. A folding model, which uses a glass tube protected in a stainless steel case, is extremely accurate and is the instrument of choice for those who service ovens. Used for spot checks at timed intervals, it isn't left in the oven throughout the cooking period. Because of its high quality, it is considerably more expensive than other models.

Recipes and Related Information
Candy and Confection, 94; Deep-fry, 174; Freeze, 242;
Ice Cream and Frozen Dessert, 308; Roast, 499;
Temperature, 575.

Steak and Kidney Pie is traditional lunchtime fare in pubs throughout England. Broiled tomatoes and a hearty English beer or ale are appropriate accompaniments.

GIZZARD

Chicken gizzard, the equivalent of the stomach in other animals, is tough but flavorful if properly prepared. It has a tough membrane that must be trimmed away. The gizzard may then be diced and browned slowly in butter with other giblets for giblet gravy, stuffing, or stew. Cajun cooks add finely ground cooked gizzards and black pepper to steamed rice to make dirty rice. Fresh gizzards should be plump and shiny, without an off-odor.

Recipes: Roast Turkey With Giblet Gravy, 474.

HEAD

Recipes for pig's, lamb's, goat's, or calf's head are common in many cuisines. Mexican families may roast a whole goat, including its head, as a celebration dish; Greek families do the same with goat or lamb. Whole heads may be boned, laid flat, and wrapped around a stuffing; they may be halved and baked with vegetables until tender; or they may be boned, poached, and served hot with vinaigrette, *salsa verde* (Italian parsley and caper sauce), or fresh tomato salsa and hot tortillas.

Ask the butcher to remove the eyes and to bone or split the head, as the recipe requires. Soak the head in several changes of acidulated water to draw out blood. Keep in acidulated water if cooking that day; otherwise, pat dry, wrap in plastic, and refrigerate for up to three days.

HEART

The deep-red heart muscle is richly flavored but tough if not properly handled. To prepare heart, trim away any visible fat, fibrous tissue, and tubes. Large beef hearts may be stuffed, tied, and braised whole. In Peru beef heart is served as an appetizer, after being cubed, marinated, skewered, and grilled over coals. Hearts can be braised with wine, herbs, and vegetables or cut in julienne strips and stir-fried with vegetables and soy sauce. Poultry hearts can be minced, sautéed in butter, and added to stuffings or gravy. To keep large hearts tender, they should either be sliced thinly and cooked quickly or kept whole or in large pieces for slow braising.

where lamb is popular, lamb's feet are simmered until tender and served with egg and lemon sauce. Chicken feet are used by cooks all over the world to give body to chicken stock. Chinese cooks braise duck feet with black beans and serve them as dim sum, a tea-house snack.

Select feet that are moist; avoid those that are sticky, dry, or blemished, or that have an off-odor. Scrape or singe off any stray hairs. Some recipes call for feet split lengthwise; a butcher can easily do this for you.

Recipes: Menudo, 591.

FRIES

The testicles of lamb, pigs, beef, and veal are known as fries. They are also sometimes referred to as mountain oysters; beef and veal fries are sometimes also known as Rocky Mountain oysters or prairie oysters. Fries should be plump and firm, with their outer skin intact. To prepare, slit the three layers of skin with a small sharp knife without slitting the flesh; pull off the skin. Soak fries in several changes of acidulated water to draw off any blood. Cover fries with cold salted water, bring to a boil, and simmer until firm (6 to 7 minutes). Drain and pat dry. They may then be sliced, coated with egg and bread crumbs, and fried; dipped in fritter batter and fried; browned slowly in butter and spices; or simmered in a highly seasoned tomato sauce. Fries are highly perishable.

KIDNEY

Lamb and pork kidneys consist of a single lobe; beef and veal kidneys are multilobed. Beef, lamb, and pork kidneys are dark red; veal kidneys are slightly lighter. Kidneys have a rich flavor and firm texture and are appealing on their own or added to other dishes. English cooks have many kidney dishes in their repertoire, including the famous Steak and Kidney Pie and kidneys broiled with bacon or braised with mushrooms and cream. The English also find a place for kidneys on the breakfast table. Chinese cooks stir-fry pork kidneys with vegetables; French cooks braise kidneys with mustard or mushrooms and cream, or grill them with herb butter.

Beef, veal, and pork kidneys should be plump, firm, and encased in a shiny membrane. Lamb kidneys are often sold encased in their fat, which should be off-white. Avoid kidneys with a strong odor.

To prepare kidneys, trim away any fat and connective tissue and pull off the outer membrane. Beef and veal kidneys should be halved to allow for easier removal of fat and tissues.

■ STEAK AND KIDNEY PIE

Some of the most typical and enjoyable English foods can be found in pubs (public houses), especially at noontime. There you are likely to find well-prepared cold plates, fine cheeses, and exceptional meat pies such as this well-known preparation. The pie may be assembled in advance (through step 3), covered, and refrigerated for several hours before baking. Accompany Steak and Kidney Pie with a green vegetable and a crisp salad. The pastry is easily made from frozen puff pastry shells, available in the freezer cases of specialty food stores and well-stocked supermarkets. The frozen shells will thaw to a consistency suitable for rolling in about 20 minutes.

   6 tablespoons flour
1½ teaspoons salt
  ¼ teaspoon *each* **ground pepper, dried**
     thyme, chervil, marjoram, and summer savory
  2 pounds boneless top round steak, cut in
     ½-inch cubes
  ½ pound beef or lamb kidneys, sliced
  ½ pound mushrooms, quartered
  2 tablespoons butter or margarine
  ½ cup dry red wine or Beef Stock (see page 560)
     or regular-strength canned beef broth
  6 frozen puff pastry patty shells (10-oz package),
     thawed
  1 egg, beaten with 1 teaspoon water

1. Preheat oven to 325° F. In a large bowl mix flour, salt, pepper, thyme, chervil, marjoram, and savory. Mix in steak cubes and kidney slices, coating well with flour mixture.

2. Sauté mushrooms in butter until lightly browned.

3. Place half the beef and kidney mixture in a 2-quart, 2-inch-deep baking dish. Top with mushrooms, then with remaining meat. Pour on wine or stock.

4. Arrange the patty shells, overlapping slightly, on a floured board or pastry cloth. Roll out pastry into a slightly larger shape than the top of the casserole. Lay pastry over meat mixture; trim and flute edge, sealing it to baking dish. Pierce or slit top in several places to allow steam to escape. Trim with pastry scraps cut into decorative shapes, if desired.

5. Brush pastry with egg mixture. Bake until meat is tender (insert a long wooden skewer to test) and pastry is well browned (1½ to 2 hours). Serve immediately.

Serves 6 to 8.

LIVER

Appreciated by cooks throughout the world, liver has a rich flavor and smooth texture. Beef, veal, pork, lamb, duck, and chicken all have delectable livers that may be used in countless ways. Beef and veal livers can be roasted whole but they are usually sliced and pan-fried. Calf's liver with onions is a popular Venetian dish. Chicken livers can be fried with bacon and served with rice or pasta. Duck livers make an unctuous, savory mousse or a rich topping for pasta. Chopped liver, that staple of the Jewish delicatessen, is usually made with beef liver but may also contain chicken liver; it is served as an appetizer with crackers or as a sandwich filling. German cooks make delicate calf's liver dumplings to float in soup. Chinese cooks stir-fry pork liver with green onions and mushrooms. Goose liver is made into a rich, creamy spread by Middle European cooks. The famous fatted goose and duck livers of France (foie gras) are one of the world's greatest delicacies, served cold in the form of a terrine or pâté, or sliced, pan-fried, and served hot.

Liver should be firm and moist, with a shiny appearance, and without any off-odor. True calf's liver is easy to distinguish from beef liver by appearance: Calf's liver is a pale reddish brown; beef liver is a dark reddish brown that verges on purple. To prepare livers, trim away any visible fat and tough connective tissue. Calf and beef livers, if purchased whole, both have a thin exterior membrane that should be pulled off. Liver is sometimes soaked in milk for one hour before cooking to "sweeten" it. Cook liver briefly and quickly; overcooked liver is dry, tough, and disagreeable.

Recipes: Curried Chicken or Duck Liver Pâté in Aspic, 416; Chicken or Duck Liver Mousse, 372.

SWEETBREADS

The thymus glands of calves or young lambs, sweetbreads gradually shrink as the animal ages. They are delicate in taste, smooth and soft in texture, and are considered a delicacy by many diners. Calf's sweetbreads are readily available from most specialty butchers, either fresh or frozen. Lamb sweetbreads may require special ordering. Sweetbreads should be plump and firm, with the exterior membrane intact.

Soak sweetbreads in several changes of cold water for one hour to draw out any blood. Then blanch in simmering acidulated water for 3 to 5 minutes (depending on size) and plunge into cold water to firm them. When cold, drain them and trim away any membranes and connective tissues. If serving whole, chill several hours under a weight to firm and shape; otherwise, separate with hands into smaller lobes.

Sweetbreads may be braised with peas or with mushrooms and cream; wrapped in bacon, skewered, and grilled; or braised in butter and served atop spinach or sorrel purée. They are also sautéed, poached, and broiled.

■ **SWEETBREADS AND MUSHROOM-MARSALA SAUCE**

The exuberance of Marsala and the luxury of sautéed mushrooms unite in a light, buttery sauce that bathes sweetbreads in a warm, rich Italianate glow. Serve with French-fried potatoes to dip in the sauce, and follow with a tartly dressed green salad.

   ½   **cup unsalted butter**
   1   **small onion, minced**
   1   **medium carrot, finely diced**
   2   **tablespoons minced shallot**
   ¼   **cup finely diced mild cooked ham**
   ½   **pound mushrooms, sliced**
  1½   **to 2 pounds sweetbreads, soaked, blanched, trimmed, weighted, and sliced if pieces are large (see page 589)**
     Salt and freshly ground pepper, to taste
   ½   **cup Marsala**
   1   **cup Beef Stock (see page 560) or canned consommé**
   ¼   **teaspoon dried marjoram**
   3   **tablespoons minced parsley**
  1½   **tablespoons flour**

1. Preheat oven to 350° F. In a flameproof, heavy-bottomed, 2-quart casserole, melt 3 tablespoons of the butter over low heat. Add onion, carrot, shallot, and ham; cover and cook over low heat until tender (about 10 minutes). Uncover and add mushrooms and 3 more tablespoons butter. Set remaining 2 tablespoons butter aside to soften. Increase heat under casserole to medium and sauté vegetables until mushrooms darken and begin to soften.

2. Season sweetbreads with salt and pepper. Combine with vegetable mixture in casserole. Pour on Marsala and stock; add marjoram, 2 tablespoons of the parsley, and additional salt and pepper to taste. Cover and bake 45 minutes.

3. Remove casserole from oven. With a slotted spoon, remove sweetbreads and most of the vegetables to a bowl. Set a colander over bowl and invert bowl over casserole so that liquid from sweetbread mixture drains back into casserole. Set sweetbread mixture aside in bowl, covered, and keep warm.

4. Over highest heat, boil down liquid in casserole until reduced by ½ to 1 cup, stirring frequently and scraping sides and bottom of casserole. Meanwhile, work remaining 2 tablespoons butter together with flour to make beurre manié. When liquid has reduced, add beurre manié to casserole. Lower heat to medium, and cook, stirring constantly, until butter melts and sauce thickens (about 1 minute). Correct seasoning. To serve, spoon sweetbreads onto a serving dish or individual plates. Pour on sauce and garnish with remaining parsley.

Serves 4 to 6.

TAIL

Beef tails (usually identified as oxtails) and pig's tails are appreciated by many diners for their rich meat and gelatinous texture. Slow braising tenderizes them and softens the gelatinous cartilage. Both oxtails and pig's tails may be stewed in wine with herbs and aromatic vegetables. The pieces can also be braised, then coated with butter and bread crumbs and broiled.

Fresh oxtails are almost always sold pretrimmed and sliced. They should have bright red meat and white fat. Pig's tails are available from ethnic markets; the meat should be firm and rosy red, the fat creamy white.

Recipes: Sherried Oxtail Soup, 501.

TONGUE

Fresh tongue—whether beef, veal, lamb, or pork—should be firm, and with no off-odor. Tongue has a rich flavor and firm meaty texture and is appealing on its own or in combination with other foods. Small whole lamb tongues can be pickled or preserved in aspic. Whole tongue can be poached and served hot or cold with mayonnaise, vinaigrette, or *salsa verde* (Italian parsley and caper sauce); it may be braised with wine and vegetables and served hot in a rich sauce. Poached tongue may also be cubed and tossed with cold vegetables and a vinaigrette for a salad. Whole tongue may be corned or smoked, thinly sliced, and served in sandwiches, traditionally on rye bread with mustard.

Fresh tongue should be soaked in several changes of cold water for two to three hours to draw out blood before cooking. A corned tongue should then be blanched 5 minutes and rinsed to remove excess salt. Poach fresh or corned tongue in court bouillon until tender (1½ to 2 hours for beef tongue, 30 minutes for lamb tongue). Drain; when cool enough to handle, trim away fat and gristle and peel off skin, which is easier to remove while tongue is hot.

Recipes: Boiled Dinner Bolognese, 530.

TRIPE

The muscular lining from two of the four parts of a ruminant's stomach is called tripe. Beef tripe is the most common; some butchers may be able to obtain veal and lamb tripe by special order. Smooth-textured tripe comes from the first stomach; honeycomb tripe, which owes its name to its appearance, comes from the second stomach. Fresh tripe should have an ivory color and no off-odor. By the time it appears in the market, it has already been cleaned, soaked, and precooked. It should be rinsed in cold water and patted dry.

Tripe is extremely bland, which is partly its virtue. During long, slow cooking with vegetables, herbs, and gelatinous meat such as calf's feet, it absorbs their flavor and becomes tender. Tripe can be cooked as little as one or two hours, but it is often encased in a tightly sealed container and braised slowly for up to 24 hours. French cooks braise tripe with onions, carrots, and cider for at least 12 hours to make *tripe à la mode de Caen*. Spanish cooks braise tripe with tomato and sweet peppers or simmer it with chick-peas and *chorizo* to make a one-dish meal. Italian cooks braise tripe in tomato sauce and then garnish it with basil and Parmesan cheese.

■ MENUDO
Tripe soup

To hear Mexicans talk of the beneficial effects of menudo, one would expect to find it included in the pharmacopoeia, along with other medicines and remedies, instead of in a cookbook. It has the reputation for fighting the ailments of the *cruda*, or hangover, and is therefore traditionally served on New Year's Day.

    1 calf's foot, cut into pieces
    3 pounds tripe, washed, trimmed of fat, and
       cut into 1-inch squares
    4 quarts water
    2 teaspoons salt
    3 ancho chiles (see Note)
    1 fresh Anaheim chile (see Note)
    1 large onion, chopped
    3 cloves garlic, crushed
    1 teaspoon freshly ground pepper
    2 cans (29 oz each) hominy, drained, *or*
       5 cups cooked hominy
    ½ cup cilantro
       Lime wedges, chopped onion, fresh mint, dried
       oregano, salsa, or sliced jalapeño, for garnish

1. Place calf's foot, tripe, the water, and salt in a large stockpot. Bring to a boil, reduce heat, and simmer, uncovered, for 2½ hours, skimming occasionally.

2. Remove and discard stems and seeds from chiles; crumble chiles into a blender or electric minichopper, and process until finely ground.

3. Remove calf's foot from pot. Remove any meat remaining on the bones and discard the bones. Coarsely chop meat and return it to soup. Add onion, garlic, pepper, and ground chiles, and continue to cook, uncovered, for another 2½ hours.

4. Add hominy and bring soup to a boil; reduce heat and simmer 1 to 2 hours. Soup will be finished in 1 hour, but an additional hour of cooking will improve the flavor. Stir in cilantro during the last 30 minutes of cooking.

5. Serve soup with garnishes passed separately.

Serves 8.

Note Two to three tablespoons mild ground red chile without spices may be substituted for the *ancho* and Anaheim chiles.

VEAL

The meat of young calves, usually no more than four months old, is the source of veal. (After six months, calf meat is considered beef.) The palest, most delicate veal is from milk-fed calves. Even young calves, if fed a grass diet, will develop red meat with stronger flavor. Veal is prized for its tender texture and mild flavor and subsequent versatility in the kitchen.

Use The delicate flavor of veal is appreciated by European cooks, with Italians having perhaps the widest repertoire of veal dishes: veal scaloppine (thin cutlets), veal stews and braises, stuffed whole breast of veal, and veal stuffings for pasta. French cooks also have a way with veal stews and sautés; Austrians are famous for their breaded veal cutlets. In Spain veal is stewed with sausage and peppers, and veal kidneys are cooked with sherry.

Veal bones are high in natural gelatin and are thus preferred by many cooks for making stock (see STOCK AND SOUP). A stock made with veal bones and some meaty veal pieces will have the rich body and mild flavor that is desirable in many French sauces.

Quickly cooked Veal Chops With Tarragon make a delicious foil for the subtle flavors of a Pinot Noir. An assortment of fresh vegetables will complete the meal nicely. The recipe is on page 593.

Selection   Because veal comes from young animals, it lacks the extensive intramuscular fat (marbling) typical of good beef. The best indication of quality in veal is its color. Look for veal with pale meat and white fat. Its texture should be fine, not coarse.

Successful veal cookery requires selecting the right method for each cut. Despite the fact that this meat comes from animals with underdeveloped muscles, all veal is not necessarily tender. It lacks the intramuscular marbling that acts as shortening by coating the muscle fibers and making them easier to cut. In addition, some cuts of veal are high in collagen, a protein which can be softened by long, slow cooking but which toughens if improperly handled. See Cuts of Veal at left.

Storage   Follow storage directions for BEEF.

Preparation   Trim off or slash the membrane that surrounds each veal scallop to prevent the meat from curling in the pan. In most recipes, scallops are pounded before cooking to flatten them as thin as possible (see POUND).

Cooking   Veal is generally cooked by moist-heat methods because it does not have enough natural fat to baste itself. Even when roasted, veal is either basted with a liquid or cooked in a covered pot in order to develop moisture in the form of steam. In many recipes, veal is paired with a sauce to compensate for its lack of flavorful fat. Veal chops, although lean, can be broiled or grilled; watch carefully to see that they don't overcook and get dry. Boneless roasts are braised or roasted in the oven. See BRAISE, BROIL, ROAST.

CUTS OF VEAL

The primal cuts of veal are similar to those of a full-grown beef steer (see page 38), but there are fewer of them. The rump, round, and hind shank, for instance, are all considered a part of the leg, and the breast is a single cut.

Ground veal   The breast and/or the shoulder are the cuts that are ground. Unless it has been mixed with beef suet, it contains only 20 percent fat or less. If the veal has not been ground with a meat grinder, it is relatively difficult to process at home; the meat is too slippery to shred well in a food processor.

Leg of veal   Most commonly, the leg is boned and sold as a roast. Butchers also divide the leg into its separate muscles and then slice the muscles thinly to make cutlets and scallops; the center cut of the leg (which is often labeled as a round) is probably the major source of these prized cuts. (More reasonably priced veal scallops can be cut at home from a boned leg.) Occasionally one finds other versions of leg of veal: Veal "round" roasts may actually be from the leg rather than the shoulder, as are bone-in rump roasts (cut from the area where the leg joins the hip). These and the center cut leg, are more tender than the shank half leg, which is occasionally sold as a roast but should really be braised.

Loin of veal   The loin includes numerous smaller cuts, not all of them available from a typical meat case. Loin chops are, of course, the most familiar, and can be sautéed, broiled, braised, or baked. The next most common cut from this section is the boneless rolled loin roast. This and several cuts from the leg are perhaps the most suitable cuts of veal for genuine roasting; all require basting. The rolled loin can be unrolled, filled with stuffing, and rerolled (tied in several places with kitchen twine) for an elegant roast. A bone-in loin includes the T-bone, and is a V-shaped cut that's also suitable for roasting.

Shoulder of veal   This cut is much more tender than the corresponding part of a steer, although tougher than the rib, loin, or leg. The shoulder is excellent for stewing and braising. Although this cut contains many membranes, long, slow cooking breaks down the chewiness. Boneless shoulder is often sold as a roast as well. Veal neck, a cut from the shoulder, is quite tough and must be cooked slowly by moist heat. Shoulder of veal is sometimes cut into steaks, which, despite the steak designation, should be braised, rather than grilled.

Veal breast   Although tough, bony, and (for veal) rather fatty, the breast is always economical. With the bone in, the breast can be cut into riblets and grilled. More popular are boned breasts, with a pocket cut in them for stuffing. Ground veal is usually made from this cut. It is much less fatty than other ground meats.

Veal foreshank   Usually this cut is sold under its Italian name, *osso buco*. Although tougher than the hind shank (which is often sold as part of the leg), and full of membranes, it is perhaps the richest-flavored cut when cooked slowly in liquid long enough to dissolve the sinews. The bones also yield delicious marrow. Veal foreshank is a common ingredient in meat stocks (and the sauces and soups based on meat stocks), yielding the gelatin that makes stocks rich and substantial. This cut is usually sold at a very reasonable price, but it has a very high ratio of bone to meat. As meat for stock, however, where the bones play a major role as a thickener, it's a superb value.

Veal rib   Occasionally veal rib is sold as an entire rack or a crown roast for use as a roast. More often, the rib section is cut into tender, flavorful chops.

Veal sirloin   Not common in butcher shops, veal sirloin is the portion of the loin next to the leg. It's a delicious cut, but since a calf is so much smaller than a steer, it's a bony one; as a result, this cut yields relatively little meat for its premium price. Veal sirloin chops are high-priced and delicious. Many butchers also cut the boned sirloin into veal scallops, although genuine veal scaloppine is supposed to be cut from the center portion of the leg.

■ **SPINACH-STUFFED BREAST OF VEAL**

Breast of veal, a large and dramatic-looking dish, is actually cooked covered for part of the time to keep the meat moist. With its meaty stuffing of ground beef, spinach, and cheese, this baked veal breast is frankly Italian. Accompanied by a salad or green vegetable, it will serve a large group economically and well.

    1 breast of veal (3 to 3½ lb)
    2 tablespoons olive oil or vegetable oil
    1 cup *each* Chicken Stock (see page 560) or
      full-strength canned chicken broth and
      dry white wine

Ground Beef and Spinach Stuffing

    ½ pound ground beef
    1 medium onion, chopped
    1 clove garlic, minced or pressed
    ¼ pound small mushrooms, thinly sliced
    1 package (9 or 10 oz) frozen chopped spinach,
      thawed and squeezed dry
    ½ cup soft bread crumbs
    1 cup grated Monterey jack cheese
    1 egg, slightly beaten
    ½ teaspoon *each* salt and dried basil
    ⅛ teaspoon freshly ground pepper

1. Have butcher cut pocket in veal breast for the stuffing. Preheat oven to 325° F.

2. Fill pocket with stuffing and fasten open end with small metal skewers. Place meat in large roasting pan. Brush with oil. Pour on ¾ cup each of the stock and the wine. Cover with foil and bake until meat is very tender (2 hours). Increase oven temperature to 350° F and continue baking, uncovered, for 25 to 30 minutes longer. Brush occasionally with pan drippings to brown meat. Remove meat to heated platter and keep warm.

3. To loosen pan drippings, add remaining ¼ cup each of broth and wine, stirring over high heat until liquid is reduced by about one third. Serve sauce separately. To carve veal, cut between rib bones.

Serves 6 to 8.

Ground Beef and Spinach Stuffing Crumble ground beef into a large frying pan and brown it in its own drippings. Mix in onion, garlic, and mushrooms. Cook, stirring occasionally, until onion is soft and begins to brown. Remove from heat; mix in spinach, then bread crumbs, grated cheese, egg, salt, basil, and pepper.

■ BLANQUETTE DE VEAU

This is the classic French white stew. Although it appears to want color, do not leave the carrots in for the traditional presentation. The recipe can be made almost completely in advance and finished just before serving (see Note). Serve over rice pilaf or steamed potatoes.

> 1 **pound mushrooms**
> 2 **tablespoons fresh lemon juice**
> 4 **tablespoons butter**
> ½ **teaspoon salt**
> ½ **teaspoon white pepper**
> 3 **tablespoons brandy or**
>   **Brown Veal Stock (see page 560)**
> 5 **cups Brown Veal Stock (see page 560) or**
>   **additional water**
> 3 **cups cold water**
> 4 **pounds veal shoulder, trimmed of fat**
>   **and cut into 2-inch cubes**
> 2 **medium onions, cut in quarters**
> 6 **carrots, cut in quarters**
>   **Bouquet garni (see page 56)**
> ½ **pound small onions**
> 3 **tablespoons flour**
> ¼ **cup whipping cream (optional)**
> 2 **egg yolks (optional)**

1. Toss mushrooms with lemon juice. In a medium skillet sauté mushrooms in 2 tablespoons of the butter over medium heat 1 to 2 minutes. Season with salt and pepper. Remove mushrooms with a slotted spoon and set aside. To avoid possible flare-ups, remove pan from heat, then add brandy, stirring to remove any cooked bits. Reserve liquid.

2. In a 6-quart kettle add the 5 cups Brown Veal Stock, 2½ cups of the cold water, and cubed veal shoulder. Bring mixture to a boil; add remaining water and remove from heat. Skim away any scum that has risen to the surface and return kettle to heat; add onions, carrots, and bouquet garni. Reduce heat to low and simmer, covered, for 1½ hours.

3. Bring 1 quart of water to a boil. Blanch small onions for 1 minute. Trim the root end, slip off the skins, and cut an *x* in the root end of each onion. Heat remaining butter in a small skillet and sauté onions over low heat until barely browned (about 15 minutes); remove onions with a slotted spoon and reserve buttered skillet.

4. Remove onion and carrot pieces from stock; set aside. In the small skillet, whisk flour into melted butter and cook briefly. Whisk 1 cup of stock into flour mixture. Return flour-stock mixture to veal, stirring thoroughly to combine. Add reserved mushrooms, their cooking liquid, and small onions to veal. Simmer for 15 minutes.

5. In a small bowl stir cream and egg yolks (if used) together; whisk into veal, and cook over low heat for 1 to 2 minutes (do not allow to boil or yolks will curdle).

Serves 8.

Note The recipe can be made through step 4 up to four days ahead. Refrigerate covered. When ready to continue, bring back to a simmer and continue with step 5.

■ VEAL CHOPS WITH TARRAGON

If pale pink, milk-fed, eastern veal is available in your area, by all means try this simple, elegant treatment. The redder, beefier-tasting veal typical of the West can be prepared the same way.

> 4 **veal rib chops, ¾ to 1 inch thick**
> 2 **or 3 sprigs fresh tarragon, plus leaves**
>   **for garnish (see Note)**
> 1 **teaspoon kosher salt**
> ¼ **teaspoon freshly ground pepper**
> ½ **cup unsalted Chicken, Brown Veal, or Beef Stock**
>   **(see page 560) or ¼ cup canned broth mixed with**
>   **¼ cup water**

1. Trim excess fat from chops. Finely chop half the tarragon and combine it with the salt and pepper. Rub salt mixture over both sides of chops.

2. Heat a large skillet (nonstick or well-seasoned cast iron) over medium heat. Add chops; cook until center springs back readily when pressed with a fingertip (3 to 4 minutes per side). Remove chops to a warm platter or to individual plates.

3. Deglaze skillet with stock, scraping up any browned drippings. Add remaining tarragon leaves. Reduce sauce by half, taste for seasoning, and correct if necessary.

4. Spoon sauce over chops, decorating each with tarragon leaves.

Serves 4.

Note If fresh tarragon is unavailable, substitute 1 teaspoon crumbled dried tarragon leaves to season the chops and omit the additional tarragon from the sauce and as the garnish. Or, use tarragon leaves packed in vinegar (available at specialty shops), well drained, in place of fresh leaves.

Meats such as veal or poultry that lack natural fat are sometimes wrapped in a layer of exterior fat to keep them moist during cooking. This technique is called barding.

▪ VITELLO TONNATO

Because this dish of cold, sliced leg of veal with tuna sauce must be made in advance, it works beautifully for a buffet. To serve, fan veal slices on platter and spoon sauce over meat. The piquant, creamy sauce—sparked with anchovy, garlic, capers, and vinegar—needs to refrigerate for a day to marry the flavors and the veal also needs to chill overnight.

     1 can (6½ oz) tuna, drained
     2 anchovy fillets
     1 clove garlic, sliced
     ¼ cup olive oil
     2 tablespoons white wine vinegar
     1 tablespoon whipping cream
     1 tablespoon capers, drained
       Leg of veal (4 lb), boned and rolled

1. Preheat oven to 350° F. In a blender or food processor purée tuna, anchovies, garlic, olive oil, vinegar, and cream. Stir in capers; chill (this sauce is better when made a day in advance so flavors can blend).

2. Place veal on a rack in an 8- by 12-inch roasting pan. Roast about 45 minutes (to an internal temperature of about 140° F). Cool briefly and refrigerate overnight.

3. To serve, slice veal ¼ inch thick, arrange on a platter, and pour tuna sauce over pieces.

Serves 8 to 10.

▪ WIENER SCHNITZEL

Any thin slice of meat is a *schnitzel* in German, but veal is the meat of choice. This preparation—Viennese (Wiener) style—consists of paper-thin veal scallops coated with seasoned crumbs and sautéed until golden brown. To keep the bound coating from slipping off in the skillet, the cutlets must sit 30 minutes before cooking. See variations at end of recipe for other classic veal scallop dishes. Use milk-fed veal from the leg for these quick sautés. When pounded to an even ⅛-inch thickness, the little scallops cook through quickly and remain tender.

     2 pounds veal scallops
     1 egg
     1 tablespoon water
     1 teaspoon salt
     ½ teaspoon freshly ground pepper
     1 cup dry bread crumbs
     4 tablespoons unsalted butter
     2 tablespoons vegetable oil
     1 lemon, for garnish
       Red Cabbage With Apples (see page 75),
       for accompaniment
       Boiled parsleyed potatoes, for accompaniment

1. Lightly pound veal cutlets with a wooden mallet to tenderize and flatten to about ⅛ inch thick, or have the butcher do it for you. In a shallow, small bowl, beat egg with the water. In another shallow, small bowl, mix salt, pepper, and bread crumbs.

2. Dip veal slices in beaten egg to coat thoroughly, then dip in seasoned bread crumbs. Place on a plate and chill 30 minutes.

3. In a large skillet sauté one half of the veal in 2 tablespoons butter and 1 tablespoon oil over medium heat 2 minutes; turn and cook second side 2 minutes. Reserve in 200° F oven while preparing remaining veal with remaining butter and oil. When all are cooked, remove to a serving platter and drizzle with lemon juice. Serve with Red Cabbage With Apples and boiled parsleyed potatoes.

Serves 6.

Schnitzel à la Holstein   Prepare veal as above. Prepare Basic Poached Eggs (see page 199) or Basic Fried Eggs (see page 200) and serve on top.

Veal Marsala   Prepare as for Veal Scaloppine (below), reducing cooking time to 20 to 30 seconds on each side (they will finish cooking in the sauce). Transfer cooked veal to a plate. Add 1 tablespoon butter and 1 tablespoon finely minced garlic to skillet; sauté until fragrant, then add ¾ cup Marsala wine. Bring to a boil and reduce until about half original volume. Remove pan from heat, swirl in 3 more tablespoons butter, cut into small pieces. Season to taste with salt and pepper. Return veal to pan briefly just to warm through. Divide scallops and sauce onto dinner plates and garnish with minced parsley.

Veal Parmigiana   Prepare veal as above, adding 1 teaspoon dried basil and 1 teaspoon dried oregano to bread crumb mixture. Prepare 4 cups Basic Tomato Sauce (see page 516). Place veal on an ovenproof serving platter, coat each piece with ½ cup tomato sauce, place a 1-ounce slice mozzarella cheese on each piece, and bake in a preheated 400° F oven until cheese melts (about 3 minutes). Serve immediately.

Veal Picatta   Prepare as for Veal Scaloppine (below); reserve in a 200° F oven while preparing lemon sauce. Over very low heat, add 6 tablespoons fresh lemon juice and ¼ cup minced parsley to skillet and scrape all browned bits from sides and bottom of pan. Add 4 tablespoons butter and stir until butter melts. Remove veal to a serving platter, pour sauce over, season with salt and freshly ground black pepper to taste, and garnish with lemon slices and minced parsley.

Veal Scaloppine   Pound veal and lightly sprinkle with salt and freshly ground black pepper. Dredge veal lightly in flour, shaking off excess. Sauté in butter and oil quickly on both sides (less than 1 minute per side). Serve immediately.

> ***Recipes and Related Information***
> *Brown Veal Stock, 560; Osso Buco, 58; Saltimbocca, 505.*

VEGETABLE

The American vegetable marketplace has expanded dramatically in the recent past. Today's supermarket stocks a much greater variety of vegetables than consumers could have imagined just 10 years ago.

The new marketplace owes its breadth in part to a curiosity about other cuisines. Many supermarkets carry a wide assortment of Chinese vegetables and Latin chiles in addition to Japanese mushrooms, Thai eggplants, and Belgian endive. Americans have also begun to demand the variety of vegetables that they find in restaurants: baby squash and squash blossoms, radicchio, and wild mushrooms. Growers, aided by progressive seed companies, have taken an interest in supplying markets and restaurants with these unusual and exotic vegetables. Another factor affecting the growth of the marketplace is the increased interest in nutrition—in reducing intake of meat, and in raising the proportion of high-fiber foods in our diet. All these recent developments provide challenge and constant delight for the curious cook.

Baby vegetables include both special miniature varieties of common vegetables and regular varieties picked when immature. Fully mature miniatures add natural sweetness and a whimsical touch to a dish; regular varieties harvested when young may or may not have fully developed flavor.

For helpful information on purchasing, storing, and preparing most of the vegetables currently available, check the individual vegetable entries in this book.

Use Although most Americans think of vegetables as secondary to meat, in many cuisines vegetables take center stage. In China vegetable stir-fries are embellished with a small amount of meat rather than the reverse. In India, even among nonvegetarians, meals based on vegetables are common.

Around the world, vegetables are appreciated at all times of the day, from breakfast through dessert. Ethiopians often eat a breakfast of boiled beans flavored with onions and tomatoes; the English enjoy baked or stewed tomatoes in the morning, and the American coffee-shop breakfast wouldn't be complete without fried potatoes. At the other end of the day are the vegetable-based desserts, ranging from carrot cake and sweet potato pie to sugar-dusted Italian squash-blossom fritters.

Vegetables are served in salads, casseroles, sautés and stir-fries, stews and braised dishes, pickles, pasta, soups, and side dishes. Some vegetables are so highly prized that they are often served as a separate course: steamed asparagus, sautéed wild mushrooms, sliced beefsteak tomatoes, whole steamed artichokes, or hot corn on the cob can launch a meal in simple but memorable style. Other vegetables are usually given a supporting role: Onions and garlic, for example, are appreciated more for the aromatic qualities they lend to other dishes than as dishes in themselves.

Baby vegetables can be used in all standard preparations; they are particularly appealing served whole.

Availability   Buying vegetables in season is the best way to get superior quality. When prices are lowest, quality is usually at its best because the domestic harvest is at its peak. Vine-ripened autumn tomatoes from a local supplier have little in common with midwinter tomatoes shipped green from Mexico. Learn to enjoy vegetables to the fullest during their season and to forgo them at other times of the year. The good cook takes pleasure in following the seasons and the well-ordered parade of colors in nature. The first asparagus, June peas, and the first sweet corn of summer give way to the sunset colors of peppers and tomatoes, followed by the earthy winter comfort of mushrooms, rutabagas, and fennel.

The season for most farmed baby vegetables corresponds with the season for the regular varieties.

Selection   Without exception, vegetables are best the moment they are harvested. The longer it takes to get a vegetable from the field to the market, the more flavor and texture suffer. For best quality, patronize local farmers' markets; most likely the vegetables were grown nearby and picked within the previous 24 hours. Alternatively, look for a market that knows how to care for its vegetables by keeping them cool and neatly trimmed, and by making an effort to stock locally grown produce. Fresh vegetables have good, bright color and firm texture. Carrots, celery, and root vegetables should feel firm, not spongy; leafy greens should be crisp, not wilted; asparagus and beans should be sturdy, not limp.

Crudités—raw fresh vegetables—are always welcome as part of an hors d'oeuvres buffet. Throughout the year, the produce market yields a varied palette of fresh vegetables. Choose the best the season has to offer, prepare them in bite-sized pieces, and arrange them in an eye-catching still life, with a dip or two alongside.

Storage   The more quickly you use the vegetables you buy, the better. Some vegetables, such as peas and corn, quickly convert sugar to starch after harvest; they should be cooked the day they are purchased. Others, such as hard-shelled winter squash, can withstand long storage but do not improve in flavor after harvest.

Most vegetables, including baby vegetables, which are particularly perishable, should be refrigerated until use, preferably in a vegetable bin. Potatoes, garlic, onions, and shallots are exceptions, however; refrigerating them encourages rot. Store them in a cool, airy place. Hard squashes can be refrigerated but don't require it; they will keep in a cool, airy place for several months.

Preparation   For most vegetables, wash and dry; peel and trim as necessary. Some baby vegetables, such as carrots and potatoes, have very delicate skins that do not require peeling.

Cooking   See BLANCH, BOIL, BRAISE, BROIL, GRILL, MICROWAVE OVEN, PARBOIL, PUREE, STEAM, STIR-FRY.

VEGETABLE COOKING SPRAY

Most pan sprays are made of vegetable oil, alcohol, lecithin (a vegetable compound used as an emulsifier), and a propellant. They are a boon to those on low-calorie or low-cholesterol diets because they eliminate the need to grease baking pans or skillets. Most commercial brands instruct the user to apply the coating while the pan or skillet is cold.

Stored in a cool place, cooking sprays will keep indefinitely. Widely available in supermarkets, they are usually stocked next to the cooking oils.

VERTICAL ROASTER

To a great degree, food cooks by conduction—the slow, molecule-by-molecule transfer of heat from outside to center mass. If heat could somehow reach both the interior and the exterior at the same time, cooking time would be faster and food would cook more  evenly. That's why dense or delicate cake batters are often baked in tube pans and why a baked potato will be done sooner with a nail tapped through the center. It's also the clever idea behind the vertical roaster for poultry.

These open, upright frames of stainless steel wire conduct heat to the internal cavity of fowl set on them. When roasted this way, poultry cooks faster and stays juicier than with conventional methods because the metal frame is an excellent heat conductor that promotes cooking from the inside as well as the outside. The frames are available for chickens and Rock Cornish game hens (see Mustard Madness, page 381).

VINEGAR

When a naturally fermented alcohol—such as sherry, wine, or apple cider—is attacked by a type of airborne bacteria called acetobacter, the alcohol is converted to acetic acid, creating vinegar. Winemakers take precautions to keep acetobacter from attacking their wine, but vinegar manufacturers take the opposite approach. Most encourage the growth of acetobacter by inoculating their base material with a starter culture. By this method, manufacturers can promote a consistent and desirable flavor.

The variety of vinegars available to consumers has increased dramatically in recent years. Formerly, distilled white vinegar, apple cider vinegar, and wine vinegar were the only readily available options. Today, well-stocked supermarkets and specialty shops offer a variety of herb-flavored vinegars, such as tarragon and dill; fruit vinegars, such as raspberry and blueberry; Champagne vinegar; sherry vinegar; Japanese rice vinegar; malt vinegar; and the famous Italian *aceto balsamico* (balsamic vinegar), made from wood-aged wine. See Availability for descriptions of specific vinegars.

The commercially available flavored vinegars are generally expensive, yet flavored vinegar is easy to make at home (see JAM, JELLY, PRESERVE, AND CONDIMENT).

Use   High-quality vinegar has a fruitiness and refreshing acidity that give a lift to many dishes. Perhaps the most common use for vinegar is in salad dressing. Almost any type of salad—whether of mixed greens, cold vegetables, cold rice, or shellfish—benefits from the jolt of acidity that vinegar provides. Vinegar also acts as a tenderizer in meat marinades by denaturing the surface proteins. Vinegar in egg-poaching water (about 2 tablespoons per quart) will keep the whites from spreading and make the eggs more tender. In a Hollandaise sauce or related sauce, vinegar keeps the protein in the egg yolk from coagulating when the sauce is cooked. Vinegar acts as an antioxidant, slowing the browning of foods such as avocado and celery root, and as a preservative, preventing the growth of harmful bacteria in pickles.

The flavor of vinegar is essential to many dishes around the world. Most pickles wouldn't be pickles without the vinegar that preserves and flavors them. American diners, especially those from the Deep South, like to flavor cooked greens such as spinach with vinegar. English fish and chips are always served with strong malt vinegar as a condiment. Japanese salads get their distinctive taste in part from mild, slightly sweet rice vinegar. Italians enrich sauces with the mellow balsamic vinegar; the finest balsamic vinegar is used, drop by drop, as a table condiment. Modern French cooks add sherry vinegar to sautéed calf's liver and pair raspberry vinegar with duck livers. The basic dressing known as vinaigrette derives its name from the French word for vinegar (*vinaigre*); usually made from 3 parts oil to 1 part vinegar, this versatile sauce is used to dress green salads and salads of cold vegetables, leeks, fish, and grains. Champagne vinegar with minced shallots and black pepper is a popular condiment for raw oysters in France. In China black vinegar made from rice is used to dress cold noodle dishes and to enrich stir-fries.

Availability The following are among the most widely used vinegars today; they are sold in supermarkets and specialty stores.

Apple Cider Vinegar Made from the juice of apples, apple cider vinegar has an aroma and flavor that distinctly suggest the fruit. Its fruity quality is appealing in dressings for cabbage salads and fruit salads. It is also widely used in pickling.

Balsamic Vinegar Made from the juice of a white grape, balsamic vinegar is aged for several years in wood barrels. The vinegar is dark brown, with a mellow sweet-and-sour character that is greatly appreciated by Italian cooks. In Italy balsamic vinegar enriches stews, dresses salads, and even perks up the flavor of strawberries. The finest balsamic vinegar is carefully aged for decades and is extremely expensive.

Distilled White Vinegar The flavor of distilled white vinegar, which is made from grain alcohol, is too coarse for most salad dressings, but it is widely used in pickling.

Raspberry Vinegar Macerating raspberries in white wine vinegar and then straining the vinegar produces raspberry vinegar. The fruit imparts a pale raspberry color and an unmistakably raspberry flavor and aroma. The fruity character is appealing when with chicken, duck, and liver, and in salads with a fruit component.

Rice Vinegar Used in Chinese and Japanese cookery, rice vinegar is clear to pale gold in color, with a mild and subtly sweet flavor. Asian cooks use rice vinegar in noodle dishes, salad dressings, dipping sauces, and pickles.

Sherry Vinegar A fragrant, slightly nutty vinegar made from Spanish sherry, it is best in salad dressings; with green beans, asparagus, and chicken or duck; or to deglaze the skillet after sauteing chicken or calf's liver.

Wine Vinegar Either red or white, good-quality wine vinegar has a pleasing aroma and is pungent without being harsh. Generally, red wine vinegar is used with dark meats, in marinades, and in salads where its color is not objectionable. Use white wine vinegar with fish, in potato salads, or in pickles where a clear vinegar is preferred.

White wine vinegar is the base for many commercial herb vinegars.

Storage Keep bottles of vinegar tightly capped; store in a cool, dark place for up to six months.

■ PORK ADOBO

The famous adobo is a classic dish of the Philippines. Like the curries of other countries, adobo probably originated as a way of preserving meat. In this case the preserving agent is vinegar, not chiles or other spices. The following version calls for boiling cubes of pork in a vinegar and garlic mixture until the liquid evaporates and the cubes begin to fry in their own rendered fat. Use pork with some visible fat, either from the shoulder or the nearby section of the loin (usually sold as "country-style spareribs").

> 1½ pounds boneless pork, in 1-inch cubes
> ½ cup rice vinegar
> 6 cloves garlic, minced
> 3 tablespoons soy sauce or fish sauce
> ¼ teaspoon freshly ground pepper
> 1½ cups water
> 1 bay leaf

1. In a bowl combine pork cubes, vinegar, garlic, soy sauce, and pepper; marinate 1 to 3 hours in the refrigerator.

2. Transfer all ingredients to a non-aluminum saucepan, add 1 cup of the water and bay leaf, and bring to a boil, uncovered. Adjust heat so meat cooks at a lively simmer but does not boil too rapidly.

3. Cook until liquid is nearly gone, then reduce heat further. Mixture will sizzle and pop as the last bits of water evaporate; then the pork cubes will begin to brown in the remaining fat. Turn cubes to brown evenly and remove from heat if mixture shows signs of scorching.

4. Remove pork cubes to serving dish. Add ½ cup of the water to pan and bring to a boil, stirring to scrape browned bits from pan. Pour over pork. Serve with rice.

Serves 4 with other dishes.

Variation Follow Pork Adobo recipe. Use a mixture of chicken, cut into braising pieces (1 to 2 inches long with bones), and boneless pork. Cook only until liquid is reduced to ½ cup, then brown meats in a separate pan: In a large skillet add 1 to 2 tablespoons vegetable oil (enough to coat bottom of pan). Heat oil over medium-high heat and brown chicken and pork pieces well. Transfer browned meats to a warm platter and cover with sauce.

> #### *Recipes and Related Information*
> *Fran's Raspberry Vinegar, 323; Herb Vinegar, 323;*
> *Raspberry Vinegar and Shallot Dressing, 521;*
> *Vinegar Dressing, 233.*

TIPS

COOKING WITH VINEGAR

Because vinegar is highly volatile, its flavor dissipates with heat and air. To retain its pungent character in a cooked dish, add vinegar to the dish only after removing it from heat. If a less pungent flavor is desired, add the vinegar while the dish is cooking and allow vinegar to boil off slightly.

WAFFLE AND PANCAKE

A thin mixture called a pour batter—the amount of liquid and dry ingredients are about equal and are wet enough to be pourable—forms the base for waffles and all types of pancakes. Most pour batters are classified as quick breads because they use a leavening other than yeast; blini, a buckwheat pancake, is the exception since it is yeast leavened. Like all quick breads, pour batters are fast to assemble and cook. Pancakes and waffles are popular breakfast foods; crêpes and blini appear on hors d'oeuvres trays as first courses, as desserts at elegant dinners, and on the menus of the trendiest restaurants.

INGREDIENTS AND METHOD

Dry ingredients include flour, baking powder or soda, salt, sometimes sugar, and often spices. These are blended and then combined with the liquid additions: milk, oil or melted butter, and eggs. For a light and delicate finished product, the eggs can be separated into yolks and whites: The yolks are added with the liquids and the whites beaten and folded into the batter as the final step.

Frequently, the same batter can be used for either pancakes or waffles; the difference is in how the batter is cooked. For pancakes, spoonfuls of batter are dropped onto a preheated griddle or skillet and cooked on both sides until golden brown. For waffles, the batter is poured onto the grids of a preheated waffle iron and baked until crisp and golden brown. See specific recipes for information on other food products.

Although pancakes, waffles, and other types of pour-batter products cook quickly, it is important not to rush them. When underdone, they are brown on the surface and unpleasantly liquid on the inside. To cook, the pan or appliance should be preheated to the proper temperature: For nonelectric pans, a drop of water will jump when it hits the hot pan; for thermostatically controlled devices, a light signals readiness. Flip pancakes when the surface appears dry and the bubbles around the edge have set. Cook waffles until steam is no longer given off or until the indicator light on an automatic waffle maker denotes that the waffles are ready.

EQUIPMENT

Although drop batters and doughs are stiff enough to hold their shape, a pour batter requires a special pan or iron if it is to have a distinctive form or imprint (see WAFFLE IRON AND PANCAKE PAN). Otherwise, when spooned onto a flat cooking surface—a griddle or skillet—the batter will spread in a gradually widening circle until set by heat.

A new griddle or skillet should be seasoned before use (see MATERIALS FOR COOKWARE). A well-seasoned pancake griddle or waffle iron should not be washed after using. Wipe away any clinging bits with a little oil and a paper towel, and store in a dry place. If the pan you are using isn't reserved only for pancakes, and isn't seasoned, you may need to add a thin coat of oil to it during preheating; if the batter contains fat, this may not be necessary.

Other equipment useful for making pancakes, waffles, and similar products includes pancake turners, whisks or wooden spoons for mixing the batter, an electric mixer for beating egg whites, and a mixing bowl. If you make these foods often, you may want to look for a batter bowl, which is an oversized liquid measuring cup with a 2-quart capacity; it is large enough to hold the batter and has a convenient pouring lip.

■ BASIC WAFFLES

If you are using a stove-top waffle iron, cook batter at least 1 minute for crisp waffles, preferably 2 minutes, after steam stops rising from iron. The top should lift without resistance. Serve waffles immediately after cooking for best texture and flavor, accompanied with butter and maple syrup, fresh fruit, or even ice cream. If they must be held, keep them warm in a 350°F oven 3 to 5 minutes. Serve on warm plates and warm any sauce served with them as well. Don't stack waffles or they will lose their crispness and get soggy. Extra waffles can be frozen, well wrapped, and toasted, but they won't have the same crispy flavor as when freshly made.

> 1¾ cups flour
> 1 tablespoon baking powder
> Pinch salt
> 2 tablespoons sugar
> 2 cups milk
> 3 eggs, separated
> 6 tablespoons butter, melted
> Pinch cream of tartar (optional)
> Butter and warm maple syrup, for topping

1. Sift together flour, baking powder, salt, and sugar into a medium bowl. Make a well in center of mixture. In another bowl combine milk, egg yolks, and melted butter. Pour into well in flour mixture; stir until smooth and creamy. This can also be done in a blender or food processor, but don't overwork or batter will be tough.

2. Preheat waffle iron according to manufacturer's directions or until a drop of water sizzles and bounces when placed onto hot iron.

3. In another bowl beat egg whites to soft peaks (if not using a copper bowl, add cream of tartar to whites when just foamy). Fold one third of beaten whites into batter to lighten, then fold in remaining whites.

4. Pour enough batter onto lightly oiled waffle iron to spread into corners (about 1 cup batter for a 4-square waffle iron). Cook 2 minutes after moment when steam stops escaping from sides of waffle maker. When waffles are cooked sufficiently, iron should release them easily. Serve immediately with butter and syrup.

Makes 4 cups batter, four 4-square waffles.

Cornmeal Waffles Prepare Basic Waffles, but substitute ¾ cup cornmeal for 1 cup of the flour. Spread with cream cheese and chopped jalapeño chile, and serve with soup or eggs.

▨ BUTTERMILK WAFFLES

This batter makes a light, tender waffle. Also try one of the variations: pecan, blueberry, or chocolate.

1¾ cups flour
  1 teaspoon baking powder
  1 teaspoon baking soda
  2 tablespoons sugar
  2 cups buttermilk
  ½ cup butter, melted
  2 eggs, separated
    Pinch cream of tartar (optional)

Prepare as for Basic Waffles.

Makes 4 cups batter, four 4-square waffles.

Blueberry Buttermilk Waffles Fold 1 cup washed and dried blueberries into batter before cooking.

Chocolate-Pecan Waffles Substitute ¼ cup unsweetened cocoa powder for ¼ cup flour called for in recipe. Use a total of 6 tablespoons sugar. Mix in 1 teaspoon vanilla extract to buttermilk mixture. Fold in 1 cup chopped pecans to batter before cooking.

Pecan Buttermilk Waffles Fold 1 cup pecan pieces into batter before cooking.

▨ BELGIAN WAFFLES
WITH BLUEBERRY SAUCE

Yeast-leavened Belgian waffles are rectangular and have an extradeep grid made with a special waffle iron (see page 603). They can also be made in a regular waffle iron.

  1 package active dry yeast
  ¼ cup warm water
  2 cups flour
  ¼ cup sugar
  ¼ teaspoon salt
  ¼ cup butter or margarine, melted and cooled
  2 tablespoons vegetable oil
1½ cups water
  ½ teaspoon vanilla extract
  2 eggs, separated
    Whipped cream (optional)

Blueberry Sauce

  ⅓ cup butter
  ⅔ cup sugar
  3 tablespoons light corn syrup
  ¼ cup water
  2 tablespoons grated lemon rind
  ¼ teaspoon freshly grated nutmeg
1½ cups fresh or frozen unsweetened blueberries

1. Sprinkle yeast over the ¼ cup warm water in a small bowl; let stand about 5 minutes to soften. In a large bowl mix flour, sugar, and salt. Beat in butter, oil, the 1½ cups water, and vanilla until smooth. Then beat in egg yolks and yeast mixture.

2. Beat egg whites until they form soft peaks; fold gently into batter. Cover and refrigerate several hours or overnight; stir down batter.

3. Place a seasoned 6- by 7½-inch Belgian waffle iron directly over medium heat, turning it over occasionally, until a few drops of water dance on grids (or preheat an electric model). Spoon about ½ cup batter onto lightly oiled iron, spreading it just to cover grids.

4. Close iron and turn occasionally until waffle is well browned (4 to 5 minutes in all). Transfer waffles to wire rack unless served immediately.

5. If waffles are made ahead, cool, wrap in aluminum foil, and freeze. Reheat in a preheated 325° F oven, uncovered, in a single layer on baking sheets until hot and crisp (about 10 minutes).

6. Serve hot, with Blueberry Sauce. Top with whipped cream (if desired).

Makes 9 waffles.

Blueberry Sauce Combine butter, sugar, and corn syrup in a medium saucepan. Cook over medium heat, stirring, until mixture boils. Stir in the water and boil 2 minutes. Add lemon rind, nutmeg, and blueberries. Cook, stirring, until mixture boils.

Makes about 1¾ cups.

Belgian waffles have deep grids, the better to trap delicious syrups and sauces. Blueberry Sauce, shown here, is served hot and is flavored with fresh nutmeg and grated lemon rind.

■ BASIC PANCAKES

Making pancake batter yourself is almost as easy as using a mix and always tastes better. For quick breakfasts, you can have the dry ingredients combined, all ready to stir into the egg mixture. Do this while the pan is heating. If the batter thickens too much upon standing, thin with a little extra liquid. Leftover batter can be stored in the refrigerator in an airtight container overnight, but the pancakes made from it won't be as light because the baking powder will have lost some of its punch. Always preheat the skillet or griddle before pouring on the batter. Test for readiness by shaking a few drops of water on the pan surface. The pan is ready to use if the water skips, sizzles, and quickly evaporates. Pour batter onto griddle or pan, and cook until the bubbles that form begin to burst and the edges look dry. Turn and cook on the other side.

    1¾ cups flour
    ¼   cup sugar
    2   teaspoons baking powder
    ½   teaspoon salt
    2   eggs
    4   tablespoons butter, melted
    1¼ cups milk
        Butter and warm maple syrup, for topping

1. Sift flour, sugar, baking powder, and salt into a medium bowl. Add eggs, butter, and milk and beat until smooth and creamy; set aside.

2. If using an electric skillet, preheat to 350° F; preheat lightly oiled griddle or skillet over medium heat until a few drops of water dance on the surface. For each pancake pour ¼ cup batter onto hot griddle and cook on first side until bubbles that form begin to pop and edges look dry. With a spatula, turn and cook until second side is a rich, golden brown.

3. Serve at once with butter and syrup.

Makes 8 to 12 four-inch pancakes.

Buckwheat Pancakes Prepare batter with 1¼ cups all-purpose flour and ½ cup buckwheat flour.

Whole-Grain Pancakes Prepare batter with 1 cup all-purpose flour and ¾ cup whole wheat flour.

■ BUTTERMILK PANCAKES

The addition of buttermilk provides a little tang and makes these pancakes extratender.

    1   cup cake flour
    2   teaspoons sugar
    1   teaspoon baking powder
    ½   teaspoon baking soda
        Pinch salt
    1   egg
    1   cup buttermilk
    2   tablespoons butter, melted, or vegetable oil
        Butter and warm maple syrup, for topping

1. Sift flour, sugar, baking powder, baking soda, and salt into a medium bowl. Add egg, buttermilk, and butter, and beat until smooth and creamy; set aside.

2. If using an electric skillet, preheat to 350° F; preheat lightly oiled griddle or skillet over medium heat until a few drops of water dance on the surface. For each pancake pour ¼ cup batter onto hot griddle and cook on first side until bubbles that form begin to pop and edges look dry. With a spatula, turn and cook until second side is a rich, golden brown.

3. Serve at once with butter and syrup.

Makes 8 to 12 four-inch pancakes.

Blueberry Buttermilk Pancakes Fold ½ to 1 cup rinsed and dried blueberries into batter before cooking.

■ BUTTERMILK BLINTZES

Unlike crêpes, which are cooked on both sides, the pancakes for blintzes are browned on one side only. They are then wrapped around a sweetened cheese filling and fried to brown the outside. Making blintzes is a lengthy operation. If you make them ahead, you can cover and refrigerate the filled blintzes for up to 24 hours. When ready, brown quickly and serve hot. The name for this Jewish dish is from the Yiddish *blintse*, which in turn evolved from the Russian *blinets* (diminutive of *blin*, or pancake). Note that the batter must chill for one hour before using.

    ¾   cup flour
    ¾   teaspoon baking soda
    ½   teaspoon salt
    2   tablespoons sugar
    1   cup buttermilk
    ½   cup water
    3   eggs
    2   tablespoons vegetable oil
    3   to 4 tablespoons *each* butter or margarine
        and vegetable oil, for frying
        Sour cream and cherry preserves, for topping

Cheese Filling

    1   package (8 oz) cream cheese, softened
    1   egg
    2   tablespoons confectioners' sugar
    ½   teaspoon vanilla extract
    ¼   teaspoon ground cinnamon
    2   cups (1 lb) pot cheese (also called farmer cheese)

1. In blender or food processor, combine flour, soda, salt, sugar, buttermilk, the water, eggs, and the 2 tablespoons oil. Whirl or process until batter is smooth, stopping motor once or twice to scrape flour from sides of container. Cover and refrigerate for at least 1 hour before using.

2. Make blintzes in a lightly oiled 6- to 7-inch crêpe pan, but brown them on first side only and cook until top surface is dry to touch. Stack blintzes to cool.

3. To fill each blintz, place about 2 tablespoons of Cheese Filling in center of browned side of each pancake. Fold in opposite edges about 1 inch, then fold in remaining edges to enclose filling, overlapping in center to make a slightly rectangular envelope. Set blintzes aside, folded side down.

4. In a large frying pan over moderately high heat, melt 2 tablespoons butter with 2 tablespoons oil. Fry filled blintzes without crowding until golden on each side (1 to 1½ minutes on each side). Add more butter and oil to pan as needed.

5. Drain blintzes well on paper towels and serve on warm plates, topped with a dollop each of sour cream and cherry preserves.

Makes 20 to 24 blintzes.

Cheese Filling In a large bowl beat cream cheese with egg, confectioners' sugar, vanilla, and cinnamon. Then beat in pot cheese.

Makes about 3 cups.

SWEDISH PANCAKES

These small, moist, delicate pancakes are traditionally made in a *plett,* a cast-iron griddle with shallow, 3-inch-diameter depressions to hold the batter (see page 604). If you don't have this pan, the pancakes will taste just as good. Serve them in the Swedish manner, with butter and lingonberry preserves, or with your favorite fruit-flavored syrup. Imported lingonberry preserves can be found at specialty food shops and well-stocked supermarkets.

- ⅔ **cup flour**
- ½ **teaspoon baking powder**
- ⅛ **teaspoon salt**
- 2 **eggs, separated**
- 1 **cup milk, at room temperature**
- ¼ **cup half-and-half**
- ¼ **cup butter or margarine, melted and cooled**
  Butter and lingonberry preserves or syrup, for topping

1. Sift flour, baking powder, and salt onto a square of parchment paper or waxed paper; set aside. In a large bowl beat egg yolks with milk and half-and-half. Beat in melted butter, then add flour mixture. Stir to combine.

2. Beat egg whites until stiff peaks form. Carefully fold into batter.

3. Set a lightly oiled Swedish pancake pan, griddle, or skillet over medium-low heat until a few drops of water dance on the hot surface. Use about 2 tablespoons batter for each pancake. Cook pancakes until golden brown on each side, turning once very carefully with a spatula. Serve hot with butter and lingonberry preserves or syrup.

Makes about 2 dozen 3-inch pancakes.

DUTCH BABIE

This oven pancake is said to have originated at a small family restaurant in Seattle. Very similar to Yorkshire pudding, it uses eggs, flour, and milk, although the proportion of eggs is much higher. The recipe can be doubled or even tripled, as long as it is baked in a shallow pan in a 425° F oven.

- 4 **eggs**
- 1 **cup milk**
- 1 **cup flour**
  Pinch *each* salt and sugar
- ¼ **cup butter**
  Confectioners' sugar, fresh lemon juice, and fruit in season, for garnish

1. Preheat oven to 425° F.

2. In a blender combine eggs and milk on high speed. Add flour, salt, and sugar in two batches, blending well after each addition until smooth and creamy.

3. Place butter in a 12- to 14-inch shallow ovenproof pan or skillet and set in oven to melt. Swirl pan to coat evenly with butter and pour in batter. Bake until puffy and golden brown (20 to 30 minutes).

4. Serve immediately in baking pan, dusted with confectioners' sugar and sprinkled with lemon juice. Accompany each serving with an assortment of fresh, seasonal fruit.

Serves 6 to 8.

Buttermilk Blintzes should be made, filled, and folded ahead of serving time and refrigerated. They can be browned later, and served hot with cherry preserves and sour cream.

HOW TO MAKE CREPES

Pour batter into greased pan, tilting pan so batter forms a thin, even covering over entire bottom.

Cook crêpe 45 to 60 seconds. Small holes will be visible on top side; bottom will be browned. Turn and cook other side.

Remove crêpe to a platter, board, or sheet of waxed paper to cool.

▉ BLINI

Yeast-risen buckwheat pancakes were a fixture on the tables of imperial Russia, served dripping with butter and caviar, or with sour cream and smoked fish. Made in a smaller cocktail size, they are novel topped in many different ways: with sour cream and chutney, with sour-cream herring, with crème fraîche and smoked trout, with a slice of grilled sausage, with melted herb butter and tiny shrimp, or with melted butter and smoked oysters. Serve piping hot, with chilled vodka, Champagne, or cocktails. They may be made ahead of serving time.

    2 **cups all-purpose flour**
   ½ **cup buckwheat flour**
    1 **package active dry yeast**
    2 **teaspoons sugar**
    2 **egg yolks**
    3 **cups lukewarm (100° F to 105° F) milk**
    3 **egg whites**
    2 **tablespoons unsalted butter**

1. In a medium bowl sift together all-purpose and buckwheat flours. In a small bowl, dissolve yeast and sugar in ½ cup warm milk and set aside to soften a few minutes. Make a well in flour and add egg yolks. Gradually stir in yeast mixture and remaining milk, incorporating yolks and flour.

2. Cover bowl with a towel and place in a warm area. Let rise until doubled in bulk. Beat egg whites to soft peaks and fold into batter.

3. Melt butter on griddle or in large skillet. Form Blini by dropping heaping tablespoons of batter onto hot griddle. Cook on both sides until golden brown.

Makes 2 dozen Blini.

▉ BASIC CREPES

In France, their country of origin, crêpes are served as a snack, a lunch or supper dish, or—depending on flavoring and embellishment—a dessert. Wrap hot-off-the-griddle crêpes around a number of mixtures: tiny shrimp warmed in a saucepan with a little sour cream, chopped tomatoes, shallots, and thyme; sausage and cheese; crumbled blue cheese and chopped walnuts; or grated Gruyère and crumbled bacon. Use cooled (but not chilled) crêpes to wrap around pencil-thin asparagus, or spread with chutney, then top with paper-thin slices of smoked ham or turkey and roll up.

    1 **cup flour**
   ¾ **cup water**
   ⅔ **cup milk**
    3 **eggs**
    2 **tablespoons vegetable oil**
   ¼ **teaspoon salt**

1. In blender or food processor, combine flour, the water, milk, eggs, oil, and salt. Whirl or process until batter is

smooth, stopping motor once or twice to scrape flour from sides of container.

2. Cover and refrigerate batter for at least 1 hour. Blend batter well before making crêpes.

3. Add just enough batter to make a thin coat to a lightly oiled 6-inch pan. Cook each crêpe until set (about 60 seconds); turn and cook other side (about 45 seconds). Transfer to a sheet of parchment or waxed paper. Do not stack crêpes until they are completely cool.

Makes 16 to 20 crêpes.

Make-Ahead Tip Completely cooled crêpes may be stacked, wrapped in aluminum foil, and refrigerated for up to five days or frozen for up to two months. Thaw in cool oven.

▉ CREPES SUZETTE

A quick-witted French chef transformed a failure into what has become a culinary classic—crêpes suzette. While the chef was preparing a dessert of crêpes with a liqueur sauce, the sauce caught fire. After tasting the sauce, he realized that the flames gave it extra depth. The dish was served in triumph. The batter makes enough crêpes for a double recipe. Extra pancakes can be frozen for later use. They are delicious with any fruit filling or ice cream.

    6 **eggs**
    6 **cups half-and-half**
    1 **cup water**
 1¼ **cups milk**
    2 **cups flour**
    2 **tablespoons butter, melted**
    1 **tablespoon sugar**
    1 **teaspoon salt**
   ¼ **cup brandy or Cognac**
      Additional butter, for cooking crêpes
   ½ **cup brandy**

Orange Butter Sauce

    6 **tablespoons butter**
      Grated rind of 2 oranges
      Grated rind and juice of 2 lemons
      Juice of 4 oranges
   ¼ **cup sugar**
   ½ **cup orange-flavored liqueur**

1. In a large bowl combine eggs, half-and-half, the water, milk, flour, melted butter, sugar, salt, and brandy. Whisk together well. Batter will be slightly lumpy. Transfer batter to blender in batches and blend until smooth. Let batter rest at room temperature 45 minutes or refrigerate overnight before using.

2. Heat a nonstick 7-inch skillet or crêpe pan over moderately high heat. Add 1 teaspoon butter and swirl to coat pan. When butter foams, add 3 tablespoons batter and quickly tilt pan to coat bottom of skillet thinly.

Cook crêpe until set (60 seconds); turn and cook other side (about 45 seconds). Transfer to a sheet of parchment paper or waxed paper. Continue with remaining batter.

3. To make Orange Butter Sauce: Melt butter in chafing dish or large shallow pan. Add orange and lemon rinds and juice and cook over medium-low heat until reduced by one third. Add sugar and stir to dissolve. Add orange-flavored liqueur and heat through.

4. To assemble: Reduce heat under sauce to low. Using 18 crêpes altogether and freezing remainder for another use, lay crêpes one by one in pan and coat with sauce. Fold each crêpe in half, and then in half again, making small triangles. Arrange triangles, overlapping them around edge of pan. Continue until all have been coated, folded, and arranged in pan.

5. Pour brandy over warm crêpes and carefully ignite, shaking pan to distribute sauce throughout dish. As soon as flames subside, transfer crêpes with sauce to warmed plates.

Serves 6.

Make-Ahead Tip Completely cooled crêpes may be stacked, wrapped in aluminum foil, and refrigerated for up to five days or frozen for up to two months. Thaw in cool oven.

WAFFLE IRON AND PANCAKE PAN

Some fascinating utensils have been designed to produce uncommon pancakes and waffles. If you enjoy varying your breakfast and brunch repertoire, you will probably want to purchase one or more of these. For more information on seasoning pans, see MATERIALS FOR COOKWARE.

WAFFLE IRONS

The iron in which waffles are baked and which gives them their distinctive gridlike pattern may be round, square, or rectangular. Some are electric; others are designed for use on top of the range, either gas or electric. In any case, the grids of a waffle iron—like the surface of a crêpe pan or a pancake griddle—should be seasoned well and then never washed. Season the grids before first use, as you would a cast-iron pan (see MATERIALS FOR COOKWARE), or if finished with a nonstick surface, follow the manufacturer's directions for seasoning. If you don't use the waffle iron often, brush grids lightly with vegetable oil or spray with vegetable cooking spray before heating iron.

Belgian Waffle Iron Belgian waffles, the hit of the 1964 world's fair in New York, are thick, with deep pockets. At the fair they were piled with fresh strawberries and whipped cream, but they are equally delicious with ice cream or fruit sauces. Belgian waffle irons come in stove-top and electric models, and with plain and nonstick grids. They are of cast aluminum.

Electric Waffle Makers A built-in thermostat takes the guesswork out of making waffles: It heats the unit to a predetermined temperature and signals you that it's ready to use. Pour on the batter, close the lid, wait a few minutes, and the light on the appliance will go on again when the waffle is ready to eat. The grids are made of cast aluminum, either plain or with a nonstick finish, and in regular or Belgian-waffle style. Some models feature reversible grids that become a griddle or have embossed disks for making *pizzelle*, thin, crisp Italian wafers.

Heart-Shaped Waffle Iron Like the *plett* (used to make Swedish pancakes, see page 604) this utensil is from Scandinavia. Circular, with five interlocking hearts, it is made of aluminum, usually with a nonstick finish. To use, the iron is first preheated, then the batter is poured over the grids. The iron is set on the burner of the stove to cook for several minutes, then is turned to finish on the other side.

PANCAKE PANS

Another name for pancakes is griddle cakes because they are best made on a wide shallow griddle. If you make pancakes frequently, consider buying a rectangular griddle. Its shape is well suited for making several servings of pancakes at a time instead of the one or two possible in a round frying pan (see COOKWARE). The following are pans for specialty pancakes.

Blini Pan A blini pan is so small some people mistake it for a one-egg frying pan. It has a bottom diameter of 3½ to 4 inches in order to shape the diminutive Russian pancakes. Otherwise, it is like a standard crêpe pan and should be seasoned and cared for in the same way.

Crêpe Pan Although a crêpe pan resembles an omelet pan in that it is fashioned of rolled steel, it differs in one important respect—it has a flat, well-defined bottom to give the crêpe a sharp edge. The sides of an omelet pan, on the other hand, curve gently into the bottom. Season as you would a cast-iron pan. Reserve it strictly for crêpes and you will never need to wash it. After each use, wipe away any crumbs with a paper towel dipped in a little oil; store in a dry place to prevent rust. Before the next use, rub a little oil over inside surface of sides and bottom as pan heats.

Crêpe pans range in size from 5 to 8½ inches (diameter of pan bottom, not top edge). Most recipes specify 6- to 7-inch crêpes.

A Breton crêpe griddle is notable for its larger size—11 to 15 inches in diameter. Not as deep as smaller crêpe pans, it has a shallow, upturned rim that contains the crêpe batter. Made of cast aluminum or cast iron, it also can be used as a griddle for modest conventional pancakes and grilled sandwiches.

Waffles and pancakes are made from batters that take on the shape of the cooking pan. Shown clockwise from top left: electric waffle iron with nonstick grids, stove-top heart-shaped waffle iron, stove-top Belgian waffle iron, Swedish pancake pan (plett), crêpe pan.

Swedish Pancake Pan (Plett)   Designed to shape the small, delicate, eggy pancakes from Scandinavia, this pan can also be used to make blini. In one respect a *plett* is even more convenient than the standard blini pan because it can accommodate several pancakes at a time. The pan is a large (about 10 inches in diameter) cast-iron griddle containing seven shallow, 3-inch-round depressions. Season and treat it as you would any other cast-iron pan.

> ***Recipes and Related Information***
> *Batter, 27; Waffle and Pancake, 598.*

WALNUT

The walnut is an ancient food of undetermined origin, although most scholarly speculation centers on Persia. Today, it is second only to the almond in world popularity. The edible portion of the nut is encased in a semi-hard, light brown, two-part shell. The meat inside consists of a pair of irregularly shaped halves connected, "back to back," near their midpoints. Of the several walnut species, only two are of commercial importance: the mild-flavored English walnut and the native North American black walnut, which has a stronger, richer flavor but is quite difficult to shell.

Use   Toasted shelled walnuts can be served as a cocktail snack or incorporated in a cocktail mix of buttered, roasted, and salted nuts. Walnuts in the shell are a traditional after-dinner companion to port. Toasted walnuts add nutty flavor and texture to green salads, vegetable dishes, breads, cakes, pies, and cookies. In sufficient quantity and finely ground, they take the place of flour in some cakes. Italian cooks make a sauce of ground walnuts and cream for stuffed pasta squares known as *pansotti*. Turkish cooks make a smooth ground walnut sauce for cold shredded chicken. In Iran cooks stew chicken or duck in a sweet-and-sour pomegranate sauce with ground walnuts. Bulgarian cooks make a refreshing cold soup, called *taratòr*, with cucumber, ground walnuts, yogurt, garlic, and dill. In America cooks use the native black walnut in ice cream and quick breads.

Availability   Fresh English walnuts in the shell are sold in many supermarkets and specialty markets in the fall. Packaged English walnut halves and walnut pieces are available in supermarkets all year; bulk shelled English walnuts are carried the year around by some supermarkets and health-food stores. Shelled black walnuts are available from mail-order sources. The difficulty of shelling them makes them hard to find commercially.

Selection   Fresh walnuts in the shell should feel heavy for their size.

Storage If stored in a cool, dry place, fresh walnuts in the shell will keep for several months. Shelled walnuts should be refrigerated or frozen because they go rancid quickly. They will keep for about two months in the refrigerator, about one year in the freezer.

Preparation Toasting brings out the flavor of walnuts; for toasting directions and times, see NUT.

■ GREEK WALNUT TORTE

A torte is a light cake, with nuts and/or crumbs substituting for part or all of the flour. Here, flour is omitted altogether, replaced by ground walnuts and dry bread crumbs. The torte is delicately scented with orange, both in the cake itself and in the whipped cream frosting. Since egg whites are the only leavening agent, it is important to beat them properly and to fold them into the batter without deflating them (see EGG, Beating Eggs, and FOLD).

      1 pound shelled walnuts
      6 tablespoons dry bread crumbs
      9 egg yolks
      ¾ cup sugar
      2 teaspoons finely grated orange rind
      2 tablespoons strained fresh orange juice
      9 egg whites
      ¼ cup sugar
      3 tablespoons orange-flavored liqueur
   1½ teaspoons finely grated orange rind
         Candied orange rind, for garnish

Chocolate Glaze

      1 to 2 ounces semisweet chocolate
      ¼ cup unsalted butter, clarified

Orange Chantilly Cream

      1 teaspoon unflavored gelatin
      2 tablespoons cold water
   1½ cups whipping cream
      ¼ cup sifted confectioners' sugar
      1 tablespoon orange-flavored liqueur

1. Preheat oven to 350° F. Butter and lightly flour two 10-inch-diameter by 2-inch-high cake pans or two 9½-inch-diameter by 3-inch-high springform pans. Line bottoms with circles of parchment or waxed paper.

2. Finely grind walnuts, 1 cup at a time, with 1 tablespoon of the bread crumbs, in food processor or small jar of blender. Bread crumbs and ground walnuts should equal 4 cups.

3. In large bowl of electric mixer, lightly beat egg yolks. Gradually add the ¾ cup sugar, and beat until mixture falls from beater in a ribbon and leaves a slowly dissolving trail on the surface (ribbon stage). Beat in orange rind and orange juice. Stir in walnut mixture.

4. In a large bowl, beat egg whites until they form peaks; gradually add the ¼ cup sugar and beat until they are stiff but still glossy. Stir one fourth of the whites into batter to lighten it. Gently fold in remaining whites. Whites should be completely incorporated but not deflated.

5. Divide batter equally between two cake pans. Bake until cake is springy to the touch and begins to pull away from sides of pan (30 to 40 minutes). Cool in pan 5 minutes, then remove sides of pans (if using springform pans) and allow to finish cooling on wire racks.

6. To assemble cake: Split each cake layer in half horizontally with a long, serrated knife. Place one layer on cake plate; brush with 2 teaspoons orange-flavored liqueur. Spread one third of Chocolate Glaze evenly over cake and sprinkle ½ teaspoon orange rind over glaze. Repeat these steps for the next two layers. Top with fourth layer of cake; brush with remaining orange-flavored liqueur. Ice sides and top of cake with Orange Chantilly Cream. Place remaining cream in a pastry bag fitted with an open-star tip. Decorate border with rosettes of cream or a chain of shells. Refrigerate until ready to serve. When ready to serve, place a 1-inch piece of candied orange rind in the center of each rosette to mark each slice.

Serves 10 to 12.

Chocolate Glaze In a double boiler melt chocolate over hot (not boiling) water. Remove from heat and stir in clarified (tepid) butter. Cool mixture to tepid (86° F).

Orange Chantilly Cream Soften gelatin in the cold water; in a double boiler stir over hot (not boiling) water until gelatin dissolves; cool until syrupy. Beat whipping cream until slightly thickened; add dissolved gelatin, confectioners' sugar, and orange-flavored liqueur. Continue beating until soft peaks form and hold their shape when beaters are lifted from bowl. Do not overbeat; cream should look soft and glossy.

> ***Recipes and Related Information***
> *Braised Celery With Walnuts, 109; Walnut-Apple Strudel, 222; Your Own Bridge Mix, 59.*

WASABI

A variety of aquatic plant unique to Japan, *wasabi* comes from an edible root that has a tough brownish green skin and a pale green flesh. The flesh is finely grated to make a pungent condiment similar to horseradish.

Use Wasabi is most often encountered in sushi bars. Sushi chefs put a thin swipe of wasabi atop the rice and underneath the fish when making Nigiri Sushi (see page 233). They also serve a small mound of wasabi with sashimi (thinly sliced raw fish), which the diner mixes to taste with soy sauce to make a dipping sauce for the sashimi. Similarly, wasabi is often served with cold noodle dishes, to be added to the dipping sauce. Japanese cooks also pickle vegetables such as eggplant with wasabi and mustard.

Availability Fresh wasabi is rarely if ever seen in this country. Powdered wasabi in tins is sold in many supermarkets and in all Japanese markets. Wasabi paste in tubes is available in some Japanese markets.

Storage Powdered wasabi, stored in a cool, dry place, will keep indefinitely. Wasabi paste should be refrigerated after opening.

Preparation For powdered wasabi, add just enough tepid water to powder to form a paste. Mix until smooth. Let stand 10 minutes to develop flavor. Paste wasabi is ready to use right from the tube.

WATER CHESTNUT

A tuber that grows in east Asian marshes, the water chestnut is now cultivated in the southeastern United States. It has a squat round shape with a pointed tip. Underneath its dark brown skin is cream-colored flesh as crisp and sweet as that of an apple. Young, fresh water chestnuts are best; flavor becomes starchy and less sweet with age.

Use Water chestnuts, essential to Chinese cooking, add texture to countless soups, stir-fries, and stuffings. Chinese steamed dumplings are typically filled with a mixture of seasoned minced shrimp or ground pork and water chestnuts. The refreshing, clean taste and crisp texture of water chestnuts make them an appealing nibble at the start of a meal. American cooks sometimes wrap them in bacon and broil them to serve as an appetizer.

Availability Fresh water chestnuts are occasionally available in Chinese markets. Canned water chestnuts, both whole and sliced, are sold in supermarkets and Chinese markets.

Selection Fresh water chestnuts should feel rock hard and should have a smooth, not wrinkled, exterior.

Storage If firm, fresh water chestnuts will keep up to two weeks refrigerated in a plastic bag. Canned water chestnuts, once opened, should be transferred to an airtight nonmetal container and covered with fresh water; they will keep for two to three weeks if the water is changed every few days.

Preparation Fresh water chestnuts may be muddy. Rinse well just before using; peel. Unless using immediately, cover peeled water chestnuts with cold water to prevent discoloration. Canned water chestnuts can be blanched for 15 seconds in boiling water, then shocked in cold water, to rid them of their canned taste.

◼ SHRIMP WITH SNOW PEAS AND WATER CHESTNUTS

This Chinese stir-fry is a study in crisp textures and complementary colors. Splitting the shrimp lengthwise causes them to curl into spirals when cooked.

½ **pound shrimp, peeled and split lengthwise**
   Pinch salt
2 **tablespoons Shaoxing wine or dry sherry**
   Oil, for stir-frying
1 **tablespoon minced fresh ginger**
½ **pound snow peas, stems and strings removed**
½ **cup sliced water chestnuts (preferably fresh)**
1 **tablespoon soy sauce**
½ **teaspoon cornstarch, dissolved in ¼ cup water or stock**

1. Toss shrimp with salt; add wine; marinate for 20 minutes to several hours.

2. Drain shrimp and reserve marinade. Heat wok over high heat; add oil. Add ginger, stir-fry until fragrant, and add shrimp. Stir-fry until shrimp are mostly opaque (2 to 4 minutes, depending on size).

3. Add snow peas and water chestnuts; stir-fry until just heated through. Add reserved marinade, soy sauce, and cornstarch mixture. Bring to a boil and cook until sauce thickens. Serve immediately.

Serves 4 to 6 with other dishes.

WATERCRESS

A member of the mustard family, watercress grows wild and profusely in shallow, slow-moving creeks. For the commercial market, it is cultivated in streams and harvested by waders. Watercress has small, round, dark green leaves on stems slightly thicker than parsley. The leaves and stems have a peppery taste.

Use Watercress makes a peppery addition to green salads and sandwiches or a lively base for chicken or egg salad. In France cooks make watercress soup, thickened with potatoes and cream. The English put a sprig of watercress on dainty tea sandwiches.

Availability Fresh watercress is sold by the bunch in most supermarkets the year around. Supplies peak in late spring and early summer.

Selection Look for watercress with healthy green leaves; avoid any bunches with yellowing or slimy leaves.

Storage Untie bunch at home and remove any bad sprigs; wash gently in cool water, dry thoroughly, then wrap in paper towels, overwrap in plastic, and refrigerate. Use within two to three days.

Preparation Cut away any overly thick stems.

THE TIGER
Third sign of the zodiac
Magnetic, aggressive, adventuro
and an unpre

Stir-fried Shrimp With Snow Peas is even better when made with fresh water chestnuts, available in Chinese markets and some specialty markets.

■ COUNTRY WATERCRESS SOUP

This creamy soup, which can be served hot or cold, is lightly thickened with potato. Serve the soup hot with Garlic Croutons (see page 506) or cold with French bread. This soup thickens as it chills. If it becomes too thick, gradually stir in another 2 to 3 tablespoons of cream or milk just before serving.

  2 medium leeks
  2 bunches watercress (10 oz total)
  1 medium potato
  2 tablespoons butter
  1 medium onion, sliced
1½ cups Chicken Stock (see page 560)
    Salt and white pepper, to taste
1½ cups milk
 ¼ to ½ cup whipping cream
    Freshly grated nutmeg

1. Wash and trim leeks. Cut white and light green parts of leeks in thin slices; reserve dark green part for other uses. Thoroughly rinse watercress, discard large stems, and reserve only upper, leafy third of each bunch. Reserve 8 to 12 attractive watercress leaves for garnish. Plunge bunches of watercress into large saucepan of boiling water. Bring back to a boil, drain immediately, and rinse under cold running water. Drain thoroughly and squeeze dry. Peel potato and cut in thin slices.

2. Melt butter in heavy saucepan over low heat. Add onion and leeks and cook, stirring often, until soft but not brown (about 10 minutes). Add watercress bunches and cook, stirring, for 2 minutes. Add potato, stock, and a pinch of salt and pepper, and bring to a boil. Reduce heat to low, cover, and simmer, stirring occasionally, until potatoes are tender (about 20 minutes).

3. Purée soup through a food mill, or in a blender or food processor. Strain to remove stringy parts of watercress.

4. Return soup to saucepan and add milk. Bring to a boil, stirring occasionally. Add ¼ cup cream and bring again to a boil. If soup is too thick, stir in remaining cream. Add nutmeg. Taste and add salt and pepper, if needed.

5. Prepare garnish by dipping a small strainer containing reserved watercress leaves into a small saucepan of boiling water for 30 seconds. Rinse under cold water to stop cooking and drain.

6. Serve soup hot or cold. To chill hot soup, cool slightly, then cover and refrigerate until thoroughly cold (several hours or overnight). Ladle soup into bowls and garnish with blanched watercress leaves.

Makes 4 to 5 cups, serves 4.

> ***Recipes and Related Information***
> *Cream of Watercress, 563; Watercress Dip With Green Onions and Basil, 521.*

WHIP, TO

To beat rapidly in a circular motion in order to increase the volume of a mixture by incorporating air into it; done with a whisk, rotary beater, or electric mixer. The action is vigorous—the whisk doesn't move around the mixture, but enters and leaves it so as to pull in the maximum amount of air.

Essentially, whipping is stirring; instead of using a single spoon, however, you use a beater or whisk consisting of 12 to 25 wires bent into a bulbous shape. Therefore, each stir represents a dozen or more stirs. The whisk has become such a standard tool for this procedure that the term *to whisk* has come to mean *to whip*.

Recipes and Related Information
Cream, 160; Egg, 194; Whisk, 608.

WHISK, TO; WHISK

To beat rapidly to incorporate air into a mixture (see WHIP); also the utensil used to perform this task. Like spoons and spatulas, whisks are beating tools, used to smoothly incorporate ingredients. Unlike them, however, whisks perform an additional function—that of  incorporating air, which causes a mixture to lighten or expand. Whisks are made of stainless steel wires in a range of thicknesses, shapes, and sizes depending on how they will be used. They are traditionally an integral part of the French chef's *batterie de cuisine;* in American home kitchens the electric mixer and food processor have taken over many of their functions—particularly for beating egg whites and whipping cream. However, the open design of the whisk is still invaluable for mixing sauces, batters, and dressings. Although using a whisk is more labor-intensive, many cooks prefer to whip egg whites and cream by hand. Studies indicate that egg whites whipped in a copper bowl with a balloon whisk produce the greatest volume and the finest, most stable foam.

Whisks are available with wires that are flexible or rigid, thin or heavy-gauge, and gathered in an open, elongated, or flat shape; match the whisk to your purpose. As a guideline, use a balloon whisk, which resembles an oversized light bulb and has anywhere from 12 to 25 thin, flexible wires, when you want to incorporate as much air as possible—as when beating egg whites and whipping cream. For blending, use one with a less open shape. Thinner wires work well for light mixtures and for aerating flours and other powders; heavier wires will stand up in denser batters and sauces. A flat whisk, which looks like a standard whisk cut in cross section, is angled for mixing in shallow dishes or pans, and is particularly useful for beating eggs and reaching around the edges of a saucepan to draw any lumpy portions of a sauce into the mixture.

Don't use a fine-gauge whisk or one with wires joined close together for heavy batters; they lack the strength to move easily through a thick liquid, and the wires will trap the batter inside the whisk. Check construction to make sure that food can't collect where wires and handle meet. A whisk with a stainless steel handle can go in the dishwasher; one with a wooden handle must be washed by hand, but tends to be more comfortable to hold.

Recipes and Related Information
Copper Egg-White Bowl, 155; Egg, 194.

WINE IN COOKING

Apart from its pleasure as a beverage, wine has an important place in the pantry. Wherever wine is enjoyed at the table, cooks have learned to take advantage of its special properties in the kitchen. White or red, sweet or dry, wine can enhance a range of different dishes.

Use Wine has three main uses in the kitchen: as a marinade ingredient, as a cooking liquid, and as a flavoring in a finished dish.

Selection So-called cooking wines sold in stores are unsuitable for most culinary purposes. They have been salted to the point that they are unfit to drink so that they may be sold in stores without liquor licenses or in dry states or localities. It is far better to use an unadulterated table wine or a fortified wine (such as sherry or Madeira).

Storage All wines should be stored in a cool, dark, well-ventilated place with moderate humidity. They should preferably be stored on their sides to keep the cork moist; a dry cork will shrink and allow air to enter. Ideal storage conditions are less important if the wine will be used within a few weeks; the longer you plan to keep the wine before using, the more important it is to store it properly.

Leftover table wines can be refrigerated and used for cooking if held for only one or two weeks. If you have at least a half bottle of wine left over, pour it off into a clean half bottle, cork it, and store in the refrigerator. Without air space at the top, the rebottled wine will keep for up to one month.

WINE AS A MARINADE

Marinating food—especially meat and poultry—in wine contributes flavor and tenderness. As well as adding a flavor of its own, wine helps food absorb the flavors of herbs, vegetables, or spices. The moderate acidity of wine also helps penetrate and tenderize meats.

Both red and white wines are suitable for marinades. It's unnecessary to use a fine wine, although you should use a well-flavored wine you wouldn't hesitate to drink. Dry wines are traditional for savory marinades, but a sweet wine can add an appealing flavor to game birds, such as squab or quail.

Wine is also used as a marinade in fruit desserts. In this context, fruits are said to macerate in wine. Peaches macerated in red wine or strawberries macerated in sparkling wine make refreshing summer desserts. Generally superfine sugar is added to taste in order to balance the acidity of the wine (see MACERATE).

WINE AS A COOKING LIQUID

Cooking directly in wine adds flavor and necessary moisture. Fish poached in white wine or chicken braised in red wine are just two examples among many of wine as a cooking medium. Poaching in wine is ideal for delicate foods, such as fish. The poaching liquid may be a simple court bouillon of wine and water flavored with aromatics or a fumet, a wine-based fish stock. Fruits, too, are often poached in a wine syrup, made by boiling wine and water with sugar and such flavorings as cinnamon or vanilla bean. Wine syrups can also be drizzled over whole just-baked cakes as a flavoring and glaze.

Steaming in wine is a technique most often used with shellfish. Clams or mussels are put into a pot with white wine, shallots or onions, and herbs; the pot is covered and the liquid brought to a boil. The shellfish open as they steam in the wine and are imbued with its flavor.

Braising meats and poultry in wine—first browning the meat or poultry in oil or fat, then adding wine and cooking slowly in a covered pan—is a technique common to some of the world's most satisfying dishes. Not only does the wine moisten and tenderize tougher cuts of meat, but its distinctive flavor also enhances the sauce. The long, slow cooking and the typical final reduction of the sauce concentrate the flavors of the wine.

This concentration, however, can be a mixed blessing. Red wines, especially, can dominate a sauce and should be used with caution. Sometimes a concentrated flavor is desirable, as in the classic Burgundian coq au vin or in dishes made with game or red meats. But with other braised dishes, even if you plan to serve a red wine, cooking with a white wine may produce the best flavors.

WINE AS A FLAVORING

Fortified wines such as sherry and Madeira are often stirred into soups at the last moment or even at the table. A spoonful of sherry or a dash of Madeira are the classic finishing touches for some consommés and cream soups. Usually the soup is not cooked further after the wine is added to avoid dissipating the flavor of the wine.

Wine is also used to deglaze a roasting pan or a skillet in which foods have been roasted or sautéed. Deglazing is

the first step in creating a delicious assortment of sauces. Whether you are working with a beef roast, pan-fried chicken, or sautéed fish fillets, the deglazing procedure is the same: Pour off excess fat, add aromatics if desired (herbs, onions, garlic), then add wine and bring it to a boil, scraping drippings loose from bottom of pan. After alcohol has boiled out of wine, other liquids such as cream or stock may be added and reduced to make a sauce.

Most recipes for wine sauces call for reducing, which simply means boiling down the sauces until the volume has been cut by about half. Reducing is an essential technique to many great sauces. Reducing a wine-based sauce eliminates the alcohol while it concentrates the flavor of the wine. Such sauces must be made with care. Reducing a wine sauce too far can make it too acidic and boil away most of the flavor.

Good cooking begins with the best ingredients. Good, inexpensive wine from a high-quality winery is an important pantry item.

Sautéed Chicken Breasts With Sherry, Cream, and Mushrooms (see page 611) is a fine complement to Chardonnay or other full-flavored white wines. The sauce lends itself to endless variations; in place of the mushrooms, try almonds or other nuts, artichoke hearts, or even a mixture of raisins and unsweetened coconut.

2. Combine ground spices, wine, vinegar, onion, garlic, and ginger in a glass, ceramic, or stainless steel bowl large enough to hold poultry.

3. Marinate whole or cut-up birds in refrigerator, covered, overnight, or for up to three days. Turn birds frequently to marinate them evenly.

4. Remove birds from refrigerator 30 minutes before cooking. Drain thoroughly and discard marinade. Roast, grill, or broil (stuffed or unstuffed) according to any standard recipe.

Makes about 1 cup (enough for a whole fryer or duck or for 2 or 3 Rock Cornish game hens).

■ PORK ROAST WITH WHITE-WINE MARINADE

Two days of marinating in a mixture of white wine, spices, and herbs gives roast pork a little of the flavor of wild boar. Be sure to marinate the pork in a nonaluminum container such as stainless steel, ceramic, or glass.

- 1 teaspoon fennel seed
- 2 teaspoons coriander seed
- 1 teaspoon black peppercorns
- 1 teaspoon salt
- ¼ teaspoon ground ginger
- 1 pork loin roast (about 3½ lb with bones)
- 1 cup Gewürztraminer or Sauvignon Blanc
- 1 large sprig fresh sage *or* ½ teaspoon dried sage
- 1 large sprig fresh thyme *or* ½ teaspoon dried thyme
- 1 bay leaf
- 8 small new potatoes

1. Two days ahead: Coarsely grind fennel, coriander, and pepper in a clean coffee grinder, electric mini-chopper, or with a mortar and pestle. Combine ground spices with salt and ginger. Rub this mixture all over pork roast. Put roast in a stainless steel, ceramic, or glass bowl, pour in wine, and crumble herbs into bowl. Marinate roast in refrigerator, turning it several times a day to marinate it evenly.

2. On cooking day: Remove roast from refrigerator at least 1 hour before cooking. Preheat oven to 450° F. Drain roast thoroughly and discard marinade.

3. Pat roast dry with paper towels and place it, fat side up, on a rack in a roasting pan. Put roast in hot oven, reduce heat to 325° F, and roast to an internal temperature of 170° F (25 to 30 minutes per pound). Add potatoes to roasting pan for the last 30 minutes to roast in drippings.

4. Let roast rest about 15 minutes before carving into ½-inch slices. Serve with roast potatoes and a full-flavored dry white wine or a lighter red wine.

Serves 4.

■ SPICY RED-WINE MARINADE

This recipe, similar to the white-wine marinade (at right), but based on a red wine, is especially good for roasted, broiled, or grilled poultry. For a sweeter taste, use ruby port instead of a dry wine.

- ½ teaspoon *each* whole coriander, fennel, black pepper, and juniper berries
- ¾ cup dry red wine
- 2 tablespoons red wine vinegar
- ½ onion, sliced
- 2 or 3 cloves garlic, minced
- 1 tablespoon minced fresh ginger *or* ½ teaspoon ground ginger

1. Grind coriander, fennel, pepper, and juniper berries together in a clean coffee grinder, electric minichopper, or with a mortar and pestle.

◼ STEAMED CLAMS

When simply steamed in a seasoned broth, clams, mussels, or oysters make a tasty first course. Serve in shallow bowls with crusty bread to scoop up the juices. Steam the clams (or other shellfish) in a nonreactive saucepan so the acid in the wine will not impart a metallic flavor.

 4 pounds (about 32 medium) clams
 8 cloves garlic, minced
 2 large shallots, minced
 ½ teaspoon salt
 1 cup dry white wine
 6 to 8 sprigs parsley, minced, for garnish

1. Wash clams, scrubbing exterior, to remove any sand. Place clams in a deep, 4-quart, nonreactive saucepan. Add minced garlic and shallots to saucepan with clams. Sprinkle with salt and add wine.

2. Bring to a boil, reduce heat, and simmer for 2 minutes. Discard any clams that fail to open. Garnish with parsley.

Serves 4.

◼ BEEF BRAISED IN RED WINE

This is not a dish for subtle wines; it works best with a full-flavored wine with ample acidity. A Petite Sirah or a Zinfandel with plenty of character will fill the bill nicely. Serve the same type of wine as a beverage. Although braised beef can be cooked on top of the stove, it is easier to maintain the slight simmer in a low oven. A slow cooker or other covered electric cooker also works well, but you will still need to do steps 1 through 3 on top of the stove.

 2½ pounds boneless chuck roast
 1 tablespoon oil or chicken or duck fat
 ⅓ pound shallots, peeled and left whole
 ½ bottle dry red wine
  Bouquet garni of parsley, bay leaf, thyme, and celery leaves
 ½ teaspoon salt
 ½ teaspoon freshly ground pepper
 4 dried tomato halves, chopped, *or* 8 dry-cured olives, pitted and chopped

1. Preheat oven to 225° F. Cut meat into large cubes (2 to 2½ inches), trimmed of excess fat and gristle. Dry cubes of meat with a paper towel. (This allows them to brown more easily.)

2. Heat oil in an ovenproof casserole over medium heat. Brown cubes of meat a few at a time. (Don't try to brown too many at a time or they will stew rather than brown.) Transfer cubes to a plate as they brown and add more as space allows.

3. When all meat has been browned, brown shallots in the same fat. Pour out any fat remaining in pan. Add wine, bring to a boil, and reduce heat to a simmer. Return meat cubes to pan. Add bouquet garni, salt, pepper, and tomatoes.

4. Cover pan and place it in oven. Bake 3½ to 4 hours, adjusting heat, if necessary, so sauce barely simmers. Meat should be very tender and should absorb flavor of sauce.

5. Turn off oven. Remove cooked meat and shallots to a serving platter and return them to oven to keep warm. Discard bouquet garni and bring sauce to a boil on top of stove. Reduce sauce by a third. Taste and correct seasoning.

6. Pour sauce over meat and serve with buttered noodles, steamed potatoes, or polenta.

Serves 6.

◼ CHICKEN BREASTS WITH SHERRY, CREAM, AND MUSHROOMS

If you are serving a first course before this dish, you can cook the chicken breasts first, then hold them in the oven for 15 minutes or so. The sauce will only take about five minutes to prepare, so you will be able to sit down and enjoy the first course before serving the entrée.

 4 chicken breast halves, boned and skinned
 ¼ cup flour
 ½ teaspoon salt
 ½ teaspoon pepper
 2 to 4 tablespoons butter
 2 tablespoons vegetable oil
 ¼ pound mushrooms, sliced
 1 tablespoon chopped garlic
 1 green onion, chopped
 ¼ cup dry sherry
 ½ cup whipping cream

1. Preheat oven to 200° F. Trim all bits of fat and membrane from chicken breasts. In a shallow bowl combine flour, salt, and pepper. Dredge breasts in seasoned flour and shake off excess. Have a warm, ovenproof plate ready.

2. In a large skillet over medium heat, heat butter and oil together. Add chicken breasts and cook just until the thickest part springs back when pressed (about 3 minutes per side). Remove to warm plate, cover loosely with aluminum foil, and keep warm in oven while you prepare sauce. (Recipe may be prepared to this point up to 15 minutes ahead of serving time.)

3. If butter has browned, pour it out and add another 2 tablespoons butter to pan. Add mushrooms, garlic, and green onion, turn heat to high, and sauté until mushrooms begin to soften. Add sherry, bring to a boil, and reduce by half. Add cream, bring to a boil, and reduce to a thick sauce. Taste for seasoning and correct if necessary.

4. Return chicken breasts to skillet to coat them with sauce. Serve topped with mushrooms and sauce.

Serves 4.

TIPS

COOKING WITH WINE

Wine can be used in place of part or all of the cooking or marinating liquid in countless recipes as long as you remember the following.

- *Boiling down wine concentrates its flavors, including acidity and sweetness. Be careful not to use too much or the finished dish may be excessively sweet or sour, or taste too strongly of wine.*

- *Whether quickly making a deglazing sauce or simmering a dish over a long period, allow enough cooking time after adding the wine for the alcohol to evaporate. Boiling a sauce rapidly in a shallow pan will cook off the alcohol in 1 or 2 minutes, but slow simmering in a deeper pan may take 15 minutes or more. Taste sauce before serving to be sure. Avoid adding wine to a sauce just before serving, or the dish may taste unpleasantly alcoholic. The last-minute addition of wine to some soups (see Wine as a Flavoring, page 609) is one delicious exception.*

- *Remember that wine does not belong in every dish. More than one wine-based sauce in a single meal can be monotonous. Use wine in cooking only when it has something to contribute to the finished dish.*

The elegant appearance of Rosé Pears in Chocolate Bath belies its ease of preparation.

■ ROSE PEARS IN CHOCOLATE BATH

Poach the pears and mix the sauce ahead of time; then assemble this elegant dessert just before serving.

> 2½   cups red table wine
> ⅓   cup sugar
> ½   cinnamon stick, broken
> ⅛   teaspoon ground coriander
> 3   whole cloves
>   Grated rind of ½ orange
>   Grated rind of 1 lemon
> 4   Bartlett pears, peeled
> 1   cup Old-fashioned Chocolate Sauce
>   (double recipe; see page 523)
> 2   to 3 tablespoons Cognac, orange-flavored
>   liqueur, or almond-flavored liqueur
>   Mint sprigs, kiwifruit slices, or
>   candied violets, for garnish

1. In a medium saucepan combine wine, sugar, cinnamon, coriander, cloves, and orange and lemon rinds. Bring to a boil. Add pears, reduce heat, and simmer just until tender (8 to 10 minutes).

2. With a slotted spoon remove pears. Halve and core if desired. Place one pear upright in each of 4 champagne or sherbet glasses.

3. Mix chocolate sauce and Cognac. Pour around pears and garnish as desired.

Serves 4.

Nut-Filled Pears in Chocolate Bath   Poach pears as directed in steps 1 and 2. Halve pears horizontally, cutting in a sawtooth pattern to flute. Core, and stuff each half with a mixture of chopped nuts, raisins, dried dates, and dried apricots. Reassemble pears and surround each one with Old-fashioned Chocolate Sauce.

Rosé Pears and Ice Cream   Poach pears as directed in steps 1 and 2. Halve vertically and core. Place a scoop of ice cream, sherbet, or frozen yogurt in each of 4 champagne or sherbet glasses. Lean 2 pear halves against each scoop.

Rosé Pears in Vanilla Cream   Poach pears as directed in steps 1 and 2. Mix 1 to 2 tablespoons Cognac into 1 cup Stirred Custard (see page 168). Whip 1 cup whipping cream and fold into custard. Place cream in bottom of serving glasses. Add pears and garnish with mint.

> ### Recipes and Related Information
> *Boeuf Bourguignonne, 43; Cheese, 110; Choucroute Garni, 75; Classic Beef Consommé With Vegetable Julienne and Madeira, 562; Fresh Fruit in Wine, 347; Game Hens Coq au Vin, 58; Marinade, 349; Stilton Crock With Port Wine, 114; Sweetbreads and Mushroom-Marsala Sauce, 590; Veal Marsala, 594; Wine Court Bouillon, 450; Winter Fruit Compote, 186.*

WORK, TO

To stir or knead a mixture; implies manipulation and resistance. This is a common term used in recipes for bread doughs: "Work the flour into the dough" is a typical instruction. Although it most often refers to hands-on processes, it more generally can mean any vigorous blending of somewhat stiff, resistant mixtures whether by hand or by machine.

> ### Recipes and Related Information
> *Knead, 326; Yeast Bread, 613.*

YAM

The true yam, *Dioscorea*, is a tuber cultivated in Africa and Asia. (For information on the vegetable Americans call yam, see SWEET POTATO.) There are several varieties of *Dioscorea* in various shapes, sizes, and colors, but all have a high starch content. The Japanese mountain yam looks like a large old bone. It is usually peeled, grated, and eaten raw; when grated, it has a gluey consistency and mild flavor. The African giant yam or white yam may grow to weigh 100 pounds. It has a barklike skin, a white flesh, and a mild, starchy flavor.

Use   The Japanese yam serves as a binder in some processed foods and as a garnish for noodle dishes and rice. The giant yam is a staple in Africa. In West Africa it is pounded into a paste called Fufu, which may be made into dumplings or used as a thickener for soups and stews. African cooks also slice yams and deep-fry them like potato chips, boil them in milk, or slice and bake them like potatoes with sliced onions, bread crumbs, and cheese. In the Caribbean, yams may be simply steamed and buttered, or grated, bound with egg, and fried in oil.

Availability   True yams are occasionally found in Japanese, African, or Latin markets in this country. Some African and Latin markets also stock canned white yams from West Africa.

Selection   Yams should be firm, unblemished, and unwrinkled. Smaller ones are preferable.

Storage   Keep in a cool place or in the refrigerator for up to one week.

Preparation   The Japanese yam should be peeled and finely grated. The yam may be irritating to sensitive skin; wear gloves while peeling or peel under cold running water. African or Caribbean varieties should be peeled and cooked. Cut peeled yam into chunks or slices and add to stews or boil in salted water until tender.

Cooking   See BOIL, DEEP-FRY, STEAM.

YEAST

Although wild yeasts have existed since the origins of civilization, their actions were not fully understood until the work of Louis Pasteur in the 1850s. Pasteur's studies of fermentation made it possible for scientists to cultivate yeasts. Today cultivated yeast strains are made and marketed expressly for breads, wines, and beers.

Use   Yeast makes bread rise and is responsible for the fermentation of grape juice into wine and barley mash into beer. The yeast feed on the sugars in the dough or the juice, converting the sugars to carbon dioxide and alcohol. In the case of bread, the carbon dioxide gas is trapped within the dough and makes it rise. In the case of wine, the carbon dioxide escapes but the alcohol remains. In beer making, trapped carbon dioxide provides natural carbonization. For the home cook, the principal value of yeast is as a leavening agent in breads.

Availability   Yeast for baking is widely stocked in supermarkets, packaged either as active dry yeast or as fresh yeast in moist cakes. One yeast cake is equivalent to one ¼-ounce package active dry yeast (1 tablespoon dry yeast). Some health-food stores also carry active dry yeast in bulk. Recently available in the market is quick-rise yeast, a high-activity yeast strain that makes doughs rise up to 50 percent faster than regular yeast does.

Selection   Check expiration date on package.

Storage   Fresh yeast is more perishable than dry; refrigerate and use within three weeks of purchase. Bulk dry yeast should be stored airtight in a covered container. Both packaged and bulk dry yeast should be kept in a cool, dark, dry place and used within six months.

Preparation   To activate dry yeast, sprinkle it over a bowl of warm (about 110° F) liquid; let soften 1 minute. Stir with a fork to dissolve yeast. Set aside to proof 5 to 10 minutes. Proofing verifies that yeast is still active. Within 10 minutes, yeast should produce a foamy layer on surface of water. If not, discard yeast and liquid, and begin again with a fresh package. To activate fresh cake yeast, place it in a bowl of warm (about 110° F) liquid; mash with a fork to blend and stir until smooth. Set aside to proof 10 minutes. Discard if yeast does not begin foaming within 10 minutes.

About Proofing: In the days when the effectiveness of commercial yeast was less predictable, proofing was essential. However, the baker's yeast produced today is extremely reliable and, if used before the expiration date on the package, should not require proofing. Indeed, many modern recipes call for adding dry yeast directly to bread dough.

Recipes and Related Information
Fermentation, 219; Leaven, 338; Proof, 479.

YEAST BREAD

Making fresh yeast-leavened bread at home is a pleasure that, if planned, can fit into most schedules. The rewards are many: the warm, relaxed kneading and shaping; the wonderful yeasty aroma that permeates the air during baking; and finally, the delight of biting into a fresh, full-tasting bread.

The world of bread is a temptingly varied one, and is much more inviting than the standard sliced white loaf frequently associated with the word *bread*. The slender, crusty French baguette and rich brioche, the dark, fragrant German rye, and the simple, chewy Italian loaf are just a few of the forms that bread takes in other cultures.

TYPES OF YEAST BREADS

All yeast breads are made from a soft dough; approximately 3 parts flour to 1 part liquid is the usual ratio. This proportion can vary somewhat as flours differ in their capacities to absorb liquid, which is why most bread recipes give a range for the amount of flour. At its most basic, bread is a combination of flour, yeast, salt, and a liquid. With the addition of eggs, sugar, milk, butter, spices, nuts, raisins, and other ingredients, the basic dough becomes richer, sweeter, and more cakelike. Flours ground from grains other than wheat also impart a special characteristic to a bread; rye, cornmeal, and oats add texture and distinctive flavor to the dough.

Examples of a straightforward yeast bread are the familiar white or whole-grain loaf. Brioche is a golden bread rich in eggs and butter and a favorite for breakfast when spread with more butter and homemade preserves. Babas and savarins also are abundantly buttery and are so sweet that they are served as a dessert, drenched in liqueur. Croissants, Danish pastries, sweet rolls, babas, and savarins are yeast leavened, but because of the high proportion of butter to flour in their doughs, they are as much a pastry as a bread.

Breads vary in shape as well—from the familiar loaf to free-form rounds and braids, to those molded in special fluted or flared tins. What these varied breads have in common is that they use yeast as a leavener. In a dough, yeast gives off carbon dioxide gas, which, along with the steam produced by liquid ingredients, causes the dough to expand and rise. Quick breads are leavened chemically; they use either baking powder or baking soda (or a combination of the two) rather than yeast (see QUICK BREAD).

INGREDIENTS FOR BREADS: WHAT EACH DOES

Most bread recipes call for the same few basic ingredients—flour, liquid, yeast, and salt—often plus shortening, eggs, and sugar or other sweetener. The nature of the ingredients, their proportion, and the way they are combined make all the difference in the final product.

TIPS

WORKING WITH YEAST

Yeast requires warm, moist conditions to multiply. Excessive heat (above 140° F) will kill it; excessive cold (below 80° F) will slow it down and reduce its leavening capability. Salt also hampers yeast growth. Many recipes call for making a salt-free starter (a mixture of starch, yeast, and liquid) to give yeast a head start; the salt is added later, with the remaining ingredients. Sugar provides food for yeast, thus speeding its growth (although excessive sugar can do just the reverse). Many recipes call for adding a pinch of sugar to the liquid used for activating yeast.

The ingredients that go into a loaf of bread are simple—flour, other grains and cereals, yeast, eggs, milk, and sugar and honey. But their combined effect is wonderfully complex.

(compressed) and active dry yeast (standard and quick-rise). Yeast is very heat sensitive: Too little heat and it will not multiply; too much and it will die. The optimum temperature varies according to the type of yeast. Both cake yeast and active dry yeast are most effective at about 110° F. Quick-rise active dry yeast will tolerate a range of temperatures from 90° to 115° F. See YEAST.

Salt In addition to flavoring bread, salt also helps to control the rate of fermentation of yeast breads and to make the dough easier to handle. In very hot weather, an environment that may cause a yeast dough to rise too rapidly, the addition of extra salt will slow down the reaction.

Sugar From sugar, a yeast dough gets sweetness and an immediate source of food for the yeast; sugar also imparts tenderness to the crumb and color to the crust.

Fat Butter, margarine, shortening, and oil are the usual forms fat takes in a yeast dough, although their addition is optional. Fat helps produce a tender loaf with a nice, brown crust.

Eggs A dough made with one or more eggs has a rich flavor and color.

BREAD-BAKING EQUIPMENT

The *batterie de cuisine* for baking bread ranges from the simplest baking sheet or loaf pan to a sleek heavy-duty mixer. Here are some of the basic tools many bakers use regularly.

Food Processor This appliance is good for mixing and kneading dough. More and more bread recipes are offering a variation for preparing doughs this way. Check the instructions for your machine to determine the capacity for heavy dough. Placing too much dough in the machine can damage the motor.

Measuring Utensils Have both liquid and dry measuring cups, and two sets of measuring spoons (one for liquids and one for powders). A spatula will come in handy to level off dry ingredients or to loosen baked breads from pans. A dough thermometer (also called an instant-read thermometer; see THERMOMETER) is helpful to determine that the liquid used in a yeast bread is at the proper temperature.

Mixer A heavy-duty mixer takes much of the work out of the labor-intensive task of making bread. Its strong motor can beat a fairly heavy dough to develop sufficient elasticity so that the dough requires less kneading later. These mixers often are equipped with a special dough hook, designed for yeast breads; many practiced bread makers use the dough hook of the mixer to knead the dough until it is almost ready to set aside to rise, then finish the job with a minute or two of hand-kneading to be sure the dough feels just right.

Flour This is the fundamental component—the foundation—of most breads. Wheat flours have the ability to make gluten, an elastic protein that gives structure to breads and all baked goods. Gluten is formed when liquid combines with two of the proteins contained in wheat flour. Beating, stirring, or kneading develops the gluten further into a strong cellular network to hold the gases and steam that are given off during the bread making and baking processes and inflate the finished product and make it light. Nonwheat flours have little or no gluten and produce breads that are dense and low rising; they are often combined with wheat flour for best results. See FLOUR and GRAIN.

Liquid In some form, liquid is present in most breads. It helps to distribute the yeast evenly in the flour and is a medium in which sugar and salt can dissolve. Doughs made with water generally yield crisper breads with more crust than doughs made with milk. Used in yeast breads, milk adds richness, makes a bread with a finer crumb and softer crust, and can help retard staling. Before pasteurization, milk used in a bread recipe was first scalded; this was thought to destroy some enzymes that adversely affected bread quality. However, scalding isn't necessary with pasteurized milk (see MILK).

Yeast When fed the correct amounts of food, moisture, and warmth, yeast, which are tiny plants, multiply rapidly. A small amount of sugar supports the growth of yeast, but too much sugar slows the rate. For this reason, rich doughs with a high proportion of sugar take longer to rise than leaner ones. Yeast is sold in two forms: cake

Molds Breads can be baked in a variety of pans, including the traditional loaf pans and fluted brioche molds, or they can be shaped by hand and set on a flat baking sheet. As with other cookware, a heavy metal pan made of a material that will absorb and hold heat well, will produce the best product. Clay is also well-suited for baking bread; some baking surfaces are soaked in water before baking so that the steam released in the oven will produce a crisp crust. For more information, see BAKING PANS.

Other Utensils A pastry brush is useful for applying glazes, wire racks are necessary for cooling the finished bread, and a serrated knife is the proper tool for making clean slices without tearing the crumb.

PREPARING YEAST DOUGHS

All ingredients should be at or near room temperature, about 72° F, since yeast thrives in a warm environment. The liquid is usually somewhat warmer, 105° to 115° F. On a cold day, rising time may be speeded if the mixing bowl is warmed in a low oven before use.

Often the first step in a recipe is to soften the yeast in warm water with some sugar; the yeast sits for about 5 minutes and then other ingredients are added. Some recipes specify proofing the yeast by leaving it longer, for 10 to 15 minutes; if within 10 minutes the surface bubbles and foams, the yeast is alive and can be used successfully. If a reaction fails to occur, the yeast and liquid should be discarded, and the process repeated with a fresh package. However, commercial yeast is reliable enough that, if a package is used before the marked expiration date, proofing shouldn't be necessary. Some recipes mix in the yeast directly with the dry ingredients.

KNEADING THE DOUGH

Flour is added last and then the dough is manipulated by hand, with a wooden spoon, in a heavy-duty electric mixer, or in the work bowl of a food processor. Working the dough disperses the ingredients and develops a strong network of gluten. Kneading continues until the dough takes on a silken elasticity and fine bubbles or blisters can be discerned just below the surface. More flour is added to bring the dough to a workable consistency. See KNEAD for a further discussion of this technique and information on using a food processor for making yeast doughs.

THE RISING PERIOD

When the dough has been sufficiently kneaded, it is set aside to rise. Confusingly, this stage is also called proofing (see PROOF). During rising the yeast continues to grow, giving off carbon dioxide gas that gently and slowly expands the dough. The first rising takes 1 to 1½ hours; during that time the dough generally doubles in bulk. The second and third risings, if called for, are for shorter periods. Some recipes have only one rise. However, flavor

improves and a finer texture results if the dough has several long, slow risings.

For rising, the dough is shaped into a ball and placed in a lightly oiled bowl, then turned to coat the entire surface. This light covering of oil keeps the dough moist and prevents it from forming a skin that will inhibit expansion. The bowl is covered with plastic wrap or a clean kitchen towel and set in a warm, draft-free place, the environment needed for yeast doughs to rise to maximum volume (usually about 80° to 85° F). Commercial bakeries have special proofing ovens; at home doughs rise nicely in a gas oven warmed by a pilot light or in an electric oven that has been turned on at 200° F for 1 minute, then turned off. As a test to determine if the dough has risen sufficiently, dent it gently with your index finger. If the dent remains, the dough is ready. If the depression fills up and nearly disappears, the dough needs more time.

SHAPING THE DOUGH

When the dough has doubled, it is punched down or deflated by hitting it with your fist or by gently picking it up and setting back down into the bowl. This step keeps the dough from overstretching and subsequently breaking the gluten network and creates a bread with a more even grain by widely distributing the bubbles of carbon dioxide that developed during the rising period. The dough is then shaped (see Shaping Loaves and Rolls at right), set in a pan or on a baking sheet, and usually left to rise a second time. Baking pans and baking sheets should be well greased; they also may be lightly dusted with flour or sprinkled with cornmeal. After rising and before baking, loaves are sometimes slashed with a sharp knife or a razor blade, or snipped with scissors. This is done both for decorative effect and to allow excess gas, which would otherwise cause the dough to tear, to escape during baking.

BAKING, COOLING, AND STORING YEAST BREADS

Within minutes after being placed in a preheated oven, a yeast dough rises dramatically. This expansion, called oven spring, continues until the yeast is killed by the heat and the structure of the bread sets; some doughs may increase in volume by almost 80 percent during this time. A light, crispy bread can be produced by baking directly on a high-fire baking stone or on an unglazed quarry tile, the home version of a commercial brick oven (see BAKING STONE). Commercial bakery ovens produce breads with superior crusts by injecting a fine spray of water into the oven cavity. Home bakers can approximate this mechanism by setting a pan filled with hot water on the floor of a gas oven or on the lowest shelf of an electric oven. In addition, spray the oven interior several times during the first 10 minutes or so of baking with a fine mist of water. Remove the pan of water toward the end of baking time in order to allow the bread to dry and brown.

SHAPING LOAVES AND ROLLS

Forming a standard loaf Shape dough into a rectangle that is as long as the loaf pan and slightly less than twice as wide as it is long. At narrow end, roll dough tightly, jelly-roll style. Pinch ends and seam to seal; turn ends under, if necessary.

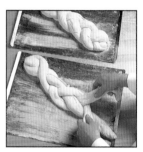

Making a braid Place ropes across baking sheet. Braid, tapering to a rounded point at both ends. Pinch ends to seal; turn ends under, if necessary.

Shaping rolls Bowknots: Tie strands of dough loosely into knots. Cloverleaf Rolls: Arrange 3 balls of dough in each cup of muffin pan. Fantans: Lay stacks of dough strips horizontally in each cup of muffin pan as shown here or vertically as shown in photograph, page 618. Parker House Rolls: Fold circles of dough in half.

The Italian flat bread called focaccia is a popular children's snack but it can also accompany a meal. Serve this onion-and-herb version with soup or salad for a casual lunch.

FOCACCIA

By most accounts, *focaccia* is reckoned to be Italy's oldest bread—a simple yeast dough flattened and baked on a stone slab in a wood-fired hearth. Quite likely, it's the grandfather of the famous Neapolitan pizza. Today's cooks can easily make this versatile country bread at home, even without the stone and the hearth. Garnished as you like— here, with sautéed onions and basil—it can partner salads and soups, sliced tomatoes and cheese, or cocktails.

    1¼ **cups warm (105° to 115° F) water**
    ¾ **teaspoon sugar**
    1 **package active dry yeast**
    2¾ **cups unbleached flour**
    3 **tablespoons unsalted butter**
    ½ **cup minced onion**
    ⅓ **cup minced fresh basil**
    1½ **teaspoons coarse salt**
    ½ **teaspoon freshly ground pepper**
    2 **tablespoons olive oil, plus olive oil for greasing and drizzling**
      Cornmeal, for dusting

1. In a large bowl combine ½ cup of the water, sugar, and yeast. Set aside 10 minutes to let yeast soften. Stir in ¾ cup flour, cover, and let rise 2½ hours.

2. While dough is rising, heat butter in a skillet over low heat. Add onion and sauté until onion is soft but not browned (about 15 minutes). Remove from heat and stir in basil, ½ teaspoon of the salt, and pepper. Reserve.

3. Mix in remaining 2 cups flour to dough. Combine the 2 tablespoons olive oil and the remaining ¾ cup warm water; add to dough. Beat until dough forms a mass. Turn out onto a lightly floured surface and knead until dough is shiny and smooth (8 to 10 minutes). Transfer dough to a lightly oiled bowl and turn to coat all sides with oil. Cover and let rise until doubled in bulk (about 1½ hours).

4. Preheat oven to 450° F. Punch dough down into a 13- by 15-inch rectangle. Transfer to a baking sheet sprinkled with cornmeal. Spread top with onion mixture. Drizzle with additional olive oil. Sprinkle with remaining coarse salt and bake until golden (about 15 minutes). Cool slightly on a rack; serve warm.

Makes one 13- by 15-inch rectangle.

PUMPERNICKEL

Dark and hearty, this free-form loaf makes wonderful sandwiches and provides a filling and satisfying accompaniment to robust soups.

    2 **packages active dry yeast**
    2 **tablespoons sugar**
    ½ **cup warm (105° to 115° F) water**
    4 to 5 **cups dark rye flour**
    2 **cups whole wheat flour**
    1 **teaspoon salt**
    2 **cups warm (105° to 115° F) milk**
      Oil, for greasing
    2 **tablespoons butter, melted**

1. In a small bowl dissolve yeast and sugar in the warm water and set aside to soften a few minutes. Sift together 4 cups rye flour, whole wheat flour, and salt; set aside.

2. In a large bowl combine milk and yeast; add flour mixture, one cup at a time, until a smooth dough forms (add additional rye flour, if needed, to make smooth dough). Turn out onto a lightly floured surface and knead until smooth, satiny, and elastic (10 to 12 minutes), or dough can be kneaded in a heavy-duty electric mixer.

3. Place dough in a lightly oiled bowl, brush with melted butter, cover with plastic wrap, and let rise in a warm place until almost doubled in bulk (about 1 hour). Punch down and knead lightly 2 minutes. Divide dough in half and shape into two free-form loaves. Set loaves on a greased or parchment-lined baking sheet, brush again with melted butter, and let rise until almost doubled in bulk (about 45 minutes).

4. Preheat oven to 375° F. Bake loaves until they are well browned and sound hollow when tapped (about 30 minutes). Cool on wire racks.

Makes 2 loaves.

■ SWEDISH RYE BREAD

This dark, fragrant rye bread from Sweden is perfumed with orange, fennel seed, and honey.

> 2 packages active dry yeast
> ½ cup warm (105° to 115° F) water
> 4 to 5 cups all-purpose flour
> 2½ cups rye flour
> 1 tablespoon salt
> 2 cups warm (105° to 115° F) milk
> ¼ cup honey or molasses
> ¼ cup firmly packed brown sugar
> ¼ cup unsalted butter, softened
>   Finely grated rind and juice of 2 large oranges (approximately ¾ cup juice)
> 1 tablespoon fennel seed
>   Oil, for greasing

1. In a large bowl of a heavy-duty electric mixer, combine yeast and the water and set aside to soften a few minutes. Sift together 4 cups all-purpose flour, rye flour, and salt; set aside.

2. Stir milk, honey, brown sugar, butter, orange rind and juice, and fennel seed into yeast mixture. Add flour mixture, one cup at a time, to yeast mixture, mixing well after each addition, to make a soft, pliable dough (add additional all-purpose flour, if needed, to make a soft dough). Knead 5 minutes in mixer or by hand on a lightly floured surface until smooth, satiny, and elastic (10 to 12 minutes). If prepared completely in mixer, turn out and knead 1 to 2 minutes. Place dough in a lightly oiled bowl, cover with plastic wrap, and let rise in a warm place until doubled in bulk (about 1 hour).

3. Punch down dough; turn out onto a lightly floured surface and knead gently 1 minute. Divide dough in half and shape into 2 round loaves. Set loaves on greased or parchment-lined baking sheets. With a sharp knife or razor blade, slash a cross about ¼ to ½ inch deep on surface of each loaf. Let rise until almost doubled in bulk (35 to 45 minutes).

4. Preheat oven to 350° F. Bake bread until it is golden and sounds hollow when tapped (50 to 60 minutes).

Makes 2 loaves.

■ BATTER BREAD

Batter breads are among the simplest to prepare because they aren't shaped. Instead, they bake in a pan.

> 1 package active dry yeast
> ½ cup sugar
> ½ cup warm (105° to 115° F) water
> 4 cups flour
> 1 teaspoon salt
> ½ cup warm (105° to 115° F) milk
> ¼ cup unsalted butter, softened
> 3 eggs
>   Oil, for greasing

1. In a small bowl dissolve yeast and sugar in the warm water and set aside to soften a few minutes. Sift together flour and salt; set aside.

2. In a large bowl combine milk, butter, and eggs; stir in yeast mixture. Slowly add flour, one cup at a time, until a soft dough forms. Turn out onto a lightly floured surface and knead for at least 5 minutes by lifting and throwing the dough down as for brioche (see KNEAD), or use a heavy-duty electric mixer.

3. Place dough in a lightly oiled bowl, cover with plastic wrap, and let rise in a warm place until doubled in bulk (about 1 hour).

4. Generously butter an 8- or 9-inch round cake pan. Punch down dough, knead lightly, and place in pan. Let rise until almost doubled in bulk (35 to 45 minutes).

5. Preheat oven to 375° F. Bake until bread is golden and sounds hollow when tapped (50 to 60 minutes).

Makes 1 loaf.

■ BEER BREAD

Beer in the dough acts as an additional leavening agent; use dark beer for a bread with a greater depth of flavor.

> 2 packages active dry yeast
> 1 teaspoon sugar
> ½ cup warm (105° to 115° F) water
> 4 to 5 cups all-purpose flour
> 3 cups whole wheat flour
> 2 cups beer (Guinness or other dark beer)
> ⅓ cup molasses
> 4 tablespoons butter, melted
> 2 teaspoons salt
>   Oil, for greasing bowl and baking sheet
> 3 tablespoons warm water, for brushing

1. In a small bowl dissolve yeast and sugar in the warm water and let soften briefly. Sift together 4 cups all-purpose flour and whole wheat flours.

2. In a large bowl combine beer, molasses, butter, and salt; stir in yeast mixture. Add flour, one cup at a time, to make a soft dough (add more all-purpose flour, if needed, to make a soft dough). Turn out onto a lightly floured surface and knead until smooth, satiny, and elastic (5 to 10 minutes). Or, mix and knead 5 minutes in a heavy-duty electric mixer, and then finish kneading by hand.

3. Place dough in a lightly oiled bowl, cover, and let rise in a warm place until doubled in bulk (about 1 hour). Punch down, knead lightly, divide, and shape into two loaves; set on greased baking sheet. Brush lightly with warm water and let rise until almost doubled in bulk (about 45 minutes).

4. Preheat oven to 400° F. Bake until loaves are well browned and sound hollow when tapped (30 to 35 minutes).

Makes 2 loaves.

■ **CLASSIC BRIOCHE**

Here is a good brioche: It is fine textured, light, and tastes of butter and eggs. It can be baked as a loaf or in small brioche molds. After the first rising, you can also use this dough to make delicious raised doughnuts (see page 183). Brioche dough is sticky and can be difficult to knead. Try the method suggested in the recipe, or the one described in KNEAD, Kneading Pastry, Biscuit, and Rich Yeast Doughs. Like all breads, brioche can be made to suit your schedule. After the dough has had its first rise, you can punch it down and refrigerate it for up to a few days before forming and baking, if desired.

      1 package active dry yeast
      2 tablespoons sugar
      ½ cup warm (105° to 115° F) milk
    1½ teaspoons salt
      2 eggs
      2 egg yolks
    3¼ to 3½ cups flour
     12 tablespoons butter (softened if mixing
        by hand, chilled otherwise)
      1 egg mixed with 2 teaspoons water, for glaze
        Oil, for greasing

To Mix by Hand

1. In a large bowl sprinkle yeast and sugar over warm milk, stir, and let stand a few minutes to dissolve.

2. Add salt, eggs, and egg yolks and mix well.

3. Add 2 cups of the flour and beat vigorously until batter is smooth and heavy. Drop in softened butter, 1 table-spoon at a time, and beat after each addition until incorporated. If some tiny lumps of butter remain, don't worry; they will blend in later.

4. Add 1 cup of the remaining flour and mix well until a rough mass forms, then scrape out onto a lightly floured surface. Knead for a couple of minutes, sprinkling on a little more flour as necessary to keep dough from being too sticky. Stop kneading and let rest for about 5 to 10 minutes. Continue kneading for a few minutes more, until dough is smooth and elastic.

5. Place in a greased bowl, cover, and let rise until dough is puffy and slightly more than doubled in bulk (about 1 hour).

6. Punch down dough. Cover and refrigerate for one or two days at this point, if desired. (The dough will continue to rise until it is thoroughly chilled; just punch it down every hour or so.)

7. *To make brioches:* Cut dough in half, and on a lightly floured surface shape each piece into an even rope about 10 inches long. Cut each rope into 7 pieces, each about 1½ inches long. Plump each piece of dough into a smooth ball by holding it in one hand as you tuck the edges underneath with the fingers of your other hand, thus forming a tight round with a seam on the bottom.

Cover with a towel and let rest for 10 minutes. To form brioches, generously butter 14 brioche molds or muffin tins. Pick up a piece of dough and pinch it with your fingertips, gently stretching the ball to elongate it slightly as you pull away a marble-sized piece of dough—but don't detach it completely. To form the topknot, place dough on floured surface, lay your index finger on top of the stretched portion, then roll your finger back and forth, to pull out the small end of dough about another inch. Twist the topknot 3 or 4 times and press it firmly back into the larger base. The final shape resembles a tiny snowman with a fat body and a tiny head. Place in one of the prepared molds, pressing down firmly around the edges. Form the remaining balls the same way. Place filled molds on a baking sheet, cover loosely with a towel, and let rise until a little more than doubled in bulk and puffed well over the tops of the molds.

To make a loaf: Butter a 9- by 5-inch loaf pan. Form dough into a smooth loaf and place it in pan. Cover and let rise until doubled in bulk (about 1 hour). After rising, use a sharp, pointed knife or razor blade to make a ½-inch-deep slash lengthwise down the center.

8. Preheat oven to 375° F. Before baking, paint top of each brioche (or the loaf) with egg glaze, taking care not to let it run down into molds.

9. Bake small brioches (on a baking sheet) for about 20 minutes, turning pan once or twice during baking if they brown unevenly. Bake loaf for about 50 minutes; if it browns too much, cover loosely with a tent of foil for the remainder of the baking time.

10. Remove from oven and turn out onto racks (if any stick, pry them out with a knife point) to cool completely before wrapping for storage or freezing. To reheat, place on a baking sheet in a 350° F oven for about 10 minutes.

To Mix With a Processor

1. In a small bowl sprinkle yeast and sugar over warm milk, stir, and let stand a few minutes to dissolve.

2. Pour yeast mixture into bowl of a food processor fitted with steel blade. Add salt, eggs, and egg yolks and whirl for a few seconds.

3. Add 2 cups of the flour and process again until smooth. While blade is turning, drop in chilled butter, 2 table-spoons at a time. Continue to process until smooth.

4. Add another 1½ cups of the flour. Process again until dough comes together and forms a rough ball that revolves around the bowl; process for 30 seconds more. Continue with step 5 of To Mix by Hand for the rising and forming. (Some food processors tend to strain while kneading a dough. If yours labors or stalls, remove dough and continue kneading by hand.)

Makes fourteen 3-inch brioches, or 1 loaf.

■ SAVARIN

This wonderfully rich yeast cake was said to be named for the French gastronome, Brillat-Savarin. It is prepared in a ring mold, soaked with sugar syrup, and served with the center filled with whipped cream and fresh fruit. Cubes of fresh pineapple are suggested here, but any seasonal fruit will be equally flavorful and attractive. Babas au Rhum (see variation) are almost identical to a savarin, but have currants mixed into the dough, are made in special cup-shaped molds, and receive a special drenching in rum. Be sure to butter the molds well.

   1   **package active dry yeast**
   ¼   **cup warm (105° to 115° F) water**
   ¼   **cup sugar**
  1⅔   **cup flour**
   1   **teaspoon salt**
   3   **eggs**
   ½   **cup unsalted butter, softened, plus butter for greasing**
   ¼   **cup rum, plus rum for sprinkling**
   1   **cup whipping cream, whipped, for accompaniment**
   1   **cup fresh pineapple cubes or other fresh fruit in season**

Soaking Syrup

   2   **cups sugar**
   2   **cups water**

1. In a small bowl dissolve yeast and sugar in warm water and set aside to soften 5 minutes. Sift together flour and salt; set aside.

2. In a large bowl combine eggs, butter, and the ¼ cup rum. Add yeast mixture, then slowly add flour, 1 cup at a time; mix to a smooth batter. Knead by slapping dough against side of bowl with hand (see KNEAD, Kneading Pastry, Biscuit, and Rich Yeast Doughs), or with a heavy-duty electric mixer and flat beater attachment. Cover batter with plastic wrap and let rise in a warm place until doubled in bulk (about 1 hour).

3. Preheat oven to 375° F. Generously butter a 10-inch savarin mold. Punch down dough, knead lightly, then place in prepared mold. Let rise again until almost doubled in bulk (30 to 40 minutes). Bake until golden brown and high (30 to 40 minutes).

4. Let cool in pan on wire rack 10 minutes; turn out from pan onto a rimmed plate or large, square baking dish. Pour hot Soaking Syrup over bread; sprinkle with rum to taste. Pour off any excess syrup. To transfer to a serving plate, cover bread with savarin mold and invert. Lay serving plate on surface of bread and invert; bread will drop out onto plate.

5. Fill center of Savarin with whipped cream and fresh fruit. Serve at room temperature or chilled.

Serves 6 to 8.

Soaking Syrup Place sugar and water in a medium, heavy-bottomed saucepan. Dissolve sugar in water over low heat, stirring; increase heat to medium-high and boil 3 minutes.

Babas au Rhum Prepare Savarin up through kneading dough, step 2. Mix 1 cup currants into dough, cover with plastic wrap, and let rise until doubled. Punch down and divide dough among 10 to 12 well-buttered baba molds, filling each approximately two thirds full. Let rise until dough fills mold (25 to 30 minutes). Bake in a 375° F oven until golden brown and high (about 20 minutes). Cool in molds 10 minutes, invert, and soak with hot Soaking Syrup. Cool, then sprinkle with rum, to taste; drain off excess syrup and serve at room temperature or slightly chilled.

Makes 10 to 12 Babas.

Rich, cakelike brioche display their characteristic topknots. Shown are four stages of individual brioches: balls of dough; dough elongated to form topknots; unbaked brioches with topknots in place; and baked brioches.

Flaky croissants are shaped from triangles of butter-flecked dough that are rolled from the wide end toward the point, then curved into a crescent.

CROISSANTS

With so many steps, croissant making might seem like quite a difficult task at first glance—but it's really not hard, perhaps just a bit time-consuming. The technique of building thin layers of butter between layers of yeast dough will be familiar if you have ever made puff pastry, and even if you haven't, instructions are detailed enough for beginning bakers. Follow directions carefully and you should not have any trouble producing the lightest, flakiest croissants you've ever had.

    1 package active dry yeast
1¼ cups warm (105° to 115° F) milk
    2 teaspoons sugar
1½ teaspoons salt
2¾ cups flour
    1 egg mixed with 1 teaspoon water

Butter Mixture

1¼ cups cold butter
   3 tablespoons flour

1. In a large bowl sprinkle yeast over warm milk, add sugar, stir, and let stand for a few minutes to dissolve. Add salt and flour, then mix vigorously but briefly, just until you have a rough, sticky dough that holds together. Set aside for about 5 minutes while preparing Butter Mixture.

2. Wipe work surface clean, sprinkle it generously with flour, and turn dough out onto it. Flour the dough, which is quite soft, and push, pat, and roll it into a rectangle about 10 by 14 inches. Unwrap Butter Mixture and place it on bottom half of dough, leaving about a 1-inch border on 3 sides. Lift up the top of the dough, working it loose with a spatula or scraper if it sticks to work surface, and flip it over the butter. Pinch edges to seal. Give the dough a quarter turn, so sealed flap is to your right.

3. Using smooth, even strokes, roll to a 9- by 17-inch rectangle. Check to see if it is sticking and sprinkle with flour if necessary—don't be afraid to pick it up and look. Fold bottom third of dough up over the middle, then flip top third down to cover it. Turn again so flap is to your right and roll out again to 9 by 17 inches. Fold in thirds as before, flour lightly, wrap in plastic wrap, place in a plastic bag, and chill for about 30 minutes. At this point, the first two turns are finished.

4. Roll chilled dough again to 9 by 17 inches, fold in thirds, wrap in plastic wrap and a plastic bag, and refrigerate for 45 minutes. (If at any time dough becomes soft and resists rolling out, or if butter breaks through in large, smeary patches, stop working, dust dough with flour, then slide onto a baking sheet and chill for about 20 minutes.)

5. Roll out and fold dough again, thus completing four turns. Wrap and chill for at least 1 hour (or for a few hours or overnight if it's more convenient) before forming croissants.

6. Roll dough out to 10 by 20 inches, keeping sides as even as possible. With a sharp knife, cut in half lengthwise, then cut each half into four 5-inch squares. Cut each square in half diagonally to make 2 triangles.

7. Working with one triangle at a time, pick up the 2 closest points, at the base, and gently stretch them out to about 7 inches. Hold these 2 points down with one hand and use the other hand to wiggle and stretch the other, farthest point out to about 7 inches or more. Starting at the base, roll up stretched dough just like a crescent roll. Pull points down, toward one another, to form a crescent shape.

8. Place croissants about 2 inches apart on baking sheets. Cover with a towel and let rise until puffy and doubled in size (about 1½ hours). If you've used 2 baking sheets and your oven can hold only 1 sheet on the same rack, chill 1 sheet for the first hour or so, to slow rising, so baking times are staggered.

9. Preheat oven to 425° F and place a rack on middle level. Brush each risen croissant with egg mixture and bake until well browned and puffy (12 to 15 minutes). If they are not browning evenly, quickly turn pan around from front to back once or twice during baking. If some are done before others, just remove them with a spatula. Transfer croissants to a rack to cool for a few minutes before serving. Wrap and freeze what you won't use in a day. (To reheat, unwrap and set on a baking sheet, still frozen, and place in a 400° F oven for about 7 minutes.)

Makes sixteen 4-inch Croissants.

Butter Mixture   Cut butter into tablespoon-sized bits, dropping them onto work surface, then sprinkle with flour. Tear off two good-sized sheets of waxed paper and set aside. Begin mashing butter and flour together by smearing across work surface with the heel of your hand; gather butter mixture into a pile with a spatula or pastry scraper, then repeat smearing a couple of times, until butter is smooth and workable, but still cold. With floured hands form butter into a small, rough rectangle and place it between sheets of waxed paper. Roll and pat butter into a larger, 6- by 8-inch rectangle, keeping sides as even as possible. Set aside while you roll out yeast dough.

DANISH PASTRY DOUGH

Danish pastry dough is slightly richer than croissant dough because it contains eggs and a little more sugar.

> 2 **packages active dry yeast**
> 1 **cup warm (105° to 115° F) milk**
> 2 **eggs, at room temperature**
> 2 **teaspoons salt**
> ¼ **cup sugar**
> 3¼ **cups all-purpose flour**

Butter Mixture

> 1½ **cups cold butter**
> ¼ **cup all-purpose flour**

1. In a large bowl sprinkle yeast over warm milk, stir, and let stand a few minutes to soften. Add eggs, salt, and sugar and mix well. Pour in flour and mix briefly, just until you have a rough, sticky dough that holds together. Set aside for about 5 minutes while preparing Butter Mixture.

2. Scrape clean surface of work area used for Butter Mixture, sprinkle it generously with flour, and turn yeast dough out onto it (dough will be quite soft). Sprinkle top of dough with flour, then roll and pat into a 10- by 14-inch rectangle. Unwrap Butter Mixture and set it on bottom half of dough, leaving a 1-inch border on 3 sides. Gently lift up unbuttered top flap and flip it down over butter. Pinch the edges to seal, then use a wide spatula or scraper to help lift dough package and give it a quarter turn, so the sealed flap is to your right.

3. To roll out and fold dough, follow steps 3, 4, and 5 of Croissants (see page 624), except roll out Danish dough a little larger, to an 8- by 20-inch rectangle, since you are working with more dough. After you've completed all the turns, form and bake the pastries (see A Variety of Danish Shapes and Fillings, page 626)—or if it is more convenient, wrap dough in plastic wrap and a plastic bag, and refrigerate overnight before forming and baking.

Makes about 2 dozen pastries, depending on shapes.

Butter Mixture   Cut cold butter into tablespoon-sized chunks, dropping chunks onto work surface. Sprinkle butter pieces with flour. Blend butter and flour by smearing them out in front of you with the heel of your hand; gather up the mixture and smear again three or four times until butter is perfectly smooth and workable but still cold. Flour your hands and pat mixture into a rectangle about 4 by 5 inches. Place between two sheets of waxed paper or plastic wrap and pat and roll into a larger, 7- by 9-inch rectangle, keeping edges as even as possible. Set aside for a moment.

Danish pastries are the flakiest and most buttery of all sweet rolls. Shown here are icing-topped Cinnamon Rolled Danish. The recipe appears on page 626.